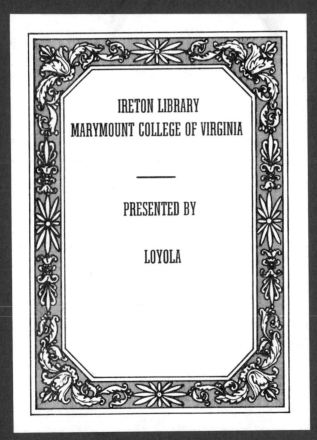

# Organizational Strategy and Change

*New Views on Formulating
and Implementing
Strategic Decisions*

# Johannes M. Pennings
## and Associates

# Organizational Strategy and Change

Jossey-Bass Publishers

San Francisco • Washington • London • 1985

85298

ORGANIZATIONAL STRATEGY AND CHANGE
*New Views on Formulating
and Implementing Strategic Decisions*
  by Johannes M. Pennings and Associates

Copyright © 1985 by:  Jossey-Bass Inc., Publishers
                      433 California Street
                      San Francisco, California 94104

&

Jossey-Bass Limited
28 Banner Street
London EC1Y 8QE

**Library of Congress Cataloging in Publication Data**
Main entry under title:

Organizational strategy and change.

  (The Jossey-Bass management series) (The Jossey-Bass
social and behavioral science series)
   Bibliography: p. 495
   Includes indexes.
   1. Decision-making—Addresses, essays, lectures.
2. Management—Decision making—Addresses, essays,
lectures.  I. Pennings, Johannes M.  II. Series.
III. Series: Jossey-Bass social and behavioral science
series.
HD30.23.075  1985        658.4'03          84-47994
ISBN 0-87589-626-X

Manufactured in the United States of America

The paper in this book meets the guidelines for
permanence and durability of the Committee on
Production Guidelines for Book Longevity of the
Council on Library Resources.

JACKET DESIGN BY WILLI BAUM

FIRST EDITION

*Code 8508*

*A joint publication in*
The Jossey-Bass Management Series
*and*
The Jossey-Bass
Social and Behavioral Science Series

# Preface

In a recent article, the *Wall Street Journal* (1983) asked a number of senior executives to describe their most difficult business decisions. Some decisions were described as difficult but relatively significant to organizations—such as the decision to dismiss a senior executive. Other decisions were difficult because the stakes were high, so that the implications for organizations were considerable. The latter type of decisions are often strategic. In the private sector, they include the entry into or exit from a market, whether to engage in vertical integration, or whether to close outmoded, inefficient plants. Many such decisions are made in the solitude of the top decision maker's office, perhaps after various associates have provided suggestions. This is most dramatically illustrated in Robert F. Kennedy's description of the loneliness of his brother John F. during the moments of choosing the naval blockade as the most appropriate course of action in the Cuban Missile Crisis. Those moments were preceded by a complex stategic game of maneuvering among the various factions of government in and around the White House. However, although some such critical consequential decisions are made by a single top decision maker, they more commonly have a distinctly collective nature, involving a multitude of individuals or groups of individuals in determining a certain course of action. Most strategic decisions have, therefore, a social quality, which renders them complex, unstructured, and political. They are certainly social if we include their implementation as part of the decision-making process.

Often, however, strategic decisions cannot be easily pinpointed, because they are embedded in an amorphous, lengthy process whose continuity defies punctuation. Their "messy" appearance might lead one to conclude that it is better to refer to *strategy, strategic change, strategic momentum,* or a *stream of decisions* that reveals a certain directionality. Nevertheless, we often witness an organization's choice for a course of action triggering particular developments, imparting an enduring disposition toward its environment, or setting off a change that acquires its own momentum. Decisions such as the naval blockade, vertical integration, or the entry into a new market set precedents for other decisions and have profound implications for an organization's identity, its position in a network of relationships, and the likelihood of future actions. It is highly desirable to identify and to study such decisions, to examine how, when, where, and by whom they were made, and to relate them to the stream of decisions that represents a sequel to such trend-setting events.

It should also be pointed out that strategic decisions are social phenomena and that, as such, they are rarely a reality "out there." After strategic decisions have been made, or when they become apparent in their consequences, they are interpreted, socially reconstructed, and cognitively enriched to render them more meaningful. Often, strategic decisions are accessible only through the selectively retained histories that reside in the heads of informants. Organizational strategy in this sense is, then, the result of creative cognitive activities of the decision makers and those who disseminate data about strategic decisions. General Motors' "Japanese strategy" and Richard Nixon's "Southern strategy" are examples of such socially constructed strategies.

Differences in viewpoints about what really should be meant by *strategy* are exacerbated by the phenomenon's being of interest to a wide diversity of researchers. Furthermore, the phenomenon is pertinent to both private- and public-sector organizations. Two streams of research and theory appear to exist in this area. Much of the literature on corporate strategy and business policy has been concerned with the *outcomes* and content of decisions—for example, whether to expand the product mix or to decrease vertical integration. Conversely, the literature on public choice has been more preoccupied with the *process* by which strategic decisions were derived or by which they were implemented. There has been little integration between those who are associated with business policy and public policy, nor has there been much communication between those involved in the content of strategic decision making and those who deal with the sequence or preconditions and intermediate choices that precede or follow a decision outcome. Thus, the area of strategic decision making is fairly disjointed. The integral theoretical and empirical literature is not very well developed. There are no well-specified models, and pertinent contributions show little cumulative character. There appears also to exist a cleavage between academicians and practicing strategic decision makers, where the former would be hard pressed to provide research-derived prescriptions for guiding the latter in the pursuit of their decisions.

The purpose of *Organizational Strategy and Change* is to expose critical theoretical, methodological, and pragmatic issues and to propose some points of resolution. The ultimate goal is to move research and practice on strategic decision making in a more analytical, theory-grounded direction. The book is organized around a set of original essays by major writers on strategic decision making. Its primary accomplishment is that it brings together a group of individuals who have made major contributions to the area and who can provide directions for research and practice. The contributors come from various disciplines, such as economics, psychology, sociology, political science, and anthropology, but they also differ in their exposure to the practice of strategic decision making. Some are actively involved in strategic decision making; others have "lived" in organizations as participant observers. Still others have examined strategic decision making under controlled, scientific conditions. The interdisciplinary nature of the book should, therefore, make it of interest to both academicians and practitioners who are concerned with strategic decision making in either the private or public sector or in both.

## Plan of the Book

This book was conceived to stimulate new lines of thinking about research and practice on strategic decision making. One of the first tasks is to examine the critical theoretical issues that underlie the concept of strategic decision making. By exploring these issues and finding some way to deal with them, we can begin to develop an interdisciplinary framework of strategic decision making. Without such a framework, research will have no direction. We do not claim that the essays in this book provide a framework. The contribution, rather, is in identifying the crucial issues that are central to the concept of strategic decision making.

The opening chapter provides a brief overview of the pertinent strategy literature and the current state of practice. It contrasts three strategy definitions—explicit, implicit, and rationalized—but deals also with other definitional problems, such as the process and content of strategy. A review of the theoretical and empirical literature leads to a conclusion that there is a lack of direction, insufficient cross-fertilization between different schools of thought, and too much hegemony for the rational model. Some disenchantment with that model is identified as well, not only in the academic literature but also among practitioners. In view of the somewhat disappointing state of affairs and because of the need to further stimulate research on and practice of strategic decision making, five issues are presented that should be of central concern in the future— the essence of strategy, the proper unit of study, the multidisciplinary nature of strategy research, the quality of strategic choices, and the selection of research strategies. These issues provide an agenda for the remainder of this book.

David J. Teece (Chapter One) does not discard the value of the industrial-organization paradigm, but he feels that it has limited value and that it has been superseded by more promising developments within institutional economics. These newer traditions include the market-failures theory (for example, Williamson, 1975) and evolutionary theory (for example, Nelson and Winter, 1982). He also presents a set of normative pronouncements ("principles") that derive from the market-failures theory, such as those that pertain to "property rights" when contractual difficulties arise. For example, firms are better off if they vertically integrate under conditions of high levels of committed investments or when know-how licensing leads to substantial spillovers to nonaffiliated enterprises. Teece discusses also the important contributions of Nelson and Winter (1982), which seek to identify a firm's distinctive capabilities. The scope of strategic choice is fostered and impeded by those capabilities and serves as another concept for integrating market structure and individual-firm behavior. These contributions are also conducive to a greater synthesis between content and process of strategic decision making. Teece's chapter presents a typical contemporary economic treatment of strategy but recognizes that older, purely rationalistic concepts and metaphors are inadequate for describing strategic behavior in institutional settings.

In Chapter Two, Colin Camerer agrees with Teece that advancing the state of the art of strategy research will require "pushing the boundaries of economic theory" but differs with him on some points of methodology. Camerer sets forth what he feels are basic shortcomings in traditional strategy research—vaguely defined constructs, inadequate testing of theories, and inductive rather than deductive theorizing—and then argues for a new approach incorporating some key features of economic thinking, including such concepts as "maximizing," "equilibrium," and "rational expectations." He concludes by proposing some specific research directions for a new "strategic economics," building on ideas from information economics and applied game theory.

Kenneth R. MacCrimmon, in Chapter Three, reviews three holistic models of collective decisions in order to analyze a well-researched strategic decision, the Cuban Missile Crisis. He contrasts the mechanistic model (routine, rule-based decision making) with the super-rational model (decision making with perfect foresight and complete information-processing capabilities) and with the so-called Machiavellian model (decision making with manipulations of the decision situation). The three models highlight different aspects of the real situation and indicate that different perspectives might be required to expose different dimensions of the decision process. Unlike Hickson and his colleagues' empirically derived classification schemes (see Chapter Five), MacCrimmon's typology is a priori derived. His a priori models force us to view organizations as monolithic units, even if strategic decisions are made within a wide latitude of negotiation and the players in the decision game are constantly interrupting the game, corrupting the process, and delaying its termination.

Sidney G. Winter (Chapter Four) takes issue with the somewhat onesided view of the mechanistic model of decision making. He argues that MacCrimmon goes too far in pointing out its deficiencies, such that two alternative and complementary models have to be advanced. Rather, he holds, we can differentiate our interpretation of mechanistic models so that they become appropriate for the description and analysis of strategic choice. Well-institutionalized decision routines have major advantages in that they economize on search and other information costs. As he and Nelson point out, "routines are the skills of an organization" (Nelson and Winter, 1982) and represent its repertoire of capabilities as accumulated over the history of its existence. These capabilities can be an unassailable source of strategic power, even though they also constrain the firm's scope of choice. Such a view contrasts sharply with the views of those who stress the ever-present capacity for strategic change and the inherent willingness to discredit or to discard hard-won routines.

David J. Hickson, Richard J. Butler, David Cray, Geoffrey R. Mallory, and David C. Wilson (Chapter Five) have developed a radically different approach to the study of strategic decision making. One could label this approach *comparative*, as they collected data on 150 decisions in a wide variety of organizations, including both for-profit and not-for-profit organizations. Theirs is an ambitious effort, covering a period of over ten years, to examine strategic decisions with respect to their duration, their antecedent conditions and outcomes, and the very processes that make up such decisions. Their study permits unprecedented conclusions about the most likely types of decisions and the processes that predominate.

For example, they have found that some decisions are highly fluid, smooth, and consistent with a mechanical, linear sequence of steps, while other decisions are discontinuous and disorderly. Such modes of research can yield decisional-process taxonomies and the conditions under which they emerge. Decisions are defined in relatively discrete terms to allow for such a comparative analysis of typal processes.

In Chapter Six, John M. Dutton argues that an organizational focus might render the analysis incomplete. The researcher has to tend to cognitive and attitudinal but also cultural and economic factors that shape the strategic decision-making process. His own research reflects this multilevel approach, and he makes a strong advocacy statement for conducting research along those lines.

In Chapter Seven, Irving L. Janis presents major additions to his previous work on "groupthink" and other defective coping patterns that characterize many cases of strategic decision making. Essentially, Janis tries to delineate the positive and negative consequences of stress on the quality of decision making. He examines several fiascoes—ill-conceived and poorly executed decisions. The reasons for such poor decisions are associated with the motivation to avoid the stress that is generated by difficult and agonizing choices. Janis does not limit himself to public policy or international fiascoes, such as Watergate and the Bay of Pigs invasion, but also includes fiascoes that strike business firms. Futhermore, he presents a complement to the discussion of groupthink and the way it can be embedded into current thinking on organizational decision making as illustrated by the so-called Japanese style of management. He indicates that groupthink can have detrimental effects on strategic, nonroutine decision making, while it can have positive effects for nonstrategic decisions. Group-based modes of decision making are most conducive to obtaining commitment to strategic decisions and foster their smooth implementation. Janis also presents suggestions for future research and theory on strategic decision making, including the possibility of complementing case studies with hypothesis-testing research designs (for example, correlational analysis and experimental research).

Deborah L. Gladstein and James Brian Quinn (Chapter Eight) challenge Janis's quest for expanding the repertoire of

research methodologies, including their commensurate conceptual
developments and theoretical maturity. They feel that one cannot
excel in all the different means of research and theory. Furthermore,
they argue that, although groupthink might be an important
concept, its theoretical and empirical, or normative, value might
differ under various strategic decision-making conditions. They
proceed to classify decision making in terms of decision rationality
(outcome oriented) and action rationality (involvement and commitment oriented). They criticize Janis for having relegated implementation and the necessary associated involvement and
commitment to the final phase, when, in fact, the involvement
might often be established during the earlier stages of the decision-
making process, even prior to the actual onset of implementation.
Commitment, which is a key concept in the theory of groupthink
and a central term for explaining its deleterious effects on decision
making, can thus be viewed in a more positive mode. Actions that
promote loyalty serve to rally the organization behind certain
strategic moves—moves that would not materialize if the commitment were absent. In an incremental spiral mode, the organization
will, over time, merge action rationality and decision rationality
and learn from the numerous iterations of commitment and involvement as it moves along.

In Chapter Nine, Richard Normann provides a framework
for organizational learning and strategic management capability.
Borrowing elements of the learning theories of Bateson (1972) and
Argyris and Schön (1978), he suggests that strategy and strategic
change can be viewed at three levels: (1) single-loop, (2) double-loop
and (3) deutero learning. If organizations learn to learn, they can
reorient themselves whenever conditions in a particular domain are
modified. The domains that he reviews are interpersonal skills,
analytical language, organizational skills, and ecological positioning. Learning in these domains will be conducive to the growth of
strategic management capabilities. These capabilities manifest
themselves in innovativeness or, to use one of his well-known terms,
*reorientation*. The role of the chief executive is of paramount
importance in generating the learning that will develop such
capabilities. Normann employs the term *statesmanship* to indicate
the conditions of high-level learning. The chief executive should be

concerned with ground rules for how power is exercised and with the design of arenas for conflict resolutions—in other words, setting the preconditions for other people's actions. Such an approach to strategic decision making requires clinical methodology in order to arrive at a theory of action that is internally consistent and that makes the observed actions of the decision makers make sense.

It is particularly with these latter comments that Lawrence B. Mohr (Chapter Ten) disagrees. For Mohr, it is virtually impossible to ascertain the reasons for individual actions. Those actions may have been induced by a variety of motives, sometimes even conflicting motives or motives that are far removed from an actor's currently accessible memory. It would, therefore, be futile to impute meaning to an actor's actions or to trace his or her goals in establishing the causes of his or her behavior. Mohr presents a rather pessimistic perspective on the feasibility of research on strategic decision making.

Andrew M. Pettigrew (Chapter Eleven) provides an analysis of strategic decision making at Imperial Chemical Industries. He traced strategic decision making over an extended period of time to discern continuities in the process of strategic change internal to the organization. Such internal strategic changes are examined in reference to changing environmental contexts, which create different power configurations, in turn generating new cultural frames of action. The researcher should simultaneously consider the content of strategic change, the context in which the organization evolves, and the concomitant processes that unfold. These three core elements become politically merged into a holistic sequence of events that display a certain persistence of change. The momentary power dynamics or political agility of handling certain change periods is less important than the vision of leadership during times of change, leadership that enjoys a certain long-term continuity and manages to merge the organization's culture with its contexts as they evolve over time.

In Chapter Twelve, Edward H. Bowman tries to place the Pettigrew approach into a more encompassing framework, containing, for example, descriptive and normative treatments. He argues that Pettigrew is highly descriptive and falls short on prescription. Shortcomings of intensive, in-depth case studies are reviewed and that most authors have focused on the process of strategic decision making and that they differ widely in defining the unit of analysis and in the discipline background that characterizes them. Yet, there is an interesting balance between chapters that display a positive or normative bias and those that reveal a strong preference for research in the process mode.

## Acknowledgments

This book is based on a symposium organized with the help of Allen Lau, James Lester, and Bertram King of the Office of Naval Research, which financed the symposium. The Strategy Research Center at Columbia University and the Jones Center at the Wharton School of the University of Pennsylvania also gave support to this endeavor. The book was compiled, revised, and edited during my stay at the Netherlands Institute for Advanced Studies. Its support is accepted gratefully. The contributors to the volume all took part in the symposium, and their chapters represent original essays in the field of strategic decision making. Their commitment and cooperation in writing and revising their essays made this book possible.

Those who worked behind the scenes, before, during, and after the symposium, also deserve mention. Philip Halperin acted as my understudy in the United States while I stayed at the Netherlands Institute for Advanced Study, where the book was compiled. Marina Voerman provided exceptional secretarial support, far beyond a secretary's usual tasks. Finally, my wife, Ria, performed monklike labor in compiling, checking, and double-checking the bibliography. To her I dedicate this book.

*Philadelphia, Pennsylvania*
*September 1984*                                      Johannes M. Pennings

# Contents

# The Authors

Johannes M. Pennings is associate professor in the Department of Management at the Wharton School, University of Pennsylvania. He received his B.A. degree (1965) from Utrecht University in sociology, his M.A. degree (1968) from Leiden University in sociology, and his Ph.D. degree (1973) from the University of Michigan in organizational psychology.

Pennings' major research activities have focused on determinants of organizational effectiveness and on aspects of the organization-environment interface. At the present time, Pennings' research deals with technological innovations, with particular emphasis on the applications of microelectronics in complex organizations. He has written on the internal and external factors that account for variations in organization designs and their effectiveness correlates, the nature and consequences of interlocking directorates, the strategic reasons for vertical information, the environmental conclusiveness of entrepreneurship, and organizational culture and environment. Pennings' books include *New*

*Perspectives on Organizational Effectiveness* (1977, with Paul S. Goodman), *Interlocking Directorates* (1980), and *Decision Making: An Organizational Behavior Approach* (1983). A new book, *Strategy Implementation*, is forthcoming.

**Chris Argyris** is James Bryant Conant Professor of Education and Organizational Behavior at Harvard University. He received his A.B. degree (1947) from Clark University in psychology, his M.A. degree (1949) from Kansas University in economics and psychology, and his Ph.D. degree (1951) from Cornell University in organizational behavior. Argyris's research has focused on the unintended consequences for individuals of formal organizational structures; ways of changing organizations, especially the behavior of executives; the role of the social scientist as researcher and interventionist; and human reasoning as the basis for diagnosis and action.

**Edward H. Bowman** is Reginald H. Jones Professor of Corporate Management at the Wharton School, University of Pennsylvania. He has been comptroller of Yale University and dean at Ohio State, as well as assistant to the president of Honeywell's computer company. He holds academic degrees from M.I.T., the University of Pennsylvania, Ohio State University, and Yale University.

**Richard J. Butler** is senior lecturer in organizational analysis at the Management Centre, University of Bradford, England. He received his B.Sc. degree (1962) from the University of Southampton in engineering and spent a number of years working in industry as an engineer. He then received his M.Sc. degree (1968) from Loughborough University of Technology in management studies and his Ph.D. degree (1973) from the Graduate School of Management, Northwestern University, in organizational behavior.

**Colin Camerer** is assistant professor in the Department of Decision Sciences at the Wharton School, University of Pennsylvania. He earned his B.A. degree (1977) from Johns Hopkins University in quantitative studies and his M.B.A. (1979) and Ph.D. (1981) degrees from the University of Chicago in finance and behavioral decision theory, respectively. Camerer's research interests include individual irrationality in markets, expert judgment, and corporate strategy.

**David Cray** is assistant professor of human resource management in the School of Business at Carleton University, Ottawa, Canada. He received his B.A. degree from New College and his M.S. and Ph.D. degrees from the University of Wisconsin, all in sociology. He is currently involved in a study of the allocation of control between Canadian subsidiaries and their American parents.

**John M. Dutton** is professor of management and organization at the Graduate School of Business Administration, New York University, where he also directs the Policy Studies Option in the M.B.A. Program and is active in the doctoral and executive education programs. He received his B.S. degree (1952) from the University of New Hampshire and his M.B.A. degree (1957) from Harvard University.

**Deborah L. Gladstein** is assistant professor of organizational behavior at the Amos Tuck School of Business Administration, Dartmouth College. She received her B.A. and M.S. degrees (1976, 1977) from the University of Pennsylvania in psychology and her Ph.D. degree (1982) from Columbia University in organizational behavior. Gladstein's main research activities have been in the area of small group performance and decision making.

**Richard J. Hermon-Taylor** is a vice-president at The Boston Consulting Group. He received his B.A. degree (1963) from Cambridge University in chemical engineering and his M.B.A. from Harvard Graduate School of Business Administration. Hermon-Taylor has been involved with research on the subject of change as part of ongoing efforts at The Boston Consulting Group in this area.

**David J. Hickson** is Ralph Yablon Professor of Organizational Analysis at the University of Bradford Management Centre, England, and an associate of the Centre for Organizational Research of the Commercial University, Milan, Italy. He qualified professionally as a corporation administrator (ACIS) in 1954 and in personnel management (AIPM) in 1958. He received a master's degree by research (M.Sc. Tech) from the University of Manchester Institute of Science and Technology in 1960, and in 1974 he was awarded an honorary doctoral degree by the University of Umea, Sweden. Hickson's primary research has centered on the structures of organizations, intraorganizational power, and the processes of strategic decision making.

**Roger Hudson** is a doctoral candidate in the Department of Strategic Management and Organization at the University of Minnesota. He received his B.A. degree in urban studies and his M.B.A. degree from the University of Minnesota. His current research interest is the formation of interorganizational relationships as a means of strategy implementation.

**Irving L. Janis** is professor of psychology at Yale University. He received his Ph.D. degree (1948) from Columbia University and recently received the Kurt Lewin Memorial Award for social psychological research from the Society for the Psychological Study of Social Issues and the Distinguished Scientific Contributions Award from the American Psychological Association.

**Paul R. Lawrence** is Wallace Donham Professor of Organizational Behavior at the Harvard Business School. He received his B.A. degree (1943) from Albion College and his M.B.A. (1947) and D.C.S. (1950) degrees from Harvard University. Lawrence's main research has been on organizational adaptation.

**Peter Lorange** is professor and chair of the Department of Management at the Wharton School, University of Pennsylvania, and director of Wharton's Center for International Business Studies. He received his undergraduate degree from the Norwegian School of Economics and Business, his M.A. degree from Yale University in operations management, and his Ph.D. degree from Harvard University in business administration. Lorange has written extensively on the subject of corporate planning and strategic management.

**Kenneth R. MacCrimmon** is E. D. MacPhee Professor of Management at the University of British Columbia. He received his B.S. (1959), M.B.A. (1960), and Ph.D. (1965) degrees from the University of California, Los Angeles, in mathematical and economic aspects of management. His current research includes experimental strategic management, generalizations of expected utility theory, problem-solving heuristics, and decision interdependence.

**Geoffrey R. Mallory** is a research fellow in the Organizational Analysis Research Unit at the University of Bradford Management Centre, England. He received his B.Sc. degree (1975) from

the University of Bradford and his M.A. degree (1976) from the
University of Leeds, and he is currently completing a Ph.D. thesis
at Bradford on speed of decision making.

**Lawrence B. Mohr** is professor of political science and public
policy at the University of Michigan. He received his A.B. degree
(1951) from the University of Chicago in English, his M.P.A. degree
(1963) from the University of Michigan in public administration,
and his Ph.D. degree (1966) from the University of Michigan in
political science. His primary research areas are organization theory
and program evaluation.

**William H. Newman** is chair of the Strategy Research Center
at the Graduate School of Business, Columbia University. He
received his B.A. degree (1930) from Friends University, Wichita,
Kansas, and his Ph.D. degree (1934) from the University of Chicago.
A past president of the Academy of Management, Newman is also
a fellow in the International Academy of Management.

**Richard Normann** is founder and chairman of the Service
Management Group, an international consulting company specializing in strategy and business development in organizations producing services rather than goods. He received his M.B.A. (1966) and
a doctoral degree in business administration in (1975), both from
the University of Lund, Sweden (where he is currently holding part-
time professorship). Normann's main research activities center
around two areas: leadership for growth and innovation and the
management of service organizations.

**Andrew M. Pettigrew** is professor of organizational behavior
at the School of Industrial and Business Studies, University of
Warwick, England. He is also on the editorial board of the
Administrative Science Quarterly and a member of the Industry and
Employment Committee of the Economic and Social Research
Council. Pettigrew received his B.A. degree (1965) from Liverpool
University and his Ph.D. degree (1970) from Manchester University.

**James Brian Quinn** is William and Josephine Buchanan
Professor of Management at the Amos Tuck School of Business
Administration, Dartmouth College. He received his B.S. degree
(1948) from Yale University in engineering, his M.B.A. degree
(1951) from Harvard University, and his Ph.D. degree (1958) from
Columbia University. He also holds an honorary degree from

Dartmouth College. Quinn's main research activities have been in the fields of formulating and implementing strategies, management of technological change, entrepreneurship, and innovation.

**William H. Starbuck** is ITT Professor of Creative Management at New York University and currently serves on the editorial boards of Administrative Science Quarterly, the Academy of Management Review, the Journal of Management Studies, and the Scandinavian Journal of Management Studies. He received his A.B. degree (1956) from Harvard University in physics and his M.S. (1959) and Ph.D. (1964) degrees from Carnegie Institute of Technology in industrial administration.

**David J. Teece** is professor of business administration and director, Center for Research in Management, University of California, Berkeley. He received his Ph.D. degree (1975) from the University of Pennsylvania in economics. Teece's main research activities are in the field of industrial organization, with particular focus on the internal economics of the enterprise. In addition, he has a long-standing interest in the economies of technological change.

**Andrew H. Van de Ven** is 3M Professor of Human Systems Management and director of the Strategic Management Research Center at the University of Minnesota. He obtained his undergraduate degree from St. Norbert College in De Pere, Wisconsin, and his M.B.A. and Ph.D. degrees from the University of Wisconsin at Madison. He is currently principal investigator of a major longitudinal research program on the management of innovation that is supported in part by a grant from the U.S. Office of Naval Research.

**David C. Wilson** is a research fellow in organizational analysis at the University of Bradford Management Centre, England, where he is currently conducting research into the strategies and structures of British voluntary organizations. He is a member of the European Group for Organizational Studies (EGOS) and is also editorial assistant of the journal *Organization Studies*. He received his B.A. (1974) and M.A. (1975) degrees from the University of Leeds in management studies and his Ph.D. degree (1980) from the University of Bradford in organizational strategy.

**Sidney G. Winter** is professor of economics and management at Yale University. He is also a fellow of the Econometric Society and founding co-editor of the *Journal of Economic Behav-*

*ior and Organization.* Winter received his B.A. degree (1956) from Swarthmore College and his M.A. (1957) and Ph.D. degrees (1964) from Yale University, all in economics. His primary research interests are in the areas of firm behavior, technological change, and the economics of organization.

# Organizational Strategy and Change

*New Views on Formulating
and Implementing
Strategic Decisions*

# Introduction:
# On the Nature
# and Theory
# of Strategic Decisions

## Johannes M. Pennings

*Strategic decision making, strategic choice, strategic planning,* or simply *strategy*—all are treated as equivalent terms for a generic organizational phenomenon. While this volume chiefly concerns the choice behavior of business firms, it will become clear that strategic choice is also discernible in other types of organizations. We believe that organizations such as those involved in health care, education, arts, government, and welfare often establish a distinct posture toward their environment, which is a decisive feature of strategy. A comparative perspective, where patterns of strategic decision making are generic rather than idiosyncratic to the great variety of organizational types, is already emerging.

    The term *strategy* originates from the military sciences. One could describe strategic decision making within the military frameworks of von Clausewitz or Mao Zedung and construe organizations as sets of fluid, mobile, and versatile resources that the strategists can deploy to obtain a decisive result. The very notion of strategy has become a frequently used analogy in economics, political science, and organization theory. The *Oxford English Dictionary* defines strategy as the "art of war" and "the art of so moving and disposing troops as to impose upon the enemy, the place and time and conditions for the fighting preferred by oneself." The implication for organizational strategy is that ideas from von Clausewitz or Mao Zedung could have validity for prescribing the action of corporate strategists.

The military analogy is limited, however, because, unlike mobile and flexible armies, organizations are comparatively sluggish, inert, clumsy, and fixed in place and time. Strongly stated, organizations are not only entrenched physically, in that they operate from within a spatial, geographic infrastructure; they are often entrenched in a particular industrial or service sector, tied to clients, suppliers, governmental agencies, and financial institutions, are saddled with plants, equipment, and labor commitments, and thus find themselves attached to a particular posture. Their prevailing "personality" or culture has the effect of further strengthening the inertial forces (Pettigrew, 1979). Applying such a military concept to organizations in order to describe their posture to the environment might therefore be a somewhat inadequate analogy.

Indeed, organizational strategy is an elusive concept that is surrounded by a good deal of ambiguity. Given its military linguistic roots, one may distinguish strategy from tactics, which presumably have a short-term and relatively minor impact on the course of events, but in the various relevant literatures, *strategy* has acquired numerous meanings: (1) It is a statement of intent that constrains or directs subsequent activities (*explicit* strategy). (2) It is an action of major impact that constrains or directs subsequent activities (*implicit* strategy). (3) It is a "rationalization" or social construction that gives meaning to prior activities (*rationalized* strategy).

As proactive behavior, strategy is typically a plan, often formalized in some document that contains a mission statement and a set of objectives and also frequently spells out a game plan with specific allocation of resources. Organizations, however, may not have formulated such a plan, even though one might discern a trend-setting action that has far-reaching effects on subsequent behavior, including the allocation of resources, definition of priorities, and patterns of behavior. Many of the conventional business policy textbooks espouse the first view and portray strategy as a linear sequel of choices triggered by a plan, which is reformulated during every planning period (compare Newman and Logan, 1955). The implicit view, which is more recent, seeks to uncover a pattern of choices, a configuration of moves, from examining an organization's history or from comparing the behavior of various organizations. One might discern a distinct trend, almost as if it were initiated by an explicit strategy, or one might discern certain differences between organizations—for example, their degree of specialization—and pretend that they are a reflection of prior planning activities. If there were strategic plans, an explicit strategy, then the notions of explicit and implicit strategy would overlap. Some organizations do not engage in strategic planning, do not have a strategic planning unit; still more frequently, organizations might have institutionalized a planning cycle with plans at the beginning, but the plans differ from what one can observe retroactively. Explicit and implicit strategy are, then, two different things (Pennings, 1985).

The third meaning of strategy—or the school of thought that stresses it—is relatively recent. There is no "objective strategy" out there, but only a cognitive representation, residing in the heads of people. It is associated with phenomenological or interpretative schools of thought, which have become increasingly in vogue. A common assumption holds that organizations consist of people whose collective experience leads to convictions that represent their image of their organization and its strategy. The strategy or the specific activities attached to it—strategic planning, budgeting, meetings—become increasingly ideational or even transformed into myths, ceremonies, and rituals. The strategy, as external posture, as organizational identity or mission, becomes a social construction of reality, to use Berger and Luckmann's (1966) term. It has been reviewed by Broms and Gamberg (1983) and Hall and Saias (1980).

The coexistence of the three meanings of strategy, clearly discernible in the literature, has also affected the state of practice. In the theoretical and empirical literature (to be reviewed shortly), one can begin to see some polarization. The explicit view is gradually being replaced by the implicit view; the recent vogue in interpretative social science is now also making inroads in the area of strategy and is beginning to obtain greater legitimacy. In the following pages, the three views will recur frequently.

In view of this conceptual disagreement, it is rather difficult to provide examples of strategy or strategic decision making. If strategy is an external posture, the result of a trend-setting plan or salient action, which locks an organization into a long-term trajectory, the example would focus on the trend-setting event or on its enduring aftermath pattern. The event might be embedded in a stream of events, and identification of the strategy shaping events might be tenuous; it might also hinge on the self-interpretative activity of the organization. Often, it may be a crisis situation that provokes a decision leading to a change in the past strategy toward a new direction in the future. Histories tend to be punctuated through such periods of transition, and they also evoke the cognitive punctuations that people use to structure their time perspectives. One might focus on cases in the public or private sector.

Consider events such as the Cuban Missile Crisis in 1962, the toppling of the Allende government in Chile, or the invasion of Grenada in 1983. Are the associated actions part of the Monroe Doctrine—an explicit strategy enunciated by President Monroe in the nineteenth century? One could construe this doctrine as a manifestation of U.S. foreign strategy in Latin America. The decision surrounding the Cuban Missile Crisis has been scrutinized by a variety of decision analysts (compare Allison, 1971; Janis and Mann, 1977; Hafner, 1977). Was the decision a strategic decision in the sense of committing the United States to one particular course of subsequent actions, such as those in Chile, El Salvador, or Grenada? Or was it a continuation of a previously articulated strategy, as conveyed by the Monroe Doctrine? If the strategy was different from its nineteenth-century prelude, one could label the Kennedy decision toward the naval blockade of Cuba as a strategic decision, in that it represented a clear shift, or so-called turnaround strategy—the Monroe Doctrine ("America for the Americans") was supplanted by a doctrine to contain the Russian influence in the

West. Decisions that reaffirm an existing external posture are not so strategically relevant.

As a doctrine, a strategy is discernible from mission statements, perhaps written down in "Pentagon papers" and possibly disseminated by public announcements (explicit strategy); it is also discernible by investigating the decisions of a Kennedy administration, including the actual diplomatic, military, and socioeconomic moves toward the foreign countries (implicit strategy). It could also be approached by a study of the collective reflections, the sense making that went on during the crises' aftermath (rationalized strategy).

The Cuban Missile Crisis triggered decisions that might be labeled strategic because they set the trend for subsequent activities. Because the crisis conditions are time constraining, tense, and extraordinarily stressful, there is often little opportunity for planning, that is, for making a long-term explicit strategy. It is often the decision provoked by the crisis situation and its subsequent aftermath that permit the identification of a strategy. Thus, the notion of implicit strategy seems more valid, or a more veridical concept. The retroactive sense making that accompanies the events during a crisis situation and thereafter adds another layer of reality to the phenomenon of strategy.

The three views of strategy can also be illustrated by cases in the private sector. Consider horizontal and vertical diversification. The first behavior pertains to the broadening of a firm's product offerings, the second to an expansion into prior or subsequent stages of a vertical chain, from raw materials to end products. In the 1920s, General Motors acquired Fisher Body (vertical integration); recently, it announced a joint venture with Toyota to produce small cars (horizontal diversification). The deliberate intentions revealed in public announcements with subsequent resource commitments can be construed as an explicit strategy. On the other hand, General Motors has incrementally diversified itself from large cars into medium-sized cars, compacts, subcompacts, and small cars. This horizontal diversification has enfolded since the 1950s, and the joint venture with Toyota is merely a small, though significant, step in a stream of decisions that led to a gradual broadening of its product mix. Similarly, the vertical integration that began in the 1920s has become very central in the relationship between General Motors and its supply lines. Presently, General Motors has absorbed many production facilities and has rendered its other suppliers highly captive by making their capital goods and equipment proprietary. In the entire pattern of events, we can infer a directionality such that we speak of an implicit strategy.

Finally, it is not difficult to find manifestations of General Motors' rationalized strategy. Many firms speculate in their annual report about their past and frequently convey some images to give meaning to that past (for example, Staw, McKechnie, and Puffer, 1983; Bettman and Weitz, 1983). Furthermore, "General Motors watchers," regardless of whether it is a clear day, add an incredibly rich array of data to the activities and communications of General Motors and its spokespeople. In short, strategy as external posture can be inferred from General Motors' corporate statements, from certain actions, or from commentaries, gossip, and public relations activities after actions have taken their course.

It is because of these coexisting meanings that it is difficult to gain a grasp on the meaning of strategic decisions. For purposes of present discussions, we consider such actions as vertical integration, market exit, joint ventures, and the like strategic decisions, regardless of whether they are preceded by statements of intent or remain largely implicit. If we focus on such relatively well-bounded decisions, we call them strategic if they have profound implications for organizations. Such decisions are often significant, unstructured, complex, collective, and consequential. Strategic decisions are *significant* because of the magnitude of resources involved. They are *unstructured* in that the problems they solve involve multiple courses of action, each one of which is hard to evaluate. They are *complex* because the solutions are multisided and uncertain in their outcomes. They are *collective* because each solution often hinges on the decisional inputs of the various interest groups that are involved in the decision-making process, whether it is during the process prior to the choice or during its aftermath. Finally, they are *consequential* because they impart distinct and relatively enduring commitments that have profound internal and external ramifications. Attached to these decisions are the collective beliefs, interpretations, myths, and symbols that help the membership to give meaning to them. The endowment with meaning will further accentuate their collective and consequential character.

Defining strategic decision is also difficult on other accounts. The definitional problems are confounded by the confusion about the agent of strategic decision making—whether the agent is an individual or an organization, for example. Furthermore, if strategic decision making is seen as being conducted by organizations, there are widely conflicting frames of reference about the meaning of organizations or the nature of their interacting participants. For example, should we construe the organization as a "machine" or as an "anarchy" (compare Thompson, 1967, and March and Olsen, 1976, respectively), or should we use another metaphor to describe organizations as instruments or arenas of strategic decision making?

Views about the nature of strategy and conceptions or myths about what constitutes an organization or its top decision maker vary with the disciplines that have been involved in strategy, such as economists dealing with organizations as machines (for example, Porter, 1980), while psychologists, political scientists, and anthropologists are inclined to the rationalized strategy notion, with organizations as loosely coupled systems, that is, as anarchies (for example, Weick, 1976).

Among the more applied research fields, we likewise see a diversity of tradition, including game theory, industrial economics, marketing, and operations research. While these fields are diverse and relatively idiosyncratic, there appears to be a growing interest among scholars and theorists in examining the concept of strategic decision making more closely and exploring the contributions in other areas. They seek to understand the process and the resultant outcomes and ultimately strive toward prescriptions for sound strategies. The literature on strategic decision making is expanding rapidly. Practitioners likewise have become concerned with understanding the process of decision making or the evaluation of its outcomes. They have not yet had much help from academic researchers. The research to date has been primarily descriptive; it has not yielded many prescriptive statements for strategic decision making. Traditional explanations for "successful" strategies are often based on conventional wisdom and what Simon (1947) has called proverbs. However, those who observe the formation of strategy are hard pressed to provide adequate answers to questions about optimal decision making. Thus, practitioners have to await further theory and research before they can achieve greater probabilities in making good rather than bad strategy.

There is a need for better delineating strategy and strategy-related attributes. We need better decision theories, which have a greater explanatory power and which can provide the underpinnings for an engineering of decisions. Should we adopt fairly narrow definitions of strategy and focus on specific, well-bounded decision events, such as the naval blockade during the Cuban Missile Crisis or the General Motors announcement of a joint venture with Toyota? Should we consider a stream of events and try to map them into a configuration, as Mintzberg (1978) and Karpik (1972) have suggested? Or should we embrace the approach of interpretive, phenomenological social scientists and consider strategic decisions as socially constructed reality, whose underlying structure has to be exposed (for example, Hall and Saias, 1980)?

From these considerations, it is clear that strategy can be defined very broadly or very narrowly. One can include all decisions that are embedded in some theoretically derived gestalt—strategic decisions in the sense of directing and constraining subsequent behaviors as well as operational or implementation decisions that are contingent upon the prior defined premises. Or one might adopt a more narrow perspective and restrict strategy to those decisions that have a subsequent constraining influence, are consequential, are unstructured, and so on. For analytical and conceptual reasons, it is preferable to define strategy more narrowly and to decompose inferred strategies into those decision chunks that are consequential for the intended or emergent strategy.

Several other issues can be raised. Before reviewing a set of issues, it may be helpful to give a brief overview of the theoretical and empirical literature and to provide a glimpse of the state of practice.

## Theoretical Literature

In spite of the growing interest in strategic decision making, the conceptual level of the pertinent literature is still in a preliminary state. There are no well-articulated theories. There is little consensus about the meaning of strategic decision making, and the number of definitions varies with the number of authors who have been occupied with the concept.

Underlying differences in the conceptualization of strategic choice are different views about the nature of decision making, which implicitly determine the theoretical delineation of strategy. In one view, strategic decision making is mostly associated with its content or outcome. Others conceptualize strategic decision making in terms of a process that leads up to a decisional outcome. Conceptualizations of strategic process also vary widely, as do the nature, role, and behavior of the decision-making agent.

In fact, in the vast body of strategic decision-making literature, there is one class that is associated with the *private sector* and deals primarily with its *content* of strategy—for example, the choice of market segments or the extent of vertical integration. A different and overlapping subset of literature is heavily associated with the *public sector* and is mostly concerned with the *process* leading to a decision, as well as its aftermath, including the implementation stage. The former is known under such labels as *business policy* or *strategic management* (Schendel and Hofer, 1979; Hofer and Schendel, 1978), while the latter is known as *public policy*. To some degree, the two subsets of literature have other contrasting characteristics. Thus, many writers in business policy depict strategic decision making as a linear, orderly set of steps with strategies executed by a rational organization (Andrews, 1980; Lorange and Vancil, 1977; Ansoff, 1965). They typically espouse the *explicit strategy* definition, as mentioned at the onset of this chapter. This view is also quite prescriptive, embodying a number of principles for strategic decision making. Organizations must conduct environmental scanning and perform thorough analyses of their own strengths and weaknesses in order to position themselves in a way that minimizes environmental threats and maximizes opportunities. Strategic decision making leads to an optimum meshing of organization and environment.

In some of the conventional literature, there is an inclination to anthropomorphize the organization by imputing rationality to it or to describe its strategic decision making as being conducted by a powerful executive who directs the organization like an ocean liner, taking audacious, risky choices to move the organization toward some future visionary state (Drucker, 1964; Hofer and Schendel, 1978; Yavitz and Newman, 1982). Issues of implementation, such as gaining commitment from relevant subunits and making corrections whenever deviations are detected, are described with mechanistic, rational metaphors. The entrepreneur is the organization, and knowing his or her choice behavior is understanding organizational choice behavior. Similar but more moderate versions of this school of thought have been articulated by critics of contingency theory, who claim that managers have considerable latitude in the choice of location, market, and other external conditions (compare Child, 1972; Schreyögg, 1980).

The image of the organizational actor as a rational, calculating being contrasts rather sharply with conceptualizations that stress the prevalence of multiple groups, subunits, and diverse individuals who are involved in strategic decision making. The organization as a holistic entity is replaced by a notion of organization as comprising diverse and conflicting components (Astley and others, 1982). This notion prevails in the public-policy literature on strategic decision making, which is mostly descriptive, seeking to document how strategic decisions are arrived at.

However, it is interesting to note a growing concern for process issues in the private-sector literature. There is a newer trend among strategic management writers to depict strategic decisions as messy, disorderly, and disjointed processes around which competing factions contend (for example, Mintzberg, 1978; Quinn, 1978, 1980; Ruefli and Sarrazin, 1981; Murray, 1978). Much of this literature is founded on the notion of cognitive limits of rationality, as described in the early publications of Herbert Simon and his colleagues (Simon, 1947; March and Simon, 1958; Cyert and March, 1963). Much influence is also due to Lindblom (Lindblom, 1959; Braybrooke and Lindblom, 1963), who conceptualizes organizational decision making as an incremental process of muddling through (as distinct from the linear rational perspective), since different subunits display a disorderly proliferation of preference orderings and divergent views of cause-effect relations. Scenarios in this area point to organizations whose participants are players in "an implementation game" (Bachrach, 1977) who, individually or jointly, are ill informed, averse to risk, parochial, rule adhering, and constrained by short-term time horizons. Strategic decision making provides the stage on which they can reaffirm their stakes, thus paralyzing their organization and preventing it from making the requisite swift moves in response to environmental contingencies. At the most, organizations can engage in "grafting procedures" (Mintzberg, 1978) in which the top decision makers can slightly modify the organization's existing momentum in response to external pressures.

The *private-public* and *rational-incremental* distinctions used to coincide with the distinction between *outcome* and *process* of strategic decision making. In the literature on private-sector organizations, many of the pertinent publications focused on the outcomes of strategic decision making, while there was relatively little concern for the process. In fact, issues of process were often relegated to the adjacent field of organization theory. The public-policy literature, in contrast, often takes the outcome of decisions for granted and focuses on the issues of implementation. The content of the decision—one might say the initial step of an implicit or explicit strategy—is often made and conveyed by a different organization—for example, the legislature, which mandates organizations to implement programs. Naturally, issues of implementation unfold analogously in private-sector organizations, but the areas of strategy formulation and implementation are only gradually merged to the extent that strategy researchers incorporate both areas in their inquiry. The above-mentioned strong trend to become less prescriptive and rationalistic and to adopt a more descriptive perspective will undoubtedly further increase efforts to understand the process of strategic decision making. Occasional attempts in this direction are incomplete (for example, Miles and Snow, 1978) or rudimentary (for example, Hall and Saias, 1980). Miles and Snow developed a strategic content typology and reviewed the probable processes that are associated with those types. However, their concern for process outweighs the discussion of content, so that a full balance is not accomplished. Only disappointing degrees of progress in theorizing about organizational strategic decision making seem to have been made.

It has been more than thirty-five years since Herbert Simon (1947) first formulated his ideas on organizational decision making. Both the conjectures about decision making and decision making itself resemble the efforts of Sisyphus in his quest to push the stone to the top of the hill. Simon quarried a stone that he and his colleagues set out to push to the crest; the stone consists of that elusive phenomenon, organizational decision making. However, there are divergent perspectives associated with different disciplines or subdisciplines whose representatives have been using discordant frames of reference. There appears little cumulative knowledge, and the crest of the hill is not yet in sight, let alone what will appear beyond the crest of the hill.

Often, the very efforts of strategic decision making in organizations resemble the endless efforts of pushing a stone to some distant and inaccessible end point. The sequential, linear, and incremental moves that are contemplated in the here and now are far removed from that terminal point about which top decision makers have only vague conceptions. Often, it is not just a single corporate Sisyphus, but a large number of his subordinates who assist him, help him in exploring various alternative routes with alternative means, thus imposing horrendous problems of coordination and conflict resolution. Within the bounded-rationality perspective, this metaphor depicts the process as evoking discordant motives, biased perceptions, and institutionalized habits, which lead to a multiplicity of sequential decisions that do not quite add up to a strategy. Furthermore, the "adding up" can often be accomplished through a near-infinite number of ways. Scholars who attempt to conceptualize this extraordinarily complex process face an *infinite regress* problem as they seek to model the numerous avenues that decision makers have or might have considered in proceeding incrementally to a strategy, whether explicit or implicit, and perhaps epistemologically accessible only in a socially constructed sense.

The history of strategic decision-making theory reveals this Sisyphean entrapment unmistakably. At the present time, the accomplishments of such authors as Lindblom (1959), Wildavsky (1979), Williamson (1975), Axelrod (1976b), and March (March and Olsen, 1976) stand out, perhaps because they draw bounded rationality and incrementalism into the core of their framework, thus acknowledging the inability to relate intermittent small steps in the decision-making process to some global terminal objective. They focus on intermediate outcomes and intermediate processes of decision making, thereby partially removing themselves from the discouraging examples set by others. Compared with rational models of strategic decision making, such models are bound to be less elegant or logically less consistent, but in the final analysis, they might be more promising and more conducive to the advancement of empirical research.

## State of the Empirical Literature

Given the limitations of this introductory chapter, it is rather difficult to give an exhaustive survey of the empirical literature, especially if we define that area broadly. Not only might we include empirical investigations in both the public and the private sectors, but we might also make reference to the contributions of management-consultant firms and the organizations that are themselves involved in the praxis of strategic decision making. From a historical point of view, it is fair to state that many of the first observations were recorded by business firms or governmental agencies or by the management-consultant firms they hired, before academic researchers became sufficiently active to make a visible contribution.

In the private sector, there were firms such as General Electric, Royal Dutch Shell, and Texas Instruments, which developed their own in-house planning and strategic decision-making heuristics. They introduced the portfolio analysis as a tool for decision making by corporate planning groups and divisions of the organization. For example, General Electric created a "business screen" for each of their divisions, which would reveal its industry attractiveness and business position as indicated by such factors as market growth, market share, or product leadership (Lorange, 1980). Royal Dutch Shell established a "directional policy matrix," which defines critical parameters such as access routes of raw materials and market position of chemical by-products (Shell Chemicals, 1975). Texas Instruments conducted research on the so-called learning curve as a key ingredient for business policy (Lorange and Vancil, 1977). These firms developed close relationships with management consulting firms, whose practice and research gave rise to various new insights about strategic decision making. While the research was highly pragmatic, it led to the formulation of decision heuristics, such as the timing of the decision—when to develop, slow down, or terminate a particular project. General Electric's notion of "business screen" became the cornerstone for the Strategic Planning Institute (SPI) and guided the collection, storage, and interpretation of Profit Impact of Market Strategies (PIMS) information (Anderson and Paine, 1978). Texas Instruments' activities had a great impact on the portfolio research of the Boston Consulting Group. Recently, academic researchers at various universities have gained access to these data archives to replicate and expand the research of the SPI staff. (Compare Anderson and Paine, 1978; Schoeffler, Buzzell, and Heany, 1974; MacMillan, Hambrick, and Day, 1982; Woo and Cooper, 1981.) Much of this recent research is data driven (that is, heavily inductive) and awaits pollination from pertinent paradigmatic developments in the decision sciences, such as economics and sociology.

In the public sector, a somewhat analogous trend could be witnessed when the experimentation of planning tools triggered a flurry of consulting and research activities that continue into the present time. The creation and introduction of tools such as "planning, programming, budgeting system" (PPBS) and "zerobase budgeting" set the stage for quasi experiments and program evaluation opportunities, which greatly enhanced understanding of the nature of organizational decision making (compare Wildavsky, 1979). While streams of research from the realm of practice to the realm of positive science are proceeding, we can characterize the realm of science as a rich mosaic of multiple perspectives around which numerous investigators have organized themselves. One can easily identify various schools of thought (for example, Allison, 1971; Jemison, 1981; Camerer, 1982). Each of the prevailing perspectives has triggered a substantial stream of empirical investigations, but few researchers have sought to combine them into more encompassing frameworks. The failure to synthesize paradigms has led to the current disarray of empirical research.

As an example of the failure to consider multiple perspectives, take the case of private-sector strategy research. There are several schools or groupings of empirical research that have refrained from cross-fertilization. These schools include those based on the *strategy-structure paradigm* (Chandler, 1962), *institutional economics* (Coase, 1937), *the bounded-rationality notion* (Cyert and March, 1963), *resource-exchange theory* (Pfeffer and Salancik, 1978), and *population ecology* (Aldrich, 1979). These perspectives have led to a flurry of empirical research activities.

Alfred Chandler (1962), a business historian, is associated with the strategy-structure paradigm. He examined the evolution of large corporations and the connection over time among environment, strategy, and organization structure. His historical analysis of four corporations suggested that increased strategic diversity, from a one-product to a multiproduct focus, was more effectively dealt with through divisional organization designs. The introduction of such designs was often impeded by organizational inertia and commitments to the status quo. His research triggered a major stream of research (for example, Wrigley, 1970; Channon, 1973; Stopford and Wells, 1972; Rumelt, 1974; Miles and Snow, 1978).

This stream of research was paralleled by industrial economists who followed the paradigm of institutional economics (Coase, 1937). The paradigm has focused on enduring patterns of industry structure, such as concentration, size distribution of firms, and height of entry barriers in relation to prevailing types of organizational conduct. Conduct is manifested in decisions such as pricing, innovation, vertical integration, and advertising. This area is vigorous in pursuing empirical findings (for example, Scherer, 1970; Caves, 1980; Porter, 1980; Teece, 1980, 1981b; Spence, 1974, 1977; Williamson, 1975; Sutton, 1980) and is somewhat akin to the emergent paradigm of population ecology, which draws its analogy from biology (compare Nelson and Winter, 1982). Institutional economics is also akin to resource-dependence research in organization theory (for example, Pfeffer and Salancik, 1978), where organizations are viewed as establishing favorable exchange relationships with interdependent actors in their external environment.

Researchers have also focused on populations of firms and their interplay over time. The unit of analysis is a community of organizational species where each one of them occupies distinct resource "niches." While the niche metaphor is often used by industrial economists to denote strategic posture, it is important to recognize that the latter impute a volitional disposition to the strategically interdependent organizations that prevail in concentrated industries. That is, organizations in oligopolies are viewed as being able to secure the necessary external control. Population ecologists have a deterministic bias and stress the ecological factors in the formation of niches and selection of occupying firms, allowing them little, if any, "strategic choice" (compare Child, 1972). A central issue in population-ecology studies is the degree of specialization, or "niche width" (McPherson, 1983), which has heuristic value in predicting the competitiveness of an organization's environment. If that environment is volatile or highly diffuse, a narrow niche width is not attractive. Naturally, the concepts of niche and niche width seem quite amenable to a description of "environmental posture" or "environmental focus," concepts that have been used to depict the content of an organization's strategy. Relevant studies include Carroll and Delacroix (1982), Brittain and Freeman (1980), Aldrich (1979), McPherson (1983), McKelvey (1982), and Miles and Cameron (1982). The Miles and Cameron (1982) study in particular represents a pioneering effort to apply concepts of population ecology to issues of corporate strategy in the major U.S. tobacco firms.

Still a different wave of pertinent research has been associated with the bounded-rationality paradigm (March and Simon, 1958). This stream has been preoccupied mostly with the process of strategic decision making, treating its final outcome as relatively secondary. In fact, the outcome is sometimes treated as a cognitive construction for retroactive sense making (Weick, 1979; Cohen, March, and Olsen, 1972). Individuals in organizations have limited capacity for storing and processing information, precluding them from considering all the relevant aspects. They "satisfice" by setting "good enough" instead of optimum standards of performance, which fit their limited views of reality. An increasing number of strategy researchers espouse this paradigm as the most viable and valid approach (MacCrimmon, 1984; Mintzberg, 1978; Frederickson and Mitchell, 1984; Davis, Dempster, and Wildavsky, 1966; Quinn, 1980). This tradition is quite akin to research in the area of cognitive social psychology, which seeks to delineate the systematic shortcomings in human judgments (for example, Tversky and Kahneman, 1973, 1974; Nisbett and Wilson, 1977; Nisbett and Ross, 1980; Slovic and Lichtenstein, 1971; Janis, 1979; Janis and Mann, 1977). These shortcomings are discernible not only from the findings of controlled research settings of social psychologists but also and even more so from the unstructured settings where strategic choices are made (Cyert and March, 1963; Mintzberg, Rasinghani, and Théorêt, 1976).

The bounded-rationality paradigm has also some affinity with political research of organizational decision making and with investigators who view strategic decision making as opportunities for consolidating or undermining the status quo. Bounded rationality and power are mutually relevant concepts for strategic-decision-making research.

This relevancy can be inferred from concepts that are related to bounded rationality, such as "suboptimization" and "quasi resolution of conflict" (Cyert and March, 1963). These concepts have an implicit if not explicit reference to organizations as being differentiated into subgroups that vie for power and whose interests are parochial and not always congruent. James Thompson's *Organizations in Action* (1967) has greatly legitimized the metaphor of organizations as machines that are designed to minimize the undesirable consequences of bounded rationality and power differentials. This view of organization is highly attractive for strategic-choice conceptualizations, as it postulates the presence of "dominant coalition," which can be construed as the agent for defining the organization's long-term posture. The concept of dominant coalition avoids the reification of an organization as a rational actor whose participants act in unison; it also suggests that organizations adopt a course of action that is the result of a negotiation among internal and external interest groups.

Perhaps the research on organizational power (for example, Hickson and others, 1971; Pfeffer, 1981c; March and Olsen, 1976; Bacharach and Lawler, 1980; Crozier, 1964) might eventually become one of the central focuses of research on strategic decision making. In view of the complexity of organizations and their environments, the cognitive limits of organizational members, and the uneven distribution of information among them, it seems quite likely that research inspired by the bounded-rationality tradition in conjunction with research on organizational power will become increasingly important. This bold prophecy is motivated partly by the extraordinary difficulties in bridging research on content and process of strategic decision making. As noted earlier, there are a nearly infinite number of avenues to realize some ideal end state, whereas organizations display an inability to absorb and to order ever-increasing amounts of data. As researchers, we are doomed to settle for middle-range research in which global objectives are decomposed into smaller, means-ends punctuations that match the human mind's cognitive capacity (Simon, 1962).

Organizations make incremental moves to eventually reach their strategic objectives. Research could uncover patterns of decision making, and that would both enhance the theory of decision making (Mohr, 1982) and develop the formulation of heuristics that will aid in the design of decision processes (Quinn, 1980; Simon, 1962). The new line of work that seems so promising would doubtless make use of the findings generated by the alternate research traditions, because much of it remains valuable and suggestive for a better understanding of this elusive concept of strategic decision making.

Although we can impose some preference order on the broad set of empirical studies and the paradigms they are associated with, we should recognize that empirical research has not advanced sufficiently to give primacy to any one of these sets of studies. Among efforts to study process or outcome phenomena, we observe competing paradigms, or models. Within the literature of public policy, this is dramatically demonstrated by Allison (1971), who, in his analysis of the Cuban Missile Crisis, contrasted "rational," "bounded-rational," and "political" models for depicting the process of strategic decision making. Allison claimed that a nonroutine, significant decision could be approached with different, mutually exclusive models, where each one exposes alternative relevant aspects of strategic decision making. From a meta-paradigmatic viewpoint, each paradigm highlights alternate dimensions.

Similarly, Mohr (1976) suggested that decision-making processes in the courts can be analyzed according to any of four decision models: rational, bounded rational, garbage can, and political. As in Allison's typology, his rational model has its roots in economic decision theory and stipulates that strategic choice follows logically from an examination of all pertinent alternatives and preferences, where these alternatives and preferences are unambiguous and clearly understood. There is full information about the consequences of actions. Finally, the model anthropomorphizes organizations by assuming that the strategic decision makers enjoy sufficient legitimate power to ensure that their choice will be the organization's choice. The other three models are "subrational," and, depending on the level of abstractness, they can be subsumed under this category. Strategic decisions are subrational because organizational members have limited information-processing capabilities and make decisions piecemeal with the aid of standard operating procedures (bounded-rational model); they often express incompatible, parochial goals and vie for power to satisfy their self-interests (political model); and, finally, these cognitive and political variables might be combined to describe strategic decisions as implicit, haphazard events that render organizations quite anarchistic (garbage-can model). The use of multiple models might have important heuristic and diagnostic values, because they provide alternative postulates about the content or process of strategic decision making. By explicitly stating these postulates, one might become sensitive to the variabilities that surface from contrasting different models. Indeed, they resemble alternate looking glasses that accentuate different aspects of strategic phenomena.

While the concurrent use of multiple paradigms might be healthy, it signals lack of direction in empirical strategy research and causes confusion if their adherents fail to establish a constructive dialogue. The popularity of the garbage-can model (March and Olsen, 1976; Weick, 1979; Pfeffer, 1982) may be due partly to its success in combining elements of several subrational models. Because it combines bounded-rationality and power concepts, it lends further credence to the earlier-stated expectation that such a research focus is more likely to advance systematic knowledge about strategic decision making.

Perhaps the underdeveloped state of the theoretical literature is such that empirical researchers are better off clinging to middle-range theories and satisfying themselves with partial explanations of strategic decision making. We feel, however, that the prevalence of multiple paradigms should not preclude their adherents from attempts to foster integration. Their combined use might lead to more valid findings and permit more prediction about the quality of strategic decision making.

### State of Practice

*Strategy* has become a key term in every major corporation and in many governmental bureaucracies. Organizations conduct "strategic planning" by establishing objectives and a course of action and by allocating resources to meet the objectives. Planning, as the activity by which strategy becomes articulated and implemented, is a multifaceted phenomenon. There is a vast literature ranging from urban economics to resources and social planning. Such a broad phenomenon cannot be discussed within the limits of this chapter. If we limit ourselves, however, to the conduct of strategic planning in organizations, we can provide a brief glance at how the state of practice relates to the current literature.

There are some very good overviews on strategic planning. In the private sector, the practice is well documented by Lorange and Vancil (1977) and Lorange (1980). In the public sector, Wildavsky (1979) has been active in describing and evaluating the planning activities of organizations. The recent public-sector literature covers mostly the shortcomings of planning efforts and seeks to identify the reasons for failure. For example, Wildavsky (1979) and his students have reviewed such systems as zero-based budgeting, where their critique centers around notions of organizational inertia, the inability of decision makers to dissociate themselves from their roles and to become proactive rather than reactive, and the difficulty in dovetailing the plans with their execution. The institutionalization and routinization of formal planning systems might lead to the crystallization of action generators that lead their own life, uncoupled from relevant strategic events (for example, Starbuck, 1983). Actions are triggered not because the planning activities required scanning the internal and external environment for information that induces such actions but by the routinized planning cycles and their rigid deadlines. The planning systems are imposed upon the organization—for example, by legislative move or by executive order—and, although the organizations at various levels are required to synchronize their planning activities, these activities become increasingly ritualized and void of strategic significance.

In the private sector, there is a vast amount of literature on the actual conduct of strategic planning. In this sector, organizations enjoy much more discretion as to whether they will adopt a strategic planning system and what type, what cycle, and what time horizon it will comprise. There are one-year, two-year, and five-year planning cycles. There are "bottom-up" and "top-down" systems; that is, the input for planning decisions might originate at the lower, operational levels and become hierarchically clustered into more encompassing inputs for the higher levels. The reverse happens when firms define strategic objectives that become hierarchically decomposed into objectives with a smaller scope, which fit the level to which they apply. The interdependence of planning among units and levels resides inside the firm. It is here that we see analogies with the public sector, where conglomerates of organizations are interdependent in their planning effort: private firms also synchronize the planning at various levels and units (divisions, departments, or "groups") and integrate the results of planning at various levels and at various time points.

Corporations have disclosed how they have institutionalized the planning process (compare Rothschild, 1976, at General Electric). Among the larger, multiproduct firms, there appears to be some degree of uniformity in their conduct of strategic planning. The uniformity might have been due to the presence of some norm-setting consulting firms, such as the Boston Consulting Group, the Strategic Planning Institute, Booz Allen, or McKinsey. The activities of these firms have not been restricted to the United States but have also extended into Europe and Asia. Presently, most *Fortune*

*500* firms appear to be involved in strategic planning activities as pioneered by corporations such as General Electric.

In the typical case, these firms have developed a product matrix as a decision heuristic in which two or more attributes are used to graph the products onto a grid, a matrix, or a classification scheme. The best-known specimens are those of the Strategic Planning Institute (which originated from General Electric) and the Boston Consulting Group (Rothschild, 1976; Henderson, 1979). The General Electric case is well documented and evaluated.

The General Electric product matrix presupposes that a firm can be decomposed into subunits, called "strategic business units" (SBUs), which are defined in terms of external attributes, such as classes of customers served, organizations they compete with, and so on, and which are sufficiently unique and separate from sister SBUs that they can be treated as profit centers. The SBUs can be plotted on a so-called business screen, where one dimension is a composite of industry features, such as its growth, rate of innovation, and entry barriers, and the other dimension represents their competitive position, such as market share, proprietary knowledge, and product leadership. If one trichotomizes these dimensions, one obtains nine cells that indicate the SBUs' attractiveness for investment. In fact, it becomes the heuristic for classifying them into investment-priority categories.

The SBUs' investment-priority categories can be linked with their resource-allocation plans, and it is at this junction that corporate strategic criteria are a steering and control constraint for the so-called business strategy of each individual SBU. For example, if an SBU goes astray, as inferred from comparing its investment priorities with those that are implied by the corporate plans, intervention is called for, and the SBU will be asked to replan and to re-examine its resource allocations.

The annual planning period at General Electric itself breaks down into two chunks: a strategy-development (January–July) and a resource-allocation/budgeting (August–December) phase. The cycle begins during the first week of January, when a general managers' meeting reviews the strategic issues and the macroeconomic forecasts and arrives at a general blueprint that defines the strategic constraints for the various SBUs. The SBUs' plans are developed during the period from February through May. These plans are reviewed at successive levels, such as the sector management meetings in July. After subsequent deliberations at which sector- and corporate-level decision units settle their disagreements, there follows a preliminary budget session in August, followed by a review of the planning implementations. Final budgets for the corporation and its sectors are drawn up. The planning cycle is complete when the corporate plan is approved and "planning challenges" have been identified.

The second well-known example that merits a brief description is the product-portfolio matrix of the Boston Consulting Group (BCG). In contrast with the General Electric business screen, where the two dimensions represent conglomerates of factors, the BCG matrix is based solely on two attributes, relative market share (the share of a business unit relative to the share of the largest competitor) and market growth (rate of increase of market demand). By splitting these attributes into low and high (at 1 and 10 percent, respectively), one can classify business units as "stars" (high market share–high growth), "cash cows" (high market share–low growth), "question marks" or "problem children" (low market share–high growth), and dogs (low market share–low growth). Naturally, the "stars" are likely candidates for preferential treatment in resource-allocation decisions, receiving cash inflows from "cash cows," whose excess profits are not reinvested there but transferred to "star" units and possibly to "problem-child" units. "Dogs" are prime candidates for divestments. The BCG matrix serves as a heuristic for determining the interdivisional cash flows that underlie the strategic shifts in a corporation's product portfolio. Those shifts are induced partly by the life cycle of the various products, such that older and more mature products are succeeded by newer ones.

In contrast to the business screen, this matrix evokes a much more pronounced external orientation, focusing the attention of strategic decision makers on environmental conditions, such as the rivalry with competing organizations. The General Electric approach and the related sequel of the Strategic Planning Institute are more concerned with internal issues, such as how to dovetail the plans of the various SBUs and how to secure their managers' commitment to corporate strategic objectives. Both approaches to planning, however, can be criticized as being somewhat mechanical and rationalistic—a critique that was also articulated by two employees of a competing management-consulting firm, McKinsey. In their *In Search of Excellence,* Peters and Waterman (1982) wage a vendetta against the rational model of strategic planning, which presumably has been abandoned by the excellent companies. The model is flawed, because it prevents common sense from entering into the definition of strategic plans. Rather, it allows "numerical" analyses to dominate the planning process, so that the chosen alternatives are based on "detached, analytical justifications for all decisions" (p. 20). Naturally, they then proceed to propose a "new theory," which relies on the ideas of Bateson (1972), March and Olsen (1976), and Weick (1979).

Among the corporate executives, there is also a tendency to question the strategic planning activities of the past two decades. It is remarkable, for example, that a recently appointed chief executive officer at General Electric has made several speeches in which he expresses his skepticism about the virtues of well-institutionalized strategic planning systems, which he considers an impediment to organizational innovation and in-house entrepreneurship. One may also note that Richard Hermon-Taylor, one of this volume's contributors, is re-examining the approach of the Boston Consulting Group in its recommendations for strategic change.

By way of contrast, it is also interesting to examine the efforts of various European consulting firms who have tried to dissociate themselves from "mechanistic" models of planning in favor of a more organic approach. Examples include the Service Management Group (Normann, 1984) and Descours, Lecerf, and Parker (Broms and Gamberg, 1983). This latter firm has adopted the assumption that organizations are systems of symbols, values, and myths that can be examined on their deeper logical structure. The methodology is akin to that of structuralism in anthropology, which presumes that all cultures have a deeper structure that revolves around patterns of opposition, such as good-bad, male-female, and rational-mythical. In the same way that a psychoanalyst seeks to uncover the deeper structure of a person's mind, a structuralist exposes a system's culture to its base configuration of polar opposites. The knowledge of the prevailing opposites helps explain how people interpret their reality and how their culture shapes their behavior. Strategic planners and their management consultants ought to likewise analyze their firm's culture by explicating its rudimentary configurations. Strategic change is accomplished by modifying the configurations of organizational values and symbols, because it is through such alterations that people in organizations will acquire new cognitive schemata, which in turn will alter their behavioral dispositions to their work. Strategic plans ought therefore to evolve into a "mantra"—a form of mythical thinking, a "code, that transports everyone's mind onto a mythical plane of what should be, ought to be or what would be good for the company or the organization" (Broms and Gamberg, 1983, p. 490). The strategic planning cycle is therefore a device for managing an organizational culture and, by implication, a device for managing the private cognitive models of strategy that people in organizations carry around in their heads.

Such ideas not only have been expressed by nonconventional European authors but have also obtained increased legitimacy in the United States. This is illustrated not only by Peters and Waterman (1982), in whose book *culture* is a key concept, but also in other publications where culture becomes integrated with the concept of strategy (for example, Deal and Kennedy, 1982). The popular business press has also reported on the increased popularity of the concept of culture, and *Fortune* in 1983 referred to "culture vultures" when it reported that many management-consulting firms have expanded their service offerings by advising on matters of corporate culture.

It is also interesting to note that the recent interest in organization symbolism and cognitive, interpretative views of strategy is legitimizing the practitioners' view of strategy as rationalized strategy at the expense of proactive strategy interpretations, which are associated with explicit or implicit strategy definitions.

## Critical Issues in Strategic Decision Making

Across the various approaches exhibited in this book, the reader will recognize common themes that represent the major challenge to the conceptualization of strategic decision making.

Any new framework should explicitly deal with at least five problems—the nature of strategic decision making, the identification of the proper unit of analysis, the multidisciplinary character of pertinent research, the distinction between positive and normative sciences, and the choice of research strategies.

The first problem to deal with is *the nature of strategic decision making*. Any theoretical development must recognize that strategic decisions are unstructured, complex, collective, and consequential. We should also recognize that strategic decision making can be conceived of as a process, a structure, and an outcome. The notion of process entails the succession of sequentially arranged states. Sometimes authors prefer to talk about strategy as a stream of decisions, suggesting that it may only be arbitrarily punctuated into certain stages. As implied by the earlier discussion, *strategy* or *strategic choice* can be defined in rather extreme opposites, ranging from a fluid, continuous flow of events without beginning or ending to a specific behavior bridging a cognition to its subsequent action. The stream metaphor implies continuity, which is difficult to "atomize" (Mintzberg, 1978). The atomistic view, linking thought to action, suggests a focus on chunks that are lifted out of the stream; it is illustrated by Weick's (1979) so-called "interacts" or "double interacts." Strategic decision making fits the concept of structure in that the sequential steps might be arranged in certain patterns or configurations of cycles of events (Rothschild, 1976; Lorange, 1980). The prevailing cycles may occur with a certain randomness, or they may be highly rigid and predictable (compare March and Olsen, 1976). Finally, strategic decisions are outcomes, the terminal point of a process to which the organization has committed itself. In this meaning, it can be the implicit or explicit choice to commit certain resources, or it might be the decision thought to be a retroactive cognitive construction after certain resources have been allocated. Choices such as the location of a new department, entrance into a new market, adoption of computer manufacturing technology, and the novel installation of MX missiles are strategic decisions in the sense of outcomes or their content.

The second problem is the *proper unit of analysis*. Strategic decision making can be studied as an individual, group, organizational, or interorganizational phenomenon. One could even "bracket" the decision-making agent, whether this is an individual or a higher aggregate, and focus on the decision-making activities themselves. It would appear more convenient, however, to attach such activities to the actors in question. Strategic decisions are made by individuals, and we must therefore be sensitive to their cognitive activities and the judgmental distortions and biases that prevail during the scanning of their environment and the retention of information. They are, however, embedded in a social context whose role in shaping decisional processes and outcomes should enter prominently into the investigation. Recent contributions have shown, for example, that social control of one's group affects the way a strategic decision maker perceives the world (Janis and Mann, 1977). Given that strategic decisions are collective decisions, there is a need to consider the various interests that intersect at any particular choice. Strategic decision makers are constrained by internal and external interest groups and have to obtain the various commitments for endorsement and implementation. The strategic agent is often the constellation of multiple groups, units, or departments that are involved in the strategic-decision-making process. One might, then, argue that the strategic decision maker is neither an individual (say the chief executive officer, or CEO) nor a group (say the senior management team) but the organization as a configuration of interest groups who become arranged around the issues and solutions of the decision-making process. At still a higher level of aggregation, one may consider an organization that is strategically interdependent with competitors, suppliers, customers, governmental agencies, and so on.

Most of the prevailing models in the relevant literature focus on organizational or suborganizational levels of analysis and either ignore or "bracket" the organization's context. Contextual factors are considered insofar as they contribute to the explanation of internal structures or processes. The increased saliency of the industrial organization and institutional economics as well as the growing interest in interorganizational relationships will probably augment the literature that treats sets of strategically interdependent organizations, or "action sets" as units of analysis (Pennings, 1981; Aldrich and Whetten, 1981; Nelson and Winter, 1982). Different levels of analysis are legitimate (Hirsch, 1975). However, the researcher ought to be explicit about his or her unit of analysis and must also recognize that other levels of analysis may comprise aspects relevant to the understanding of phenomena that are addressed at his or her aggregation level. For example, the decision-making activities in individual firms provide some of the impetus for the interfirm dynamics in an industry; conversely, aspects of industry structure and process are antecedents for organizational decision making. Multilevel problems are clearly illustrated by Williamson's (1975) treatment of interorganizational relationships, which are cast partly in terms associated with individual-level, bounded-rationality metaphors.

A third problem involves *the multi-disciplinary character of pertinent research*. The ambiguity of the unit of analysis is aggravated by the diversity of disciplines that intersect in the research on strategic decision making. Psychologists, sociologists, economists, operations researchers, political scientists, and others are involved in the study of strategy. They are not always aware of the work going on in other areas. The field of strategic decision making is inherently interdisciplinary. It is eclectic, because it involves the study of cognitive processes, the study of intergroup conflict in organization, the structure and dynamics of the industry or market the organization belongs to, the social dynamics of groups within which decision making unfolds and the norms and values that affect it.

The interdisciplinary nature of policy research implies that what members of the contributing disciplines consider random aberrations are often central phenomena of policy research. It is only natural to expect members of the main disciplines to preoccupy themselves with the dominant paradigms and to be oblivious of some of the "disturbance terms" that pertain to central questions of strategic-decision-making research. *Disturbance term* is a metaphor from regression analysis. For example, the variance that an economic study cannot account for is "error" or is relegated to "other things being equal" assumptions. A strategy researcher is often interested in assumptions or in error variance that are left out in purely economic, sociological, or psychological studies. Ideally, the researcher should know all these disciplines. Individuals who act as go-betweens between main disciplines and policy research should beware of being unduly limited by the prevailing paradigm developments in the main disciplines when they seek to develop holistic models of strategic decision making.

An illustration is provided by game theory or oligopoly theory in economics and its concern for strategic interdependence (Pennings, 1981), as reflected in such terms as *conjectural variations* ("I anticipate," "he anticipates that I anticipate") or *mutual expected rationality* (Harsanyi, 1977). Many strategy researchers are concerned primarily with the strategic qualities of a single, focal organization (or its "strategic business units") and examine strategic interdependence solely from that organization's perspective (compare Porter, 1980; Rumelt, 1974; Hofer and Schendel, 1978). Thus, reference is made to "distinctive competence," "strategic advantage," and "preemptive moves" as attributes that can be acquired from competing firms, from learning, from consulting firms, and so on. These authors do not give enough weight to strategic interdependence considerations and the limits they impose upon the strategic leverage of individual firms. In fact, if every firm would follow Porter's recommendations to pick any of the so-called generic strategies, they would all end up being number one on the *Fortune 500* or, at least, the leader of their industry. Oblique references to "competitive advantages" do not overcome the neglect of equilibrium conditions as stipulated in game theory or oligopoly theory (Camerer, 1982).

One could stretch the argument about interdisciplinarity in policy research and suggest that any strategy researcher ought to stay abreast of any of the contributing disciplines. For example, most authors with an economic bias tend to provide a fairly shallow description of the internal organizational realities, which they envelop in mechanistic or overly rational frameworks (compare Williamson, 1975; Porter, 1980; Spence, 1974). Conversely, authors with a bias toward the behavioral sciences often consider economic realities a given and never draw them into the core of their analysis (for example, Galbraith and Nathanson, 1978; Hrebiniak and Joyce, 1983). Ultimately, the issue of eclecticism and multidisciplinary research would lead to an ambitious approach where researchers consider simultaneously the relevance of different disciplines. To a large extent, such an approach remains utopian, since it requires researchers in this field to have a thorough knowledge of all these disciplines and to synthesize that knowledge in such a way as to cover all aspects of strategic decision making. Since utopias are rarely realized, investigators must adjust their aspiration levels; but they ought at least to inform themselves about other disciplines and to establish lines of communication to ensure a well-balanced informedness.

A fourth problem involves the *quality of decisions*. This problem points to the interface between the world of research and praxis of strategic decision making. It raises the question whether academic researchers can arrive at normative pronouncements that would enhance the process or outcomes of strategic decision making. Conversely, this problem also raises the issue of whether research can benefit from the practical experiences of decision makers.

Very few have addressed the feasibility of an "engineering of choice" (March, 1978). Much of the research to date has been restricted to the description and analysis of the process of decision making or its outcomes, without making inferences about the relative appropriateness of different aspects. Would it be possible to conclude, for example, that decisions involving more research, more comprehensive analysis, more involvement by relevant parties, and greater degrees of decentralization are superior to decisions made under different conditions? Perhaps we should seek to establish contingent prescriptions when different decision designs apply to different conditions, such as availability of slack resources or amount of time-induced stress (Clarkson, 1981).

Most of the strategic decision-making literature has been limited to the documentation of the patterns of steps through which a strategic decision-making process goes (for example, Mintzberg, Rasinghani, and Théorêt, 1976; March and Olsen, 1976; Padgett, 1980). Other researchers, dealing with content, have been more inclined to consider differences in quality, perhaps because their focus has been primarily on strategic decisions in the private sector, where assessment criteria are more readily available. For example, investigators such as Porter (1980) and Rumelt (1974) have examined a number of firms and developed an empirical taxonomy of strategic types, generic strategies, and so on, where some types are superior in that they are associated with higher levels of economic performance. A different set of researchers has been examining the extensive data archives of the Strategic Planning Institute, the so-called PIMS data base (for example, Anderson and Paine, 1978; Schoeffler, Buzzell, and Heany, 1974), and tried to relate clusters of marketing variables to outcome indications, such as return on assets or return on investments.

These "content" authors, who inductively arrive at seemingly prescriptive pronouncements, typically do not address the question of how a firm becomes saddled with a particular product portfolio or how its marketing disposition was arrived at. They are a given. They do not explore questions such as the various avenues to a particular product portfolio or the equifinal ways toward a particular configuration of marketing variables. One would ask: What are those avenues, and which avenues are the most desirable (least costly, most adaptive, least disruptive or conflicting, most conducive to obtainment of commitments)?

At a more general level of discourse, this question overlaps with the never-ending debate about positive versus normative science. Most writers in most disciplines have been cautiously avoiding "Hume's guillotine." This label originated with Black (1970), who paraphrased Hume's proposition that one "cannot deduce ought from is" as implying that factual descriptive statements by themselves can entail only other factual statements and never prescriptions or normative pronouncements. A basic challenge in policy research is to overcome this sharp demarcation between the realm of facts and the realm of values. The demarcation might fade away by future research, which could uncover patterns of variation, selection, and retention (Campbell, 1969; Weick, 1979; Mohr, 1982; Argyris and Schön, 1981; Nelson and Winter, 1982) from which certain strategy modes are to be retained while others are to be discarded. Given agreement on certain obvious normative criteria, further research ought to demonstrate which modes of decision making are to be preferred over others because they minimize cognitive bias; for example, the deliterious effects of groupthink, the destructive consequences of intergroup conflict, or the malfunctioning of interorganizational coordination. The success in developing propositions about quality of strategic decisions will bridge the gap between researchers and practitioners. For example, a firm might secure a toehold in a different industry through a variety of avenues ranging from internal to acquisitive diversification. Research might reveal what modes are the most appropriate.

A fifth problem pertains to *research strategies*. All of the relevant research to date can be classified as either variance or process theory. This distinction is due to Mohr (1982), who claims that, while decision making is a process, most investigators have treated it as a final outcome. Variance research treats independent variables as both necessary and sufficient conditions. Their time ordering is immaterial; the outcome is the dependent variable. The researcher seeks to explain the variance in the dependent variable (for example, return on investment, degree of vertical integration, adoption of new programs) by an array of independent variables. In contrast, process theory treats independent variables as necessary conditions, which are binary rather than variable (that is, "states"), while the dependent variable is a "final cause." Consistent with the notion of process is the emphasis on the time ordering of the antecedents of the decision outcome.

Examples of variance research on strategy are Porter's (1980) generic strategic types or the earlier-mentioned PIMS studies (Schoeffler, Buzzell, and Heany, 1974). Process research is illustrated by March and Olsen (1976) and Miles and Cameron (1982) as they conceptualize strategy in terms of a succession of events. Mohr (1982) goes on to argue that most decision-making research of the variance type is contradictory, conflicting, and inconclusive, because it imposes the wrong study design. Decision making is equifinal, with interactions among the independent variables. Although he is not explicit, one can surmise that we should therefore utilize process methodologies, including time-series analysis (for example, Grabowski and Baxter, 1973), clinical case studies (March and Olsen, 1976), simulations (Cohen, March and Olsen, 1972), and historical, ideographic techniques (Chandler, 1962; Pettigrew, 1973). The question remains, however, whether research on the outcomes of strategies could not continue to use variance theory. Mohr answers this question negatively, claiming that the detection of numerous interaction effects among independent variables will remain an endless effort. In view of the equifinality of decision-making processes, there will be a virtually infinite number of possible interactions among antecedent variables, a situation that strengthens the recommendation to use methodologies that fit the process phenomenon.

In addition to the variance-process research distinction, there is also the frequently mentioned contrast between highly theoretical and heavily empirical research. This contrast, which can be related to the induction-deduction distinction, has preoccupied many philosophers and continues to stir debates among contemporaries such as Karl Popper and Thomas Kuhn (compare Blaug, 1980). Simply stated, in deductive research, conclusions are logical extensions of the premises or assumptions that are formulated in the proverbial armchair, while inductive research exposes the researcher to the facts such that his or her conclusions are inferred from empirically derived premises. Naturally, the distinction is not so sharp, since the most arrogant deductionist still employs factual examples, while the most pronounced data-driven empiricist is still guided by some a priori hunches about data and interpretations (Gergen, 1978). Strategy research has ranged from highly formal models, with their internal normative logic, abstract theories with reference to facts, operationalism, and dustbowl empiricism, to highly concrete experiential narratives of events in field settings.

Nevertheless, the preoccupation with logical consistency versus realism has pervaded all areas of research, including research on strategic decision making. Abstract theoreticians, such as representatives from game theory or economics (for example, Schelling, 1978; Williamson, 1975; Spence, 1977), are quite far apart from empirically biased researchers, such as Rumelt (1974), Pettigrew (1984), or Hickson and others (1985). The distinction between economics and the behavioral sciences coincides largely with the distinction between abstract theories and empirical research. The former enjoy more esteem and are generally believed to have greater potential for the advancement of knowledge. However, there can be no induction without deduction, and vice versa, so that both types of academic research should be considered legitimate (Gergen, 1978). Research in strategic decision making not only is interdisciplinary but also should draw very heavily from conjectures as they have been developed by abstract efforts as in game theory, as well as from rich descriptions as they have been provided by anthropologists and other scientists who excel in documenting decision-making activities at a level of phenomenological concreteness and reality that seemingly defies any infusion of abstract and artificial conjectures.

These five issues are believed to be among the most critical ones. Process-biased researchers are inclined to stress them somewhat differently from content-biased ones. Representatives from different disciplines will also reveal a diversity of accentuations. In the present volume, the issues were articulated to evoke further reflections on that elusive phenomenon, organizational strategy.

# ❦ ONE ❦

# Applying Concepts
# of Economic Analysis
# to Strategic Management

## *David J. Teece*

The basic idea behind strategic management is that a firm needs to match its capabilities to its ever-changing environment if it is to attain its best performance (for an excellent recent statement and development of this, see Miles and Snow, 1978). This will typically involve the formulation and execution of plans relating to the establishment and deployment of a firm's assets. It would seem on its face, therefore, that resource allocation issues are involved in strategic management and that there ought to be a well-known set of economic principles to guide strategic management decisions. But this is not the case. Economic analysis employing standard economic theories of the textbook variety is virtually unknown in strategic management. The purpose of this chapter is to explore why economics until recently has contributed so very little to

*Note:* I wish to thank Sidney Winter of Yale University for helpful discussion on many points in this chapter. The second section of the chapter is drawn in part from Teece and Winter (1984). I have also benefited from useful discussion with Richard Rumelt and Richard Caves.

strategic management, to outline some existing contributions, to identify the types of economic analysis likely to prove most useful in the future, and to attempt an assessment of the contributions of economic analysis relative to other approaches.

## Orthodox Economic Theory and Strategic Management

The concept of strategy itself, at least as used in the field of strategic management, is somewhat alien to economic thinking. The term rarely appears in microeconomic texts, except in game-theoretical discussion of pricing and advertising policies and the like. It is, therefore, in need of some translation before it can be examined in terms that most economists will find meaningful.

The notion that a firm can choose from a finite set of strategies (for example, low-cost, high-volume strategies versus high-cost, innovative-product strategies) implies that a firm's resources and capabilities are not completely fungible and generalizable, certainly in the short run, if not in the long run. Particular strategies imply particular investment decisions, particular organizational structures, and possibly particular organizational cultures. Put differently, the concept implies that certain factors of production "are assumed to be semi-permanently tied to the firm by recontracting costs and, perhaps, market imperfections" (Caves, 1980, p. 65). The assumption that resources are immobile and heterogeneous is implicitly if not explicitly embedded in the strategic manager's view of the world. However, this world view does not sit comfortably with the models and theories contained in most microeconomic texts, although the tension is not as great with the industrial organization literature. The problem is that the microeconomic theory of firms and markets was not developed with the education of business managers in mind. Indeed, in some contexts, economists will point out that their characterizations of rationality do not pretend to describe how decisions are actually made or ought to be made. The discipline of economics in general, and formal economic theory in particular, is shaped by a concern with normative questions in public policy that are very different from the problems general managers must face. In addition, economics as an empirical science has long been determinedly oblivious to the problems of predicting behavior of the individual decision unit and has focused its attention on and developed its specialized tools for the statistical analysis of patterns of behavior of whole populations of economic actors. The fact that very different success criteria and information resources are associated with the normative study of the problems of the individual entity is often missed and, when noted, is often underestimated in importance. Finally, and perhaps most importantly, the dominant mode of theorizing in contemporary microeconomics tends to remove the discipline from management problems, with the important exception of problems relating primarily to the functioning of organized auction markets operating under high-information conditions (that is, finance). The dominant mode combines unquestioning faith in the rational-behavior paradigm as a framework, relative indifference to the delineation of the empirical phenomena that are thought to require theoretical explanation, and a delight in the construction of "parables of mechanism." Such parables provide a sharply defined view of an imaginary world in which the logic of a particular economic mechanism stands out with particular clarity. The insights generated by this method often seem valuable and compelling, but, unfortunately, there is often no attempt to bridge the vast gulf that separates the simple imaginary world with its isolated mechanism from the complex real world, in which some analogous mechanism may, perhaps, operate.

Without doubting the legitimacy or importance of the concerns and objectives that have shaped mainstream economics, one can doubt very seriously that the discipline thus shaped makes a wholly constructive contribution to strategic management. The following section examines some areas where such doubt seems particularly well justified.

*Treatment of Know-How.* The production and utilization of technological and organizational knowledge is a central economic activity that is handled in a most cavalier way within economic theory. By far the most common theoretical approach is simply to take technology as given, ignoring entirely the fact that the options open to a manager almost always include an attempt at some degree of innovative improvement in existing ways of doing things. On the occasions when this pattern is broken by explicit attention to technology change, the treatment of states of knowledge and the changes therein is often simplistic and undifferentiated. It is common to assume that technology is uniformly available to all or, if technology is proprietary, that it is embedded in a "book of blueprints." However, in reality, know-how is commonly not of this form. It is often tacit, in that those practicing a technique can do so with great facility, but they may not be able to transfer the skill to others without demonstration and involvement (Teece, 1981b). To assume otherwise often obscures issues relating to the generation and transfer of know-how.

In general, the fact that technological and organizational change is such an important and pervasive aspect of reality and yet so peripheral in economic theory may be the single most important consideration limiting the contribution of orthodox economics to issues in strategic management.

*Focus on Static Analysis.* Strategic management issues are centrally concerned with dynamics. Economic theory, on the other hand, deals almost exclusively with equilibrium analyses, which are very often static. In recent years, much greater attention has been given to theoretical formulations that are dynamic in nature, but formal modeling endeavors of this kind are often exceedingly difficult to perform. Accordingly, only very simple problems can be dealt with mathematically, and certainly not the kinds of problems of concern to managers. While comparative statics is one way to get at dynamic issues, it suffers from inattention to the path to equilibrium. These matters are usually exceedingly important. Managers are often as concerned with the journey as they are with the destination when industries and markets are being transformed.

*Focus on Equilibrium.* Economic analysis widely employs equilibrium analysis. (An equilibrium is a state where "the intended actions of rational economic agents are mutually consistent and can, therefore, be implemented"; Hahn, 1973, p. 2.) In fact, almost all of the central propositions of economics rely on the assumption that markets are in equilibrium. Clearly, equilibrium is a fictitious state. The justification for its use is the supposed tendency toward equilibrium, which is, however, an empirical rather than a theoretical proposition. Indeed, G. B. Richardson argues that "the general equilibrium of production and exchange

. . . cannot properly be regarded as a configuration toward which a hypothetical perfectly competitive economy would gravitate or at which it would remain at rest" (Richardson, 1960, pp.1-2). His argument is the obvious one, that for equilibrium to be attained, firms need information about each other's investment plans. In the absence of collusion, however, this is not going to be fully and accurately revealed. Accordingly, "it is difficult to see what but an act of faith can enable us to believe that equilibrium would be reached" (Richardson, 1960, p. 11). Indeed, as Hahn has pointed out, the basic purpose of the famous Arrow-Debreu model of equilibrium is "to show why the economy cannot be in this state" (Hahn, 1973, p. 4). While equilibrium analysis yields valuable insights into certain public-policy issues, it is of rather limited utility to managers of the strategic process. Indeed, it may obscure as well as clarify. It certainly distracts attention from process issues.

*Inadequacy of the Theory of the Firm.* With little exaggeration, we can assert that, until very recently, economics lacked a theory of the firm. To be sure, textbooks contain chapter headings labeled "the theory of the firm," but on closer examination, one finds a theory of production masquerading as a theory of the firm. Firms are typically represented as production functions or, in some formulations, production sets. These constructs relate a firm's inputs to its outputs. The firm is a "black box" that transforms the factors of production into usually just one output. Firms are thus single-product in their focus. If multiproduct firms exist, then they are flukes in that they have no distinct efficiency dimensions (Teece, 1980).

The boundaries of the firm—the appropriate degree of vertical, lateral, or horizontal integration—thus lie outside the domain of traditional economic analysis. Moreover, the theory is completely silent with respect to the internal structure of the firm. In short, the firm is an entity that barely exists within received neoclassical theory. The only dimensions of its activities that are given much play are the volume of its output and the price at which that output is sold.

*Suppression of Entrepreneurship.* Because equilibrium analysis has such a dominant position within received theory, and because change is so often modeled as a movement from one equilibrium condition to another, the role of entrepreneurship tends to be downplayed, if not outrightly suppressed. In fact, "it may be said quite categorically that at present there is no established economic theory of the entrepreneur. The subject area has been surrendered by economists to sociologists, psychologists, and political scientists. Indeed, almost all the social sciences have a theory of the entrepreneur, except economics" (Casson, 1982, p. 9). Casson goes on to identify two villains. One is "the very extreme assumptions about access to information which are implicit in orthodox economics . . . simple neoclassical models assume that everyone has free access to all the information they require for making decisions" (p. 9), an assumption that reduces decision making to the mechanical application of mathematical rules for optimization. This trivializes decision making and makes it impossible to analyze the role of entrepreneurs. Moreover, the Austrian school, which does take the entrepreneur more seriously, is trapped by extreme subjectivism, rendering predictive theory building impossible. A predictive theory of the entrepreneur is impossible with the Austrian school, because "anyone who has the sort of information necessary to predict the behavior of entrepreneurs has a strong incentive to stop theorizing and become an entrepreneur himself" (p. 9). The need for a theory of entrepreneurship—or at least a theory that does not suppress the process of entrepreneurship—is of considerable importance to strategic management.

*Stylized Markets.* In neoclassical theory, transactions are performed by faceless economic agents operating in impersonal markets. However, markets are not nearly so anonymous. Even traders on the New York Stock Exchange—supposedly the most "objective" of all markets—know a good deal about each other. Reputation effects, experience ratings, and the like are the very stuff that permits markets to operate efficiently. To strip such considerations out of the theory renders it impotent before many strategic management problems. Where managers know each other, trust relationships abound, and fly-by-night operators can generally be exposed.

Not only are markets characterized by a variety of information conditions, but they differ widely in the frequency with which transactions and the opportunities for and costs of disruption occur (compare the sale of nuclear power plants with the sale of a bushel of wheat). Intermediate markets and relational contracting (Williamson, 1979) are virtually absent from the textbooks and most advanced theorizing. By neglect of the institutional foundations of market structure, the conventional tools of economic analysis are rendered impotent before many strategic management problems.

*Assumptions About Decision Makers.* Economic analysis commonly assumes a form of behavior that has been referred to as superrational or hyperrational (Simon, 1978b). Decision makers are supersmart, don't have problems with memory loss or memory recall, and can instantly formulate and solve problems of great complexity. Even their expectations are rational. This is, of course, a caricature of real-world decision makers. The abstraction may be appropriate for framing certain problems, but it is generally an approach that managers find quite unhelpful. It is not a characterization of individual behavior and even less one of organizational behavior. Little can be learned from treating firms in this fashion.

*Behavior of Cost.* In microeconomic theory and in practically all textbook treatments, costs in the short run are considered to rise with increasing output because of the law of diminishing returns. While the empirical evidence generally contradicts the assumption of increasing short-run marginal cost, the rising marginal-cost curve persists in the textbooks because it must, if much of the rest of the paraphernalia of neoclassical microeconomic theory and welfare economics is to survive. Without the rising marginal-cost curve, it is often harder to derive industry equilibriums and to arrive at normative conclusions; hence, the reluctance to push it into the appendixes, where it might well belong.

That is not to say that economists have not been involved in an important stream of research on alternative cost structures, particularly the progress function. In essence, the progress function implies that unit costs fall with cumulative volume, because of learning-by-doing efforts. T. P. Wright, working as chief engineer and general manager at Curtis Aeroplane in Long Island, played a catalytic role in developing, applying, and diffusing the progress function concept (Dutton, Thomas, and Butler, 1983). After the war, industrial engineers and production managers pushed the construct empirically, while economists explored some of the theoretical implications (Alchian, 1959; Hirschleifer, 1962). In the 1960s, the concept was applied (and sometimes misapplied) by the Boston Consulting Group and others to strategic management. (Alchian's research was performed at RAND in the late 1940s, but the classified nature of sources prevented publication until much later.)

The progress function and various derivative concepts have proved quite valuable in linking cost behavior to strategic choices. But the literature on it within economics remains somewhat enigmatic and apart from mainstream treatments of cost. The concept has meanwhile become an important, though perhaps overused, concept in strategy management. In fact, Richard Pascale has invented the term "Honda Effect" to describe how consultants, academics, and executives have tended to squeeze reality into the straitjacket of the experience curve and other parables, "to the neglect of the process through which organizations experiment, adapt, and learn" (Pascale, 1984, p. 3). Pascale juxtaposes the Boston Consulting Group's (BCG) parable of Honda's entry into the British and American motorcycle industry with the reality as seen by Honda's management team. The BCG paradigm imputes coherence and purposive rationality when, in Pascale's view, the opposite was closer to the truth.

*Assessment.* Orthodox microeconomic theory, useful as it is for understanding many important economic and public-policy issues, is of little value to the strategic manager. Indeed, it can be suggested that received theory, standing alone, tends to saddle the practitioner with perceptual blinders that block peripheral vision. However, economics is a very diverse discipline, and within the field of industrial organization, broadly defined, greater realism is permitted to operate, although several of the central problems just surveyed are still pervasive. Since the field is developing very rapidly, the potential for positive contributions is considerable. Therefore, a brief journey through several of the streams of research in industrial organizations that seem to be relevant to strategic management appears to be warranted.

### Contributions from Industrial Organization

Industrial organization is that field of economics that has traditionally dealt with the structure of markets, the behavior of firms, and the social benefits and costs associated with various forms of market structure and firm behavior. As one text puts it, "the field of industrial organization is about: (1) how enterprises function within a variety of market structures, and (2) how well the outcomes fit the public interest" (Shepherd, 1979, p. 4). As the author of the leading text points out, "the name is a curious one . . . [as the field] has little or nothing to say about how one organizes and directs a particular industrial enterprise" (Scherer, 1970). Rather, the focus of much of the industrial-organization literature is on how particular forms of price and output behavior by firms affect consumer welfare.

There is now sufficient variety within the industrial-organization literature, however, that it is extremely difficult to characterize it as a whole. While research continues within the traditional structure-conduct-performance paradigm, interest is also being shown by economists within a variety of other traditions. These include transactions cost, game theory, and evolutionary theory. There are a number of other related fields, as well, such as information theory and agency theory, that are possibly relevant. I will discuss the contribution from several traditions, particularly those that either are already visible or offer considerable promise for future contributions.

*Structural Analysis of Industries*

*The Structure-Conduct-Performance Paradigm.* The first and most visible contribution from industrial organization to strategic management has come, not surprisingly, from employing the first and most visible paradigm in industrial organization, namely, the structure-conduct-performance paradigm. The most notable early developers of the structuralist paradigm were Edward Mason at Harvard during the 1930s and Joe Bain at Berkeley during the 1950s. Within the paradigm, the performance (profitability, efficiency, and so on) of firms in particular industries or markets depends upon the conduct of buyers and sellers in matters such as pricing practices and policies, tacit and overt interfirm coordination and cooperation, research and development commitments, advertising and product-line strategies, investment in production facilities, and the like. Conduct, in turn, depends upon the *structure* of the relevant market, as determined by features such as the number and size distribution of buyers and sellers, the degree of product differentiation, the existence of barriers blocking the entry of new firms into the industry, the degree of vertical integration, and the ratio of fixed to variable costs associated with the industry's technology. Market structure and conduct are also influenced by various fundamental or basic conditions. On the demand side, these include the price elasticity of demand at various prices, the availability of substitutes, buyers' practices, and the like. On the supply side, basic conditions include the nature of access to raw materials, characteristics of the industry's technology and production processes (fixed or flexible, continuous flow or batch, and so on), product durability, and shipping and inventory costs. Other basic conditions include aspects of the regulatory and community environment. The causation runs from structure to conduct to performance, although most treatments recognize feedback effects and some stress circumstances under which causation may run the other way, that is, from performance to structure. The basic theme, though, is that the market structure is the critical factor, and the paradigm focuses on exploring its many facets and tying those to conduct and performance.

The trick that has been used to apply this paradigm to strategic analysis is to treat the normative theory of industrial organization as a positive theory of strategic management. The principal focus becomes not one of how to select antitrust and regulatory policies to increase consumer welfare by enhancing competition but, rather, how to increase profits (and, if necessary, reduce consumer welfare) by containing or restricting competition. The principal weapon is the erection of various forms of entry barriers. As Michael Porter has explained, "public policy makers could use their knowledge of the sources of entry barriers to lower them, whereas business strategists could use theirs to raise barriers, within the rules of the game set by anti-trust policy" (Porter, 1981, p. 612).

The essence of strategic management in the structuralist framework is thus to shield the firm, to the maximum extent legally possible, from competitive forces. (The structuralist approach is in marked contrast to the transactions-cost paradigm, outlined later in this chapter, which focuses on economic efficiency as the mechanism to achieve advantage against one's rivals. It could be argued that some forms of strategic positioning that the structuralist paradigm helps identify involve contrived barriers to entry and are contrary to the public interest, whether or not they violate the antitrust laws.) In Porter's words, "The goal of competitive strategy for a business unit in an industry is to find a position in the industry where the company can best defend itself against these competitive forces or can influence them in its favor. Since the collective strength of the forces may well be painfully apparent to all competitors, the key for developing strategy is to delve below the surface and analyze the sources of each. Knowledge of these underlying sources of competitive pressure highlights the critical strengths and weaknesses of the company, animates its positioning in its industry, clarifies the areas where strategic changes may yield the greatest payoff, and highlights the areas where industry trends promise to hold the greatest significance as either opportunities or threats" (Porter, 1980, p. 4). This is simply a translation, redirection, and refinement of the Mason/Bain structure-conduct-performance paradigm of industrial organization, made visually apparent by comparing Porter's approach, as presented in Figure 1, with the basic industrial organization (structuralist) paradigm, as summarized by Scherer, in Figure 2.

Besides refashioning existing constructs, this tradition has also made considerable progress in refining the concept of entry barriers, which has led to the related concept of mobility barriers and strategic groups. Consider entry deterrence through the erection of industry entry barriers. Such barriers are exposed to free rider "abuses" and, hence, underprovision. In order to overcome this problem, collusion among incumbents is needed. Overt collusion is, of course, illegal in many industrial settings, although tacit is not. Tacit collusion is legal and possibly viable if firms' reactions to each other's strategic moves are predictable. This is conceivable where spatial elements in markets make some incumbents closer rivals than others. Hence, behavior by certain groups of firms to deter rival incumbents may be more viable and valuable than deterring potential entrants through the erection of entry barriers at

**Figure 1. Forces Driving Industry Competition.**

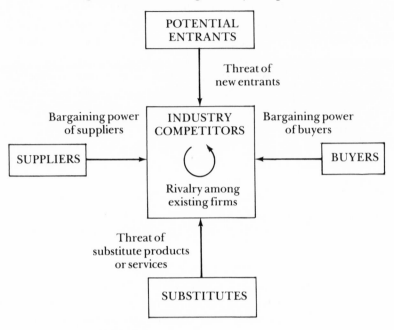

*Source:* Porter (1980).

the industry level. One can thus arrive at the concept of *strategic groups.*

Committed strategic choices and industry heterogeneity obviously underlie the strategic-group concept. Fine-grain differences in market requirements, firm capabilities, and transactional relationships allow for differentiation among strategies. Firms occupying the same market niche are likely to be more aware of each other's behavioral reactions than of the behavioral reactions to be expected by others. Mobility barriers separate the various groups from each other. According to Caves (1984), the concepts of strategic groups and mobility barriers "do not add up to a tight formal model. Rather they serve [as] . . . a dynamized add-on to the traditional structure-conduct-performance paradigm."

With the redirection and refinement of structural analysis, a good start has been made toward the systematic understanding of the competitive environment of an industry. However, despite the

**Figure 2. A Model of Industrial Organization Analysis.**

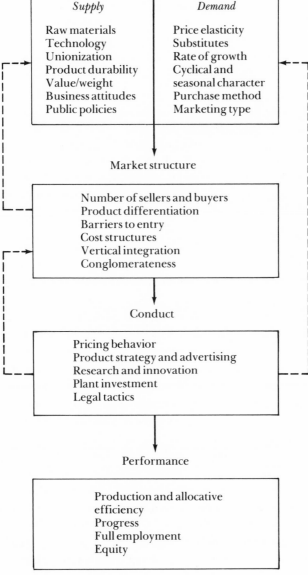

Basic Conditions

| *Supply* | *Demand* |
|---|---|
| Raw materials | Price elasticity |
| Technology | Substitutes |
| Unionization | Rate of growth |
| Product durability | Cyclical and |
| Value/weight | seasonal character |
| Business attitudes | Purchase method |
| Public policies | Marketing type |

Market structure

Number of sellers and buyers
Product differentiation
Barriers to entry
Cost structures
Vertical integration
Conglomerateness

Conduct

Pricing behavior
Product strategy and advertising
Research and innovation
Plant investment
Legal tactics

Performance

Production and allocative
efficiency
Progress
Full employment
Equity

*Source:* Scherer (1970).

useful work on strategic groups, this tradition does not provide much of a framework for assessing the capabilities and behavioral responses of individual firms, so that if the essence of formulating a competition strategy is relating a firm to its environment, the structuralist paradigm has dealt with only half of the problem. As will be shown later, recent work on the theory of the firm within a somewhat different industrial-organization paradigm is helping to redress this deficiency. The complementary nature of these endeavors does not appear to have been fully recognized and exploited at this point in time.

*Contestability, Sustainability, and Committed Competition.* In the last few years, some old ideas have been repackaged and some new ones developed that, while often advanced by a group of scholars rather distinct from the structuralist school, nevertheless have a structuralist overtone. Some of these developments will be briefly surveyed and assessed with respect to their relevance to strategic management.

Consider, first, the concept of contestability (Baumol, Panzar, and Willig, 1982). A perfectly *contestable* market is one that is accessible to potential entrants and has the following two properties: (1) The potential entrant can serve the same market and has access to the same technology on the same terms as incumbent firms. Thus, there are no entry barriers, if entry barriers are defined in the sense of potential entrants facing greater costs than those incurred by incumbent firms. (2) The potential entrants evaluate the profitability of entry at the incumbent firms' pre-entry prices. A *sustainable* industry configuration or structure involves prices and outputs such that supply equals demand and there are zero excess profits available to potential entrants if they take the prices of incumbent firms as given. Clearly, only sustainable industry configurations are consistent with contestability and equilibrium. Contestability, of course, requires that potential entrants have available to them the same technology as does the incumbent, and on the same terms and conditions.

It is clear that the classical case of a perfectly competitive market satisfies the condition of perfect contestability, but so might a natural monopolist if potential competitors have access to the same technology and costs as does the incumbent. Thus, markets may be natural monopolies and remain contestable, thereby earning zero economic rents for the incumbents. One example may be small airline markets where demand is satisfied before economies of scale are exhausted. Consider two small towns where the demand for travel is sufficient only to support a single daily nonstop flight. It is a natural monopoly market, and yet, because air transport equipment is highly mobile and can thus be redeployed ("flown") at low cost, entry into *and* exit from the market ought to be easy. If the incumbent sets prices so as to capture higher-than-competitive returns, an entrant need only deploy an aircraft to the market and undercut the incumbent's price. Should the incumbent lower prices to competitive levels, the new entrant can exit as effortlessly as it entered, so long as there are other hit-and-run opportunities, or so long as there is a well-developed aircraft leasing market, as is apparently the case. It ought to be clear that the reversibility of "sunk" costs, which include the costs of shutting down and opening up plants (or, equivalently, the nonexistence of transaction-specific assets), and the absence of customer loyalties are essential for contestability. A contestable market is thus one subject to "hit-and-run" entry. Were it not for such exposure, some firms might want to lower their output and raise prices. However, the threat of hit-and-run entry prevents the exercise of market power.

The utility of the concept of contestability for short-to-medium-term strategy formulation is limited by the widespread existence of some degree of investment irreversibility. The assumptions may be met in some transportation industries and in various other service industries, for example, circuses. But whenever irreversible investments in physical and human capital must be made, a market is unlikely to be contestable. Thus, while contestable-market theory is useful for sharpening one's appreciation of the role of costs, technology, and potential competition, it is of limited applicability, as it suppresses the role of irreversibilities, strategic interactions, and demand variability. Nevertheless, it is a lens through which one can view certain types of service industries. Where entry barriers lack durability, it is a framework that has applicability for evaluating the long run as well as the short run.

A concept orthogonal to and more relevant than contestability is *committed competition*. Whereas contestability assumes that investments are reversible, committed competition assumes that they are not. As suggested earlier, the concept of entry barriers implicitly rests on irreversible commitments by industry incumbents. Entry barriers are therefore exit barriers as well (Caves and Porter, 1977).

Recent research on entry deterrence has identified ways in which it may pay to expand the commitment of irreversible investments in order to make entry unfeasible. Expanding production capacity ahead of demand, advertising outlays, brand proliferation, and the like may sometimes be effective. Whether such strategies can be profitable is another matter.

*Transactions-Cost Economics*

Within a somewhat different tradition of industrial organization, sometimes referred to as the transactions-cost, or markets and hierarchies, literature, an important set of new ideas and theories has emerged with strong normative implications for several central strategic management issues, including the degree to which a firm should integrate (backward, forward, lateral, multinational, and conglomerate) and the appropriate internal structure for the large enterprise. The first set of issues can be labeled efficient boundary issues and the second, internal organization issues.

The transactions-cost approach starts with Coase's (1937) observation that markets and hierarchies are alternative organizational mechanisms for supporting transactions and that the choice of the one or the other ought to be made according to which is the more efficient way to support the transaction in question. Thus, arm's-length transactions in markets, such as when one firm purchases an input from another, and "in-house" production, as with vertical integration, can be thought of as alternatives. Table 1 identifies several market forms and their corporate equivalents. Note that the economic transactions conducted within the corporate form could conceivably take place in a market. One must, therefore, investigate why it may not always be desirable to push economic activity into the market, and vice versa. In order to do so, one must explore the nature of market processes in some detail. The development below owes much to Oliver Williamson (1975, 1979, 1981).

**Table 1. Organizational Alternatives.**

| Market Form | Corporate Form |
|---|---|
| Intermediate product markets | Vertical integration |
| Capital markets | Conglomerate |
| Markets for know-how | |
|     Horizontal | Multinational firms |
|     Lateral | Lateral diversification |

One feature of markets is that they are informationally economical. If prices are left free to clear markets, they will often do so quickly. However, the adjustment features of markets are often illustrated in the textbooks with markets for highly standardized commodities, such as wheat or cloth. But in modern industrial societies, some rather unique and nonstandardized products often need to be procured or traded; for instance, electronic switches in the telecommunications network, weapons, aircraft engines, low-sulfur crude oil, and experienced scientists and engineers. Unassisted spot markets, such as those used to trade wheat, do not always work as well as some alternative arrangements. To see why this is so, one must zero in on the properties of transactions.

A transaction occurs when a good or service is transferred across a technologically separable interface, as when a firm buys an input from an independent supplier. The attributes of transactions that are of special interest are (1) the frequency with which they recur, (2) the uncertainty to which they are subject, and (3) the degree to which the transfer of technological and managerial know-how is involved (Williamson, 1979, 1981; Teece, 1977; Monteverde and Teece, 1980). In most textbook descriptions of the functioning of markets, it is usually assumed that transactions are frequent, uncertainty is low or nonexistent, transaction-specific investment is not involved, and the commodities traded are tangible or at least can be packaged and clearly labeled as to their performance features. But in the real world, commodities are not always that standardized. Let's see how it matters.

Infrequent exchange prevents purchasers from building up an experience rating on particular suppliers, such as when a new company offers an (allegedly superior) microprocessor to board designers and manufacturers. Uncertainty means that writing, executing, and enforcing contracts that are anywhere near complete is extraordinarily difficult, since many contingencies cannot be identified and responded to during the contract-negotiation period. As a result, exchange is governed by incomplete contracts, as unexpected contingencies will surely arise—a potentially hazardous situation for all of the parties. Asset specificity can arise because of locational imperatives (as with iron and steel production, residuum and petroleum manufacture, and research and development and first commercialization of complex petrochemical processes), physical asset specificity (as when specialized tools and dies are needed to produce a component), or knowledge specificity (as when research and developed knowledge are generated that are specialized to a particular firm's requirement). The reason asset specificity is critical is that, once the investment has been made, it is largely irreversible, so that buyers and sellers may be operating in a bilateral exchange relation for a considerable period thereafter. To the degree that the value of highly specific capital in other uses is, by definition, much smaller than the specialized use for which it has been designed, the buyer is "locked in" to the transaction to a significant degree. The buyer and seller must thus make special efforts to protect the relationship, since both can be injured if it breaks down.

The criterion for organizing commercial transactions is assumed to be cost minimization. For analytical purposes, this can be broken down into two parts: minimizing production costs and minimizing transactions costs (Williamson, 1981). The former are fairly well understood and will not receive much attention here. Rather, it is the relatively poorly understood transactions costs that will be emphasized.

It is convenient to assume that transactions will be organized by markets unless market exchange gives rise to contractual difficulties and, hence, transactions costs. In other words, the presumption is that economic activity is best organized by markets, as this seems to reduce various bureaucratic distortions to which internal exchange may be subject. Furthermore, there are obvious production-cost advantages associated with using markets. For instance, scale economies can be more fully exhausted by buying rather than making if the firm's own needs are insufficient to exhaust scale economies. Furthermore, markets can aggregate uncorrelated demands, thereby achieving intertemporal efficiencies. Finally, contracting out may avoid diseconomies of scope when a particular firm's requirement is only one of several that can be produced using the same equipment. Accordingly, we should presume that firms will contract out unless contractual difficulties can be anticipated. There are a number of such regularities that can be used to derive several principles of organizational design (several of these are from Williamson, 1981, some are derived from my earlier work, and some are presented here for the first time).

*The Sunk Cost Principle.* If a firm, in order to minimize costs, must put in place specialized and, hence, dedicated assets in order to keep costs to the minimum, then it ought to protect itself against the possibility that the supporting transactions will be upset in an opportunistic way by suppliers, purchasers, or rivals. Thus, if an aluminum smelter is to some degree dedicated to a particular grade or type of bauxite, then the owner of the smelter ought to be sure that the ore will be available on competitive terms. Integration generally affords more control than relying on arm's-length contracts with unaffiliated enterprises. Accordingly, the supply relationship should involve a progressive degree of vertical integration as the extent of the dedication increases. (Where the input in question is a specialized component, the buyer may be in a position to demand that the seller license out its know-how so that the component in question can be second-sourced. In some cases, this will overcome the need for vertical integration.) Hence, the following principle: *Principal 1: As asset dedication increases (so that once committed, investment decisions involve some degree of irreversibility), the supporting transactions should be brought under tighter control, vertically integrating if necessary to ensure the continued supply of raw materials and other inputs necessary to keep the specialized asset fully employed.*

*Quality-Assurance Principles.* (For an earlier treatment, see Teece, 1976.) For many goods and services, the provision of product quality has economic value to the consumer, enabling the quality product to support a higher price. With some products, such as the camshaft of an engine, the buyer may not be able to establish the quality of the good by inspection of the final product and may not even be able to screen for quality with trial use. If the potential damage caused by utilization of a substandard good is great, it is essential that quality be checked before the buyer takes delivery. This is a special case of the more general proposition that the seller of a product has material advantage over the buyer in screening for product quality, because the seller is one step closer to the producer and may, in fact, be the producer. Information about product quality is generated naturally as a joint product of the production process and accrues in the first instance to the person supervising production. The costs of quality control may be reduced significantly by drawing upon this information instead of replicating its discovery at a subsequent stage.

For the intermediate product, there are three main strategies available for giving assemblers confidence in the supplier's quality control. The first is simply to build up confidence through successful experience through frequent trade between the same buyer and seller. The second strategy is for the seller to agree to the buyer supervising the production of the component/product in question, and the third is for the buyer to integrate backward into the manufacture of the component, that is, to bring the production process in-house, where the buyer has maximum access to information and is able to take remedial measures without having to negotiate with an independent enterprise. The argument is also symmetrical in the sense that a seller who feels that it will be slow or difficult to build up confidence among buyers may decide to integrate forward into the user's business. This suggests the following principle: *Principle 2(a): Producers of high-quality products ought to be vertically integrated into component production when the costs of product failure are high, when limited opportunity exists to develop an experience rating on suppliers, and when effective in-plant monitoring of the supplier's production activities involves significant contracting costs.*

Quality-assurance issues also explain the incentive to integrate forward in situations where the activities of individual distributors affect one another (rather than the manufacturer, as in the situation just considered), as when one retailer's poor service injures the product's reputation and limits the sales of other retailers. Independent forward integration or, possibly, franchising will thus tend to displace independent distributors as the most efficient mode of organization, leading to the following principle: *Principle 2(b): Franchising and forward integration become progressively desirable as spillover effects among retailers become more significant* (see Williamson, 1981).

*The Systemic-Innovation Principle.* As discussed earlier, uncertainty makes contractual relations especially complex, since it is unlikely that many of the contingencies that may occur can be realistically written into a contract. One of the activities in which a corporation may engage that gives rise to uncertainty is innovation. Innovation by its very nature involves uncertainty. Costs and outcomes of the innovation process are never clear until commercialization and significant market penetration have occurred.

Technological innovations vary enormously in nature and characteristics. For present purposes, it is useful to distinguish between two types of innovation: autonomous, or "stand-alone," and systemic. An autonomous innovation is one that can be introduced without modifying other components or items of equipment. The component or device in that sense "stands alone." A systemic innovation, on the other hand, requires significant readjustment to other parts of the system. The major distinction relates to the amount of design coordination that development and commercialization are likely to require. Examples of systemic innovation are electronic funds transfer, instant photography (it required redesign of the camera and the film), front-wheel drive, and the jet airliner (it required new stress-resistant airframes). An autonomous innovation does not require modification to other parts of a system for first commercialization, although modification may be necessary to capture all of the advantages of the innovation in question. The transistor, for example, originally replaced vacuum tubes, and the early transistor radios were not much different from the old ones, although they were more reliable and used much less power. But one did not have to change radio transmission in order to commercialize transistor radios. Another example is power steering—the automobile did not have to be redesigned to facilitate the introduction of this innovation, although it did permit designs that placed more weight over the front wheels. A faster microprocessor or a larger memory would be further examples. The third principle of efficient organizational design relates the firm's boundaries—the degree of vertical integration, in particular—and the rate and direction of technological innovation. *Principle 3: A structure that displays common ownership of the various organizational units that must participate in innovation is the structure that, ceteris paribus, is the most likely to facilitate the innovation in question.* Corollaries to this principle are: (1) Autonomous innovations do not require complex transactions among organizational units and will proceed efficiently in (small) unintegrated enterprises. (2) Systemic innovations require transactions among several organizational units and will proceed most efficiently in (integrated) enterprises whose boundaries span the various participating organizations.

When technological interdependencies are important, it is likely that the commercialization of an innovation will require complementary investments in several different parts of the industry. Thus, suppose that a cost-saving (equipment) innovation has been generated that can enhance efficiency if successfully introduced into an industry, and suppose that introduction into one part requires that complementary investments be made in other parts. If the subparts are independently owned, cooperation will have to be obtained in order for the innovation to be commercialized.

There are two powerful reasons why common ownership of the parts will speed both the adoption and the subsequent diffusion of the innovation. Where there are significant interdependencies, introduction of an innovation will often result in differing benefits and cost to various parties. This effect makes it difficult, if not impossible, to coordinate the introduction of such an innovation. While a system of frictionless markets could overcome this problem—the firms obtaining the benefits could compensate those incurring the costs so that the introduction of the innovation would not depend upon the degree of integration in the industry—it is commonly recognized that it may be extremely difficult to engineer a workable compensation agreement, in part because all relevant contingencies are not known when the contract is drawn up.

For example, inasmuch as innovation involves uncertainty and difficulty in measuring costs and benefits, the *distribution* of costs and benefits cannot be evaluated as accurately as the net total effects, and it is this distribution among separate firms that would underlie any agreement to introduce the innovation and the requisite adjustments in the production process. Thus, genuine differences can arise among the parties in their assessment of cost and benefits. Moreover, even if the costs and benefits are perceived similarly by the parties involved, differences in risk preferences may affect the manner in which the risks are priced. These problems will make it difficult to reach agreement, with attendant delays in commercialization. Even if an arrangement for sharing costs and benefits is devised, initial terms and conditions can be circumvented, and unforeseen contingencies—of which there are likely to be many—can be interpreted opportunistically. By rendering distributional and contracting issues irrelevant, integration reduces contractual problems and facilitates the commercialization of innovation, which affects several stages of production or several parts of an operating system.

Therefore, in the absence of integration, commercialization can be slowed or completely stalled. Considerable cost disparities can open up between old and new methods, yet the new method may not be implemented because the individual parties cannot agree upon the terms under which it will be introduced. There can be a reluctance on the part of both parties to make the necessary investments in specialized assets and to exchange information about each other's needs and opportunities—even if cooperation would yield mutual gains and certainly if the gains would go to one party at the expense of the other. Hence, in the absence of integration, there can be a reluctance on the part of one or more of the parties in an industry to develop or commercialize a systemic innovation requiring the participation of two or more firms.

To summarize, integration facilitates systemic innovations by facilitating information flows and the coordination of investment plans. It also removes institutional barriers to innovation where the innovation in question requires allocating costs and benefits or placing specializing investments into several parts of an industry. In the absence of integration, there will be a reluctance on the part of both parties to make the necessary investments in specialized assets, even if this would yield mutual gains. One reason is that both parties know that the exercise of opportunism might yield even greater benefits to one of the parties. Hence, in the absence of common ownership of the parts, there will be a reluctance on the part of one or more of the parties to adopt a systemic innovation.

*The Appropriability and Efficient Technology-Transfer Principle.* Successful firms possess one or more forms of intangible assets, such as technological or managerial know-how. Over time, these assets may expand beyond the point of profitable reinvestment in a firm's traditional market. Accordingly, the firm may consider deploying its intangible assets in different product or geographical markets, where the expected returns are higher, if efficient transfer modes exist.

The arm's-length market for know-how and other intangible assets is, however, riddled with transactional difficulties and costs. There are problems of both recognition and disclosure—potential trading opportunities may go unrealized because it is difficult to fully publicize the availability of certain forms of highly proprietary know-how, and when publicity is attempted, the buyer may thereby be able to obtain much of the know-how without actually paying for it. The buyer often needs to be fully informed about the technology before being able to value it, but once all the pertinent aspects of the technology needed to evaluate it are known, the buyer no longer needs to purchase it! Accordingly, it is often risky for the seller to rely on licensing to nonaffiliated enterprises as a mechanism for appropriating the returns to its intangible assets. However, if the "buyer" is an affiliated enterprise, such as a foreign subsidiary or another domestic division selling in a different market, the spillover effects mentioned above will wash out and will not affect the overall returns to stockholders unless divisional profits are taxed differently in different markets. This suggests the following principle: *Principle 4: When know-how licensing leads to significant transactions cost and substantial spillovers to nonaffiliated enterprises, the firm ought, ceteris paribus, to adjust its boundaries so as to internalize the transactions in question. This implies foreign direct investment when the markets in question are international and lateral integration when the markets in question involve modification of the primary production process.*

*The Hierarchical Decomposition Principle.* (See Williamson, 1981.) If a transaction is moved in-house, there is no necessary assurance that the activity will be effectively organized thereafter. Decision making must be factored into relatively independent subsystems, each of which can be designed with only minimal concern for its interactions with the others. The other operating parts must be grouped into separable entities, the interactions within which are strong and between which are weak. The strategic function, involving lower-frequency interactions, needs also to be separated and associated with higher levels in the organizational hierarchy. The hierarchical decomposition principle can thus be stated as follows: *Principle 5: The internal structure of an enterprise should be designed so as to effect quasi independence between the parts. Operations and strategic planning should be clearly distinguished, and incentives should be aligned so as to promote global profitability rather than group or divisional goals.*

*Other Contributions*

The two streams of research previously identified are the most developed in terms of their applicability to strategic management issues. As mentioned earlier, there are a number of additional streams that appear promising in terms of their potential contributions to economic science and to strategic management. Prominent among them is an evolutionary theory of economic change that has recently been outlined by Nelson and Winter (1982). The Nelson and Winter framework is significant because it promises to address an important deficiency in the existing literature: lack of a theory that can delineate the firm's distinctive capabilities. Existing theory is almost completely silent on this matter, and the field of strategic management often succumbs to an ad hoc approach. Yet the whole concept of strategy involves matching the firm's capabilities to its environment, so that in the absence of an adequate theory of the firm's capabilities, one lacks an adequate theory for addressing important issues in strategy formulation.

The firm in evolutionary theory is conceived as having a distinctive package of economic capabilities of relatively narrow scope. The information required for the functioning of the enterprise is stored in routines, in which much of the underlying knowledge is tacit, not consciously known or articulable by anyone in particular. As Nelson and Winter point out (1982, p. 124), "Routines are the skills of an Organization." Prevailing routines define a truce, and attempts to change routines often provoke a renewal of conflict that is destructive to the participants and to the organization in routine operation, but it is a flow that is continuously primed by external message sources.

For such a system to perform production activities, some highly specific conditions must be satisfied, and these will be different in particular cases. The specific features that account for the ability of a particular organization to accomplish particular things are reflected in the character of the collection of individual members' repertoires and the possession of particular collections of specialized plant and equipment. Restaurants have chefs and kitchens, while universities have professors, research laboratories, libraries, and classrooms. Central to productive activity is coordination, and central to coordination are individual skills and the existence of an information and control system that enables the right skills to be exercised at the right time.

What emerges is a conception of the firm with a limited range of capabilities based on its available routines and physical assets. There is no "shelf of technologies" external to the firm and available to all industry participants. A firm's capabilities are defined very much by where it has been in the past and what it has done. History becomes important, as the firm's performance is a function of deeply engrained repertoires.

Nelson and Winter's concept of routines thus cuts across orthodox notions of capabilities (the techniques that a firm can use) and of choice and treats these as similar features of a firm. To view firm behavior as governed by routines implies that what a firm is currently doing or has recently done defines its capabilities more appropriately than the set of abstract possibilities that an external observer might conceive to be available to the firm. (This is unlikely to be news to strategy practitioners, but it does bear an uneasy tension with textbook treatments of the firm's technological choice set as contained in most microtheory texts.) Thus, a firm's flexibility is constrained not only by the irreversible investments that it may have made but also by its limited range of available routines. Identifying these for a firm and its rivals thus becomes an important part of strategy formulation. This view also suggests, however, that the strategy lever may not be as powerful as is commonly supposed. If a firm has only a limited range of repertoires, its range of strategic choices is correspondingly limited. However, if its distinctive skill—be it innovation, service, or quality—is not readily imitable, it can be an almost unassailable source of above-normal profits.

Evolutionary theory also directs one's attention to the process and mechanisms of imitation (Nelson and Winter, 1982, pp. 123-124). The interest in imitation arises because it often happens that a firm observes that some other firm is achieving the success that it would like for itself. The envious firm may then try to duplicate this imperfectly observed success. Assuming that the envious firm does not have open access to the target firm's internal operations, then the target firm's routines are not available as a template, so that when problems arise in the copy, it is not possible to resolve them by closer scrutiny of the original (the target). This implies that the copy may constitute a substandard mutation of the original. At one extreme, the target routine may involve so much idiosyncratic and difficult-to-unravel tacit knowledge that, even if the organization tried to replicate itself, success would be highly problematical, and imitation from a distance would be completely impossible. This may be at the heart of what Lippman and Rumelt (1982) refer to as "uncertain imitability." Uncertainty in their model arises from ambiguity as to the factors of production and how they interact. If the precise reasons for success and failure cannot be discerned, even ex post facto, then replication is impossible. Given uncertain imitability, the average firm with positive economic profit and incumbents will be more efficient than new entrants. With uncertain imitability, new entry activity will be essentially a function of market growth rather than industry profitability. High levels of profitability in stable markets may well signal incumbents possessing difficult-to-imitate skills that deter entry.

At the other extreme, the product in question may be a novel combination of highly standardized technological elements, so that engineering may suffice for successful imitation. Even vague rumors from good sources may provide enough clues to permit almost complete replication.

The theory of imitation, which may be lurking here, can be linked back to the structuralist concept of entry barriers and its group-level equivalent, mobility barriers. Individual firms as well as groups or industries may be insulated from competition by the high costs or impossibility of imitation. Richard Rumelt has used the term *isolating mechanism* to refer to phenomena that limit the ex post facto equilibration of rents among individual firms. Isolating mechanisms include patents, trade secrets, and tacit knowledge. The importance of isolating mechanisms in business strategy is that they are the phenomena that make competitive positions stable and defensible. They may appear as first-mover advantages that can be undone only by changes in the environment that cause the value of the underlying inimitable assets to dissipate.

## Assessment

The economic theory of the firm and of markets is to the point where, if correctly applied, it can have a constructive impact on the field of strategic management. As a robust theory of the firm with strong normative implications develops, as the structural analysis of markets improves so as to focus more attention on the fine-grained aspects of structure and conduct, and as theorists and practitioners find ways of blending together the theories and various findings of research and best business practice, the possibility arises that economics can make an increasingly positive contribution to certain aspects of strategic management, especially questions relating to the design of business strategies. (Aaker, 1984, p. 167, points out that major contributions or potential contributions to strategic management are emerging from a host of disciplines, including marketing, organizational behavior, finance, accounting, economics, and law, in addition to the strategy field itself. He further notes that "the almost incredible reality is that these developments in separate disciplines have been emerging independently," with little cross-fertilization between disciplines.) However, it is most important that the analysis of strategic positioning, to which economic analysis has much to contribute, be balanced with concern for the building of distinctive competencies and with strategy implementation and execution. In fact, some argue, correctly in many instances, that the execution *is* strategy (Peters, 1984). One thing is clear. It is not enough to choose fundamental competitive strategies that *assume* the performance of the production system. In some instances, one may be able to attain superior performance by reorganizing existing competencies or by positioning business units more advantageously. In general, however, it is critically important to focus on the building of distinctive competencies. Thus, in suggesting that there are important contributions to management to be derived from economic analysis, particularly through employing a heterodox theoretical framework, I do not mean to suggest that this is a priority matter for the field of management. American management is more in need of sharpening basic skills in the management of innovation and human resources in a global context.

# Thinking Economically About Strategy

## Colin Camerer

In Chapter One, David Teece examines "orthodox" economics and finds it not very useful for answering questions about organizational strategy. In this chapter (and in Camerer, 1984), I examine "orthodox" strategy research and find it lacking in economic rigor. Teece and I end up endorsing remarkably similar research agendas, though we take opposite paths to our conclusions.

First, the philosophical bases and shortcomings of traditional strategy research are examined. Then, some foundations of a more rigorous approach to strategy research are proposed, by separating the useful from the absurd in economic theory. Finally, a critique of Teece's paper is offered (halfheartedly), and some specific research directions are proposed that are mostly complementary to those that Teece advocates.

### Shortcomings of Traditional Strategy Research

*Confusion About Basic Concepts.* Most policy and strategy texts contain "definitions" that, if not obviously circular, have their teeth nipping at their tails. For example, *strategy* is defined as the means to achieve ends, which are either vague or defined circularly as "strategic objectives." Inevitably, checklists, typologies, or "approaches" loosely constructed from such flimsy definitions are ambiguous, debatable on petty semantic grounds, and difficult to teach convincingly without dictatorship. Disbelieving readers should ask their students to define *strategy* and *policy:* many will insist that strategy is what top managers formulate, while others will argue that policy is the occupation of top managers. Bright students quickly become bored with this debate, recognizing it as a mindless matter of conventional definition, and so should we.

Efforts to reform the fuzzy language of policy by declaring arbitrary conventions—replacing *strategy* with *planning*, for instance—are superficial solutions, because the problem is deep: English is a poor grammar for strategic management. Better to invent an artificial grammar, customized to serve the job at hand and to enable us to "file" ideas in our minds and in journals, neatly and without confusion. The time-tested jargon of economic theory is one such grammar.

*Failure to Test Models Stringently.* Even when variables can be clearly defined or measured, traditional approaches or taxonomies are rarely subjected to the usual positivist scientific criteria of proof. The first "test" is a useful but lazy one: Does a checklist "seem sensible"? Occasionally, a second test is run: Does a theory make good predictions? Prediction is appropriately demanding, because after-the-fact explanation of events is too easy for facile minds and glib tongues. But even many predictive tests are too easy, because a good theory should predict more accurately than *competing* theories, not only more accurately than some innocuous null hypothesis. The "product life cycle" is a good example. Of course, products grow and fade in popularity, but predicting the length of stages in a life cycle is very difficult; and traditional strategy theories of product life cycles probably predict no better than the intuitive competing theories that managers use, implicitly, every day.

When extensive empirical work has been done in policy, it often results in hypothesis generation disguised as conclusive hypothesis testing. A classic example is the well-known market share–ROI correlation (Schoeffler, Buzzell, and Heany, 1974). Early studies documenting this correlation, and later replications, are taken as evidence of the "direct effect" of share on ROI (Return on

Investments)—leading to radical advice such as "get market share or get out" (Gale and Branch, 1979). But the finding of a *correlation* does not disprove the existence of a "stochastic effect" (such as "permanent" luck) that simultaneously causes *both* share and ROI (Lippman and Rumelt, 1982). It takes very clever tests to pit the "stochastic effect" theory against the "direct effect" theory (Wensley, 1982; Camerer and Fahey, 1985), but the difficulty of such clever tests is no defense for not doing them.

*Strategy Research: Art or Science?* Successful sciences should cumulate knowledge: Einstein's physics generalizes Newton's, and the "core" of a cooperative market game generalizes the notion of perfectly competitive equilibrium in economics. These sorts of quantum advances in understanding are unheard of in strategy research. Old planning matrixes are replaced by new matrixes without being encompassed by the new (perhaps because no clever tests pit the old and new directly against each other on an empirical battlefield), much as Picasso replaces Rembrandt without encompassing him, but unlike Einstein's grand replacement of Newton. Of course, arts need not progress to be successful, but sciences must, and I think that strategy researchers wish to be scientists.

*Why Induction Often Leads to Bad Strategy Research.* Much of the blame for the doldrums of strategy research might be laid to methodology—specifically, to the tendency for researchers to casually *induce* hypotheses rather than carefully *deduce* them. Induction is the unconstrained imagining of general rules from considering specific cases. Deduction is the specification of narrow assumptions that yield irrefutably true theorems about generalities. In both cases, the goal is the same—generality—and pieces of induction are a natural part of the machinery of deduction, and vice versa.

Induction is bad because it is difficult to argue with. For instance, Bower (1978, p. 324) states that capital allocation within firms "is a far more disciplined resource allocation process than the capital markets provide," a belief that he probably induced from consideration of a large number of cases (at least five). While I disagree with Bower, if he chooses to be stubbornly "inducto-centric," then no amount of data or rhetoric can logically persuade him that my inducted faith in capital market allocation is more accurate than his. By contrast, deductive arguments are either valid (internally consistent) or not, so a competent deducer can always convince another of his or her claim, and disputes between equally valid theorems can often be resolved by proving even more general theorems, based on more general assumptions, encompassing both of the equally valid theorems.

Thomas Kuhn (1970) hints, in an obscure passage (pp. 36–37) of his famous book, that solving deductively posed "puzzles" may yield scientific progress more quickly than pondering inductive "problems," which "can be a distraction." Formal theorem proving begins with unrealistic proofs of obvious claims and builds to counterintuitive, useful assertions (ideally), while induction begins with realistic synthesis of cases and ends with an equally valid realistic synthesis of cases. It is not necessary to know a lot of mathematics in order to do good formal deductive theorizing, but it helps. Mathematics is the magic that makes impossible leaps from premises to conclusions possible.

## Foundations of a New Approach

Economic thinking seems to be the most suitable basis for a deductive, formal tradition of thinking about strategy. Economic theory has its own grammar, so there is little debate about definition; the positivist tradition of testing theories is deeply ingrained in economics; and economic theories progress (if slowly), with later theories encompassing earlier theories as "special cases." Some key features of economic thinking should be imported to modern thinking about strategy.

*Maximizing and Equilibrium.* Economists make assumptions of extreme rationality, because such assumptions give their theories closure. By assuming that people maximize utility, for instance, one can take derivatives of utility functions and derive precise solutions, which are used as falsifiable predictions. If people "satisfice" (Simon, 1957c), predictions about individual choice are broader and almost impossible to disprove. Since unfalsifiable theories never progress on the basis of empirical observation, such theories are unscientific and illegitimate. But since they yield precise predictions, theories based on assumptions of maximizing are laudable *on methodological grounds,* even if they are unrealistic or obviously wrong.

The logical counterpart and result of individual rationality is market *equilibrium.* It too, is useful on methodological grounds—equilibriums are precise predictions—even if a never-ending series of "exogenous shocks" makes the actual existence of equilibrium fleeting or practically impossible.

*Rational Expectations.* The bold extension of traditional assumptions of maximizing to decision making under uncertainty has led to the extreme idea of "rational expectations," the assumption that agents in a theoretical world know the underlying economic theory and use it to form expectations about the future. For instance, a finance theory that predicts that shares of small firms yield higher risk-adjusted returns to investors than shares of large firms do is inconsistent with rational expectations, since any agents knowing that theory would rationally buy small firms and sell large ones until the difference in returns was driven to zero. Since such a theory is inconsistent with rational expectations, financial economists are puzzled about the empirical "size effect"—small firms *do* seem to return more—and they are currently busy hypothesizing why such a size effect cannot be cheaply arbitraged away. As another example, Peters and Waterman (1982) observe that "excellent" firms have strong corporate cultures, treat employees well and inspire them, worry obsessively about product quality, and so on. But if managers have rational expectations about how important these organizational features are, then they are *already* "investing" in them, until their marginal benefits barely outweigh the marginal costs; so advice such as "worry more about product quality" is not good advice.

In assuming that expectations are rational, economists are being extremely (and uncharacteristically) humble. Any theory that yields unexploited profit opportunities or good advice must be wrong if people have rational expectations. Thus, the assumption of rational expectations is useful for disciplining academics who are not humble. For instance, researchers who found market share–ROI correlations in the PIMS (Profit Impact of Marketing Strategies) data have claimed that firms can earn a higher ROI by simply increasing their market shares. Such a theory is clearly inconsistent with rational expectations among managers, because managers who know of the alleged causal link between market share and ROI would "bid up" the cost of gaining share—advertising more aggressively, and so on—until ROI would not automatically increase after hard-fought market share increases. While Biggadike (1979, p. 109) rejects the assumption of rational expectations, suggesting that "perhaps there is still a widespread lack of awareness of the relationship between profitability and market share," this relationship is so elementary that smart managers surely know about it; so advising them to "get share or get out" can only lead to disastrous "share wars" that yield losses for everyone. Belief in rational expectations suggests that researchers should find an explanation for the share—ROI correlation that doesn't depend upon managers stupidly underestimating the importance of share (see Camerer and Fahey, 1985).

*Game-Theoretical Rationality.* In game theory, players are assumed to be rational and to know that others are rational. This strong, often unrealistic assumption of "mutual expected rationality" can be a useful reminder to strategists that their opponents are probably more like them—smart, careful, rational—than different. If so, how can a rational conglomerate sell a "dog" business for more than it is worth? (They can't.) If they can't, why should they sell it? (Perhaps they shouldn't.) Humble thinking suggests that the Boston Consulting Group's matrix variables for determining business spin-offs or acquisitions—expected growth and market share—are bad rationales if competitors can project expected growth or measure market share as accurately as we can. But belief in game-theoretical rationality suggests two important analogous dimensions (Wensley, 1982): Businesses should be sold only (1) if the seller has some private information about the true worth of the business (and this private information had better be "secret," so that competitors do not know that the seller has inside information) or (2) if the business doesn't fit well into a conglomerate's mix of businesses (the portfolio of businesses has no "economies of scope").

*Beyond Rational Expectations to Strategy.* Taken too seriously, rational expectations can be a crippling assumption for students of strategy, just as humility can cripple the competitive spirit. In one telling joke, a naive disbeliever, walking along with a believer in rational expectations, spots what appears to be a ten-dollar bill on the ground. As the disbeliever rushes to pick up the currency, the purist says, "Don't bother; if it was a ten-dollar bill, somebody would have picked it up, so it is not a ten-dollar bill." The story is a little unfair, since rational expectations theories do allow for random shocks that provide profit opportunities, perhaps even to naive companions of economists. But the point is that believing too strongly in rational expectations or ignoring the possibility of random unexploited profit opportunities can be stifling. Rational expectations are assumed in order to derive predictions about equilibrium; and in equilibrium, the purist would be right about the apparent ten-dollar bill. But the world that strategy researchers worry about is never in equilibrium, and the very process of getting there—squeezing all the profit opportunity from a "shock"—is what strategic management is about.

### Thinking Economically About Strategic Issues

At this point, Teece and I can join hands. We began oppositely—Teece argues persuasively that economics needs more strategic content, while I contend that strategy needs more economic thinking (but not too much)—but we reach strikingly similar conclusions about what the resulting "strategic economics" might consist of. In so doing, Teece says many sensible things that are too-rarely noted; but with our methodological kinship duly noted, let me stress some disagreements.

*Elements of a Strategic Theory of the Firm.* Teece begins, as do most "strategic economists," by assuming that there are assets or skills that are anchored to firms in the short run. Since machines and buildings are easy to move, this emphasis on what makes firms-full of people stick together points swiftly and appropriately to assets that are difficult to trade and, especially, to human capital (or "know-how"). With our consciousness thus raised, the excitement stops; Teece busily catalogues the many ways in which microeconomic theory ignores such considerations and thus says nothing interesting about strategy.

Teece politely calls the revival of interest in "industrial organization" (IO) among strategy thinkers a "good start," though he laments the traditional ignorance of IO theorists of firm-specific factors. He notes in passing that applying concepts from industrial organization to strategic management is debatably ethical, like teaching criminals about law-enforcement technique, since entry barriers—the golden fleece of Porter's (1980) book—almost always fleece consumers. This point deserves elaboration, and I am thrilled that Teece raised it, especially since there are many ways to approach strategy—such as Teece's—that stress general improvements with no consumer harm, by shifting resources to better uses or simply innovating.

Teece mentions recent work on "contestability," which is mostly a sensible clarification of the old IO disagreement about whether entry barriers are created by sunk costs or by fixed costs. Baumol, Panzar, and Willig (1982) contend—rightly, I think—that sunk costs are more important, but the debate is unnecessarily fierce, because, in practice, fixed costs are so often sunk as well. Teece notes that "entry barriers are therefore exit barriers as well," a simple truth that is widely misunderstood, but he doesn't add the reverse, that "anticipated exit barriers are entry barriers as well."

Teece mentions "sustainability," but the impossibility of "intertemporal sustainability" (Baumol, Panzar, and Willig, 1982) seems worth noting, too. The idea is that competitors who intend to build plants and then later modernize or expand can only deter current entry by recouping the later marginal costs of modernizing only through future revenues; but, in the future, newcomers building from the ground up can undercut the competitor's prices, because their per-unit costs will undoubtedly be lower than the competitor's per-unit costs of modernizing. This seems like a much more natural, and blameless, explanation for the succession of American "smokestack industries" by the Koreans, the Japanese, and others than currently popular theories assuming myopic management, union greed, or overregulation.

*Transactions-Cost Economics.* Transactions-cost economics is an important new way of thinking about one simple issue—organizational structure—and Teece's exposition of this is excellent. Transactions costs stemming from ex ante anticipation of ex post contracting problems—and resulting supply disruption—are a key reason for vertical integration, and the view advanced by Williamson (1979, especially) and extended by Teece and others hardens the soft old idea that "supply assurance" is what integration provides.

However, when trapped in the Procrustean bed of marginalism, transactions-cost economics can be whittled down to "merely" an innovative application of the idea that an activity—organizing hierarchically—will be pursued until its (rising) marginal costs equal its benefits (Coase, 1937). But the marginal-cost part of the clever transactions-cost economics argument is not well developed. As Grossman and Hart (1984) note, the fact that integration sometimes remedies contracting problems between separate parties provides a rationale for the existence of integrated firms but does not clearly limit the firm's boundaries—why not one huge integrated firm, centrally planned?

Of course, transactions-cost economists have some ideas about why marginal costs of organizing rise—control is lost, information distorts, and free riding and shirking are more rampant in larger hierarchies (see Teece's "principle five")—but these ideas need to be more carefully developed. Indeed, their neglect might be traced to the emphasis in transactions-cost economics on ceteris paribus comparative static statements (see Teece's five "principles") without emphasis on deriving equilibrium firm sizes or scopes. In most economic theory, the equilibrium horse is put before the comparative static cart, and that is one methodological tradition worth preserving.

In advancing research into the contracting problem that transactions-cost economics dwells on, and especially into why the costs of organizing rise at the margin, the explosion of work on agency relationships and contracting under incomplete information seems to be a useful source of ideas and formalism.

*Horizontal Integration.* To my mind, transactions-cost economics has effectively solved the puzzle of *vertical* integration (though compare Grossman and Hart, 1984), but Teece's own work (1980, 1981a, 1981b) has concentrated on solving the puzzle of *horizontal* diversification, especially by firms marrying businesses that make (seemingly) unrelated products. The gist of Teece's solution is that information or human capital, analogous to machinery in the case of vertical integration, is the common element in production of related products—Procter & Gamble's marketing savvy, IBM's legendary sales force, and so on—and horizontal integration is needed to avoid the overwhelming problems of trading or renting these skills in a secondary market.

Teece also uses the problem of trading know-how as a useful recasting of old arguments about foreign direct investment versus international licensing. But the big question in that debate is why direct investment seems to happen in waves, and any answer probably involves some financial considerations—stickiness in adjustment of real returns to capital across countries, for instance—along with transactions-cost considerations. Teece's emphasis on "know-how" begs crucial strategic questions: After they've organized them, what should a firm do with its skills? How can it best develop them? He lauds Nelson and Winter (1982) for promising to address a closely related question, the delineation of the firm's distinctive capabilities, but their theory *starts* with an arbitrary assumption about the distribution of nontransferrable (or "uncertainly imitable") skills and tells a derivative evolutionary story, so it hardly *delineates* firm capabilities (though perhaps it "promises" to do so).

*Corporate Culture.* Some answers to strategic questions about the development of firm skills might be found by focusing on the magic synergy of teamwork (which Teece does mention) as an explanation for why competitors cannot replicate Procter & Gamble's success or IBM's sales force. (Furthermore, since teams are harder to trade than individuals, teams may be more tightly "anchored" to firms and hence may form a more solid foundation for development of competitive advantage.) Most important is the elusive "corporate culture" that circumscribes individual behavior and has a metaphorical life of its own beyond the lives of human agents passing through the firm. As Pennings indicates in the introductory chapter, the importance of culture is certainly recognized; so the tough question is how to study it.

Most thinking about corporate culture has been done by organization theorists with sociological training and some acquaintance with anthropology. I suggest that culture is a strategic tool—

albeit an unruly one—that evolves by chance or is designed by cleverness to achieve the profit-maximizing aims of the firm. Thinking economically, it is natural to define culture as the unwritten aspects of contracts among managers, employees, stockholders, and directors who constitute a firm; with such a definition, notions from the burgeoning economics of agency and contracting become useful. And just as organizational structure may balance costs and benefits, achieving an equilibrium, so may there be "equilibrium" cultures—sets of beliefs that, if widely held by members of a firm, are fulfilled. But since some equilibrium cultures are more efficient than other cultures, such a theory can still yield interesting prescriptions.

*Reputation.* Much of a successful company's culture revolves around its reputations—for equity (and justice), for product quality, for attracting the best employees, and so on. Reputation is thus an important asset, which can figure prominently in strategic decisions. For instance, in a recent merger, Dean Witter's "rental" of a Sears "asset," customer trust, was internalized, because renting Sears's reputation outright was impossible. Applied game theorists have recently found elegant mathematical ways to model reputation (for example, Kreps and Wilson, 1982a), which should be brought to bear on strategic-level problems. Ironically, the strong assumptions of rationality and foresight in such models yield predictions of complicated strategic behavior that is richly "behavioral," providing a refreshing link between good description and deductive prescription in economic theory. Economic thinking about personal reputation might provide some rigorous basis for political theories of the firm (for example, defining one's reputation as a sort of "currency") and, hence, for theories of corporate control, directorship, and strategy implementation.

## Conclusion

I began by describing some philosophical reasons why the state of the art in strategy research is unimpressive: Basic constructs are vaguely defined and confusing; testing of theories, if done at all, is undemanding; and induction of theories based on extensive case evidence leads to inefficient argument and stifles theoretical progress. I advocate the introduction of economic concepts—especially the ideas of maximizing, rational expectations, and equilibrium—with some formalism (probably mathematical) and some moderation as a way of addressing many strategic issues. Teece and I agree that such an effort will require pushing the boundaries of economic theory, and we agree on many of the places to push.

However, we disagree on some things. Teece's nice exposition of transactions-cost economics is more useful than the theory's predictions are, since they address (deeply) only a narrow strategic question—how to organize the firm. However, Teece has brought human skills into transactions-cost economics by a carefully drawn analogy to vertical integration, thus helping explain horizontal integration into (seemingly) unrelated product lines. But badly needed in transactions-cost economics are fresh accountings for organization costs and for the creation and allocation of human capital (including culture and reputations); and some of these holes can be patched with work based on fundamental new ideas in information economics and in applied game theory.

# ぐ THREE ら

# Understanding Strategic Decisions: Three Systematic Approaches

## *Kenneth R. MacCrimmon*

Everyone is affected by organizational decisions. The impact of decisions made by political and business organizations is especially pervasive. Whether, as scientists, we wish to explain decisions or, as managers, we wish to make better decisions, we need to have a systematic way to understand organizational decision making.

Understanding begins with good description. An ideal description will be complete and unbiased. Organizational decisions, however, are far too complex for any description to be truly "complete." More crucially, no description can be truly "unbiased." Even the most conscientious attempt to be objective will encounter the limitations of language and viewpoint. Our attempt to cope with these problems here involves using a variety of "languages" and taking different viewpoints (Kuhn, 1962; Stretton, 1969).

A first step in systematic description and explanation is determining the *structural* perspective to take with regard to the organization that is making the decisions. The basic issue is whether to treat the organization holistically or as an aggregation (Gellner, 1956; Nagel, 1961). A *holistic* approach involves viewing the organization as a whole, rather than focusing on its constituent parts. Obviously, any organization has a number of components, and the components have a differential effect on the outcomes. A top-level manager can be expected to have more impact on a major decision than a factory worker; the finance people can be expected to have more impact on terms of a new loan than the marketing people. While a knowledge of these relationships can be valuable, we can often learn a great deal about a decision without studying the relationships among the components.

Even when we want to focus on the components, it is not easy. Social units larger than small groups are very complex; indeed, the dynamics of small groups are complex. Hence, it becomes necessary at some stage to treat social units as wholes—if not whole organizations, then bureaus, or if not bureaus, then work groups. We cannot account for the behavior of hundreds of millions of people in studying major decisions taken in the United States or the Soviet Union. At a first cut, then, it seems reasonable to treat an entire organization (including a nation) as a whole. In fact, this is the most common practice. For example, on one page in a newsweekly ("Periscope," p. 19), we see "the Iranian Government carefully screens citizens," "a kind of debtor's cartel has haunted Western bankers," and "Venezuela has already signalled its indifference to Western wishes." The reference to "Western wishes" is particularly mind boggling.

In this chapter, we will restrict attention solely to a *holistic view*. Although component views are important and have usefully been developed by others—for example, Janis (1972) and Anderson (1983) develop such models and apply them to the Cuban Missile Crisis—space precludes the treatment of component models in this chapter. Such models have been discussed by MacCrimmon (1973).

Adopting a holistic view, we will discuss the characteristics of decision making and explore the use of a "covering-law" approach to explaining decisions. In the process, we will present a *decision logic*. Then, we focus on the disposition premise of this logic and consider four aspects of disposition: rationality, informedness, social motives, and manipulativeness. These characteristics become important when the decision environment is characterized by high complexity, uncertainty, scarcity, and mistrust, respectively. We show how the characteristics of the decision maker can be combined to provide a systematic basis for developing holistic models. We select extreme combinations for the disposition premise and form them into three models that can be used as guides in understanding any organizational decision.

The three models are presented in the latter part of the chapter. First, we describe the *mechanistic model*, in which the decision unit does not deliberate but simply acts as it always does in such situations. Then comes the *super-rational model*, in which the decision unit acts with perfect foresight of the consequences and has an unlimited capacity to process all necessary information. Finally, we consider the *Machiavellian model*, in which the decision unit uses its capabilities in manipulating the situation to further its own ends, which may include deliberately making others worse off.

In presenting these models, we will describe the similarities and differences with the work of others, especially Graham Allison and Oliver Williamson, as well as pointing out the places in which current research in economics, game theory, and psychology can be directly drawn upon. We will give short examples from a variety of political and business situations, especially the Cuban Missile Crisis, to contrast our models with Allison's (1971) analysis in *Essence of Decisions*.

## A Decision Logic

There are four major characteristics of any decision maker. First, there will be a *disposition* to act in a particular way. The disposition may be toward careful calculation, toward exploiting others, or toward hasty emotional responses. Second, there will be a set of *goals* to achieve. Third, there will be a set of *beliefs* about the decision environment, particularly with regard to uncontrollable events that can affect the outcome of the decision. Finally, there will be a set of *options* made possible by the available resources (MacCrimmon, 1970).

Hempel (1959, 1963) and Dray (1963) have used a "covering-law" approach to explain social behavior. This approach can be adapted to help direct our understanding of decision making by using the four main characteristics of decision makers as premises from which we will develop a "conclusion"—the decision itself. This *decision logic* is specified as follows:

- *Disposition Premise:* The decision unit is disposed to act in manner D.
- *Goal Premise:* The decision unit seeks to attain goals G.
- *Belief Premise:* The decision unit holds beliefs B about the environment.
- *Option Premise:* The decision unit's resources make options O available.

From these premises, we would deduce a conclusion, as:

- *Conclusion:* The decision unit took action X.

Clearly, the conclusion is the decision that we are trying to understand.

To reach the conclusion, though, in addition to the four premises listed above, we need a *law premise* of the form: "A decision maker disposed to act in manner D, when trying to attain G, with beliefs B, will take action X when the available options are O." In the social sciences, we are not far enough advanced to focus on the law premise, as would be done in the physical sciences (Ryan, 1970). Usually, the law premise would be whatever was necessary to make the other premises fit with the conclusion. Obviously, the more we could generalize from the particular circumstances, the more lawlike we become. So, instead of the covering "law" being of the form "in the 1962 crisis over missiles in Cuba, the strong stand taken by the United States forced the Soviet Union to back down," it would be preferable to be able to say "in serious confrontations between the superpowers, in which nuclear war seems possible, at least one of the parties will back away." On the other hand, we need a larger sample than only one case to make such generalizations (Smoke and George, 1973). In the remainder of our discussion in this chapter, we will not focus on the law premise but will assume that it takes the form consistent with the other premises.

In using this decision logic, we can proceed either forward or backward. The *forward* approach would involve determining the disposition, goal, belief, and option premises, and combining these with the law premise to make an induction about the behavior that could be expected (that is, the conclusion). This prediction could then be compared with the behavior. If it did not match up, then the premises would be changed to find a set that did predict accurately. The *backward* induction approach, however, is the more common one. Some behavior occurs, and one then tries to pin down the premises. Thus we ask: What could the decision unit's goals have been? What were its beliefs? What options must have been available for it to choose as it did? What does the behavior tell us about how it was disposed to act? Clearly, we cannot ask all these questions at the same time; there are too many degrees of freedom. We need to develop a well-specified model from which we can infer the unspecified parameters (Swinburne 1974).

In general, if we are trying to infer goals, we cannot simultaneously be inferring beliefs; if we are trying to infer disposition, we cannot simultaneously be inferring options. In careless inference processes, little attention is given to the need to specify a subset of premises before inferring the premise of interest (often the goal premise).

In the remainder of this chapter, we will use this decision logic to help develop a set of holistic models to guide us in explaining organizational decisions.

## The Disposition Premise

There are many ways to characterize the disposition of individual decision makers. Study of the literatures on decision making (primarily from economics and psychology), along with an analysis of well-documented decision situations, leads us to focus on four main aspects.

First, decision makers may differ considerably in the degree of *rationality* they bring to the choice. At one extreme is very high rationality that requires infinite processing capacity and infinite memory. At the other extreme is a total lack of ability to retain or process information. Second, decision makers may differ in the degree of *informedness*. At one extreme is perfect knowledge and perfect foresight; at the other extreme is a complete lack of information. Third, decision makers differ in the degree of *social interest* exhibited in their decisions. The "midpoint" is a lack of concern for others, that is, complete self-interest. At one extreme is high positive concern (altruism), while at the other extreme is high negative concern (the desire to "do others in"). Fourth, decision makers may differ in the degree of *manipulativeness* they exhibit. At one extreme, the decision maker is completely trustworthy; at the other extreme, the decision maker is scheming and will do whatever is necessary to attain objectives. In the following paragraphs, we shall briefly examine each of these aspects.

*Rationality*. Rationality is inseparable from decision making. Winter (1969) identifies a dozen or so concepts of rationality, including consistency, congruence with norms, and suitable choice of means and ends. Our focus here is on rationality of the means to a particular end, rather than on judging the rationality of the ends themselves (the choice of ends is considered under "Social Interest"). We will discuss rationality as if it were a continuum from high to low, but, clearly, it can be multidimensional. One can exhibit high rationality in one area and not in another.

The most developed theory of rationality is expected-utility theory. Axioms of rational behavior are specified, and a theorem of maximizing expected utility is derived (Von Neumann and Morgenstern, 1947; Savage, 1954). A main advantage of this theory is the preciseness with which it is stated. Contrary to some popular beliefs, it is refutable as a positive theory. If the underlying axioms (which are necessary and sufficient) do not correspond with reality, the whole theory has deficiencies (MacCrimmon and Larsson, 1979). The theory has been generalized by Chew and MacCrimmon (1979).

Theories of partial rationality have perhaps been most forcefully stated by Simon (1957b). Many subsequent formulations by Lindblom (1965), Cyert and March (1963), Etzioni (1968), Liebenstein (1976), Steinbruner (1974), Quinn (1980), and others have augmented Simon's earlier work.

*Informedness.* Economic theory is often attacked because it seems to require perfectly informed economic agents. Consumers know their preferences and budgets as well as the prices and availability of all goods of interest to them. Producers know their production function and the demand and supply conditions of the factor and product markets. Recent work on rational expectations and signaling suggests how some of this information can be inferred from actions of others given particular rationality assumptions (Spence, 1974). Economics and decision theory also address the question of when to collect more information utilizing concepts such as the expected value of "perfect information" (Howard, 1968).

Some behavioral theories emphasize the limited information available to real-world decision makers. These theories usefully emphasize that decision makers not only are limited by the lack of information "out there" but also may be unable to retrieve from memory information that they supposedly possess. They also draw attention to strategies for collecting information (Newell and Simon, 1972; Simon, 1979).

*Social Interest.* Biologists and various social scientists have been concerned about the social motives of various species and the evolutionary implications of motives such as altruism or competitiveness (Wilson, 1978; Campbell, 1975). Studies of animal behavior from an evolutionary perspective ask how altruism has survival value. A focus on a range of social motives has received even less attention in economic models than has limited rationality. Economic theories are attacked for ignoring the range of human motives beyond self-interest. While it is true that little specific attention is directed toward motives, it should be noted that antagonism toward others is ignored as much as is altruism.

*Manipulativeness.* In addition to the motives of decision makers toward others, we need to consider the range of actions they are prepared to use. To what extent will they employ unethical means such as lying, cheating, or stealing? Less obtrusively, are they completely straightforward in their dealings with others, or are they manipulative? Seymour Hersch (1983) has claimed that Henry Kissinger was supplying Democratic Party secrets to Richard Nixon during the 1968 campaign at the same time as he was offering the Democrats inside information on Nixon. The Watergate scandal of the 1972 presidential campaign revealed a range of unethical behavior that in scope and level was beyond what most people had contemplated, even in politics.

What we have in mind by "manipulativeness' is related to Williamson's (1975) concept of "opportunism." However, opportunism implies exploiting one's special position (for example, having "first-mover" advantages when recontracting) rather than creating the special position by misrepresentations, threats, and so on. Manipulativeness implies opportunism, but not the converse.

*The Four Dispositional Characteristics.* We have identified four primary dispositional characteristics: rationality, informedness, social interest, and manipulativeness. These four characteristics are neither mutually exclusive nor exhaustive. Despite interrelationships among these factors, they are conceptually distinct. Although many more characteristics of decision makers could be identified, these four factors are the major ones, and adding more factors to the list would unduly complicate the discussion.

It should be observed that we have directed our attention to cognitive aspects of decision. That is not to say that "affect" is unimportant but rather that it is ignored from direct consideration here (for a discussion, see Argyris, 1973). Note, though, that all four characteristics (and especially social interest and manipulativeness) have indirect affective implications.

*Individual Versus Environmental Characteristics.* One obtains only half a picture by focusing on the decision maker. The complete picture is obtained by viewing the decision maker in the decision *environment.* What does it mean to say that a decision maker has low rationality without considering whether the environment is simple or complex? What may seem like high rationality in a very simple environment is seen as low rationality in very complex environments. Clearly, characterizations of low or high rationality must be made relative to a level of environmental *complexity.*

Similarly, informedness by itself says little without a knowledge of how uncertain the environment is. The *uncertainty* may be very high in situations that have not been encountered before or when dealing with the long run. High uncertainty can also arise from the inability to predict what other decision units will do.

The characteristic of social interest depends upon the *scarcity* of resources in the environment. On the one hand, the environment may be so favorable that, when you are pursuing only your own self-interest, you make others better off. This needs to be distinguished from the situation in which, because of scarce resources, pursuing one's self-interest makes others worse off. When everything is scarce, one's instincts for positive concern for others tend to be lessened.

Finally, manipulativeness will not stand out in an environment where lack of trust is the norm, so we need to relate manipulativeness to the social culture. The degree of *mistrust* depends partially upon the relationships among the agents and upon the form and outcome of their previous transactions.

Thus, we need to consider the four dispositional characteristics in conjunction with the associated environmental characteristics: rationality in conjunction with complexity; informedness in conjunction with uncertainty; social interest in conjunction with scarcity; and manipulativeness in conjunction with mistrust.

### Developing Holistic Models

*The Disposition Premise as a Model Parameter.* In using the decision logic described earlier to explain decisions, we cannot infer all the premises simultaneously. The most straightforward use of the logic is to specify all the premises except one and then to infer the remaining premise from the conclusion and the other premises. In principle, we could leave any premise unspecified, but we will treat the premises asymmetrically. Specifically, we single out the disposition premise for special treatment and develop some standard cases for the disposition premise, on the basis of the dispositional characteristics that we have discussed. Then we use these cases as models to help throw light on the other premises. With the disposition premise thus used as a parameter, we focus on making inferences about the remaining three decision premises. Assumptions can be made about two of these premises, and the third can be inferred. Thus, for any given model, defined by a particular disposition premise, three types of inference can be made: inferences about the decision maker's goals, beliefs, or options. The various possibilities are shown in Figure 1.

**Figure 1. Inference Modes.**

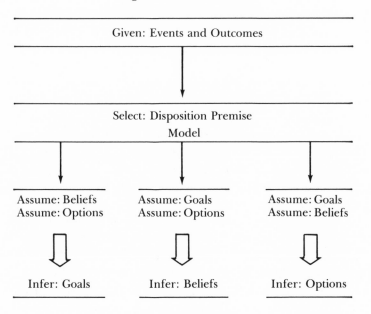

The particular form of the model will depend upon what values we choose for the disposition premise. Some assumptions about the disposition premise will lead to insightful inferences; others will not. Some assumptions about the disposition premise will make subsequent assumptions about goal, belief, and option premises more or less interesting. In our discussion, we will take these interdependencies into account by labeling the inference patterns that seem most useful as "primary," while the others will be labeled "secondary."

Since different sets of parameters for the disposition premise will give different insights, it is important to avoid trying to select a single "best" set. It is our contention that much can be learned by selecting very different models and using several models instead of just one.

*The Composition of Holistic Models.* We now want to examine combinations of the dispositional characteristics that we have identified. Even four dispositional characteristics, however, can generate hundreds of possible combinations. With four characteristics and four levels for each of the characteristics, we could have 256 possible combinations. Some of these combinations would seem unreasonable and would be unlikely to increase our understanding of strategic decisions. By restricting the number of levels and by eliminating some combinations, we can rule out these cases, although we run the risk of excluding some potentially interesting ones.

For simplicity, we will consider only two levels of rationality, high and low. We realize that this is a major simplification. In fact, to take into account the complexity of the concept, not only would rationality have to be measured on a continuous scale, but it would have to be multidimensional as well. To some extent, the multidimensional nature is reflected by combining rationality with informedness. We shall consider three levels of informedness: perfect informedness, high but imperfect informedness, and low informedness. We add the "perfect" level to the usual "high" and "low" to focus attention on the extreme case of omniscience. By combining rationality with informedness, we rule out the unreasonable combination of low rationality/perfect information as well as high rationality/poor information. (That is not to say that these cases never occur but just that they seem less interesting.) We allow the middle level of informedness, imperfect informedness, to be combined with either high or low rationality.

We need to consider three levels for social interest: negative social interest (such as hostility and competitiveness toward others), neutral social interest (that is, self-interest), and positive social interest (such as cooperation and altruism). Manipulativeness is considered at two levels, high and low, although it could be treated as a continuous scale. Its multidimensional nature is reflected when it is combined with social interest. By combining manipulativeness and social interest, we can eliminate the unlikely combination of high manipulativeness/positive social interest as well as low manipulativeness/negative social interest. The neutral level of social interest, self-interest, can combine with either high or low manipulativeness.

Figure 2 shows the sixteen cases (of the thirty-six that are possible with this number of factors and levels) that we are allowing. It would be confusing and redundant to consider all

**Figure 2. Models Defined by Dispositional Characteristics.**

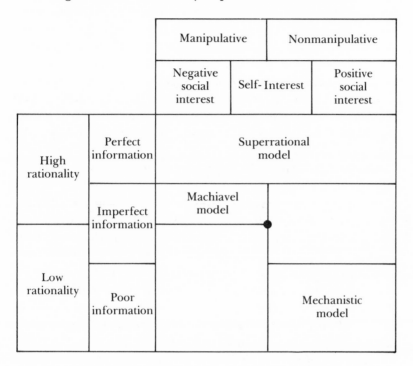

sixteen combinations, so we shall restrict attention to a few key cases. In selecting such cases, there is a strong tendency to take into account the capabilities of ordinary people and collectives and thus to propose something "reasonable." Real people do not have a high order of rationality, are not perfectly informed, are not totally manipulative, and do not have a high negative social interest. Thus, it seems reasonable to focus on the middle level of the four characteristics (at the dot in Figure 2). However, these reasons are exactly the ones that suggest that we should not focus on the middle levels. We do not want to "be reasonable"; we want to stimulate insights into collective decisions.

The extreme cases allow more precise predictions than the reasonable cases. It is less important that these predictions be right than that they be specific enough that they can serve as benchmarks. The "reasonable" forms can be spun into reasonable stories but often need considerable work before they can yield specific predictions. Watkins (1953, 1970) has emphasized the usefulness of extreme cases or "ideal types" against which actual behavior can be measured. In this sense, building a model is like constructing a meter measuring rod. Few of us can visually assess a meter, and even with a measuring rod we may make mistakes (as we find out on the last corner of our homemade picture frame), but we want a standard against which to judge behavior. With a demanding standard, we can highlight deviations and obtain increased understanding.

### Three Holistic Models for Explaining Organizational Decisions

We shall focus on three paradigms of decision at the holistic level. These three cases were chosen from the sixteen possible combinations in Figure 2 on the basis of utilizing extreme characteristics (to provoke thought) but retaining simplicity (so that characteristics would not be confounded). Our three "pure" types are: (1) the *mechanistic* model, characterized by *low rationality* and low informedness, (2) the *super-rational* model, characterized by *perfect information and high rationality,* and (3) the *Machiavellian* model, characterized by *high manipulativeness* and high (but imperfect) informedness. The primary (defining) characteristics of the three models are the italicized ones. The secondary characteristics could have been specified either more narrowly or more broadly.

In the following discussion of these three models, remember that, when we focus on the goal, belief, or option premises, the disposition premise is implied by the model: The decision unit may be disposed to act either mechanistically, super-rationally, or Machiavellianly. In applying these models to actual decisions, we are not asserting that the decision unit really was mechanistic, superrational, or Machiavellian. Our purpose is rather to examine the implications of making that assumption and to contrast these implications with what actually occurred. Space is limited, so one cannot be very systematic, but an indication can be given of what the models are and how they can be used.

*The Mechanistic Model.* The defining characteristic of the mechanistic model is low rationality. By low rationality, we mean either the lack of ability to reason or failure to use the ability.

Among the characteristics of a decision unit with a low level of rationality are limited goals, limited beliefs, and limited options. Indeed, goals and beliefs are not directly considered in this model. While at least two options have to be present for a decision situation to exist, the mechanistic decision unit does not think in terms of choices; in fact, we wouldn't characterize it as thinking at all. It simply does what it has always done. Even if the decision unit doesn't think in terms of goals, we as observers may still try to infer goals. In this case, we should keep it simple. To the extent that goals could be discussed, only a single goal would be considered. If it appeared that over time several goals were relevant, we assume with a mechanistic decision unit that they would never be considered jointly. There is no check by the decision unit to see whether they are inconsistent.

Beliefs are not directly considered. There is not constant monitoring of the environment; only occasional checks for changes are made, and they will be used only when the new situation is very different from the familar patterns. The change would have to exceed some high threshold. The mechanistic decision unit does not adapt to new situations. Situations are perceived in standard ways. Problems are classified into regular categories for which there is a routine response. No checks are made for whether the environment is being misperceived. The framing of the situation depends upon the routines available. The decision unit is subject to standard biases. It anchors on available facts. It acts independently of probabilities, appearing to misestimate them but, in fact, ignoring them. It does not adequately revise beliefs in accord with new information. It avoids uncertainty and ambiguity. Only standard scenarios are considered.

A standard alternative, the focus of attention, is used repeatedly in many situations even when it is inappropriate. Habit is the byword. Standard operating procedures (SOPs) are built up and comprise the set from which responses to new situations will be made. Only very extreme changes in the environment will lead to changes in the SOPs, and even then, the changes will be minor. Any search for information or options will be confined to the neighborhood of the old solutions or problems. The processing capacity is very limited, and the memory is slight. No calculations are made.

Correct deductions from a set of premises are not directly made. Complex environments cause confusion. The decision unit will be purely reactive. It will not actively seek to solve problems. When problems can no longer be avoided, it will be forced to cope with them. Its orientation is remedial. Large organizations, even more than individuals, depend heavily upon unchanging routines for accomplishing tasks. Standard operating procedures are the hallmark of a bureaucracy, and the term *bureaucracy* has developed a pejorative meaning because of its lack of responsiveness and accommodation to different circumstances.

The main disciplines from which the mechanistic model is drawn are psychology and sociology. In particular, the view of the behaviorists, such as Watson (1913) and Skinner (1974), is the appropriate basis for this model. The TOTE ("test, operater, test, exit") model of Miller, Galanter, and Pribam (1960) is highly mechanistic. Mischel (1968) and Ryle (1949) focus on the differences between patterned behavior and reasoned behavior.

The mechanistic model is intended as much more routinized than the "satisficing" of Simon. Simon (1957b) has sometimes referred to the "satisficing" person as intendedly rational—our mechanistic person doesn't form intentions toward rationality or anything else. Similarly, Braybrooke and Lindblom's disjointed incrementalism (1963) or Etzioni's mixed scanning (1968) is a step above mechanistic behavior. The actions of Hollis's (1977) "plastic man" are determined according to strict rules based on conditions. To the extent, however, that "plastic man" follows complex rules, he has moved beyond our mechanistic model.

The level of rationality of the mechanistic model is similar to but lower than that in Allison's (1971) "Model 2." Remember, though, that Allison's "Model 2" is not a holistic model. In moving from his "Model 1" to his "Model 2," Allison both changes the level of analysis from holistic to component and changes strong rationality to weak rationality. However, Allison's emphasis on SOPs does have a suitably mechanistic flavor. The SOPs that he identifies can be considered as SOPs for the Soviet Union as a whole rather than for some subunit.

In illustrating his "Model 2," Allison has provided a number of examples of the use of standard routines in the Cuban Missile

Crisis. Despite the supposed concern with secrecy, the Soviet Union built the missile sites in the standard slash pattern that the United States was aware of. The "civilian advisers," although they did not wear uniforms, marched in formation along Cuban roads and constructed the Red Army Star insignia outside their barracks. Tanks and antitank equipment were sent to Cuba along with other supplies, not because of a careful calculation of the costs and benefits of their use but because such equipment was always transported with the associated army division. The United States was not free from such routines. The air force presented a full-scale air-strike plan in response to a request for a "surgical" strike because the full-scale plan was one of their SOPs. The navy used their standard plans for antisubmarine warfare with little concern for modifying them to the situation.

Thorson and Sylvan (1982) model Kennedy's behavior during the Cuban Missile Crisis as a production system with rules for which action to take under various possible conditions. This is a holistic approach that corresponds to our mechanistic model when the rules are very simple, such as "launch an air strike," no matter how the Soviet Union responds. With more complex rules, the model goes beyond the mechanistic model.

The usual focus of inference in the mechanistic model is on the options. From outcomes (and implicit goals and beliefs), options are inferred. The effect of goals and beliefs is slight, since it is assumed that they are not directly considered. It would be possible to infer goals from outcomes and beliefs (or to infer beliefs from outcomes and goals), but only the simplest goals and beliefs would be considered.

The mechanistic model may be summarized thus: The decision unit will do what it always does. Little or no direct attention will be paid to goals or beliefs.

*The Super-Rational Model.* Rationality models have often been used as targets for those taking potshots at the unrealistic demands that theories of decision require of human beings. Simon (1957c) developed his "satisficing" approach as an alternative to utility maximization. Braybrooke and Lindblom (1963) present utility maximization as a "synoptical" model, which they attack in establishing the reasonableness of their disjointed-incrementalism model. Even with these positions in mind, we will present here a rationality model more demanding than almost any of its predecessors.

Our super-rational model is defined by the characteristics of (1) the highest rationality and (2) the highest informedness. In our model, the decision unit is allowed to have a very complex set of goals, which are not necessarily independent and which can be pursued simultaneously. It has consistent beliefs, and, even more strikingly, it has perfect knowledge of the outcomes of its actions. With such omniscience, there is no need for it to maximize "expected" utility, since it knows for certain what will occur. To handle these complex goals and beliefs, it has an unlimited processing capacity and memory. Thus, from the set of options available to it, it chooses the alternative that will yield the preferred outcome. This does not imply that it can do whatever it wishes; it still will have resource limitations. We don't need, however, to speculate on whether the decision unit wanted the outcome that occurred. There is no element of chance; whatever happened was anticipated, and the resulting outcome was the best that it could have hoped for.

The standard rationality models stem from economics, both the classical utility-maximization models and the more modern expected-utility models. The model is consistent with the recent research on "rational expectations," since it is assumed that one's opponents will take the best course of action available to them and that all participants know "how the system works." All the axioms of utility theory are satisfied, but the probabilistic aspects are irrelevant. Allison (1971) develops a "rational-actor" model, but our super-rational model is more extreme. Allison's rational actor makes careful calculations, based on available information, to determine the best action to take. However, he or she doesn't assume that outcomes are known. Similarly, our model is more extreme than the revision of Allison's rational-actor model that was applied by Weil (1975) to the decisions of North Vietnam.

The inference process for the super-rational model is very straightforward. Given the occurrence of an event (for example, the Soviet Union placing missiles in Cuba), we do not need to speculate on the beliefs of the decision unit—they knew what was going to happen. Hence, in the Cuban missile case, we do not consider whether the Soviet Union thought that it could establish a missile base in Cuba to narrow the missile gap (as Allison concludes in his rational-actor model). Under the super-rational model, it knew that the missiles could not stay in Cuba. It knew that it would be necessary to withdraw them when the United States imposed the blockade and threatened air attacks. Note how different, then, this model is from Allison's rational actor.

With perfect foresight, the belief premise becomes uninteresting: the decision maker believed that what did happen was going to happen. Attention is thus shifted away from beliefs to goals and options. But doesn't this present a paradox? If the Soviet Union knew that it would have to withdraw the missiles from Cuba, what could have been its purpose in putting them there in the first place? At first glance, such a supposition seems ridiculous, yet it forces us to stretch our minds to create explanations that we might otherwise ignore. For example, consider the following possible goals of the Soviet Union. First, it may have wanted to conduct a logistics exercise. Since missiles had never been sent out of the Soviet Union before, it wanted to work out routines for efficiently sending missiles abroad. More broadly, the Soviet Union wanted to develop procedures for sending arms of all kinds to allies in the West. Second, it may have wanted to mobilize support for increased defense expenditures. The crisis made clear that the "missile gap," despite the Democratic rhetoric of the 1960 United States presidential campaign, was actually one in which the Soviet Union was behind. Demonstrating United States superiority would allow large increases in expenditures for missiles and other armaments so that the Soviet Union could "catch up."

A "wilder" explanation involves the Soviet Union's goals for future American actions. After the disastrous 1961 attempt to help exiles invade Cuba (the "Bay of Pigs" episode), the United States seemed to become more isolationist. While this might have some advantages for the Soviet Union, it also meant that the United States was unlikely to get involved in future disastrous escapades in foreign countries, namely, Viet Nam. If the self-confidence of the United States could be built up, then it would be more likely to engage in costly foreign military operations. What better way to overcome the demoralization over the Bay of Pigs than to show that

American military operations and threats could force the Soviet Union to withdraw missiles from the very same Cuba? To test the possible relevance of this hypothesis, simply reflect on the effect of the financial, political, and social costs of the Vietnam War to the United States.

In the preceding explanations, we have focused on possible goals. Alternatively, we can focus on options. If we assume a particular goal, such as the worldwide spread of Soviet influence, we ask what the range of Soviet options could have been such that placing the missiles in Cuba (and having to remove them shortly afterward under United States pressure) was the best alternative available to it. What does this imply about its underlying resources (which determine the set of options)? Consider the following inferences. By shipping missiles to Cuba, even if they were later to be withdrawn, the Soviet Union gave the United States and other countries a concrete demonstration of Soviet worldwide operations more effectively than threatening Berlin or Turkey or other standard options would have done. In addition, because Castro insisted upon visible support to deter future U.S. attacks, the missile shipment guaranteed that Cuba would be a long-run Soviet ally.

We are not asserting that the super-rational model gives "better" explanations than other "rationality" models. However, it should be clear that the form of the model raises questions and forces consideration of issues ignored by models such as Allison's. In addition, the systematic focus on the three premises (in addition to the disposition premise that defines the model) of the decision logic provides a systematic way to attend to goals, beliefs, and options.

Allison's rational-actor model, on the other hand, has considerable ambiguities from a "rational" point of view. First, in considering the initial Soviet decision, he focuses solely on goals and gives no attention to beliefs. However, when he examines the United States, he takes goals for granted and still ignores beliefs but focuses on the range of options. Second, if it truly is a rational-actor model, why would such an actor have only a single goal? Yet Allison tries to ascertain which of a range of reasonable (and not inconsistent) goals was the Soviet Union's "goal." Third, since no direct attention is paid to the Soviet Union's expectations about the

United States response, not only did the "rational" actor have less than perfect foresight; it doesn't seem to have any concern about what the uncertainties are. Our super-rational model, then, is different from Allison's rational actor, as the application to the Cuban Missile Crisis should make clear.

The super-rational model may be summarized thus: The decision unit knows what the final outcomes will be. Hence, it chooses that alternative, from the set of options, that will give it the most preferred outcome of those available.

*The Machiavellian Model.* The term *Machiavellian* conveys perhaps better than anything else the essence of the model. The defining characteristics are (1) the highest degree of manipulativeness and (2) a nonpositive concern for others. The decision unit not only is opportunistic but has no ethical concerns in doing whatever it can get away with in turning a situation to its advantage. The goal may be to further its own self-interest with a total disregard for anyone else or may even be more hostile—the explicit desire to profit at someone else's expense.

In *The Prince,* Machiavelli (1961) provides a guide for the attainment of political ends through the use of the most expeditious means. The willingness to engage in manipulative practices depends upon the state of trust that exists among the environmental units. When others are engaging in or are perceived as engaging in deception, then the propensity for one to be manipulative increases. "Do unto others before they can do unto you." To be manipulative implies a reasonable degree of rational calculation; after all, you need to figure out what misrepresentations are to your advantage. On the other hand, the model does not require that you be able to anticipate the responses of others. One may be manipulative solely to further self-interests without harboring a desire to do others in. On the other hand, it is likely that the deception implied by this model is going to hurt others, especially those who rely on the misrepresentations. So, even though a Machiavelli may not start out with an intention to harm other's interests, he must be willing to tolerate that inevitable result.

Williamson (1975) makes opportunism a central concept in his model involving a transactions-cost approach. People seek contractual positions by gaining first-mover advantages, for instance. Our concept of manipulativeness is not too dissimilar, but we want to emphasize that the decision unit is not simply taking advantage of opportunities that arise; it is often creating them by misrepresentations and deceit. Similarly, our Machiavellian model implies a more pervasive manipulativeness than the mini-Machiavellian leadership strategy discussed by March (1978) or the bargaining behavior described by Schelling (1960) and Raiffa (1982).

A great deal of work in political science in general allows for behavior consistent with the Machiavellian model. While Allison does not emphasize manipulativeness, it presumably could be part of his governmental-politics model. The bureaucratic-politics model described in Allison and Halperin (1972) and Halperin (1974) also incorporates manipulativeness, but not to the extent of our Machiavellian model.

Important work in social choice, initiated by the studies of Gibbard (1973) and Satterthwaite (1975), has focused on the conditions under which people misstate their true preferences. Under general conditions, there is no way to guarantee that someone would not gain by misrepresenting his or her preferences (and, undoubtedly, there will be some who will do so). The term *strategic behavior* has been used to describe such misrepresentations, although this usage tends to distort a useful term.

Game theory focuses on the use of threats to achieve ends, although recent research has limited the scope to occasions on which a person would be motivated to actually carry out the threat (Kreps and Wilson, 1982b). Other recent research has dealt with the notion of "reputation" and the short-term sacrifices that might be entailed in gaining a good reputation (Milgrom and Roberts, 1982). The prisoners' dilemma indicates the difficulty of enforcing trust. A defecting strategy is dominant when considered individually, although, when each player chooses his or her defecting strategy, everyone is worse off. A common response in such situations is tit-for-tat, in which one acts cooperatively if others do. Since no one, however, has any gain by acting cooperatively on the last move, the whole process tends to unravel (Snyder and Diesing, 1977).

The focus of the inference process for the Machiavellian model is on beliefs and options. In the extreme form of the model, we consider that goals are less relevant, since it is assumed that the decision unit will either act solely in its own interest or act to do another party in. While this distinction is interesting, the primary focus needs to be on beliefs, for, unlike the super-rational model, the Machiavellian model does not assume perfect knowledge.

In applying the Machiavellian model to the Cuban Missile Crisis, we can assume that the Soviet Union was acting solely for its own ends. So why did it place the missiles in Cuba? To begin with, the Soviet leaders probably thought that they could get far enough along in the installation process before being caught if they continued to deny sending the missiles and to misrepresent the situation in any way that would be of advantage to them. Even if they took into account the possibility of a U.S. attack on Cuba, it would not after all, be an attack on the Soviet Union. Furthermore, such an attack might justify further Soviet intervention in Berlin, Turkey, or other places in which the U.S.S.R. had more pressing concerns. So what if Cuba had to pay the price? Mihalka (1982) considers examples of Soviet deception in this situation, as well as in many other international crises. A similar Machiavellian model could be developed for the actions of the United States.

To summarize the Machiavellian model, the decision unit will take whatever actions are available to further its ends, with no regard for the ethics of the behavior.

## Summary and Conclusions

In this chapter, we have systematically developed a set of holistic models to provide explanations of decision behavior by organizations. We have presented a "decision logic" as an extension of the covering-law model for explanation. The logic is based on four premises: a disposition premise, a goal premise, a belief premise, and an option premise.

We singled out the disposition premise of the logic to serve as a basis for defining a set of decision models. The dispositions used as defining characteristics were rationality, informedness, social interest, and opportunism. By restricting consideration to two or three levels of each of these characteristics, and by ignoring unlikely combinations, a set of sixteen possible models was defined.

We confined our attention to the development of three of these models: the mechanistic model, the super-rational model, and the Machiavellian model. The central focus of the mechanistic model is: "What standard operating procedures are available?" The central focus of the super-rational model is: "Since what happened was anticipated and represented the best possible choice, what goals were being pursued?" The central focus of the Machiavellian model is: "What misrepresentations were believed to yield an advantage?"

The three models were deliberately chosen to be "extreme cases" so that deviations from the models would be most apparent. It should be clear that the three models are conceptually distinct; the examples showed that the models provide different explanations. We believe that a deeper understanding of decisions results from considering a variety of systematically generated explanations than from trying to force the facts to fit some single model, no matter how reasonable the model seems. It would be easy to develop and trace through the other models implied by different combinations of our dispositional characteristics.

Decisions form the basis for outcomes in all spheres of activity. Although organizational decisions are usually the result of actions taken by many people, we can learn a great deal by thinking of the organization as a monolithic unit. In adopting such a holistic focus, we need to use systematic models to enhance our understanding. In this chapter, we have provided an illustration of such models.

# ❧ FOUR ❧

# The Case for "Mechanistic" Decision Making

## Sidney G. Winter

In Chapter Three of this volume, Kenneth MacCrimmon offers us a sample from a larger project on strategic collective decisions. It is possible that the sample is not representative, and this poses a problem, since I find the chapter marked by a certain imbalance in its concerns. Perhaps the balance is righted or the appearance of imbalance shown to be illusory in some other section of the complete work. I have little choice but to accept the risk that this is the case and go ahead and discuss the chapter as it stands, by itself. However, I will hedge the risk a bit by devoting a substantial portion of my attention to the topic of routinized, or "mechanistic," decision making. I think I am safe in inferring from the contents of Chapter Three that my own perspective on this topic is quite different from that presented in MacCrimmon's forthcoming book.

If I understand him correctly, MacCrimmon's contribution in his chapter is an endorsement and development of the idea that extreme hypotheses are a valuable tool in the study of decision making, particularly when the study involves an attempt by an external observer to explain the actions of a complex organization. The word *holistic* in his chapter signals that he is relatively unimpressed by the familiar objections to treating complex organizations as unitary actors. The main body of his discussion is organized around three "provocative models," each of which embodies an extreme hypothesis about the characteristics displayed by the hypothetical "decision unit." His "mechanistic" decision unit is extremely nondeliberative in its choice processes. His "super-rational" decision unit is extremely foresighted concerning the consequences of its actions. And the "Machiavellian" unit is extremely unconstrained by any notion of adherence to the rules of the game. Since the extreme positions are taken on different dimensions, the models are not mutually exclusive, as MacCrimmon notes. But they compete for the observer's attention in terms of their ability to make the known facts of a decision episode fall into place.

In this context, as elsewhere, an extreme hypothesis is a theorist's gauntlet thrown before the empiricists, especially before those who keep discovering that the facts cannot be accommodated comfortably in any of the available theoretical boxes. "Show me the ones that don't fit!" roars the theorist, thereby providing productive employment to the empiricists. In the end, the empiricists generally respond to this sort of challenge effectively, and it has to be acknowledged that there are some—perhaps many—facts around that simply will not fit in the box defined by the extreme hypothesis. But in the meantime—the story goes—more facts will have been found or better confirmed, and the relations among the facts will have become better understood. Even the facts that don't fit will have acquired a meaningful identity. Instead of being a motley assortment, they will be assimilated to the main structure of knowledge under the heading "Facts that don't fit in the $H_x$ box."

Personally, I confess to being a theorist of the sort that prefers to construct a roomier box. It seems to me that we already know more than enough about decision processes in organizations to be able to reject most extreme hypotheses outright. Indeed, I believe that we even know enough to be able to identify the likely areas of weakness of theoretical schemes that attempt to be quite accommodating toward the facts. The task of making sense of what we already know is a challenging one, and, in my view, it is not much furthered by considering extreme hypotheses that demand a "willing suspension of disbelief" at the very outset of the discussion. We would be better advised to try to make statements that will sound credible to a moderately diverse audience of informed observers of the human scene.

I would concede, nevertheless, that there is considerable merit in the case for the value of extreme hypotheses sketched previously. Many episodes, in many different sciences, seem to illustrate the power of the extreme hypothesis to focus attention and effort on narrowly defined issues and thus to promote the rapid advance of knowledge. I suspect that the basic mechanism that produces this effect is akin to the one that empties the benches in an otherwise tranquil baseball game when a fight breaks out on the field. The confrontation of forces of stylized good and evil brings into play energies that would otherwise go untapped.

MacCrimmon's three models can also promote understanding in quite a different way, by serving as emphatic and detailed signs warning the observer-explainer away from uncritical acceptance of basic assumptions about the course of action to be explained. Observers might be tempted to assume that the action was intentional in the sense of being the outcome of a deliberative choice process; the mechanistic model warns of the possibility that it was entirely reactive and just the sort of thing that the routines and procedures in place would be likely to produce. They might be tempted to assume that the result of the action was unforeseen; the super-rational model warns of the possibility that it was a foreseen outcome achieved in the furtherance of a deep and subtle purpose. The Machiavellian model warns them not to unthinkingly ascribe to the decision unit under scrutiny an unrealistically high degree of respect for the values that they themselves hold. The dangers of falling into these errors of interpretation are both real and important; the warning signs are well placed.

The many analyses and speculations concerning the tragedy of Korean Airlines (KAL) Flight 007 provide vivid illustrations of the importance of these interpretive issues and of the tendencies of some observers to jump into particular interpretive frameworks without visible signs of serious prior reflection. Was the destruction of the plane simply illustrative of the routines of the Soviet air defense forces, perhaps triggered by interaction with routines of KAL, KAL pilots, or the CIA? Was the uproar a foreseen outcome, anticipated by a hawkish cabal (on one side or the other) as contributing to the demise of the intermediate-range-missile talks? Or perhaps it was an effort to remind the world that the Soviet Union is not to be trifled with. Is it safe to assume that, if the Soviets had been convinced that it was a passenger plane only accidentally off course, the plane would not have been shot down? Arguably, a serious attempt to explain the event ought to include consideration of all of these questions; with MacCrimmon's contribution before us, we can extend this by saying that the explanatory effort should include at least a preliminary probe with each of the three models.

Clearly, however, there is much more to the task of finding a convincing explanation than generating *possible* explanations. It is at this point that I have a problem, or at least a sense of puzzlement, with the methodological stance that MacCrimmon takes in his chapter. I have suggested earlier that MacCrimmon's case for his three "provocative models" has much in common with the familiar case for the value of an extreme hypothesis. But, ordinarily, the proponent of an extreme hypothesis believes that the hypothesis is true or substantially true—or at least gives a convincing simulation of such belief. He or she is prepared to haggle quite strenuously about the percentage of truth that it contains. It is the fact or convincing appearance of sincere advocacy that raises hackles and leads to productive intellectual conflict. The same results will not likely follow from the announcement "here is a far-out idea that we could toss around." But MacCrimmon signals very clearly that he does not advance any one of his extreme hypotheses as true but only as productive of "insight."

What, for example, are we to make of such an extreme construct as MacCrimmon's "super-rational" model and such illustrative applications as the notion that the Soviet objective in placing missiles in Cuba was to enhance the U.S. feelings of confidence and efficacy and thus the probability that the United States would get bogged down in foreign quagmires such as Vietnam? (If we continue along that thread of speculation, we discover that the reason that it was useful to get the United States bogged down in Vietnam was that it would greatly diminish the Americans' sense of confidence and efficacy and thus *diminish* the likelihood of serious commitment in such quagmires as Lebanon and El Salvador.) Are our hackles supposed to rise or not? Should we go off and comb the record for evidence that the Soviets didn't want the United States involved in Vietnam, probably because they feared that such involvement would lead either to a U.S. win or to a wider conflict in which they might be involved? Suppose that we do that and come back with such evidence, which we invoke in a stern denunciation of MacCrimmon's grossly misleading model. Will MacCrimmon then retreat into the combination super-rational and Machiavellian model—long familiar as the basis of "conspiracy theories"—and maintain that the Soviets are capable both of perfect foresight and of totally consistent dissembling about their objectives and intentions? Or will he simply advise us that we have taken him too seriously?

According to my understanding of the chapter, he will advise us that we have taken him too seriously. He offers the super-rational model not for its truth but for the sake of the "useful insights" that it may generate—of which his speculation about Soviet motivation in Cuba may or may not be a good example. He contends that the model is useful because it is provocative. It certainly is provocative, but not nearly as provocative as it would be if he claimed it to be true.

There is an alternative way of classifying the central methodological inspiration of MacCrimmon's paper, and that is to view it as an application of the "method of multiple working hypotheses." This method of inquiry was expounded in 1897 in a delightful essay by the American geologist T. C. Chamberlin (1897), and its application in social science is beautifully illustrated by Graham Allison's (1971) well-known study of the Cuban Missile Crisis. In pursuing this method, the investigator does his or her best to take seriously more than one major organizing hypothesis or framework for his or her study. Frequently, the various hypotheses under consideration will be partially inconsistent or at least incongruent. Also, conceptual frameworks provide a form of heuristic guidance to inquiry that is difficult to exploit without a degree of psychological commitment to the task. For both of these reasons, it is difficult or impossible to employ multiple working hypotheses except by taking each in turn and attempting to use it as effectively as possible. This sequential approach is taken in Allison's book and in MacCrimmon's discussion of the missile crisis.

A major virtue of the method of multiple working hypotheses is that diverse lights are thrown upon the subject matter. Facts that seem insignificant in one framework may seem highly significant in another. Reliance on a single framework risks overlooking the high coherence that the facts (including presumptively insignificant ones) might have when appraised from a different angle. On the other hand, it is impossible to operate without employing a framework, since without one there are no criteria of significance at all. The method of multiple working hypotheses seeks a rational balancing of the risks of being trapped in a framework and the risks of being without one. This desirable goal presumably is part of the motivation for MacCrimmon's proposed triumvirate of explanatory models.

But a key question is what happens after the diverse lights have been thrown. One possibility is that the investigator may want to declare that one hypothesis has clearly triumphed in the sense that it can readily subsume all the valid insights provided by the others, while offering correct predictions on matters where the others are wrong or silent. More likely, however, the issue of which is best will remain unsettled. In that case, further progress requires some mix of development of "critical tests"—to determine which hypothesis is correct—and amalgamation of the hypotheses into a broader scheme that captures the best insights of each.

The question of what to do at this stage is inevitably a difficult one, but whether one is seeking to develop critical tests or to develop a more comprehensive explanatory scheme, it would seem that the dominant heuristic has to be an effort to determine "what is really going on" in a sense that transcends the original hypotheses. MacCrimmon offers no guidance on how this stage of inquiry is to be pursued and appears to argue that it would be premature to attempt to move beyond the use of models for the generation of insights and inferences to the development of predictive laws. This stance may well represent an appropriate humility so far as the present power of descriptive social science is concerned, but it certainly offers little comfort to decision makers who need to anticipate the behavior of other actors in their environments. One would not bet a career, a company, or a country on a model that had no claim to attention beyond its ability to generate provocative insights.

In addition to the foregoing concerns about the methodological basis of MacCrimmon's approach, I have reservations on a number of more substantive points. For example, while I agree with MacCrimmon that "holistic" models are useful, this is mainly because information on the internal workings of the observed decision unit is sometimes entirely lacking. The question of what should be done when there are at least some strong hints about those internal workings is an important one and deserves more serious attention than MacCrimmon gives it. But space does not permit a full discussion of all such issues, and I choose to concentrate my attention here on one major one.

My strongest reservations about MacCrimmon's framework relate to his development of the "mechanistic model." It is clear that he takes a dim view of mechanistic decision making, ascribing to it a long list of drawbacks and limitations but few if any virtues. Even the obvious virtue of placing low demands on the decision maker is left implicit and not very clearly distinguished from the vice of sloth on the part of the decision maker. Thus, for example, MacCrimmon says, "The mechanistic decision unit does not think in terms of choices; in fact, we wouldn't characterize it as thinking at all. It simply does what it has always done." "The [mechanistic] decision unit is subject to standard biases. It anchors on available facts. It acts independently of probabilities, appearing to misestimate them but, in fact, ignoring them." Consistent with this appraisal is the fact that all of the illustrative applications of the mechanistic model as a generator of explanatory hypotheses are proposed explanations for *counterproductive* actions.

MacCrimmon is certainly not alone in this negative assessment of decision making that is "mechanistic"—or, in synonymous or near-synonymous terms, "routinized," "habitual," "programmed," or governed by "standard operating procedures," "standard plans," or "rules of thumb." Indeed, this is a very common attitude among normative analysts and critics of decision

making of every sort of background and disposition, from the
meanest faultfinder and scapegoat seeker to the most sophisticated
decision analyst. I shall argue that this is a very limited and limiting
point of view. In a more provocative mood, I might argue that it
is little more than a prejudice. The effect of this prejudice is to
divert attention from important considerations and deep dilemmas
that are relevant to the understanding of all sorts and instances of
decision making and action taking—including instances that are
superficially remote from the domain of MacCrimmon's mechanistic model. Consider, for example, the advance of science. According
to the analysis of Thomas Kuhn (1970), the practitioners of "normal
science" are following a standard operating procedure (SOP) defined by the currently accepted paradigm. The fact that this SOP
may take years of advanced education to pick up does not make it
less susceptible to some of the drawbacks of mechanistic decision
making. "Situations are perceived in standard ways. Problems are
classified into regular categories for which there is a routine
response. No checks are made for whether the environment is being
misperceived." Although this statement was made by MacCrimmon in Chapter Three, it could easily have been made by Kuhn. Of
course, Kuhn recognizes that there are advantages as well as
disadvantages to this way of proceeding.

To place mechanistic decision making in a less prejudicial
and more informative perspective, I will examine here a number of
commonly assumed oppositions between the properties of mechanistic decision making and desirable (or allegedly desirable) properties, arguing in each case that the claimed opposition is at best an
unbalanced appraisal and at worst an inversion of the truth.

*There is no necessary opposition between mechanistic deci-
sion making and the rationality properties of the formal decision
models of economics and management science.* The shortest argument in support of this claim is to note that, in the context of those
formal models, the results of rational analysis of a decision problem
are summarized in an optimal decision *rule.* Like any other sort of
rule, an optimal rule can be followed mechanistically; indeed, so far
as the formal analysis of rationality is concerned, once the analysis
is done, there is little else to do. The same point is reflected in
management practice when optimization techniques are actually

employed in the development of organizational routines: one does not expect to see expensive talent looking in the bin to determine whether the inventory of item $i$ is down to $s_i$ or not.

Of course, many organizational routines do not emerge from explicit optimization calculations. They derive their claim to authority not from being legitimately born of a large computer but rather from the accumulated experience of the organization. The details of this experience may have been forgotten, and the processes by which it becomes relevant to current choices may not be fully articulable. The extent and nature of suboptimality in such learned patterns of organizational behavior are interesting, important, and subtle questions but are not within the scope of the formal models of rationality. So far as that theory is concerned, an optimal rule is an optimal rule, and the provenance of rules is not at issue.

It should also be noted that the overwhelmingly dominant concern in formal models of rationality is with the characterization of a purely *subjective* optimality. The analysis relates to behavior that is "rationalizable" as the consistent pursuit of some set of objectives given some set of beliefs about the action opportunities available and about future states of the world. Comparatively little attention has been given to the role of direct experience of the world and of communication with others about their experience and its interpretation in the formation and modification of preferences and beliefs. (Learning from experience and from consultation and comparison with others is the operational basis of what counts as "objective" as opposed to "merely subjective" in the real world. It is the neglect of these influences that properly identifies a model as concerned with subjective rationality, regardless of whether the author of the model so identifies it or takes note of the issue at all. Frequently, the exposition of an economic model does not include any reference to the issue.) Although, in some respects, the rationality of the formal models represents an unattainable ideal, in its extreme subjectivism it sets a low standard for human performance. A test for rationality that involves nothing more than checks for internal consistency is a test that mechanistic decision making will often pass with flying colors. (This by itself is not very reassuring as to the merits of mechanistic decision making, since much the same observation could be made about the world views held by the certifiably insane.)

*There is no necessary opposition between mechanistic decision making and effectiveness as that term is commonly understood, that is, as adequate to superior performance at a given task in a given environment.* Here (as in chapter 4 of Nelson and Winter, 1982) I argue that individual skills provide a useful metaphor for organizational routines. I am behaving quite "mindlessly" as I type my draft of this comment, in the sense that I am not attending at all to the motions that my fingers are going through and very little to the individual letters that I am putting down. My conscious thought is mostly at the level of words, phrases, and sentences, while the actual mechanics of typing seem to flow automatically from my purpose. This is not a flaw in my typing, nor it is a flaw in my calculus skills that I can differentiate $a.x^2$ without thinking about *that*. Similarly, the fact that organizations make most of their "decisions" without "thinking"—without top management being involved in something it identifies as a decision situation—is not a flaw in organizational decision making. On the contrary, taking action "without thinking at all" is often a symptom of high effectiveness, a characteristic of complex behavior patterns that are highly adapted to the environment in which they take place. Conversely, the sort of thinking that ranges over levels of analysis (or of an organizational hierarchy) in an unstructured way is characteristic of the *attempt* to *become* adapted—of troubleshooting or of new learning under way. While attempting to become adapted is more exciting, actually being adapted is more effective.

Typically, rapid processing of large amounts of information is an important element in the effectiveness of mechanistic decision making. A recent article in *Scientific American* emphasizes how true this is of typing skill. A century after the typewriter came into use, it is still not clearly understood how it is possible for skilled typists to type as fast as they do (Salthouse, 1984). MacCrimmon, following tradition on this matter, says quite the opposite: the mechanistic model is characterized by "low informedness." "The processing capacity is very limited, and the memory is slight. No calculations are made." This appraisal is akin to the common observation that a highly skilled performance "looks easy." When you are learning to type or to drive a car, the fact that the activity uses a lot of processing capacity is reflected in conscious attention devoted to the task. When the skill has been acquired, the actual amount of processing going on per minute is probably larger (since the activity is being carried on faster), but it has become "decentralized" and unconscious. When your checkbook doesn't balance and it turns out that the *bank* made the error, you may remember that the bank, too, has to process information to get it right—as it usually does. Absent the reminder provided by an error, the bank's processing capabilities are taken for granted. The same point holds over a vast range of activity where things are done very routinely and at least reasonably well.

One can find all this routinized competence interesting or uninteresting; regardless, there is little basis in reality for the view that routinized decision processes are necessarily or typically information poor. The real situation is very nearly the opposite. Because rationality is bounded, it is not possible for individuals or organizations to *improvise* the effective use of large amounts of information. Such use is possible only as a result of prior investment in some sort of system (or skill, habit, routine, or program) that "mechanistically" picks out, from the enormous range of possible processing activities, the actual processing that the information is to receive.

*Mechanistic decision making does not necessarily diminish the opportunities for genuine, deliberate choice.* By "genuine, deliberate choice" I mean that selection of the action to be taken is done in full conscious (central, top-level) awareness that there *is* a choice and that it deserves some deliberation. Such choice is non-mechanistic by definition, so clearly there is a valid opposition between mechanistic decision making and genuine, deliberate choice *about exactly the same matters.* But suppressing genuine choice about some matters may be the only way to make genuine choices available with regard to other, possibly more important matters. As was suggested earlier, this is true partly because suppressing choices about what to do with available information is the only way to get it processed in time for it to be useful as an input to deliberate choice. An analogous point holds for the control of the effectors of an organization. The wealth of options represented by the full range of logical possibilities for action taking in a complex system is like the wealth of Midas, unconvertible to the real benefits that wealth ordinarily confers. Absent some prior structuring (and hence restriction) of the action options, the processes of choice and implementation are unmanageable.

Computer programs provide a useful analogy here. At one extreme, there are programs that are connected directly to clocks or sensors and provide no scope for genuine (human) choice at all. One step from that extreme are those that present only the choice of whether to run the program or not. At the other extreme, there is no program at all; again, there is no choice, apart from the choice of setting out to create or locate a program. In one sense, the options are then as numerous as the set of possible programs, but, in the more immediate sense, they are nonexistent. A statistical package illustrates the intermediate range where significant issues arise as to whether the user is actually better served by expanding the range of available options or by restricting it.

*Mechanistic decision making does not preclude effective monitoring for environmental change.* The monitoring issue exists at two different levels, according to what "monitoring" is presumed to entail. At the first level, even the most routinized effort to detect change in the environment is monitoring. At this level, the earlier remarks on information intensiveness are relevant. Far from precluding effective monitoring, mechanistic decision making facilitates it by providing an operational definition of the objectives that sensors and processing routines are to serve, a role similar to the one that definite hypotheses, formulated in advance, play in a well-designed statistical study.

At the second level, monitoring for environmental change might be understood to be activity that relates only to types of environmental change that are *not* routinely detected and responded to by the operating system. It is directed to the domain of change events characterized by some combination of low frequency, low probability, and Knightigan uncertainty, but with potentially large implications for decision outcomes.

Here, the genuine and subtle problems posed by mechanistic decision making begin to emerge. Defensive driving provides an everyday example. The skilled driver has a lot of information-processing capacity available that the novice must employ in controlling the vehicle and responding appropriately to the high-frequency part of the spectrum of hazard contingencies, such as traffic lights changing to red. This capacity could be employed in monitoring the environment for early signs of low-probability hazards that the driver's ordinary skills might fail to handle in time; this is defensive driving. However, that capacity could also be employed watching for street signs, carrying on a conversation, preparing for the crisis awaiting the driver at the destination, or daydreaming. These activities do not supplement the driver's normal skills, and they may occasionally impair the exercise of those skills. If an accident occurs that defensive driving would have avoided, should it be attributed in part to the fact that drivers' normal skills permit them to cope with a very wide range of driving situations without thinking about what they are doing?

"Yes and no" is the answer to that question, and the conundrum illustrated by this example is a basic one, present in every decision-making environment. Routinized competence clearly does not *dictate* inattention to considerations that fall outside of the scope of the routines; in fact, it should make possible higher levels of attention to such considerations. But the wider the range of situations subsumed by the routines and the better the routinized performance, the fewer reminders there are that something besides routinized competence might on occasion be useful or even essential to survival. Not only is the door opened to irresponsible or slothful inattention, whose consequences are made to seem tolerable, but rational economic calculation itself dictates a reduction in nonroutine monitoring when the marginal benefits to such monitoring are diminished as a result of the improvement of routines. If the routines are perfect, being alert to their possible limitations is, of course, wasteful. Most likely, the routines are not perfect. Most likely, also, appraisals of the gains to improvement of routines typically fail to allow for the decline in diffuse alertness that is thereby induced (appropriately or not) and for the consequences of the attendant vulnerabilities. Such appraisals may not even be made, since the improvement of routines is often brought about by learning that is the automatic consequence of doing and thus is nondeliberate in itself.

The foregoing review of familiar indictments of mechanistic decision making yields the clear implication that there is no necessary relation between the fact or degree of routinization in a decision process and the quality of the decisions made. The quality of decisions is a matter of the match between the actions taken and the environmental states in which they are taken. Routinization can contribute in important ways to the achievement of good matches. Because rationality is bounded, and the set of conceivable environments is of infinite range and complexity, no feasible decision process, routinized or not, can promise to deliver good matches in every conceivable environment. Routinized processes are, of course, distinctively vulnerable to significant change that is "unforeseen" in the sense that the routine itself comprises no method for foreseeing it. In many cases, this vulnerability poses a problem that is minor, tractable, or both. Frequently, the answer to the problem is not to limit routinization but to enhance it, to modify routines so that troublesome contingencies are diagnosed earlier and responded to systematically.

However, in a world in which the pace and diversity of change place comprehensive, routinized foresight far out of reach, there are some major vulnerability problems to which more and better routinization is not an adequate answer. Such hazards affecting business decisions take a variety of forms. One very important category is that the company may find itself among the victims of a wave of Schumpeterian "creative destruction" (Schumpeter, 1950); its markets may disappear or its product prices decline precipitously as a result of a technological innovation that introduces a substitute for the company's product. When such a threat arises from a technological quarter remote from the company's own concerns, or when the fact that the new product is a substitute for the company's own is not apparent until actual buyer behavior reveals it, timely warnings are unlikely to be generated by the company's own routines. There are other obvious categories of hazard arising from the external environment, such as political or regulatory change. But it is also true that organizational routines provide only a stylized and limited account of the organization's *internal environment,* with regard, for example, to its capabilities in activities different from those that it is routinely pursuing. Critical misjudgments of the company's likely competitive strength in new areas of endeavor may result, leading the company to pursue illusory opportunities or to overlook real ones. This hazard interacts with the vulnerability arising from new competitive threats, since, in maneuvering to outflank such threats, the company may well find itself on unfamiliar paths.

It is easy enough to observe that the way to mitigate these hazards is through the business-strategy counterpart of defensive driving. Not being blessed with the perfect foresight of MacCrimmon's "super-rational" decision maker, the best that actual decision makers can do is to devote some time and resources to maintaining diffuse alertness toward threats and opportunities that are only vaguely visible on the horizon. But this prescription hardly suggests the difficulty of the problem. Alertness that is totally diffuse will yield only an ever-growing list of dreams and nightmares. What is needed is some basis for identifying and dealing with those concerns that deserve management attention at levels well above that devoted to simple monitoring of the mass media, the business press, and the industry grapevine but perhaps well below that devoted to final choice and implementation of new strategic moves.

Since MacCrimmon's principal concern is with the problem of understanding decision behavior from the position of a relatively poorly informed external observer, the subtle normative problems of how to allocate scarce managerial attention to cope with an imperfectly understood environment are not directly relevant to his undertaking. But if part of the concern is to explain why serious errors in decision making occur—and that appears to be the major role envisaged for the mechanistic model—then the explanatory scheme should at least make room for the fact that those normative problems frequently *are* subtle. Even the most diligent and responsible decision makers, determined to attend to and deliberate about every choice that is worth making, can go badly wrong when it is difficult to identify the choices that are worth making. The likelihood of such error is strongly dependent upon the historical path that led to the situation from which a flawed decision may emerge. The hazards depend largely upon how prevailing organizational routines reflect the organization's experience—the lessons that experience has taught and the ones it failed to teach.

# ❦ FIVE ❦

# Comparing 150 Decision Processes

## David J. Hickson, Richard J. Butler
## David Cray, Geoffrey R. Mallory
## David C. Wilson

To William Shakespeare, life was but a play in which each player frets his hour upon the stage and then is gone. This metaphor has become fundamental to sociology, and it is fundamental also to the comprehension of strategic decision making in organizations. The making of a decision is a game among the players on an organized stage of play, each of whom sweats his hour upon the stage and then is gone—though, in most cases, not gone permanently but just moved on to another concurrent game or awaiting the beginning of the next. Here the view of an Elizabethan English playwright blends with that of contemporary French sociology in the writings of Michel Crozier (Crozier, 1964, 1976; Crozier and Friedberg, 1980). To him, what else is an organization, what else is a bureaucracy,

*Note:* The research for this chapter was supported by the British Social Science Research Council, the University of Bradford Management Centre, and the Netherlands Institute for Advanced Study in the Humanities and Social Sciences.

114

but an "ensemble des jeux"? It is an array of overlapping games of decision and power.

The conversation of those at the top of organizations is full of allusions that indicate that, to them, this is a very real perspective. "You can't win them all," they say. Or "I don't know what the next move should be," or "it's all politics in this game," or "I can't follow what their game is," or "it's a matter of gamesmanship," or, cynically and despairingly, "it's a dirty game in this business." They do not mean, and it is not meant here, that these are games played for amusement during jocular interludes in the working day! The analogy of a game is expressive for those involved and enlightening to researchers who watch and enquire, but the games are serious all through. Strategic decisions are serious for individuals personally involved, since they become settings for career struggles, and they are serious for the organization as a whole—that is, for all the others with stakes in it, including its employees—since they set its future course.

Decision-making games at the top are therefore rarely played to destruction. They may strain the organization, but they do not tear it apart, for without it there would be no decision-making games in which to play. Those involved pursue the "logiques d'action" (Karpik, 1972; Weiss, 1981) of their interests within "rules of the game" (Crozier and Friedberg, 1980), which guide them in the moves to make and in just how far they may go. These are games of restrained maneuver in which there is "quasi-resolution of conflicts" (Cyert and March, 1963) between interests whose representatives survive to conflict again another day. The play is for positions in the game and in games to come, rather than for all or nothing (Crozier, 1976), and "schismatic tendencies" (Morgan, 1981) are held in check—unless, of course, the final fateful issue arises of whether to merge with another organization, whether to accept or to resist a takeover, whether to keep going somehow or to close down.

The significance of these decision-making games is not only in their consequences for the organizations in which they take place. Their consequences are wider, since organizations are forces in economic and social change, and their major managerial decisions can be vital to society (Colignon and Cray, 1980). Successive decisions reveal their strategies, and to understand these decisions, it is necessary to understand the processes by which they are reached and the influence of the interests involved.

Because an organization is a shifting multiple-goal coalition of stakeholders (Cyert and March, 1963), numerous interests are drawn into strategic decision making—internal departments, divisions, and subunits of all kinds and external customers or clients, suppliers, government departments and agencies, and so on, all of which can exert influence. It is therefore not surprising if the "trajectory" (Hage, 1980, p. 116) followed by the matter for decision is sometimes, if not always, erratic as it ricochets from one to another in formal meetings and corridor encounters and telephoned interventions. It may run into "interrupts" and "recycle" again and again (Mintzberg, Rasinghani, and Théorêt, 1976), while "sequential attention to goals" (Cyert and March, 1963) swings the emphasis first one way, then another. Those who play on toward a decision probably follow the tactics of "logical" though "disjointed" incrementalism (Quinn, 1980; Braybrooke and Lindblom, 1963) and may even arrive at an outcome that is not only "satisficing" (Simon, 1960) but partially "uncoupled" (Cohen, March, and Olsen, 1972; March and Olsen, 1976) from what they thought they were doing. So we have a caricature of strategic decision-making games at the top as being politically imbued maneuverings tugged hither and thither in spasms of action and inaction that shove them little by little toward semiunforeseen decisions—an insightful caricature, an exciting and, from some angles, slightly comic caricature, but one more vivid in outline than solid in form.

To ask the absolutely basic question, are there differences? Most of what is written is written just about "decision making," as if it were all the same. Surely the game is played differently in different organizations or with different decision topics. Are there any clues as to what is most associated with organization and what is most associated with the characteristics of the decision? Notable case-study analyses, such as those by Cyert, Simon, and Trow (1956), by Allison (1969, 1971), and by Pettigrew (1973), have accumulated over the decades but have not had nearly enough follow-up by comparative research. There have been projects that brought together sets of cases recorded separately by different individuals, the pioneering work by Mintzberg, Rasinghani, and Théorêt's (1976) students, which gave a lead in comparing twenty-five processes, and the typically vigorous presentation of thirteen cases by March and Olsen (1976) and their colleagues. There have been attempts to use questionnaires, such as Axelsson and Rosenberg's (1979) comparison of views of decision making in twenty organizations and the sixty-four mailed questionnaires returned to Stein (1981a, 1981b) from unspecified managers and organizations. But difficulties of comparison across cases remained, samples were small, and the meaning of mailed questionnaire data on decision making must be in doubt. Encouragingly, Drenth and others (1979) widened the coverage dramatically to no fewer than 103 cases, though they report only the influence of hierarchical echelons; at the same time, Quinn (1980) achieved appreciable depth of coverage by talking to managers in nine business corporations.

The Bradford studies are an attempt to develop the area in both depth and breadth and, by doing so, to begin to meet the need outlined by Mohr (1982, p. 156) for characteristics of process that can act as independent variables for the explanation of outcomes. They combine intensive study of detailed case histories with comparison of a larger number of shorter narratives of events, all guided by the same concepts, and add both a wider variety of organizations and a larger sample of decisions in each organization, which is vital to any investigation of what effects are due to organizational type and what to the nature of the decision.

This chapter offers only partial answers to some of the simpler questions (full results appear in Hickson and others, 1985). If the course of a decision-making game follows an unsteady, wavering trajectory, then how long does it go on? That is, how long does it usually take to arrive at a strategic decision? If each game reflects underlying issues that surface as matters for decision, then what matters are these? That is, what topics are strategic decisions usually about? If numerous players take part, then what interests do they represent? That is, what internal and external interests usually become involved? If influence is exerted, then how much, and by whom? That is, what is the usual influence of different kinds of interests? It must be acknowledged that even these straightforward questions are often bigger than the answers that can be offered and that these studies in their turn share methodological weaknesses in an empirically difficult field of research, but substantial data have been obtained.

## The Bradford Studies

*Sample and Data Collection.* A data base of 150 cases of strategic decision making was built up by interviewing, and six of the same cases were traced by intensive case-study methods. Data collection, all in Britain, took place from 1974 to 1980, especially in the years 1977 to 1980. The origins of the decision-making processes described often reached back to earlier years and most were concluded by the time of the data collection, so that they occurred over periods from the mid-1960s to the late 1970s.

Organizations were first approached by letter to the chief executives, supplemented by telephone calls as necessary. Of those approached, two thirds—that is, thirty organizations—cooperated. They range in size from 100 to over 50,000 employees. Seventeen are privately owned (manufacturers, financial institutions, road transport, and so on), and thirteen are publicly (state-) owned (health service districts, universities, utilities, and so on). There are eleven manufacturing (metal components, glass, chemicals, breweries) and nineteen service (banking, insurance, airways, local government, and so on) organizations. Most are relatively prominent, a large proportion being national or international leaders in the private or public sectors and household names, which prevents publication of some details in case histories. They were chosen from published directories, with the aim of as even a coverage as possible over a selection matrix that offset private and public ownership categories against manufacturing and services categories, to reflect as far as practicable the diversity of contemporary organizations. However, the resulting set of organizations depended upon personal managerial collaboration, because those at the top who were centrally involved in cases of decision making had to be willing to give considerable information about decisions that were still important to them and that had occurred sufficiently recently to be readily recalled. They also had to be willing and able to give time to researchers. As in all this sort of research, any biases introduced by self-selection are beyond knowing.

In an initial interview, the chief executive reviewed the history of the organization, its outputs and basic structure, and its external relationships and was asked to nominate major decisions involving more than just one department or section and with widespread effects, including, when possible, one each concerning inputs, outputs, core technology, personnel, and reorganization, but there was no hard-and-fast sticking to these categories.

Interviews about each case were then conducted with centrally involved "eye-witness" informants; for example, managing directors and function directors in firms, vice-chancellors and deans in universities, management-team members in health districts, and chief officers in local government. Since what was wanted was information about *processes* of decision making that take place at top managerial levels, middle-management or lower employees or unions were not approached, as they would know nothing firsthand of the inner workings at this level. Interviewees were informants giving information about events, not respondents talking about themselves; each was interviewed at length, often more than once. There was an average of six informants per organization; in one third of the cases, there were two or more informants. When the direct account was from one informant only, many interviews were joined by managerial colleagues, who were asked to add to what the informant could say.

Each interview began with a historical narrative of the sequence of events as they had unfolded. This was followed by numerous open-ended questions about particular aspects of the story, which led the informant to elaborate on certain features of what had happened. Seven of these features were then rated on five-point scales (for example, of influence and of prevalence of delays). These ratings provided precise summings up, while the narrative notes gave them meaning.

In each of three organizations, a public utility, a university, and a private manufacturer, two cases were studied in far greater depth by intensive methods. Three were followed concurrently as they happened, and three were traced historically, by interviews, casual discussions, lunchtime contacts, and document searches throughout management across departments by a researcher who spent hours or days weekly in the organizations over two or three years. These six case studies are fully reported by Wilson (1980, 1982).

*Model of Strategic Decision Making.* The research design was guided by a model of strategic decision making that is diagramed in Figure 1. First comes power. In both the private and the public sectors, the ultimate power holders—those who have the final financial and legal throw when the chips are down—establish and maintain the organization as a setting in which decision making can take place. By doing so, they set implicit or explicit limits on what may be considered and what may be decided (Bachrach and Baratz, 1962) and introduce unquestioned assumptions inherent even in the language of managerial decision making itself (Lukes, 1974; Clegg, 1975). From the perspective of decision making, it is appropriate to see an organization not as a "bureaucracy" or as a "labor process," which it is from other points of view, but as a framework of rules of the game. Its very existence, constituted by or by leave of the laws of the land for given purposes, circumscribes the play. In particular, it sets the permissible and the impermissible, the practicable and the impracticable, in what topics may surface for decision.

The topics that arise, such as proposed new products or reorganizations, pose problems and implicate interests that together shape processes, a theory expressed in earlier formats by Astley and others (1982) and Butler and others (1979-80). The multiple features of decision *problems* are embraced by using the term *complexity* very broadly to include features such as their rarity (or novelty), the seriousness of their consequences, the endurance of those consequences (how far decision makers look ahead into a more uncertain and complex future), and the complications of involving diverse interests. Problem complexity represents the view of decision making as task centered, facing dynamic and novel problems (Axelsson and Rosenberg, 1979; Kirsch and Kutschker, 1982, pp. 474-475, who extract a complexity factor; Hage, 1980, pp. 109-129) within the limits of human cognitive abilities (Simon, 1960; March and Simon, 1958). The multiple features of decision *interests* are embraced by using the broad term *politicality* (or, more narrowly, *cleavage;* Astley and others, 1982) to include, for example, the pressure or weight of influence, the balance of influence, and the contention of

**Figure 1. Model of Decision Making for the Bradford Studies.**

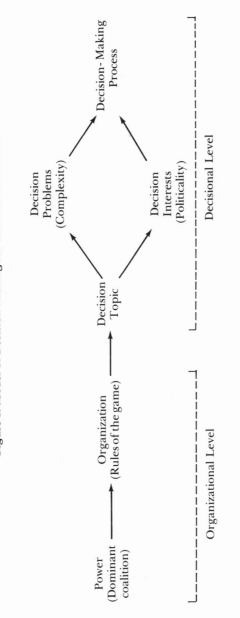

objectives, all of which flow from the complexity of interest involvements. Interest politicality represents the view of decision making as inherently political, manipulating, and contending with the interests of the influential and the less influential (as, for instance, in Pettigrew, 1973; Bacharach and Lawler, 1980; Hage, 1980; pp. 109–129; Pfeffer, 1981c).

Complexity and politicality constitute dual explanations of the nature of the game and the process it follows (Astley and others, 1982), for into the organizational "garbage can" go complex problems, and in it, awaiting them, are political interests (March and Olsen, 1976). "From this point of view, an organization is a collection of choices looking for problems, . . . solutions looking for issues to which they might be the answer, and decision makers looking for work" (Cohen, March, and Olsen, 1972, p. 2). Small wonder that the processes that ensue in the "garbage can" can be characterized in a vast number of different ways: for example, by their duration (Hage, 1980, p. 117; Astley and others, 1982, p. 363; Mallory and others, 1983, p. 199) or their amount of negotiation (Hage, 1980, p. 117; Astley and others, 1982, p. 363) or their continuity (Butler and others, 1979–80, p. 15; Astley and others, 1982, p. 363) and so on, almost indefinitely.

More of the many questions raised by this model are examined in Hickson and others (1985). As has been said already, this chapter must be restricted to a few that are comparatively straightforward.

## The Course of the Game

What do we know, or think we know, about the course of the game? It follows a path, or "trajectory," that bounces around like that of a molecule in a bubble chamber, on some occasions running along the branches of the hierarchy and on others veering away into a "network" pattern (Hage, 1980, pp. 110 and 119). As it does so, it often runs again along pathways that it has followed before, repeating "routines" of recognition or diagnosis or search and the like (Mintzberg, Rasinghani, and Théorêt, 1976) and recycling through "bargaining zones" (Abell 1975) until the final choice of what is to be done ends its cavorting.

How long does this endure? Or is it more pertinent to ask how long those involved endure it? Are all such processes interminable, like that recorded by Pettigrew (1973) in a British retail business where choosing replacement electronic data-processing equipment seemed to drag on for something like seven years? Probably not, for the twenty-five Canadian cases reviewed by Mintzberg, Rasinghani, and Théorêt (1976) ranged to something over four years (the full duration of the longer cases was not known), and the twenty-nine "strategic" and twenty-seven "tactical" decisions studied in three organizations in the Netherlands by the DIO International Research Team (1983, Table 2) averaged seventy weeks, a year and a half.

The chances are that it does take about a year to make most strategic decisions, for the mean of the 150 Bradford studies cases is just over twelve months (12.4 months, to be overprecise with less than precise data), and the mode is just under six months. This is defining the decision-process time as running from "first proposal" (Hage, 1980, p. 117) or when "a stimulus for an action is perceived" (Mintzberg, Rasinghani, and Théorêt, 1976, p. 58) to "final decision outcome" (Hage, 1980, p. 117) or when "the commitment to the action is made" (Mintzberg, Rasinghani, and Théorêt, 1976, p. 258). Periodizing history is always debatable, as any historian will admit, for the choice of the start and the end is arbitrary. But, then, so is all empirical research, which must cut pieces out of an uncomprehended existence. For the purposes of the Bradford studies, the rule was to define the process from the first recalled deliberate action that began movement toward a decision (when, for example, the matter was discussed in a meeting or a report was called for) to the approved choice (when the decision and its implementation were authorized).

This period is obviously followed by implementation, but, less obviously, it is often, perhaps always, preceded by a time of comparatively covert interactions. This is a time when the possibility of raising the matter may be casually mentioned, perhaps more than once in conversations over the years, but nothing is done to move toward a decision. The possible functions of this "gestation time," as it can be called (Mallory and others, 1983, p. 199), are discussed elsewhere (Hickson and others, 1985).

Though a deliberate process time of usually a year or less does not seem unduly long for arriving at a decision that can shape the future for years to come, some decisions do take much longer. There is a wide range about the mean (standard deviation 10.6 months), which goes up to a maximum of 48 months, or four years. As if to ridicule the popular image of hard-driving, no-nonsense, quick-action private enterprise, two of the longest processes were both in the same private manufacturer, and one of the shortest was in a public bureaucrary, a municipal authority. It showed how the personal commitment of influential individuals can accelerate a novel decision through an administrative and political structure that was not evolved to deal with it. It gets by potential impediments before they are ready for it, so to speak.

Indeed, the accidents of personal encounters can be momentous. It happened that the leader of the controlling political party in the municipal council took his holidays one year in a coastal resort in the warmth of Devon, in the southwest of England. But, though he left his industrial metropolitan area behind, it did not leave his thoughts. Budget restrictions were pressing. So when, during his holiday, he met a promoter of lotteries who talked persuasively about the painless money-raising potential that lay unexploited pending someone having the initiative to try out a municipal public lottery, he was all ears. Here was a way to transcend all the difficulties of raising the level of local taxes (called "rates" in England). He may not have realized that the process of making a decision would also transcend the slowness of the procedures evolved over the decades to deal with public funds. The committee procedures were appropriate to the detailed scrutiny and political controversy associated with raising funds by taxation. A proposal for a lottery was unique, unprecedented. Despite the reservations of the members of some churches, which cut across party lines, the lottery promoter visited the municipality immediately following the holiday resort encounter, the party leader and an equally enthusiastic colleague introduced the proposal, and it shot through the hands of officials and committees in the August-to-October period when numbers of councilors were still away traveling. Its strategic value lay in opening up a source of revenue beyond the immemorially fixed set of traditional sources.

Yet, in a prominent and highly successful British-owned multinational company with an outstanding record in technical advancement and product innovation, senior managerial echelons took no less than four years to decide to invest in a huge new plant using new technology and almost as long to assess the chances of a revolutionary product use before they went ahead. These decisions would have gratified the writers of management textbooks. They moved carefully from planning committees to financial committees to divisional committees to divisions and group boards and back again, passing on the way through innumerable working parties and project teams and generating multitudes of reports and written evaluations. Indeed, this was an organization with manuals that listed strings of technical and other specialist committees, far more than any other of the organizations studied.

It can be inferred from this that search costs time. Finding and evaluating information makes the months go by—beneficially, perhaps, for the quality of judgments made, suggesting that following the textbook may work well for major "computation" type decisions (Thompson and Tuden, 1964) such as these two examples, when numerate information can be gathered and totted up, given always that time is available, but warning that, when time is short, the textbook and the exhortations of management trainers must be pushed aside to allow freedom to "fly by the seat of your pants"— an acrobatic that Lindblom (1959) believes is more comfortable anyway.

What should not be inferred is that committees inevitably cost time, as is commonly supposed. Mallory and others (1983) pick up the couplets printed by Downs (1967, p. 160):

> Committees of twenty
> deliberate plenty.

> Committees of ten
> act now and then.

> But most jobs get done
> by committees of one.

Certainly committees—and that label is used here generically to include boards, standing committees, and temporary working parties or project groups—take the time of those individuals who perspire within them on long, hot afternoons, not to mention murky grey mornings. But that is not the same as saying that decision processes that pass through committees take longer. They don't. There is no correlation between the number of committees in a process and its length from start to finish ($r$ = 0.08), though it should be noted that this is the number of separate committees and not the number of times each one met or how long it met for. That is, committees are as likely to speed a process toward its conclusions as they are to hinder it.

At the lower end of the range, some of the decisions studied were made in just a few months, and a few even in as little as about a month. What is it that marks out these from the others? There is not much to go on. Time correlates with very little else. Perhaps fast decisions are pushed by the powerful. Perhaps they "fly by the seat of their pants" without stopping to gather or to assimilate fresh information. The case material on this is still being analyzed.

### The Focus of the Game

Fast or slow, what are the games of strategic decision making about? Power, it is averred (Crozier and Friedberg, 1980; March and Olsen, 1976), because each game is played for itself and for position in the next. Yes, indeed; that borders on a truism. Oddly, less is known at a more ostensible level. What decision topics arise? Are strategic decisions mainly financial ones? Are they mainly takeovers and mergers?

Early favorites for researchers were decisions on whether or not to buy a computer or which brand to buy (for example, Cyert, Simon, and Trow, 1956; Carter, 1971; Pettigrew, 1973). These may have been barely strategic in the full sense of that word, but, relative to the organizations in which they occurred, they did commit both funds and the form and administration of the organization for years ahead, and so they can be given the benefit of any doubt. After all, there is no exact and accepted definition for what is and is not strategic. Later, March and Olsen (1976) included six reorganization decisions among the thirteen reported by themselves and their colleagues; but Mintzberg, Rasinghani, and Théorêt (1976) went in another direction, with only one case out of twenty-five concerning the form of the organization itself, a merger, but eleven concerning investment in new equipment of one kind or another, from new planes and runways for airlines and airports to new data-processing systems (still a favorite) and new buildings. If this is put beside the sixteen "medium-size capital investment" decisions among the twenty-nine classed as strategic from those studied by the DIO team (DIO International Research Team, 1983), it looks very much as if the typical strategic decision is about a financial commitment to equipment or buildings. Is this supported by the balance of the 150 Bradford cases? It is, at first sight, for the category tops the list of topics of decision in order of frequency:

| | | |
|---|---|---|
| Technologies | 23 | (investment in equipment or premises) |
| Reorganization | 22 | (internal restructurings) |
| Controls | 19 | (planning, budgeting, and requisite data processing) |
| Domains | 18 | (marketing and distribution) |
| Services | 16 | (new, expanded, or reduced services) |
| Products | 12 | (new products) |
| Personnel | 12 | (job-assessment schemes, unionization, and so on) |
| Boundaries | 11 | (takeovers, mergers) |
| Inputs | 9 | (financial and material supplies) |
| Locations | 8 | (site of major plants or of headquarters) |
| | 150 | |

A topic is the label attached by those involved to the choice made when an issue becomes the subject of a decision-making process (Astley and others, 1982, p. 373). The subject is referred to as "the Swedish plant" decision or the "takeover of the new subsidiary" decision, and, though each will have other ramifications, this label denotes how the decision presents itself to and is recalled by executives centrally concerned at the time. Topics arise from issues, persisting problems or opportunities (Astley and others, 1982, p. 373) that may give rise to more than one decision in the course of time, each labeled as a separate topic.

The topics of decision of the 150 Bradford cases were classified by two members of the research team into the preceding ten categories according to their labeling by the managerial informants. It is a classification that could be shuffled differently. Categories could have been combined—for example, products and services could become "outputs"—but in this and other instances, they were kept separate so as to be able to see any differences between them in decision-making processes. Other categories could have been split—for example, technologies into equipment versus buildings—but in this and other instances, it was not thought that further differentiation would be of interest. In general, categories were kept as broad as possible consonant with meaningfulness so that each would include a reasonable number of cases for comparison.

Hence, although at first it may appear that technology topics best represent what strategic decisions are about (23 of 150 = 15 percent), this may not be so. Both manufacturing and service organizations are frequently embroiled in decisions over whether to venture new products or new services, and if these two categories are put together as "outputs," then there are 28, or 19 percent. Similarly, the 22 reorganization topics, concerned with internal structure, and the 11 boundaries topics, concerned with the external structure or limits of the organization, make up 33 in all, or 22 percent, on "organization." Probably, therefore, strategic decisions are most often about the form of the *organization* itself or the goals inherent in its *outputs* and *investment* in technology, topics that among them make up more than half the 150 Bradford cases. This is a reassuringly commonsense picture into which biases both toward organization topics and toward technology topics in previous research can be fitted.

Since, as mentioned earlier, the interviewers preferred, whenever possible, a spread among the five topics chosen in each organization, there will be some small bias toward variety, and, therefore, the bulk concerning organization, outputs, and investment in technology could even be underrepresented. At the same time, the rest of the topics should not be forgotten. There is a bewildering array—for example, whether to move a company's huge headquarters from one end of England to the other (they stayed put), whether to launch a stock issue and for how much (they did, the biggest ever in its day), whether to resist unionization (they did, in a bitter struggle), whether adopting a common name or names with a common component for each of a group of companies would enhance the common image or would lose business (they risked it and renamed), what the shape of the business plan and budget should be (they were cautious), and many more. In general, it looks as if almost anything *can* become strategic in the eyes of those who take part.

Some topics are more familiar, of course. One decision may cause little stir because its like has been seen before, whereas another may be much more of an event because nothing like it has happened, yet both are major matters. Even if "familiarity breeds contempt," as the saying goes, so that there is less excitement over the familiar topic, it is no less important for the organization. Comments obtained by asking "How often do decisions of this nature arise?" showed that the most precedented topics were inputs decisions, about either funds or materials, and new-products decisions. On financial inputs, although a big stock issue, for example, may be vital, similar decisions may have been made before. On products, a new one may affect the whole future by its success or failure, as did the well-known cases in American industry of IBM's computer, Du Pont's Corfam shoe, and Ford's Edsel car, which Hage (1980, pp. 120–121) classifies as examples of high risk, but most firms are used to new-products decisions and have made many before. Senior managers know how to go about them, and procedures have evolved for handling them.

Not so with the most infrequent and, by implication, novel category of topics, internal reorganizations. Inserting a regional level into the hierarchy between local and national offices or merging prominent departments may be a unique matter, and even if something of the sort had arisen in the past, it was very rare. Reorganizations, then, appear to be the most unprecedented difficult-to-handle decisions, a finding that, as Cas Vroom of the Royal Military Academy at Breda in the Netherlands has pointed out to us, augers well for everyone researching and teaching on organizational problems. Further, there is a possible clue here to differences in decision-making processes in response to the characteristics of decision problems that is being followed up (Hickson and others, 1985).

## Players in the Game

*Involvement.* As Cohen, March, and Olsen (1972, p. 1) put it, there is "fluid participation. Participants vary in the amount of time and effort they devote to different domains; involvement varies from one time to another." Each decision topic draws in a variety of "players." They may be the staffs of internal specialist departments, asked to examine some aspect and to report to the chair or to the marketing subcommittee or to the capital-investment committee. They may be members of such committees. They may represent outsiders, such as large customers who are asked whether they would welcome a new design or service, an industry or trade association whose experienced advice is sought, or a government department that is consulted or asked for a financial grant. This complexity of involvement, or "extensity of participation" (Hage 1980, p. 117), is to be expected from the view of organizations as coalitions of interests developed by Cyert and March (1963) and from the examples of the differing demands made upon an organization by outside interests given by Rhenman (1973, pp. 38–39).

Analysis of the 150 Bradford studies cases confirms that top management is very much concerned with the external environment in the course of decision making. Informants named no fewer than 422 different external units involved in the decisions in some way at some stage, both fleeting and sustained contacts, comprising 40 percent of all involvements. The other 60 percent were internal departments, sections, and the like (informants listed the units, as well as often mentioning them in narrative accounts; the totals are of the numbers listed, irrespective of the amount or importance of the involvements). Involvements external to executive management were broken down as follows:

| | |
|---|---|
| Auditors, trade associations, shareholders | 112 (11 percent) |
| Government departments and agencies | 108 (11 percent) |

| | |
|---|---|
| Suppliers | 79 (7 percent) |
| Competitors | 45 (4 percent) |
| Customers, clients | 43 (4 percent) |
| Trade unions | 35 (3 percent) |
| | 422 (40 percent) |

So that the units could be grouped in this way, they were classified by their *interests* in the functioning of the organization, following the lead given by Katz and Kahn (1966), who formulated a more abstractly defined classification. Reading upward through the list, the interest of the unions is in employment, of customers in outputs, of competitors in (comparative) performance, of suppliers in inputs, of government in public standards, and of auditors in private (that is, privately set) standards. This is self-evident except for these last two, most frequently involved groupings, especially the last, which brings together otherwise disparate units by their common form of interest.

The top two positions in the list are occupied by the two classes of "regulatory" interests—first, the auditors, trade associations, and shareholders, interested in conformity to privately set standards, and, second, government departments and agencies, interested in conformity to publicly set standards. This demonstrates what has long been believed, that top managements are not wholly free agents even in their most crucial internal decision making, for regulatory hands reach in and mark the ultimate limits. They also bring advice (from trade associations, for example) and assistance (state subsidies), of course.

But are these involvements influential? Do they noticeably affect the decision? Whose influence does management feel? That of unions and of government is of special interest.

*Influence.* If politics "is the study of power in action" (Pfeffer, 1981c, p. 7), then in this context that means *the exercise of influence in decision making.* This is active influence as experienced by those influenced, whether or not the influencing party was aware of the effect achieved. "Politics refers to the active influence process, but power is latent, referring to the ability or capacity to influence" (Miles, 1980a, p. 184). The narrative summaries of cases of decision making indicated the influence of the more prominent interests, informants subsequently listing all involved interest units and then rating their influence on a five-point scale running from "a little influence," rated 1, to "a very great deal of influence," rated 5 (following Tannenbaum, 1968, and Hinings and others, 1974, who studied internal subunits only). The ratings were not disembodied figures, therefore, but assessments in the context of a particular history of events that had been brought to mind.

As for trade union influence, unions are weak. The mean rating for all instances of union influence is 2.26, probably lowest of all the categories of interests and comparing with a mean for all interest units, internal and external, of 3.05 ($N$ = 1,021). It is averaged over thirty-five unions, in twenty-nine cases of decision making. (In twenty-six decisions, one union only was named as exerting an influence. In the three remaining decisions, which were all public sector—in a National Health Service district organization and in a polytechnical school—there were respectively two, three, and four unions. Wilson and others, 1982, report the trade union data in full.) As already pointed out, this rating reflects the view of those influenced, top managers and administrators. Whether union officials would have rated themselves differently is a moot point, but, since the known tendency for raters to overrate their own influence is slight, the presumption is that they would not have seen things very differently. Moreover, overrating of their influence by the unions themselves would not alter the perceptions of those influenced.

In more detail, there was any union influence at all in only 29 of 150 decisions. Second, that influence was small and less than that of most other interests, the low average reflecting ratings of merely 1, 2, of 3 out of 5 for the unions in 20 out of the 29 decisions (Wilson and others, 1982, Table 2). Third, in only one case did the union initiate the decision-making process. That was in a university, where the dominant national union, the Association of University Teachers, submitted a letter to the governing university council drawing attention to grievances over hiring and firing and urging reforms (which were eventually made, apparently ineffectively).

As Fox (1974, p. 280) argues from a critical standpoint: "What many see as major conflicts in which labor seems often now to have the advantages are conflicts only on such issues as management deems it realistic to contest, and these never touch the real roots of ownership, inequality, hierarchy, and privilege." Nor do unions seem to seek anything more. Long-standing managerial prerogatives of virtually complete control of decisions about new products or services, markets, and inputs seem unchallenged, and the decisions about which unions are consulted or, perhaps, told usually involve matters of personnel, equipment, and organization (Wilson and others, 1982, Table 1). This meshes perfectly with European research revealing negligible employee influence and not much more influence for unions when they participate in formally constituted representative bodies (Teulings, 1985; IDE International Research Group, 1981).

Yet what of the nine decisions not referred to so far, in eight of which the influence of a union was considered to be "a great deal" (rating 4) and in one of which it was considered to be "a very great deal" (5) (Wilson and others, 1982, Table 3)? Although these appear to tell a different story, a closer look reveals that a superficial impression is misleading. It is crucial to know from the narratives of the decision making what the influence was exerted for and whether it was successful. This enables the figures of influence to be understood as they should be.

In three of these situations, the union just defended its members' interests without attacking the decision itself, and the decision went through. In three more, it resisted outright the decision that was being made—and lost. That leaves three decisions only, of 150, in which the unions had it more or less their way. These were a transport service's reorganization, a health service district's policy on radiographers, and a police force's change of its staff-appraisal system. At first sight, it seemed that union power had won the day. A second look gave a different interpretation. In each case, the management either were not averse to the union view or positively wanted the same! In short, the unions "won" only when there was no one to beat.

Hence, unions can be regarded as marginal to the making of strategic decisions. These continue to be the preserve of management, even during the years of full employment and expansion when the decision-making cases studied took place. This contradicts the instant impressions created by the mass media of a Britain torn by union strife and dominated by union influence. It shows unions with little hand in decision making. They are on the receiving end. So is it at the late stage, when decisions are already made and implementation is beginning or under way, that unions make their presence felt? Media pictures show conflicts about decisions that have been taken and are being put into effect, not conflicts during the making of decisions. The closure of a factory is announced, and then the resistance gathers and the television cameras come in, but they are not there during the decision making leading up to that announcement. So the evidence is that the role of unions is reactive, delaying or modifying implementation but not changing the decisions themselves.

Does government fare any differently? In an industrialized, often said to be "de-industrializing" liberal democracy, is private business free to ride in any direction it chooses, freewheeling through its strategic choices unrestrained by the influence of the state? In Western Europe, there have been times when the state was all but omnipotent. Teulings (1982) harks back to the way in which the imperatives of survival under a foreign military regime during the Second World War brought the leading Dutch industrial firm, Philips, gradually into military production for that regime, using forced labor. Even in Britain, there was a growing corporatism in the private and public sectors during the times when the decisions that were studied were made. Nonetheless, despite attempts at incomes policies, national price freezes, continual meetings between industrial figureheads and government ministers, and discussions within the framework of the National Economic Development Office (NEDO), private business continued to be private business.

The Bradford studies data offer a glimpse within the privacy of that business's decision making. They do not show any effects of generalized government exhortations or actions, of course, since these are a common given for all the organizations; what they hold is a range of examples of influence through direct contact. In the thirty organizations studied, there are sixteen private or non-state-owned businesses—seven manufacturers of a variety of metal and chemical products, two breweries, and seven commercial firms in finance, banking, insurance, entertainment, and road transport.

Eighty instances of decision making, five in each organization, were covered. In these, governmental influence is on a narrow front. It is reported in fifteen of the eighty cases, or barely one in five.

Or does almost one in five seem quite a lot? If government can directly affect a fifth of all decisions in a parliamentary democracy, would it not have a heavy hand on the levers of power? Perhaps it would, but whose is the hand? Mostly, it is no more than a light touch from the Department of Industry or the Health and Safety Executive and Factory Inspectorate. There are ten instances of contacts with the Department of Industry over possible grants or subsidies in the long-depressed old industrial areas of the north of England and two instances of the Health and Safety Executive and Factory Inspectorate being concerned with potential pollution should a decision be made to expand. These are the run-of-the-mill contacts with governmental departments and agencies under standing legislation. The executives who report them rate them a mean influence on the ensuing decision of only 2.4, even less than that of the unions.

It should not be concluded that this level of state intervention is useless. Though a subsidy for industrial renewal may be only a lesser consideration during decision making, it is still a consideration. Moreover, the average conceals two cases when the Department of Industry was felt to have influenced decisions on expansion "a great deal" (ratings of 4), in the one case by a financial grant and in the other by making available factory premises built by the state to entice manufacturers to enter or to stay in the area.

Even more significant are five cases of intervention that were not run-of-the-mill in quite the same way. The Treasury (which wanted deflation) and the Department of Environment (which wanted to encourage house building and ownership) both successfully influenced a decision by a leading national financial institution to reduce interest rates in collaboration with its peer institutions; the Department of Employment (which wanted to raise performance levels) influenced a decision on a pioneering productivity agreement; an Arts Council's grant from public funds was crucial to a decision on the future of an entertainment organization; and behind a finance company's decision on a credit service lurked the possibility of investigation by the Monopolies Commission.

These five governmental interest units rated influences of 5, 5, 5, 4, and 3, respectively, giving a mean of no less than 4.4. This is an average of only five figures, but it does show that departments and agencies can and do heavily influence private enterprise in a small number of vital decisions.

This inside view, unaffected by any pretentions that the representatives of the state themselves may have about their standing and effectiveness, suggests, first, that broad semiroutine governmental involvement does play some part and, second, that selective stronger action can be very influential. Government can and does influence the direction taken by decisions in the private world of private business. Possibly, government is more effective than it sometimes seems to be from broad economic analyses.

If that is so, how much more should it be so in the public sector, where the state owns the reins? Public-sector data are being examined (Hickson and others, 1985). There are also questions to face on the interpretation of influence. What does it mean if there is said to have been high influence and yet a decision is made that is counter to that influence? Should the influences upon a negative decision—a decision not to do something—be interpreted differently from those upon the more frequent positive decision? Examples of such cases still await more detailed study.

### The Game and Its Framework

What is shown by the few features that have been described of decision-making "games," this most serious of pastimes? First, they are not so protracted as they may have seemed to be. Although they can go on for four years or more, they are commonly brought to a conclusion in a year or less. Organizations are not normally bestrewn with half-finished decisions begun long ago and never concluded, though, certainly, some decision making can be found in that condition.

Second, while strategic decisions are most often about organization, new outputs, and technology, they include such a variety of topics that it is probably safest to assume that almost anything can loom up and take on major significance to the top managers and administrators personally involved. There is no sweeping simplicity, such as that most strategic decisions are about new products or even that all new-product decisions are strategic. Strategic meaning is in the eyes of the decision makers in line with their view of the organization, rather than automatically attached to the topic.

Third, while such decision making is the province of internal management and administration, it involves external interests over and over again along the way. It is surprising, perhaps, that, while these interests do include suppliers, customers or clients, and even competitors and sometimes unions, these are not the most often involved. The interests most often involved are those concerned with privately set and publicly set standards, such as auditors and trade associations and government departments.

Fourth, these last interests, the government departments and agencies concerned with public policy, have influence far beyond the organizations in the public sector. They distinctly affect the decisions of "private enterprise," both in a low-profile manner, by, for example, financial grants to stimulate industry, and, more conspicuously, when they intervene during the making of specific major decisions, not by pushing in unannounced but by being consulted or informed under known arrangements and their views then being taken into account. Trade unions are less well placed, however, and if they exert any effective influence, it is probably upon the implementation of decisions and not upon their making.

There is nothing here to contradict the caricature of strategic decision making as politically imbued maneuvering that has been drawn by published research and was referred to at the beginning of this chapter. Rather, this fills out the picture to show that the making of such decisions is not necessarily protracted, is about matters much more varied than investments and electronic data processing, and is indeed highly externally oriented and externally influenced.

As has been mentioned, many other features are under analysis. So also are intriguing questions of explanation: Why does one episode of decision making differ from another? The ingredients of explanation implied by the model in Figure 1 are too many and too complex to be discussed here. The most that can be done is to raise this question: *Which counts for most in explaining the*

*process of reaching a conclusion, the organization or the decision?*
Do managerial decision makers respond most to their organization
or to the decision that they face?

The model assumes that processes of decision making are
responses to decision topics that emerge in an organizational
framework. As has been said, that framework sets the rules of the
game. Among the many questions is whether it so affects the process
of decision making that, within any one organization, all decisions
are handled in much the same way, which would mean, for
example, that a university would process both an investment
decision and a reorganization decision similarly, and a business
firm would also process both similarly, but in a different way than
would the university. The popular images of dynamic private
enterprise versus stultified public bureaucracy rest on this assumption. Alternatively, different topics might be processed in the same
way no matter what kind of organization was making the decision,
so that a university would process an investment decision in much
the same way as a business firm did, and both would process a
reorganization decision differently from that.

On the side of "the organization counts for most," a contrast
has been drawn between the two organizations first included in the
Bradford studies, both doubly covered by interview and by intensive
case-study methods. These are a "paralytic" public utility and a
"politicking" university (Butler and others, 1977–78; Hickson and
others, 1978). The utility, an electricity board, is tightly restricted
in the strategic choices open to it. It is constituted by an act of
Parliament to supply electricity and electrically operated appliances
(and nothing else) in a delineated region (and nowhere else); it
obtains its electric current from a single national, state-owned
corporation that runs all electricity-generating plants; and its
prices are regulated. It works with a well-understood and stable
product and technology. Its decision making is therefore predicted
to be uneventful, for "Internal meetings are anything but a jostling
for power. . . . There is no suggestion of politicking, competing for
resources, or pushing new activities" (Hickson and others, 1978, pp.
33–34).

In contrast, the researchers' experience of the university was
much nearer the vividly named "garbage-can model" (Cohen,

March, and Olsen, 1972). To Cohen and March (1974, pp. 82–83), "The properties of universities as organized anarchies make the garbage-can idea particularly appropriate to an understanding of organizational choice within higher education. Although a college or university operates within the metaphor of a political system or a hierarchical bureaucracy, the actual operation of either is considerably attenuated by the ambiguity of college goals, by the lack of clarity in educational technology, and by the transient character of many participants." As Butler and others (1977–78, p. 55) comment: "This is the fabric for politicking." Baldridge (1971) had already found it so in an American university, and March and Olsen (1976) and their colleagues found much the same in Norway and Denmark. In the "politicking" university, therefore, decision making would be predicted to be a comparative maelstrom in a system that has evolved a whole panoply of committees to cope with its built-in politicality by allowing all (or most) to have their say.

Business firms might not be quite like the "paralytic' utility, but their decision making is reputed to be less ebullient than that of universities. "Business organizations are, for the most part, less overtly political than organizations in the non-profit or public sectors such as governmental agencies, hospitals, and universities" (Pfeffer, 1981c, p. 77). Though Pettigrew's (1973) account of a decision in a retail business describes political activity, it is an activity dominated by hierarchy, swayed by a boss who had authority simply to override two contending departments that reported to him and to shut them off from his superiors. The business firm hierarchy can also be seen at work in the summary of a new-product decision in a chemical company presented by Hickson and others (1981, p. 183), where the matter passes smoothly around the hierarchy between specialist departments and rises level by level to the managing director for decision.

These examples imply that decision making does differ greatly from one organization to the next, and presumably that applies to all decisions, no matter what they are about. Assuming for the moment that this is so, then how is it done? What does organization most affect?

It is too soon in the analysis of the Bradford studies data to write of conclusions about organizational effects, but the following conjecture is offered. The purposes (for example, manufacture or education) and associated professionalization (for example, business staff or university faculty) of organizations shape the structures that set the rules of the game for decision making, in ways that first and foremost affect access to the game, who and which interests come in at what stage and how they get in, and the parts played by hierarchy and by mechanisms of involvement such as committees. Primarily, *organization affects access to and authorization of decision making.*

Yet what of the kind of decision that is being made? Differences between decision topics can be sharp, sometimes sharper than between organizations. With five cases in each organization, the Bradford studies data offer a chance to explore such differences, controlling for organizational effects. They certainly appear to be replete with differences between one decision process and another, some being smooth and fast but others disrupted and slower, some being quiet and orderly but others alive with interaction and negotiation. Analysis is under way to see if there are common types of decision-making process, some "agitated," some "fluid," that could result from the differing complexity and politicality of decisions (Cray and others, 1983; Hickson and others, 1985).

There is the outline of an encouragingly simple and comprehensible grouping of processes that could be the foundation of a typology of ways of making strategic decisions. This would begin to distinguish one pattern from another within the insightful but too sweeping generalizations that have been common currency so far, such as that decision making is incremental and political. Certainly, it is clear that some processes are much more "agitated" or "sporadic" than others. The historical narratives and interviewees' elaborations of them lead to the characterization of a variant of decision making that is comparatively more disrupted and impeded, drawing on a greater range of sources of expertise and generating wide informal interaction over a prolonged period, amounting usually to some years, and culminating in authorization at the highest level. This mode of reaching a conclusion typifies perhaps one third of all cases and differentiates them from those that were more placidly "fluid" in nature.

This can be seen in the contrasts between two decision-making processes that took place in the *same* chemical manufacturing company (Wilson and others, 1984; Wilson, 1980). They differed *despite* both being nominally new-product topics, bound up with the company's reasons for existence. The first was initiated by requests from existing customers for a new chemical. The sales department assessed the possible market and arranged a market survey, and, after some hesitation, the idea was put to the board of directors, which approved pilot manufacture. A special committee was set up to examine what new plant would be required, and eventually, despite difficulties over insurance and in obtaining the capital internally, production was authorized. This briefest of summaries shows that, despite some obstacles, it was a fairly fluent and apolitical process.

Not so the decision on whether or not to generate electricity (more fully recounted by Wilson, 1982). During this, the same managers in the same firm were swept into a political vortex. It began peaceably enough when the engineers and, notably, the production (or factory) director sought ways to use surplus high-pressure steam. One possibility was to use it for the generation of electricity, a near-unique idea at which the state-owned electricity monopoly referred to earlier looked askance. It would be peculiar for a chemical company to also become an electricity producer, even for its own consumption, and even the company's own capital control committee was unconvinced that it was what the firm was in business for, that it would be technically reliable, or that it would pay. That might have been the end of it. But then the managing director announced his forthcoming retirement. The production director, who favored the electricity scheme, and the purchasing director, who opposed it, were each candidates for the succession. The former realized that, if he could win a decision on the electricity question, his chances of promotion would be enhanced. He reopened it with fresh figures, and there followed a prolonged period of escalating and more and more personal conflict, with both parties trying to gain support from other departments and outsiders, such as the electricity industry and the Confederation of British Industries. This highly political, turbulent process ended with a decision in favor of electricity generation; shortly afterward, the production director did indeed become managing director.

Though both these decisions were about what the company should be doing, the first dealt with a familiar topic, product innovation. The second not only was highly unusual but became hyperpoliticized as a personal career struggle.

It can be conjectured that for such reasons—indeed, for many possible reasons—different decisions can precipitate very different kinds of process. In short, *the matter for decision affects the mode of process*, as Mohr (1982, p. 158) has begun to suspect. Should that be so, much greater attention would have to be paid to the characteristics of each topic than to decision making in general or to decision making in kinds of organizations, such as private business or public administration. The meaningfulness of the sort of generalized assertions on which the contemporary view of decision making is based would be shown to be limited. All decision-making processes are not highly political, disjointed, or repetitive: some are, some are not; some are more, some are less. Nor even are all decisions in "organized anarchies" (Cohen, March, and Olsen, 1972) likely to be arived at in the same garbage-can fashion: some will be, some will not be; some more so, some less so.

The question implicit in Figure 1, which we have raised previously (Astley and others, 1982), is which is which? So far, rather than eye-catching organizational styles of decision making, there seem to be differences due to the topic under decision, the complexity of the problem, and the interests being accommodated. The answer to "tell me how this decision is likely to be made" is "first describe to me what kind of decision it is." The day when the likely characteristics of the route of arriving at a decision can be forecast is not come, not by any means, but it may be coming nearer.

# ⚘ SIX ⚘

# Toward
# a Broadly Applicable
# Strategic Framework

## *John M. Dutton*

The Bradford studies (Chapter Five of this volume) emphasize how organizations' strategic problems become entangled in political influences. Using a Shakespearean analogy, the authors argue that the game's the thing, with top executives fretting and flitting their way through an endless stream of strategic decisions. Much ado about nothing? Perhaps. But Shakespeare was not pointing to leaders' games as inconsequential. Instead, he pointed out how leaders may have limited strategic understanding and how this human failing may manifest itself in deeply felt emotions—especially in times of strategic failure. For instance, Macbeth's fortunes and feelings varied dramatically. At the moment when he made the metaphor of a player (act 5, scene 5), he had reason to feel somewhat reduced in spirit, changed from acclaimed general and ascendant king to a widower surrounded by bloodthirsty foes craving vengeance.

*Note:* The author wishes to thank John E. Butler and Roger L. M. Dunbar for their comments on an earlier draft of this chapter.

Shakespeare's grasp of human affairs was profound, as another way of understanding this scene is to invoke the current population-ecology view of organizations, where executives are gripped by forces outside their control (Hannan and Freeman, 1977) and, because of bounded rationality (Simon, 1955), beyond their ken. Unlike Hannan and Freeman, however, Shakespeare also captured the emotional mood accompanying the ongoing strategic game. And extending current theory along this direction could lead to interesting research. But the authors do not pursue this lively argument further. Instead, having dramatized the possibly illusory nature of top-management strategic decision making, they settle down to the more prosaic task of comparative organizational analysis.

As a commentary on the Bradford studies research efforts, this chapter closely follows the Bradford studies report outline, developing observations along the way. The Bradford studies embrace many different research efforts, and these strike sparks in different directions. Thus, this commentary is not constructed around its own central theme but instead plays a counterpoint role. The reader may therefore want to review this commentary against the Bradford studies report.

## Scope and Content of the Inquiry

The Bradford studies propose a duality of rational and political organizational behaviors, two independent factors that together determine the strategic decision-making process of organizations. Their model parallels in form the structure-strategy-conduct-performance portrayals of earlier industrial economics (Bain, 1956), and the structural-functional models of organizational sociology (Blau and Scott, 1962), combined with more recent information-processing treatments of organizations (Galbraith, 1977; Nadler and Tushman, 1977). Once power, organization, and decision topic (or domain) are known, the decision process can be defined. The remainder of the chapter then explores this proposed rational-problem (complexity) and decision-interest (politicality) duality comprising the study's underlying argument.

In part, the discussion summarizes findings from three intensive case studies reported on elsewhere (Butler and others, 1977-78; Hickson and others, 1978, 1981; Wilson, 1980). These studies contrast strategic decision processes in a public utility, a university, and a chemical manufacturer, focusing on the effects of power structures on organizations' strategic decisions. The discussion is also preliminary to further analysis of data from a field survey of 150 strategic decisions in thirty British organizations between 1974 and 1980, each decision involving more than one subunit and having widespread effects. Included in these data are the three aforementioned case studies. Stating their reasons for undertaking this large project, the authors emphasize the need for broader and deeper understanding of the determinants of organizations' strategic decision processes and their outcomes. Thus, the Bradford studies cast a wide net over a diverse sample of organizations, seeking to obtain variation in type of organization, decision topic, decision complexity, decision interest, and decision process— using a time frame long enough for encapsulating strategic decisions. From the data thus collected, the researchers want to obtain generalizations about mean and variation across organizations on variables such as decision time, decision pathways, and decision influences.

So far, so good. These are worthy design goals. But what findings can and cannot be expected from such a study? One study constraint stems from the inevitable inquiry trade-offs pointed out by Weick (1979). Thorngate (1976) postulated that inquiry cannot simultaneously be general, accurate, and simple. Any two of these attributes can be combined, but only at the expense of the third. Translating this postulate into the Bradford study context, it might be expected that what is generally true across all the organizations studied, for a variable such as decision-time variance, may be accurate in no specific case or that the number of contingencies needed to reach accurate conclusions, say, regarding decision process for an organization may be so difficult and ambiguous as to preclude simple description. Starbuck (1981) points out the seemingly endless debates over the "true" meaning of the Aston studies because of the enormous number of potential measures and comparisons involved. Such studies run the risk of creating the Bonini

(1963) paradox of being so complex that they not only defy understanding but may be more complex than the phenomena that they seek to capture.

Firms included were chosen to reflect the "diversity of contemporary organizations." Public and private service and manufacturing organizations were approached so as to obtain a representative sample in these categories. As the authors point out, obtaining such a variety of organizations for study is no small problem. And the resulting sample varied widely in characteristics such as size of organizations (100 to 50,000 employees) and public prominence (likely to be collinear with size?).

Since the authors proceed to use the sample, two consequent questions are (1) of what population are these firms representative and (2) does the sample possess unknown characteristics that will confound analysis of its behavior (Berkowitz and Donnerstein, 1982; Mook, 1983; Weick, 1969a)? For instance, do firms listed in published directories have special features? Are they listed because they have survived long enough to attract the attention of directory compilers? And are some members listed because they want to be? Furthermore, why did one third of the firms approached not cooperate? Are they different in ways important to this research? And so on. Making inferences from samples of unknown characteristics is a tenuous affair. In studying strategic decision making in British organizations, Grinyer and Norburn (1975) paid careful attention to sample design, attempting to control for unwanted biases and to obtain wanted variation. They were thus able to control, for instance, for size, financial performance, and industry type in carrying out their statistical analyses.

Known sample characteristics may also constitute a problem in analyzing data. All 150 decisions studied were based on the self-perceptions of executives and were therefore subjectively defined. But self-perception by executives became mixed with the researchers' perceptions: Upon inquiry, the chief executives in the thirty cooperating organizations cited several major decisions for their firms. Then these executives were asked, "when possible," to nominate decisions in five researcher-defined categories—one each concerning (1) inputs, (2) outputs, (3) core technology, (4) personnel, and (5) reorganization. The Bradford researchers do not seem to see this mixture of reference frames as a problem. But others might (Shrivastava and Mitroff, 1983).

Attempting to spread decisions across at least these five preselected categories both enhances and restricts the analysis. It enhances the variance across these categories and thus adds leverage to analyzing their effects on decision complexity and politicality. But it restricts making statements about strategic decisions generally. For instance, the authors use these data to make general inferences regarding average length of time for reaching decisions (approximately one and a half years in most cases), to discern decision pathways (highly variable), and to enumerate decision topics (ranging from twenty-three on technologies to eight on locations). But such conclusions regarding frequency or mean of occurrences are questionable when using a nonrandom sample of decisions. The decision topics volunteered by executives do have wide variation, however, and thus provide a natural data base for relating other variables to these topics.

Still another prospective problem with the Bradford studies is using variance-analysis methods for studying organizational decision-making processes. As Mohr (1982) points out, decision processes are nonlinear and recursive, with many interactions present among independent variables. Variance analysis, even when using decomposition approaches such as path analysis, is often unable to disentangle such time-dependent and interactive processes. Somehow, dealing with this inherent contradiction between the phenomena being studied and the study methods employed may confront the Bradford studies.

### Conceptual Framework of the Inquiry

The Bradford studies aim at gaining a better understanding of organizations' strategic decision making. But the conceptual framework employed may sidestep this goal. A basic role of top managers is seen as shaping organizational objectives and strategy, with strategy intervening to define organizations' relations with their resource environments, thus acting as an important determinant of organizations' performance outcomes (Ackoff, 1970; Andrews, 1980; Ansoff, 1965; Child, 1972; Hofer and Schendel, 1978; Mintzberg, 1973b). But the Bradford inquiry framework stops short of analyzing such outcomes, making the decision process itself the final result of organizations' strategic decision-making behavior. In the theater, the play may be the thing, and real games often are played for their own sake. But in the world of organizations, top-management decisions often do have consequences—for top managers as well as for their organizations.

As such strategic outcomes tend not to be assessed, strategic management researchers may treat the Bradford studies lightly, not integrating them into their own inquiries. This result would be unfortunate, because the Bradford studies promise major implications for understanding organizational outcomes—for instance, the extent to which the influence of political interests on managers' perceptions of their decision problems may effect decision-making processes and, therefore, organizational decisions and their consequences.

A related question regarding the scope of the Bradford studies inquiry is: what constitutes strategic issues for organizations? Discounting prescriptive approaches to strategic management—especially those lacking bias-free, validating evidence—there remains a kernel addressing two themes: (1) managing organization-environment relations and (2) managing organizations' resource-allocation behaviors. Both these themes are grounded in a substantial social science and systems-theory literature, and both draw upon related work in natural, physical, and mathematical sciences (Aldrich, 1979; Bower, 1972; Buckley, 1968; Caves, 1980; Mayr, 1966; Meyer and Associates, 1978; Pfeffer and Salancik, 1978; Sahal, 1982).

Can the Bradford studies be related to this work? The evidence is mixed. On the favorable side, the study topics include those relating the organization with inputs and output environments. On the other hand, the Bradford studies organizations' environments are not systematically identified and compared. Thus, those exogenous influences for which the authors explicitly argue at the outset are neither overtly examined nor neutralized via sample design. In short, a recognized influence dominating the fate of organizations is seemingly not directly recognized in these studies.

To be sure, top-executive turnover is a widespread phenomenon (*Business Week*, Dec. 19, 1983). But the authors' contention that top-executive games usually continue with different players belies the evidence. The most likely fate for organizations, especially young ones but also old ones, is extinction—through complete dissolution, with redistribution of their physical, social, and financial assets; through being swallowed up by another; or through massive reorganization (Starbuck and Nystrom, 1981). Some organizations may be temporarily shielded from these fates, perhaps reflecting national policies or extraordinary reserves of resources (Wynne and Zaleznik, 1972). But, surely, great age is an exception for organizations.

### Interpreting Strategic Decision Topics

Seeking to assemble an overall view of their field data, while acknowledging potential biases, the researchers classified their 150 decision cases into ten categories showing high frequencies for decisions on (1) financial commitments, (2) investments in plant and equipment, (3) outputs of products and services, and (4) organization structures. In their emphasis on defining relations with key external economic and technical environments, these findings are congruent with the strategic management literature (Ansoff, 1979a; Cohen and Cyert, 1973; Drucker, 1946; Guth, 1971a; Hofer and Schendel, 1978; Miles and Snow, 1978; Thompson and Strickland, 1980). These findings are also consistent with analyses pointing out the relation among variables having larger effects on organizational outcomes, variables capable of measurement, and variables over which managers exercise more control. On the basis of an evaluation of sixty American and European firms, Guth (1971a) pointed out that growth and profitability are both highly visible and measurable outcomes and that allocation of financial resources and strategy formulation are input variables relatively visible, measurable, and controllable by top managers. Hence, they receive disproportionate emphasis in top management and decision making.

Top managements' preoccupation with organizational structure as a decision variable has been explored in the case of business organizations by Armour and Teece (1978), Burgelman (1983a, 1983b), Chandler (1962), Miles and Snow (1978), Mintzberg (1979),

Rumelt (1974), Scott (1973), Sloan (1963), and Thorelli (1977), all
arguing for close relationships between strategy and structure. Still
more basic is the efficient-market position that formal organizations
are a substitute for market transactions in accomplishing economic
exchanges, an argument making structure and strategy often one
and the same (Chandler, 1977; Nelson and Winter, 1982; Williamson, 1975). Other studies take a contrasting position, seeing much
slippage among strategy, formal structure, and organizational outcomes (Grinyer and Norburn, 1975; Guth, 1971b; Cohen, March,
and Olsen, 1972; Galbraith, 1973; Miles, Snow, and Pfeffer, 1974) or
the existence of external constraints sharply limiting managers'
latitude in exercising strategic choices (Aldrich, 1979; Porter, 1979).

Reconciling these differing views, by providing new simplifying theories or by establishing conditions supporting a wider
array of narrower theories, is an unfinished task, one to which the
diverse range of organizations included in the Bradford sample may
contribute. Arguing against the potential of the sample for this
purpose are the limitations of the data gathered. For instance,
subjectively or objectively defined overall strategies or structural
data were apparently not collected for the the thirty organizations
studied. Nor were systematic subjective or objective data collected
on these organizations' environments. Hence, comparing strategies
and structures might be difficult. The researchers might argue that
the studies' specific focus on the relations between decision complexity and politicality made these data irrelevant. But the studies'
focal variables then assume a disembodied aspect, not being related
to contextual strategic and structural variables, internal and external to their organizations. Or, if they are seen as related, then such
factors need neutralizing. But the need for such control was not
overtly described in the sampling-design discussion.

In fact, the "bewildering array" of topics encountered by the
researchers supports at least three current approaches to organizational decision making, namely, the "garbage-can model" of Cohen, March, and Olsen (1972), the market-structure models of
industrial economics (Bain, 1956; Coase, 1937; Caves, 1980; Porter,
1979), and the population-ecology arguments of Aldrich (1979) or
Hannan and Freeman (1977). Albeit for different reasons, each of
these approaches views organizations as reacting to issues and

problems laid before them by often less-than-benign circumstances. At least implicitly, the Bradford studies assume a similar stance in accepting decision problems and interests as arriving "over the transom," so to speak, with top managers doing little to anticipate their organizations' strategic problems or to define their organizations' resource environments.

During the period 1970–1980, when the decision problems studied for the Bradford studies organizations were emerging, macroeconomic effects may have played a major role in defining issues for many British organizations. At a national economic level, this was a period characterized by slow economic growth, monetary inflation, loss of overseas markets, and technological stagnation for major sectors of the British economy. But, as a consequence of North Sea oil discoveries, other sectors of the economy were benefiting from major capital investments. Strategic issues for many public and private organizations were sharply influenced by these macroeconomic conditions.

Portraying organizations' strategic behaviors in this way is consistent with a selection-by-consequences (Skinner, 1981), or ecological, view of organizational outcomes. But, if that is the researchers' position, then organizations' decision processes truly are a random game, whose function is providing natural experiments from which the environment blindly selects more successful responses. And given this perspective, whatever the studies' findings are, the strategic game does not matter.

### Interpreting Players, Influences, and Frameworks

The Bradford studies found widely varying involvement in strategic decision making, with participation differing for decision topics and over time with respect to individuals and interest groups, both within and outside organizations. Such fluidity may suggest that involvement in strategic decisions contains random elements, with coalitions often made unstable by chance exposure to events, perceptual influences, and shifting political alliances (Cohen, March, and Olsen, 1972; March and Olsen, 1976). Perhaps where organizations are characterized by weak central controls, high but diverse levels of individual expert knowledge, loosely coupled units, and normative cultural controls (Cohen and March, 1974; Etzioni, 1975; Meyer and Rowan, 1977; Weick, 1976, 1979), such fluidity may be especially pronounced, a finding the Bradford studies might clarify and strengthen when further analyzing their field data.

The fluid nature of individual and interest-group involvement in organizational decisions also may be explained by choice of unit of analysis (Freeman, 1978). Using an analogy from the field of thermodynamics, the random movements of and collisions between gas molecules in a fixed enclosed space give rise to stable pressure and temperature conditions for the space as a whole (Sahal, 1981). The entropic effects of randomness thus produce stability for the system as a whole. If organizational rationality is as severely bounded as has been argued by some (Simon, 1955, 1956; March, 1978), then randomness may be a stabilizing response at the level of populations of organizations, as it is with animal species (Mayr, 1966).

The consistently high involvement of top executives with external environmental constituencies contrasts with other, apparently more random interactions surrounding strategic decisions. Both more traditional and recent managerial strategy and policy literature (Newman and Logan, 1959; Mintzberg, 1973b) and studies of organizational boundary spanning and information gatekeeping support this finding (Adams, 1976; Aldrich and Herker, 1977; Galbraith, 1973; Jaques, 1951; Kahn and others, 1964; March and Simon, 1958; Miles, 1980b; Miles and Cameron, 1977; Miller and Rice, 1967; Pettigrew, 1972). Heavy involvement by top executives in dealing with external constituents is also consistent with the legal and quasi-legal, transaction-cost, and internalized-contracting portrayals of Chandler (1962), Coase (1937), Jones (1983) Nelson and Winter (1982), Ouchi (1980), Wilkins and Ouchi, (1983) and Williamson (1975). These researchers view formal organizations as efficient substitutes for auction markets, acquiring specialized abilities in completing economic transactions, performing physical transformations requiring large-scale facilities, and carrying out services requiring interdependent individual skills. Top managers supervise contract design and monitor the relations involved in delivering contract specifications, activities requiring their close and relatively constant attention. Top managers also monitor their environments for competitors' contracting initiatives and innovations and for opportunities for initiating new contracting opportunities themselves, acting as classical entrepreneurs (Kirzner, 1973; Schumpeter, 1950).

Here, variance analysis might yield results illuminating the bases for organizational dependence on top managers' boundary-spanning, gatekeeping, and information-processing roles. And such a project might also show how organizational outcomes are related to the kinds of information-processing behaviors Grinyer and Norburn (1975) discovered in their study of firms' strategic planning by ninety-one executives in twenty-one British firms.

Their study of influences on strategic decisions indicated to the Bradford researchers the constraints bounding top-management actions, a conclusion further confirming the external-control view of organizational behavior proposed by Pfeffer and Salancik (1978). It may be significant that, in the decisions facing them, the Bradford studies top managers seemed dependent upon their environments for defining their issues, often seeming prisoners of their pasts (Starbuck, 1983). With one notable exception (the electricity-generating case), top managers did not appear to be proactively identifying new strategic issues or synthesizing original, new activities for their organizations (Alexander, 1964; Kirzner, 1973; Zaleznik, 1966). But such behavior may be partly a function of managerial beliefs reflecting organizational cultures and executive norms as much as objectively determined restrictions on managerial actions (Mason, 1969; Mitroff and Kilmann, 1975; Shrivastava and Mitroff, 1983; Zaleznik, 1966).

Assessing governmental and union influences, the Bradford researchers find their effects weak insofar as their data are concerned. This conclusion is puzzling and may be hasty. In collecting their organization sample, the researchers deliberately included governmental agencies. Yet they do not conclude that these government organizations were more constrained in making decisions than others in their sample. What the researchers may be implying is that organizations generally are loosely connected, often playing mixed games of cooperation and competition with one another. Metcalf (1981) explicitly pursues this idea in exploring precarious partnerships between organizations not hierarchically related but nevertheless bound to interdependence by common fates. By implication, such circumstances may be widespread among the organizations included in the Bradford studies and may provide valuable data for exploring joint, cooperative relations among organizations.

The apparently low influence of unions may reflect the ways in which the Bradford researchers constructed their analysis. As observers have noted (Selekman, Selekman, and Fuller, 1958), management-labor relations are an ongoing phenomenon reflecting slow evolution rather than dramatically punctuated periods of change. Although such evolutionary processes change at slow rates, their longer-term effects may be very pronounced. With their attention monopolized by sharp discontinuities in their current environments, top managers may be insensitive to such long-term, slower-acting effects. This insensitivity may have been amplified by the subjective-ranking techniques used by Bradford researchers to elicit largely current assessments as strategic topics and influences. In the longer term, gradual, evolutionary effects have rendered entire industrial sectors noncompetitive, as inflated wage rates and other costly features of negotiated contracts created competitive disadvantages for firms in international markets. Such effects unquestionably have objective strategic implications for top managers, whatever may be their temporal, subjective views of unions' influence.

Manager and researcher unit of analysis may also govern perceptions of union influence (Freeman, 1978; Roberts, Hulin, and Rousseau, 1978). Union locals are often subordinate units in a hierarchical national organization with strong, aggressive leadership. Thus, an appropriate focus for analyzing unions may be at the national level. At this more aggregate level, unions may target whole industries, rather than individual firms, for contract gains. Toward this end, unions may pursue strong party affiliations, thus creating both legislative and administrative constituencies for themselves in governments. In these ways, unions can indirectly but powerfully influence individual firms by creating legislative and regulatory mandates dictating conditions for many organizations. Such coalitions provide unions with other, sometimes more effective avenues for gaining advantage than do direct union-management negotiations. Thus, the Bradford conclusion that unions exercise low influence upon organizations' strategic decisions may be distorted by their conceptual framework.

## Defining the Frameworks for Strategic Decision Making Games

As to defining their gaming frameworks, organizations do sometimes initiate new strategies, and in ways that alter their overall strategic contexts. Burgelman's (1983a, 1983b) studies of induced versus autonomous strategic behavior and internal corporate venturing show how, at least occasionally, firms may act in "negentropic" ways (Sahal, 1982), redefining critical aspects of their external resource environments and altering their internal political and task structures to suit such newly emergent self-concepts (Mason and Mitroff, 1981b). In the venture into electrical generating by a chemical manufacturer (Wilson, 1982), the Bradford studies appear to have captured a case virtually identical to those postulated by Burgelman. In this company, internal corporate venturing and product championing by the production director and his engineers led to electricity generation as a new line of business activity. And in the ensuing contest for leadership, the production director became managing director of an organization possessing a redefined strategic context (Burgelman, 1983a, p. 65). The currently expanding literature linking strategic management and organization theory may be fruitful territory for the Bradford researchers to explore for explaining their results and for further integrating their findings.

## Studying Organizational Strategies

A number of plausible paradigms, each of which enjoys substantial theoretical, empirical, and social support, are currently being explored in the arena of strategic management combined with organization theory. These include views of strategy as a problem in synthesis of form rather than one of scientific analysis; as equilibrium-maintaining or equilibrium-shifting phenomena; as reactive or proactive organizational behaviors; as externally or internally determined; as reflections of organization-environment niche-filling behavior; as rational or nonrational; as interactions among different units of analysis or part-whole relationships; as evidence of evolutionary processes taking place in larger organizational systems; and as intelligent logical incrementalism reflecting bounded human rationality.

Fortunately or unfortunately, the wide net cast by the Bradford studies has caught evidence supporting many if not most of these viewpoints. How one may proceed in the face of such mixed evidence is a question confronting the entire field—not just the Bradford studies. One response to this ambiguity is to attempt logical integration to resolve this problem of having overdetermined explanations for a single phenomenon. Another is to design empirical experiments aimed at having multiple theories compete with one another in explanatory power. Still another is to attempt sharper differentiation among phenomena and to formulate differentiated theories to explain these independent effects. Yet another is to encourage even stronger efforts at capturing the dynamic, longitudinal, time-dependent behaviors seemingly central to understanding organizations' strategies. As the Bradford researchers seem to have concluded, intensive case studies tracking organizational events over time—often using methods drawn from social anthropology—may illuminate stable and general effects over organizational space and time sufficient for constructing a science of organizational strategy.

At present, the field enjoys no consensus on such general effects. Thus, a greeting that long-time students of strategic management might offer newer entrants from social science fields, whether their study orientation is prescriptive or descriptive, observer or participant, subjective or objective, cross-sectional or longitudinal, is "Welcome to the game of capturing and taming the strategic behaviors of modern organizations!"

# ❦ SEVEN ❦

# Sources of Error in Strategic Decision Making

## *Irving L. Janis*

Practically every social scientist who has studied strategic decision making in complex organizations emphasizes that making strategic organizational choices is a very fuzzy business. It is pervaded by uncertainties, doubts, and all sorts of complications stemming from clashing vested interests and misguided efforts to reduce the chaos by relying on contradictory proverbs or heuristics based on salient prior decisions, some of which are pointed to as cautionary tales, while others are alleged to be precedents for adventuresome lack of caution. And when outside experts are consulted, they almost invariably disagree.

### Disagreement Among Social Scientists

It is not a very closely guarded secret within the social sciences that much the same can be said about theory and research

*Note:* Much of this chapter is from the author's forthcoming book, *Crisis Management and Mismanagement in the Nuclear Age.* The studies described from the author's current program of research are supported by a grant from the National Science Foundation.

on organizational policy making. Experts in the field of organizational behavior and change certainly do not agree with each other. Just take a look at any of the recent symposium volumes in this field. A typical example is *Perspectives on Organization Design and Behavior,* edited by Andrew Van de Ven and William Joyce (Van de Ven and Joyce, 1981). Several of the contributors, including the two editors, give loud congratulatory applause to new developments that are redirecting mainstream theory and allegedly will soon lead to big improvements in the way strategic decisions are made. But their exuberant noises are drowned out by the booing section.

One loud and clear voice in the booing section is Jeffrey Pfeffer's (1981a). As one of the final commentators on the conference, he distilled his reactions to the presentations in the form of general laws of organizational research. One is "the law of unresolvable ignorance," and another is "the law of unrequited effort." Cogent reasons for these laws are provided by James March (1981a), another leading expert in the booing section. March asserts that "there are no clear universals": Individuals and groups in organizations often, but not always, appear to "satisfice" rather than maximize. Their actions frequently are incremental, yet on occasion they make "heroic leaps." Sometimes they act strategically when it seems required; sometimes they fail to do so. Certain of their new decisions reflect learning from past mistakes; others do not. As to the conditions under which they do one thing or the other when making policy decisions, existing theories of organizational choice do not tell us very much. Nor are we ever likely, according to March, to have any major breakthrough in this field to enable us to make precise forecasts about how policy decisions will be made. Even in the long run, he says, we cannot expect anything more than a theory that contributes "marginally to ordinary knowledge . . . analogous to the contribution of a good consultant, or possibly a minor poet" (March, 1981a, p. 236).

My own view about our present state of knowledge is a bit less modest, and I am less pessimistic about future prospects for developing theoretical propositions. I think that there are a few rays of hope for substantial progress in the near future. One promising line of research and theory construction, which I shall discuss in later sections of this chapter, involves specifying the conditions under which individuals and groups who make strategic policy decisions are likely to make gross miscalculations, poor implementation plans, or other errors that greatly reduce the chances that a new policy will be carried out successfully.

### A Cautionary Tale: Unremoved Missiles in Turkey

The disagreements among experts are not by any means restricted to broad theoretical propositions or efforts to set up paradigms to direct research on organizational decision making. Demoralizing disagreements are to be found even for particularistic conclusions about even a single historic decision.

Consider, for example, the well-known failure of the United States government to remove American nuclear missiles in Turkey during the months prior to the Cuban Missile Crisis, despite the fact that the president of the United States had made a clear-cut policy decision to dismantle those missiles and had issued explicit orders to implement the decision. The story has repeatedly been told of how surprised and annoyed President Kennedy was during the harrowing days of the Cuban Missile Crisis when he discovered that his orders to remove the obsolete and vulnerable Jupiter missiles from the U.S. bases in Turkey had not been carried out by the State Department and Defense Department officials. President Kennedy was enraged because the Soviet demand to remove those missiles in exchange for removing the Cuban missiles would be seen as confirming European suspicions that the United States would sacrifice defense of its allies to safeguard its own security, and this could wreck NATO and the entire Western Alliance. At one point, he shouted "get those frigging missiles off the board." Afterward, he "reflected sadly on the built-in futilities of big government." This is the way the story is told in Elie Abel's definitive book on *The Missile Crisis* (1966, pp. 191–193).

Essentially the same story appears in the memoirs of two of the presidential advisers who participated in the White House meetings during the Cuban Missile Crisis, Robert Kennedy (1969) and Roger Hilsman (1967). The story has been retold by Graham Allison (1971) and by Morton Halperin and Arnold Kanter (1973) as a prime instance of how a noncompliant bureaucracy, adhering to its own routines and parochial goals, can conceal from the president their failure to implement one of his policy decisions. This story appears to highlight the danger that the bureaucrats who are counted upon to implement the chief executive's policies may, as Allison (1971) says, set the drumbeat to which the chief and the entire organization must march.

Surely in the repeated accounts given by the numerous experts who have described and commented on the Turkish missiles episode, we have a reliable example of how a policy can be made surreptitiously by the bureaucrats who are charged with implementing it—an example that deserves to be featured in political science textbooks and administrative sciences handbooks. But no! Along comes another expert, Donald Hafner, who has made a much more intensive case study (1977) of the episode, and he concludes that all those other experts have been promoting a myth. According to Hafner, the officials charged with implementation were not recalcitrant or narrowly bureaucratic in executing the president's policy decision, but, rather, they ran into major obstacles to implementation that had not been foreseen when the policy decision was made. They encountered strong objections from the leaders of the Turkish government and informed President Kennedy about those objections. Furthermore, about one week before the Cuban Missile Crisis started, Kennedy was reminded that the U.S. missiles were still in Turkey by an official complaint about their presence from the Soviet government, to which Kennedy made reference in a news conference.

Hafner concludes that, in light of the historical record, there is no evidence that the episode illustrates anything at all about bureaucratic politics arising from the self-serving parochialism of bureaucrats in complex organizations. Nor does it warrant, Hafner says, Allison's interpretation in terms of the detrimental effects of bureaucratic routines on the implementation of presidential decisions. One of the main implications that Hafner draws from his revised interpretation of the episode is that, when a chief executive and his aides are highly sensitive to the evils of bureaucratic politics, they are likely to see bad motives and shortcomings in the bureaucrats who execute policy decisions. They are likely to overlook the compensatory gains to be expected from the participation of bureaucrats who can help clarify the tasks of implementation. The chief executive not only must be aware of the possibility that his policy decisions might be distorted by bureaucratic implementers but also must guard against becoming a "victim" of his own "distorted perceptions of organizational behavior of the sort reflected in the Turkish missile myth" (Hafner, 1977, p. 328).

Fortunately, we can get along without this alleged example of the undermining of a chief executive's policy decision by bureaucratic implementers. There are plenty of other examples, including the U.S. Navy's unauthorized bombing of Soviet submarines and other episodes that occurred during the Cuban Missile Crisis, that will probably withstand the jaundiced scrutiny of would-be revisionists.

### Values and Limitations of Case Studies

The main point I want to make about the missiles-in-Turkey story is a methodological one. When we are trying to describe a typical source of error and to identify the conditions under which it is most likely to occur, we cannot rely upon anecdotes that seem to conform to a pattern expected on the basis of one or another current hypothesis or theory. Instead of merely picking up salient bits and pieces of case material that suggest a memorable story, we need to examine the available records intensively and systematically to find out what story, if any, is really warranted by the evidence.

In the early discovery phase of research, some genuine advances can be made by carrying out systematic case studies. When studying sources of error in policy making, we should certainly look for whatever explanatory determinants we can find. But whenever we think that we have spotted one of them, we should treat it as an untested hypothesis that needs to be checked out as thoroughly as possible by available case-study documents, observational reports, minutes of meetings, memoirs, and testimony by the executives and aides who participated in the policy-making deliberations. Systematic case studies can help to resolve some unproductive disagreements among experts and may even prevent some of those disagreements in the first place. In later stages of the research, the hypotheses derived from intensive case studies can be examined by diverse methodological approaches, including series of comparative case studies, questionnaire surveys of executives, content analyses of archival records, and laboratory and field experiments on the effects of changing the antecedent conditions that are expected to affect the quality of decision-making procedures (see Janis, 1982b; Tetlock, 1983). Since each method has its unique strengths and weaknesses, converging findings from studies using different methodological approaches provide the most dependable evidence for verifying hypotheses about psychological determinants of defective policy making.

Behavioral scientists have good reasons to be reluctant to take seriously the conclusions derived from case studies. The example I have just cited concerning the myth about why the U.S. missiles in Turkey were not removed illustrates some of the most extreme deficiencies—lack of standards for evaluating evidence, selective attention to seemingly confirmatory items and neglect of contradictory evidence, failure to examine rival hypotheses, and exploitation of the "certainty-of-hindsight" tendency described by Fischhoff and Beyth (1975). But case studies do not need to be that bad. Distinctions should be made among case studies in terms of the degree to which efforts are made to avoid obvious sources of bias and overinterpretations of fragmentary evidence. At one extreme is the purely casual, impressionistic type of case study in which anecdotes and details are selected by the storyteller. At the other extreme is the highly systematic type of case study in which the behavioral scientist conscientiously answers a series of pertinent questions by carefully examining all the available evidence bearing on the questions and takes account of the judgments about the case materials by independent observers. I have attempted to provide an example of the latter type of case study in my analysis of the Watergate cover-up (Janis, 1982a).

One of the main features of the systematic type of case study is that the behavioral scientist commits himself or herself to be nonselective in examining and appraising the available records and is answerable to the community of scholars for overlooking or distorting any important piece of evidence. This expectation of criticism acts upon the behavioral scientist as he or she carries out and reports the case study, increasing conscientiousness in dealing with evidence, just as it does for experimental scientists and professional historians when they know that fellow experts will examine their methods, will be watching for errors of commission or omission in the evidence cited, and will challenge dubious inferences from the evidence.

I am strongly emphasizing the need to use the best possible methods of case-study analysis because it seems to me that relying on such methods can advance the study of strategic decision making, which at present is still in a stage of infancy. Intensive case studies can provide valuable clues to the antecedent conditions—including leadership practices and standard operating procedures—that reduce the chances of gross miscalculations and defective implementation plans when executives in a large organization arrive at a strategic decision. As knowledge of the antecedents increases, prescriptive hypotheses for improving the quality of policy making can be formulated and tested, using other methods of research, including large-scale correlational studies and controlled experiments.

### Should We Use the Coroner as a Model?

Michael Scriven (1976) has described a methodological approach that I believe can be applied fruitfully in research on policy fiascoes resulting from defective strategic decisions. He has analyzed in detail the logic of the coroner who investigates the probable cause of death of each individual case brought to the morgue, using nonexperimental evidence to draw fairly dependable inferences about the causal sequences. He describes the coroner's "modus operandi" approach, which is also used by many detectives, historians, auto-repair mechanics, structural-engineering troubleshooters, and aeronautics specialists who investigate the probable causes of death and injury in each air crash, all of whom have found ways of determining the probable cause of undesirable events with fairly high certainty even though the data available to them do not come from controlled experiments or even quasi experiments. Essentially the same modus operandi approach used by the coroner can be used to determine the probable causes of disastrous decisions by top-level executives that can lead to severe losses or the death of an organization.

Basically, the approach involves formulating all the known causal sequences that might account for the observed outcome—whether it be a death, a crime, or a policy fiasco—and then attempting to find out which of them appears to be implicated. This requires careful scrutiny of every shred of evidence that might provide telltale signs indicating the step-by-step ways in which each of the alternative causes is most likely to operate. Working backward from the observed effect, the investigator watches for a pattern of indicators of mediating processes that connect antecedent conditions with the observed outcome.

Scriven points out that historians and others who use this modus operandi approach seldom formulate explicitly the entire list of causal sequences that they have in the back of their minds, and they often work with lists that are quite incomplete. But he argues that, even with nonexhaustive lists that include speculative causal chains that have not yet been shown to have the postulated effect, valid inferences about the probable causes can still be made. From his reconstruction of the logic of the modus operandi approach, he offers four rules for drawing a causal inference, after the investigator has checked carefully for the presence of indicators of each of the known possible or potential modus operandi (MO) sequences:

1.  If there are indicators for only one MO sequence, that is the most probable cause. The more complete the evidence for all the steps in the MO sequence, the higher the certainty.
2.  If there are indicators for more than one MO sequence, the one that is most complete is the most probable cause.
3.  If two complete MO sequences are detected, the two are to be regarded as co-causes.
4.  If no indicators of any of the known MO sequences are found, none of the MO sequences in the original (obviously incomplete) list can be regarded as the probable cause.

The fourth rule can undoubtedly be expected to hold sway for initial investigations of puzzling outcomes when we do not as yet know enough to construct rich lists of MO sequences to work with. But it seems to me that the frustration of the case-study investigator when he or she encounters the type of negative results specified in the fourth rule can nevertheless be a goad to creative discovery. The investigator can examine all the case material once again, looking for a new MO sequence that is not yet on the list of known ones.

Scriven points out several implications for the social sciences that follow from his reconstruction of the modus operandi approach. One is that new investigations can benefit from making explicit the implicit knowledge of causal lists possessed by research workers and practical specialists who have accumulated a great deal of tacit knowledge from a rich backlog of experience. Another is that research workers should be alert to opportunities to observe "telltale signs" that expose distinctive characteristics of the causal sequences they are investigating; whenever they use experimental designs, they should incorporate appropriate "tracers" or "signature arrangements." The most important implication of all is Scriven's (1976, p. 108) conclusion that "the time has come to change our orientation in the development of social science away from the goal of abstract, quantitative, predictive theories toward scientific, qualitative, explanatory checklists and troubleshooting charts." Like the coroner, the detective, and the engineering troubleshooter, the social scientist in new fields of research has the opportunity, according to Scriven, to draw plausible and useful conclusions from arrays of relatively weak qualitative bits of data by using in a sophisticated way the modus operandi approach.

Should the approach recommended by Scriven be taken seriously in the fields of research bearing on strategic decision making? I believe that it should be, particularly when working on problems that cannot be investigated by means of controlled experiments. With regard to the central problem with which I have been concerned—sources of error in arriving at new strategic decisions—we already know a fair amount about a few of the causal sequences, and these should be formulated much more explicitly than has been done so far. One well-known sequence involves the unproductive bickering that occurs when a decision-making group is composed of hostile factions engaged in internecine warfare. A second involves the collective monologues that fail to make use of the cognitive resources of the group when it is composed of members with nonoverlapping expertise who do not use the same kinds of vocabulary and rhetoric and therefore cannot communicate adequately with one another. Other causal sequences involve overdependence of the members of the group on the leader. The most familiar one occurs when a powerful, autocratic leader induces conformity to his or her idiosyncratic position, stifling all dissent, skepticism, and cautionary information from the members by making it clear that anyone who does not completely go along with the leader's foregone conclusions will be fired or subjected to other punitive actions. Commenting on findings from group-dynamics research bearing on various determinants and consequences of conformity, Hatvany and Gladstein (1982, p. 217) point out that: "Unexpressed doubts make it likely that group members will feel no real commitment to the adopted solution. If resistance to or discomfort with a decision can be brought into the open, then either a new and perhaps superior decision can be made, or commitment to the early decision will be the result of true acceptance rather than simple overt compliance."

The few sequences that are well known, such as the ones I have just mentioned, may occur only rarely, especially since they are frequently described as avoidable pitfalls. They are often featured in textbooks on effective management and in cautionary tales that are recounted among executives as part of the local culture of many large organizations.

In line with Scriven's recommendations, I believe that social scientists should make a concerted effort to specify as fully as possible the causal sequences that are the most frequent sources of error in strategic decision making. We need to elaborate, it seems to me, the faint glimmerings we have obtained so far concerning such sources of error as bureaucratic politics, misperceptions arising from cognitive-consistency strivings, stress-coping patterns that interfere with effective problem solving, misuse of analogies, oversimplified decision rules, faulty heuristics, and stereotypes of opponents or other out-groups. Initially, intensive case studies are needed, incorporating the modus operandi approach in order to specify step-by-step sequences that link antecedent conditions (such as structural features of the organization, design and composition of the decision-making group, and norms of the organization affecting leadership practices) with the quality of decision-making procedures used in arriving at strategic decisions. A series of such case studies could help us to formulate *descriptive* hypotheses concerning the conditions under which each source of error is most likely and least likely to occur. Insofar as subsequent research findings are confirmatory, they could be used to formulate *prescriptive* hypotheses, which specify when, where, and how to reduce the likelihood of each of the various types of error. In the later phases of the research designed to test both the descriptive and prescriptive hypotheses, the full range of behavioral research methods could be brought to bear, including comparative case studies using "blind ratings" of the variables.

### Criteria for Judging Quality of Decision-Making Procedures

One of the first requirements that I felt to be essential for starting to carry out research on defective policy making was to specify criteria that can be used as dependent variables. In my earlier research (Janis, 1972; Janis and Mann, 1977), I reviewed the extensive literature on decision making and extracted seven major criteria to use in judging whether a decision made by a person or group is of *high quality*. Such judgments pertain to the decision-making *procedures* that lead up to the act of commitment to a final choice (compare Etzioni, 1968; Hoffman, 1965; Maier, 1967; Simon, 1957a; Taylor, 1965; Young, 1966; Wilensky, 1967). As applied to decision-making groups, the seven procedural criteria or requirements are as follows: The group (1) thoroughly canvasses a wide range of policy alternatives; (2) takes account of the full range of objectives to be fulfilled and the values implicated by the choice; (3) carefully weighs whatever is found out about the costs or drawbacks and the uncertain risks of negative consequences, as well as the positive consequences, that could flow from each alternative; (4) intensively searches for new information relevant for further evaluation of the policy alternatives; (5) conscientiously takes account of any new information or expert judgment to which the members are exposed, even when the information or judgment does not support the course of action they initially prefer; (6) re-examines the positive and negative consequences of all known alternatives, including those originally regarded as unacceptable, before making a final choice; and (7) makes detailed provisions for implementing the chosen policy, with special attention to contingency plans that might be required if various known risks were to materialize.

These criteria or requirements can be used to judge the quality of decision-making activities even when executives are pursuing the goals and interests of their own subunit, which may be concerned only with purchasing, sales, or fund raising (see Pennings and Goodman, 1977). The seven criteria can also be applied when executives arrive at strategic decisions by adopting a "logical incrementalism" approach, making a series of tentative or partial decisions pertinent to only one subsystem within a large organization. As Quinn (1980, p. 17) observed in his study of managers of multi-billion-dollar corporations, "In the hands of a skilled manager, such incrementalism was not muddling."

Elsewhere (Janis and Mann, 1977), I have pointed out that, although systematic data are not yet available on this point, it seems plausible to assume that when the top managers of an organization are making a fundamental strategic decision, their failures to meet the criteria are symptoms of defective decision making that increase the chances of undesirable outcomes. In order to assess the frequency and intensity of such symptoms displayed by members of a policy-planning group for any given decision, it is necessary to examine the available records of the group's formal and informal meetings.

So far in my research, I have been using the seven criteria for assessing the quality of decision making in an impressionistic way by making qualitative clinical judgments based on the available case materials. In subsequent studies, I plan to use the criteria more systematically and objectively by obtaining ratings from trained research assistants who are kept as blind as possible with regard to the outcome of the decisions and all other variables under investigation.

## The Groupthink Syndrome

My research in recent years has concentrated on several causal sequences that are much less well known as sources of error in group decisions than the ones I mentioned earlier (involving internecine warfare, nonoverlapping expertise, and conformity out of fear of recriminations induced by an autocratic leader). One major source of defective policy making has been described in my prior research on fiascoes resulting from foreign-policy decisions made by top-level governmental advisery groups (Janis, 1972, 1982a). I call attention to a *concurrence-seeking tendency* among moderately or highly cohesive groups. When this tendency is dominant, the members use their collective cognitive resources to develop rationalizations in line with shared illusions about the invulnerability of their organization or nation and display other symptoms of concurrence seeking (referred to as "the groupthink syndrome").

A number of historic fiascoes appear to have been products of defective policy planning on the part of misguided government leaders who obtained social support from their in-groups of advisers. My analysis of case studies of historic fiascoes suggests that the following groups of policy advisers were dominated by "groupthink": (1) Neville Chamberlain's inner circle, whose members supported the policy of appeasement of Hitler during 1937 and 1938, despite repeated warnings and events indicating that it would have adverse consequences; (2) Admiral Kimmel's in-group of naval commanders, whose members failed to respond to warnings in the fall of 1941 that Pearl Harbor was in danger of being attacked by Japanese planes; (3) President Truman's advisory group, whose members supported the decision to escalate the Korean War in 1949 despite firm warnings by the Chinese Communist government that United States entry into North Korea would be met with armed resistance from the Chinese; (4) President John F. Kennedy's advisory group, whose members supported the decision to launch the Bay of Pigs invasion of Cuba in May 1961 despite the availability of information indicating that it would be an unsuccessful venture and would damage the United States' relations with other countries; and (5) President Lyndon B. Johnson's "Tuesday luncheon group," whose members supported the decision to escalate the war in Vietnam during the mid-1960s despite intelligence reports and other information indicating that this course of action would not defeat the Viet Cong or the North Vietnamese and would entail unfavorable political consequences within the United States. In all these groupthink-dominated groups, there were strong pressures toward uniformity, which inclined the members to avoid raising controversial issues, questioning weak arguments, or calling a halt to softheaded thinking. Other social psychologists (Green and Conolley, 1974; Raven, 1974; Raven and Rubin, 1976) have noted similar symptoms of groupthink in the way Nixon and his inner circle handled the Watergate cover-up during the early 1970s. Drawing on their work and my own detailed analyses of the unedited Nixon tapes, I have recently completed an additional case study of the Watergate cover-up and have used it to elaborate on the theory of groupthink (Janis, 1982a).

Eight main symptoms of groupthink run through the case studies of historic decision-making fiascoes (Janis, 1972, 1982a). Each symptom can be identified by a variety of indicators, derived from historical records, observers' accounts of conversations, and participants' memoirs. The eight symptoms of groupthink are:

1.  An illusion of invulnerability, shared by most or all of the members, which creates excessive optimism and encourages taking extreme risks;
2.  Collective efforts to rationalize in order to discount warnings that might lead the members to reconsider their assumptions before they commit (or recommit) themselves to a policy decision;
3.  An unquestioned belief in the group's inherent morality, inclining the members to ignore the ethical or moral consequences of their decision;
4.  Stereotyped views of rivals and enemies as too evil to warrant genuine attempts to negotiate, or as too weak and stupid to counter whatever risky attempts are made to defeat their purposes;
5.  Direct pressure on any member who expresses strong arguments against any of the group's stereotypes, illusions, or commitments, making clear that this type of dissent is contrary to what is expected of all loyal members;
6.  Self-censorship of deviations from the apparent group consensus, reflecting each member's inclination to minimize to him-

or herself the importance of his or her doubts and
counterarguments;

7. A shared illusion of unanimity concerning judgments con-
forming to the majority view (partly resulting from self-
censorship of deviations, augmented by the false assumption
that silence means consent); and

8. The emergence of self-appointed "mindguards"—members
who protect the group from adverse information that might
shatter their shared complacency about the effectiveness and
morality of their decisions.

Taking account of prior research findings on group dynamics, I have formulated a set of hypotheses concerning the conditions
that foster concurrence seeking on the basis of inferences from my
case studies of groupthink and from comparative case studies of
well-worked-out decisions made by similar groups whose members
made realistic appraisals of the consequences. One of these counterpoint case studies is of the main decision made by the Kennedy
administration during the Cuban Missile Crisis in October 1962.
Another deals with the hardheaded way that planning committees
in the Truman administration evolved the Marshall Plan in 1948.
These two case studies indicate that policy-making groups do not
always suffer the adverse consequences of group processes, that the
quality of the group's decision-making activities depends upon
current conditions that influence the group atmosphere, including
leadership practices.

*Conditions That Foster Groupthink and Ways of Counteract-
ing Them.* My main hypotheses concerning the causes and consequences of concurrence seeking are summarized in Figure 1. This
chart is a condensed representation of the causal sequence that links
defective decision making with a set of antecedent conditions
(involving a cohesive group of decision makers in an organization
characterized by certain types of structural faults when the members
are exposed to certain types of provocative situations). It can be used
to carry out the type of modus operandi analysis described by
Scriven (1976). In order to determine whether the groupthink
hypothesis can help to account for any given policy fiasco, the
investigators must examine all the available evidence to determine

Figure 1. Theoretical Analysis of Groupthink.

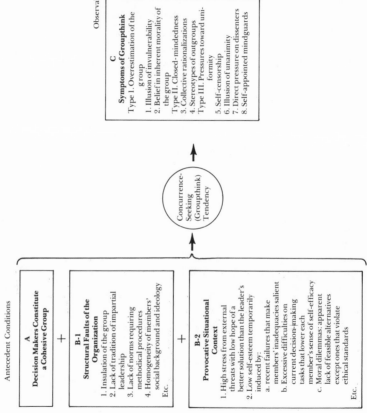

whether the entire pattern represented in Figure 1 is present. It does not suffice merely to see whether a few of the symptoms can be detected. Rather, it is necessary to find out whether practically all the symptoms were manifested and to see whether the antecedent conditions and the expected immediate consequences (the symptoms of defective decision making) are also present.

*Groupthink and Clanishness in Business Firms.* The groupthink syndrome is likely to occur in a wide variety of situations, including the meetings of top management groups in all sorts of business firms. Likely examples are to be found among notorious fiascoes of the past in the manufacturing industry—such as the Ford Motor Company's ill-conceived decision to produce the Edsel, a costly big car loaded with extras, at a time when the market had already started to shift to more economical compacts, which resulted in a loss of more than $300 million.

A more recent example of a fiasco in which groupthink may have a role was the disaster in 1972 that resulted from the decision by the Buffalo Mining Company in West Virginia to ignore warnings about the unsafety of their massive piles of coalwaste refuse that were damming a stream in Buffalo Creek. Their own dam inspectors as well as their insurance underwriters and numerous engineers repeatedly warned the company that this dam might burst at any moment and was a grave threat to all the small communities downstream. After each warning the company executives decided to do nothing and to continue the dangerous, old Appalachian practice of heaping slag to dam up the creek. On the morning of February 26, 1972, the dam broke, just as the experts predicted it would, creating one of the worst man-made disasters in American history. Over 125 people were killed, thousands were made homeless, and property damage came to more than 50 million dollars. In 1976 the company was ordered by a court to pay 26 million dollars in damages to the survivors [Wheeler and Janis, 1980, pp. 192–193].

At present, we do not know what percentage of major fiascoes among business firms and other organizations are attributable to groupthink or how often groupthink leads to undesirable outcomes that could have been avoided. All that can be said from the case studies analyzed so far is that the groupthink syndrome sometimes plays a major role in producing ill-conceived decisions that entail avoidable losses and that are promptly regretted by the executives who are responsible.

The likelihood that groupthink will occur in any cohesive group of managers depends to a considerable extent upon how many of the antecedent conditions listed in boxes B-1 and B-2 in Figure 1 are present. One of the most potent conditions is insulation from direct contact with men and women in the same organization who are not members of the in-group of top-level policy makers. For example, an insulated group of executives is likely to receive only brief and unimpressive summaries of warnings about the insurmountable difficulties of implementing a strategic reorganization or a new method of production that is under consideration. The top commanders of the organization may end up concurring on a course of action that many middle-level and lower-level personnel on the firing line could have informed them in advance would not be feasible. Or, as a result of being insulated, they may fail to take account of a change in the market. A vivid example is given by Starbuck (1983) from his study of Facit AB, a large manufacturing company that produced mechanical calculators and other business machines in factories located in twenty cities in five different countries. The company nearly went bankrupt because the top managers did not realize that there would be a switch in demand for electronic rather than mechanical calculators. They kept relying mainly on information from satisfied customers and did not learn about the new trend in the market from others in their own organization who knew about it. "Although some lower-level managers and engineers within the company were acutely aware of the electronic revolution in the world at large, this awareness did not penetrate upward, and the advent of electronic calculators took Facit's top managers by surprise" (Starbuck, 1983, p. 92).

Suppose that a cohesive group of policy-making managers could establish a communication climate that overcomes the tendency of people at the top of a hierarchy to be insulated from others in the rest of the firm: Would there no longer be any danger of the group's strategic decisions being adversely affected by groupthink? According to my analysis, the likelihood of groupthink would be somewhat reduced, but the danger would still be there if one or more of the antecedent conditions listed in Figure 1 were present, including any of the structural faults of the organization other than insulation (listed in box B-1) and/or any of the provocative circumstances (listed in box B-2). The more of those conditions that are present, the higher the probability that groupthink will impair the quality of the policy-making group's strategic decisions by giving rise to serious errors that could be avoided.

This view of the dangers of groupthink is somewhat at variance with the position taken by William G. Ouchi (1980, 1981) in his account of the advantages to be expected if business firms were to foster a "hierarchical clan" (or "type Z") form of organization. This type of organization characterizes many of the large industrial corporations in Japan and, according to Ouchi, is also prevalent among some of America's leading companies, such as Hewlett-Packard, IBM, Kodak, and Proctor and Gamble. The clan type of organization, in his view, is highly efficient because it is a culturally homogeneous organization in which cohesive face-to-face working groups are linked together. A clan form of control develops as a result of the socialization of the members, which is so complete that the goals of each individual tend to coincide with the goals of the organization, and everyone is strongly motivated to serve the organization. This is achieved mainly by three types of organizational practices—providing stable, long-term employment, disseminating an organizational philosophy, and arranging for collective participation in decision making.

In Japan, Ouchi informs us, implementation of decisions is fostered in the clan type of organizations by making use of the *Ringi* system for arriving at a consensus on strategic decisions. "When an important decision needs to be made in a Japanese organization, everyone who will feel its impact is involved in making it. In the case of a decision where to put a new plant, whether to change a production process, or some other major event, that will often mean 60 to 80 people directly involved in making the decision. A team of three will be assigned the duty of talking to all 60 to 80 people and, each time a significant modification arises, contacting all the people involved again. The team will repeat this process until a *true consensus* has been achieved. Making a decision this way takes a very long time, but once a decision is reached, everyone affected by it will be likely to support it" (Ouchi, 1981, p. 37).

The clan type of organization, according to Ouchi and Price (1983, p. 574), is "homogeneous with respect to values and beliefs." Note that this is one of the structural faults that I have listed in Figure 1 as being conducive to groupthink. Ouchi and Price (1983, p. 574) add that such organizations are characterized by "consensual decision making" and that the members tend to be "hostile to deviant views, including those that may be important for future adaptation and survival." Thus, these authors acknowledge that the clan type of organization could have some costly drawbacks along with the expected gains.

Other observers of the clan type of Japanese business firm raise serious questions about its overall effectiveness and its applicability to firms in America or Europe; they claim that there are additional defects (see Golden, 1982; Lambert, 1982). For example, Lambert asserts that "the fear of group pressure and reprisal both kills ideas and allows faults to go unquestioned" (p. 41).

Perhaps Ouchi will prove to be correct about the value of a clan type of organization for increasing productivity by fostering employee loyalty, commitment, and implementation of new decisions under routine circumstances. But my analysis summarized in Figure 1, based on comparative case studies of policy-making groups, leads me to expect that the top management group runs a grave risk of making defective strategic decisions, especially when a serious crisis arises, unless special precautions are taken to avoid groupthink.

When groupthink occurs in a top management group, is it always likely to be detrimental for the organization? Not necessarily. In my book on *Groupthink* (Janis, 1982a), when discussing the kinds of decisions to which Figure 1 is applicable, I specify two general types of circumstances in which groupthink can be expected to have predominantly *favorable* effects.

Longley and Pruitt (1980) call attention quite correctly to the potentially positive effects of concurrence-seeking under certain very special conditions, which are entirely different from the circumstances of the groupthink-dominated decisions I have been talking about. Their point is that when consensus is reached *after careful deliberations,* the *brief* appearance of symptoms of groupthink could enable the group to stop discussing the problem they have just finished solving and move on to other pressing matters. This point is essentially the same as a view presented by Janis and Mann (1977) about what happens to vigilant decision-makers when they reach the final stage of commitment, after they have already gone through all the essential earlier stages for sound decision-making—carefully surveying alternatives, exhaustively searching for information, examining the pros and cons for each alternative in an unbiased way, and finally, facing up to the question, "which course of action will best meet all the essential requirements to solve the problem?" After doing all that, according to Janis and Mann (p. 194), a vigilant decision-maker is likely "to bolster, in a highly biased way, the one [alternative] he regards as best"; "the decision-maker's pattern of vigilance may give way to defensive avoidance at the point where he loses hope of finding a better solution" than the one he has so painstakingly arrived at. Janis and Mann (pp. 284–286) add that the bolstering (or cognitive dissonance reduction) that occurs as a result of the defensive avoidance pattern in this final stage, just prior to implementation of a new decision, can have the functional value of stabilizing the decision, enabling the decision-maker to become more fully committed to it, to implement it wholeheartedly, and to continue to act in accordance with it despite the deterrence of minor setbacks.

Since Janis and Mann state that groupthink can be "a collective form of defensive avoidance" (p. 129),

their position is compatible with the point emphasized by Longley and Pruitt: the symptoms of groupthink would have a positive function if they were to
occur after a *mature* consensus has been reached at the
end of thorough deliberations that include vigilant
search and appraisal of the alternatives. But I must
emphasize that the model of groupthink in the Figure
pertains *only to instances where the symptoms of
groupthink pervade most or all of the group's deliberations on the problem at hand, which makes for
premature consensus characterized by the symptoms
of defective decision-making* (box D in the Figure)
[Janis, 1982a, p. 298].


Lawrence and Lorsch (1967) have called attention to two
different processes, both of which are essential for effective policy
making in the long run. One of them they label "differentiation,"
which involves proliferation of ideas and debate within the policy-
making group. The other they label "integration," which pertains
to the members' efforts to achieve and maintain unity. Whenever
groupthink predominates, according to Longley and Pruitt (1980),
decision making suffers from too much integration too soon, at the
cost of too little differentiation. Thus, the members, having become
all steamed up with high esprit de corps, are likely to implement
the group's newly agreed-upon strategic policy in a wholehearted
way, but that new policy is likely to be ill conceived as a result of
the group's failure to meet the criteria for sound decision making.

Another point mentioned by Longley and Pruitt (1980) is
that when the group is required to make a relatively routine or
minor (nonstrategic) decision, the groupthink syndrome can prove
to be more helpful than harmful. Commenting on this point, I have
suggested that "the more trivial the issue, the greater the likelihood
that groupthink will have the beneficial effect of making for a
speedy consensus on an acceptable, or at least harmless, solution,
which can avoid wasting the precious time of high-level executives"
(Janis, 1982a, p. 299). In addition, as I have already repeatedly
emphasized, groupthink makes for prompt and conscientious im-

plementation, which is generally advantageous for nonstrategic decisions that do not require careful search, analysis, or planning.

In summary, the groupthink syndrome is expected to have detrimental effects for a business firm (or for any other type of organization) only under special conditions, notably: *"when it pervades the group's deliberations on a consequential policy choice.* It is for such choices that the figure indicates that when a chief executive and his advisers engage in defective decision-making (box D) as a result of the symptoms of groupthink (box C), their failure to engage in adequate search and critical appraisal is likely to have the *detrimental* effect of decreasing the group's chances of attaining its goals and of avoiding fiascoes (box E)" (Janis, 1982a, p. 299).

*Preventing Groupthink.* Not all cohesive groups suffer from groupthink, though all may be vulnerable from time to time (Janis, 1972, 1982a). A cohesive group of competent people is not only characterized by *commitment* to the group's decisions and *conscientious implementation* but is also *generally capable of making better decisions than any individual in the group who works on the problem alone* (see Hatvany and Gladstein, 1982; Steiner, 1982). And yet the advantages of having policy decisions made by a cohesive group are often lost when the leader and the members of the in-group are subjected to stresses that generate a strong need for unanimity. The striving for concurrence fosters lack of vigilance and reliance on shared rationalizations that bolster the least objectionable alternative. That alternative is often the one urged by the leader of the policy-making group at the outset of the group's deliberations about a strategic decision. When groupthink remains dominant throughout all the meetings, the leader's initial biases are likely to remain uncorrected despite the availability of impressive evidence against them.

> For constructive thinking to go on, a group must have a fairly high degree of like-mindedness about basic values and mutual respect. The members must forgo trying to score points in a power struggle or to obtain ego gratification by deflating rivals. These basic conditions are not likely to be created until the policy-making group becomes at least mod-

erately cohesive. But then the quality of the group's deliberations may deteriorate as a result of the concurrence-seeking tendency that gives rise to the symptoms of groupthink. Consequently, the problem of preventing costly miscalculations and lapses from sound thinking in decision-making bodies is complicated: How can policy-makers benefit from the cohesiveness of their group without suffering serious losses from groupthink? This sort of intricate psychological issue has been called a pretzel-shaped question and it may require pretzel-shaped answers [Janis, 1982a, p. 260].

In order to prevent groupthink, I have suggested a set of somewhat convoluted recommendations. Altogether, there are ten prescriptive hypotheses for counteracting the conditions that foster groupthink (Janis, 1982a):

1. Information about the causes and consequences of groupthink will have a beneficial deterring effect, if presented in a way that is neither unduly optimistic nor pessimistic.
2. The leader, when assigning a policy-planning mission to a group, should be impartial instead of stating preferences and expectations at the outset. This practice is likely to be effective, however, only if the leader consistently allows the conferees the opportunity to develop an atmosphere of open inquiry and to explore impartially a wide range of policy alternatives.
3. The leader of a policy-forming group at the outset should assign the role of critical evaluator to each member, encouraging the group to give high priority to airing objections and doubts. This practice will not be successful, however, unless it is reinforced by the leader's acceptance of criticism of his or her own judgments in order to discourage the members from soft-pedaling their disagreements.
4. At every meeting devoted to evaluating policy alternatives, one or more members should be assigned the role of devil's advocate. In order to avoid domesticating or neutralizing the

devil's advocates, however, the group leader will have to give each of them an unambiguous assignment to present the opposing arguments as cleverly and convincingly as he or she can, as a good lawyer would, challenging the testimony of those advocating the majority position.

5.  Throughout the period when the feasibility and effectiveness of policy alternatives are being surveyed, the policy-planning group should from time to time divide into two or more subgroups to meet separately, under different chairpersons, and then come together to hammer out their differences.

6.  Whenever the policy issue involves relations with a rival organization or out-group, a sizable block of time (perhaps an entire session) should be spent surveying all warning signals from the rivals and constructing alternative scenarios of the rival's intentions.

7.  After reaching a preliminary consensus about what seems to be the best policy alternative, the policy-planning group should hold a "second-chance" meeting, at which every member is expected to express as vividly as he or she can all residual doubts and to rethink the entire issue before making a definitive choice.

8.  One or more outside experts or qualified colleagues within the organization who are not core members of the policy-planning group should be present at each meeting on a staggered basis and should be encouraged to challenge the views of the core members.

9.  Each member of the policy-planning group should discuss periodically the group's deliberations with trusted associates in his or her own unit of the organization and report their reactions.

10. The organization should routinely follow the administrative practice of setting up several independent policy-planning and evaluation groups to work on the same policy question, each carrying out its deliberations under a different chairperson.

All of these and related prescriptive hypotheses, such as the procedures recommended by George (1980) for ensuring "multiple advocacy," must be validated before they can be applied with any confidence. Each of the proposed remedies may prove to have undesirable side effects and other drawbacks. But these hypotheses appear sufficiently promising to warrant the trouble and expense of being tested as potentially useful means for counteracting group-think whenever a small number of policy planners or executives in any organization meet with their chief executive to work out new policies.

The last three prescriptions (8, 9, and 10) might not only help to avoid groupthink but also prove to be valuable for overcoming some of the resistances that interfere with implementation of new strategic decisions throughout the organization. These require the members of the top management group to consult with knowledge-able people outside of their own in-group. Information from middle- and lower-level managers who are on the firing line can correct original misconceptions and influence even the earliest stages of strategic decision making. The policy makers can discard at the outset those proposed alternatives that they discover are not going to be feasible from an implementation standpoint; later on in their deliberations, they can make use of what they have learned from the implementers to choose the best available course of action that will meet all the major objectives of the strategic decision (which should always include the objective of avoiding the hidden as well as the apparent costs of implementation difficulties). Some of the other anti-groupthink procedures might also help to coun-teract initial biases of the members, prevent pluralistic ignorance, and eliminate other sources of error that can arise independently of groupthink.

### Patterns of Coping with the Stresses of Decision Making

In my collaborative work with Leon Mann (Janis and Mann, 1977), the groupthink syndrome is treated as a special case of one particular defective coping pattern—defensive avoidance. Our work focused on a major problem that requires theoretical analysis and empirical research: Under what conditions does stress have favora-ble versus unfavorable effects on the quality of decision making? Our conflict-theory analysis attempted to answer this question as well as broader questions concerning the conditions under which people will use sound decision-making procedures to avoid arriving at choices that they soon regret. We described, on the basis of the extensive research on psychological stress, the different ways that people deal with the stress of making vital decisions. When a person is preoccupied with a decisional conflict, the main sources of stress include fear of suffering from the known losses that will be entailed by whichever alternative is chosen, worry about unknown things that could go wrong when vital consequences are at stake, concern about making a fool of oneself in the eyes of others, and losing self-esteem if the decision works out badly. Vital decisions involve conflicting values, and often decision makers realize that any choice that they make will require sacrificing ideals or other goals. As a result, the decision makers' anticipatory anxiety, shame, or guilt is increased, which adds to the level of stress.

In assuming that stress itself is frequently a major cause of errors in decision making, we do not deny the influence of other common causes, such as ignorance, defective use of analogies, prejudice, and bureaucratic policies. We maintain, however, that a major reason for many ill-conceived and poorly implemented decisions has to do with the motivational consequences of decisional conflict, including attempts to ward off the stress generated by agonizingly difficult choices.

Our analysis deals with five basic patterns of coping with the stress generated by any realistic challenge (threat or opportunity) requiring a person to make a vital choice. Each pattern is associated with a specific set of antecedent conditions and a characteristic level of stress. These patterns were derived mainly from an analysis of the research literature on psychological stress bearing on how people react to warnings that urge protective action to avert disasters or other serious threats (Janis and Mann, 1977, chapter 3). The five coping patterns are:

1.  *Unconflicted adherence (or inertia):* The decision maker complacently decides to continue whatever he or she has been doing, ignoring information about the risks.
2.  *Unconflicted change:* The decision maker uncritically adopts

whichever new course of action is most salient or most strongly recommended, without any concern about costs or risks.

3. *Defensive avoidance:* The decision maker evades the conflict by procrastinating, shifting responsibility to someone else, or constructing wishful rationalizations that bolster the least objectionable alternative, minimizing the expected unfavorable consequences and remaining selectively inattentive to corrective information. (This pattern usually seems to be dominant among the members of a policy-planning group when they display the symptoms of groupthink.)

4. *Hypervigilance:* The decision maker, in a paniclike state, searches frantically for a way out of the dilemma, with rapid shifting back and forth between alternatives, and then impulsively seizes upon a hastily contrived solution that seems to promise immediate relief. He or she overlooks the full range of consequences of his or her choice because of emotional excitement, repetitive thinking, and cognitive constriction (manifested by reduction in immediate memory span and simplistic ideas).

5. *Vigilance:* The decision maker searches painstakingly for relevant information, assimilates information in an unbiased manner, and appraises alternatives carefully before making a choice.

While the first two patterns are occasionally adaptive in saving time, effort, and emotional wear and tear, especially for routine or minor decisions, they often lead to defective decisions when decision makers must make a choice that has serious consequences for themselves or for their organization. Similarly, defensive avoidance and hypervigilance may occasionally be adaptive in certain extreme situations but generally reduce the decision makers' chances of averting serious losses. Consequently, all four are regarded as defective patterns of decision making. The fifth pattern, vigilance, although occasionally maladaptive if danger is imminent and a split-second response is required, is more likely than the others to lead to decisions that meet the main criteria for sound decision making.

Even when a decision maker is vigilant, we can expect that he or she will sometimes make erroneous appraisals and choices as a result of relying upon rules of thumb and other cognitive shortcuts that people use to deal with the multiplicity of judgments that they make in everyday life. Considerable evidence from psychological research shows that all sorts of people, including statisticians and scientists, often make various types of cognitive errors, such as overestimating the likelihood of events that can be easily and vividly imagined, giving too much weight to information about representativeness, relying too much on evidence from small samples, and failing to discount evidence from biased samples (see Nisbett and Ross, 1980; Tversky and Kahneman, 1974). All of these types of cognitive errors probably increase whenever a person's motivational state is not conducive to doing the difficult mental work required to prevent sloppy, uncritical thinking and premature closure.

Whenever a decision maker's dominant coping pattern is unconflicted adherence or unconflicted change, the person is so unaroused by the risks to be expected that he or she resorts to "lazy" ways of making judgments because of lack of motivation to engage in careful information search, appraisal of alternatives, and implementation planning before deciding what action to take. When the dominant coping pattern is defensive avoidance, the decision maker is motivated to avoid the tasks required for vigilant decision making. If the decision can neither be evaded by passing the buck nor postponed, because the decision maker is clearly held responsible for making the choice and a deadline is at hand, the defensively avoidant person usually makes a rapid choice to get the painful decision over with and engages in wishful thinking; he or she bolsters the choice with rationalizations that play up the positive reasons and play down the negative ones (as described in studies of cognitive-dissonance reduction). When his or her coping pattern is hypervigilance, however, the decision maker is very highly motivated to search for relevant information and to deliberate about alternative courses of action. But in a near-panic state, he or she temporarily suffers from loss of mental efficiency and from informational overload as a result of being indiscriminately attentive to all sorts of information, whether trivial or vital. The informational

overload and sense of imminent catastrophe contribute to the
hypervigilant decision maker's tendency to fall back upon simple-
minded decision rules, such as "do whatever the first expert you ask
says is the best thing to do."

Among the main theoretical questions we addressed in our
analysis of the coping patterns were: What are the conditions that
make for vigilance? How do they differ from those that make for
each of the four defective coping patterns? Preliminary answers to
these questions are presented in Figure 2, which is a schematic
summary of the Janis and Mann (1977) conflict model of decision
making. This model, based on the research literature on psychological stress, specifies the psychological conditions that mediate the
five coping patterns and the level of stress that accompanies them.

The coping patterns are determined by the presence or
absence of three conditions: (1) awareness of serious risks for
whichever alternative is chosen (that is, arousal of conflict), (2) hope
or optimism about finding a better alternative, and (3) belief that
there is adequate time in which to search and deliberate before a
decision is required. Although there may be marked individual
differences in preference for one or another of the coping patterns,
all five patterns are assumed to be in the repertoire of every person
when he or she functions as a decision maker. In different circumstances, the same person will use different coping patterns, depending upon which of the three crucial conditions are present or absent.

In our review of social-psychological studies bearing on
premature closure, postdecisional regret, and a number of other
aspects of decisional behavior (Janis and Mann, 1977, chapters
4–12), we call attention to case studies and scattered experimental
findings consistent with propositions about the behavioral consequences of vigilant versus nonvigilant coping patterns, from which
we conclude that our theoretical analysis is plausible. We also
describe a few of our own social-psychological experiments that
were designed to test prescriptive hypotheses derived from our
conflict model. These include studies of the effectiveness of a
balance-sheet procedure, stress inoculation, and a number of other
interventions that counteract the beliefs and perceptions specified in
Figure 2 as being responsible for defective coping patterns. Some of
the interventions can probably be incorporated into standard oper-

Figure 2. The Conflict-Theory Model of Decision Making.

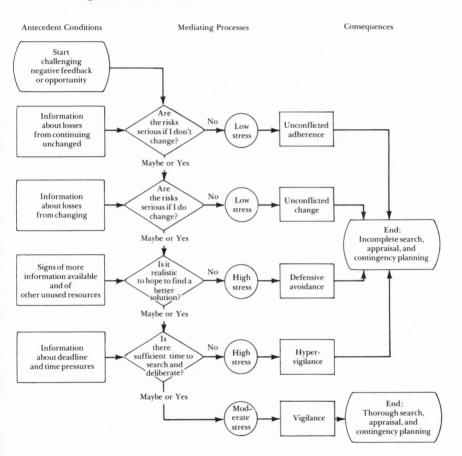

*Source:* Janis and Mann (1977).

ating procedures to be followed by executives when they participate in making strategic decisions.

Most of the evidence that illustrates and supports the Janis-Mann model comes from studies of personal decisions concerning career choices or health problems. Some, but not much, of the evidence comes from case studies of policy makers in small organizations, such as those who developed the plan for desegregating the city schools in San Francisco. Recently, Leon Mann and I have started to explore the applicability of our model to strategic decisions by large business or industrial firms and public welfare organizations, as well as national governments.

## Current Research on International Conflicts

Most of my current research focuses on two central questions that need to be answered: Is the Janis-Mann model applicable to governmental policy decisions on momentous issues involving international conflict? If so, does the available evidence indicate that the theoretical formulations need to be supplemented or modified? I am now carrying out intensive case studies of about two dozen major international crises faced by the United States government since the end of World War II. This research includes comparative analyses, using the "disciplined-configurative" approach recommended by Sidney Verba (1967), as elaborated by Alexander George and Richard Smoke (1974) in their description and applications of the "focused-comparison" method. The main hypotheses are formulated in terms of testable relationships between independent and dependent variables, which are derived from the theoretical models of causal sequences represented in Figures 1 and 2 and from whatever new causal sequences are suggested by individual case studies of defective decision making that cannot be fitted to known sequences. This initial phase is preliminary to a later phase of the research, in which I plan to carry out correlational analyses using fairly large samples in order to test whatever hypotheses survive after the first phase and also to test any new ones that emerge.

As a strong proponent of the experimental method for testing hypotheses about causal relationships, I am keenly aware of the shortcomings of case studies and correlational analyses based on historical narratives and archival documents. But, despite all the methodological difficulties, I expect that valuable evidence can be obtained. By developing empirically based theory to elucidate the conditions under which misjudgments or miscalculations are made by top-level executives in situations of crisis, I hope that this research will also provide useful guidelines for executives who want to avoid gross errors when making crucial decisions about momentous policy issues.

For purposes of investigating sources of error in strategic decision making, it will be worthwhile to apply Scriven's modus operandi model of analysis to each defective pattern of coping with stress, each leadership practice and organizational defect that interferes with group effectiveness, and each of the potentially misleading heuristics and decision rules. That is to say, an analytical flowchart should be worked out for every known source of error, showing the antecedent conditions, the mediating processes, and the specific effects on quality of decision making. Some sources of error may affect only one of the seven criteria for effective decision making, while others affect several. A few (such as hypervigilance) may affect all seven criteria. In order for the flowcharts to be useful for analyzing the probable causes of defective decision making in any given case, it will be essential, of course, to specify in detail the telltale signs for each step in the causal chain.

### The "Unsqueaky-Wheel Trap"

Once the flowcharts and telltale signs are worked out for a variety of cognitive and motivational sources of error, it should be possible for policy analysts as well as social scientists to use the list of causal sequences whenever they are analyzing any major policy failures. Such lists should help them to extract more valid "lessons of history" than can be inferred on the basis of the impressionistic analyses now being used. In some instances, as I mentioned earlier, more than one casual sequence may be found to play contributory roles as sources of error. In other instances, we can expect to find that the list of known causal sequences is incomplete, because none fits the case at hand, which can lead to the discovery of causal sequences that have not yet been explicated.

Recently, I encountered an example of a causal sequence involving serious defects in implementation planning that I had never previously encountered in any of my prior research or in the social science literature. The case study deals with the decision by President Carter and his advisers in April 1980 that led to the ill-fated attempt to use military force to rescue the American hostages in Iran. The news media called it a fiasco comparable to the Bay of Pigs. Government spokespersons claimed that it was all a matter of unforeseeable accidents and bad luck that helicopter failures forced the military commander to abort the entire mission on the desert sands of Iran hundreds of miles from Teheran. Some informed critics, however, say that the plan was ill conceived.

I tried to find out how many of the seven symptoms of defective decision making could be discerned in the White House deliberations that ended with presidential approval of the military rescue mission. So far as the present evidence goes, however, no dependable answer can be given, because details about the secret meetings in which the rescue mission was planned and approved have not yet been released, and the available bits of testimony are somewhat contradictory. But I think that I have learned something important about one specific type of defect in planning the mission.

One major source of information is the memoirs of Zbigniew Brzezinski (1983), the national security adviser, who for many months had been urging the president to restore America's honor by launching a military attack rather than continuing to try to negotiate. Contrary to the reports of governmental investigative committees, Brzezinski conveys an image of the decision to launch the Iranian rescue mission as having been very carefully worked out, with full exploration of the alternatives. But his overall claim that the rescue mission was thoroughly worked out is contradicted to some extent by his detailed account of how it failed. From what he says, it is apparent that the major risks of the first crucial phase of the rescue plan—the rendezvous and refueling of the U.S. aircraft in the Iranian desert—had hardly been examined at all by President Carter and his key advisers. For example, Brzezinski acknowledges that "my concern over the possible failure of the mission did not pertain to something like what finally happened—its early abortion—but rather to . . . its execution in Teheran" (p. 488).

Brzezinski's memoirs make it clear that the top policy makers in the White House group had not envisaged the possibility either that the mission might have to be aborted because several of the helicopters might malfunction or that the mission might be compromised as a result of being observed by Iranians in passing vehicles on the nearby road. Apparently, certain of the crucial implementation plans were not examined carefully enough by the president and the key members of his advisery group for them to become aware of these risks. The high-level military review group's report to the Joint Chiefs of Staff concluded that the flaws could have been corrected if the plan had been reviewed by experts outside the small secret circle of planners (reported in the *Los Angeles Times*, August 24, 1980, p. 1). For example, more helicopters could have been added to the mission. The same report also faults the planners for having failed to arrange to have the desert rendezvous "fully rehearsed" in advance and also for having neglected to set up an identifiable on-scene command post with adequate communication and control in the event of unanticipated difficulties (Middleton, 1981, p. 112). If these additional implementation and contingency plans had been worked out, the chances of a disaster such as the accidental crash of U.S. aircraft in which eight men were killed might have been considerably reduced.

From the available accounts, I surmise that a major reason that questions about the risks of the first phase of the mission were not raised within the top-level planning group is because the most obvious risks of the rescue mission were in the later phases—the enormous chances of invading U.S. forces being detected and attacked when they approached Teheran, of the hostages being killed before their would-be rescuers could get to them, and of U.S. aircraft being shot down as they attempted to depart from Teheran. Evidently, as the old saying goes, it is the squeaky wheels that get the oil; any unsqueaky wheel is neglected. When grappling with a complicated multistage plan, policy makers are likely to focus their implementation and contingency planning on the steps that pose the most obvious risks. Perhaps there is a contrast effect whereby the least risky steps tend to be labeled safe and easy to handle—"that's not where our troubles will be."

The main point is that, even when decision makers are quite vigilant in their approach to the problems of working out or checking on a feasible plan that takes account of the risks, their tendency may be to focus their information search, appraisals, and implementation planning entirely upon the steps that are known from the outset to be fraught with danger, the "squeaky wheels." If so, they will tend to overlook the more subtle or hidden risks in any relatively nondangerous or routine step in the plan. This is what I refer to as "the unsqueaky-wheel trap."

In another case study that I have been working on, I have encountered what I think is another clear-cut example of the unsqueaky-wheel trap. In this case, the defective implementation planning occurred in a business organization and involved a new policy for recruiting executives. The new policy entailed several very difficult problems (involving recruitment of well-qualified candidates) and one minor one (involving assessment of the personality and character of each qualified candidate). The minor problem proved to be the neglected unsqueaky wheel, which resulted in the appointment of a seemingly well-qualified but unconscientious manager as head of a new department. A few months later, the manager had to be fired after causing considerable losses to the firm and much adverse publicity. I suspect, therefore, that the unsqueaky-wheel trap might sometimes prove to be a detectable source of error in decision making in business firms and other organizations that are phenotypically quite different from the governmental body that made the errors in planning the ill-fated Iranian rescue mission. Perhaps the tendency to neglect the unsqueaky wheel could be counteracted if policy makers were to assume that every wheel is potentially squeaky and could lead to failure if one complacently assumes that it will be trouble free.

## Sources of Implementation Failures in Business Firms

For any strategic decision involving major changes in the way managers are expected to carry out one or another of their functions, we can expect to find that some hitherto dependable routines are undermined, often in subtle or unexpected ways. If the unsqueaky wheels that need attention are not discovered soon enough, the managers who start to implement the decisions may discover through bitter experience that they can no longer carry out certain of their tasks as effectively as they used to. This can become a major source of resistance among implementers, even when they initially approve of the new policy and have started off honestly trying to live up to the new requirements.

Sometimes, the middle- and lower-level managers who are expected to apply a new policy announced by the top managers can see right off that it is going to conflict with long-established operating procedures, which they are not likely to abandon unless specifically ordered to. If those experienced implementers are not consulted in advance, the top-level policy makers fail to make adequate provisions for dealing with such conflicts. Then, when they discover that the new policy is not being implemented as planned, they are likely to blame the managers for sabotaging it. Perhaps I should mention here that, from the small sample of the voluminous literature on implementation problems that I have read so far, I have the impression that there is a very heavy emphasis on implementation failures arising from shortcomings of the middle- and lower-level managers. They are described as misunderstanding strategic decisions made by the top management, as being unwilling to change their established routines, or as clinging to their territorial imperatives and parochial interests without regard for the needs of the organization as a whole. You will recall that the president of the United States and everyone else responsible for national security and foreign policy were forced to march to the drumbeat of the reluctant bureaucratic implementers—so ran the moral of the original myth about those "frigging" unremoved missiles in Turkey that irritated John Kennedy so much during the Cuban Missile Crisis.

All these sources of resistance to implementing new policies undoubtedly are present to some extent in every large organization. But I wonder whether organization analysts are neglecting the genuine obstacles and conflicts encountered by the implementers that could be alleviated if the policy makers were to work out appropriate implementation and contingency plans beforehand to take them into account. Perhaps if I read more extensively in the management sciences literature, I will find that my impressions are wrong and that I have merely rediscovered the unsqueaky wheel.

With regard to the problems of implementing strategic decisions, I think that it could be enlightening to examine in detail the types of conflict that typically are engendered in the implementers of strategic decisions. From intensive interviews of eighty-one middle-level managers in two large industrial corporations, in a study I conducted in collaboration with Cyril Sofer, we learned something about their dilemmas. For one thing, there are always unknown dangers along with worrisome ambiguities about the applicability of any new policy to the concrete, day-to-day administrative problems that the managers must deal with (see Sofer, 1970). In attempting to resolve the dilemmas, the managers often anticipate more punishment from dashing ahead in accord with a new policy than from dragging their feet. They expect that if they were to change the procedure in line with the new policy and it worked out badly, they would be held responsible for not doing the traditionally expected thing, for misapplying the new requirements, or for failing to proceed cautiously before the bugs have been eliminated. If they deal with the ambiguities by deciding just to keep right on doing what they have been doing, the social punishment is very mild, because everyone knows that administrative practices cannot be changed overnight, and it takes time to work out new ones.

Similarly, unequal rewards are anticipated for successful outcomes if a manager's decisions turn out well. When the successful decisions are in line with the new policy, it is the top management policy makers who are expected to get the main credit. But when a decision is not in accord with the new policy and proves to be successful, the deviant manager gets the credit, if others in the organization are getting poor results from trying to apply the new policy. So managers typically expect that if they wait for strongly worded reminders before starting to implement a new policy, their immediate superiors will see them as sensible executives who use their own good judgment. They might even become outright heros who are applauded for saving the organization from suffering the dire consequences of yet another ill-conceived strategy concocted up on Mount Olympus without any awareness of the way things actually work among mere mortals in the real world.

Now, what I have just been talking about is the lore about differential punishments and rewards that we picked up in our interviews of middle-level managers. I do not know how widespread this lore may be or to what extent it is based on reality. But if that is what many managers within an organization believe, the policy planners need to take it into account, perhaps by making explicit the positive incentives for adhering to their new policy decisions as well as by reducing ambiguities as to when, where, and how each of the new requirements is intended to be applied.

Perhaps some implementation planning could also be designed to increase the chances that new policies will be carried out by middle- and lower-level managers in a sensible and sensitive way. Special steps might be taken to enable them to make full use of their experience and intellectual resources to work out adequate solutions to whatever unforeseen implementation conflicts might arise. To some extent, eliciting participation of the implementers during the planning stages and obtaining feedback from them by pretesting a new policy before putting it in operation contribute to this objective.

Another way that policy planners might facilitate effective implementation is by trying to establish the conditions that will promote vigilant decision making among the implementers, rather than defective ways of dealing with decisional conflicts. Earlier in this chapter, I discussed the essential conditions that emerge from the Janis and Mann (1977) analysis of various patterns of coping with decisional conflict, such as unconflicted inertia, defensive avoidance, and hypervigilance (see Figure 2). It follows from this analysis that, in order to facilitate vigilant decision making among middle- and lower-level managers who have to make decisions about when, where, and how to implement a new strategic decision, the top-level policy makers need to accompany the announcement of each strategic decision with supplementary communications containing three main messages. One such message should attempt to counteract complacent inertia by highlighting the unfavorable consequences of continuing business as usual in the face of whatever new threats or opportunities constitute the challenge that induced the policy makers to work out the new strategic decision. A second message should be designed to counteract procrastination, passing the buck, and other defensive reactions by conveying a sense of optimistic hope and self-confidence in the implementers. The message could contain hints about how to use the organization's resources as well as their own resources to work out good solutions to whatever implementation dilemmas they may encounter. Above all, it could give cogent arguments to refute any specific reasons that the managers might have for feeling pessimistic about being able to live with the new policy. The third message should try to prevent an undue sense of time pressure that can evoke paniclike feelings, impulsiveness, and unproductive vacillation. Often this can be done by emphasizing in a reassuring way what can be accomplished before deadlines are at hand. The message could also help to counteract hypervigilance by calling attention to the flexibility of those deadlines that are likely to be negotiable and extendable if it turns out that many managers have indicated that they do not feel there will be sufficient time to arrive at sound implementation decisions.

When implementation decisions are to be made by a group of managers working together, additional, auxiliary messages might be included to prevent the conditions that foster groupthink, which leads to premature choices that fail to meet the requirements for high-quality decision making (see Figure 1). Earlier, I listed a set of suggested prescriptive steps that organizations can take to prevent groupthink among the top policy makers. With slight modifications, all those prescriptive recommendations are likely to be equally applicable to groups of middle- or lower-level executives who have the responsibility for applying new strategic policies when making their own administrative decisions.

### Concluding Comments

In the preceding section, I focused mainly on one particular type of failure on the part of top-level policy planners—namely, failure to work out adequate implementation and contingency plans when they select what they believe to be the best available policy option in terms of anticipated benefits and costs for the organization. (This is one of the seven requirements for high-quality decision making listed earlier.) In line with what I said about using Scriven's modus operandi approach, we need to work out in detail the sequence for each of the known causes of failure to meet this requirement, specifying the telltale signs for identifying the mediating processes that connect the observable antecedent conditions with the observable indicators of the policy makers' failure to work out adequate implementation and contingency plans. Our knowledge about those sources of error would undoubtedly increase if behavioral scientists also set themselves the task of working out the causal sequences that lead them to *succeed* in meeting this same requirement. We might then discover that the contrasting sets of conditions leading to success versus failure in meeting the requirements are not mirror images of each other, because there are interaction effects among the antecedent causal factors.

Our knowledge of effective decision making will be advanced, it seems to me, if we encourage (and carry out) the same type of inquiry for each of the other six criteria for high-quality decision making. Of course, as I have already indicated, certain of the psychological sources of error in decision making reduce the chances of meeting all seven of the criteria. Examples of such causal sequences from my own research were presented in my discussion of the groupthink hypothesis (Figure 1) and of other defective patterns of coping with decisional conflict (Figure 2). Obviously, much more work needs to be done on these general sources of error, as well as on the more specific sources pertaining to each of the seven criteria. We might then be able to develop somewhat more comprehensive middle-range theories that take account of the interacting antecedent conditions. The development and testing of such theories should enable us to formulate more sophisticated— and I hope more valid—prescriptive recommendations. Ultimately, it should be possible to arrive at sound prescriptions for counteracting all the various psychological and sociological sources of error discussed or mentioned in this chapter—internecine warfare, conformity out of fear of recrimination, groupthink, bureaucratic politics, reliance on misleading heuristics, oversimplified decision rules and stereotypes, defective patterns of coping with the stresses of decisional conflict, and the unsqueaky-wheel trap. And the same can also be said about sources of error that I have not mentioned— including all those that remain to be discovered.

# EIGHT

---

# Making Decisions
and Producing Action:
The Two Faces
of Strategy

## Deborah Gladstein, James Brian Quinn

We would like to congratulate Janis (Chapter Seven of this volume) on undertaking the complex topic of "specifying the conditions under which individuals and groups who make strategic policy decisions are likely to make gross miscalculations, poor implementation plans, or other errors that greatly reduce the chances that a new policy will be carried out successfully." The topic is a broad one, and thus Janis, in fact, has written several subchapters. We will concentrate on two of his main themes, which in a broad sense seem to embrace the others: (1) appropriate methodologies for studying strategic decision making and (2) the relationship between "rational" decision making and group effectiveness.

*Note:* The co-authors thank William Joyce and James Walsh for their helpful comments on earlier drafts.

Our orientation is one of integration and consolidation. It is our belief that theorists often get too caught up with defending or attacking specific models for research or strategy formation and lose sight of the higher goal of furthering and communicating understanding. The physical sciences often progress by establishing competing models of the same phenomena and searching for proof of one over the other (Kuhn, 1970). But in the policy realm, different models may have validity under different sets of conditions. This is especially true in the realm of strategic decision making, where no agreed-upon taxonomy exists. Arguments over models may be taking place from different perspectives representing different kinds (or aspects) of decisions in different situations. Here, we shall adopt the catholic view that Janis takes early in his chapter and highlight the appropriateness of various research methodologies and decision analogues under particular conditions. The goal is to match models with conditions so that more constructive analysis and greater progress occur.

### Research and Analytical Methodologies

Janis begins his chapter by discussing a variety of methodologies that are appropriate for studying strategic decision making. We agree with many of his major arguments that center on fitting analytical methods both to the state of the art and to the particular problems at hand: for example, his points about using well-formulated cases as an analytical base during the early stages of research, then using alternative methods, such as laboratory and field experiments, to do confirmatory testing. Janis demonstrates commendable flexibility in (1) using multiple case studies to build an argument, (2) employing as laboratory subjects real individuals deciding real issues to improve external validity, and (3) utilizing the modus operandi approach as an alternative way of exploring causality.

*Insights from the History of Science.* A careful review of the history of scientific progress in other fields suggests that scientific knowledge (or "truth") is also built by a complex of research stages and processes. For each of these, a different set of research methodologies and skills is usually appropriate. The framework for this approach is currently perhaps most identified with the works of

Kuhn (1970) and Kaplan (1964). Both suggest that scientific knowledge is not an abstract truth established for all time and for all occasions but rather that it emerges in a series of partial truths that are useful for a period and for a purpose. Scientific models may be useful though not strictly true (the atom as a whirling ball of electrons around a nucleus) or true in detail but ignored as not very useful for most purposes (the atomic nucleus as a complex collection of mesons, quarks, and so on) (Dubin, 1968).

Kuhn argues that scientific knowledge advances through periodic establishment of broad "new paradigms" in eras of "scientific revolution." Interspersed are lengthy periods of "normal science," in which researchers add brick by brick to the edifice provided by a dominating paradigm yet erode its specific validity in detail drop by drop. (Newtonian physics provides an excellent example.) During "normal science" periods, these latter (contrary) observations are accommodated by expanding, modifying, or acknowledging fuzziness in the paradigm rather than abandoning it. The paradigm is eventually overthrown when the weight of post hoc observations and anomalies becomes a burden, and some new, simpler, or more satisfying propositions adequately account for the expanded body of data. Thus, the historical school argues that the accepted scientific truths of an era are established by a kind of social process that incorporates certain aesthetic—even political—judgments about (1) what are allowable deviations from the dominating paradigm and (2) the range of deductive inferences one can legitimately draw from experimental data.

*Insights from Epistemology.* Within this broad historical framework lie certain procedures that derive from the philosophical field of epistemology. This tradition traces back at least to Bacon (1620), who discussed the role of proposing alternative explanations and then conducting explicit tests to distinguish between their validity. This theme has more recently been influenced strongly by Popper (1959, 1962) and his followers, notably Platt (1964), who argue for "proof by disproof." While a hypothesis can never actually be proved true—since future events, though currently unknown or unmeasurable, could conceivably provide contrary evidence—they can be proved incorrect by observations that fail to fit their predictions. True scientific knowledge, in their view, can advance only by the rejection of previously tenable hypotheses about the real world. They claim that this "strong inference" approach characterizes most successful research. Baconian or Popperian hypothesis testing is regarded by many—particularly in academia—as the only legitimate form of research and scientific knowledge building. This is the current "dominating paradigm" of academic research and is at the heart of many conflicts among biologists and ecologists; epidemiologists, doctors, and microbiologists; and economic theorists and policy researchers.

*Problems in Policy Research.* Neither tradition deals with truth and prediction in the normative proximate sense that frequently faces analysts of large-scale systems or policy makers. Many situations are unique. The researcher must often live with the problems inherent in a sample of one and the vagaries of the incomplete, biased, and often contradictory information available to a historian. The number of potential variables is so great that it is impossible to either monitor or measure all of them in detail. Policy systems often require rapid decisions under pressure and later defy reasonable experimental replication. Even when time allows careful analysis, predictions about relationships or outcomes in policy situations must be probabilistic and thus cannot be falsified by single contrary observations in the Popperian sense. And even a macro failure of a policy—or a policy process—to produce a predicted outcome may not invalidate an underlying analysis, theory, or decision rule but may merely indicate that several low-probability events combined in unusual ways to dominate the statistically expected norm.

In researching and analyzing policy systems, measurement problems abound. Some most important relationships may be true, but their causal inputs may not be reliably measured independently of results (for example, "stable democracies persist"). On the other hand, some insights about policy systems may have important predictive values, even if they are not demonstrably true in a given case (for example, a key player lacks integrity). Those variables that are measurable and predictable may be trivial in impact. Single dominating (but totally unpredictable or unknowable) events can render all other system parameters impotent (for example, the Nazis invent and build an atomic bomb before the Allies do, or vice versa).

A true null hypothesis (absence of any effect from a given force) may be meaningless or impossible to test in the real world. And so on.

Policy research seems more affected by such factors than research in other areas. Indeed, there are many recognized hazards in applying traditional experimental and hypothesis-testing approaches to the analysis of large-scale systems or predictions of their outcomes. Consequently, there is constant pressure to deny legitimacy to policy research because it cannot satisfy these supposed mainstays of the "scientific method." Perhaps the field must of necessity rely more on other well-recognized—but less generally espoused—methods of generating understanding.

*A Structure of Knowledge-Generating Processes.* One is considerably less humbled by this problem when one reads the history-of-science literature carefully. Even the physical sciences do not advance solely—or perhaps even primarily—by scientists generating hypotheses and then testing them through controlled experiments. Other processes make major contributions in the "hard sciences" and deserve much more recognition and legitimization in other realms—particularly in large-scale systems, organizational, or policy research—where they can be similarly fruitful. There are perhaps some seven definable research activities, each frequently having its own particularly skilled practitioners and appropriate information-generating techniques. These activities are briefly outlined here, along with a single physical sciences analogue (classical biology) that makes the point.

1. *Exploration and description (creating a data base):* One must know validly what is there before a hypothesis or test is meaningful (Homans, 1950). In many cases, assembling adequate data narrows the zone of conjecture sufficiently to specify an otherwise nonobvious solution. Especially early in the development of scientific knowledge, this stage can define truth as adequately as experimentation and testing. For example, Charles Darwin's systematic observations on the Beagle expedition provided essential knowledge about species throughout the world. And it is probably the use of this powerful field data base in his arguments that most distinguishes Darwin as a scientist from earlier proponents of biological evolution, notably Buffon, Erasmus Darwin, and Lamarck.

2. *Cataloguing and classification (developing a taxonomy):* Communication about complex systems, replication of data or results, and generalizations to wider systems are inpossible without an adequate nomenclature. For example, Darwin's careful structuring of his data (on coral reefs, geospizid finches, lepadid and balanid barnacles, orchids, and so on) was a major step in developing a systematic worldwide biological science and a major contribution in itself. The lack of a similarly powerful taxonomy has confused many research fields, including our own, for decades. The skills and procedures used by a taxonomist are quite different from those of an explorer or a laboratory experimentalist.

3. *Extension of observations into generalized patterns (defining subsystem laws):* Defining new patterns in data (creative induction) is often a major contribution in itself (Kemeny and Snell, 1972). These observations are precursors of what Kaplan calls "simple," "extensional," and "intermediate" generalizations leading to laws. Generalizations from laws become "theories" (Kaplan, 1964) or paradigms (Kuhn, 1970). Like policy scholars, scientists are usually able to study any given system only under a small number of specific conditions, from which they must attempt any wider generalizations (Kaplan, 1964). For example, in an early application of the modus operandi approach, Darwin recognized that bill and limb sizes and shapes in a small sample of a single genus of finches differed from one another, probably as a result of specific adaptations to the food and habitats available to them. He proposed that all the birds—through adaptive radiation and later speciation—had come from a common ancestor species. Yet these conclusions defied explicit experimental tests at the time—and perhaps now. Similarly, cross-case patterns in nonstatistical samples can be useful to policy analysts in identifying new areas for controlled research and even as predicting mechanisms for systems outcomes (although they might be nondominant or nontestable in specific situations).

4. *Proposing hypotheses (suggesting causal mechanisms):* This is often called the "creative act" of science (Einstein, 1934; Kaplan, 1964). At its best, this stage creates new "revolutionary paradigms" and separates the scientific greats from the elegant practitioners. But two important caveats should be noted: (1) In many cases, the hypothesis follows the data-gathering step (or

experiment) that led to it. (2) At the time most major paradigms are proposed, they can rarely be fully tested. Kuhn (1970) estimates an average of twenty-five years between the initial statement of a "revolutionary paradigm" and its first definitive test. Nevertheless, well-formed hypotheses—though testably incomplete—can advance a science far more than most of the specific experimental tests that later prove them "correct" or "wrong" at the margin and cause their incremental modification. For example, to provide the causal mechanisms behind his "patterned observations" of adaptive radiation and speciation, Darwin hypothesized the process of "natural selection." After 100 years, Darwin's proposed explanations are still being modified, and only a handful of examples exist where the complete linkage from environmental stress to mutation of individual genes is completely understood in an experimentally verifiable sense.

5. *Tests of hypotheses (experimenting and testing):* Although an important aspect of the total research process, formalized hypothesis testing may not be possible or meaningful in specific situations, as has been noted earlier. The technology may not exist to test a hypothesis unambiguously at the time it is proposed or, indeed, ever. Scientists themselves have noted the tyranny and inadequacies of formalized hypothesis testing in specific situations (Lewin, 1983a, 1983b). Trivial questions with small ultimate benefits are tested repeatedly, while more important issues—where small insights could allow large leverage—are ignored. The imprecisions of extrapolating laboratory measurements to live systems can be greater than the added precision that laboratory conditions contribute to the experiment. And so on. One should, of course, perform formal hypothesis tests when the situation warrants. But this is by no means always possible or desirable in policy or large-scale natural systems. The fact that one can unambiguously test only one set of proposed mechanisms (for example, cancer from saccharin) while being unable to test others (slow obesity through increased sugar use) can lead to fallacious conclusions (such as the Delaney Amendment) in policy settings.

6. *Synthesis (merging theories for new paradigms):* Some of the richest developments in science have occurred by the combining of seemingly disparate disciplines. Haldane, Dobzhansky, and Mayr

merged Darwin's theories with classical genetics to create the "New Synthesis" in the 1930s and 1940s. Fisher and Wright combined emerging statistical and mathematical techniques with Mendelian genetics to forge the basis for modern population genetics. And, recently, biochemistry has merged with genetics in recombinant DNA investigations. Similarly today, active participation of other specialties in policy research could yield far more beneficial insights than highly refined, quantitatively rigorous measurements at the margin of defined disciplines. As Gordon Orians says, "Asking the right new questions can ultimately lead to interestingly new answers though the answers are currently untestable. The field learns little from much more elaborate testing of uninteresting questions." Yet faculty structures and tenure practices actively impede such interactions in many universities.

7. *Manipulation for a purpose—interactive development (technology and diffusion):* Technology often precedes science, answering previously unanswered scientific questions and defining new ones as relevant (the steam engine preceded thermodynamics). Various studies have shown that much scientific discovery and innovation occur as knowledge users interactively develop their first applications (Von Hipple, 1977). Similarly, one of the richest arenas for policy research continues to be action research on the struggling attempts of major organizations to solve their own new problems (Argyris, 1980). Establishing an interactive learning relationship between theory builders and real-systems users can increase the quality of the knowledge for both parties. Kaplan (1964) strongly emphasizes the interactiveness of "logic in use" and "reconstructed logic" in developing valid new theory. Each poses and resolves issues for the other. (For example, feedback from the actual marketplace showed that L dopamine was not as effective for its intended purposes as phase-one and -two laboratory tests suggested, but it was (surprisingly) effective against Parkinson's disease. Yet academia often discourages the kinds of publication, hands-on policy participation, and interactive consulting that are necessary to generate policy knowledge at this interface.

Professionalism requires that each activity level be honored and well performed. Within any healthy area of inquiry, all levels typically occur simultaneously and interactively. No single level or approach should have legitimacy to the exclusion of all others. Each should be used as a support and check for all others. Yet textbook descriptions of scientific method—and faculty screening procedures—deal almost exclusively with processes 4 and 5. The effect in some schools has been devastating for the development of both broad concepts and younger faculty.

Just as no single research approach satisfies all steps of knowledge development, no single rational-analytical or behavioral construct will be appropriate in all strategic situations. A model of strategic decision making that can embrace the wide variance in different types of such situations seems politic. Given the present state of the art in strategic process knowledge, it is most important to recognize when different elements of various potential constructs apply and how to marshal these for specific situations. Despite the important tolerance that Janis applies in evaluating policy research approaches, we do not believe that his discussion in Chapter Seven displays the same breadth in relating various possible strategic models to different strategic situations. The processes and culture inherent in "groupthink" may be destructive in some situations, helpful in others.

### Policy Processes and Outcomes

Central to Janis's model of policy fiascoes is a process-performance relationship. Essentially, his argument is that poor decision-making processes in top management groups account for a greater likelihood of "gross miscalculations and poor implementation plans." Janis argues that if these top decision-making groups follow the normative model of (1) thoroughly canvassing a wide range of policy alternatives, (2) taking account of the full range of objectives to be fulfilled and the values implicated by the choice, (3) carefully weighing negative and positive consequences, (4) intensively searching for new information relevant for further evaluation, (5) accounting for new information, (6) re-examining positive and negative consequences of all known alternatives, including those originally regarded as unacceptable, and (7) providing detailed provisions for implementation, then organizational outcomes will improve. If, however, cohesiveness, threat, and isolation cause concurrence seeking in the group, "groupthink" will occur, and performance will probably suffer. Thus, Janis is proposing that groups should try to improve what Brunsson (1982) refers to as decision rationality.

Other researchers argue that when commitment and motivation are the primary outcomes of interest, "action rationality" (Brunsson, 1982) should guide the process of the top decision-making group (Pfeffer and Salancik, 1978; Starbuck and Hedberg, 1977). Action rationality differs from decision rationality in that the aim may be not to arrive at the "best" decision in some abstract sense but to involve people in the decision-making process so as to gain their input in molding the decision and their cooperation in implementing it. The issue is less one of organizational effectiveness (whether what is being done should be done) and more one of efficiency—how decisions can best be carried out (Pfeffer and Salancik, 1978). The emphasis is on implementation, how to get organizational members to follow through on decisions.

Action rationality specifies a decision-making process (see Table 1) that differs from Janis's normative model of vigilant decision making. The top decision-making group will probably be heavily involved in symbolic management (Pfeffer and Salancik, 1978), influencing and creating acceptability for the group and for its activities. This is done by providing explanations, rationalizations, and legitimizing arguments for chosen courses of action both inside the group and externally. Myths, symbols, and images—even if they are stereotyped images—are used to legitimize the organization's purposes in the larger context. The objective is to influence the beliefs and sentiments of organizational members in ways that motivate people, mobilize internal support, and favorably affect external views of the company (Pfeffer and Salancik, 1978). Rationalizations, stereotyping, and illusions of unanimity are important tools in building commitments within the group so that its members can enthusiastically help steer other employees in appropriate directions. Top decision makers display appropriate attitudes and priorities to influence decision making in desired directions (Peters, 1978). This modeling behavior is facilitated when fellow team members support both these directions and each other (Festinger, 1956; O'Reilly, 1983).

Table 1. Principal Characteristics of Processes.

| | Decision Rationality | Action Rationality |
|---|---|---|
| Goals | Effectiveness | Efficiency |
| Group | Heterogeneous outlook | Homogeneous outlook |
| Groupthink | Clear estimation of group Open-mindedness | Overestimation of group Closed-mindedness Rationalizing of behavior Stereotyping of outsiders |
| | Diversity | Uniformity |
| Process | Thoroughly canvassing a wide range of policy alternatives | Looking at only a small number of alternatives (one or two) |
| | Taking account of the full range of objectives to be fulfilled and the values implied by the choice | Using predicted consequences to evaluate alternatives, account for implementation |
| | Carefully weighing negative and positive consequences | Bolstering alternatives with positive information |
| | Intensively searching for new information relevant for further evaluation | Searching for new information that supports alternative desired |
| | Accounting for new information | Accounting for new information |
| | Re-examining positive and negative consequences of all known alternatives, including those originally regarded as unacceptable | Readjusting alternative to account for new information, not going back to original alternatives left behind |
| | Providing detailed provisions for implementation | Continuing to back chosen alternative and modifying action and direction slowly over time |

Note: These are intended to be indicative, not complete, definitions. Obviously, overlaps occur between the two.

Action rationality has important consequences for the way top decision makers proceed. Processes that are often termed irrational and ineffective under conditions of decision rationality are now considered useful. These include (1) seeking information that solely bolsters particular alternatives, (2) viewing group decisions as more favorable than is objectively warranted, and (3) making suboptimal decisions to avoid conflict or to maintain cohesion (O'Reilly, 1983). Under conditions of action rationality, few alternatives should be analyzed, a narrow range of potential consequences should be used to choose among alternatives, and implementation issues should be dominant throughout the entire process.

Janis (1982a, Chapter Seven in this volume), too, has identified the usefulness of action rationality (or integration as opposed to differentiation) for nonstrategic decisions and for bolstering decisions after a "mature consensus" has been reached. These procedures may also be optimal for strategic decisions, as when a serious threat requires rapid cohesive action, continuing unity is more important than other consequences, the top group has significantly more information than the organization, and so on. The consideration of multiple alternatives could evoke dysfunctional uncertainty. This uncertainty can increase and conflict take hold when both positive and negative consequences of alternatives get equal attention. At some point in any decision process, perhaps even before a mature consensus is reached, bolstering of a few alternatives (rather than continued discussion of all pros and cons) is necessary to help implant group support behind the feasible set (Brunsson, 1982).

Janis's normative model suggests that analytically derived objectives should be used as criteria for choice. Lindblom (1959) argues, however, that, for producing action, it is better to use consequences as criteria and to state or announce these as objectives afterward. Group members may conflict substantially over goals but may find that they can agree on a program to achieve those goals. Once that program has been carried out, there is something tangible around which consensus can be developed, and objectives can then be formulated retrospectively to justify the action (Weick, 1969a). For example, a group of military personnel may disagree permanently on the goals for which a ship is built, but they can all agree that it should be built. Later groups faced with creating a naval blockade can identify military preparation as an objective that they believe was met by having the ship built earlier.

Finally, Janis's sequential listing of seven criteria of effective decision making and his references to "this final stage [choice of an alternative] just prior to implementation of a new decision" imply that implementation is the final phase. This can be quite disadvantageous from an action standpoint. The relationship between participation and commitment is well documented (compare Bass, 1970; Coch and French, 1948; Lawler and Hackman, 1969). Barring situations where an individual's championship or charisma is important, premature disclosure could endanger needed secrecy, or rapid response outweighs all other considerations, those implementing the decision should be generally brought in early in the process.

As Janis's account of the attempt to rescue the hostages in Iran demonstrates, feasibility and commitment in implementation should also be important criteria for evaluating possible alternatives. For example, in a recent interview on *This Week* with David Brinkley, Margaret Thatcher was asked whether she liked Ronald Reagan's suggestion of having the United Nations meet half the year in New York and half the year in Moscow so that delegates could compare the two systems. Thatcher replied (approximately) that she thought the question was irrelevant. "It doesn't make any difference whether I like an idea. If it can't be done, there's no point in spending time on it." She thought that the expense and difficulties of moving the United Nations across the world were too enormous to consider. To extend the argument further, an enthusiastically implemented alternative with a lesser "expected value payoff" will often achieve higher gains than a less committed organization's performance of an alternative with a higher calculated payoff. This is the whole argument behind "champions" in innovations and new ventures.

The quality of a strategic decision is also influenced by the quality of the information that goes into it. Often, those deep down in an organization have much better information about specifics than those at the top (for example, in high-technology organizations). Strategic managers can simultaneously tap this information base and create initial enthusiasm for specific proposals by early involvement of the line people who will carry out the decision. By getting these people to make proposals, endorsing some of these as experimental projects, and supporting task forces with increasing resources as their ideas begin to favorably shape the strategy, top managers can have a decision half implemented—with correspondingly lower time and organizational costs—before it is even made final.

## A Synthesis

We have outlined two different kinds of decision processes represented in the literature. They can be fitted together into a more complete view of the decision-making process. Both descriptive and normative models of strategic decision making in large organizations have suggested a circular (interactive-learning) as opposed to linear (preformulated-sequential) process (Mintzberg, 1978; Quinn, 1980). Mintzberg (1978) writes that such decisions resemble the process of fermentation in biochemistry rather than an industrial assembly line. A managed strategic process can perhaps better be illustrated by a spiral (see Figure 1), where the top management group, over time, cycles through various phases of formulation and implementation, moving from the general to the specific, from determining direction to gaining supportive action.

The process begins with problem sensing, which is triggered by an opportunity, problem, or crisis (Mintzberg, Rasinghani, and Théorêt, 1976; Mason and Mitroff, 1981a). At this point, the decision-making group usually has little understanding of the decision situation that it faces or the route to solution. Individuals may have only a vague idea of possible solutions and how they might be evaluated. This is decision making under ambiguity, "a wicked problem" (Mason and Mitroff, 1981a) characterized by novelty, complexity, and open-endedness (Mintzberg, Rasinghani, and Théorêt, 1976).

The best one can do in such situations is to forecast the forces most likely to impinge on future events, estimate the probable nature and strength of potential impacts, and broadly define a desired and feasible vision of success. Then the top group must build a resource base and strategic posture that are so strong and flexible in selected dimensions that they ensure that the organization can come as close as possible to its goals, despite the unknowability of all forces and their potential interactions. The organization moves step by step from early generalities to later specifics, further clarifying the strategy incrementally as new information emerges and organizational or political constraints permit or dictate (Quinn, 1982).

Figure 1. Model of Strategy Development.

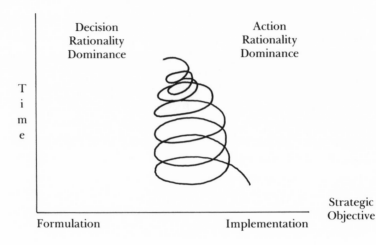

This kind of strategic incrementalism proceeds slowly, tumultuously at times, but logically and proactively, as the top management group maintains its options and moves from broad visions toward final specific positioning strategies (Quinn, 1982). As initial positions become clarified through discussion or investigation of alternatives, champions may appear to lead specific strategic thrusts, or component organizations may build internal momentums around partial decisions. The choice and selective nurturing of these champions and groups will inevitably shape the directions of the strategy itself, as the values, imaginations, and talents of key players screen or suggest options that top management itself might not have considered. As individuals and teams move toward generally accepted goals—those at the top of the vortex—they may modify elements in their segment of the corporate concept and ultimately shape the concept itself in new ways. For example, IBM's PC group, by using an open architecture and standard components—an alternative not envisioned or espoused by top management—will shape the entire "low-end" strategy of IBM and hence, its overall strategic balance.

These groups shift general management's visions and policies in the very acts of participation and implementation. Champions, or group managers, in turn will go through similar experiences as they build organizational awareness, commitment, and consensus around their desired directions (which are simultaneously being formed and carried out from below). Overall strategies typically emerge after a long process of realignment in both the formal and informal organizations and as individuals and opportunities present themselves (Nadler and Tushman, 1977; Quinn, 1982). Yet, being aware of this process, top managements can proactively guide it, utilize the organization's total talent pool to best advantage, and maintain ultimate approval authority over its output. In essence, a manager merely operates like an expert brewmaster, not like the master of a slave ship.

The lines between strategy formulation and implementation constantly blur; some parts of the strategy are in the building stage while others are being refined. Commitment to a few key thrusts may be developed through discussion, argument, myths, slogans, or symbols (Siehl and Martin, 1982), yet a complete new structural system is not introduced until sufficient political and emotional support can be obtained for and from key power figures.

This spiraling process of continually increasing specificity and commitment for a new strategic focus requires great skill on the part of the top managers. They must constantly move back and forth between decision and action rationality. The process is not neatly broken up into choosing the best alternative, gaining commitment for that alternative, and moving on to implementation. The group is constantly cycling through this process. True managerial artistry is needed to determine when to crystallize viewpoints and when to maintain more open options. While building commitment and consensus from below, the group needs to bolster what it considers desirable alternatives, emphasizing positive thrusts while diverting or killing unwanted options and rationalizing decisions and behaviors so that a coherent view is both achieved and presented. At times, a biased picture of the world may have to be presented—for example, stereotyping the "enemy" to build support from within. As Janis points out, some groupthink symptoms may be quite beneficial at key points. In order to lead the organization in coherent directions, top management and upper echelons may consciously induce groupthink (that is, develop the illusion of unanimity), and group members may try to minimize extraneous conflicts and rally round the cause. There comes a time when continued probing of the pros and cons in possible new directions can destructively diffuse enthusiasm and create unnecessary uncertainty.

A true danger occurs if this "cohesiveness behavior" becomes over-routinized in group norms. For continued success, a group must be able to switch gears when entirely new stimuli appear and creative thinking is needed. The networks put in place to provide only positive reinforcing information will need to be circumvented to surface potential negative scenarios and legitimize new options. The heuristics that so neatly foreclosed decision alternatives and helped program actions toward a common group response need to be challenged when a new problem arises that requires a different approach. The group must be able to swing back from its action rationality to a more objective analytical approach. Here, group-think characteristics will clearly impair critical investigation and damage the quality of resulting decisions. Thus, both decision and action rationality are required; the major issues are knowing when it is optimal to change and whether the group is able to make that change.

## Organizational Evolution

The previous section suggests the spiraling developing of a typical complex corporate strategy and the necessity for top managers to shift from a process dominated by decision rationality to one of action rationality and back again. This section identifies different phases of organizational development that may require a greater use of action rationality or the analytical model.

*Convergence Versus Reorientation.* Current models of organizational evolution indicate that organizations move from periods of convergence around a particular strategy to periods of reorientation, when the organization must readjust to a changing environment (compare Romanelli and Tushman, 1983). The core task of the top management group shifts in these different periods. During periods of inertia, the leadership must maintain commitment to strategies and structures instituted during prior reorientation periods. Romanelli and Tushman (1983) state that this time of inertia corresponds to one in which the top management is primarily concerned with symbolic decisions, and, thus, action rationality should prevail. They further argue that the longer the inertia period lasts, the more successful and older the organization, the more likely it is that the leadership will become insulated and uncoupled from the organization's competitive environment. As Janis predicts, this insulation, coupled with other group properties, reduces the probability that problems will be accurately perceived and/or acted upon (Staw, Sandelands, and Dutton, 1981). If the organization faces new challenges or threats, a reorientation is necessary.

During reorientation, groupthink could be a disaster. As the organization tries to align itself with a significantly changed environment, both substantive and symbolic management is necessary (Romanelli and Tushman, 1983). Not only do norms and decision premises need to be changed, but typically so do structures, work flows, products, markets, and dependency relationships. As the top group attempts to move toward reorientation, it must shift the balance between decision and action rationality, with increasing emphasis on the former. If the group has been entrenched in a convergence phase for too long, it may not be able to shift processes. Partial suupport for this comes from a number of studies that indicate that major new corporate strategy shifts often require a new top management team (Hofer, 1980; Starbuck and Hedberg, 1977).

*Smaller Organizations and Entrepreneurship.* Mintzberg (1973a) argues that three modes of strategy making exist: entrepreneurial, adaptive, and planning. The first is most characteristic of small, young firms or those with strong leadership. The second tends to be present in moderate-sized established firms, while the third is most prevalent in large companies. The entrepreneurial firm tends to be more proactive in its approach, constantly analyzing and searching to satisfy its need for growth and resources in a very uncertain environment. But much of this search occurs at the very top level of the concern. Many entrepreneurial managers are very rational-analytical in their approach to opportunity search and to decisions. Nevertheless, the scale of their enterprises and the pressures on their time may not allow them to use the same level of specialists' skills or highly formalized planning as somewhat larger enterprises.

If uncertainty in these organizations is sufficiently high, action rationality may have to become an important component of internal management in order to gain cohesion. One of the recognized advantages of a small company or team is its capacity to quickly rally emotional support behind a chosen direction. This response capability comes in large part from the perceived threat of extinction, the commonly held goals, and the cultural norms of cooperation often found in such groups. The group itself frequently does not operate in an opportunistic scanning mode but responds rapidly because of some characteristics contained in the groupthink model.

Thus, small entrepreneurial groups also frequently display a balanced mixture of rational-analytical planning—though not quite in the "planning mode" suggested by Mintzberg (1973a)—and groupthink characteristics. In entrepreneurial companies (especially smaller ones), the top management team is likely to have a higher percentage of the relevant information needed for decisions and the lower groups are more closely interconnected to the top than in larger organizations. Therefore, the spiraling decision process described—though often present—tends to be very flat, representing the lack of tiers of information and commitment needed in these organizations.

In sum, both action and decision rationality are predicted to be important processes for top management teams. The spiraling incremental development of a strategy requires that the team move back and forth between formulation and implementation, substantive and symbolic management, and, therefore, decision and action rationality. The balance varies, however, depending upon the stage of organizational development and organizational mode. During times of reorientation, decision rationality will play a more major role, but when convergence is necessary, action rationality should dominate. In the entrepreneurial mode, organizations will go through fewer iterations between action and decision rationality, since the spiraling process of strategy development is flatter. However, both forms of rationality are still present.

# ❧ NINE ❧

# Developing Capabilities for Organizational Learning

## *Richard Normann*

Interest in strategic management is rising again among managers and researchers. Many of the normative models promoted by glamor companies and glamor consultants are beginning to look increasingly inadequate, and this inadequacy is aggravated by what is perceived as greater complexity of strategic problems. A large number of industries and businesses are in or are entering into a period of complex change and restructuring. Many traditional manufacturing industries (such as steel and automobiles) are in zero-growth situations, where the choice is either to get out, to get involved in an industrywide restructuring process, or to make creative reinterpretations of the business. In new high-technology businesses, such as genetic engineering and information, knowledge frontiers are moving so fast and blind alleys are appearing so suddenly that attempts to "analyze" the situation will be something of a guessing game, and the consequences of strategic moves are extremely difficult to evaluate. Service industries, playing a predominant role in today's society that has not yet even begun to be recognized, have their specific strategic problems.

A further reason why practitioners are now looking for new advice is their increasing realization that actual change does not automatically follow from good strategic decision making. In particular, they are beginning to see a strong relationship between strategic decisions and what is popularly called implementation of a strategy. I have seen many examples of strategies that have been deemed unsound when, in reality, it was not the conception of the strategy that was at fault but rather an inability to anchor it in the organization and to create the focused and powerful action necessary for putting it into practice. Perhaps this phenomenon is particularly highlighted in service industries, which tend to have highly scattered organizational structures, where a changed strategy is put into practice by the concrete individual actions of thousands of people out in the field. The outcome depends not only on whether a particular decision was "good" or "bad" but also on the ability to raise sufficient human energy and enthusiasm to move ahead with force—and to adapt creatively when more information is generated as a result of action.

A third reason why managers and theorists are looking for good theory on strategic change (and finding the state of the art less than satisfactory) is that they are increasingly aware of the importance of a long-term view. It is fine if a specific strategic situation is well handled—resulting in a good strategy, well implemented— but in today's complex and changing business context, there is a tendency for situations requiring strategic skill to appear more and more frequently. Business success is becoming the result of a succession of good strategic actions over time. The ability to achieve good strategic action on a longer-term, repeated basis is what we would call strategic management, or strategic action capability.

Single successes or failures in the strategic positioning of a company can have various explanations—they can be the result of luck, smartness, serendipity, bad judgment, or accident. Studying them can provide insights into a strategic process, but understanding the nature and conditions of good strategic management requires more than an analysis of isolated actions. I find that, while interest in the process of decision making and in inventing more creative strategy outcome types persists, there is an increasing interest in *the basic preconditions for a successful strategic manage-*

*ment process;* that is, for strategic action capability. More and more managers ask themselves not only how they will be able to take good individual strategic actions but also how they can ensure conditions within the organization that will raise the probability of a high-quality strategic management process on a long-term basis.

From a theoretical perspective, there have been many approaches to strategic decision making and strategic management. One view, stressing the cognitive aspects of the process, is the so-called rationalistic one, perceiving a strategy as the outcome of a rational process of information gathering, analysis, formulation of alternatives, and choice. This view presupposes that the process is governed by a decision maker or a fairly clearly identifiable center of decision making. Other views tend to emphasize formal decisions and decision makers as more or less the victims of chance and circumstances in a complex network of multiple internal and external influences. While the former models emphasize cognitive processes, the latter stress influences of internal politics, culture, and limited information. Such models of strategic decision making, focusing on cognitive, political, and social processes of strategic action, can be further enlarged by bringing the realm of psychological processes, at the individual and group level, into the analytical framework.

As a consultant to managers, I accept the validity of all these views. It is clear that they all treat different and relevant aspects of the problem. It is also clear that, taken one by one, the approaches are insufficient, since they are only partial, and this probably should be interpreted as a need for a "grander," more integrated framework of strategic decision making and strategic management. But it is also a matter of perspective and of research. The perspective of this chapter is to develop knowledge that can be used for making strategic action more effective, that is, that can be used by the actors themselves and by interventionists, such as consultants, whose aim is to increase the strategic action capability of their clients.

Strategic action results from actions of individuals, and we need normative models of the decision-making and strategic action process as well as of outcomes or "ideal types" of strategies in different situations. It is true that decision makers are the victims of circumstances, but they are also able to influence circumstances.

Managers and change agents want a normative, rationalistic view, since it tells them what to do. But they also need this view to be tempered by an understanding of the whole system of influences on this process, whether we call these influences rational or not. We need to understand and take into account both the individual actors and the context they are working in and how they can best use and handle that context to enhance the quality of the strategic management process and the strategic outcomes.

I would hasten to add, though, that those with a rationalistic, normative view must not fall into the trap of oversimplification. In my view, many rationalistic and normative models of strategic decision making and action fail to capture the inherent logic of strategic action. There are two points that are absolutely crucial in understanding the logic of strategic action and that must be reflected in any normative framework. The first of these points is that strategic action is rarely a simple sequence of "first decision, then action." This "sequence myth" has done a lot of damage to many business companies and probably to researchers as well. Instead, we can observe how strategies evolve as a result of a process that has at least three key elements: the formulation of a *vision; action* based on that vision; and interpretation and *reflection* based on the action and its outcome. Then the sequence starts again: The vision is further clarified, new action is taken, there is food for more reflection, and so on. There are very few instances of strategic change that are not best described in terms of such a spiraling process (compare "the process view of planning," Normann, 1977).

Of course, there is nothing "antirationalistic" about such a process, although it sometimes seems as if managers do not like it because it tends to deprive them of a heralded self-image of being able to master plan a strategy and then implement it. The view merely reflects the inherent logic of strategic change, and this brings me to the second crucial point. Strategic change is inherently not so much an analytical, deductive process as an open-ended, inductive, *synthetic process.* A strategy is a piece of architecture; it is the result of creative-design thinking. We know that design, innovation, and creation result from a combination of analysis and synthesis, of systematic and open-ended thinking, and of consciously bringing an element of the unknown and of surprise into the process. Any design process is an iterative process, and therefore my conclusion is that models of strategic change and of developing strategic management capability must reflect this inherent logic. From one point of view, we would like to see the organization as a machine able to continuously synthesize and create. A theory of how to develop strategic action capability must account for this.

Therefore, there is close relationship between strategic action and organizational innovativeness. The development of strategic management capability is closely related to the organization's ability to learn and be creative. It is this link between organizational learning (learning in a proactive sense, including the ability to synthesize and innovate) and strategic management capability that I want to explore in this chapter. The quality of an individual strategic action and of a series of strategic moves over time is a function of how well the organization has learned to identify and respond to new situations and to take a proactive position vis-á-vis its environment. *High learning capability, then, is an underlying variable explaining performance in strategic action.*

I will also argue that we need to apply two sets of criteria to determine what is such action. One outcome of effective strategic action obviously is the substance of the organization's strategy—expressed, for example, in such terms as product market configuration, overall "mission," and competitive positioning. The other set of outcomes of good strategic action would be preservation of the organization's strategic action capability and the maintenance and enhancement of the basic preconditions for proactive learning.

An ultimate aim is to formulate an *action theory for learning strategic management capability.* The purpose of such an action theory would be to give actors (I prefer that term to *decision makers*) better tools to influence the course of events—both by being able to conceive of better, more innovative outcome categories (business strategies) and by better being able to influence the process of setting a course of action and implementing it.

A theory of action implies an analysis of events in the light of a fundamental understanding of the beliefs, world views, and rationales of the actors. Therefore, the best methodology for arriving at such a theory of action is a clinical methodology. (These concepts and some of their implications are brought up later in this chapter.) Thus, two fundamental and closely related questions that will be addressed are: (1) Are there any basic overall properties of organizational structure and management that increase the likelihood of an effective strategic action process? (2) How can we design an increased learning capability—where "learning" is understood as the development of appropriate action skills—into the organization, so that it not only adapts more effectively to the course of events but actually increases its capacity to innovate, in terms of both strategic process and strategic outcome?

## Learning Theory and Organizations

Although much has been said about individual learning, surprisingly little systematic research and conceptualization have taken place in the area of *organizational* learning, where new knowledge is manifested in new structural arrangements, new culture, and new collective action. The approaches so far can be divided into three types.

One approach has borrowed concepts from general systems theory, including analogies from biological systems (Buckley, 1967; Dunn, 1971). Buckley lists the following four conditions as necessary for a social system to achieve "morphogenesis" (structural change): (1) some degree of "plasticity" and "sensitivity" or *tension* vis-à-vis its environment such that it carries on a constant interchange with environmental events, acting on and reacting to them; (2) some source or mechanism providing for *variety*, to act as a potential pool of adaptive variability to meet the problem of new or more detailed variety and constraints in a changeable environment; (3) a set of *selective* criteria or mechanisms by which the "variety pool" may be sifted into those variations in the organization or system that more closely match the environment and those that do not; and (4) an arrangement for *preserving and/or propagating* these "successful" mappings (Buckley, 1967, p. 63).

A second line of approach, which is certainly not a homogeneous one, is concerned with the ability of organizations to innovate (in most cases, understood as their ability to conceive and develop new products). Most of the fundamental observations in this area were made in the study by Burns and Stalker (1961), who recognized the superiority of organic, as opposed to mechanistic, structures to promote the outward orientation, result orientation, and general climate conducive to sensing environmental change and producing the appropriate action. It was observed that the political system of an organization tends to move it in the mechanistic direction but that the "code of conduct" visibly displayed in action by top management (and, most importantly, by the person at the top) was highly contagious and could counter such forces. Among important later contributions developing some of these themes further and operationalizing them is that of Lawrence and Lorsch (1967).

The third direction has its roots in individual and social psychology. Argyris and Schön (1981) distinguish among three levels of learning. The simplest is *single-loop learning*, which implies a change of action that does not violate a pre-established norm of effectiveness. The second level, *double-loop learning*, leads to a change in the very norms defining effective behavior. At a third level, they distinguish—borrowing, I believe, the concept from Bateson (1972)—the notion of *deutero learning*, a still higher-level learning process whereby an individual or an organization is able to reflect on its ability to learn and influence it. Deutero learning is the art of developing a viable theory of action on how to learn— learning how to learn. If we link these three levels to the concept of strategy, single-loop learning would roughly correspond to operating decisions within a given framework, double-loop learning to single strategic actions, and deutero learning to strategic management. An organization with a high capability of deutero learning can be expected to deliver a series of good strategic actions over time.

Using a framework developed primarily to account for individual learning process, Argyris and Schön (1981) try to bridge the gap between the individual or small group and the organization as the unit of analysis by introducing the concept of "maps" (p. 17), denoting, "for example, diagrams of work-flow, compensation charts, statements of procedure, even the schematic drawings of office space." Such maps "describe actual patterns of activity, and they are guides to future action."

## Types of Learning and Strategic Action

Let us make a closer formal examination of these levels of learning as they pertain to action in organizations. This can be done by enquiring into two crucial dimensions—the cognitive processes involved and the internal power system implications for the organization (Normann, 1971).

Single-loop learning, corresponding to decisions within a basic strategic posture, takes place within a given frame of reference and with no change in the criteria of effective performance or governing variables. A steel mill facing projected lower demand, applying a single-loop learning framework, would typically react by selecting an appropriate mix of price adjustment, production-capacity adjustment, and perhaps more aggressive selling in marginal markets as appropriate tools to handle the situation. All these actions would take place within the existing organizational structure and action programs of the company. In our terminology, we would hardly call this action "strategic," at least not unless this kind of action has deliberately been chosen as an alternative to other, consciously evaluated options derived from fundamentally different ideas of strategic positioning.

Double-loop learning is something quite different and is characterized by a change in the basic conceptualization of what the organization is doing. Here we can talk about a change in the governing variables (criteria of effectiveness) and positioning of the company in its environment—even of a paradigm shift, to use Kuhn's (1962) terms. Such a shift requires a new cognitive perception of the situation, or the discovery of a new logic. Examples of such a paradigm shift in two large, established organizations will illustrate this.

During the general airline recession, one major international airline had tried to survive a decrease in profitability by slashing costs and saving on every conceivable item not related to security. Some people inside the airline began to talk about the "no-olives policy," indicating that serving olives to passengers with their dry martinis was unnecessary. In an enormous effort to change not only the attitudes but also the concrete behavior of all employees of the airline, a new president started a program aimed at giving more value to customers at constant or lower prices. Behind the effort was a fundamental reinterpretation of what would bring success in the business. In our terms, the governing variable against which people were now asked to measure their performance was "satisfaction of the customer" rather than "cost saving." As a result, costs for services went up, but increased customer loyalty, leading to a larger market share in relevant market segments, more than compensated. Persuading people to measure their performance in terms of client satisfaction rather than cost saving might seem like a simple idea, but it required enormous effort and talent and is, in our view, a good example of a real strategic move and double-loop learning.

The pharmacy system of one of the European welfare countries, a federation of independent pharmacists, had a monopoly on the retail distribution of drugs in their country. They were not immediately threatened by other organizations, but they realized that privileges of the kind they had could not possibly be retained in the long run, with increasing pressure to control health care costs. "Noblesse oblige!" With visionary persistency, this very successful organization started a fundamental reorientation process. It was one thing to decide that they should change their mission from being a drug distribution organization to being a health promotion one, but to find the necessary concrete content in this concept and to bring many hundreds of individual pharmacists/ businessmen who all owned their respective units into this change process was again an exceedingly difficult and challenging aspect of the strategic change.

The established theories held in both organizations on how the system they were operating in functioned and on how success was best achieved were fundamentally changed. This mental jump is in itself very significant, but it is far from all there is to a process of strategic change. In fact, in both of the organizations mentioned, the "new" strategies did not represent a major cognitive breakthrough, since the ideas characteristic of the new strategies had been known and even advocated for years by some managers. As Kuhn (1962) points out, and as has been shown empirically in research about major innovation and major strategic change (see, for example, Burns and Stalker, 1961, and Normann, 1971), a genuine change of strategy—a reorientation—is always accompanied by internal politics and changes in the distribution of power. Every organization is characterized by a "battle of ideas," and it is only when there is a sufficiently strong confluence of the cognitive strength of a new logic and sufficient power to back it up that a paradigm shift will take place. As soon as we enter the realm of double-loop learning, paradigm shifts, and strategic decision making, we cannot avoid bringing the concepts of power and politics into our frame of reference.

Deutero learning, in this context, can be described only as the ability to achieve repeated double-loop learning, which means a continuous process of testing and creatively developing the cognitive maps of the organization, as well as the ability to shift organizational power as the need evolves. Such an organization would have good strategic management.

### Action Skills for Organizational Learning

Knowing some of the preconditions for learning, we should be able to use that knowledge for staging learning processes. Since proactive learning is by definition an open-ended process characterized by elements of synthesis and creativity, we shall never be able to pinpoint precise cause-effect relationships but must be satisfied with a pragmatic approach, aimed at increasing the likelihood that the desired design processes will occur by acting in certain ways.

What we are looking for is a theory of action to enhance organizational learning and strategic action capability. On the basis of learning theory and also, to a great extent, of empirical observations and clinical experience, I would like to suggest four domains of action skills necessary for organizational learning. These four domains, summarized in Table 1, are (1) the domain of interpersonal skills, (2) the domain of analytical language (cognitive frame of reference), (3) the domain of organizational skills, and (4) the domain of ecological positioning.

*Interpersonal Skills.* The first area, that of interpersonal skills, will be only briefly mentioned here, since it has been so thoroughly analyzed by Argyris and Schön (1978 and 1981). These authors identify the search for valid information, free and informed choice, and internal commitment to action strategies taken as the

Table 1. Domains of Skills Necessary for Staging
Proactive Organizational Learning.

| Type of Learning and Corresponding Strategic Action | Domain of Required Action Skills | | | |
|---|---|---|---|---|
| | Interpersonal Skills | Analytical Language Skills | Organizational Skills | Ecological Interfacing Skills |
| Action within a strategy (single-loop) | Few necessary | Diagnostic ability within given cognitive framework | Unchanged structure | Effective signal system with present environment sufficient |
| Strategic paradigm shift (double-loop) | "Model II" behavior[a] | Alternative framework | Structural change (as effect or cause) | Exposure to new demands and impulses |
| Strategic management (deutero learning) | "Model II" behavior[a] | Continuous management of "battle of ideas"; certain overriding values in focus | Constitution conducive to structural and cultural change | Continuous confrontation with new demands and segments of environment |

[a]Argyris and Schön (1981).

three key governing variables, and they outline action strategies in interpersonal situations to maintain those standards. A major blockage to learning is the common phenomenon of "nondiscussibility" of key issues and assumptions. Argyris and Schön continuously stress the necessity to make the basic assumptions on which action is based visible and testable, in order to maintain long-term congruence between espoused theory (what actors say they are doing and why) and "theory-in-use" (the actual behavior as formed by the assumptions they are really holding) to avoid getting into unfruitful, "self-sealing" processes in which assumptions are hidden and cannot therefore be challenged. This is relevant for higher-level learning (double-loop and deutero learning).

*Analytical Language Skills.* A second category of skills needed for higher-level learning consists of the ability to perform a *creative cognitive analysis* of a strategic situation and of having access to or being able to formulate a set of strategic directions.

Access to relevant data is, of course, necessary for this, but of greater interest is the ability to conceptualize and arrange data in fruitful categories that yield innovative interpretations. Much of the theory on strategy consists of classifications of strategic situations and strategic action according to some framework. Ansoff's product-market matrix (Ansoff, 1965), the Boston Consulting Group's experience curves and portfolio matrix (Henderson, 1979), and Porter's (1980) competitive strategy analysis are three examples of frameworks that have had an important impact on management thinking and practice.

It may be an open question whether a switch from one strategy to another (say, from product-based diversification to market-based diversification in Ansoff's model) represents a paradigm shift and, therefore, higher-level learning. Even if a specific theory may define a new line of action as a strategic change, it could be argued that no paradigm shift, or double-loop learning, has taken place, since the shift in strategic posture may be in well-defined categories within the framework of the old theory. The strategy may be new, but the theory may well be old. To be sure that real learning has taken place, we might posit as a condition that the theory held by the actors has changed, so that we are not dealing just with conditioned responses within the framework of an old theory. Even an agile movement over a longer time within an established strategy matrix could be interpreted as a sign of little or no genuine learning; there is learning when the matrix itself is challenged—when there is movement *of* rather than within the matrix.

What are the action skills necessary to change or develop a theory or a framework of analysis held by the dominant actors of an organization? In practice, these skills may be very difficult to isolate from the domains of skills related to the organizational structure and ecological interaction as elaborated later, since changing a frame of reference is rarely a purely (or even primarily) cognitive process. However, in terms of a model, it would be hard to argue for a better one than "scientific method." The essence of scientific method, of course, is extreme perceptiveness to any discrepancies between the theory held and observed data, combined with high intellectual and moral integrity in recognizing and interpreting such discrepancies. What we learn from analysis of the evolution of science, as well as of the evolution of business companies, is that there are multiple blockages, including those related to issues of power and vested interests in existing structure, that moderate the assumed rationality of the development of knowledge.

I would like to make two additional observations about the relationship between language and learning in organizations. One has to do with the need for a relatively "rich" frame of reference, the other with the apparent need for a number of overall governing variables, which in our experience should be so integrated with an organization that they become part of its "culture." One precondition for learning that we often find missing is the existence of a rich and substantive communication *language.* Too many organizations—perhaps as an inheritance of the golden days of conglomeratism of the late 1960s—are dominated by a poor figure-oriented language, focusing on budgets, profit-and-loss performance, and procedures but not on the substance of the business. As one of the key officials of a large multinational company told me, suddenly getting a flash of insight: "We had this long and nice dinner with the managing directors of two of our largest subsidiaries, one corporate vice-president, and myself. And suddenly I realized that we had been together for three hours, talking about the company every minute, but not once had anybody used the words *clients, product,* or *people.* The only things we talked about were budgets, return on investment, and the company's long-range planning procedure. We do have profit problems—but *talking* about profits and procedures will not solve any of them!"

Our diagnosis was that, among several problems of this company, it had fallen into the trap of defining good management as procedure and profit oriented. At all the big meetings with the key executives from various countries, it was always the procedures and planning schemes that were in focus, and this made it virtually impossible to raise the more substantive issues of who the clients were, what was actually delivered to them, how the quality of products and services was to be improved, and how the multitude of experiences of the subsidiaries in about twenty of the major countries in the world could be shared and built upon to give the

Figure 1. A Vicious Learning Circle Maintained by Poor
Communication Language.

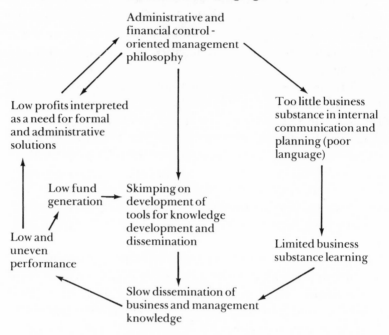

corporation a lead against the competition. Cross-unit learning was inhibited, since the available communication-channel capacity was occupied with procedural rather than substantive problems. A vicious circle, depicted in Figure 1, emerged and locked the company into its bad performance.

Closely related to the concept of language and, to some extent, covering the borderline between language and structure is the presently very popular idea of culture. Perhaps culture could be defined as the institutionalized language and values of an organization, together with their symbolic and structural manifestations. Culture has two absolutely crucial functions in any organization: It acts as a *symbol and storage of past learning,* and it works as an *instrument to communicate this learning* throughout the organization. The latter is important when success becomes more and more dependent not only on taking the right grand strategic measures but also on the focused, concerted efforts of motivated individuals.

Every organization learns, and every organization has a set of dominating ideas (Normann, 1977). They may be more or less consciously formulated and more or less visible, and they may represent good or bad interpretations of what has led to past success or failure, but they are always there. If they are not espoused—in Argyris and Schön's terms—they at least exist as "theory-in-use." Some are translated into organizational charts, others into formal strategies, and still others into symbols, language, rituals, norms, and taboos; standards of evaluation; and styles of interpersonal communication. The concept of culture stands for many of the more "soft" aspects of dominating ideas in an organization, which are difficult to translate into concrete maps (such as organizational charts) or manuals. I would interpret the increasing interest in the concept of culture as really an increasing interest in organizational learning—in understanding and making conscious and effective as much as possible all the learning that has taken place in an organization. To be aware of culture is to increase the likelihood of learning. Only when the basic assumptions, beliefs, and success formulas are made conscious and visible do they become testable and open to reinforcement or modification.

Culture, to a great extent, is imposed upon an organization from the outside world—from society at large, from a specific region, from a specific profession or industry. But part of culture can also be molded from within the company, as an act of will and conscious choice by significant leaders who impose their beliefs and theories of action on the organization and its structure and language. We might call this internally imposed, consciously chosen part of the total culture of a company its *philosophy* (Normann, 1984). Corporate philosophy, then, would cover and be another expression for the dominating ideas, or theory of action, of a company as regards strategic decision making, strategic management, and learning-capability development.

Against this background, let us take a brief look at corporate cultures and corporate philosophies, as we encounter them, and how they tend to influence learning. A common aspect of philosophy is that of business mission—a statement of what the company is good at and what it is not good at and therefore what kinds of business logics, products and market types it should deal with. It is well known that many such "mission formulations" are mere wordplays: pompous, empty, and noncommittal decorations. One that is valid and useful can be recognized because it is firmly rooted in practical (positive and negative) experiences, has a unique and creative touch to it, and gives day-to-day guidance of behavior.

Equally common is the management philosophy whose roots are founded in assumptions and beliefs about how people function. There is no doubt that more and more of the consistently successful companies have assumptions about people that approach those of McGregor's (1960) "Theory Y" (people-oriented management style) while at the same time being quite demanding and extremely task and efficiency oriented. Good companies are people oriented but not "soft." There is probably no area where we find such a discrepancy between "theory espoused" and "theory-in-use" as management philosophy and assumptions about people. I do not know of any one company admitting to a non-"Theory Y" philosophy about people, but there are fairly few who practice it.

Having a clear-cut philosophy is a double-edged sword. It is also a constraint in that it implicitly defines beliefs that are not held and territories that are not to be entered. However, it seems that those problems must be taken care of by other measures, and the fundamental attitude of a philosophy is that it must define focus but it must not mean imprisonment. Philosophy can be changed, but only by the weight of experience reflected upon.

A clearly distinguishing feature of the philosophy of successful companies that we meet is that there is a very strong commitment to excellence and that, therefore, mediocrity is recognized and handled. First of all, this excellence orientation has the customer relationship as its point of departure—value for money and satisfied customers who come back for repeat purchase are simple and reliable criteria (Normann, 1980, 1984). Although managements with a high learning capacity are very result oriented (including profit oriented), they see profit and growth not as ends in themselves but as the inevitable results of excellence. Therefore, they tend to pursue the objectives of excellence and satisfied customers rather than profit. But, as witnessed by the Japanese art of quality management, quality is best pursued by looking not only at the end product but also at the process and the resources by which it is produced and delivered. Value, high quality, and excellence therefore are pursued in all aspects of organizational life—from the company canteen to the appropriateness of office decoration—via the quality of planning procedures.

*Organizational Skills.* We next come to the third domain of necessary conditions and action skill for learning, the *organizational skills.* From the science of biology we can infer that the structure of an organism—its complexity, its differentiation of functions, the layout of its physical sensory and motor capacity, its availability of tissue with nonspecialized functions but adaptive capabilities—will highly influence its capacity to adapt to new situations and handle, for example, structural changes in its ecological niche. All these conditions for learning have their equivalence in the world of social organization, but here the restrictions are fewer, and the possibilities for action and, therefore, *learning by design* higher. An individual cannot add six more fingers or substitute them for a kidney to increase his or her learning capability, but the analogous task seems less formidable to a business organization.

As we said earlier, the simplest kind of learning, single-loop, takes place within an unchanged cognitive framework and overall organizational structure, but a paradigm shift entails a change of structure and power relationships. The cause-and-effect relationship is twofold, so that a change of structure could be effected with the aim of creating increased learning and a paradigm shift. Usually the "strategy-structure" model (I believe first developed by Chandler, 1962) is seen within a one-way sequential framework, so that a strategy is supposed to have been formulated first, and then an appropriate structure is formed to reflect and implement it. However, this does not at all have to be the case. Following are a couple of examples where structural change has preceded strategic change and has been used as a *tool* to create a new strategy. In both situations, it was felt that there was a need for increased learning and probably for a new long-term strategy, but no such strategy had yet been clearly conceived or formulated.

A vertically integrated company in the chemical industry had developed a high level of technical excellence and had come across a great number of interesting by-products and technologies that some members of the board thought could be better exploited. However, new strategic ideas tended to drown in the company's main business, and, besides, there were many arguments about which of many seemingly possible directions diversification should take. Finally, several of the new embryonic businesses were made into profit centers of their own, physically separated and staffed with some entrepreneurial people. A period of experimentation started, and some of the original ideas were wiped out, while others developed, were transformed, and proved their viability. After this structural experiment, management thus had a wealth of healthy experiences to interpret, and a few years later, the group was once again reorganized. This time, however, the aim of the reorganization was to achieve focused support and resource coordination in the two new strategic business areas that had proved most viable during the previous period.

We saw the same type of process in a bank, where the entering new chief executive officer felt that things were moving too slowly and that the bank somehow needed to get stronger and more focused but where nobody really could come up with enough substance for a viable new strategy. An intensive campaign with the general aim of market orienting the bank, along with some restructuring to give the most entrepreneurially oriented people more power and freedom of action, as well as the creation of a small new company in a different but growing financial services industry, were the significant steps taken. In this case, also, the effect was a rapid increase in the amount of learning and generation of business alternatives; two or three years later, a significant strategic change that could hardly have been conceived of earlier was under way.

In these cases, it is clear that the managers involved were able to recognize the true nature of the process of strategic evolution. Rather than using a "strategy first, then structure" model, they understood and acted according to the iterative-process view referred to earlier. A need for change was felt, but it was recognized that the level of preparedness and understanding of strategic opportunities was such that a clear strategy formulation would have been based on insufficient information and therefore would have been premature. Instead, given the best vision that could be formulated, action—including structural change—was taken to generate more information and to experiment with new patterns of behavior; the results of these courses of action were interpreted and, in turn, generated new and more crystallized visions, and so on.

So organizational change is closely connected with strategic change, and in a complex interrelationship. Organizational structure influences learning and, therefore, the emergence of strategy via various mechanisms. The structural map of a company defines much of the world view for the members of the organization, channeling their energies, influencing their images of reality, redefining their interaction patterns, and changing career paths, values, and priorities. But the most interesting question here is whether it is possible to use structure to promote deutero learning, our highest level of learning related to long-term strategic action capability. We have seen that structural change can be used as a tool for a paradigm shift, but is there any relationship between structure and the ability to achieve continuous paradigm shifts?

I have to be extremely cautious and suggestive here, but I would like to suggest that long-term strategic management capability is related to and can be enhanced by not only the formal structure but also the higher-level *constitution* of any organization. An organizational structure defines operating relationships and power relationships between parts of an organization; an organizational constitution is a set of higher-level rules that may allow, within themselves, a variety of structures. In fact, a constitution could be seen as a framework for structural change, a set of ground rules about how power is supposed to be shifted and structure supposed to be changed in different types of situations. The most important aspects of a constitution define rules for how and under what conditions power can be shifted.

A tentative empirical observation about good constitutions is that they prescribe several power centers and that they allow power to be shifted among these. Many organizations that have been successful in the longer run have been highly conscious about their constitutions. Companies such as Texas Instruments and 3M have tried to institutionalize innovative change by higher-level rules and arrangements—"metarules"—that permit and are supposed to create tension and structural change, with a few overall values and governing variables as the stable pillars. Hattori, the Seiko watch-makers, have built strong tensions and even conflicts into their organization (by having fierce competition between development and production units as to who is going to supply the marketing organization) but have taken great care to define the rules of the game and the area of conflict to focus on the crucial issue of merging technical proficiency with market insight. Some companies with complex matrix-type structures, such as IBM or Ericsson, have likewise been able to recognize and fruitfully exploit tension within a system where rational action leads (via internal politics) to gradual shifts in the focus of tension and conflict, leading to learning, strategic adjustment, and structural change. In all such cases, there has been high flexibility, with a few overriding, generally accepted, and strongly enforced values and ground rules.

The business-management literature is much too scarce in the area of relating business strategy with organizational power and politics, especially over the long run. We need better analyses of the governing variables and crucial metarules of a system able to achieve strategic change on a continuous basis.

One structural aspect that is often brought up when discussing learning and strategic change capability is that of centralization versus decentralization of power. Is an organization with a high learning capacity centralized or decentralized? There are more and more indications that the centralization-decentralization dichotomy is not a fruitful one. In working especially with service business organizations, we have been struck by the need for decentralization—by, for example, the power of recreating the small-scale business conditions in every office of a bank or in every one of 7,000 McDonald's outlets around the world. At the same time, successful service organizations tend to be extremely centralized, and one conclusion must be that a successful structure, at least in this type of business, must be simultaneously very centralized and very decentralized (Normann, 1980). The seeming contradiction in this statement can be resolved by analyzing more closely what realms of operation should be left decentralized and what realms under central control. The conclusions so far are that items that should be centralized, at least in service organizations are: quality and excellence standards related to what is delivered to clients and how it is delivered; control over factors closely related to quality, including basics of human resources management, such as recruitment, reward, promotion, and internal education policies; and control of key aspects of "image management" related to what customers and society, including potential employees in the recruitment market, expect from the company.

If these factors, which are all strongly related to the quality of operating efficiency, are under central control, but the policy is to give a lot of freedom of action in all other respects, local initiatives and local experiments at all levels of the organization can be expected to thrive, forming important variety and learning material that can be interpreted and, if promising, reinforced by power centers.

*Ecological Interfacing Skills.* A fourth and very powerful condition for learning is the *choice of what part of the environment to interact with*—what we call ecological interfacing. One of the most fascinating features of social organizations, with their relatively flexible structure and a certain discretionary freedom as to what they choose to do, is that, within very flexible limits, they can pick out what part of the environment they can interact with and what external demands they want to expose themselves to. They can consciously make use of the fact that any social or biological system will tend to "map" into itself the requirements of the environment.

How does this mechanism of ecological interfacing work? Although exposure to new demands and environments moderates the evolution of biological organisms or species only gradually, the process can be much more rapid for social organizations. Perhaps the mechanism can best be illustrated by an empirical observation that I first made on professional service organizations, such as management consultants, but that seems to be equally true of virtually all organizations: No company is any better than its most skillfull and demanding customer.

By selecting the most difficult markets and the most demanding customers, an organization not only makes life more problematical in the short run but really significantly increases the probability of long-term success. Handling difficult environments weeds out mediocrity and promotes excellence. It raises the level of ambitions of an organization. It makes an organization more attractive to the best professional resources in the environment, thus creating a "good circle" whereby excellence breeds excellence. It increases the likelihood that the organization will be confronted with (and thus have to cope with and learn about) new technological frontiers, new needs, new ideas in general.

At the level of double-loop learning, or strategic change, it can easily be seen how an action strategy of submitting the organization to new types of stimuli and difficult demands can pave the way for strategic reorientation. At the level of deutero learning, we would expect such an action strategy to be a way of life of an organization—a kind of institutionalized globe-trotting. Of course, there is no guarantee that exposure to new environments with their demands and ideas will in itself promote learning and strategic capability; I have seen many examples of such action strategies that have become mere rituals, where there has been no underlying commitment and preparedness to genuinely take the intellectual and financial risks involved in such interfacing.

How this action strategy was used, at least at level-two learning, can be illustrated by a simple example. The chief executive of an ailing bank described how they started a conspicuous turnaround process: "We realized that there was no other way but to raise the level of ambition. The first thing we did was to pick out the most successful banks we could find and visit them. But we realized that this would not be enough, so we also picked out the best service companies of any kind that we could find out about and looked at them. Next, we invited some knowledgeable consultants for brief sessions. And we selected the most knowledgeable potential customers in the country and tried to sell something to them. After that, we really had quite a different frame of reference. It was no longer a question of trying to do as well or almost as well as the other local banks, but we felt we were now about to play in another league."

The foregoing might seem like an overly simplistic way of dealing with the problem—there is no way that study trips and consultants can substitute for the real experiences of the marketplace and the clients—but we find time and again that high ambition level, choosing the best companies in either one's own industry or some related industry that one can identify with, and working in the most demanding markets and together with the most demanding clients who themselves have the highest ambitions are necessary preconditions for learning.

### Strategic Change: Social Reality and Action Theory

Translating a strategic idea into action may be achieved by a combination of many different means, such as acquiring other companies, employing new managers, redeploying resources, and so on. Generally, to achieve real change—a reorientation, or paradigm shift—throughout an organization, a number of conditions must be fulfilled, and they consequently must be seen as intrinsic to good strategic management. From experience, I would say that these conditions are:

1. A *direction*, in the form of either a clearly understood desired state or a hazier but challenging and motivating vision.
2. *Power* to back up the strategy or vision and to mobilize resources in its direction, in competition with other interpretations of the situation.
3. Strong *driving forces,* in the form of either personal ambitions or crisis stemming from extremely bad performance or overt external threats.
4. *Cognitive ability* to analyze the situation and to invent appropriate action strategies and structural arrangements to effectively move and reshape the organization.
5. *Leadership* that can make the change credible and attractive to the organization, mobilizing energy and directing focus of efforts through effective communication.

A good action theory of strategic management must include the ability to make all these factors appear simultaneously; otherwise, we may be left with brilliantly conceived analyses and decisions but no change. It would bring us too far in this context to analyze each of the conditions, but I would like to comment on the last one, the need for leadership and effective communication. There is a huge class of strategic changes that are highly dependent upon the ability of top management to influence, rapidly and with lasting effect, the attitudes and behavior of the personnel. The realization of the American car industry that increased and consistent quality of the products was necessary to gain customers back may seem like a simple operating decision rather than a strategic one. However, actually getting the message across to affect the concrete behavior of hundreds of thousands of people who can influence quality is a gigantic task.

If dominating ideas of culture and philosophy are explicitly stated and well known throughout the organization, this can contribute to effectiveness in several different respects. First, it will contribute to coordination and concerted action. It is like the functioning of a successful soccer team, where the players are tied together by an invisible but commonly held set of behavior patterns and mutual expectations guiding their joint action. Second, as we discussed previously, it also increases the possibility and probability of learning, since only known and visible ideas can be subjected to testing and even to opposition. If performance is below par and if the theory of action has been stuck to, there is no other choice but to question the theory of action; if there is no stated and commonly held theory of action, including performance standards, the first prerequisite for learning—perceived difference between actual and desired performance—is absent.

The art of making the dominating ideas and values known and accessible to everybody in an organization seems to be gaining ground among managers (this may have something to do with the increasing awareness of the special conditions of service businesses, where, to a very high extent, "production" tends to take place by a social network of highly dispersed individuals). A rather appropriate term for it is *visible management,* which is in itself becoming part of a predominant theory of action for managers. Setting norms and standards, picking out and displaying role models, using symbols, and making heavy use of personal example are among the methods used in the practice of visible management.

Such a management style seems to work best when it includes a somewhat paradoxical combination of two elements. One of these, which could be termed "management by simplicity," is characterized by extremely clear and simple signals about the few key norms and overriding values that bring success, according to the current theory of action. But the cognitive aspect of making a theory of action known and therefore testable by visible management has a complementary counterpart, with more emotional overtones. A business or any other organization is not a bloodless mechanism; it is a system where emotional identification and hard work can and will in the longer run have a tremendous impact on effectiveness and learning. Enthusiasm creates energy, which increases initiative and the likelihood of learning. In addition to visible "management by simplicity" becoming part of the general theory of action for managers, we see a corresponding increase in deliberate intervention into the social and symbolic reality of an organization. For lack of a more scientific term, I would like to call this aspect of management practice "management by magic."

Visible management means managing the internal images that people—employees but also others—have of an organization. In the broadest sense, image is the same as inner reality, a model that we carry about our situation and the phenomena around us. Image therefore affects the way we see things and the way we act. If our images can be influenced, our actions will also be changed, and this insight is now giving rise to the increasing use of *image as a management tool* to guide expectations and enthusiasm among employees and in the marketplace (Normann, 1984).

The tremendous power of image and expectations can be illustrated by a small example from the airline mentioned earlier, which had, for several years, been cutting back on its customer service and had therefore begun to lose passengers and money. In an effort to get out of the vicious circle, a number of changes were made to increase value to the client. Passengers soon began to marvel at the attitude changes that they could see among the personnel. However, when I interviewed an air hostess and asked how it was possible that the personnel and their attitudes had changed so dramatically in such a short time, she reflected and said: "No, we have not changed. But it really is fantastic how our customers have changed! They have become enthusiastic and appreciative, and it's simply great fun to work with them." Here we saw the positive reinforcement of mutual expectations caused by skillful management. A "good circle" is created in the customer contact, with increased perceived value to the customer and increased emotional rewards for the personnel.

Thus, managing image and social reality to influence people's expectations and actions can be a conscious tool to achieve self-fulfilling prophecies and, therefore, to create reality. Obviously, image management takes skill and must not be abused, since there is a fine line between achieving the self-fulfilling prophecies and losing credibility. If an image is promoted that does not correspond to reality, and if there is not sufficient content and "magic" to create the necessary reality change, people will sooner or later feel frustration and cynicism. "Management by magic" must therefore be accompanied by very conscious efforts to maintain the credibility of management by achieving actual results.

### Statesmanship and Strategic Management: The Role of the Chief Executive

An organization equipped with the ability to make not only one but a series of good strategic decisions and, in addition, capable of actually accomplishing strategic change has the capability of strategic management. It will be able to interpret new situations as they emerge, as a result of either external influences or its own action; make its frame of reference—its strategic paradigm—evolve; and invent the tools to get from analysis to action and implementation. We have proposed a number of hypotheses about the action-skill requirements for deutero learning and some for going from analysis and decision making to implementation and change. Some of the relationships are depicted in Figure 2. No doubt, these hypotheses still comprise, at best, an incomplete and suggestive framework, but, apart from that, the question remains how such properties can be built into and maintained in an organization in the first place. To this question, I have no other reply than "through good leadership." In another context (Normann, 1977), I have referred to this type of leadership as metamanagement, or statesmanship.

The primary task of leaders at the statesmanship level is to ensure that the basic preconditions for deutero learning exist. At the structural level, we would expect such leadership to be concerned particularly with constitutional issues, that is, the ground rules for how power is exercised and shifted and the design of suitable arenas

Figure 2. Linkages Between the Learning Process Logic
and Action Skills.

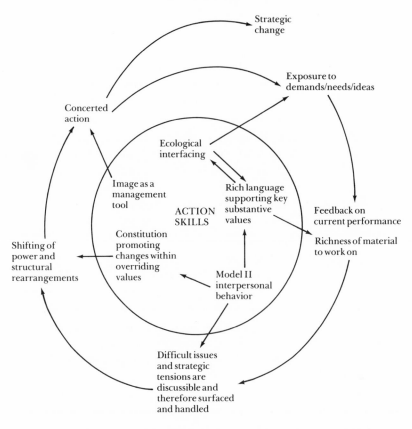

for the playing out of internal tension and conflict. Organizational culture should be characterized by some overall values, such as focus on relationships with clients and on emancipatory social technology (Normann, 1984; Crozier, Normann, and Tardy, 1982), that bring out the best resources in people; such values will then function as important and fruitful arbitrators of conflict. Predominant language should be checked for richness in substance and for reflecting values of excellence. Interpersonal relations and conflict resolution modes should fulfill the requirements for learning and effectiveness posed by Argyris and Schön (1978). It must be ensured that the organization is subjected to the demands and variety of difficult environments.

A crucial part of the role of the chief executive as a metamanager is to diagnose action genuinely leading to the preconditions for learning and change, as opposed to action that only seems to do so since it has become ritualistic. Companies and managers also learn how to play games, often without even being aware of it. Is the open and confrontative style of executive board meetings a sign of effective problem solving, or is it a comfortable routine performance? Is the large international research project on new human technology, with its multinational advisory board of distinguished scientists, a sign of real questioning and commitment to change and new ideas, or is it a pastime activity and escape for some executives? Is the famous planning system, widely admired in business journals, really still effective, or is it primarily a game that people have learned to play inside the organization? Do top managers really back up the acclaimed and published philosophy with their personal behavior, or is it something one merely talks about? These are typical questions that must be addressed by the statesman, and they are difficult, because there is such a fine line between rituals and games, on the one hand, and genuine struggle with the difficult issues, on the other.

Metamanagement can intervene to develop and maintain such ground rules of structure, culture, and positioning, but it can also intervene more directly. A fascinating example of such statesmanship has been the Swedish Wallenberg group, where for generations some "statesmen" have led and gradually restructured a number of extraordinarily successful (over the long run) business companies. In addition to being involved in understanding the overall changes in society giving rise to business opportunities and to restructuring needs, the Wallenbergs seem to have been highly concerned with the cultural features of the companies in the group. Their direct interventions often have aimed at infusing an organization with new dominating ideas and values as it has reached some new stage of strategic development (Danielsson, 1974). An example of this process is the case of Atlas Copco.

The international growth of this very successful company was based on an innovation that has followed the typical life cycle of business ideas, as depicted in Figure 3 almost to the book, the "Swedish method" for drilling tunnels. As the method and its associated equipment had been developed and tried out, "metamanagement" realized the international potential and the need for a new style of management. Thus, a new chief executive, known for his international contacts and experience, was appointed. His task was to develop an international organization and the human resources necessary for taking advantage of the innovation on an international scale. In a third stage, a person known for his marketing experience became the new chief executive; his job was to animate the network and the resources to achieve a rapid market penetration. With the successful completion of that stage, Atlas Copco was now a major international company in its field, with a complex network structure functioning in a large number of local markets in different stages of development, with several of the international companies developing identities and ideas of their own—in other words, it was now a mature multinational corporation with a multitude of products, markets, technologies, and organizations with their own will. The management problems of that stage were, again, mapped by the choice of a new chief executive, who was expected to garden and prune the complex multidimensional matrix while maintaining the outgoing energy of its people.

We do not know much about how such metamanagers or statesmen develop their abilities. Sometimes, as in the Wallenberg case, their skills are localized in power centers largely outside the realm of day-to-day operations of a company, but at other times, we must assume that they somehow develop inside an organization and become part of its culture. I would expect companies that have a long-term record of success and strategic change, spanning over generations of managers, such as IBM and Volvo, to possess such qualities. This is an important topic for future research.

### Clinical Research for a Theory of Strategic Action

Where, then, does this point in terms of research needs in the future? No doubt, we still need research on industry dynamics and competitive game situations to formulate analytical models and ideal-type strategic postures. This is an area that I have deliberately

**Figure 3. The Business Idea Life Cycle and Its Associated
Management Problem.**

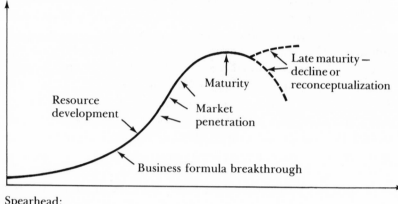

Spearhead;
developing a new
business formula

*Source:* Normann (1977) (slightly adapted).

chosen not to go into in this chapter. Particularly in industry
situations mentioned initially, such as extremely dynamic new
high-technology industries and service industries, the field is still
open for conceptualization.

In the field covered in this chapter—a theory of action useful
for managers with strategic management aspirations—and with the
frame of reference outlined, there is a great deal of ground to be
covered. While the work of Argyris and Schön (1978) has done much
to clarify the social and interpersonal skills necessary for organizational learning, and while a whole range of theories focusing on the
cognitive aspects of strategy formulation exist, we are not as well
off in understanding the relationship between organization and
learning. The myth that strategy precedes structure (or, ideally,
should do so) can easily be shattered, and the idea of structure as
a tool to develop strategy should be both recognized and elaborated.
Of particular interest is the notion that certain overall structural-
cultural ground rules could contribute to some kind of consistent
dynamic properties of an organization, increasing the likelihood of
appropriate strategic changes over time. This idea is not new—it

can, for example, be traced back to the work of Burns and Stalker (1961), and recent works such as those of Peters and Waterman (1982) and Normann (1977 and 1984) approach the issue. However, the dynamic interrelationships among phenomena such as internal politics, key cultural values, formal constitution, and statesmanship remain to be better conceptualized before we can formulate an action theory and specify the "governing standards" necessary to maintain a state of deutero learning and strategic management.

Similarly, a theory of strategic management needs to take into account and integrate the concept of strategy implementation on change. Theory of strategic decision making is considerably less interesting than theory of strategic change. Again, what we need is an action theory for implementation—for mobilizing and focusing energy throughout an organization.

What are the characteristics of a theory of action, and how does one arrive at such a theory? Researchers tend to be interested in explaining behavior and the course of events and—if their research interest goes further—in constructing theories and tools that will make it possible for practitioners to act more effectively. If we want to explain strategic action, such as how a particular strategic decision is arrived at or how action to build strategic management capability is taken, we can do so only by referring to the theory of action that the actor holds and by investigating how that theory makes the actor adapt to the particular situation to produce a specific outcome. To explain action, we therefore need to reconstruct the invisible theory that the actor holds. To learn about the theory of action at work, we can ask the actor about his or her beliefs, but experience tells us that this is not enough. By interviewing the actor, we may get insufficient, irrelevant, or even distorted data. As Argyris and Schön (1978) have pointed out, there may be a more or less important divergence between the theory espoused by the actor and the actual theory in use. Moreover, a theory of action can very well exist without being espoused at all or even while being mostly unconscious (Polanyi, 1969). An espoused theory is not necessarily the same as the actual theory of action. A bicyclist, a piano player, a physician, or a manager all act partly on the basis of conscious, crystallized principles that we may not even have the language to express.

This is where the idea of a clinical theory and methodology enters. In reconstructing a theory of action, the researcher must go beyond what can be expressed by the actor. There is not any clear-cut, mechanical, scientific method for this—only a methodology for getting deeper toward reality, which in itself requires great skill and a complex, only partly espousable theory of action. The method, which has been termed the hermeneutic-dialectical method, consists of two parallel processes. The first is the pulling together of evidence and fragments of evidence from various realms, such as expressed theory and intentions, observed behavior, and research into historical influences and events that seem to have affected the ideas and capabilities held by the actors. From such scattered evidence, the researcher will try to reconstruct and formulate a theory of action against two criteria: It should be internally consistent, and it should make the observed actions of the actors make sense—that is, they should be consistent with the reconstructed theory.

The second process of the hermeneutic-dialectical approach normally is to interact with the object under research, the actor, by presenting to him or her various explanations and hypotheses about his or her behavior. Such an increase in the actor's own consciousness can trigger him or her to respond and thereby bring additional improvements, which can be inputs for the next turn in this upward spiral of increased understanding of the actor's theory and explanation of behavior in terms of that theory.

A theory of (effective) action implies a normative, design-oriented research interest. Clinical study of actors (actor systems) who have come close to satisfying the criteria for good strategic management that we have outlined would therefore seem to be the most effective method of getting closer to the normative theory of strategic action, integrating the areas of higher-level learning and implementation into our definition of such a theory.

# ❧ TEN ❧

# Forces
# Influencing Decision
# and Change Behaviors

## *Lawrence B. Mohr*

Normann (Chapter Nine) has imported a *process* flavor to the study of strategic decision making. It seems to me that the continued emphasis of this perspective, as a supplement to if not a replacement for the *variance* approach, cannot help but abet the systematic understanding of strategic change. Variance-oriented analyses seek to explain why a variable takes on certain values by specifying parameters and the values of other variables hypothesized to be causal. Process-oriented explanations, on the other hand, illuminate the occurrence of an event by specifying the series of prior events that must take place over time in order for the focal outcome to occur (see Mohr, 1982, pp. 35–70). One is easily persuaded by Normann's analysis that too much is missed in this area through the variance approach, in which a certain amount of forcing is necessary to capture a dynamic process; strategic decision making develops in important ways over time, and its essence is lost without analytical tools that appreciate and highlight the dynamic property.

First, any strategic decision must be preceded by an experience of double-loop learning, a "change in the basic conceptualization of what the organization is doing" (see Chapter Nine). With this rather simple formulation, strategic action comes alive as the culmination of a dynamic process in which key organization members perceive the functional interface of the organization with its environment, recognize that a repositioning is, in essence, demanded for the sake of a satisfying fit, and proceed through the diplomatic and political steps that are necessary to bring about a paradigm shift in organizational self-perception. Second, we see that strategic decision making is merely the beginning of another process, in which a difficult stage of implementation must be executed in order for durable change to be realized. Lastly, the truly desirable organizational capability at issue here depends upon strategic management, which leads the organization through a series of strategic changes over time and which depends not upon double-loop but upon deutero learning—development of the capacity to view the environment continuously as an evolving niche that calls for a corresponding adaptive evolution in organizational function (see Chapter Nine). Seeing strategic change in these process-oriented terms, Normann is able to propose the series of skills and leadership behaviors that will enhance the organization's potential for proceeding successfully through the chain of stages that his analysis has revealed.

Still, what Normann has offered is not process *theory*. It is not presented so as to conform to the demanding format of that type of universal explanation exemplified by diffusion theory, by the "garbage-can" model of organizational choice (Cohen, March, and Olsen, 1972), and by prominent theories in the biological sciences. The process-theory format requires, among other elements, both necessary preconditions and the probabilistic confluence of streams of independent events. If not classical process theory, however, exploration might reveal that Normann's view constitutes a "descriptive quasi theory" of substantial merit, that is, a process description "in which (1) the fit to reality, though not stable, is either quite common or otherwise intriguing, so that a justifiable claim to importance can be made, or (2) the potential for constructive normative application is auspicious" (Mohr, 1982, p. 166). I will argue in subsequent sections, and especially in the final one, that the potential for constructive normative application, at least, is unfortunately relatively small.

In exploring further whether Normann's analysis constitutes successful descriptive quasi theory, it is necessary to recognize that strategic decision making is a motivated behavior, so that to explain, predict, or control it successfully, it is essential to find the proper role of *motives* in the analysis (Mohr, 1982, pp. 71–101). Normann has not taken the common path of including, either explicitly or implicitly, a set of specific motives whose presence or strength is responsible for observed values of the outcome—here, strategic decision making. Instead, he has presented an analysis that conforms either to what I have labeled (Mohr, 1982) a "summary motivation" approach or to a "ceteris-quietis" approach. The two are similar. In the first, one simply assumes that the necessary motives for taking an action (strategic decision making) are in place, recognizing that they may be different for different actors or even for the same actor over time. The main body of the explanation or description is given over to the variables or events other than motives that serve to illuminate the behavior. In the second, one assumes that a given, single motive or small motivational set is constant in the "on" position and that all others are quiescent, and one then proceeds with nonmotivational factors, as in the summary-motivation approach. In the present case, the constant, assumed motive would be the desire for organizational success or effectiveness.

Taking either a summary-motivation or a ceteris-quietis approach can be an excellent strategy, because, without such simplifying devices, dealing with specific motives as elements of explanation or understanding is likely to be extremely troublesome. One must ask, however, whether in this case a variety of motivational elements might need actually to be included instead of controlled and, even if they need not, whether strong theory or quasi theory is produced by assuming either an unspecified but positive summary of motives or, alternatively, a dominating and constant organizational-effectiveness goal. My answers to these questions will be (1) that there is no point in including active motivational variables or events in the explanation of strategic decision making but (2) that the strength of Normann's analysis as descriptive quasi theory tends to be undercut by the significance of fundamental motivational forces running counter to strategic change. For that reason, his model tends to be lacking in a characteristic of strong descriptive quasi theory that would be highly desirable in this instance—a high potential for constructive normative application. The next two sections contain elaborations of these two answers. That is, I will try first to show why Normann's avoidance of a variety of specific explanatory motives is tactically correct and next to make a case for giving prominence to the counterforces that undercut the utility of his summary-motivation or ceteris-quietis approach.

## Motives as Causes

As a point of departure, consider a frequently recurring theme in the literature on strategic decision making that is summed up by Normann (Chapter Nine) with the words, "Theory of strategic decision making is considerably less interesting than theory of strategic change." There would seem frequently to be a connection between decisions and change, but it is apparently neither an invariable nor a simple one. This theme, to me, stimulates more general questions about the connection between decisions and behavior and, ultimately, about the role of motives in both. I suggest that an understanding of strategic decision making and strategic change would best be developed in light of an explicit conceptualization of the relations among motives, decisions, and behavior. I will present such a conceptualization in this section and then discuss some of its implications for strategic decision making in the concluding section.

In the work cited previously (Mohr, 1982), I tried to demonstrate that motives are in general unacceptable as causes in potential general laws of human behavior. The argument was a lengthy one, but it depended at its core on a "fundamental assumption on motivation and behavior," namely, that "any motive may, in principle, be a condition for any behavior." This means that we cannot in general rule out the possibility that some individual, somewhere, at some time, has performed or will perform behavior $B$ for some reason $M_{n + 1}$, which is different from the $n$ motives already incorporated in the aspiring universal law. Thus, a universal law of behavior depending upon motives for explanation can never be complete. Furthermore, the record appears to indicate that such attempts at explanation are invariably very far from complete; actual operation of the fundamental assumption is strong and pervasive. I tried further to demonstrate that explanatory generalizations about human behavior cannot be valid *without* resorting to motives as determining forces. In the present context, this analysis implies that a universally or even a nearly universally applicable generalization explaining the occurrence or nonoccurrence of either strategic decisions or strategic change cannot be found; that is, we will never have a dependable rule for predicting the behaviors in question.

Although they would put it differently, a great many philosophers of science and social science would agree with the analysis and conclusions just reviewed. All (including myself in the cited book) appear to accept, however, that motives *are* or can be causes of behavior in the individual case. Individual human action, in fact, is best explained, even indispensably explained, in terms of motives. I would now like to amend the latter view, proposing that it can be and has been quite misleading and that the true relation of motives and behavior is more complicated and less intimate. In brief, motives do not cause behavior. In the present context, this implies that motives should not be relied upon for an understanding of strategic decision making or change, even in very limited populations and, ultimately, even in the case of the individual organization or chief executive.

A recent article has catalogued 102 separate definitions of the term *motive* as they appear in the books and journals of a variety of disciplines (Kleinginna and Kleinginna, 1981). The one common thread that may be said to run through this long and disparate list is that there is a certain large category of behavior ("motivated" behavior) that must have an internal cause, and, although its nature cannot yet be identified very far beyond the specification that it is a neural state, that ill-understood causal construct is nevertheless given a legitimizing label, the label *motive*. Having begun with the question whether a motive can be a cause, if we now infer a cause and label it *motive*, we have only a circular conclusion. Existing definitions of *motive* then, do not help us decide whether a motive can be a cause of behavior.

An element that is surprisingly missing from all of the definitions is whether this neural construct labeled *motive* is conscious. That issue seems, in fact, to be avoided. Peters (1969, p. 35) did note the distinction, but it is clear from his very brief discussion that he considers an unconscious motive to have the same linguistic form and logicorational foundation as a conscious one. It simply receives no attention. It is identified as a possible motive by the observer or behavioral analyst with exactly the same linguistic conventions that the actor would use in identifying it as a conscious motive. The actor might say that he "wanted to impress his boss," for example, while the behavioral analyst suggests that "he really wanted to impress his boss's secretary." That is, somewhere down underneath, the actor had a motive that was in perfect linguistic form but that remained unverbalized in his thoughts. Peters's usage parallels that of Freud, whose views on unconscious motives are analyzed at some length in Peters's book (1969, pp. 53–71). We will see momentarily that this is unlikely to be valid, that is, unconscious behavioral stimuli are unlikely to depend upon the linguistic processes of the conscious human mind; they apparently have another, far less intelligible form.

Let us use the simpler term *verbal* as a synonym for *language dependent* or *dependent upon linguistic expression*. For our purposes, the distinction between verbal and nonverbal causes of behavior should be pursued, because it helps greatly to clarify the possible explanatory role of motives. It raises the dual questions (1) can a verbal thought cause behavior? and (2) can a nonverbal cause be usefully employed to explain behavior? If the answer to both questions is no, and if motives are defined in part as verbal thoughts or expressions, one is led to eliminate motives, in social science, as explainers of individual acts. I suggest that the answers are indeed no.

Let us then, for a trial, make the distinction and require that what we will call a *motive* must be something that is conscious and dependent upon language. A motive is a desire for a state, conscious and verbal, that is considered capable of generating instrumental behavior. It is appropriate to deal with a concept so defined, whether it is called a motive or not, because, unless the behavioral stimulus is somehow both conscious and rendered into language, there is little possibility of measuring it, apart from its associated instrumental behavior, in social science. (Inferring the content of the motive only from its associated behavior is, of course, unsatisfactory, because it would destroy by circularity the possibility of determining whether it is indeed the motive that causes the behavior.)

We emphasize that a motive must be conscious and verbal rather than conscious alone. It seems quite certain that some thought is conscious but not language dependent (see, for example, Shepard and Cooper, 1982, pp. 1-5). Visual thoughts or images appear to fit in this category (Shepard and Cooper, 1982, pp. 5-14). So may instantaneously realized "paragraphs." It is possible, as well, that conscious but nonverbal thoughts are capable, in some sense, of causing behavior. What must be important for the present purpose, however, is that such thoughts are, without language, inaccessible to social science. They may be intelligible in some nonlinguistic sense to the observed subject, but their content is not currently transmissible to the observer—that is, measurable—without linguistic rendering; on that ground, they are excluded here in the consideration of "motives." When such conscious thoughts become measurable in content without resort to language, the thesis of this chapter will require review to determine their status as possible determinants of behavior in social science explanations.

Just as we accept that a motive is conscious and language dependent, let us also accept that there are indeed nonconscious—or perhaps conscious but nonverbal—drives, needs, goal states, and other stimuli of behavior; but to the extent that these stimuli are in no way articulated through language in the conscious mind, of either the actor or the observer, we will simply refer to them as "stimuli." A motive, then, is the conscious, language-dependent version, if it exists, of a presumed behavioral stimulus.

Are motives, so defined, the causes of behavior? Let us begin by suggesting that what we have called "stimuli" do exist and are the true causes of behavior. Observe that lower animals do not require motives; they behave without the benefit of motives—that is, they require only nonconscious or nonverbal stimuli. To the evolutionary biologist, it would be ridiculous—contrary to a mountain of related evidence—to suggest that all of this complex, nonverbal neurological and endocrinal system of behavior determination, elaborated and refined over the entire phylogenetic tree, was suddenly lost in the evolution of our own particular species. On the contrary, this fact provides a strong presumption for accepting that the elemental determiners of human behavior, as well, are something other than conscious, language-dependent thoughts.

Relevant motives may indeed exist before a potential behavior. For example, "I hate this commuting. I would love to live within ten minutes of the office." Later, if the same person is house hunting in a new city, the remembered antipathy to commuting might be expected to motivate a choice of residence that is close to the workplace. Other motives do not pre-exist but are more uniquely tied to a current, potential behavior. They arise only in reaction to ongoing behavior. "I would love to rest a while." "I wish my shoelace were tighter." "I'd hate to antagonize *her*." How are these various kinds of motives related to the stimuli that, we may continue to presume, must be the true causes of behavior? Two possibilities that tend to preserve verbal motives as causes are that they actually cause the stimuli or that they are accurate reflections of the effective stimuli. However, even if the attitudinal or sensory experiences cause some of the stimuli that cause behavior (for example, experiences such as the discomfort of commuting or of loose shoelaces), we will see that the *motives* relating to those experiences are at best only poor reflections of the set of effective stimuli.

The comparison of human beings to lower animals provides reason to believe that something other than motives are the causes or, at least, the immediate causes of behavior. There is also strong reason to believe that motives *cannot* be the causes of behavior; there must be something that is quite different, at least a large portion of the time, and, therefore, that "something" most likely operates all of the time. The reason is the following: Over and over again, the set of apparently operant motives is internally inconsistent (March, 1978). (The "risky" situation is a frequently recurring example; one knowingly desires to obtain some of the possible consequences of a behavior but to avoid other possible consequences of the same behavior.) If motives determined the behavior of a person, that person would, by definition, find it impossible to behave *at all* in the face of inconsistent motives. He or she would have almost nothing to do but expire. Sometimes, indeed, a person or animal shows temporary signs of extreme agitation, apparently because of true inconsistency in the underlying behavioral stimuli. Sometimes long-term illness or neurotic behavior may result. In the main, however, human beings are past masters at behaving in the teeth of what can only be discerned as totally inconsistent motives. It simply cannot be done, yet we do it every day, all the time. A person, for example, wants to eat a lot and yet wants to be thin. How can he decide what to do when confronted with a doughnut? He cannot. But he does! Then, he looks in the mirror one day and says, "Well, it is now clear that I would rather eat than be thin," but there may have been absolutely no way to determine this at any time, even after the fact, from an examination of his motives alone. The motives cannot be the cause of this behavior; something on that level is either missing or wrong (probably both).

The complete and correct set of stimuli, on the other hand, is somehow constituted and weighted so as to be internally consistent, thus permitting behavior. Presumably, these nonverbal stimuli are precise. What happens to motives, however, through language and conscious thought is that they become broad and sloppy, overly generalized and overly durable. Wanting to be thin, or to be wealthy, or to be prestigious, or to avoid commuting—with constant linguistic rendering, each of these varies not only in its strength from time to time but also in its nature, its content. What does it actually mean to be rich or to be thin or to want an effective organization? By being so imprecise and generalized, language-dependent motives continually bump into one another. The underlying stimuli, not burdened with words, shifting, going and coming constantly, are fine and sharp and so tend to avoid one another; if they do happen to conflict momentarily, they are generally joined by others, which tip the balance toward one behavior or another.

When the individual should be tied up in inconsistent motives, as far as can be discovered by introspection or elucidation, and yet behaves, the set of motives identified cannot be the determinant of the behavior. (Those motives that cannot be identified as such, if they exist at all, should be considered as stimuli rather than motives; motives are verbal and conscious.) But further, even when there is no inconsistency, the conscious, language-dependent motive is too imprecise to be considered the cause of behavior. This is true because, no matter how fully a motive set is specified, there is more than one behavior that will satisfy it. The instruction, in other words, is so ambiguous that the neurological system would not know how to carry it out. Sometimes it is indeed the behavior itself that clarifies or reveals preferences to the consciousness—preferences, as noted by March (1978), are frequently endogenous. The chief executive tells himself and his secretary that he would like to talk to Smith, the vice-president for sales. If Smith, having been summoned, were then observed to come in for a talk, little light might be shed on the present issue, but if Smith came in and the two went down to the bar off the lobby to talk, much more might be revealed to the (surprised) observer about motives *versus* stimuli. Let us say, for example, that the chief usually has his "talks" in the bar. This time, was he impelled in part by wanting a drink? If he chose to talk in the office, was he impelled by wishing to *avoid* drinking? Nothing about drinking, privacy, or atmosphere was included in the original statement of motive. How is the neurological system to know that having a talk means going to the bar? To someone else, it would surely mean remaining in the office. Furthermore, if drinking did happen to be included among the original motives, there is in principle always something else that was not—for example, drinking scotch or bourbon, taking a curt and efficient or a relaxed and expansive tone, avoiding showing an opinion in Smith's disagreement with Brown, and so on. Always, there is ambiguity owing to overly general terms and insufficiently specific content.

In sum, it is unlikely that motives cause behavior. The best that may be said is that motives are sometimes close in content to conscious thoughts of a nonverbal nature that either themselves affect behavior or are somehow related to operative nonconscious stimuli. We will see in a moment that motives considered by an individual to cause his or her behavior may actually be quite irrelevant to it. Thus, being noncausal, being several steps removed from operative stimuli, being dependent upon an imprecise modality of realization, and possessing a strong bias toward incompleteness and ambiguity of scope, motives are untrustworthy and crude as bases of explanation.

The above analysis is supported by experimental evidence showing how easy it is for motives that are inoperative to coexist with operative stimuli having quite radically different content. Indeed, this evidence suggests that the articulated motives may always actually be inoperative, even if they happened somehow to be quite similar to the operative stimuli. In these experiments, described and in some cases conducted by Nisbett and Wilson (1977), subjects were unable to report accurately on processes that truly caused their own behavior. Experimental conditions were made to create an operative behavioral stimulus, but subjects rarely seemed to be aware of this. When called upon, they singled out other causal mechanisms instead, if any at all.

Complete stimulus sets with regard to the outcome behaviors in each of these experiments may well have been complex, variable across individuals, and, in fact, probably unique to each individual included in a given study. Nevertheless, the experimental procedure (randomized experimental and control groups; manipulated intervention) guaranteed within statistical limits that the experimental and control groups were equalized with respect to their potential for that outcome behavior, except for the one stimulus that constituted the experimental intervention. This one stimulus was strong enough, in the context of the various stimulus sets represented by individuals who received each experimental treatment, to produce a behavior that was different from that displayed, on average, in the corresponding control groups. In most cases by far, however, subjects were not able to report accurately the role of this experimentally determined stimulus; in fact, each subject tended to deny that it had any role at all in his or her case. Instead, subjects seemed to search for plausible explanations ("a priori causal theories") for their behavior and to conclude erroneously that these were the operative, critical factors. Thus, the stimulus inferred on the basis of the experimental design to have been highly instrumental in causing the behavior existed on an unaware level insofar as its causal role was concerned. At the same time, many subjects' heads were filled with conscious thoughts that seemed to be causally operative but that probably were not, while other subjects could find no conscious motive at all for the behavior in question.

Only a few of the many studies reported by Nisbett and Wilson deal directly with the issue of effective motives versus effective stimuli (others deal with problem solving, perception, and belief formation). Moreover, those studies that are directly pertinent do not demonstrate that salient motives, when they exist, do not ever cause behavior. They do, however, show how flimsy and even how totally erroneous an explanation based on motives can be. They constitute a powerful demonstration that stimuli that are critical in the process of behavior determination are frequently unavailable to the conscious mind and are, instead, quite smoothly replaced there in role by completely unrelated motives.

Thus, one cannot attribute behavior to certain motives, even in limited populations or individuals, without high risk of error. It is too easy to mistake the strength and nature and applicability of the corresponding underlying stimuli and to miss a great many of them altogether. Perhaps the motives seized upon add up to the same acts as the true configuration of underlying stimuli, but knowledge of the latter would cast the behavior in a different light. It would cause it to be interpreted differently and therefore to be, in the sense that behavior is defined by intention, a different behavior (Peters, 1969).

A decision is a behavior like any other, except that it may take place entirely in the mind and need not necessarily be articulated in speech or writing. Thus, a decision is caused by some set of subconscious stimuli, just as any other act. Some decisions appear to cause an associated behavior—the "carrying-out" behavior. In a sense, there may be a kind of causal connection, because the remembered fact of the decision may feed, in certain ways, into the set of stimuli determining the behavior. It provides a set of pre-existing motives. Nevertheless, it is well accepted that behavior is not in general determined by decisions. One initial way of stating the true relationship is that it is spurious, in the technical, statistical sense of that term. That is, the same variables—the underlying stimuli—cause both the decision and the behavior. That is close but incorrect in principle, because neither a stimulus, a decision, nor a behavior is a variable. They are qualitative events. More precisely than "spurious," then, a decision is related to an associated behavior in the sense that the two are caused by overlapping sets of stimuli.

That the two sets are overlapping, however, does not mean that they are equivalent. That would be a great oversimplification for at least four important reasons. (1) As has been pointed out by Normann and others, behavior, including strategic change, frequently takes place in the absence of any discernible prior decision to perform the acts observed. (2) There are frequently certain benefits of announcing or revealing a decision, even if it is never carried out. This has been documented well in organizational behavior (Christensen, 1976), and the same applies to individuals. In particular, an announced decision may improve relations with certain other people for the time being; the others may be brought to feel that the decider is on their side in a conflict, for example. Decisions are a way of revealing and reinforcing values that may be at issue; they frequently do not need to be implemented to achieve this end. A strategic change might be agreed to, for example, in order to buy time and tranquility. The proponents may go away, change their minds, or be placated in a different manner before the necessity to implement falls due. *Revealing* a decision, on the other hand, may indeed have a causal effect on later behavior in one way that should not be overlooked. The decision may have an impact on the environment, which then may affect behavior by supplying new stimuli. For example, it is harder to begin smoking again if one has announced the intention to quit to one's friends than if one had simply kept it to oneself. Announcing a strategic decision in an organization can set in motion many expectations and structural changes, as Normann convincingly argues, that then become strong, autonomous determinants of strategic change. In this sense, then, strategic decision making is not a negligible target of understanding and explanation. (3) In the process of making a decision, an individual or group frequently attempts to simulate in thought the stimuli of the implementation stage. One imagines doing the thing versus not doing it and decides which course to take on the basis of the benefits and costs that seem to come up. The behavior stimuli would in this sense be causing the decision, as well. This process clearly may be far from exact, however, both because some implementation stimuli simply are not thought of and because thought itself is not a reliable way to render the strength and content of associated stimuli. (4) Situations change. By the time implementation is to begin, the world is a different place, and the new set of pros and cons may be significantly different from the old one.

Thus, because acts without prior decisions are quite common and because the stimuli affecting behavior can be quite different from those affecting decisions, the study of strategic decision making in itself would not seem to be worthwhile. On the other hand, the overlapping of the two sets of causal stimuli may be very extensive at times, and, further, decisions often affect the environment in critical ways that constrain later behavior and make implementation more probable. In this perspective, decision making would seem to be a productive target of attention.

Either way, it is important to remember that decisions are behaviors and, as such, are governed not by motives but by what we have been calling "stimuli," or "subconscious stimuli." As with strategic change, then, the student of strategic decision making should not expect profound understanding, of either the general or the individual case, to come from the analysis of motives or possible motives. Interest in strategic organizational behaviors reflects an interest in organizational effectiveness, success, and adaptability. These could be motives, but they are crude, overly generalized motives at best, utterly mistakenly imputed to management at worst. In the space that remains, let us deal with the extent to which the idea of stimuli, rather than motives, can contribute to an understanding of both strategic decision making and strategic change.

Normann suggests that learning is an important factor in the determination of strategic change, as well as interpersonal skills, structure, constitution, culture, philosophy, change of management personnel, visible management, and statesmanship. Each of these may indeed be important at times. They are, however, a sort of miscellany. They suggest by implication the stimuli that may be affecting or may potentially affect diverse actors at diverse times. To understand why they may sometimes be quite important, and what other kinds of things might be important, it will be helpful to keep in mind that we are concerned with the behavior of many individuals where, in each case, behavior is a continuous flow of acts governed by a unique, continuous flow of stimuli. We cannot hope to know what all of the latter are; indeed, it is hard enough to know what any of them might be. In this perspective, what can be said?

## Accentuating the Negative

Almost all of the writings in the applied area under examination suggest that the single most important characteristic of strategic change is that it is *change*. Why should anyone change? Presumably, in terms of the rough model of behavior we are now using, a pattern of behavior somehow recognizable as recurrent has been in use. If change is about to occur, then the subset of stimuli reinforcing the pattern has presumably become weaker than the subset tending to divert it. What sorts of stimuli might these all be? One must immediately assume that they may be infinitely diverse and, therefore, that broad generalizability—even for one sort of applied behavior, such as strategic change—will not be possible. Moreover, they are numerous, interacting, and obscure, so that even the study of one individual would have problematically valid results. I propose that one device well worth trying, both for some degree of generality and for individual or single organizational analysis, is to look toward fundamental forces that may be evoked by the situation, that is, inclinations that may be highly characteristic of the species, on the one hand, and that have a high probability of being strongly evoked in the behavioral setting at issue, on the other. The advantage of such fundamental forces in potential explanations is that, if they are evoked, we can sense or understand that they have a common meaning, rooted in the biology of the species, so that the linguistic terms used are less like themes for interpretive variation and more like code words that attempt to signify the raw stimuli themselves. In the human species, some of these forces may be status in a group, security, conferrable resources, and, I propose, behavioral inertia. It is doubtful that such forces are at work in the potential strategic change situation on the positive side, the side impelling toward change. Those stimuli appear to have more to do with individual and contextual factors, such as ego satisfaction, commitment to certain organizational goals or groups, severity of financial crisis, and availability of information about the change. Innovation research has dwelled mostly on the positive side—the motives for change—and that is one possible reason for its poor track record, its inability to come cumulatively closer over time to some agreed-upon explanations (see Downs and Mohr, 1976). We would have done better, perhaps, to accentuate the negative (see Charters and Pellegrin, 1972). It is possible that some of the fundamental forces of which I speak do operate to *keep* executives from embarking on strategic change programs. Instead of seeking to understand strategic change, where broadly applicable insights are unlikely to be attained, it may ultimately be better to take the roundabout and admittedly less satisfying tack of seeking to understand the nonevent, the declination to change, the failure even to see the possibilities. (I have in mind as actor here primarily the chief executive or controlling management team; the status stimulus might surely impel other, upwardly mobile managers toward changes that would enhance their own positions.) Starbuck (1983) takes a similar course when he notes that very little organizational activity is of the problem-solving variety; there is little activity in response to current organizational needs. Instead, actions are generated by such sources as established performance programs, tradition, and dogma. It should not be surprising that there is little action in response to problems. The discomfort from the problem may be fairly strong, but the stimuli toward specific, substantial changes are weakened by uncertainty. It is unclear what changes to make. Several may vie for selection, so that the stimuli are crowded and diffuse. All potential changes probably have uncertain outcomes in terms of solving the current problem without generating more and perhaps worse ones. One prime type of "worse one" is the lack of expertise to deal with substantially changed operations; the current top managers may sense that they won't look as good—as much in control—and may have to share de facto authority more widely, which generally tends to undermine a status position.

On the other hand, the stimuli that militate *against* strategic change may be expected in general to be strong. There seems, especially, to be a generalized, fundamental behavioral inertia that is probably adaptive for our species and for others whose behavioral responses to current environments are not highly programmed. A pattern of behavior that works is a precious commodity; to change it frequently, even experimentally, is likely to be extremely disadvantageous. This inertia at the stimulus level easily results in "superstitious learning" at the conscious level (Lave and March, 1975); one performs certain acts and seems to get along well, so one attributes the getting along well, often quite mistakenly, to those acts. This sort of learning can be monumentally difficult to dispel or disassemble.

The learning that has most impact on strategic change may in fact be superstitious learning rather than double-loop learning (Chapter Nine; Argyris, 1976c). The latter is so close to strategic change itself that it has always been difficult for me to see it as other than a behavior; the state of double-loop learning is governed by a set of stimuli that would have to overlap almost completely with that governing strategic change. What these writers call "deutero learning," on the other hand, is a significant possibility. This is a flexibility, a readiness always to see the environment in new terms. It is difficult to imagine that such a state could develop in a very stable environment or could long persist in an environment that has become stable for an extended period of time. It could, however, develop in individuals who have needed to cope persistently with rapid and radical environmental change. If our entire species were subjected to such an environment over a long period, deutero learning might become a fundamental source of stimuli, but stability and moderate change are still more the rule than the exceptions. Performance programs and behavioral inertia would still seem to be adaptive, both for particular situations at the level of the individual person (as a part of culture) and as a general force at the species level (as a part of biological adaptation).

There can be no question but that financial crisis, visions of new success, the fear of being fired, certain organizational or decision structures, and the like can and will produce strategic change even when the need for it is not constantly repeated but only occasionally crops up. More frequently, however, there is a tendency to be swamped by behavioral inertia, for better or worse. When there would seem to be a strong need to do things differently, but an organization exhibits stagnant behavior, the stagnation will most likely be permanent. As Starbuck (1983) points out, organizations do die of this disease in great numbers. An obvious solution in this case, one that is commonly sensed in the organizational world, is to change executives—to import new management that is not worse in other respects and that does not internally associate the past methods and outlook of the company with getting along well and even with achieving substantial success. The literature, including Normann's examples, does suggest that there may not be another solution.

The above analysis might be interpreted as reductionist, as attributing everything to a few basic drives. Two comments should be made about this possibility: (1) There is no thought here of trying to stretch this sort of explanation beyond its true limits of validity. This is itself a ceteris-quietis sort of analysis. That approach is useful only when the stimuli considered constant and "on" are very common across individuals (have a high probability of existence), which is why fundamental forces are sought, and are likely to be evoked with substantial strength in the applied context of concern. It must be recognized that the playing out of these forces as if in isolation from others of their kind may not always occur in the real world, but the presumption is that it is helpful to know what must commonly be going on in the individual beneath the surface—tending to happen—even if that is submerged from time to time by situational forces that happen to be more potent. (2) The sort of explanatory thrust that is traditionally employed to explain change has not had and will not have the kind of payoff we seek as scholars. It is inherently unstable, ad hoc, and misleading. One must therefore seek alternatives; if not this one, then some other. (Structural solutions that will channel effort toward strategic change when indicated constitute another possibility; I have neither confidence nor space enough to explore it here and so leave the territory to others.)

Lastly, it seems correct to me to emphasize, as Normann does, that the problem of strategic change does not end when top management acts in that direction. The stimuli at the stage of implementation are far different from those at both the decision and the initial-action stages, especially on the negative side. In implementation, there is frequently a need to act in such a way as to get many other people, nearly simultaneously, to do what they do not want to do. The stimulus sets of executives at this point are no doubt infinitely diverse and not reliably dominated by any fundamental forces.

What is perhaps more reliable is the behavior of the rest of the organization, at least those members with some stake of status or comfort in the old ways—the ones to be modified or abandoned. Behavioral inertia will be strong there, too. Why change? Certainly, not because of the vision of a changed organizational environment and the need for new goals; most members below top management levels, most of the time, would have neither the information, the perspective, nor the feeling of responsibility to decide upon the need for radical change and act upon it. Thus, a great many stimulus sets in the organization will be heavily weighted on the negative side. One significant counterweight, perhaps the only one, would be the recognition that resistance will lead to negative performance appraisals (including or, perhaps, especially including the informal ones that arise out of interactions across hierarchical lines). Persistence and strength are needed by the managers of change to make the new outlook felt and get it taken quite seriously. This is why the qualities that Normann calls "visible management" and "statesmanship" are so important. One must make sure that the new goals and procedures are well known, as well as the serious intention of top management to implement them, come what may. What is highly problematical is whether bringing all of this to the attention of managers and exhorting them to be persistent, visible, and statesmanlike will do any good. The behavior of each is determined continuously by a unique set of stimuli. Motives that come from information and exhortation will feed into the set, but what impact they will have on it is difficult to say at a distance—and certainly impossible to say for the general case.

Thus, change can be difficult—not only for the manager, which has long been well known, but also for the analyzing scholar. There are few reliable, stable pegs in this realm on which one might hang the beginnings of a robust model. Behavioral inertia is one such peg, although it does not by any means guarantee the development of theory. I suggested in a recent publication that social science cannot explain with stable generalizations everything that is interesting in social behavior. It is too soon to tell just how well we will do in the area of strategic change, but I submit that all hope lies in the direction of nontraditional rather than traditional approaches.

# ❧ ELEVEN ❧

# Examining Change
# in the Long-Term Context
# of Culture and Politics

## *Andrew M. Pettigrew*

Descriptively and prescriptively, the starting and finishing points of this chapter are the same. Theoretically sound and practically useful research on strategic decision making and change should involve the continuous interplay among ideas about the *context* of change, the *process* of change, and the *content* of change, together with skill in regulating the relations among the three. Stated in this way, it would take a bolder person than I to say, "and here's the answer to the problem of relating context to process, to the content of strategy." There is, of course, no simple way of answering such a broad analytical question, but, as we shall see, using those three classes of variables and their relationship as a starting point does ensure that some consequential and perhaps, at this time, more answerable questions are posed about the what, the why, and the how of strategic decision making and change.

*Note:* The research reported in this chapter was supported partly by a personal research grant awarded by the British Economic and Social Research Council.

In general analytical terms, it is clear from the developing literature on strategy over the last two decades both that the context in which strategy is said to be formulated and implemented is variously defined and that a whole plethora of different process theories have evolved and are evolving to explain choice behavior. In the meantime, as Schendel and Hofer (1979) and others often tell us, there are innumerable working definitions of what strategy and strategic management are. Furthermore, the literature on the content of strategic decision making and change (Hofer and Schendel, 1978; Porter, 1980) has developed rather separately from the more behavioral theories of choice and yet relies on a rational theory of choice long since discarded by process analysts as being divorced from the empirical reality of how decisions and changes are actually made. The process theorists, in consequence, have abandoned artificial distinctions between the formulation and implementation of strategy, while those more interested in the content of strategy struggle to develop yet more sophisticated analytical techniques, which often flounder in the political and cultural mosaic of large organizations. Meanwhile evolving in parallel with this literature, there has also emerged that rather precious subculture of theory and practice about change labeled organization development (Bennis, 1969; French and Bell, 1973). The organization-development literature, which itself has not been well connected with existing work or novel theoretical developments going on in organization theory and behavior, or with advances conducted by sociologists and anthropologists in thinking about change (Zald and McCarthy, 1979; Geertz, 1973), has rarely been used to inform thinking about strategic change, even though recent writing by, for example, Beckhard and Harris (1977) and Beer (1980) could be used with profit to grapple with some of the practical problems of creating and managing strategic change.

This chapter will use the terms *strategic decision* and *strategic change* almost, but not entirely, as interchangeable notions. Strategic decisions and changes will be viewed as streams of activity involving individuals and groups that occur mainly but not solely as a consequence of environmental change and that can lead to alterations in the product-market focus, structure, technology, and culture of the host organization. *Strategic* is just a description of magnitude of alteration in, for example, structure and organizational culture, recognizing the second-order effects or multiple consequences of any such changes. Analytically, of course, decisions and changes can both be understood in terms of broad questions of context, process, and content. A single strategic decision can of itself lead to strategic changes, but, as we shall see, the focus here will be to treat both decision making and change as continuous processes whereby strategic changes can be a product of and enabler of many consequent decisions. The chapter does make some attempt to combine description and analysis with prescription, and the reader may find that prescriptive thoughts fit better into the language of strategic change than of strategic decision making, although the chapter does report theoretical and empirical ideas of a descriptive character about strategic change.

Given the author's previous research (Pettigrew, 1973, 1977, 1979, in press) and the predisposition to approach decision making and change as continuous processes, the chapter begins by examining some of the currently available process theories of choice. Necessarily brief reflections are offered on process theories using the language of rationality, incrementalism, "garbage-can" theory, and politics. Some attempt is made to highlight the analytical power of each of these approaches as separate views of the same organism, but overlaps between these process theories are also identified, and space is taken to indicate in particular how so-called political and cultural analyses of process may be profitably combined and refined. This section of the chapter ends with a warning: Beware of the singular theory of process or, indeed, of social and organizational change. Look for continuity and change, patterns and idiosyncracies, the actions of individuals and groups, and processes of structuring. Give history and social processes the chance to reveal their untidiness. To understand strategic decision making and change, examine the juxtaposition of the rational and the political, the quest for efficiency and power, the role of exceptional people and of extreme circumstances, the untidiness of chance, and the enabling and constraining forces of the environment and explore some of the conditions in which mixtures of these occur.

Thus warned by Gianfranco Poggi's stricture that a way of seeing is a way of not seeing (Poggi, 1965, p. 284), the trap to avoid is the opposite dilemma of trying to see everything and thus seeing nothing. The author's frame of reference, heavily reflected by the concern with political and cultural analysis, is then developed by revealing the preference for contextualism as a mode of analysis. Central to this research on strategic change is an attempt to specify some of the language and conditions that link the multilevel analysis and processual analysis of organizational phenomena in a contextualist analysis. Such an analysis draws on phenomena at both vertical and horizontal levels. The vertical level refers to the interdependencies between higher or lower levels of analysis and phenomena to be explained at some further level, for example, the impact of social and economic trends on organizational functioning. The horizontal level refers to the sequential interconnectedness among phenomena in historical, present, and future time. An approach that offers both multilevel, or vertical, analysis and processual, or horizontal, analysis is said to be contextualist in character.

A view is taken that the study of strategic change is now at the stage where theory and knowledge are required not so much to unravel particular changes but to reveal the dynamics of changing in alternative contexts, using a framework of analysis that can incorporate different levels of analysis with varying degrees of explanatory immediacy and distance from the change processes under examination. In order to do this, the field has to move beyond the useful but mechanical statements of contingency theory, which emphasize the interconnections between a state of the environment and certain requirements for structure, behavior, or change, and begin to examine how and why changes occur in different organizational cultures and political systems, under different socioeconomic conditions, through time. The interest is both in catching reality in flight and in embeddedness—a return to context as a principle or method—in seeing long-term processes of continuity and change as a complex dynamic system with a mixture of processes occurring at different levels and at various rates. It is in the dialogue between trends and forces in a multilevel and changing context and the systems of value and meaning, actions, and initiatives between powerful groups and individuals seeking to adjust and manage contexts to meet their ends that much strategic change—its origins, mechanism and forms—can be located and understood.

Having established the frame of reference and mode of analysis for this research, the chapter then moves on to consider some illustrative examples from a comparative and longitudinal study of strategic decision making and change in Imperial Chemical Industries PLC (ICI). ICI is one of Britain's largest manufacturing firms and in 1981 ranked as the fifth largest of the world's chemical companies in terms of sales in U.S. dollars, after Du Pont and the big German three of Hoechst, Bayer, and BASF. The research examines ICI's attempts to change their strategy, structure, technology, organizational culture, and the quality of union-management relationships over the period 1960–1983. An important and unusual feature of the research strategy has been the collection of comparative and longitudinal data. Interviews and documentary and observational data are available from four divisions and the head office of the company. These data have been assembled from a continuous real-time study since 1976 and from retrospective analysis of the period 1960–1975.

The study explores two linked continuous processes. The initial focus of the research was to examine the birth, evolution, demise, and development of the groups of internal and external organization-development consultants employed by ICI to help initiate and implement organization change. This analysis of the contributions and limitations of specialist-led attempts to create change has led to the examination of broader processes of continuity and change in ICI as seen through the eyes and activities of the main board of the company and the boards of ICI's four largest divisions—agricultural, Mond, petrochemicals, and plastics.

The full findings and theoretical developments of the research are published in Pettigrew, 1985. The reader will, I hope, bear with me in my frustration at not being able to report here the rich description and analysis available from such an extended stream of time-series comparative case-study data. Instead, all that can be achieved in the limited space available in this chapter is to reveal some of the key empirical themes about strategic decision making and change that have emerged from one part of this study. Brief illustrative data are reported on ICI's main board's attempts to change the top governance and culture of the company over the period 1972-1982. These data are briefly linked back to earlier discussions in the chapter about alternative process theories of decision making and change, to various features of intraorganizational and socioeconomic context, including changes over the ten-year time period in those contexts, and to the content and outcome of some of the strategic change processes.

The chapter ends with some very brief observations of what the ICI data can tell us of the practice of managing strategic change. Here the chapter's theoretical focus on political and cultural analysis of organizations and the methodological emphasis on understanding change not as discrete change projects or episodes but as long-term processes of continuity and changing lead us prescriptively to consider managing development processes in terms of keying into the natural processes of changing going on in an organization and its contexts. The question of strategic change is posed less in terms of how this change project or proposal can be foisted on this system and more in terms of how existing processes can be speeded up, how the conditions that determine people's interpretations of situations can be altered, and how contexts can be mobilized to achieve practical effects along the way to move the organization, perhaps additively, in a different strategic direction.

## Alternative Process Theories of Choice and Change

In a broad review of the literature on organization change made elsewhere (Pettigrew, 1985), the point is made that, with a few limited and noteworthy exceptions (Kervasdoué and Kimberly, 1979; Berg, 1979), much research on organizational change is ahistorical, aprocessual, and acontextual in character. In this respect, the area of organizational change merely reflects the biases inherent in the social sciences generally and in the study of organizations in particular. There are remarkably few studies of change that actually allow the change process to reveal itself in any kind of substantially temporal or contextual manner. Studies of innovation are therefore often preoccupied with the intricacies of particular chan*ges* rather than the dynamics of chan*ging*.

Where the change project is treated as the unit of analysis, the focus is on a single event or a set of discrete episodes somehow separate from the immediate and more distant antecedents that give those events form, meaning, and substance. Such episodic, or project and program, views of change not only treat innovations as if they had a clear beginning and a clear end but also, where they limit themselves to snapshot time-series data, fail to provide data on the mechanisms and processes through which changes are created (Bowers, 1973; Franklin, 1976). The point here, of course, is that the research findings on change are method bound. Time itself sets a frame of reference for what changes are seen and how those changes are explained. The more we look at present-day events, the easier it is to identify change; the longer we stay with an emergent process and the further back we go to disentangle its origins, the more likely we are to identify continuities. Where we sit influences not only where we stand but also what we see.

As will become apparent, similar arguments can be made against much of the literature on strategic decision making, where the concern is often with concrete decision events, the front stage of decision making and power, rather than back-stage processes of non-decision making (Bachrach and Baratz, 1962) and overarching features of organizational control (Lukes, 1974; Brown, 1978) that provide the paradigmatic frameworks within which the very meaning of such actions as making decisions is defined. Even given these observations, however, real progress was made in the 1970s by authors such as Bower (1972), Allison (1971), Pettigrew (1973), Mumford and Pettigrew (1975), March and Olsen (1976), Mintzberg (1978), and Quinn (1980) to rescue the research on strategic decision making and change from its prevailing concern with rational analytical schemes of intentional process and outcome and to see decision making and change in a variety of process modes.

The kinds of process theories of choice and, sometimes, change proposed by the above authors tend in the main to use as a whipping boy the rational deductive view of problem solving propounded by the neoclassical theory of the firm and its equivalents in the strategy literature (Andrews, 1980; King and Cleland, 1978). In essence, the neoclassical theories of the firm take as given what the incremental, political, and garbage-can views of process seek to explain. Predating these behavioral theories, the so-called managerial theories of the firm (Baumol, 1959; Marris, 1966; Williamson, 1964) have also explored how the absence of tight markets or shareholder discipline on management decision making has enabled managers to exercise discretion in the face of previously assumed exogenous forces. More recently, Williamson's (1975) important market-failures approach to discussing firm behavior has further liberated the organization, as distinct from the impersonal forces of the market, as a unit of analysis and helped to provide a language of analysis that is stimulating contact among industrial economics, organization theorists, and business strategy teachers and researchers.

As applied to the formulation of strategy, the rational approach describes and prescribes techniques for identifying current strategy, analyzing environments, resources, and gaps, revealing and assessing strategic alternatives, and choosing and implementing carefully analyzed and well-thought-through outcomes. Depending upon the author, explicitly or implicitly, the firm speaks with a unitary voice or can be composed of omnipotent, even heroic general managers or chief executives, looking at known and consistent preferences and assessing them with voluminous and presumably apposite information, which can be organized into clear input-output relationships. With that as the intellectual rabbit, it is no wonder that so many empirical and processual foxes have set off in search of such an easy lunch! However, having devoured the rational rabbit with such apparent ease, the process foxes may in turn have failed to see either the rational elements of their own theoretical approaches or even those aspects of real-life decision processes that can be interpreted in rational problem-solving terms. But more of that reflection later.

The empirical process research on strategy by authors such as Bower (1972), Mintzberg (1978), Miller and Friesen (1980a), and Boswell (1983) made a number of descriptive contributions to the understanding of strategic decision making and change. Strategic processes were now accepted as multilevel activities and not just the province of a few or even a single general manager. Outcomes of decisions were not just a product of rational or bounded-rational debates but were also shaped by the interests and commitments of individuals and groups, the forces of bureaucratic momentum, gross changes in the environment, and the manipulation of the structural context around decisions. With the view that strategy development was a continuous process, strategies could now be thought of as reconstructions after the fact, rather than just rationally intended plans. The view of a linear process from strategy formulation to strategy implementation was questioned, and, with increasing interest in enduring characteristics of structural and strategic context (Bower, 1972; Burgelman, 1983a), Chandler's (1969) dictum that structure followed strategy was modified by evidence indicating why and how strategy followed structure (Galbraith and Nathanson, 1978).

Analytically, however, the Bower and Mintzberg research was weakened by a number of factors. Chief among these was, first, the treatment of decision making just as front-stage behavior and the lack of concern with non-decision making and, second, the lack of development of a specified process theory to explain the descriptions of process and outcome. Quinn's (1980) publication, however, tied itself to a very specific interpretation of process. Drawing on the work of Lindblom and Braybrooke, Quinn interpreted his case-study data on strategic change as displaying patterns of logical incrementalism. This is described as a jointly analytical and political process in which executives are recommended "to proceed flexibly and experimentally from broad concepts to specific commitments, making the latter concrete as late as possible" (Quinn, 1980, p. 56) and are described as so doing. Strategic change is thus seen as a cautious, step-by-step evolutionary process, where executives muddle through with a purpose.

Quinn's (1980) style of presenting his ideas, moving easily from description to prescription, makes his book extremely attractive as a teaching medium, but the clarity of his belief in the prescriptive value of logical incrementalism means that it is not always easy to disentangle what he has discovered empirically from what he would like to see. Certainly, Mintzberg's (1978) finding that incremental change takes place in spurts, each followed by a period of continuity, tends to contradict Quinn's (1980) finding or view that strategies emerge in a continuous incremental and thereby additive fashion. Perhaps because Quinn's (1980) work is presented in the language of change rather than of decision making, and because he is interested in prescription, he does make the extremely important point that, in the management of strategic changes, there are process limits to consider as well as just cognitive limits. These process limits, the concern with the timing and sequencing of action and events in order to build awareness, comfort levels, and consensus for strategic change, were also a crucial part of the strategic change process in ICI.

Although the characterization and description of process in Quinn's (1980) work are a good deal richer than anything offered by the bounded rationalists, as in the works of Simon (1957a) and March and Simon (1958), the underlying rationalist perspective that there is an element of "conscious, foresightful action reasonably autonomously constructed to achieve some goal or value" (Pfeffer, 1982, p. 7) is shared by Quinn and the bounded rationalists. No such rationalistic perspective is at the bottom of another process theory developed in the 1970s, the so-called garbage-can view of action and choice (Cohen, March, and Olsen, 1972). In this view of organization, individual and group interests are only partially understood and acted upon, actors walk in and out of decision processes, solutions are generated without reference to problems, and outcomes are not a direct consequence of process. In this anarchical picture of organizational life, behavior can be predicted neither by intention nor by environmental constraint; instead, decisions appear out of foggy emergent contexts when people, problems, and solutions find themselves sharing the same bed. Fundamentally, "rationality cannot guide action in this view, because rationality, goals, and preferences are viewed as emerging from action rather than guiding action" (Pfeffer, 1982, p. 9).

This is a very attractive view of process precisely because it is such a counterpoint to the rationalists, but one wonders whether the view of anarchy has not been overstated—there are greater consistency and continuity of action, clearer beliefs in self- and group interests and action derived from those interests, and generally firmer cause-effect attributions in connecting perceptions, information, interests, and preferences to action and outcomes than are implied by the garbage-can theorists. In addition, most of the empirical examples used to support this garbage-can approach to choice are taken from educational organizations (March and Olsen, 1976), where the theory may fit a context widely assumed to contain hapless citizens confused and conflicted about means and ends, confronted by multiple systems and centers of leadership, and unclear about their responsibilities and accountabilities.

The preceding necessarily synoptical account of the rational, bounded-rational, incremental, and garbage-can approaches to choice and sometimes change will have given a flavor of the variety of perspectives now available to the student of strategy, some of the strengths and weaknesses and overlaps of each, and a few of the empirical findings that those alternative views of process have encouraged. A task that remains is to sketch out the meaning and utility of a process view of choice and change that combines a political and cultural analysis of organizational life.

## Political and Cultural Perspective

Earlier in this chapter, I issued a warning to the reader and myself—beware of the singular theory of choice and change. Behind this warning was the obvious desire to avoid premature theoretical ethnocentrism, especially as we have shown that the analyst of process does actually have a choice of perspectives, if not theories, available. In terms of how conceptual and empirical developments in the study of strategic choice and change could take place, there are obviously a number of alternative strategies even within the process type of research favored here. One approach is to discount ethnocentrism and pursue and refine any particular process the-ory—if I can be forgiven another metaphor, to clip a single powerful lamp onto the miner's helmet and take that down into the data mine. A second strategy is to be ostensibly a more reasonable person and go into the mine lights ablaze, looking from many perspectives of process, and hope to see and explain without being blinded by all the distractions and reflections. A third strategy is to keep in mind the different process theories and work toward making contingent statements of, for example, where and when the different theories of process may be more or less appropriate. This strategy, of course, is already bearing some fruit, with incremental theories perhaps fitting easily alongside programmed or repetitive budgetary decisions (Davis, Dempster, and Wildavsky, 1966), political process theories seeming to be compatible with the complexity and uncertainty of innovative decisions (Pettigrew, 1973), and garbage-can approaches fitting the anarchistic, loosely coupled character of educational organizations (for example, March and Olsen, 1976; Weick, 1976). A fourth strategy, and the one favored here, is to try to develop a more unified theoretical analysis, not only by, in this case, combining political and cultural views of process but also by clarifying a methodological approach to process analysis—labeled here *contextualism*—that seeks to engage a process analysis of action with features of intraorganizational and social, economic, and political context. This section of the chapter tries to briefly present a unified view of political and cultural analysis as it can be applied to strategic choice and change, and the following section discusses contextualism as a mode of analysis.

The frame of reference used to inform this research is a continuation and development of the author's previous work on organizations as political systems (Pettigrew, 1972, 1973, 1977) and the politics of organizational change (Pettigrew, 1975a, 1980). Considering the organization as a political system directs attention toward the factors that facilitate and hinder change and toward the reasons why political energy is often released within the firm at even the prospect, never mind the reality, of change. Political processes within the firm evolve at the group level from the division of work in the organization and at the individual level from associated career, reward, and status systems. Interest groups form in organizations around the particular objectives, responsibilities, and intentions of functions or business areas; they also form around differences between groups at varying hierarchical levels or around collectivities such as newcomers versus old-timers or progressives versus conservatives. Interest groups may also form around the issues of the day: whether to grow or not to grow, whether to diversify or not to diversify, whether to bring in new technology or to continue to use old methods and procedures. Indeed, a key part of the political process of the firm may have to do with which issues become a focus of individual or group interest and attention and move onto the stage of decision making and which issues are suppressed or otherwise immobilized and left in the wings, waiting for changes in the power balance of the firm and/or environmental adjustments to redirect the attention of organizational participants.

These interest groups are likely to have different goals, time orientations, values, and problem-solving styles. In short, they may have different *rationalities,* which provide the motive forces for their actions and reactions, along with the language and styles of behavior to express those actions. As the author has argued elsewhere (Pettigrew, 1977), strategy formulation and change processes in organizations may be understood in part as the outcome of processes of competition between these rationalities expressed through the language, priorities, and values of technologists; of accounting and finance—the bottom line; or of the rather more diffuse perspectives adopted by specialist groups from planning, operational research, organizational development, or personnel.

Given the present interest in time and social process and contextual analysis, the clear implication is that neither are such interest-group relationships set in concrete, nor is their development bounded just by intraorganizational forces. While at any point in time an organization may be dominated by a particular rationality—expressed, perhaps, through the interests and power positions of scientists or technologists or finance or marketing groups—that dominance is always subject to intraorganizational and environmental changes. The micropolitics of the firm are inextricably linked to the macropolitics of the firm. Nowhere is this more clearly expressed at the moment than in tracing how the economic policies of the Thatcher and Reagan governments are altering the resource base of many public organizations in the United Kingdom and the United States and releasing new waves of micro- and macroorganizational politics.

While the concern for organizational resources is likely to be a continuing feature of organizational life and may be expressed differently in one organization than another, politics in organizations breed in times of change. The point about organizational changes is that, to a greater or lesser degree, they are likely to threaten the existing distribution of organizational resources as they are represented in salaries, promotion opportunities, and control of tasks, people, information, and new areas of a business. Additional resources may be created and appear to fall within the jurisdiction of a group or individual who had previously not been a claimant in a particular area. This group or its principal representative may see this as an opportunity to increase its power, status, and rewards in the organization. Others may see their interests threatened by the change, and needs for security or the maintenance of power may provide the impetus for resistance. In all these ways, new political energy is released and, ultimately, the existing distribution of power endangered.

These processes are likely to receive their more volatile expression not, as is often imagined, during the implementation of changes but during the decision to go ahead with the change (Mumford and Pettigrew, 1975). Constraints are set during the decision stage that can make resistance and maneuvering at later stages of the change mere ritualistic gestures. The issue, therefore, is less one of where and when political energy is likely to be released than one of the extent to which it will be released within the change process. Among other factors influencing the extent of political behavior will be how aware individuals and groups become about resources during early discussions of the change, the actual objective redistribution of resources consequent to the change, how critical the change is to any group, and that group's capacity to mobilize power to protect its interests.

There is, of course, a considerable difference between awareness by an interest group of the impact of change on its position and its ability to translate that heightened awareness into effective action. Consciousness of the implications of a change may have to be tied not only to the awareness that the interest group has of its potential power resources but also to the tactical manner in which those resources are used in negotiating the parameters and processes of implementation of change. It has been suggested elsewhere (Pettigrew, 1975b) that the power resources of expertise, control over information, political access and sensitivity, assessed stature, and group support may be of considerable importance in making and preventing changes from happening.

More recently (Pettigrew, 1977, 1979), this resource view of power and political process has been complemented by another perspective on organizations, which seeks to draw out the synergy between a political and a cultural analysis of organizational life.

The acts and processes associated with *politics as the management of meaning* represent conceptually the overlap between a concern with the political and a concern with the cultural analyses of organizations. A central concept linking political and cultural analysis is legitimacy. The management of meaning refers to a process of symbol construction and value use designed both to create legitimacy for one's actions, ideas, and demands and to delegitimize the demands of one's opponents. Key concepts for analyzing these processes of legitimization and delegitimization are symbolism, language, belief, and myth.

In the pursuit of our everyday tasks and objectives, it is all too easy to forget the less rational and instrumental, the more expressive social tissue around us that gives those tasks meaning. Yet, in order for people to function within any given setting, they must have a continuing sense of what that reality is all about in order for it to be acted upon. Culture is the system of such publicly and collectively accepted meanings operating for a given group at a given time. This system of terms, forms, categories, and images interprets a people's own situation to themselves. Indeed, what is supposed to be distinctive about human beings compared with other animals is their capacity to invent and communicate determinants of their own behavior (White, 1949; Cassirer, 1953). While providing a general sense of orientation, culture treated as a unitary concept in this way lacks analytical bite. A more useful approach is to regard culture as the source of a family of concepts and to explore the role that symbolism, language, belief, and myth play in creating practical effects.

Language provides order and coherence, cause-effect relationships—rationales—in times of confusion and transition. Contextually appropriate words may be used to give legitimacy to faded causes and new ideas or to breathe life back into established practices that are under threat. In a competitive situation, there is clearly a point where ideas for change may become unsupportable, and the issue becomes not one of mobilizing power for the pre-existing idea but one of seeing how the idea can be modified and connected to rising values and environmental priorities, so that its power requirements can be assembled. Metaphors and myths help to simplify—to give meaning to—complex issues that evoke concern. Myths serve also to legitimate the present in terms of a perhaps glorious past and to explain away the pressures for change that may be caused by the discrepancies between what is happening and what ought to be happening. In these various ways, it may be possible for interest groups to justify continuity in the face of change and change in the face of attempts to preserve continuity.

One of the logical problems that the political and cultural view of process shares, potentially at least, with other process theories is the difficulty of demonstrating that the process does in fact produce the observed outcome. In some cases—for example, maximizing and "satisficing" explanations—no process information is actually offered. The reader is expected merely to accept that outcomes have been produced as a result of "black box" notions such as maximizing and "satisficing." Political explanations of outcomes can likewise end up as tautologies if, for example, it is merely inferred that the possession of a power resource such as wealth means that some individual or group is powerful. A more satisfactory explanation would, in this case, have to demonstrate how the possession and tactical use of some resource—for example, wealth—was connected to the achievement of some practical outcome. The challenge with the political and cultural view of process is, however, much greater, for what is being proposed here is not a framework to examine just front-stage decision making and power but also back-stage decision making and, therefore, *control*. The front-stage view of decision making and power closely resembles Lukes's (1974) one-dimensional and two-dimensional views of power, while the interest in deeper processes of control confirms to Lukes's third dimension of power. As Hardy (1983) has succinctly put it, a concern with both power and control as explanations of, in this case, choice and change process would in effect correspond to two uses of power—power used to *defeat* competition in a choice or change process and power used to *prevent* competition in a choice or change process. In both of these processes, there would be an explanatory role for unobtrusive systems of power derived from the generation and manipulation of symbols, language, belief, and ideology—from culture creation—and from the more public face of power expressed through the possession, control, and tactical use of overt sources of power, such as position, force, or expertise.

There are two further essential points to derive from this way of thinking about process. The first is that structures, cultures, and strategies are being treated here not just as neutral, functional constructs connectable to some system need, such as efficiency or adaptability; those constructs are viewed as capable of serving to protect the interests of dominant groups. This means that not only can the existing bias of the structures and cultures of an organization in general terms protect dominant groups by reducing the chances of challenge, but features of intraorganizational context and socioeconomic context can be mobilized by dominant or aspiring groups in order to legitimize existing definitions of the core strategic concerns, to help justify new priorities, and to delegitimize other novel and threatening definitions of the organization's situation. These points, as we shall see, are as pertinent to understanding processes of choice and change as they are to achieving practical outcomes in strategic change. As Normann (1977, p. 161) has so aptly put it, "the only way to bring about lasting change and to foster an ability to deal with new situations is by influencing the conditions that determine the interpretation of situations and the regulation of ideas."

The preceding political and cultural view of process gives a central place to the processes through which strategies and changes are legitimized and delegitimized. The content of strategy, the other leg of our three-legged stool of content, context, and process, thus is ultimately a product of a legitimization process shaped by political/cultural considerations and expressed in rational/analytical terms. But no amount of theoretical interest in legitimization processes for new and old ideas or in the mobilization of contexts and languages to achieve practical effects will help us to study choice and change empirically unless we can temporarily locate human beings seeking to adjust social and organizational contexts to meet their ends. The following section, on contextualism, sketches out a way of trying to do that.

### Contextualism as a Mode of Analysis

One of the differences in the social sciences between so-called quantitative and qualitative research approaches is that the techniques and methods of the quantitative work have been so much more effectively turned into procedures that can then be described, learned, and practiced. Given that the types of problems and kinds of questions asked by qualitative researchers are, by their nature, likely to be more indefinite and the kinds of approaches used to tackle those problems more likely to require craft rather than technician skills, it may be unreasonable and certainly unrealistic to expect the methods of qualitative researchers to be as readily proceduralized as have been those of scholars using quantitative approaches. But the fact that the task of describing the craft of qualitative research is difficult does not absolve the researchers working in this way from the responsibility of trying to describe what they do. This is so not only because, if there is more than the average amount of intuition, interpretation, and structuring through language in the qualitative research process, then it is perfectly reasonable for process researchers to be hoist with their own petard and asked what process they went through to attain their outcome, but also because younger scholars interested in doing research the qualitative way may actually derive some benefit from appreciating the theory of method practiced by more experienced qualitative researchers. The December 1979 edition of the *Administrative Science Quarterly* has helped to draw out some of the ideas about theory of method that may be useful, but Chris Argyris (1970, 1982) and Donald Schön (1983) are rare among scholars in consistently and creatively thinking and writing about the craft and, some would say, crafty process of intervening in systems for the purposes of qualitative research and consultancy.

I offer this glimpse of my own theory of method as a modest attempt to sketch out a way of thinking about doing process research, and I hope that others will do the same. Presented here, it may appear as an intendedly rational strategy conceived before action, but, in fact, much of it was conceived and organized as the result of a series of research projects using longitudinal processual analyses (Pettigrew, 1973, 1975a, 1979, 1985). However, what follows should be treated as an idealized view, never to be completely realized and certainly to be tuned according to the vagaries and surprises of different contexts.

A contextualist analysis of a process such as strategic decision making and change draws on phenomena at vertical and horizontal levels of analysis and the interconnections between those levels through time. The vertical level refers to the interdependencies between higher or lower levels of analysis upon phenomena to be explained at some further level; for example, the impact of a changing socioeconomic context on features of intraorganizational context and interest-group behavior. The horizontal level refers to the sequential interconnectedness among phenomena in historical, present, and future time. An approach that offers both multilevel, or vertical, analysis and processual, or horizontal, analysis is said to be contextualist in character. Any wholly contextualist analysis would have the following characteristics: (1) It would require a clearly delineated but theoretically and empirically connectable set of levels of analysis. Within each level of analysis and, of course, depending upon the focus of explanation, there would be specified a set of cross-sectional categories. (2) It would require a clear description of the process or processes under examination. Basic to the notion of a processual analysis is that an organization or any other social system may profitably be explored as a continuing system, with a past, a present, and a future. Sound theory must, therefore, take into account the history and future of a system and relate them to the present. The process itself is seen as a continuous, interdependent sequence of actions and events that is being used to explain the origins, continuance, and outcome of some phenomenon. At the level of the actor, the language of process is most obviously characterized in terms of the verb forms *interacting, acting, reacting, responding,* and *adapting,* while at the system level, the interest is in emerging, elaborating, mobilizing, continuing, changing, dissolving, and transforming. The focus is on the language systems of becoming rather than of being—of actors and systems in motion.

Any processual analysis of this form requires as a preliminary the set of cross-sectional categories identified in point (1). Change processes can be identified and studied only against a background of structure or relative constancy. Figure needs ground.

(3) The processual analysis requires a motor, or theory or theories, to drive the process, part of which will require the specification of the model of human beings underlying the research. Within this research on change, strong emphasis is given both to

humans' capacity and desire to adjust social conditions to meet their ends and to the part played by power relationships in the emergence and ongoing development of the processes being examined.

(4) Crucial, however, to this whole approach to contextualist analysis is the way that the contextual variables and categories in the vertical analysis are linked to the processes under observation in the horizontal analysis. The view taken here is that it is not sufficient to treat context either just as descriptive background or as an eclectic list of antecedents that somehow shape the process. Neither, of course, given the dangers of simple determinism, should structure or context be seen as just constraining process. Rather, this approach recognizes that processes both are constrained by structures and shape structures, either in the direction of preserving them or in that of altering them. In the past, structural analyses emphasizing abstract dimensions and contextual constraints have been regarded as incompatible with processual analyses stressing action and strategic conduct. Here an attempt is being made to combine these two forms of description and analysis, first of all, by conceptualizing structure and context not just as a barrier to action but as essentially involved in its production (Giddens, 1979; Ranson, Hinings, and Greenwood, 1980) and, secondly, by demonstrating how aspects of structure and context are mobilized or activated by actors and groups as they seek to obtain outcomes important to them.

In this analytical approach to understanding the origins, development, and implementation of organizational change, the interest, therefore, is in multilevel theory construction. An attempt will be made to formulate models of higher-level factors and processes, lower-level factors and processes, and the manner in which they interact. It is recognized that each level often has its own properties, processes, and relationships—its own momentum—and that, while phenomena at one level are not reducible to or cannot be inferred from those at another level, a key to the analysis is tracking the interactions between levels through time.

The above represent some broad principles informing a contextualist analysis of process. But how might those principles be translated into a series of practical components to inform data collection and analysis in any particular study? Figure 1 lays out in

Figure 1. Components of Analysis: Context and Process.

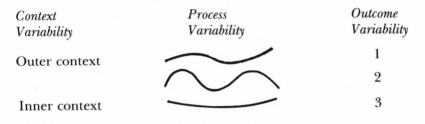

| Context Variability | Process Variability | Outcome Variability |
|---|---|---|
| Outer context | | 1 |
| | | 2 |
| Inner context | | 3 |

highly simplified diagrammatic form a possible series of interlinked components in a contextualist analysis.

Figure 1 indicates that there are three basic elements to a contextualist analysis: the process component, the context component, and the outcome component of the process under investigation. In terms of the practical research questions of gathering data and sorting those data into broad categories for analysis, the basic steps may be described as follows:

1. Describe the process or processes under investigation, which, for example, may be processes of conflict, decision making, or changing.
2. Expose in these descriptions any variability or constancy between the processes. This variability is represented in Figure 1 by the curved lines.
3. Begin the analysis of these processes by using existing theories of process or developing novel ones.
4. Begin the task of pinpointing the levels of analysis in the context and some of the categories or variables in those different levels of analysis. Are, for example, the levels in the context to be restricted to features of the intraorganizational context through which the processes immediately flow, or is the analysis to include aspects of the other context, such as the social and economic conditions surrounding the organization at any point in time?
5. Having established the levels of analysis and categories in the

context, begin the task of describing and analyzing any variability across the contexts through which the processes are
unfolding. Seek also to describe and analyze trends and developments in the various contexts through time.

6.  Begin to consider the alternative criteria that can be used to
    judge the outcome of the process under study. This is a difficult
    practical research problem. Good sources to assist reflection on
    this problem are contained in the literature seeking to assess the
    success and failure and other outcomes of social movement
    organizations (Goldstone, 1980; Gamson, 1980).

Important as the uncovering of the above components is to
the success of the contextualist analysis, the key to the analysis lies
in positing and establishing relationships among context, process,
and outcome. In short, what are the relationships, if any, among
variability in context, variability in process, and variability in
outcome? It is in the craft skills of unraveling and establishing
relationships among those three components of the analysis that the
major benefits and principle problems of this kind of contextualist
mode of analysis lie.

### Strategic Change in Imperial Chemical Industries

Researchers who choose to conduct processual analyses have
usually decided to trade off generality over actors and systems for
realism of context and scope for theoretical interpretation. What
they have usually also committed themselves to is presenting their
findings in book-length form, especially if the research was conducted on a comparative and longitudinal basis. Even by collapsing
the time scale of the ICI research by half and using only the head-
office corporate-change process as a case, what follows is a very
limited treatment of the context, content, and process of strategic
change in ICI. For those who would like to read a further and more
appropriate description and analysis of the divisional and corporate
strategic changes in ICI, I can only suggest that they read Pettigrew
(1985). In the meantime, this description and interpretation of
the ICI corporate-change process between 1972 and 1982 should be

regarded as highly selective illustrations of much more complex processes of strategic change.

This case illustrates how much the formulation of strategic change is dependent upon managing its context and process. The process skills at the most general level involve handling the relationship between the content of strategy and its context. The case illustrates the deep-seated organizational cultural and political roots of strategy and the existence of dominating rationalities in organizations that provide the frame of reference by which individuals and groups attach meaning to and make sense of intraorganizational and socioeconomic action and trends developing around them. The case also points to the enormous difficulties of breaking down such dominating rationalities once a particular marriage of strategic content, context, and process has become established. The breaking down of established patterns of strategic content, context, and process is seen as a long-term conditioning process influenced by the interest and, above all, persistence of visionary leaders, the changing patterns of competition between individuals and groups representing different rationalities, and the massive enabling opportunities created by environmental change, changes in the power distribution of the company, and the connecting of what are perceived to be coherent solutions at particular points in time to culturally legitimate problems.

Regarding strategic decision making and change as continuous processes means that breaking into the process to note a beginning is an arbitrary act. The year 1972 has been chosen as a starting point for examining a period of continuity and change in ICI because it was in that year that the main board of ICI, the ultimate decision-making body for ICI's worldwide interests, decided to set up a board organization committee as a subcommittee of the main board, which was to examine the organization of the board and its method of working and the top management structure of the group; to consider the organization that would be appropriate regarding the changes that were expected to take place in the group's business over the next decade; and to make recommendations.

In fact, the beginnings of high-level pressure to change ICI's top governance system and structure had probably been in 1967, when one of the deputy chairman candidates in the election for chairman of ICI had tied his campaign for election to a program of strategic change to reduce the complexity and increase the responsiveness of ICI's top structure. This deputy chairman badly miscalculated the mood of the main board, and he and his ideas for change were rejected.

Exactly the same fate befell the board organization committee's report prepared in 1973. The committee of a deputy chairman and three executive directors took evidence from executive and nonexecutive directors, division chairmen, the heads of some overseas companies, and the main United Kingdom general managers. Their report contained much criticism of ICI's top structure and the culture surrounding its operation. The report recommended a form of organization that would have been more compatible with a move by ICI to develop markets in North America and continental Western Europe than with their existing preoccupation with the nine United Kingdom divisions. It also suggested that executive directors and, therefore, the main board should spend much more time on strategic thinking about the size and shape of ICI's worldwide interests and recommended a smaller main board, the end of deputy chairman status as a distinct level in the structure, and wider involvement of division chairmen in matters that affected them.

An executive director reported that, at the main board meeting called to consider these recommendations, the organization committee's report "sank at the first shot," or, as another executive director put it, the organization committee "presented the parcel to the board, and the board unwrapped it and threw the parcel out of the window." Both executive directors blamed the failure of this change attempt on individual directors' fears of this degree of radical change and the inadequate process adopted by the committee: "It had done just about everything you could have done to get it wrong. It had taken massive amounts of evidence and so aroused massive expectations. It had barely reported back to its colleagues, and it had not really carried its chairman with it. . . . Also, it doesn't take a genius to see that a hell of a lot of executive directors would have been out of a job if this change had gone through. So again the working through had not been done." "There was little lobbying, persuasion, or involvement of other people by the organization committee."

Someone close to events at that time also pointed out the poor process plan of the committee and the fact that, with the financial results as good as they were in 1973, there was no desire to rock the boat that fundamentally: "In that sense, the process was wrong—it was a misdiagnosis of the power structure in the board and the readiness for fundamental change. They [the organization committee] were really talking about a culture change. People could give lip service to bits of it, but when it was put back in terms of 'prove this is better than what we have,' why upset the company? There was no external crisis, no business problems, so it was theory against theory."

Nine years later, in the quite different business, economic, and political conditions of 1982, and with a different cast of characters on the ICI main board, nearly all the recommendations presented as one person's solution in 1967 and as a subgroup's perception of a problem and solution in 1973 were now more universally accepted as a problem and a solution that fitted a context. By 1982, therefore, the strategic changes raised some ten to fifteen years earlier could now go ahead. Those nine years between 1973 and 1982 can be understood as a long, meandering conditioning process, whereby a small number of key people on the main board, assisted by a few internal and external organization development (OD) consultants, raised the level of concern and dissatisfaction with the status quo in ICI and helped to create flows of information, meetings, organization mechanisms, and processes whereby a critical mass of senior people in ICI then began to acknowledge that questions of organization, systems, and management culture and processes were legitimately connectable to issues of business environment, strategy, and business survival. Throughout this process of questioning the old and flag-waving for the new, and increasingly supported by a change caucus on the main board, two executive directors, Richard Nelson and Tony Woodburn (personal names used in this section are fictitious), always persistently, sometimes right out in the open, but often of necessity implicitly and quietly, in turn pushed for the initiation of strategic change and then, in the face of opposition, backed off, until the environment changed to the point where a marriage of convenience was possible among the content, context, and process for creating strategic change.

In the depths of ICI's business difficulties of late 1981, Richard Nelson was appointed chairman. A main board director not normally associated with the "for change caucus" on the board during the 1970s had this to say why Nelson got the chairman's job: "The events of the last three years have shown that ICI's old way of doing things and old approach to a number of questions haven't served it terribly well. Whether it would have been possible to have done things differently, had clearer foresight, and taken better avoiding action I think is exceedingly debatable. But with hindsight, the way we had done things hadn't served one terribly well— there could be no argument about that. Therefore, there was a realization that things needed to be different, and the man to my knowledge for the last eight years in Millbank who has said most persistently and consistently, and without too much regard for how the message was received—there are a lot of things we ought to be doing differently—was Richard. Change was needed; the obvious change agent was given the job."

*A Context that Created a Culture of Inertia: ICI in 1973.* Richard Nelson was promoted from his position as chairman of ICI's petrochemicals division onto the main board in March 1973. In 1972, when the board organization committee was created, ICI was not only Britain's biggest industrial company; it was, according to the prevailing rates of exchange, the biggest chemical company in the world. Sales in 1972 were £1.694 billion and assets £1.869 billion. ICI had 350 subsidiaries and was active in all major industrial and most nonindustrial countries. However, in spite of this international spread, ICI was in culture and management almost entirely British. The British factories were by far the most important part of ICI's manufacturing interests. £2.91 billion of ICI's overseas sales of £9.18 billion in 1972 were exported from the United Kingdom, which accounted for 63 percent of total sales. Counting subsidiaries, ICI employed 132,000 people in 1972. About two thirds of the total work force were employed in Britain.

ICI was divided into nine largely autonomous and profit-accountable divisions, answering to the main board and monitored through a system of central planning and budget controls. Some of the divisions were and are substantial businesses in their own right—Mond, for example, employed 17,000 people and had sales of £3.40 billion in 1972, ranking it thirty-second among Britain's largest companies.

ICI's head office was and still is at Millbank, London SW1. The main board and executive directors were resident at Millbank and maintained effective strategic control at the center over the divisions and subsidiaries through two main elements of reserve powers. The main board had final say over the investment decisions that determined ICI's future shape and also was the final arbiter of personnel policy.

In 1972, because of a combination of the growth of existing markets and the creation of new markets by the invention of new products, the chemical industry in the United Kingdom was growing at twice the rate of manufacturing industry as a whole. ICI was producing an enormous diversity of products, ranging from fertilizers to artificial fibers, explosives, paints, plastics, petrochemicals, and pesticides. More than half of ICI's sales in 1972 were accounted for by products not on the market fifteen years before.

Since its creation in 1926, as a buffer against the size and strength of the large U.S. and German companies, ICI had more than demonstrated its capacity to create new products and invent and absorb new technological processes, but in the 1970s, ICI discovered that more than technology changes. During the 1970s, ICI slowly came to terms with their up-to-then dependence on an inflation-ridden and declining British economy and a worldwide chemical industry where the premium of chemical growth over general growth rates was reduced and in some sectors eliminated. By the end of the 1970s, there was massive overcapacity in the European fibers, petrochemicals, and plastics industries, and throughout the 1970s, ICI, like all other large British manufacturing firms, had to learn to live with the rise and then increasingly confident use of trade union power and government intervention in business affairs. Finally, the arrival of the Thatcher Conservative government on the scene in 1979, pursuing as it did strict monetarist economic policies, meant high interest rates, a recession in industrial production, and mounting unemployment. The further fall in

ICI's United Kingdom customer base and, worse still, the sharply rising value of sterling in 1980 and 1981 in relation to the U.S. dollar and the deutsche mark meant cheaper chemical imports from continental Western Europe and North America and a trend for British chemical prices to move out of line with those in continental Europe. These various environmental pressures and the ways they were seen, interpreted, and acted upon produced, between 1970 and 1982, the business results shown in Table 1.

There is not space here to analyze and interpret these figures, except to note that the expected cyclical low points in the chemical industry of 1971 and 1975 were reflected in ICI's figures and to pinpoint that ICI's considerable fall from grace in 1980 was sustained through 1981 and 1982. It is also worth noting that the board organization committee was constituted in a relatively poor year following the 1971 downturn, and the radical strategic changes recommended and repulsed in 1973 coincided with all but the best ratio of trading profits to sales in the 1970s and early 1980s.

ICI's core strategy in the 1970s was to try to reduce its dependence on United Kingdom and Commonwealth markets by

**Table 1. ICI Worldwide Sales and Trading Profit,<br>1970–1982 (in Millions of Pounds).**

| Year | Total Sales | Trading Profit | Ratio of Trading Profit to Sales |
|------|------------|----------------|----------------------------------|
| 1970 | 1,462 | 159 | 10.9 |
| 1971 | 1,524 | 130 | 8.5 |
| 1972 | 1,694 | 141 | 10.0 |
| 1973 | 2,166 | 329 | 15.2 |
| 1974 | 2,955 | 461 | 15.6 |
| 1975 | 3,129 | 325 | 10.4 |
| 1976 | 4,135 | 514 | 12.4 |
| 1977 | 4,663 | 545 | 11.7 |
| 1978 | 4,533 | 497 | 11.0 |
| 1979 | 5,368 | 634 | 11.8 |
| 1980 | 5,715 | 332 | 5.8 |
| 1981 | 6,581 | 425 | 6.4 |
| 1982 | 7,358 | 366 | 5.0 |

acquiring and creating assets and increased market share in North America and continental Western Europe and by majoring in a number of strategic business sectors, such as petrochemicals, plastics, and general chemicals, where it had competitive market, technological, and production strength. The fact that ICI imperfectly realized that strategy in the 1970s was felt by the authors of the 1973 board organization report and by the likes of Nelson and Woodburn to be attributable largely to the top structure and culture of ICI. The focal point of Nelson's persistent pressure for strategic change in the 1970s was therefore on the top governance and culture of ICI and the dominating rationality of the period—the twin obsessions with fixed capital and cash management. The problem that Nelson and the change caucus faced was that ICI in the 1970s still had a structure and culture that fitted Anthony Sampson's 1960s view of ICI as "the Slumbering Giant."

The point has been made that ICI has been very much a British-based and -managed multinational company. There was a reduction from 52 percent to 43 percent in the percentage of total group sales attributed to United Kingdom customers between 1963 and 1973, but between 1973 and 1981, that percentage fell only another 4 percent, to 39 percent. In 1973, 66 percent of ICI's worldwide employees were working in the United Kingdom divisions, and, notwithstanding interests in North America and Western Europe, the main board and Millbank were heavily preoccupied with the United Kingdom Divisions. ICI was often referred to in the press as Britain's largest manufacturing company, and its prestige offices in London SW1 were within ten minutes' walk of Parliament, Whitehall, and the main government departments and the headquarters of the two major political parties. When and if ICI executive directors left the company, they often became chairpersons of large but lesser United Kingdom companies or played prominent roles in employers' organizations, such as the Confederation of British Industry. The financial fortunes of ICI were regarded as a barometer for more general upward and downward movements in the stock market, and, certainly outside the company, there was the view that ICI was a British institution and had to behave and be seen to behave in an appropriately ethical, regulated, and stable fashion.

The tradition in ICI had, of course, been to recruit first-class scientists and engineers and turn them into managers. The requirement from the company's beginning to develop new products and processes and to turn product out in volume into well-regulated markets meant that technologists and people with production experience were pre-eminent. As one person put it, "things were produced, and chaps were told to sell them. You didn't really closely follow the market." The combination of engineering and production bias and the location in the British national culture were two key determinants of inertia in ICI. "The line of succession [to top positions] has been 90 percent technologists of one sort or another, all coming out of the same kinds of schools, playing rugby together at the same kinds of places, and having the same kinds of orientations to life. . . .The marketing free-swinging businessman or the very innovative science type, as distinct from the good scientific analyst—the free-swingers and entrepreneurs have been in a minority in this company in strategic positions. Put that in the British culture, and you get a reinforcement for the inertia, because the British culture is not an entrepreneurial culture, it is an inventing culture."

Many of the people interviewed talked of ICI as a traditional, conservative organization, with images of the "great ship plowing through waters and not needing to change" and of well-tried and stable systems, layers of management hierarchy, bureaucratic stops derived from compartmentalization, and at the center a heavily functional or disciplinary organization. ICI was also described as an intellectual culture, and, while this had its plusses, "one of the minuses was that people tend to overintellectualize. We have wonderful seminars about almost everything." A further consistent theme was the difficulty of innovating. "There's a sense of continuity in this place that is old, traditional. It's a hard place to innovate. Change has to be evolutionary rather than revolutionary. The revolutionary is tolerated but seen as a bad boy." A main board director's summary view of the ICI culture picked up many of these points: "If you have an organization, which has been by and large successful, it's fifty years old, it's hierarchical, it's almost totally inbred, it advances layer by layer, rank by rank, it has to be very, very conservative. And unless it falls off a cliff as it did in 1980, then people feel just as they would in a plant control room on a Friday afternoon, 'keep your hands in your pockets, don't touch anything, it's Friday, the plant's running well, isn't it?' "

If conservatism was a theme often mentioned to describe the ICI culture, then consensus decision making was the key theme in discussions of the main board culture of the 1970s. ICI twice had dynamic, autocratic chairmen, once before, during, and after the Second World War in the persona of Lord McGowan, and then again between 1960 and 1968 with Sir Paul Chambers. Reader (1975) describes how the ICI main board effectively curbed McGowan's executive powers as managing director in the late 1930s but allowed him to continue as chairman with his autocratic inclinations trimmed by a series of committees. Sir Paul Chambers grew in power while he was chairman to the point where he was effectively able to make appointments to the board, and so his personal strategy for ICI became the strategy that ICI acted upon. Chambers's maxim of growth, caught in the catchphrase he is supposed to have recited to division chairmen, "Give me a good profitable project, and I will get you the money," eventually led to ICI's cash crisis of 1966, the rise of planning as an activity in the company, and Chambers's exit from ICI in 1968, two years earlier than planned. The tenure of each of the next four chairmen did not exceed four years, and all behaved as first among equals, thus reaffirming a consensual style of board decision making.

Without doubt, the 1970s pattern of giving each chairman a three- to four-year term acted as a brake on change. One executive director remarked: "If you have a chairman who has a three-year stint in office, the first year he's not going to lash about him too much because he wants to establish himself. The second year is a year when he can lash about, but the third year he's already saying, 'I don't want to prejudice the position of my successor,' and guys on the board are not wanting to take big risks, because there's always one or two competing to be the next chairman. So if you analyze the thing, you find that you only have one year in three— rather like elephants—when you can mate and make it happen." Division chairmen who became executive directors in the 1970s talked of entry onto the main board as "a numbing experience after being a chief executive." One said, "it was the nearest thing to

Devil's Island I'd known, boredom, not brutality. . . ritual dancing time and time again, failure to take the decision, walking away from decisions. Continual frustration through the consensus board, where one or two strong and opinionated voices could stop the whole thing stone dead.''

Overlaid on this was the two-tier system of having a chairman and three or four deputy chairmen acting as an inner cabinet in relation to the remaining executive directors. ''We had a two-tier system of a chairman and three deputy chairmen, which wasn't clear, and I felt that, well, you can't be let out on your own yet, and your instinct was to go on and continue doing a division chairman's job, but this just drives the layer below you potty.''

This tendency for executive directors to continue to try to act as superoperators alongside the operating units caused frustration and defensiveness with the chief executives of those units. But, more importantly, the policy group's system and ICI's top-level obsession with capital expenditure and cash management meant that the board became more and more involved with monitoring the operating units and capital-expenditure decision making and less and less with the strategic direction of the ICI group. One executive director summed up the problem in these terms: ''There were two obsessions, one the obsession with fixed capital, and the other—and by obsession I mean the thing the mind is always on—the other was a fear of running into another cash crisis like the one in 1966. There was an enormous cultural force pressing people's minds onto fixed capital and cash management. Anything very quickly boiled back again to the capital program and what are we going to do six months hence—and when you'd had that capital expenditure, the six months after that. The key constraint was how much money it would be prudent to spend in the ensuing twelve months. This was something the treasurer's department and planning department worked on quite closely, with the finance director putting in rules of prudence and the treasurer's and planning departments using that to make recommendations on the total size of the fixed-capital program.''

In this atmosphere, the planning department worked on the annual cycles of finance and capital and helped create mechanisms such as the business ranking system and strategic business sectors to allow the board to distinguish between the operating units more or less deserving of additional capital. Capital in a world full of technologists and powerful production people became a "virility symbol," and division chairmen and policy group directors measured one another by their success in acquiring fixed assets. Enormous "sectoral pressure" was put on the board by policy group directors pressing for their territorial or product area. Given the consensus style of the board, this led to a lot of "I'll support you in this proposal if you support me in that one." An executive director explained how the drive for board consensus managed to ally itself with the sectoral pressure coming onto the board from the policy group system and the policy group directors: "Those that got to the top in the divisions and came onto the main board were very clear that fracturing in a division was highly undesirable. They were equally strong-minded people who were not going to be done down. So you had to have a situation where strong-minded people wouldn't be done down and there would be no fracturing, and this produces a tremendously strong force for consensus—not because people tremendously want consensus, but because anything else is unthinkable."

This "smoothing rather than problem-solving culture" eventually led to some inadequate selection of capital and left an undue capital burden in some very embarrassing places. More significantly, perhaps, the obsessions of capital and cash meant that "the concept of explicit longer-term strategies in which individual capital expenditures were steps really was absent."

The Millbank head-office culture was, of course, dominated by two features: the chairmen and executive directors on the sixth floor and the general managers or their equivalents—the nine "barons"—with their functional or disciplinary departments. One executive director thought "the whole Millbank thing" to be wrong: "It gives a feeling of comfort, of immutability, permanence, lack of change, hierarchical organization. . . . If I appear in the cafeteria for a pie and a pint, it's almost as if spaceman has appeared. . . . On the sixth floor, every door is shut. There's the affectation that no one had their name on the door—you could find people wandering around this bloody floor for hours trying to find somebody!"

Another executive director was less concerned with the atmosphere of hierarchy and status in Millbank than with the feelings of lack of identity and purpose in the head office compared with a division: "There's no identity in this building in the way there is identity in a division from its production operations and its desire to make money out of its products. There is a highly functional organization in this building, with not much interpenetration between those functions. There aren't the policy, the objectives, the singleness of purpose you have in a division."

Given the functional organization at Millbank, it was natural that people should acquire much of their consistent identity from the floor that they were on and the pattern of work that came from their expertise in their function. Millbank, with all its highly intelligent functional experts, epitomized the intellectual side of ICI's culture. A departmental head in Millbank described what the norms were in the 1970s in these terms: "Be a good chap—say some interesting things in an intellectual way that are stimulating and challenging, but don't expect that anything will happen as a result of them. You will get a name for being a bright boy with all sorts of ideas. But don't push things too far." The final part of that quotation indicates what the central taboo was: "Don't rock the boat, don't dig too deep, we're pretty well all right, thank you, we know most of it. You can dig too deep, too fast. This boat has stood the test of time."

An executive director summarized how the intellectual atmosphere in Millbank, the concern for stability, and the smoothing, risk-aversive culture at board level and among the general managers all contributed to influence the pattern of decision making at the center: "The whole physical environment was structured to dealing in a very hygienic way—a splendid paper, a limited discussion, perhaps not an entirely open discussion, leading to a decision. There are many topics where perhaps one wants to talk to people for longer, and in more depth."

These, then, were some of the critical features of the structure and culture of the ICI top governance system in the 1970s—the short-tenure, non-chief-executive chairmen, the two-tier main board, and executive directors with portfolios allocated by product, territory, and function; the consensus style of decision making on the main board; the cultural obsession with cash management and capital expenditure; the game playing between the operating units and the main board and among the policy group directors over the annual capital-expenditure allocation process; the power of the policy groups and the influence of the planning and treasurer's departments and the limited time the main board spent formulating macroplans and strategies on the shape, size, and growth of the group; the compartmentalized and intellectual culture of Millbank; and an expectation that, with continuing financial success but not necessarily brilliant financial results, the great ship would continue to plow its way through the waters. The question was: Could this smoothing rather than problem-solving culture be convinced that issues of organization and culture could influence business effectiveness, and, if that could be accepted at an intellectual level, was it possible for the ICI collegial board system to radically change itself?

*The Process of Strategic Change.* Before Richard Nelson formally became an executive director in April 1973, he was asked to join the 1972 board organization committee. The failure of that committee to influence the board did not deter him from seeking what he felt were appropriate top-level changes. Interviewed for the first time in this study in 1976, Nelson described his change philosophy on entering the board in these terms:

> In my view, the ways in which we have tried to change our organization in the past have been wrong— because the approach has been to wait until some bit is evidently hurting and then to move in on that bit. . . . It then takes quite a while for that change to become effective. If, as is usually the case, you are trying to change attitudes, you are in for a four- to five-year haul—you're too bloody late, you are dealing with the symptoms of the last war. . . so I see my role, since I became organization director, as being to stop trying to frig around with bits of the company and really concentrate on getting some major changes in the board. . . . I believe we need to: (1) try to read the environment about five years ahead and (2) try to aim

our objectives five years ahead and only then to start
intervening organizationally. In the meantime, you
have to make some interventions. . . but you have to
make sure that these changes will be reinforcing to the
big changes you are trying to aim for. . . so that the
initiative has been and still is to try to make the board
change.

But, tactically, how was he to achieve that objective? Clearly, with
the board organization committee of 1973 now stone dead, he
realized that he would have to wait until the encumbent chairman
retired, seek in the meantime to plan to influence the incoming
chairman, and use his board responsibility as organization and
services director "to legitimately roam all over the place. . . in a
fairly structured way in order to get some of the real dissatisfactions
of ordinary guys with the performance of the board recognized."

In highly synoptical form, these are some of the core elements of the strategic change process between 1973 and 1982:

1. During late 1973 and on into 1974, Nelson encouraged a
number of things to happen, some of which were conventional
moves to create change and others decidedly counter-cultural. He set
up a room on the directors' floor at Millbank where "anybody could
put up a chart to bring the bad news to the attention of the board
without having to stand up and say 'boo.' . . . I got a number of
studies done of views of where the board was going. . . and I started
a real effort to try to get the staff in Millbank to operate better and
again put pressure on the board."

2. More significantly, perhaps, in terms of the long-term
structural development of ICI, Nelson was able to use his role as
board liaison director for the petrochemicals division to set up a
petrochemicals products directors' advisory committee. This was
the first mechanism to pull together all the chairmen of divisions
connected with petrochemicals and the first tangible move on the
chess board toward creating a heavy-chemicals business organization in the United Kingdom.

3. While all of these moves were being made, Nelson and an
internal OD consultant, Stewart Dudley, began to meet once every
three weeks to share, first of all, views about the organization

problem that ICI had at that time and then "to prepare a strategy for opening up a discussion with the main board" about those problems. The essence of their strategy was not to try to influence the outgoing chairman, Sir Ronald Lee, who was due to leave in March 1975, but to try to influence the next chairman, whom they expected to be Derek Roberts. Dudley wrote a paper, "A Look at ICI in 1974," to be used as the vehicle to draw the board into a serious discussion about organization matters. Dudley takes up the story: "We understood that Derek Roberts's appointment would be announced round about September 26, 1974. Our plan was to influence a group of directors by going to them individually with the 'ICI in 1974' note, rewriting it if they didn't agree with it, but slowly building up a note that was acceptable to a critical mass of directors on an individual level. We then planned to give that note to Derek Roberts immediately after his appointment, but before he formally became chairman in April 1975. We wanted to try to capture him in the period between knowing he was going to be chairman and his actually taking the job, in that pause period. Then we hoped he would pick up and validate the things that were being said to him." This carefully planned tactical exercise went badly astray when Nelson's secretary, in the absence of both Nelson and Dudley decided the "ICI in 1974" note was meant for a board agenda item titled "Review Company Progress" at a Monday-morning directors' meeting. She circulated Dudley's draft note to the chairman and all executive directors.

Nelson's report of what happened next "was that this produced the most fantastic explosion—absolutely marvelous. The chairman sent for me white with rage, lost his temper, and commanded that I withdraw it and fire Stewart. I said, 'no way, poor devil. I've asked him to do this. If you don't like it, fire me.' That was a real breakthrough in its own way, but it hadn't been designed. It meant that we were able to get Ron Mercer (an external OD consultant) to the chairman; it also meant that we were able to raise the pain level on the board so that, when Derek Roberts became chairman, he did his trips around the company to talk to people at various levels, and this again increased the pain level and began to open up the possibility of change."

Evidence that Sir Ronald Lee received Dudley's note with shock and bewilderment can be seen from his memorandum of August 6, 1974, to Richard Nelson. "Much of what is said in it is contrary to the impression I have gained traveling at home and abroad among the ICI organization. . . . Are you, or whoever, trying to tell me that my thirty-nine years have been totally wasted? Are you seeking to destroy my faith? Or are you making a bid for a new era launched by enlightened men?"

Mercer, the external consultant, was invited to see Sir Ronald Lee and then requested to write down his diagnosis and discuss his paper at a board meeting. Mercer remarked when he met the board as a group, "There were various degrees of belief and disbelief, but this helped to motivate what Derek Roberts was going to do when he took over." The minutes of the meeting ended, however, on a none-too-optimistic note: "An improvement in the general area covered by the discussion was most likely to be achieved by a fairly low-profile approach from the top, aiming at gradual rather than sudden or dramatic change."

There had been some movement, at least, in legitimizing changes in organization and top-management behavior as a topic for board discussion and also in opening the way for Mercer to work with the board in the future, but would any action follow this opening?

4. These processes, redirected by the secretarial error, nicely characterize the role that chance, opportunism, and environmental preparedness can play in hastening processes of change. But concrete change was still a long way off. The new chairman was persuaded to go out into the divisions and use diagnostic slice meetings to take the company pulse. More significantly, he practiced some norm breaking by taking the executive directors away for a two-day informal meeting to discuss the top structure and operation of the ICI group and then followed this up by setting up board task groups to examine a different aspect of organization change. The chairman was also persuaded to set up a board resource group, composed of Nelson, another executive director, and the internal and external consultants, Dudley and Mercer, "to provide personal support to the chairman when he is faced with the personal risk of validating new behavior and actions."

5. In the meantime, during the early 1970s, an informal meeting of division chairmen was formed, initially as a defensive maneuver against centrally created personnel policies and practices. This meeting of division chairmen had no position in the scheme of organization and was not recognized by the main board. Seeing that the main board was discussing the possibility of change, the division chairmen began to reach out for interpenetration with the board "so that decisions to change and thereby improve the company had our commitment."

As a result of a tortuous, subtle, and highly political process, the "shop stewards' committee" of the division chairman's meeting was eventually recognized and regulated as part of the ICI scheme of organization; and, more significantly, for the first time ever, in January 1977, a chairman's group conference was institutionalized into the ICI system of top-level governance. This conference became an important annual event, when the executive directors met with the division chairmen, the chief executives of the major overseas subsidiaries, and the United Kingdom general managers to discuss at length matters of substance about the policy, aims, and organization of the group. Subsequent chairman's group conferences became one of a series of legitimate administrative mechanisms that were used by the change caucus to sense, articulate, draw out, and in other ways mobilize illegitimate opinion.

6. The main board task groups continued throughout 1976 to agonize about the now familiar issues of the board: not spending sufficient time discussing key strategic issues, such as the long-term business strategy and shape of the group; not being able to have deep, objective discussions on key subjects and then come to crisp decisions; not being able to handle conflicts arising out of the product-territory-function matrix; spending too much time managing and not enough time directing; and spending too much time on United Kingdom affairs to the detriment of ICI's interests as an international operation. These issues, although never aired more comprehensively and openly than in 1976, were not resolved. Again they were left on the table. For all the effort, the right combination of political will and environmental pressures had not yet been assembled by 1976, and the changes that had appeared by then could still be described as cosmetic and not yet fundamental.

7. However, by 1977, the composition of the main board was beginning to change. As Mercer put it, "people were coming onto the board who were or came to be known as 'for change.'" The "young turks" were by no means uniform in their perspective or priorities for change. One stream of new thinking emphasized the importance of marketing and commercial skills alongside world-wide business strategies, as against the technical skills and preoccupations of older generations of ICI management. Another stream of new thinking, personified by Nelson and Woodburn, recognized the importance of international commercial acumen, saw that changes in the commercial sphere would also require a rethinking of the organization, the systems, and the culture of ICI, and gave some place to OD thinking and methods as the way of pushing those changes forward. But for those wishing for change, the pace was still too slow.

8. The rise of these new rationalities and the people associated with them was aided enormously by the worsening business scene of 1978 and 1979 and then by ICI's heavy-chemicals interests "falling off a cliff" in the spring of 1980. Faced with the gathering storm, the talk in ICI in 1978 was of the "vital importance of reducing costs," of "reducing group overheads." Other measures to improve profitability besides reducing numbers were also discussed. These included performing better in the marketplace, upgrading the quality of the customer base, and providing better technical service.

Signals that had been around for a while about the falling away of growth and overcapacity in the European heavy-chemicals sector began to be absorbed at the intellectual level and even contemplated at the heartfelt level. As it became clearer that ICI had been overinvesting and was continuing to overinvest for some of its markets and that there might be some very embarrassing clumps of underutilized capital around, the consensual decision-making system on the main board and the policy groups and planning systems that had produced some of those now-questionable decisions were themselves under question. The ethos of growth through strategic business sectors and capital expenditure was about to be fundamentally replaced by the rising ethos of survival through efficiency. Structural and cultural change as a solution was now legitimatized by a new context. But the difficulty remained of breaking the emerging problem into understandable, manageable, and actionable bits, of dividing the problem into legitimate packages, and of finding acceptable administrative mechanisms to focus people and energy to produce additive solutions in a form and at a pace that were politically and culturally acceptable. As one of the executive directors, still frustrated at the pace of change, put it, "Occasionally one would see the opportunity to put the ball into space and run after it."

The preceding brief process description stops short of chronicling the concrete-action phase of strategic change that occurred in ICI between 1979 and 1983. The outcomes of a long process of developing concern about a mismatch between ICI's business strategy, organization, and top governance and culture and its business and economic environment were the revolutionary changes in company ideology, structure, and strategy that finally came with the severe economic and chemicals recession of the early 1980s.

By 1979, a new and more integrated business organization and strategy had emerged for penetrating European markets. The fibers and organics divisions lost more assets and people. Assets in the two biggest loss-making divisions, petrochemicals and plastics, were closed, and then, in 1981, the two divisions were merged under a single, smaller board. Mond division took out £40 million of fixed costs by reducing the number of levels of management and cutting employees by around 30 percent in three years. The number of ICI's United Kingdom employees fell by 25 percent, from 89,400 to 67,300, between December 1979 and December 1982, as a result of the structural changes, additional changes in the service functions to the various United Kingdom divisions, and cuts in headquarters staff. With the arrival of Richard Nelson as chairman in April 1982, the ideological, top-governance, and stylistic changes that he and others had been championing for some years became manifest in changes in the role, style, and mode of operation of the main board and the decision to move out of the prestigious Millbank headquarters. Through all this, business strategy changes are becoming evident that are designed to reduce the proportion of ICI's total sales emanating from the low-growth heavy-chemicals sector, marshaling resources to buy further assets in specialty chemicals with high margins, such as pharmaceuticals, agrochemicals, and chemicals used in electronics, and the continuing talk of a big U.S. acquisition to take a dominating role in the specialty end of the U.S. chemical industry.

### Periods of Revolution and Incremental Adjustment

The preceding highly synoptical account of the corporate strategic change process in ICI over the period 1972–1983 reveals how much the politics of creating strategic change is a long-term conditioning process of breaking down the old marriage of strategic content and context and establishing the dominating legitimacy of a different pattern of relation among strategic content, context, and process. The case illustrates that the real problem of strategic change is anchoring new concepts of reality, new issues for attention, and new ideas for debate and resolution and mobilizing concern, energy, and enthusiasm, often in an additive and evolutionary fashion, to ensure that these thoughts initially considered as illegitimate gain powerful support and eventually result in contextually appropriate action. The ICI corporate-change process described here and the other cases of strategic change reported in Pettigrew (1985) also reveal the role of leadership in initiating strategic change. In this case, Nelson put new energy into a faltering change process by sensing and, at first imprecisely, articulating concerns about a mismatch or performance gap between aspects of ICI's current structure and culture and what he saw as a changing environment. This important early activity of problem finding, of developing concern about the continuance of the status quo, was also linked to another leadership activity designed to raise the level of tension in the organization—the presentation of an imprecise vision of where the organization ought to be moving in the future.

Another important feature of managerial action in strategic change is the necessity to alter the structural and cultural context in which strategy changes are being articulated. These attempts to change inner context included using new ideological posturing to challenge traditional ways of thinking and acting, setting up management-development programs to focus attention on the need for new management capabilities and skills, and creating permanent and temporary changes in administrative mechanisms and working groups to build energy and commitment around particular problems and their solution. These activities did not occur in the ICI cases as part of some grand process design. Instead, opportunities were taken as they presented themselves to break any emerging global vision of a better future into manageable bits, to find small steps on the way to larger breaks, and to use any political momentum created by a number of complementary moves to bind a critical mass of powerful people around a set of principles that eventually would allow a series of pieces in the jigsaw to be moved simultaneously.

These processes required understanding and skill in intervening in the organization's structure, culture, and political processes. As Selznick (1957, p. 70) has argued, "a wise leader faces up to the character of his organization, although he may do so only as a prelude to designing a strategy that will alter it." This kind of process management also necessitated patience and perseverance. It required waiting for people to retire to exploit any policy vacuum so created; introducing known sympathizers as replacements for known skeptics or opponents; using succession occasions to combine portfolios and responsibilities and integrate thought and action in an otherwise previously factious and deadlocked area of change; and backing off and waiting or moving the pressure point for change into another area when continuing downright opposition might have endangered the success of the whole change exercise.

The ICI corporate-change process reported here reaffirms Quinn's (1982) findings that strategic changes do not occur according to the rational-analytical schemes touted in the planning literature. There is little evidence in the ICI data of change occurring as a result of a rational linear process of calculatedly forming a strategy and then sequentially proceeding to implement it through controlled and programmatic planning. Forming and implementing strategic changes comprise not a steady, undisturbed progression from one routine to another but rather a slow and incomplete process of breaking down old marriages between strategic context and content and, in an additive, intuitive, and occasionally opportunistic fashion, building up a climate of acceptance for change.

In examining this buildup of acceptance for change in ICI during the 1970s, we see that the process led by Nelson and others of first developing concern that all was not well and then getting acknowledgment and understanding of a variety of problems began, in effect, to alter the belief systems or ideology of the top decision makers in the company, as a prerequisite for first structural and then business-strategy change. But, although the anticipatory and enabling processes of 1973–1979 produced a degree of ideological change, some alterations in structure and management culture that facilitated more integrative management processes, and, indeed, some additive changes in the content of strategic change, it took the quite dramatic change in business and economic context of 1980–1983 to unify management planning and action around now starkly clear change objectives. After the long phases of development of concern and acknowledgment and understanding of problems, environmental crisis precipitated a rapid change of gear into a phase of planning and action, with perhaps a stronger emphasis on action than on planning.

This revolutionary break of 1980–1983 in ICI was not the first of its kind; and, indeed, the more complete description and analysis of ICI's corporated development in Pettigrew (1985) indicates that strategic changes tend to occur in radical packages interspersed with longish periods of both absorbing the impact of revolutionary action and then slowly coming to terms with the fact that further changes are eventually necessary. Crucial to the timing of such periods of revolutionary change are real and constructed crises (Pettigrew, 1983), changes in leadership and power, and the transformation of organizational ideologies.

For ICI, the period from the late 1950s until 1983 featured three eras of high levels of change activity. Two of these three periods, the ones between 1960 and 1964 and between 1980 and 1983, could be sensibly labeled as revolutionary periods, in that they were characterized by ideological, structural, and business-strategy change, while the third period, between 1970 and 1973, was a period of substantial if lesser change, when further structural change was made and elements of the ideological and business-strategy changes made ten years earlier were accelerated or de-emphasized. The periods in between these packages of changes were occasions for stabilizing and acting upon the new strategic orientation of the company and, most notably between 1973 and 1979, an era when ideological justification was prepared for the revolutionary break between 1980 and 1983.

Each of these periods of high levels of change activity was associated with world economic recessions, with their associated effects on world chemical production, markets, and prices and, in turn, on ICI's relative level of business performance. Table 2 shows the peaks and troughs in ICI's profits and ratio of trading profit to sales over the period 1958 to 1982.

Since 1958, there have been five years of peak profits followed by downturns of varying severity, with each cycle lasting from four to five years. The improvement from trough to peak has been 82 percent (1958-1960), 74 percent (1961-1964), 92 percent (1966-1969), 255 percent (1971-1974), and 95 percent (1975-1979). The two periods of revolutionary change between 1960 and 1964 and between 1980 and 1983 were preceded by and further reaffirmed ideological

**Table 2. ICI Worldwide Sales and Trading Profit in Peak and Trough Years Between 1958 and 1982 (in Millions of Pounds).**

| Year | Total Sales | Trading Profit | Ratio of Trading Profit to Sales |
|------|------------|----------------|----------------------------------|
| 1958 | 463 | 51 | 11.0 |
| 1960 | 558 | 93 | 16.6 |
| 1961 | 550 | 65 | 11.8 |
| 1964 | 720 | 113 | 15.7 |
| 1966 | 885 | 99 | 11.2 |
| 1969 | 1,355 | 119 | 14.0 |
| 1971 | 1,524 | 130 | 8.5 |
| 1974 | 2,955 | 461 | 15.6 |
| 1975 | 3,129 | 315 | 10.4 |
| 1979 | 5,368 | 634 | 11.8 |
| 1980 | 5,715 | 332 | 5.8 |
| 1981 | 6,581 | 425 | 6.4 |
| 1982 | 7,358 | 366 | 5.0 |

shifts and were associated with, on the first occasion, the 1958 and 1961 economic and business downturns and, on the second occasion, the sustained recession of 1980–1983. They were also occasions when new business leadership was supplied by people who had not spent their whole careers in ICI.

Although these findings on patterns of strategic change in ICI are highly consistent with observations made by Mintzberg (1978) and Miller and Friesen (1982) that organizations have tradition-bound periods punctuated by noncumulative revolutionary breaks and that, on the face of it, there is a clear association between environmental disturbance and those periods of major change, it would not be appropriate to infer too simply a relationship between business crisis and a strategic change. While the periods of high levels of change activity in ICI were precipitated by business crisis, explanations of the processes of creating such changes and, indeed, the character and content of these changes must not be limited to objective changes in economic and business context. Such explanations must also include the role of executive leadership and managerial action in intervening in the existing concepts of corporate strategy in the firm; using and changing the structures, cultures, and political processes in the firm to draw attention to performance gaps resulting from environmental change; and leading the organization to sense and create a different pattern of alignment between its internal character, strategy, and structure of its emerging concept and its operating environment.

## Managerial Tasks in Creating Strategic Change

"A comprehensive managerial strategy of change requires a more thorough understanding of change in organizations, not a theory of how to introduce any arbitrary change, but a theory of how to direct somewhat the conventional ways in which an organization responds to its environment, experiences, and anticipations" (March, 1981c, p. 575). In this quotation and in a subsequent paper on change and reorganization in government (March and Olsen, 1982), the essentially simple and elegant point is made that any practical theory of change has to be based on contextually based knowledge and action about the factors and processes that create and sustain continuity as well as change. March and Olsen come to this conclusion on the basis of their empirical observation that, while incremental and less visible changes in government not linked to major reorganizations often succeed, comprehensive reorganizations tend to consolidate opposition and thus fail. In this view, leadership in change management requires skill in timing small interventions so that the force of natural organizational processes amplifies those interventions. This recognition that major reforms seem to require commitment, patience, perseverance, and repetition of intent and action fits well with the long-term conditioning and influence process character of strategic change described in this study of ICI. Since business strategies are likely both to be rooted in the idea systems, or strategic frames (Huff, 1982), that are institutionalized in an industry sector at any point in time and to be represented in the values, structures, and systems of powerful groups who control the firms in any sector, changing business strategies has to involve a process of ideological and political change that eventually releases a new concept of strategy that is culturally acceptable within a newly appreciated context.

But how is this done? Indeed, prescriptively, how can it be done? Is it possible to describe and codify the tasks and skills appropriate for such a contextually sensitive activity as managing strategic change? There is space left in this chapter to draw on the ICI case and a useful paper by Johnston (1978) to provide only the beginnings of an answer to that question. Evidence from the cases of strategic change in ICI reported in Pettigrew (1985) indicate that change processes are often dependent upon a few people, are reactive to the external world, and can peter out or be reversed. A way to try to prevent such regression or reversals is to conceptually understand the evolution of natural processes of change in organizations and to help establish an organization process of change with the necessary internal skills, actions, and systems to maintain development in the direction sought. In the broadest sense, this means, prescriptively, that step one in the change process should be to improve and build upon any natural processes of change by tackling questions such as how existing processes can be speeded up, how the conditions that determine people's interpretation of situations can be altered, and how contexts can be mobilized toward legitimate problems and solutions along the way to move the organization additively in a different strategic direction. Thus, any adequate approach to managing a process of strategic change must be based upon a principle of understanding and using any perceived movement in a firm's inner and outer context and building upon that movement and of identifying a trend with significant support where, more than likely, the energy for strategic change is based upon the recognition of environmental pressure and an early sensing of a gap between the organization's present and its desired future relationship with its business-competitive, social, political, and economic environments.

For all its oversimplifications, including the tendency to assume both discrete and exclusive categories and linear sequential development, Johnston's (1978) view of a natural four-stage process of change does capture elements of the ICI strategic change process and allows sensible prescriptive statements to be made about necessary management tasks at each of the following four stages:

1. *the development of concern* by a subset of people in the organization that aspects of the organization may no longer be compatible with its operating environment;
2. *the acknowledgment and understanding* of the problem that the organization now faces, including an analysis of the causes of difficulties and alternative ways of tackling those difficulties;
3. *planning and acting* to create specific changes; and
4. *stabilizing the changes* made by altering the organization's reward, information, and power systems so that they reinforce the direction of intended change.

The key management task at the stage of development of concern is to build upon the perspective, information, and contacts of the early adopters and broadly educate the organization about the need for change—in effect, to recognize the group doing the early sensing, to expand that group by helping to connect them to peers, bosses, and subordinates with similar views, and to prepare more of a critical mass of people to help influence key power figures. This educational process may involve encouraging deviants to think the unthinkable and say the unsayable; it may require setting up unusual meetings and administrative mechanisms that cross departmental and organizational boundaries and help spread information and views so that they can be integrated around particular issues or problems.

In the next stage, trying to get acknowledgment and understanding of problems and issues that are emerging, a key management task is to help the early adopters and key power figures maintain and develop any structured dialogue about the problems and avoid a tendency either to escape from the problem by, for example, projecting it onto others or to make a precipitous and ill-considered rush into action. This stage is not only critical in terms of perpetuating any ideological change now in process but is also important in rational-analytical terms for exposing alternative diagnoses of the problem, exploring causes, and generating alternative solutions that may yet become acceptable as the context around the problems changes.

The ICI study has indicated that these first two stages—developing concern and seeking acknowledgment and understanding of problems—are long processes with many iterations, blocks, dead ends, and unpredictable areas of movement. Persistence and patience in championing change seem to be necessary to initiate and perpetuate this process of conditioning and influence, and deliberative attempts to alter the structural and cultural context of decision making and capitalize on environmental disturbances seem necessary to break out from mere acknowledgment and understanding of problems into a stage of executive planning and action. Because radical changes require strong commitments and high motivations, they also presuppose the existence of ideological reorientations and, therefore, the unequivocal availability of a new ideology that precisely and enthusiastically endorses the changes. Such ideological change can emerge out of a protracted process of education and climate building. It is also facilitated by the appearance of new leaders articulating new sets of values and, of course, by the massive enabling opportunities provided by changes in business and economic environment. Gross changes in the environment of the firm can be orchestrated and capitalized upon to create opportunities for organizational learning, to destabilize power structures, and to connect previously unrelated solutions to now starkly evident problems.

The planning and acting tasks in change management have been well codified and described in the concepts and techniques reported in Beckhard and Harris (1977) and Beer (1980). In addition to accepted ideas of change management, such as clarifying the desired future state and change objectives in relation to a changing environment and the organization's present position, appointing transition managers, and encouraging the development of detailed and contextually sensitive action plans, an important role for top management at the action stage is creating and maintaining tension and pressure for change. This can be done by providing a clearly articulated rationale for change and some consistently stated change objectives and then following this up with monitoring and supporting activities with operating management who are likely to have the detailed tasks of making particular changes happen.

Strategic change is, of course, more than just making something happen. It is also a question of making changes that do happen actually stick. Here, there is the additional management task of stabilizing changes—of making sure that reward systems, information flows, and power and authority distributions support the newly emerging state. Since strategic changes are often initiated by or otherwise associated with key power figures, and changes often remain as long as those key figures remain, a critical part of the stabilization process has to do with the development and choice of successors who will want to maintain the new situation for as long as that situation is perceived to be contextually appropriate.

# ❦ TWELVE ❦

# Generalizing About
# Strategic Change:
# Methodological Pitfalls
# and Promising Solutions

## *Edward H. Bowman*

This chapter is an admixture of a commentary on Chapter Eleven of this volume, by Andrew Pettigrew, and a presentation of some studies of content analysis of annual reports. The contrast is offered as instructive in highlighting in some detail such issues as validity, replicability, generality, and operationality. The approaches are different and serve different purposes. It is perhaps fortunate that we do not all march to the same drummer.

The progress of academic people thinking and writing about managerial decision making and problem solving may appear at first blush to be minimal. The discussions seem to circle back and forth between the way problems are solved—or not solved—and the

*Note:* This chapter is a response to the draft paper presented by Andrew Pettigrew at the Arden House Symposium. The chapter therefore contains references to material no longer in the substantially revised paper by Pettigrew published as Chapter Eleven in this book.

way they should be solved. However, this chapter proposes a more hopeful metaphor, that of the helix. As the analysis moves back and forth between description and prescription, it may, as in a helix, circle to higher levels (compare Leonardo da Vinci).

A first stage in this development, marked about 1930, started with fairly mundane and pedantic description. Business schools may have labored in the farther reaches of the academic hierarchy at this stage. In the 1950s and 1960s, with the Gordon and Howell and Pearson reports for the Ford and Carnegie Foundations, which challenged schools of management to offer a better education to their students, a more advanced prescriptive stage, derivative from economics and applied mathematics, surfaced. The rational actor was in his heyday.

Somewhat later, and to some extent as a reaction to the highly parsimonious, astringent, and somewhat naive "rational man," came a more sophisticated description of managerial decision making embedded in organizations. Simon and Lindblom stand out here as major contributors—both, interestingly enough, associated with political science.

The next stage in our progression along the helix is sophisticated prescription, which seems still to be coming painfully slowly. Andrew M. Pettigrew's work under review here (Chapter Eleven of this volume) fits essentially in the third category of sophisticated description, with only the most minor forays into sophisticated prescription. As some "criticism" (as in its usage in the term *literary criticism*) will be offered here, it is appropriate to point out that our arguments are more with omission than with commission and are therefore largely a matter of taste and style.

There are numerous methods of research available for the study of corporate behavior. Aside from the interesting issue of what, if any, intellectual fields of theory and literature will be drawn on, with economics and the behavioral sciences as obvious candidates, other choices exist. Examples include normative versus descriptive, longitudinal versus cross-sectional, and person as actor versus organization as actor. The choice of individual manager versus corporate organization as the focus of study may be linked to a particular and idiosyncratic view of behavior versus a more general and structured view of behavior. This polarity is nicely captured by a quotation from Alexis de Tocqueville that Allison (1971) supplies as an introduction *Essence of Decisions:* "I have come across men of letters who have written history without taking part in public affairs, and politicians who have concerned themselves with producing events without thinking about them. I have observed that the first are always inclined to find general causes, whereas the second, living in the midst of disconnected daily facts, are prone to imagine that everything is attributable to particular incidents, and that the wires they pull are the same as those that move the world. It is to be presumed that both are equally deceived."

A tradeoff that often seems to accompany the level of focus of the study is the size of the sample or number of the units versus the details or the number of the variables and "depth" of the study. Often, one must seem to trade "richness" for "coverage," or vice versa. At one end of this scalar is the in-depth field study of one organization, requiring much time within the firm and often utilizing methods from anthropology and ethnography. Pettigrew's study falls essentially at this polar end of the spectrum. At the opposite end of this spectrum is a study of many organizations, perhaps a thousand or more, from a large data base often obtained by others, such as the Compustat data base from Standard and Poor or the Profit Impact of Marketing Strategies (PIMS) data base from the Strategic Planning Institute. No time may be directed "inside" the organization, and the methodology often utilized is that of the economist.

Somewhere between these two end positions of one versus a thousand comes the small-sample work, with a range chosen here of five to fifty. This middle ground offers the strong advantage of some comparative analysis, multiple-variable work, some qualitative richness, and possibilities of research replications for either followers or skeptics, though sometimes stretching the availability of convincing statistical tests. As counterpoise to Pettigrew's study, several examples of content analyses of corporate annual reports from this middle ground of depth and breadth will be offered here. The annual-reports content analysis will be interposed at three or four places to compare with Pettigrew's methods, theories, and findings.

Pettigrew's study falls largely into three sections: (1) a comment on the literature of managerial decision making and change, (2) advocacy of attention to culture and politics along with "contextualism" as a method, (3) a study described as strategic change at the board level. The sections of his chapter are only loosely coupled, and the longer case study at the end, in this reviewer's opinion, doesn't fully reflect the interesting ideas espoused at the beginning. As the author indicates, a book-length treatment is required (Pettigrew, 1985) to do justice to his material. The author is to be commended for his joint treatment of the theoretical and the empirical—the ideal and the real. The best of management literature does not slight either side of this couple. The very best continually moves skillfully back and forth between the two sides, using each to explicate the other.

Pettigrew's approach to organization study advocates a coordinated treatment of *context, process,* and *content* of changes or decisions and their interaction. This is further extended to his idea of "contextualism," which treats the process both "vertically" and "horizontally," as he labels the approach. *Vertically* essentially means *between levels in the organization,* and perhaps outside as well, while *horizontally* essentially means what most writers call *longitudinally*—a treatment over an extended period of time. Interestingly, this three-fold and two-fold treatment dismisses the distinction between strategy formulation and strategy implementation as "artificial" (see Galbraith and Nathanson, 1978, for strong contra argument and the need for congruency between the two) and virtually ignores the distinction between descriptive and prescriptive. Many authors, including Bowman (1974), find both of the latter distinctions useful and important. Taking only the comparisons among context, process, and content and between descriptive and normative may be instructive. Pettigrew's detailed work in this chapter deals almost entirely with one of the six boxes possible in this matrix, that of descriptive process, treating largely culture and politics and not, for instance, cognition. This is mentioned, of course, with the realization that an author has some rights of choice in his interests.

However, none of these boxes is really empty of treatment. Even normative-context can be discussed as the firm "enacting" its environment (Weick, 1979). Reginald Jones, as chairman of General Electric (USA), discussed at some length (in Wachter and Wachter, 1983, and elsewhere) the modern chief executive officer's appropriate role of working in the nation's capital with lawmakers to help shape national policy. Authors who write of normative process include Lorange and Vancil (1977), and those who write of normative content include Ansoff (1965) and Porter (1980). Those who write of descriptive process include March (1981b) and Mintzberg (1973a), and those who write of descriptive content include Chandler (1962). Finally, those who write of descriptive context include Thurow (1983) and Magaziner and Reich (1982).

The intellectual position that Pettigrew does advocate is an attractive one—include multiple constructs, multiple levels, and multiple time periods. His choice of good authors, "real progress," is also attractive—Bower (1972), Allison (1971), March and Olsen (1976), Mintzberg (1978), and Quinn (1980), as well as, later, Baumol (1959), Marris (1966), and Williamson (1964, 1975). No argument here. His favor toward careful empiricism is noted. Even his primary normative comment, "key into natural processes," is most sensible to old deans, as well as the one he borrows from March and Olsen, "persistence."

Pettigrew's limits of space in a chapter rather than a book show more in his stories than in his intellectual constructs. While he tries to incorporate his research prescriptions from the section "Contextualism as a Mode of Analysis" into the OD consultants' story, it is too brief to really show their usefulness. His story of "Strategic Change in Imperial Chemical Industries" is interesting especially in some of its points and quotations (for example, the secretary's key mistake) but doesn't fully meet the kinds of criteria he sets out earlier in the chapter. It appears to deal largely with process and politics and seems largely theory free. Though some elements of context and content are mentioned, they don't seem integral or compelling to the story of the change in organization and personae at the board level. While the story is surely told "horizontally," it misses almost the entire picture "vertically"—his contextualism is flawed. To put it differently, he seems to show a strong preference for isomorphic over paramorphic models, such that his emphasis on process may "miss the forest for the trees."

While only a third of a chapter is acknowledged here as a tough limit to draw out what the author sets as his own criteria, the exemplars of Chandler (1962) and Allison (1971) are offered. Chandler does it iteratively with his four large studies, and the

Du Pont story of reorganization affecting the board from a centralized functional company to a decentralized divisional company with the board removed from operations stands out in contrast to the brief story of ICI.

Allison captures the levels that Pettigrew recommends by dealing sequentially with the nation-state, with organization units, and with individual actors. Rather than different "models," as Allison labels them, my preference is to think of his analysis as carried out at different levels of aggregation. Allison describes and analyzes the behavior of the United States and what its goals, options, and choices seemed to be. He then describes the behavior of various organization units, such as the navy and the air force. Finally, he deals with the behavior of individual key executives, such as the secretary of state, secretary of defense, and ambassador to the United Nations. These different levels of aggregation— nation-state, organization unit, and individual actors—permit an enormously rich and complex picture to be drawn. Both contrast and reinforcement are possible with this style (or styles) of analysis.

Pettigrew stays somewhat closer to the style of the ethnographer or field anthropologist. He deals almost entirely with the roles and behavior of individual executive actors. This permits him the opportunity to offer many interesting data about the individuals over a substantial time period and under varying circumstances, but it does not offer the reader the viewpoint of the more macro forces both within the firm and between the firm and its environment. Put differently, the *strategy* elements suggested by the term *strategic decision making* are slighted.

While the *strategy* aspect of the ICI story does not come through strongly enough for a management-school teacher of strategy, this may be only a matter of taste. Included might have been ideas about enterprise strategy, corporate strategy, and business strategy (see the chapter by Igor Ansoff in Schendel and Hofer, 1979). How was the firm dealing with the wide range of constituents in its environment? What were the exchanges taking place between divisions? How were the divisions positioning themselves versus competition? What was taking place in marketing or research and development?

Somewhat more remote but still relevant might have been ideas about the apparent generic strategy of ICI (see Miles and Snow, 1978, and Porter, 1980). Was ICI essentially aiming at low-cost volume leadership permitted by market domination, or was it looking for particular product-market niches that could be made profitable? Was it essentially defending an established base, or was it continually looking for new product markets to enter? Were such generic strategies, if they existed, common to all divisions, or was there high variance within the corporation? Some effort, even to the extent of being labeled "pedantic," might be useful to show further the *interactions* across levels, including context and content. That is, over-explain to the reader, "what is the context, what is the process, what is the content, and what are their linkages."

Much of the chapter's middle section is well advocated and accepted and is not argued here. Many quotations could be given as examples, including: "In the pursuit of our everyday tasks and objectives, it is all too easy to forget the less rational and instrumental, the more expressive social tissue around us that gives those tasks meaning. Yet, in order for people to function within any given setting, they must have a continuing sense of what that reality is all about in order for it to be acted upon. Culture is the system of such publicly and collectively accepted meanings operating for a given group at a given time. This system of terms, forms, categories, and images interprets a people's own situation to themselves." Indeed, much of the first two thirds of Pettigrew's chapter develops such ideas nicely and is not subject to debate here, though he is harder on normative strategic problem solving and strategic control than I would be—what consulting help would *he* offer the CEO searching for strategic *content* or the business school student in the classroom?

One small addition to methodology offered here for understanding corporate culture beyond the anthropological-type field study of Pettigrew or the well-worn questionnaire of the academic journal is content analysis of annual reports (Bowman, 1976, 1978, 1982, 1984; Bowman and Haire, 1975, 1976). It works very nicely in large samples and is analogous to a projective test that is neither obtrusive nor intrusive. Content analysis of written documents involves coding words, phrases, and sentences against particular constructs of interest. These constructs often come from previous empirical work or developed theory. The coding can be rather simple or extend to multidimensional coding as well.

An extended quotation from an article in *Interfaces,* the professional and applied journal jointly published by the Institute of Management Science and the Operations Research Society of America (Bowman, 1984, pp. 63–64), is offered here to describe validity tests of this methodology. Though perhaps overly detailed, consider this quest for validity tests as compared to the anthropological-type field study in an industrial setting performed by one individual.

### Validity Testing of Annual Report Content Analysis

Because it is usually the case that several people read and code the written documents, and their coding can be cross-checked, consistency of interpretation can be reasonably assured. The question can still remain about the correspondence between the documents and objective reality. This may be thought to be of particular importance with corporate annual reports.

For this reason, in our work we made several tests from external independent data to assure ourselves and the reader of a reasonable correspondence with objective reality. Before describing these tests, however, it should be stated that these reports have the advantage of unobtrusive measurement and that they are written for purposes and to audiences different from the content analysts. That is, they are like a projective test taken inadvertently. In addition, while some people maintain that the prose sections of annual reports are written by public relations staffs sometimes external to the firm, the truth is that the typical chief executive officer spends considerable time outlining the contents of the report, sketching out much of it, and proofreading and changing most of it to his taste. The CEO tends to view the annual report as a major if not *the* major communication device to many constituencies, both internal and external, concerning his and the company's performance.

The tests which were undertaken in this line of projects were as follows (Bowman, 1976). The first empirical test of annual report discussion involved a search for a list of companies independently generated as outstanding in their corporate social responsibility activities. Milton Moskowitz, editor of *Business and Society,* had provided such a list in the *New York Times,* February 11, 1973. Included in his brief article were fourteen companies he considered outstandingly responsible firms. Our first test chose fourteen other companies to supply as matched pairs for comparison purposes. Each of these fourteen matched pair companies of this second set was chosen from the same industry as the corresponding Moskowitz company, and randomly selected from firms of approximately the same size. Annual reports for 1973 were obtained from all twenty-eight companies (i.e., 2 x 14). We coded each of these reports on a line-by-line basis as to whether or not the line was discussing issues of corporate social responsibility.

The test hypothesis was that the outstandingly responsible companies discussed issues of corporate social responsibility significantly more in their annual reports on a line-by-line coding basis than did the neutrally chosen matched pair companies. Recall that the annual report, though written for many purposes, is written essentially *to the shareholder,* and one should not expect unusual puffery on issues like corporate social responsibility (or international activities, something to be discussed shortly).

The test hypothesis was confirmed, as the average for the outstanding group was a 4.80 percent discussion of this topic, close to three times the average for the randomly chosen matched pair group of 1.74 percent discussion (statistically significant in binomial pair-wise comparison at the .017 level of confidence).

The second independent and completely different test of the correspondence between annual report discussion and objective reality was in the area of international activities. Similarly to the line-by-line coding of corporate social responsibility discussion, a coding on international activity discussion was made from a set of annual reports to determine the percentage of the total discussion devoted to this topic. That is, lines of annual report discussion of international activity were coded and counted. The annual reports obtained were from the food processing industry as listed in *Moody's Industrial Manual, 1973*, and restricted to those companies which are listed on the New York Stock Exchange.

For these forty companies *Standard and Poor's* provides detailed reports including in most cases the percentage of the company's business generated by international activities. The two sources of international activity measures, one from content analysis of the 40 annual reports, and one from a received source of objective reality, *Standard and Poor Reports,* could then be compared. A rank order of company international percentage activity for both lists separately were compared. This comparison of the two lists, both ranked from high to low in activity rate, offers a different test of annual report line-by-line coding. Using the Spearman Rank Order Correlation Coefficient, the list orders were significantly similar (coefficient of 0.65, level of significance beyond 0.001). That is, annual report discussion gives results consistent with *Standard and Poor* reports.

Both tests of annual reports content analysis— each with different topic, different industries, different external reality source, different statistical test—suggest that annual report discussion, line-by-line, is a reasonable surrogate for real activity. Clearly a sizeable sample, such as several dozen or so companies in an industry, is more reliable than one or two companies. For strategic analysis, as for most other questions, the limited data sources will be have to be treated sensibly given the purposes of the analysis.

As an example of how content analysis may offer insights into strategic culture, an extended quotation is given from an article in the *Sloan Management Review* (Bowman, 1976, pp. 53-54):

> In order to have a picture of how the corporations in the food-processing industry view their strategy, a number of the annual reports were once again reviewed for the purpose of abstracting some actual comments. The eighty-two annual reports were first divided into quartiles by five-year return on equity (ROE). The top quartile and the bottom quartile were chosen for investigation. Next, from each of these sets of twenty (or twenty-one) annual reports, the five reports with the most pages were chosen for detailed review. (The reports with the most pages were chosen in order to get the most material with the least amount of noise for review. The author was also subjected to time constraints which prevented him from reviewing all of the annual reports.)
>
> It turned out that all of these ten companies were relatively large, with nine out of ten in the top half of the total eighty-two companies according to size (i.e., size of company apparently correlates with length of report), and all ten are listed on the New York Stock Exchange. The median ROE (for the five years) for the top quartile five was 17.1%, and for the bottom quartile was 5.9%—a rather large difference.
>
> To reiterate, the organizing scheme here was a segmentation according to ROE. A group of companies which were least successful was to be compared to a group of companies which were most successful. Actual comments in their annual reports on various topics were to be the basis for the comparison. The statistician might be willing to call this a poor-man's discriminant analysis.

A word of caution is warranted because this methodology permitting most of the introductory declarative statements is not for the most part statistically sound. The sample is small (though fair), and the instrument is blunt. In part due to these caveats, it is necessary to draw more heavily on theory and intellectual speculation—this is not an uncommon substitute at the margin, theory for sound empirical data. At the extreme the substitution is complete—all theory and no data, not a very attractive scheme.

## The Differentiating Content

Clearly annual reports talk about many things. Profit (or loss), sales volume, products, and facilities would be high on the list. It is the purpose here to highlight the differentiating content; that is, the nature of the discussion which is different between the low-profit companies and the high-profit companies.

All quotes about a given topic were copied from all ten reports. Though no brief is offered for statistical proof, the copying was straightforward. The interpretation is speculative. The declarative statements at the beginning of this article will now be taken in their first order.

1.   "Food-processing companies that are less successful complain about the weather."

There were many (seven) different comments mentioning unfavorable weather conditions in the low-quartile companies and no mention in the high-quartile companies (and it should be repeated that the ROE figure which separates the company quartiles is an average for five years).

"The (Name) Division shares industry concern this year over the severe and unusual weather that punished major growing areas and is causing some disruption in crop yields." (4th Quartile)

". . . continued wet weather during the last season delayed harvesting and caused increased raw-product expense due to the need for additional drying." (4th Quartile)

"The primary earlier factor contributing to the poor results was the adverse weather condition experienced in the states of Arkansas and Mississippi where the Company's plants are located." (4th Quartile)

"Unusually heavy rainfalls in Central Arizona and in the Salinas Valley caused the loss of a large part of the Arizona spring lettuce crop, and inhibited planting of Salinas Valley lettuce during the winter months." (4th Quartile)

". . . Group showed a decline in earnings due principally to the effects of a severe blowdown suffered in the (Honduras) Division." (4th Quartile)

The thesis could be advanced that companies with less satisfactory results complain. More likely, it is that their basic business puts them in a situation which is more vulnerable to the occasional and persistent vagaries of the weather (and that their complaints are justified). If the business is a "commodity" business, with little "value added," there will be little margin or flexibility to cope with supply difficulties.

Of course, problems of causality, explanation, and attribution are buried in the above food-industry study. Our surmise is that the five years' poor performance is actually associated with a minimal position on the value-added chain and a low profit margin especially vulnerable to the weather. Contrarily, Bettman and Weitz (1983) use my study as support for their position of success and failure attribution—success is due to us, failure is due to external causes. Regardless of interpretation, the full set of quotations is given, the data source is unambiguous, skeptics may use, and students may replicate.

Some smaller points of alternative treatment in Pettigrew's chapter include his ignoring March's many and interesting normative recommendations for the college president following the "garbage-can model." For the reader who has not seen them, these include the following from *Leadership and Ambiguity: The American College President* (Cohen and March, 1974, pp. 206-207):

*Major Properties of Decision Making in Organized Anarchies*

1.  Most issues most of the time have *low salience* for most people.
2.  The total system has *high inertia.*
3.  Any decision can become a *garbage can* for almost any problem.
4.  The processes of choice are easily subject to *overload.*
5.  The organization has a *weak information base.*

*Basic Tactical Rules for Those Who Seek to Influence the Course of Decisions*

1.  Spend time.
2.  Persist.
3.  Exchange status for substance.
4.  Facilitate opposition participation.
5.  Overload the system.
6.  Provide garbage cans.
7.  Manage unobtrusively.
8.  Interpret history.

*A Small Beginning*

1.  First, we can treat *goals as hypotheses.*
2.  Second, we can treat *intuition as real.*
3.  Third, we can treat *hypocrisy as transition.*
4.  Fourth, we can treat *memory as an enemy.*
5.  Fifth, we can treat *experience as a theory.*

Another point is Pettigrew's emphasis on change as a *continuous* process, while Mintzberg shows and argues strongly that it is an intermittent process (pulse, then coast, or change, then consolidate)—the distinction here may be between process and content. While the *process* of learning and deciding may be more continuous, the *content* of the strategy itself may change only in a noncontinuous fashion. Mintzberg (1978) indicates that his studies show that real changes in strategy may take place only about every twenty years. Further, he indicates that a continuous/yearly attention to strategy may dull the senses to the need for real change when it comes.

Pettigrew takes to task both naive normative treatment of strategic change and "prevailing orthodoxy." It is doubted here whether the latter exists. If there is a developing orthodoxy, it comes somewhat closer to Quinn's logical incrementalism than the straw man posited. This new orthodoxy has a nice history, starting even earlier than Lindblom's (1959) "The Science of Muddling Through." James Schlesinger, a cabinet officer for both Democratic and Republican presidents, had written an interesting paper in about 1950 while an analyst at the RAND Corporation. It is cited here for its nice use of metaphor. He contrasts "Cook's Tour Planning" with "Lewis and Clark Planning." The Cook's Tour lays out a complete itinerary of date and place and transport mode before the journey even starts. On the other hand, for their Northwest Passage, Lewis and Clark had to make some rough estimates of the kinds of terrain they might cross and what some of their alternatives might be in order to load their gear for a start. Flexibility and options and general capabilities had to dominate the "plans."

One of Pettigrew's comments (made at the symposium) that strikes this reviewer as strange because of current work is, "The other features of group context relevant to explaining both the overall pattern of continuity and change in ICI 1960 and (to) 1982 and the impact and fate of the five OD groups is *outer context* level of analysis. This is the third level of analysis in the study. The one most *novel* to the analysis of organization change and analysis, and the one most difficult empirically and theoretically to handle. The outer context of level of analysis refers to the *economic performance* and competitiveness of ICI as a whole, and to each division under study, throughout the period 1960-1982" (emphasis added).

While perhaps the orientation is content rather than process, surely many studies of organization and organization change focus on *performance* as the *context* that drives *process* to change *content*. Much work on industry life cycles (for example, Porter, 1980) illustrates this. I don't believe that this is a novel orientation and offer, ad hominem, three papers out of a current stream (Bowman, 1980, 1982, and 1984). Following analysis of strategy context and content (not process) in the food-processing and computer-peripheral industries, it was discovered that, in a majority of all industries (eighty-six Value Line and fifty-four Standard and Poor Compustat), risk and return were negatively correlated between companies within industries.

Two basic possible reasons were explored by content analysis to explain this finding (a paradox from a finance and economics standpoint). One was that companies that took risks became less profitable. A longitudinal test of this explanation was not supportive. The other was that companies that had been less profitable then took more risks. This test was positively supported, and the idea was theoretically grounded from the work of Tversky and Kahneman (1981) and Kahneman and Tversky (1979) on prospect theory of risk seeking below aspiration levels at the individual-experimental level. Our work moved from this level to the corporate-field level through the content analysis of annual reports. Three longitudinal (but short-term) studies showed that food-processing companies (of ninety) that had been less profitable became more involved in acquisition activities (risk surrogate); computer-peripheral companies (of forty-six) that had been less profitable became more involved in litigation (risk surrogate); and container companies (of twenty-seven) that had been less profitable became more involved in new activities (risk surrogate). In sum, the "outer context" seemed to drive the "inner process."


Pettigrew has written numerous useful articles and books supporting his method of research. He sets tough standards, which are difficult for himself and others to meet. I am supportive of this research, not only in the spirit of pluralism, which I find attractive, but also because of the direct contribution he makes. I leave him, however, with one set of questions that he doesn't appear to address in *this* work. They are questions of epistemology. Will he generalize from one long case study? Is his method operationalized, and can his work be replicated? Does he gives us theory, and is it falsifiable? To put it more mundanely, how idiosyncratic are his work and his results, and how does the reader answer *this* question for himself or herself?

# ❦ THIRTEEN ❦

# Acting First and Thinking Later: Theory Versus Reality in Strategic Change

## *William H. Starbuck*

"Gaiety is the most outstanding feature of the Soviet Union"—Joseph Stalin, 1935.

"The only thing science has done for man in the last hundred years is to create for him fresh moral problems"—Geoffrey Fisher, archbishop of Canterbury, 1950.

"I don't believe in aeroplanes, science and progress, in railway timetables or in economic law. I cannot think of them as real, and there will be none of them in my future. There is no room for them"—Bernard Fay, philosopher, 1933.

Social science research has demonstrated a few truths quite convincingly. One of these is that people behave in very diverse ways, so that one can find at least a few instances that match or contra-

*Note:* Except where otherwise attributed, the quotations that appear throughout this chapter were compiled by Coffey (1983).

336

dict virtually any assertion about human behavior. Another truth is that realities are as numerous and different as their perceivers. Thus, social scientists should feel no surprise upon learning that other people see realities somewhat different from their own. But some realities diverge so greatly from my own perceptions that they do surprise me. Consider the following observations about organizational decision making:

• Organizations' members make conscious decisions that determine their actions. A contrasting observation attributes the power to determine organizations' actions mainly to decision making by top managers; subordinates supposedly act as their superiors decide.

• Organizations' members make decisions by engaging in problem solving, and they expect their organizations' actions to solve problems. Steiner (1969, p. 322) stated one version of this view: "A business decision is made in the course of and grows out of the lengthy, complex, and intricate process of problem discovery, exploration of methods to resolve it, and analysis of means."

• Actions that begin after the actors construct sturdy rationalizations produce more benefits than would actions lacking strong prior rationalizations. More elaborate rationalizations—such as operations-research models—yield greater benefits. For instance, Hofer and Schendel (1978, p. 5) asserted that "organizations need formalized, analytical processes for formulating explicit strategies." Similarly, Christensen, Berg, and Salter (1980, p. 13) said, "An evaluation of both the strategy itself as well as the progress of the organization in carrying out that strategy is made easier if the strategy formulation process and the underlying logic and assumptions are made explicit."

• In similar circumstances, actors (whether people or organizations) that behave in highly consistent ways get greater benefits from their actions than do actors that behave quite inconsistently. Thus, actors should increase the consistency of their actions through strategies and policies. Before taking any actions, organizations' members ought to choose strategies and policies and then use these to constrain their organizations' subsequent actions. Actions that adhere to preformed strategies yield greater benefits than actions occurring in an absence of preformed strategies or those deviating from preformed strategies. Similarly, actions that conform to preformed cross-unit policies produce more benefits than actions that occur in an absence of cross-unit policies or those that violate preformed policies. Chang and Campo-Flores (1980, pp. 29–30), for example, listed four benefits of strategy making: "Strategic actions . . . replace brute force and hasty actions. Second, strategy offers a mentality, a discipline, and a technique to manage changes. . . . Third, strategy . . . provides a systematic and decisive method of problem solving. . . . Last, strategy generates directional action."

• In similar circumstances, actors that try to predict the long-range future get greater benefits from their actions than do actors that make no long-range predictions. Newman and Logan (1981, p. 34), for instance, prescribed, "To adjust most effectively, central management should try to predict important changes before they occur." To get the benefits, however, actors must turn their predictions into formal plans and take the plans seriously; actions that adhere to formalized long-range plans generate more benefits than actions occurring without formalized long-range plans or those diverging from formalized plans. Newman and Logan (1981, pp. 537–538) said that long-range programming yields three advantages: "Long-cycle actions are started promptly. . . . Executives are psychologically prepared for change. . . . Actions having long-term impact are coordinated."

The foregoing summary is no straw man. Not only does it describe the general thrust of the literature on strategic decision making, but such a reality attracts me. I wish I inhabited it! How nice it would be to predict the future accurately, to formulate strategies that are much more likely to yield more benefits than costs, to see only rational causality in my environment, even to be sure that I think before I act. But research evidence, personal experience, and logic compel me to live elsewhere. Stated concisely, my reality looks like this:

People, including organizations' members and top managers, act unreflectively nearly all of the time, because they adhere to well-established behavior programs. Indeed, most organizational actions originate in action generators, which are automatic behavior programs that are activated by job assignments or clocks rather than by informative stimuli.

People often take actions without saying or thinking that they solve explicated problems, but some actions do arise from reflective problem solving. Problem solving can be identified by its origin—the perception of a problem. Normative theories assert that perception of a problem should instigate a unidirectional sequence of activities: a problem solver should identify alternative actions that would solve the problem and then evaluate these alternatives, choosing the best. Such tidy, unidirectional sequences occur very infrequently in actual behaviors, however.

Decision making can be identified by its termination—a decision. Thus, decision making and problem solving do not always coincide. In fact, Mintzberg, Rasinghani, and Théorêt (1976) inferred that the decision makers usually perceive no problems when decision making starts. Decisions may solve problems even though they lead to no actions; and problem solving can end without decisions having been made, if the problem solvers can find no solutions or if the problems disappear while the problem solvers are still searching for solutions.

People make many of their decisions, perhaps a great majority of them, after they have begun to act and have seen some of the consequences of their actions. When they begin courses of action, people normally see themselves as following the only sensible courses, not choosing among several plausible courses. They may not even realize that they are embarking on distinct courses, partly because organizations decompose big actions into multiple increments and partly because the individual actors in organizational actions merely follow banal programs. But looking back, the people can see that alternative courses did exist, and so they must have chosen. Thus, decisions are often retrospective re-enactments that misrepresent actual sequences of events. Because strong rationalizations make behaviors inflexible, actions that begin with only tentative and quick rationalizations produce more benefits than do actions that begin after the actors construct sturdy rationalizations. All actions evoke retrospective rationalizations, and these retrospective rationalizations grow stronger as the actions are repeated.

People and organizations do act consistently in that their actions resemble preceding and successive actions: most actions repeat familiar patterns, and most innovations are no more than incremental variations on familiar patterns. However, this consistency arises because people unreflectively follow behavior programs, because powerful people have vested interests, and because settings for action remain stable, rather than because people are striving consciously to conform to preformed strategies.

Strategies are behavior patterns that remain consistent over time, and policies are intended behavior patterns that remain consistent either through time (strategies) or across organizational subunits. To be the objects of decision making, strategies and policies have to be conscious. But very few of organizations' members and very few top managers choose strategies or policies consciously on a regular basis. The choices that do occur reflect the choosers' interests as individuals as well as their organizations' interests as collectivities. People formulate many strategies and policies, perhaps a great majority of them, only after they have acted and seen some of the consequences of their actions. The general consistency of organizational actions makes strategies and policies easy to invent. Thus, like decisions, strategies and policies are generally retrospective re-enactments.

The processes by which people articulate strategies and policies often involve rationalization. But people perceive their environments inaccurately, and logic injects large amounts of fantasy into rationalizations. So articulated strategies and policies render actions less realistic and less responsive to environmental events. Consequently, actions occurring in an absence of preformed strategies and those deviating from preformed strategies generally yield greater benefits than would adherence to preformed strategies. Similarly, actions that violate cross-unit policies and those taken in an absence of cross-unit policies generate more benefits than would conformity to cross-unit policies.

Partly because they misperceive their environments and themselves, partly because they apply rational logic to situations that lack rationality, and partly because they generate predictions through processes of social construction, people predict their alternative futures inaccurately. Predictions about long-range futures incorporate much larger errors than predictions about short-range futures. People revise formalized plans less often than informal plans, and they formalize plans through social interactions, so formalized plans incorporate larger errors than do informal plans. Thus, actions that diverge from formalized long-range plans and those taken without formalized long-range plans usually generate more benefits than would continued adherence to formalized long-range plans.

This chapter explains why I find this second reality more realistic than the first. The discussion loosely follows the sequence in which I have just summarized my views, but it is organized around the consequences of three powerful tools. Generally speaking, tools that can cause no harm also lack power, whereas powerful tools have correspondingly strong disadvantages. Three of humans' most powerful tools are rational thought, programmed behavior, and social interaction. These enhance humans' effectiveness tremendously, but they also circumscribe actions sufficiently to become serious handicaps.

## Rationality

"Prediction is very difficult, especially about the future"—Niels Bohr.

Rationality is defined by human physiology. Human brains use rational logic, although imperfectly and inconsistently; and from a human's perspective, rational logic seems to aid understanding. Indeed, human philosophers, logicians, and mathematicians have abstracted this propensity and generated rules that they prescribe normatively. But physical and social universes probably act nonrationally. There is no reason for confidence that human physiology has evolved a logic that matches the physical universe. A social system may behave nonrationally in the aggregate even if every one of its human members acts rationally at all times—an implausible assumption itself. Thus, it is an empirical question how accurately rational logic can predict the future states of humans' worlds. Experience suggests, however, that rational logic produces disappointingly inaccurate interpretations of and predictions about social phenomena.

Further, human brains often apply rational logic inappropriately. People cannot avoid revising their memories to make them match their perceptions, because brains involuntarily alter the information they already hold in order to make new information fit in (Kiesler, 1971; Loftus, 1979). And brains revise perceptions to make them match memories; laboratory experiments suggest that people update their beliefs much more slowly than statistical models say they should (Edwards, 1968). Brains also invent memories and perceptions of events that never occurred but that rational logic says ought to exist, and they resolve logical inconsistencies by creating new categories. Awareness that one has contributed to an action stimulates one's brain to justify that action (Salancik, 1977; Weick, 1979, p. 194–201).

Singer and Benassi (1981, p. 50) have concisely summarized the findings from laboratory experiments investigating how people interpret information: "When presented with an array of data or a sequence of events in which they are instructed to discover an underlying order, subjects show strong tendencies to perceive order and causality in random arrays, to perceive a pattern or correlation which seems a priori intuitively correct even when the actual correlation in the data is counterintuitive, to jump to conclusions about the correct hypothesis, to seek confirmatory evidence, to construe evidence liberally as confirmatory, to fail to generate or to assess alternative hypotheses, and, having thus managed to expose themselves only to confirmatory instances, to be fallaciously confident of the validity of their judgments." Wanting to control events and to claim credit for good results, people interpret very weak clues as indicating that their actions influence what happens—the existence of competition, the mere hypothesis that skillful actors do better, or talk about causation (Dunbar, 1981; Langer, 1975). Such clues can be injected into virtually any situation. But, despite their reluctance to concede that situations may be beyond their control, people tend to blame bad results on chance or on exogenous influences, such as people they dislike (Berkowitz and Green, 1962; Frankenberg, 1972; Langer and Roth, 1975; Maier, 1963).

"And while I am talking to you mothers and fathers, I give you more assurance; I have said this before, but I shall say it again and again: Your boys are not going to be sent into any foreign wars"—Franklin D. Roosevelt, 1940.

"In all likelihood, world inflation is over"—the managing director of the International Monetary Fund, 1959.

"Rock 'n' roll is phony and false, and sung, written and played for the most part by cretinous goons"—Frank Sinatra, 1957.

Industrialized societies promote rationalization and bureaucratization. The ideologies of these societies say that organizations should operate consistently, should make plans and monitor their progress toward fulfilling these plans, should obey hierarchical superiors, and should take only actions that they can justify (Dunbar, 1981; Meyer and Rowan, 1977). The societal ideologies also tell people to eliminate inconsistencies and disorder, to integrate their perceptions and beliefs, to look for causes, interdependencies, and implications, and to extrapolate their experiences (Beyer, 1981; March, 1973; Sproull, 1981; Thompson, 1967).

At the same time, industrialized societies make rational logic less effective. Large, complex societies flood their members with information, confound them with tangled causal relations, and assail them with numerous changes, many of which cannot be predicted with rational logic. Faced with too much information, information that comes through intermediaries, and intricate cause-effect relations, people find learning difficult, and they develop oversimplified beliefs that have little validity (Hedberg, 1981; Hewitt and Hall, 1973; Schroder, Driver, and Streufert, 1967). Simpler frames of reference omit more contingencies and make cruder distinctions.

"Nay, if a woman, even in unlawful copulation, fix her mind upon her husband, the child will resemble him though he did not beget it"—Aristotle.

Organizations, too, promote rationalization: they encourage people to make rational logic more perfect and to justify actions explicitly. Explicit rationality is the essence of bureaucracy. However, explication makes rationality more rigid; easily communicated and recorded concepts oversimplify and distort perceptions; social pressures induce people to espouse positions somewhat dishonestly; and large organizations' complexity makes it more likely that changes will produce unforeseen consequences (Axelrod, 1976a; Bougon, Weick and Binkhorst, 1977). Because organizations create buffers between themselves and their environments (Thompson, 1967), they have more scope than individual people to misperceive environmental events. Although most organizations encompass numerous and contradictory viewpoints, many organizations punish dissent and deviance, so the disparate views remain unspoken, and top managers dominate beliefs and perceptions (Dunbar, Dutton, and Torbert, 1982; Janis, 1972). Unfortunately, top managers experience most events at second hand, and their spokesperson roles encourage them to simplify their beliefs and to filter out logical inconsistencies, so they frequently have less realistic beliefs than many of their subordinates, and their public pronouncements and vested interests make them slower to accept new views (Axelrod, 1976a; Bougon, Weick, and Binkhorst, 1977; Hart, 1976, 1977; Starbuck, Greve, and Hedberg, 1978).

"I think there is a world market for about five computers"—Thomas J. Watson, president of IBM, 1948.

*Ideological Molecules.* Rational logic creates systems of interdependent ideas that resemble molecules. Each molecule integrates diverse elements—such as goals, values, beliefs, perceptions, theories, plans, expectations, labels, and symbols—that interlock through logical bonds. Advocates of rational problem solving have consistently prescribed unidirectional procedures for growing ideological molecules (Weick, 1983). For example, in their comparatively sophisticated book, Kepner and Tregoe (1965) prescribed a sequence of fourteen activities, which start with identifying whether a problem exists. People, they said, should give the label *problem* to an issue or situation only if and insofar as it involves a deviation of actual performance from desired performance; and they should identify and describe this deviation precisely. The problem definition should become the foundation for searching out possible causes of the problem and choosing the single most likely cause. The next steps ought to be laying down criteria for a desired action, developing and evaluating alternative actions, and choosing the single best action. However, the best action may produce bad side effects, so possible adverse results should be predicted, and the solution should be expanded from one action into a cluster of simultaneous actions. The final step should be making sure that actions are carried out.

Behaving quite at odds with such prescriptions, people naturally make unclear distinctions between problems and related ideological elements, such as goals, expectations, descriptive statements, threats, opportunities, and labels. Kepner and Tregoe (1965, pp. 7-17) and Maier (1963) have observed that people treat the word *problem* as interchangeable with *issue, question, trouble,* and *situation* and that people apply these concepts variously to evidence that something differs from what is desirable, to events that are causing discomfort, effort, or stress, to possible reasons why something differs from what is desirable, to possible sources of events that are causing discomfort, and to actions that ought to be taken.

Furthermore, natural behaviors flow in complex streams that environmental events stimulate and perturb. Witte (1972) and his colleagues analyzed the documents generated by 233 decision processes: only 4 of these processes flowed unidirectionally from problem definition to solution selection. Even the decision processes that approximate a unidirectional sequence include activities such as learning, experimentation, and feedback from actions to problems (Mintzberg, Rasinghani, and Théorêt, 1976); and the four unidirectional processes observed by Witte (1972) and his colleagues were no more efficient or thorough than most other processes. A new molecule may begin to form around various kinds of elements (Beyer, 1981), and, thereafter, it gains and loses elements in an erratic sequence—a plan forms; a goal fades; a relationship clarifies. Rational logic expands the molecule to include other elements that fit in, it edits out or distorts elements that are hard to integrate, and rationalization fills in the logical gaps. Thus, the molecule tends to generalize and simplify as time passes, growing more complete and more stable (Pettigrew, 1979). Each incremental change propagates through the molecule, influencing the logically adjacent elements and weakening or strengthening some of the logical bonds between elements. Because adjacent elements can remain slightly incongruent, the effects of a change attenuate as they propagate; and a sequence of changes that erode a molecule may leave fragments that become the nuclei of new molecules.

As rational logic grows stronger, bad results lose the power to instigate changes. Our current programs have strong justifications, and they would have produced good results if accidents had not happened or enemies had not acted malevolently. Rather than abandon our programs, we should strengthen them with more effort or more money and give them enough time to yield good results (Salancik, 1977; Staw and Ross, 1978).

The "fundamental business of the country . . . is on a sound and prosperous basis"—Herbert Hoover, Black Friday, 1929.

Altheide and Johnson (1980), Edelman (1977), and Manning (1977) have described explicit, intended efforts to manufacture evidence that justifies organizations' actions. The examples range from television ratings based on the reports of viewers who volunteer to participate and on periods of special programming, through military reports that portray all battles as victories and all personnel as superior, to falsified police reports. Recognizing that the people to whom justifications are addressed may discount them, organizations that seek public support sometimes go to elaborate efforts to render their justifications credible. A clean example is the research and politicking that enabled Crest toothpaste to win an endorsement from the American Dental Association, and a horrible example is the campaign of propaganda and false accusations through which the Nazis aroused hatred of Jews.

Even though people have to interact with and respond to complex and unpredictable environments, the ambiguity and inconsistency of natural behaviors pose a mystery in part. Brains' enthusiasm for rational logic suggests that people might naturally draw clear distinctions between concepts and might naturally form ideological molecules in orderly ways such as Kepner and Tregoe and others have prescribed. So what explains the deviations between prescribed rationality and natural rationality? Are the prescriptions right, and do people naturally think poorly? Or does natural behavior offer advantages over prescribed rationality?

Attempts to follow unidirectional problem-solving sequences tend to be self-defeating, because such sequences make very weak provisions for correcting ignorance, and ideological elements have meaning only in relation to other elements (Bobrow and Norman, 1975; Schank, 1975). To infer what is wrong, for example, people must perceive other aspects of their situations: they can identify $A$ and $B$ as wrong only if they can also see $C$ and $D$. And to infer what is wrong, people must consider their goals, values, and expectations; Kepner and Tregoe themselves said that people should identify problems by comparing actual performances with expected performances. But to form expectations and to set realistic goals, people need causal beliefs and perceptions. People rarely have enough information and understanding to feel certain that they have actually solved problems, so they dare not postpone taking actions until they have found solutions. Looking at alternative actions exposes the potential difficulties accompanying the actions and usually shows that the best actions differ little from other good alternatives and so makes it more difficult to take chosen actions (Brunsson, 1982). Problems defined without regard for possible solutions often have no solutions (Watzlawick, Weakland, and Fisch, 1974).

Outside of laboratory experiments and training sessions, people do not generally know that they ought to be solving problems, because they do not know whether problems exist. They simply act and do not always reflect on their actions or watch the results of their actions. Result watching, when it occurs, might take them in various directions. They may, in fact, perceive new problems, but they may see successes, threats, or opportunities instead (Mintzberg, Rasinghani, and Théorêt, 1976). They may think of potential actions and wonder whether these actions would block any threats or exploit any opportunities. They may discover causal processes or notice changes in contingency variables (Hedberg, 1981). New causal beliefs or potential actions may lead to new goals and expectations. And so on. Cyert, Simon, and Trow (1956, p. 247), for example, remarked that "the 'problem' to be solved was in fact a whole series of 'nested' problems, each alternative solution to a problem at one level leading to a new set of problems at the next level. In addition, the process of solving the substantive problems created many procedural problems for the organization: allocating time and work, planning agendas and report presentations, and so on." The diverse elements of an ideological molecule are truly interdependent, and effective thinking acknowledges this interdependence by recalculating iteratively.

Another reason for people to deviate from the prescriptions for rational logic is that rational logic itself makes them justify their actions (Salancik, 1977; Staw, 1980; Weick, 1979, pp. 194-201). For actions to seem rational, people must have ideological molecules that include and highlight "needs for action" (Brunsson, 1982). These justifying molecules may be problems, successes, threats, or opportunities.

"If God had intended that man should fly, He would have given him wings"—George W. Melville, chief engineer of the U.S. Navy, 1900.

*Some Suggested Terminology.* "Needs for action" are ideas stating that certain actions ought to be taken, or need not be taken, to correct what is wrong. "I got to get an answer back to these guys!" "Well, then, our problem seems to 've turned to how to get the maximum amount of feedback from the participants" instead of "The participants might not express their opinions." "It's my job to manage, and I must do something. How can I motivate them?" "We shouldn't count on it until they put up some money."

To avoid confusion, I distinguish needs for action from "symptoms" and from "causes of symptoms." Symptoms are ideas describing aspects of the world that are undesirable or cause discomfort, effort, or stress. To allow for positive outcomes, the concept of symptom encompasses: (1) evidence of results that are better than satisfactory as well as worse than desirable and (2) events that cause pleasure as well as discomfort. Of course, "causes of symptoms" are ideas that conjecture about the reasons symptoms exist.

The word *problem* itself denotes a distinct ideological molecule. Problems comprise one subset of continua in at least two dimensions; other subsets of these continua can be called successes, threats, opportunities. Problems justify actions negatively by emphasizing symptoms; and problems justify currently or retrospectively by emphasizing perceived or remembered symptoms. Successes also justify actions currently or retrospectively, but they justify positively by suggesting that repetition of past actions will continue to produce successes. Threats and opportunities justify prospectively by pointing to predicted symptoms or future needs for action (Staw, 1980).

Threats and opportunities offer more latitude for fantasy and social construction in that people need suppress only dissonant predictions rather than memories. But threats and opportunities may lack credibility because they are only predictions or may lack immediacy because they lie in the future. To justify strongly, threats and opportunities have to be somewhat larger than life, with the risk that they are too large to be taken seriously. Moreover, societal ideologies frown upon opportunism, so opportunities are mostly used confidentially. For external audiences, people sometimes try to legitimate their pursuits of opportunities by announcing their altruistic motives (Mills, 1940).

"The President's program will begin to bear fruit even before it is enacted"—Donald Regan, U.S. secretary of the treasury, 1981.

*Rationalizing Actions.* Many of the activities that people label "problem solving" are mislabeled in that they do not start with problems and end with solutions. At least as often as they solve problems, probably much more often, people build rationales for actions that they have taken or intend to take.

Emphasizing that people construct problems, solutions, and theories collectively, Hewitt and Hall (1973) pointed out that people often create theories by backward inference from cure to core problem to theory. The participants in "problem solving" frequently start by appraising a shared situation and stating needs for action, and they continue such appraisal talk until they agree upon a cure. They then make the agreed cure the basis for defining a core problem and construct a theory that explains why the core problem arose and how the agreed cure will solve it. The theory also distinguishes the essential, real aspects of the core problem from the peripheral, illusory aspects; incorporates widely accepted values and beliefs; and portrays the stimulus situation as a specific instance of a general class of problems. The participants build their theory iteratively, testing it against past events and concocted examples, and their interactions make extensive use of stylized language.

Such backward reasoning has roots in widespread methods of childrearing and schooling. Children learn that results are generally good or bad, not neutral; that results call for statements that actions are, or are not, needed; that results have discernible causes; that correct explanations for results have social legitimacy, whereas incorrect explanations do not; and that one can depend upon other people, especially experts, to provide legitimate explanations for mysterious results. Because adults reward or punish them frequently, small children learn that results are normally good or bad, that rewards and punishments are ubiquitous, and that adults react to results by taking actions promptly. Older children discover that results, rewards, and punishments may be delayed and subtle. Because their parents and teachers nearly always know the answers to children's mysteries, children learn that adults can see the causes of mysteries and that mysteries look mysterious mainly because of inexperience or ignorance.

Thus, as adults, people spend very little time observing and describing situations before they start judging them good or bad and start proposing needs for action; they expect to be able to discern causes, and they construct theories that arise as much from societal ideologies as from direct evidence (Beyer, 1981; Kepner and Tregoe, 1965; Maier, 1963; Mintzberg, Rasinghani, and Théorêt, 1976; Sproull, 1981). They often explain mysterious results with quasi theories—prevalent and legitimate causal attributions that are difficult to disconfirm with evidence (Hall and Hewitt, 1970; Hewitt and Hall, 1973). The quasi theory of time holds that events occur at natural or preordained times—for example, that getting visible results takes at least a minimal, but unknown, amount of time; or that organizations go through certain distinct developmental stages at appropriate, but ambiguous, times. The quasi theory of antisocial conspiracy implies, for instance, that journal editors block the publication of innovative research that would revolutionize their disciplines. The quasi theory of communication blames mistakes, crises, arguments, and wars on insufficient communication—thus, communication training is supposed to integrate into harmonious teams managers who face disparate pressures; or decisions to refuse tenure result from incomplete understanding of the merits of specific cases.

Labels and categories guide the editing of ideological molecules by helping to determine which elements fit in. Most labels and categories imply that these particular labels and these specific categories are the only right and proper ones; and some labels and categories make it improbable, even impossible, for actions to produce bad results (Golding, 1980; Leach, 1964). Who would hire a "dropout" or an "unskilled worker"? Would an "innocent" person refuse a "fair hearing" that metes out "justice"? Edelman (1977, p. 38) has observed: "Ever since it was established, the Federal Communications Commission (FCC) has given paramount weight in choosing among competing license applicants to the financial resources available to the applicant, so that wealthy individuals and successful corporations easily make a persuasive case, while people of moderate means, including minorities, dissenters, and radicals, are easily rejected. The Commission's justification is that radio listeners and television viewers will be hurt if the licensee uses poor equipment or goes bankrupt; the weighing of comparative financial resources therefore promotes 'the public interest, convenience, or necessity,' as required by the Communications Act of 1934. Paramount weight to a more equal representation on the air of political perspectives could obviously be justified on the same ground."

## Behavior Programs

"The Americans have need of the telephone, but we do not. We have plenty of messenger boys"—William Preece, chief engineer of the British Post Office, 1876.

As long ago as 1958, March and Simon (pp. 141-142) remarked that behavior programs "account for a very large part of the behavior of all persons, and for almost all of the behavior of persons in relatively routine positions." This turned out to be an underestimate of behavior programs' pervasiveness: research has subsequently revealed that behavior programs account for nearly all of the actions of all people, no matter what positions they occupy

(Mintzberg, 1973b; Mintzberg, Rasinghani, and Théorêt, 1976; Newell and Simon, 1972; Tuchman, 1973). People get their behavior programs through spontaneous habits, professional norms, education, training, precedents, traditions, rituals, and organizations' standard operating procedures. By adulthood, people have acquired large repertoires of behavior programs that comprise the essence of behavior.

Behavior programs amplify humans' capabilities greatly. When people perceive that situations fall into familiar categories— which happens most of the time—they do not waste time and effort discovering appropriate actions all over again: they simply follow familiar programs. The behavior programs demand little or no reflection by the actors, and they quickly produce actions like those that succeeded in the past (Weick, 1984). Then, when people perceive novel situations, they create new behavior programs by reassembling segments taken from existing programs. Their inventive efforts can focus on major issues rather than minor details, because reused segments fill in the details. Thus, behavior programs conserve humans' analytical resources, allowing people to allocate these resources where they can yield large benefits.

"The bow is a simple weapon, firearms are very complicated things which get out of order in many ways . . . a very heavy weapon and tires out soldiers on the march. Whereas also a bowman can let off six aimed shots a minute, a musketeer can discharge but one in two minutes"—Colonel John Smyth, advising the British Privy Council, 1591.

Behavior programs do free people from having to stay constantly alert and responsive to impinging events, but the other side of this is that behavior programs encourage people to misperceive their worlds. Firstly, much perception happens automatically, without reflection, because it is itself programmed. Organizations formalize perceptual programs in standard operating procedures, job specifications, and contracts; and they concretize them in space assignments and buildings (Starbuck, 1976). Secondly, behavior programs focus perceptions: events form natural equivalence classes corresponding to the behavior programs that they initiate, so people attend to the distinctions between classes and ignore the distinctions within classes. One consequence is that people generally fail to notice gradual trends until these have grown so large that no existing behavior program works, and these oversights occasionally turn out to be very important (Hedberg, Nystrom, and Starbuck, 1976). Thirdly, behavior programs constitute frames of reference, so people base their information gathering and interpretation on these frames of reference (Berger and Luckmann, 1966; Rosenhan, 1978; Salancik, 1977; Starbuck, 1976; Tuchman, 1973). Data tend to confirm what the programs assume to be true: the gathered data may show mainly good results even when poor results prevail, because people are gathering few data where poor results show up. For instance, people do not monitor events that they believe to be tangential or phenomena that they assume to be stable. Even with plentiful data, however, people misunderstand the causes and implications of events that violate their frames of reference (Starbuck, Greve, and Hedberg, 1978; Watzlawick, Weakland, and Fisch, 1974).

"The trade of advertising is now so near to perfection that it is not easy to propose any improvement"—*The Idler*, a newspaper, 1759.

"Atomic energy might be as good as our present-day explosives, but it is unlikely to produce anything very much more dangerous"—Winston Churchill, 1939.

*Why Programs Persist.* Rather than create new programs, people reuse existing behavior programs whenever possible (Dunbar, 1981; Hall, 1976; Newell and Simon, 1972). Consider, for example, Charlie Strothman's reactions to a research project that reduced one of his intricate behavior programs to a simple linear equation. Although not about strategic decisions, the story does show some characteristics of a real-life behavior program, and it exposes some reasons why behavior programs exhibit stability.

John Dutton and I (Dutton and Starbuck, 1971a) spent five years studying how Charlie created production schedules, including one entire year investigating how he estimated run time. Many times each day, he would look at a schedule and estimate how many hours of work it represented. We got interested in how he did this; and Charlie, who was very intelligent and had had some engineering training, took as much interest as we did. He donated his weekends to experimentation at the university, seventy miles from his home. He also made numerous useful suggestions about experimental design.

At the outset, Charlie could not say how he estimated run time. Although he had words to describe his thought processes, his words did not match what actually went on in his head. No one had taught him an explicit procedure; he had just learned from experience, and he doubted that he always used the same procedure. We and he eventually discovered that he did adhere to a single procedure. When estimating a schedule's run time, Charlie first added up the schedule's total length in feet. Then he examined several characteristics of the schedule according to a consistent sequence. One peculiarity was that he did not always estimate the number of setups, but he did always scan a column of numbers showing the length of each setup and then estimated the average length per setup. We discovered that he could estimate average length per setup much more accurately than he could estimate the number of setups without actually counting. Both estimates gave similar information in that:

$$\text{Number of setups} = \frac{\text{Length}}{\text{Average length per setup}}$$

but Charlie did not actually calculate this equivalence.

Charlie used a schedule's characteristics to select a machine speed from his memory. His memory astonished us. He had preserved his experience by memorizing approximately 5,000 machine speeds, together with the characteristics of the schedule or schedules that had produced them. Finally he would calculate:

$$\text{Time} = \frac{\text{Length}}{\text{Speed}}$$

Charlie could interpolate between the speeds in his memory, and he could make general statements about the kinds of schedules that ran faster or slower, but he had no detailed understanding of why a certain speed would occur in certain circumstances. Interpolation or extrapolation made him extremely uncomfortable, and he distrusted time estimates based on interpolated speeds. From his viewpoint, the memorized speeds were discrete observations. We, however, wondered whether there might be patterns and an implicit rationale. If Charlie's observations were accurate, we conjectured, the memorized speeds should form patterns corresponding to the machines' characteristics. Through calculations and experiments— 577 experiments—we learned that his memorized speeds fitted remarkably closely to the equation:

$$\text{Time} = A \times (\text{Number of setups}) + [B + C \times (\text{Density of material})] \times \text{Length}$$

where $A$, $B$, and $C$ represent constants. Charlie had been using two nonlinear equations and an amazing memory to compute production times that he could compute with one linear equation.

The linear equation predicted Charlie's speed estimates so accurately that he himself could not distinguish its estimates from ones he had actually made. The linear equation also provided a rationale for interpolating and extrapolating beyond Charlie's actual experiences. He had contributed as much as we to discovering the linear equation, and he understood its logic. He was no conformist, and he liked to innovate: he had introduced several innovations to his job even though his immediate superiors distrusted and criticized them. So we naively expected him to start using the linear equation in his daily work.

Not so. Six years of habit and the frame of reference that went with it were too strong. The familiar program worked, and he trusted it. Who knows what errors lurked in an unfamiliar program? The linear equation conspicuously ignored several characteristics of schedules that his familiar program took into account, and it used a strange new characteristic—density of material. Moreover, the familiar program meshed with other programs used by other people: the whole organization talked and reported data in terms of speeds, not times. Times make little sense within a speed frame of reference: to convert times to speeds, one needs to know lengths, which might be arbitrary. If Charlie were to shift to a time frame of reference, he would isolate himself from other people in his organization, and their talk about speeds would lack meaning for him. It was no accident that he had earlier told us: "When I first came to work here, I was told what the average speeds were."

*Action Generators.* Some behavior programs—action generators—are executed automatically and unreflectively and activated by job assignments or clocks. I did not get up early this morning because some problem had appeared and careful analysis had convinced me that a good solution would be to get up: I get up early every morning, even after I have gone to bed unusually late.

Although everyone has a few action generators, they seem to perform mainly peripheral functions when people are acting as individuals. Organizations, however, use action generators profusely and assign them central functions. Organizations operate to a great extent on the basis of repetition and expectations instead of analyses and communications, and programs of various types afford the main means by which organizations learn, coordinate activities, and control actions hierarchically. Action generators minimize the need to communicate, and people who are following action generators do not disobey or behave unpredictably. For instance, large organizations produce budgets and performance reports at regular intervals whether or not they face any difficulties that can be surmounted through budgets or performance reports: the organizations appoint budget specialists whose sole responsibility is to produce budgets, they set up procedures for recording performance data, they employ accountants who are supposed to tabulate performance data, and they provide budgets and floor space for budgeting. Likewise, organizations fabricate products, monitor product quality, conduct research, and advertise without regard for whether these actions can solve immediate problems.

The term *organization* homogenizes a very diverse spectrum of forms and practices. Not only do some organizations use action generators more extensively than others, but some subunits within a single organization make greater use of them. Past research suggests several hypotheses:

- Older organizations and subunits likely use more action generators, because new organizations and subunits lack programs, and formalization increases over time (Starbuck, 1965).

- Bureaucratization correlates with organizational size, and bureaucratization produces formal job descriptions and standardized procedures, so larger, more bureaucratic organizations and subunits have more action generators (Pugh and others, 1969).
- More successful organizations and subunits probably depend more strongly upon action generators, because successes breed complacency, whereas failures and difficulties encourage reflection (Hedberg, 1981).
- Action generators likely proliferate in organizations and subunits that conduct ceremonies and those that are supposed to conform to legitimate practices, because self-selection and socialization would make the members of these subunits especially respectful of societal ideologies (Beyer, 1981; Kaufman, 1960; Meyer and Rowan, 1977).
- Industrialized societies encourage programming and bureaucratization, so they also nurture action generators.

In many organizations, enough programs take the form of action generators to make unreflective, automatic action the dominant mode of behavior.

"The war in Vietnam is going well and will succeed"—Robert McNamara, 1963.

*Justifying Stability and Understanding Change.* Both individual people and organizations sometimes change their behavior programs and action generators in order to get better results. But, because behavior programs generally, and action generators especially, let people act without reflecting, they also stabilize behaviors, impede adaptation, and produce the strategies and policies that people impute to their actions in retrospect. Moreover, people tolerate extremely loose and flexible associations between actions and benefits: they may retain their programs unchanged despite trouble and turbulence (Hedberg, Nystrom, and Starbuck, 1976). Indeed, behavior programs and action generators make stability, strategies, and policies appear realistic by keeping people from seeing problems, successes, threats, or opportunities that would justify changes.

Stability is more easily justified by larger problems that have more general and more robust labels (Starbuck, 1982, 1983). For example, the United States government has fought the challenge of international Communism on many fronts: at home through loyalty oaths, Senator Joseph McCarthy, and the House Un-American Activities Committee; in Korea, Cuba, Berlin, Vietnam, Chile, Guatemala, El Salvador, Grenada, and the skies over the Soviet Union. It is hard to imagine how the United States could have justified massive expenditures on armaments, far-flung espionage, and internal-security investigations that infringe citizens' constitutional rights if the challenge had been defined less abstractly or less generally. Halberstam (1972, p. 151), for instance, observed: "It was one thing to base a policy in Southeast Asia on total anti-Communism in the early 1950s when the Korean War was being fought and when the French Indochina war was at its height, when there was, on the surface at least, some evidence of a Communist monolith, and when the United States at home was becoming locked into the harshest of the McCarthy tensions. But it was another thing to accept these policies quite so casually in 1961 (although McCarthy was gone and the atmosphere in which the policies had been set had changed, the policies remained much the same), when both the world and the United States were very different. By 1961 the schism in the Communist world was clearly apparent: Khrushchev had removed his technicians and engineers from China."

In many organizations and societies, the top managers develop central problems, successes, threats, and opportunities that are extremely stable because they are so big and so perfect in logic. Because a large, general ideological molecule picks up new elements as rapidly as it loses old ones, it just evolves instead of dissolving; and organizations and societies amplify this natural stability by creating specialized subunits that are assigned to look for new elements to add to their central molecules (Ditton, 1979). For instance, the challenge of international Communism did not diminish in 1972 when the United States recognized and began trading with the People's Republic of China, when the United States and the Soviet Union signed a nuclear-arms-limitation agreement, and when Bobby Fischer defeated Boris Spassky; for

Chile had recently expropriated the Anaconda and Kennecott copper mines, Communist athletes dominated the 1972 Olympic Games, and North Vietnam was continuing to win the Vietnam War. Partly because they have large central molecules, organizations and societies exhibit a phenomenon called unlearning: the members wait until events have explicitly disconfirmed their central beliefs before they seriously consider alternatives (Hedberg, 1981; Hedberg, Nystrom, and Starbuck, 1976).

More generally, people find reorientations difficult. Reorientations are large strategic changes that would redefine individuals' or organizations' domains in some fundamental respects. People lack experience outside their domains, so proposed reorientations evoke confusion and uncertainty. Reorientations may seem illogical and paradoxical, because they violate basic tenets of people's frames of reference (McCall, 1977; Watzlawick, Weakland, and Fisch, 1974). It is clear, however, that reorientations imply changes in power distributions, so they instigate struggles between those who have power and those who seek it (Argyris and Schön, 1978; Normann, 1971; Pettigrew, 1973; Rhenman, 1973; Wildavsky, 1972).

On the other hand, people react rather positively to variations, which are small strategic changes that appear to modify individuals' or organizations' domains only incrementally. Newman and Logan (1955) listened to business executives discussing why firms grow: the five reasons that they noted all fit the prescription that organizations should change incrementally at their margins. People can make sense of variations because they alter actions or beliefs moderately within overarching frames of reference, without challenging the frames of reference themselves (Watzlawick, Weakland, and Fisch, 1974). Variations also take advantage of experience, they do not threaten current power holders, and they can draw support from divergent interests (Lindblom, 1959; Normann, 1971). Organizations program many variations: industrial engineers discover problems that call for slightly different actions; sales personnel report on market trends within current domains. A team from McKinsey & Company analyzed ten companies that managers regard as being especially well run: the study's main conclusion was that "Controlled experiments abound in these companies. The attitude of management is to 'get some data, do it, then adjust it,' rather than wait for a perfect overall plan. The companies tend to be tinkerers rather than inventors, making small steps of progress rather than conceiving sweeping new concepts" (Peters, 1980, p. 196).

Unhappily, "small steps of progress" often fail to keep actions up to date. Even when variations are generated by random processes or mechanistic rules, people postpone reconceptualizations until the evidence piles up to uncontestable levels (Box and Draper, 1969; Edwards, 1968; Tversky and Kahneman, 1974). But people do not ordinarily generate variations randomly or mechanistically. They choose variations on the basis of their current beliefs and vested interests, so the variations do not challenge their prior beliefs or rattle the status quo; and people interpret the results of variations within the frameworks of their current beliefs and vested interests, so their interpretations support their prior beliefs and reinforce current organizational structures (McCall, 1977; Wildavsky, 1972). Misperceptions persist and accumulate. Indeed, successful people and organizations create programs to reproduce their successes, and they want these programs to operate in stable environments, so they try to choose variations that counteract social and technological changes (Starbuck, 1983). Such variations succeed only temporarily at best. One consequence is that smooth strategic trajectories made up of variations are sometimes interrupted by abrupt crises and reorientations (Hedberg and Jönsson, 1977; Jönsson and Lundin, 1977; Miller, 1982; Rhenman, 1973; Starbuck, 1968, 1973).

"The day of the battleship has not passed, and it is highly unlikely that an airplane, or fleet of them, could ever successfully sink a fleet of navy vessles under battle conditions"—Franklin D. Roosevelt, assistant secretary of the navy, 1922.

"As far as sinking a ship with a bomb is concerned, you just can't do it"—Admiral Clark Woodward, 1939.

## Social Interaction in Organizations

"Violence breeds violence, and it is predicted that by 1990 kidnapping will be the dominant mode of social interaction"—Woody Allen, 1982.

Social interaction, too, illustrates the general proposition that powerful tools can produce much harm as well as much good. Many people cooperating in an organization can achieve results far beyond the capabilities of one person, but a large organization can also constitute a complex environment that dominates its members' actions while confusing their understanding. An organizational hierarchy can smooth coordination and enable a few wise and insightful leaders to dictate their subordinates' actions, but a hierarchy can also allow a few arrogant leaders with faulty perceptions to steer an organization into disaster or let selfish superiors claim the money and credit from their subordinates' hard work and creativity. Organizations promote and enlarge the scales of rationality and programming, thus amplifying both the advantages and disadvantages of these tools.

The complexity and uncontrollability of organizational environments show up in descriptions of decision making or problem solving. Different observers have reported seeing very different behavioral sequences: Mintzberg, Rasinghani, and Théorêt (1976) alone saw seven categories of sequences that were composed of twelve categories of activities. Witte (1972) and his colleagues found that the numbers of information-gathering operations, alternative-developing operations, and alternative-evaluating operations all maximize near the ends of decision-making processes; that the minimum numbers of these operations all occur shortly after processes begin; and that processes typically incorporate numerous subdecisions rather than building to final major decisions. Cohen, March, and Olsen (1972) explained the diversity of behaviors by saying that four distinct streams interact: a stream of problems, a stream of potential actions, a stream of participants, and a stream of choice opportunities. Because people facing choice opportunities may introduce their pet problems or propose actions that bear no relationship to the visible problems, "Problems come to seek connections to choice opportunities that solve them, solutions come to seek problems they handle successfully" (Cohen, March, and Olsen, 1976, p. 31).

To some degree, the reported behavioral sequences are best explained as artifacts of the observers themselves or of the unnatural situations observed. However, the very diversity of descriptions indicates that observers are looking at a diverse range of complex phenomena, as does the prevalent observation that behaviors iterate through repetitive cycles. Numerous participants and their interactions render collective behaviors intrinsically complex and erratic. Even if autonomous individual people would follow unidirectional behavioral sequences—which seems improbable—interacting people have to respond to stimuli from their social environments. Organizational membership entails commitments to attend and respond to such environmental stimuli; and organizations increase the numbers of stimuli by integrating many people into networks, making it easy to transmit information, and creating numerous interorganizational interfaces.

Studies of decision making or problem solving start from deceptive premises by initially classifying certain activities as decision making or problem solving. Although decision-making meetings do occur, people do not enter most mundane work situations with clear expectations that new problems, successes, threats, or opportunities have arisen or that they must make significant decisions. Often, people take actions without saying or thinking that the actions solve specific problems or meet specific threats, and people may continue acting for long periods without looking at the results of their actions. When people do watch results, they often lack strong expectations beyond ambiguity. Most of the performance information that organizations collect routinely has ambiguous significance: because organizations record very little information about causal processes, and the standards for collecting and interpreting information are supposed to help managements appear successful, the recorded information impedes understanding and confounds attempts to draw practical implications (Boland, 1982; Dunbar, 1981; Garfinkel, 1967; Hopwood, 1972).

"The Harkins briefings were of course planned long in advance; they were brainwashings really, but brainwashings made all the more effective and exciting by the trappings of danger. Occasional mortar rounds going off. A captured rifle to touch, a surly captured Vietcong to look at. What was created on those trips was not an insight about the country but an illusion of knowledge. McNamara was getting the same information which was available in Washington, but now it was presented so much more effectively that he thought he understood Vietnam. Afterward Arthur Sylvester, his PIO, told reporters how many miles he had flown, how many corps headquarters, province headquarters, district headquarters he had visited, how many officers of each rank. The reporters sat there writing it down, all of it mindless, all of it fitting McNamara's vision of what Vietnam should be. Vietnam confirmed McNamara's preconceptions and specifications"—David Halberstam (1972, p. 305).

Since all situations have numerous possible interpretations, colleagues decide jointly which interpretations seem realistic (Berger and Luckmann, 1966; Ditton, 1979; Hewitt and Hall, 1973; Langer, 1975; Ungson, Braunstein, and Hall, 1981). As one consequence, observations about the stimuli that initiate decision making or problem solving tend to be tautologies. For example, Mintzberg, Rasinghani, and Théorêt (1976, p. 253) asserted, "The need for a decision is identified as a difference between information on some actual situation and some expected standard," but people can change their expected standards and perceptions. Similarly, people could interpret any situation as violating at least one of the criteria stated by Hewitt and Hall (1973, p. 368): People classify a situation as problematical when "the orderly quality of the scene is questionable. . . . People are disposed to view a situation as orderly if they can find a basis for viewing the behavior in it as typical of its members, probable under the circumstances, applicable in the light of conditions, appropriate to the goals being sought, realistic in its direction, and morally within the norms. They view it as disorderly if the behavior seems atypical, unlikely, inexplicable, technically inappropriate, unrealistic, or morally wrong." People believe that they are supposed to state symptoms, causes of symptoms, and needs for action when they are result watching, so they do state them; and it is these statements that explicate order or disorder and that define situations as problematical or successful or threatening or opportunistic. The actions that ensue from such definitions may turn the definitions into self-fulfilling prophecies (Rosenhan, 1978; Starbuck, 1976; Weick, 1983).

Social construction also frequently makes decisions, strategies, and policies the consequences of actions rather than their determinants. Cohen, March, and Olsen (1972) noted that participants in decision making may perceive that decisions have occurred in three circumstances: (1) when actions are taken, even if these actions do not solve one of the visible problems; (2) when problems are removed from choice opportunities, even if no actions are taken to cause their removal; or (3) when actions are mated with problems and called solutions. Cohen, March, and Olsen asserted that events (3) happen much less frequently than events (1) and (2). Garfinkel (1967) and Weick (1979) have pointed out how often people re-enact decisions by looking into the past and seeing that they evidently must have chosen courses of action. Process models of human behavior, whether models of individuals or organizations, have been strikingly devoid of explicit choices (Dutton and Starbuck, 1971b). The process models indicate that people seek to design the single best actions rather than to choose among alternative actions. The process models also emphasize experimentation: people try out actions to see how they work, shifting to alternatives only if they get bad results. Because behavior programs govern both the designing and the experimenting, people seem to exercise little choice even at tactical levels.

Complex social environments give people good reason to simplify their worlds, and they can do this by acting tentatively, following precedents, adhering to social rituals, speaking in stylized language, anticipating others' reactions, and choosing to whom they listen. People edit their statements before making them, and they hedge their voiced observations and proposals with disclaimers (Hewitt and Stokes, 1975). They emphasize symptoms that high-status people say are important and deviations from legitimate goals or expectations (Lyles and Mitroff, 1980). They define accidents as deviations from the predictions of authorities, and they blame people instead of rules or machines and enemies instead of friends (Dunbar, 1981). They appeal to accepted theories and quasi theories. They propose conventional and accepted actions that would harmonize with current actions, that imitate other organizations' actions, that use wasted resources, or that reinforce current power holders (Alexander, 1979; Mehan, 1984; Starbuck, 1976; Staw and Ross, 1978). They vote on proposals and endorse observations via neglect, skeptical looks, clichés, and rephrasings, among other means (Starbuck, 1983). Of course, they follow confident leaders, defer to authority or presumed expertise, and give high priority to social solidarity (Janis, 1972; Milgram, 1974). Although ritual and editing do have the intended effect of simplifying complex worlds, they also foster misinformation and misperception (Argyris and Schön, 1978).

"I won't be involved in the day-to-day operations of the team. I'm too busy with the shipping business"—George Steinbrenner, 1973.

"I thank God there are no free schools, nor printing, and hope we shall not have them these hundred years; for learning has brought disobedience and heresy and sects into the world, and printing has divulged them"—William Berkeley, royal governor of Virginia, 1670.

Hierarchies, too, simplify complexity, and the stories of Alexander the Great, Napoleon, Henry Ford, and Thomas Watson show how successful hierarchical control can be. Hierarchies generally mean that replacing just a few top managers can induce large behavioral and ideological changes. Unfortunately, top managers tend to misperceive what is happening even more than many of their subordinates do: top managers' direct personal experiences with clients, customers, and technologies occurred years ago; they receive much of their information through secondhand reports that systematically avoid displeasing them; they interpret their promotions and high statuses as evidence that they have more expertise than their subordinates; and they listen mainly to other top managers who are subjected to similar pressures (Porter and Roberts, 1976, pp. 1573-1576). Top managers' influential positions make their perceptual errors quite serious. Top managers also tend to resist, more than their subordinates do, strategic reorientations within their organizations: significant social and technological changes threaten their dominance and high social statuses; and they fear, with reason, that they will become scapegoats if current programs and strategies are judged failures (Normann, 1971; Starbuck, Greve, and Hedberg, 1978). But top managers can exert little influence upon social and technological changes beyond the boundaries of their organizations, so their efforts to regulate and decelerate change may simply steer their organizations into stagnating backwaters (Hedberg, Nystrom, and Starbuck, 1976).

"Most of the ideas in IBM have come from me personally, but our inventors did the actual inventing, and it is their names which are on the patents"— Thomas J. Watson, president of IBM, 1946 (Belden and Belden, 1962, p. 260).

## Blundering in the Dark

"I cannot imagine any condition which could cause this ship to flounder. I cannot conceive of any vital disaster happening to this vessel"—E. J. Smith, captain of the *Titanic,* 1912.

Top managers may be more prone to erroneous perceptions than some other people, but the great majority of people struggle along with numerous and large perceptual errors, and their beliefs incorporate substantial amounts of fantasy (Hall, 1976; Singer and Benassi, 1981; Starbuck, Greve, and Hedberg, 1978; Tversky and Kahneman, 1974). All people have limited ranges of experience: most have worked in one or two occupational ladders, in a few organizations, in fewer industries, over a couple of decades. Programs and buffers have blurred their perceptions. So they depend upon colleagues and schooling to extend their experiences and to provide contexts for interpreting them. They believe that they are working in competitive industries or decentralized firms or whatever, not because these judgments have firm foundations in their own experiences but because other people have told them so or because they have read it in a trade magazine. The other people, of course, have no wider personal experiences than they themselves and are mainly repeating what they in turn have heard, filtered, and rationalized. Some people do, of course, have clearer visions and more relevant experiences, or they have done careful research. But perceivers' influence probably correlates not at all with their realism—misguided leaders fill human history (Antonio, 1979), and listeners infer expertise on the basis of superficial cues, such as speakers' white coats, enthusiasm, and self-confidence (Milgram, 1974). The various pressures upon top managers might even make the influence-realism correlation negative. Social pressures and ritualistic formal-reporting systems encourage all people to tolerate observations that contradict their beliefs and to accept explanations, such as quasi theories, that explain nothing. Thus, not only do organizational and societal mythologies shape frames of reference, but these mythologies perpetuate themselves somewhat autonomously of actual events.

"Heavier-than-air flying machines are impossible"—Lord Kelvin, renowned physicist, 1890.

"X-rays are a hoax"—Lord Kelvin, 1900.

Payne and Pugh (1976) reviewed numerous studies of organizational structures and climates and contrasted objective and subjective measures. They found that organizations' members disagree strongly with each other: "Perceptual measures of each of the structural and climate variables have varied so much among themselves that mean scores were uninterpretable" (p. 1168). With understatement, Payne and Pugh (1976, p. 1167) also concluded that "Relationships between perceptual and objective measures of structural variables were not strong," although people do seem to know whether they are working in large organizations or small ones. The disagreements among people correspond in part with their different occupations and hierarchical statuses. However, the disagreements cannot be explained completely by differences in valid information and expertise, for intergroup differences are much smaller than interindividual differences, and the intergroup differences clearly include the effects of rationalization and contagion. For instance, members holding higher statuses have generally more positive views of their organizations.

"That is the biggest fool thing we have ever done. . . . The [atomic] bomb will never go off, and I speak as an expert in explosives"—Admiral William D. Leahy, speaking to Harry S. Truman, 1945.

Members also misperceive their organizations' environments. Tosi, Aldag, and Storey (1973) asked 102 middle and top managers from various firms in diverse industries to describe their environments' stabilities; then they correlated the managers' perceptions with volatility indices calculated from their firms' financial reports and industry statistics. The correlations between subjective and objective measures ranged from -.29 to .04. In a similar study, Downey, Hellriegel, and Slocum (1975) elicited the perceptions of 51 division heads in a large conglomerate and correlated these perceived environmental stabilities with the variabilities of industry projections made by the Department of Commerce. Correlations of the objective measure with various subjective measures ranged from -.17 to .11.

Research generates Rorschach inkblots—findings that people interpret differently. Tosi, Aldag, and Storey (1973, p. 35) viewed their findings as proof that the questionnaire they used to obtain subjective measures "is not methodologically adequate"; and Downey, Hellriegel, and Slocum (1975, p. 623) concluded that "the results do not support the construct validity" of the two instruments that they had used. I draw another inference—that both studies show how frequently subjective observations diverge from objective ones. Some people do perceive some facets of their worlds accurately, at least some of the time; but enough people misperceive seriously that, averaged across many people, subjective data correlate hardly at all with objective data. A later study by Downey, Hellriegel, and Slocum (1977) suggests that people's characteristic ways of thinking exert stronger effects on their perceptions than do properties of the things perceived.

"There can be no whitewash at the White House"—Richard M. Nixon, 1973.

Organizations' formal reports contribute to misperceptions and encourage people to rely on mythologies instead of on data. Quite a few studies have pointed to the misrepresentations and inadvertent biases that perforate formal reports: formal reports encourage and reflect game playing, and they mislead their readers by emphasizing financial and numerical data, by highlighting successes and rationalizing failures, and by crediting good results to superiors (Altheide and Johnson, 1980; Boland, 1982; Dunbar, 1981; Edelman, 1977; Hofstede, 1967; Hopwood, 1972). It may be that those organizations that rely primarily on formal reports either perform poorly or drift into crises (Grinyer and Norburn, 1975; Starbuck, Greve, and Hedberg, 1978). If so, the correlation probably arises not because formal reports themselves cause problems but because formal reports are so manifestly unreliable and inadequate that only very unrealistic people depend upon them.

"You can predict things only after they've happened"—Eugene Ionesco.

Numerous studies have sought to assess the effectiveness of formal planning (Armstrong, 1982; Bresser and Bishop, 1983). In spite of Armstrong's (1982) conclusion to the contrary, I believe that the results show that the worst studies find the strongest relationships between planning and performances, whereas the best studies find no significant relationships between planning and performances. In related studies, Thune and House (1970) and Herold (1972) concluded that formal planners grow faster and increase their profits faster than informal planners: both studies gathered data with mail questionnaires; Thune and House got 36 usable responses after contacting 145 firms, and Herold analyzed more data about 10 of these firms. Malik and Karger (1975) inferred that formal planners have higher sales and earnings than informal planners: they gathered their data by a mail questionnaire that "a CEO could answer in a few minutes"; after mailing their questionnaire to 273 companies in six industries, they got 38 usable responses, distributed across three industries. All three studies gathered quite superficial data concerning the formality of planning, and their response rates range from 7 percent to 25 percent.

Two studies are somewhat superior to the foregoing ones, but these studies, too, depended on questionnaires and had low response rates. Rue and Fulmer (1974) surveyed 1,333 firms about their planning practices and got 386 usable answers: 29 percent. Rue and Fulmer classified firms into four categories of formality, got financial data from the Compustat tapes, and found "no simple, across the board relationship between completeness of long-range plan and financial performance" (p. 72). Wood and LaForge (1979) asked a number of questions about specific planning practices and received 41 usable responses out of 150 banks surveyed: 27 percent. Wood and LaForge classified banks in three categories of formality and found that the comprehensive planners and the partial planners had higher profits than the informal planners, but the comprehensive and partial planners had similar profits.

Kudla (1980) had a response rate of 59 percent: 328 usable responses out of 557 firms surveyed. He, too, created three categories based on questionnaire responses, but, for no apparent reason, he discarded all of the partial planners and half of the formal planners and so ended up with only 129 firms: 23 percent. He went to considerable effort to develop credible statistics but focused on rates of return that depend upon volatile stock prices and found no differences between formal and informal planners.

Grinyer and Norburn (1975) studied only 21 firms, a stratified 30 percent of the 71 firms chosen for their sample frame; they did not say how many of the 71 firms they actually contacted. They gathered data about planning practices, goals, and organizational structures through long, structured interviews with 91 executives; then they classified planning by both formality and regularity. Grinyer and Norburn obtained a variety of performance data but focused on return on assets; they stated each firm's profitability as a Z-score relative to that specific industry. They made careful statistical calculations.

Nearly all of these studies gathered their data by mail questionnaires that could be filled out quickly and that were filled out by self-selected respondents who had little reason to respond accurately and who may not have known what they were talking about. The data concerning planning activities were extremely sketchy, and the very low response rates imply that these data were biased. In effect, the planning-is-profitable studies found that people in profitable, fast-growing firms say that they have long-range goals and plans, whereas people in unprofitable, slow-growing firms say that they are unsure of their long-range goals and plans. Is it not probable that profitability makes people confident of their futures? Because deviation from long-range plans implies disappointment with performance whereas adherence to long-range plans implies satisfaction, planning's consequences ought to be evaluated longitudinally, not cross-sectionally, and the plans should be identified before their consequences are observed. (A few studies have been interpreted as proving that strategies raise profits: because these studies identified strategies retrospectively, they show only that dissatisfied people are more likely to change their behaviors.)

In what is probably the best study of formal planning to date, Grinyer and Norburn (1975) discovered that firms' profitability correlates only very weakly with the formality of planning ($r = .22$). That is, profitable firms are about as likely to plan informally as formally, and the same is true of unprofitable firms. Profitability also correlates inconsistently and meaninglessly with the degrees to which senior executives agree about objectives or responsibilities: the correlations range from .40 to –.40. Thus, formalized plans seem to be inferior to informal plans nearly as often as they are superior, and consensus can be as harmful as beneficial when there is no way to assure that the objects of consensus are good.

Grinyer and Norburn also found that profitability correlates weakly but significantly with reliance on informal communication ($r = .40$) and moderately with the use of diverse information when evaluating performance ($r = .68$). Both correlations relate to formal reports: managers in more profitable firms make greater use of informal communication channels, whereas managers in less profitable firms communicate primarily through formal reports; and managers in more profitable firms use diverse kinds of information when evaluating their firms' performances, whereas managers in less profitable firms get their information mainly from formal reports. I know of no studies that have assessed the consequences of adhering to or deviating from long-range plans. But I can predict what they would say.

"The Nazi threat to unleash U-2 bombs on London is just a meaningless publicity stunt"—Lord Cherwell, advising Winston Churchill, 1940.

"Everyone acquainted with the [incandescent lamp] will recognize it as a conspicuous failure"—Henry Morton, president of Stevens Institute of Technology, 1880.

"You'd better learn secretarial work or else get married"—Emmeline Snively, head of Blue Book Modeling Agency, speaking to Marilyn Monroe, 1944.

So people blunder along, partially blind, acting before thinking, and fortunate to stay out of trouble. No wonder they normally avoid strategic reorientations—drawing strong inferences from undependable perceptions and faulty beliefs can lead to unpleasant surprises. Behavior programs and strategic variations keep actions close to the familiar and their consequences close to the expected. And, like whistling in the dark, retrospective decisions and strategies maintain the confidence to keep on acting. But, with perseverence, a series of variations can add up to a revolution.

"Not within a thousand years will man ever fly"—Wilbur Wright, 1901.

FOURTEEN

# In Defense of Planning as a Rational Approach to Change

*Paul R. Lawrence*

The object of William Starbuck's "Acting First and Thinking Later: Theory Versus Reality in Strategic Change" (Chapter Thirteen of this volume) is to draw upon organization theory to help clarify and explain strategic decision making. Starbuck's chapter is a colorful attack on the rational model of strategic decision making. In this, he follows the lead of other organizational research, especially the classic work of March and Simon. By citing fairly recent endorsements of the rational model in various business texts, he argues that the rational model is not a straw man. He then sketches his alternative "organization as action generator" model, making a number of useful points. I have three main troubles with his presentation. He regularly confuses the use of the rational model as a descriptive model with its use as a normative model. He does not provide a balanced analysis of the decision/change process. He generalizes about decision making in all organizations—failing to recognize that different strategic decision/change processes tend to dominate in organizations functioning in different contexts.

Starbuck bases most of his attack on the rational model on evidence that individuals tend to wander away from rational thinking. For instance, he cites the human tendency to distort facts to fit prior assumptions, the tendency to attribute causation in self-serving ways, and the tendency to perceive order in randomness. While these tendencies certainly exist, there is also evidence, not cited by Starbuck, that, under certain conditions, individuals tend to avoid these errors and make use of more rational analysis.

Along with his treatment of individual cognitive tendencies, Starbuck cites types of errors in reasoning to which groups and organizations are prone. In particular, he comments on the tendency in organizations to suppress deviant ideas and thereby cut off consideration of unpleasant facts. It is well established that organizations at times do this. However, there is also evidence, not cited by Starbuck, that, under certain conditions, groups can help individuals avoid errors in reasoning and can generate solutions that are objectively superior. Along the same line, Starbuck cites the tendency of organizations to use "backward reasoning," after-the-fact justification of action. He overlooks, however, a possible positive result of this tendency. Many actions taken by experienced people are based on implicit, intuitive reasoning. When such actions produce desired outcomes, it can be useful to reconstruct and make explicit the rational underpinning of such intuitive action in order to make it available to others. The same can be said for the value of careful postmortems in failure cases.

In discussing organizational rationality, Starbuck persistently confuses descriptive and normative models of strategic decision making. For instance, he attacks the descriptive accuracy of statements when the people he is paraphrasing (Newman and Logan, 1981; Dunbar, 1981; Meyer and Rowan, 1977) are in fact using the normative "should" in every sentence. I would submit that normative models can fairly be tested not in terms of their descriptive accuracy but rather in terms of whether their use brings managers closer to their goal of basing action on a careful analysis of cause-and-effect relationships.

Starbuck's testing of normative models in terms of descriptive accuracy is clearest where he states, "Normative theories assert that perception of a problem should instigate a unidirectional sequence of activities. . . . Such tidy, unidirectional sequences occur very infrequently in actual behaviors, however." Who but Starbuck has talked about their occurring frequently? Starbuck repeatedly attacks normative theory as nondescriptive. Again, the proper test of a normative theory is not its accuracy as description but its utility in moving behavior in the direction of rationality.

Starbuck argues on sounder ground when he asserts that formal planning rigidifies behavior and, given his premise of an unpredictable future, pushes behavior away from its goals. But, even here, Starbuck flaws his reasoning by overstating both the unpredictability of events ("people predict their alternative futures inaccurately") and the inability of people to make interim corrections in plans in order to respond to unanticipated events ("articulated strategies and policies render action less realistic and less responsive to environmental events"). I recently witnessed an interesting example to the contrary. At the conclusion of the presentation of a corporate five-year plan to a board of directors, the chief executive officer (CEO) remarked, "Tomorrow things will start to happen that we were unable to anticipate in the plan, and we had better be prepared to adjust our plans accordingly. Planning is a great thing as long as we don't feel locked in."

The tendency of Starbuck to overstatement is particularly apparent as he moves into a discussion of behavior programs and action generators. Having devoted two paragraphs to explaining that behavior programs make an essential contribution to everyday organizational life by saving time and resources, he devotes the remainder of that section to discussing the hazards of behavior programs. I would have been happier with equal air time. By focusing so heavily on the fact that people in organizations spend much more time executing behavior programs than they do in strategic planning, he begs the important question of how, if at all, the two types of behavior are balanced and related to each other. The thrust of Starbuck's argument is that people's use of programmed behavior blocks rationality. Ironically, his principal example illustrating the point, Charlie's refusal to use the newly developed linear equation, winds up demonstrating the opposite. Charlie decided, according to Starbuck's evidence, to stick to his old scheduling method because in the broader organizational context it was more cost effective. He was responding not to habit but to a rational analysis of costs and benefits.

Starbuck introduces the concept of action generators to distinguish the particular type of behavior programs that is activated by job assignments or clocks, the kind commonly found in an organization. He starts his analysis by citing the advantages of action generators as "the main means by which organizations learn, coordinate activities, and control actions hierarchically." This brief accolade to action generators is followed by several pages that, among other things, largely blame action generators for U.S. involvement in Korea, Cuba, Berlin, Vietnam, Chile, Guatemala, El Salvador, and Grenada. Clearly, action generators can, according to Starbuck, get people into trouble.

Starbuck gives a similarly unbalanced analysis of social interaction in organizations, a third powerful tool that he says can work for good or ill. Just one sentence states the positive: "Many people cooperating in an organization can achieve results far beyond the capabilities of one person." The remainder of the section provides a litany of the ways that social interaction can cause trouble. He ends with the thought that the world is becoming too complex for humans, and, although organizations can help simplify matters, they usually get it all wrong, especially when the simplification is done by top managers.

Starbuck's analysis reminds me of a series of organizational events that I observed in connection with research I was doing a number of years ago in a supermarket chain. The events themselves were anything but remarkable, but they do represent a rich example of how the action generators Starbuck emphasizes can be developed in an organization. The example shows that a variety of decision modes can be employed with a fair bit of rationality in a single sequence.

Senior managers of the supermarket had decided that providing a check-cashing service for customers would help boost sales and profits—provided, of course, that the company did not get stuck with too many bad checks. Given this tentative conclusion, they authorized some stores to begin offering check-cashing service. They asked the store managers and their supervisors (district managers) to try out different procedures and generally keep track of the process, but no systematic research was conducted.

Several weeks later, I sat through a six-hour meeting attended by several district managers, their immediate superior, and staff people from the finance office. It was announced that top management had decided that providing the check-cashing service was, on balance, a good thing and should be implemented in all stores if the group could develop practical procedures that would minimize bad checks without irritating customers. The single agenda item was the pooling of their experiences; the goal was to establish standard procedures for use in extending the check-cashing service throughout the chain. The meeting was long and drawn out, because its members had already accumulated a wealth of experience with the good and bad features of different ways of providing the service. The group began testing different procedures by checking each alternative way of providing the service against their experience. There was sporadic pulling and hauling between the finance people and operations people over their respective authority and responsibilities. New combinations of methods began to pop up. In time, the group managed to wade through these experiences and, slowly and painfully, hammer out a few simple rules to be followed by store personnel. Implementation was partially built into this process, since the district managers at the meeting were the same people who were expected to teach the store personnel about these rules, monitor their use, and be responsible for bad-check losses. I, of course, was watching the creation of behavior programs that would eventually be triggered in hundreds of employees, some thousands of times daily, by customers presenting checks for cashing (the action generators).

The point of my example is that one series of related events can involve a mix of all the various types of decision making and behavior programs that Starbuck discusses. It shows, as Starbuck stresses, that a great deal of organizational behavior was programmed, but it also shows that programs can contain a healthy amount of rationality. It shows, as Starbuck points out, that policy decisions were made retrospectively to rationalize the past, but, at the same time, they were made prospectively to guide future behavior. It shows that, even though learning was taking place by a trial-and-error, incremental process, the learnings so derived were also formalized and promulgated as general rules. It shows that, while the social interaction used as a key part of the decision making was a repetitive, disjointed, somewhat political process, it was by no means devoid of rationality. It shows that, while the resulting rules were undoubtedly suboptimal, based as they were on limited data and the limited cognitive processes of the people involved, the rules still seemed to achieve a "satisficing" level of rationality. No one could claim that the process could best be described by any normative decision model, but the participants' awareness of normative problem-solving methods may well have added an increment of rationality to the results. I remember coming away from this experience with a good deal of respect for the people and the organization involved. Looking back, I find it difficult to categorize this episode as an example of any single kind of decision process; I would have to call it a mix of methods, with an emphasis on "satisficing."

My third and final concern about Starbuck's chapter stems from his tendency to generalize. By implication, Starbuck suggests that his observations about strategic decision making, gleaned from organization theory, apply to *all* organizations. Such a sweeping conclusion is not, in my view, justified by the existing body of organization theory. To the contrary, it is exactly on this issue of how organizations vary under different conditions that organization theory has the most to offer to our understanding of strategic decision making. One of the least controversial points of organization theory is that it generally takes different kinds of organizations to survive and thrive under different environmental circumstances. Can these organizational differences help us explain differences in emphasis in strategic decision making? Starbuck has helped by laying out the full variety of strategic decision modes that are detailed in the literature, but he missed the opportunity to connect this variety to the variety of organization forms. I cannot resist the temptation to provide a tentative example of how this connection can be made by drawing on some of my own recent research.

Starbuck's chapter makes reference to four well-known modes of strategic decision making and proposes a fifth, the action generator mode. The four he cites are *incrementalism*, otherwise known as muddling through or trial and error (Lindblom, 1959), *satisficing* (March and Simon, 1958), the *garbage-can* model (Cohen, March, and Olsen, 1972), and the *political* model (Pettigrew, 1983, and Chapter Eleven of this volume). He develops a fifth, which is characterized by the dominant use of *action generators* in organizations to the virtual exclusion of all explicit decision modes. As my supermarket example indicates, it is likely that at least traces of all these descriptive decision modes can be found in every organization. It is possible and useful, however, to examine which of these modes is dominant in different organizational circumstances.

Neo-contingency theory (Lawrence, 1981; Lawrence and Dyer, 1983) provides a general framework for tentatively explaining why these different modes would tend to dominate in specific organizational and environmental circumstances. Dyer and I found it useful to characterize the relevant environment or domain of any organization in terms of the two dimensions of resource scarcity and information complexity. Figure 1 portrays the nine-celled analytical framework that we devised to show different combinations of these environmental conditions. Our earlier work posits that different forms of organization will tend to evolve and thrive in each of these nine environmental niches, even as different organizational forms will, over time, tend to generate the corresponding environmental conditions by a process of mutual adaptation. Figure 1, as a point of orientation, shows the expected location of the organizational forms identified by Mintzberg (1979). It also shows where I would hypothesize that each of the five modes of strategic decision making would, in this model, tend to be dominant. Let me elaborate a little on this hypothesis.

In area 1, with high information complexity and low resource scarcity, there is an overabundance of information to be handled but little press for conserving resources. The expected form is adhocracy, with its loosely coupled organizational units. Affluent universities and hospitals are the usual examples of organizations in this niche. Innovation can be expected, but not efficiency. It is in this context that the theory would hypothesize the dominance of the garbage-can model, with occasions for decision making used as receptacles for assorted problems, solutions, and participations. There is an abundance of differentiation but little pressure for integration, so all the various points of view and ideas are aired, but whatever resolution emerges is usually more arbitrary than rational.

**Figure 1. Neo-Contingency Analytical Framework.**

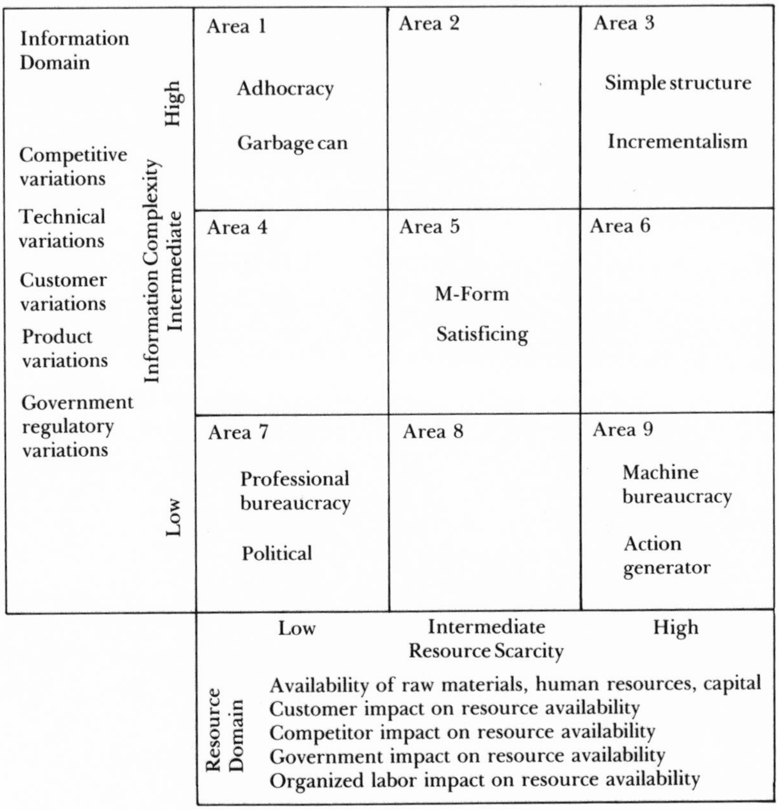

| | | Low | Intermediate | High |
|---|---|---|---|---|
| Information Domain<br><br>Competitive variations | High | **Area 1**<br><br>Adhocracy<br><br>Garbage can | **Area 2** | **Area 3**<br><br>Simple structure<br><br>Incrementalism |
| Technical variations<br><br>Customer variations<br><br>Product variations | Intermediate | **Area 4** | **Area 5**<br><br>M-Form<br><br>Satisficing | **Area 6** |
| Government regulatory variations | Low | **Area 7**<br><br>Professional bureaucracy<br><br>Political | **Area 8** | **Area 9**<br><br>Machine bureaucracy<br><br>Action generator |

(Information Complexity on the vertical axis)

|  | Low | Intermediate | High |
|---|---|---|---|
| | | Resource Scarcity | |

Resource Domain
- Availability of raw materials, human resources, capital
- Customer impact on resource availability
- Competitor impact on resource availability
- Government impact on resource availability
- Organized labor impact on resource availability

*Source:* Lawrence and Dyer (1983).

At the other extreme, in area 9, organizations must find ways to survive with few resources and a very stable information domain. It is under these conditions that the dominant use of Starbuck's action-generator mode could best contribute to organizational survival. This is where machine bureaucracies are to be expected. These organizations rely heavily on detailed behavior programs and action generators in order to minimize costs and thereby cope with the scarcity of resources. This can work as long as nothing of significance changes in the environment. These organizations have no slack resources at hand for responding to environmental change. Their learning capacity will have atrophied from lack of use and lack of resources. They are the organizations that Starbuck can cite as places where strategic decision making is virtually nonexistent.

Another relevant example is area 3, which combines a high scarcity of resources with high information complexity. These conditions lead to high mortality rates for organizations. Lots of variation exists, but no slack resources. Firms are small and simple, with no capacity for research and development work. They are pressed to rely primarily on incremental, trial-and-error ways of coping, without much time for reflection. If they hit on a successful strategic method, they can build up slack resources and move into a more benign domain.

By contrast, in area 7, with the lack of environmental challenge implicit in both abundant resources and a quiescent information domain, organizations can be expected to turn inward and make decisions on internal criteria. Power distribution among members and groups will be an overriding issue, and power will tend to flow to those with ascribed status factors and dominating personalities rather than to those who can meet environmental challenges. So strategic decision making will be predominantly political in nature. It follows that organizations that stay in this niche, without real competition, will tend to grow older and larger and more bureaucratic.

Area 5 is of special interest in our neo-contingency model. Firms in this area are facing vigorous competition for both resources and ideas but not overwhelming pressures in either regard. This area fosters organizations that are especially attractive from a societal standpoint, since they are more apt to be both innovative and efficient. It is here that we expect to find the $M$-form (multi-divisional) organization (Williamson, 1975) that can combine the strengths of decentralized, divisionalized decision making with some joint decision processes that can create synergies across divisions. It is here that we expect firms to use more elements of normative decision models, but, in descriptive terms, our theory would suggest that "satisficing" would be the dominant mode.

This application of the neo-contingency model goes beyond Starbuck's useful descriptive treatment of strategic decision making. It builds on the differences among strategic decision making modes—suggesting how these differences can be explained by incorporating them in a more complete analysis of organizations and their environments. It provides an example of how organization theory can contribute to a broader understanding of the strategic decision-making process.

# ✣ FIFTEEN ✣

# Finding New Ways
# of Overcoming
# Resistance to Change

## *Richard J. Hermon-Taylor*

About five years ago, a division of a $7 billion diversified corpora-
tion recognized a major strategic opportunity. A segment was
emerging in its market that if pursued correctly would probably
lead to a substantial increase in sales and a major new profitable
business for the corporation. In this business, the industry leader
had a well-established network of distributors, who carried a wide
line of traditional products. The division was one of three producers
of a new generation of products that appealed primarily to the
largest, most sophisticated buyers, who were more interested in a
quality product at a good price than in the services that distributors
provided.

*Note:* The author would like to express his appreciation for the
advice and help of Chris Argyris during the course of the past two years,
when the ideas and experiences in this paper were being developed.
Argyris's assistance in many hours of discussion and client contact has been
invaluable to this effort; since its impact has been broad based, it would not
be proper to identify it with any particular idea in this chapter.

The industry leader's ability to compete in this new segment was severely hampered by its previous strength—its distribution channel. Direct selling was becoming prevalent, at prices the distributors found hard to match. The door was open for an aggressive move by one of the new entrants, and the division manager made such a proposal to his corporate headquarters. The corporation, looking for growth opportunities, accepted the plan enthusiastically.

For a while, things went well, and sales and profits climbed rapidly. But the division's share-gain tactics in a fast-growing market soon led to a need for a major capacity increase. Being short of capacity in this high-growth market was extremely costly, especially because delivery was one of the keys to getting the business. Conversely, the risk of overinvesting in fixed assets was small, since the ratio of sales to fixed assets was very high. But the corporation's traditional activities were in mature, fixed-capital-intensive businesses, for which its elaborate capital-budgeting procedures were well suited. So the division manager and his planning staff found themselves making no fewer than twenty-seven separate presentations over an eighteen-month period to get approval for the capacity increase.

The old plant became overloaded, and efficiency dropped. Quality fell, customer service and delivery deteriorated, and overtime and other labor increases, attributable largely to the choked factory, began to drive direct product costs through the roof. The division's sales representatives whose compensation depended heavily upon commissions on current sales, found themselves being asked to make much larger sales with long lead times to more sophisticated customers. Not only did they fear that they lacked the requisite selling skills; the compensation system gave them no incentive to pursue the new business. Consequently, they tended to maintain a high proportion of small orders in the mix, which further choked the plant.

The corporation, alarmed at the fall in profitability and made painfully aware of the service problems by customer complaints to headquarters, withdrew the capital authorization and told the division to put its house in order before seeking further investment. Today the division—under new management—has broken back into the black, but it has lost for good its opportunity to be a major force in the industry and a much more significant part of the parent corporation. The best it can hope for is a mediocre level of profitability as a distant number three in the market.

The lesson from this story is painful, but it is repeated many times each year across American business. Strategic thrusts that require new ways of making and implementing decisions are highly likely to fail, because of the difficulty of changing the ingrained behavior of the organization, either between the corporation and the divisions, within the division, or both. There is also an important side effect. In the case just cited, the division's plan had been developed as an early prototype of a new and highly heralded corporate strategic planning process. The plan was praised as being insightful and based on sound reasoning and analysis and was even held up as an example of what a good divisional plan should look like. When the business turned sour, the planning process was simultaneously discredited. The plan was criticized as being unrealistic and naive. The planning department budgets were cut back. And other division managers throughout the corporation silently congratulated themselves on taking a less aggressive approach to their own plans. In fact, a cynical observer of the development of the planning process in this organization noted that it worked best when only fine tuning was being recommended; that it was valuable in the hands of the corporate planners as a means of enforcing attention to perennially weak businesses; but that it failed to live up to its promise whenever something original and creative was being proposed.

### Strategic Decision Making at a Crossroads

Business planning and decision making have evolved considerably in the last thirty-five years. Two major points of transition stand out, each of which accompanied significant shifts in management practice. The first transition was the shift away from centralized authority. As organizations increased in size, and their activities became more diverse and complex, the concept of the decentralized-profit-center organization developed. This increased the need for new forms of communication, both to express intent (planning) and

to monitor results (reporting and control). These needs were met by
the development of a highly sophisticated language of communication based on financially expressed values. The Du Pont formula
was perhaps the epitome of this era, and the planning and control
systems that emerged tended to be strongly oriented toward the
financial projections and results of the decentralized profit centers.

The second stage of evolution came with the realization that
the financial language of communication was causing inappropriate allocation of strategic resources. Improperly acute focus on
return on assets (ROA), whether as a measure of profit-center
performance or as a hurdle rate for project investment, led inexor-
ably to starvation of strategic opportunities and systematic overin-
vestment in mature businesses. New business opportunities with
very attractive long-run profit potential were often overlooked or
rejected because they failed to meet current ROA targets. Similarly,
research and development and quality improvements were inappropriately denied investment.

Two concepts that appeared at about this time, the business
portfolio and the notion of sustainable competitive advantage, led
to the idea of managing business units toward a defined strategic
mission. These advances introduced competition as an explicit
consideration in policy development in a way that had not been
possible before. They allowed organizations to consider alternatives
instead of having to rely on the commitments or track records of the
profit-center managers. And they promoted the development of
planning from an inwardly focused financial exercise to one that
not only included consideration of the external environment but, in
the better manifestations of the discipline, gave corporate management two important new controls on their organizations. The first
was the ability to ask for a properly reasoned basis for the results
projected by the business units submitting the plans (in place of a
negotiated commitment). Second, by asking for alternative strategies and assigning missions, management obtained more precise
and forward-looking control over the allocation of the corporation's
resources and a better handle on the shape and direction of the
overall portfolio.

This style of management decision making and planning has
emerged during the past fifteen or so years in corporate America. It

has significantly improved the quality, in those firms that have practiced it successfully, of the strategic choices made. But the realization is now beginning to emerge that this approach, too, is unsatisfactory, despite being an improvement over the former model, in that it does not always produce lasting change in strategic direction. From our perspective of participating in and being exposed to many important strategy choices, we believe that the benefits of the strategic approach to decision making may be in danger of being thrown out without due consideration of the reasons for its failure.

We may now have reached the point, in other words, where a third major transition is needed. Management must find ways to take the initiative in bringing about significant strategic change. This not only means ensuring the proper quality of analysis and business judgment in diagnosing the need for change and formulating specific proposals. It also requires explicit consideration of and development of new ways of dealing with the cultural and organizational obstacles to change that are present in almost every major corporation.

## The Nature of Change

At the heart of this question is the whole issue of change. Let us first define what we mean by change. All organizations change. They grow, their people come and go, their environments change, their product lines and customer sets evolve. A well-managed organization, whether it be the corporation or a business unit under a much larger corporate umbrella, should be able to pursue a basic strategic mission that remains constant while the tactics and programs through which it is fulfilled are continuously updated and refined to meet the changing circumstances. This kind of fine tuning of basic direction is change but typically does not meet an overwhelming amount of organizational or cultural resistance. It is, in other words, within an acceptable range of movement.

Donald Povejsil, the vice-president of corporate planning at Westinghouse Electric since 1977, refers to this kind of behavior as "the 10 percent rule." He argues that almost no manager will voluntarily commit to anything that will change overall operations by more than about 10 percent annually, though individual parts of the operation may grow faster. This planner's perspective may be shaped by the environment in which he operates, since many high-technology firms regularly grow at higher rates than Westinghouse's average of slightly over 7 percent in the past decade. But it is nevertheless probably true that, within any culture, there is a characteristic degree of change that is the norm for the organization, whether this is expressed in terms of achievable growth or significant shifts of strategic emphasis (where growth may not be the principal issue).

But change of the kind anticipated by the division described earlier is different. In this kind of change, embedded behavior patterns may need to be altered dramatically. A paper by Miller and Friesen (1980a), entitled "Momentum and Resolution in Organizational Adaptation," described a research study of twenty-six firms that tracked twenty-four structural and strategy-making variables, which together captured the essence of those organizations' cultures and management styles. The authors found that, for significant change to occur, the great majority of these variables not only were affected but had to reverse their direction.

We will refer to this kind of change as "frame breaking." Typically, a dramatic change in or reversal of a firm's external behavior—its strategy—will be accompanied by a corresponding need to change its internal behavior. The greater the strategic change, the greater the need for internal reassessment. While the threshold between acceptable and frame-breaking change cannot be expressly defined and will vary from one organization to another, depending upon its size, its degree of bureaucracy, its leadership, and a host of other variables, it is possible to observe that some degree of change will run into internal obstacles that are too severe to be overcome. Unfortunately, this threshold of permissible change is often below what is required to ensure the long-term health or even survival of the organization.

## Models of Change

Most executives manage in a way that implicitly suggests some underlying model of change that they believe to be appro-

**Figure 1. Organizational Influences on Models of Change.**

| | | Management Style | |
| --- | --- | --- | --- |
| | | Authoritarian | Participative |
| Reasoning Process | Judgmental | Control-oriented | Collegial |
| | Analytical | Logic-driven | Informed concensus |

priate. There would appear to be several such models. The features of an organization that are perhaps most influential in determining these models are the managerial style of the organization and the way in which its members reason about major decisions. The simple matrix in Figure 1 illustrates this idea.

The ways that company managements reason about key decisions, such as those involved in determining strategy, appear to fall within a spectrum. At one end of this spectrum, analysis is virtually eschewed, and the critical decisions are made by senior managers, either individually or in groups, on the basis of their intuition or experience. We refer to this as a *judgmental* style of decision making. At the other end of the spectrum, enormous effort is expended on analytical exercises designed to reduce to a minimum the area of uncertainty within which judgment has to be brought to bear. We refer to this as *analytical* decision making.

Businesses in which the major strategic decisions surround investment in capital assets frequently employ an analytical approach to decision making. Not only are the firm's resources to be irrevocably committed to fixed and frequently highly illiquid assets, but these are the kinds of decisions for which sophisticated analytical techniques have been developed, and it is only prudent for management to take advantage of such tools.

By contrast, judgmental decision making is more often (though not exclusively) found in large financial institutions, such as banks or insurance companies. This is probably because, at least historically, opportunities to develop sustained competitive advantage in such businesses have been restricted by regulation, while the risks associated with too bold a strategic approach have often outweighed any benefits (witness the Penn Square disaster). Furthermore, the assets of the business—people resources and money, for the most part—have (again, historically) been highly liquid and products fairly easily copied. Therefore, judgment, whether in underwriting insurance risks or approving loans, becomes critical to success. It follows naturally that this should be extended to strategic decision making, as successful managers are promoted to the top positions in the organization.

*Authoritarian Models of Change*

There is also a range of preferred management styles, from *authoritarian* at one end of the spectrum to *participative* at the other. Authoritarian managers believe that it is the function of strong management to ensure that whatever is decided should be made to happen by force of authority. Let us look first at the change models that this implies.

*The Control-Driven Model.* Authoritarian managerial styles combined with judgmental reasoning usually lead to a highly control-oriented model of change. The guiding belief here is that if you can explain clearly to a subordinate what you want him or her to do, and that if you can devise a suitable system for measuring his or her performance and then reward or punish him or her accordingly, the desired result, in terms of strategy execution, will be achieved. But this model of change is flawed. One major problem lies with the extent to which the goals can be articulated. In the absence of any explicit reasoning about what other key criteria are important to strategic success, financial performance is frequently emphasized. The goals to which the subordinates commit are usually expressed in terms of growth and profitability. In this model, subordinates are given the authority to run their parts of the organization as they see fit, so long as they meet these commitments.

The model of change implied by this authoritarian/judgmental quadrant of the matrix shown in Figure 1 is essentially that which was implied by the profit-center form of organization. And, as indicated earlier, in meeting the demands of the financial goals, the unit manager may either knowingly or unknowingly make trade-offs that favor the short term and harm the future. Since these are not measured, there is no countervailing balance in the system to ensure the organization's long-term health. If the environment is sufficiently hostile, no efforts on the part of the unit manager will yield the desired results.

The kinds of planning systems that tend to be found in organizations of this type may be quite elaborate in their formats, demanding in some cases detailed financial pro formas and being strongly linked to both operating budgets and the capital budgeting process. But strategic planning is generally weak or nonexistent and, in any case, clearly subordinated to the financial planning and implied budgetary commitments. Linkage between the stated strategic goals and the financial results is usually expressed in terms of strategic programs for which line-item budgets are negotiated. It is not usual to find explicit logic that explains what the cause-and-effect relationships are. Strategic planning is, in effect, regarded as something of a nuisance to be got out of the way so that the serious business of negotiating and then managing the commitments can be undertaken by the line managers involved.

*The Logic-Driven Model.* Some authoritarian companies try to counteract the negative effects of this tension between strategic planning and the budget and control process by making strategy development as analytical as possible. In the extreme case, both short- and long-term financial results are explicitly related to the strategic analysis.

To some extent, this model of change does overcome the main drawback of the control-driven model. If the analysis can be made explicit enough, a connection can be made between the financial results of the strategy and the key assumptions and logic upon which they depend. Thus, should there be pressure on short-term results, the impact on the strategy of choices made to meet these needs can be evaluated, and strategic goals can be revised accordingly. Alternatively, if the unit's performance is not living up to expectations established by the strategic logic, it is possible to go back to examine whether the cause is with the assumptions, the logic, or the execution.

Strategic planning in organizations that emphasize analysis as a basis for decision making is frequently an important function. Both corporate and divisional planning staffs tend to be large, representing a pool of analytical resources to support the various decisions being made. The object in the better of such systems is to explain why a given set of strategic actions will lead to expected consequences. The concept of competitive advantage is an important underpinning here, and the analysis focuses on the means to obtain it and how lasting it is likely to be, once achieved. Alternatives are proposed and evaluated, sometimes with considerable sophistication, as in one company we know, which has adopted a full-fledged discounted cash-flow and capital-asset pricing methodology for assessing the "warranted value" of each of its business units' plan alternatives.

Planning of this kind has considerable value in diagnosing the need for change and in formulating and developing alternatives for such change. Once a mission for a given business unit has been identified and agreed to, it becomes more possible to manage toward it to the extent that the critical plan elements and assumptions of the plan, and the logic on which it is based, are specified. These elements, in a well-founded planning system, are monitored as the plan unfolds.

*Participative Models of Change*

The basic problem with authoritarian models of change is that their top-down nature makes it inherently more difficult for the organization to "buy on" to the proposed change. This is not just a matter of "not invented here." There is also an issue of understanding, and strategies communicated from the top have a habit of suffering from considerable distortion at the operating level, especially where they represent a significant degree of change from the previous direction.

To deal with this drawback, there is a school of management thought that proposes that more effective decision making and more lasting change will result from a participative management process. This style of management seeks consensus about key decisions in a way designed to promote "ownership" of commitments or plans for change. It does this by involving those who will be parties to the implementation of these decisions in both the decision process and the design of the execution steps that follow. The basic notion is that people will behave in ways that will produce effective change if they can be made to feel part of the decision, rather than having it thrust upon them. Participative companies typically make heavy use of task-force forms of organization, especially where the decision is complex or crosses organizational lines. Resistance to change is most likely in these cases, and it is essential in this model to have the views of all parties represented so that everyone can feel that he or she has had a fair chance to participate in the decision.

Both judgmental and analytical decision-making processes are found in organizations with participative management styles. Once again, different change models are implied.

*The Collegial Model.* Where a participative management style is combined with a judgmental decision-making approach, the implied model of change is that a group of people of good judgment will achieve a reasoned consensus that will guide the subsequent actions of the participants. This collegial style is especially common in organizations where there is strong mutual dependence among key organizational subunits or functions, so that the cooperation of the members of these suborganizations is essential to forward progress. Unfortunately, it is far more common that such organizations become either frozen or, at best, able to change only incrementally. This is because the consensus building implied by the participative style must mediate among and meld the interests of many constituencies. It would be hard for any individual or subgroup to propose a frame-breaking change, no matter how visionary, because other players who felt threatened would use their judgment to oppose it.

The play of contending judgments in this environment can create disruptive organizational tension. To control such tension, participative-judgmental organizations usually practice some form of conflict avoidance. One common approach, which we observed recently in a large regional bank, is to force decisions downward. The staffs of conflicting departments then find ways to compromise so that the conflicts are not carried all the way to the official decision-making forum. The middle management in this bank had learned that this was a better outcome than allowing the conflicting viewpoints to be carried to the top management decision-making group, because, to preserve a semblance of unity at the top, the chief executive would stop the discussion and suggest that the meeting "adjourn for lunch," as he put it, which often resulted in no decision being made at all.

Strategic planning in participative organizations that rely primarily on judgment to make key decisions is generally a beleaguered function. The councils of management revolve around a weighing of experience and influence. It is rare for organizations to make strategic planning a way station on the route to top management. The planner is thus frequently not viewed as a person who has the requisite experience in the business to make judgments. As a senior officer at this same bank, when it was looking for a candidate to replace the recently departed planner, observed, "Whoever we get must have had several years' experience as a loan officer. Otherwise, he'll never be able to understand our business." Planners in such organizations tend to be either specialists, whose forte lies more with routine planning systems and their effective administration, or passed-over executives who have experience in the business but whose counsel carries relatively little weight.

The strategic planner in a participative organization where the reasoning processes are judgmental thus typically has little influence over the company's ongoing strategies except to the extent that he or she can control the agenda of the management meetings that determine the organization's strategic direction.

*The Informed-Consensus Model.* The participative-analytical approach to strategic decision making is perhaps the most complex. The implied model of change both is informed by logic and seeks to engage the cooperation of those charged with implementation. Thus, it embodies both of the main ideas for creating effective change that have characterized most organizations to date—namely, supporting the judgment of top executives with analysis and ensuring effective buy-on through a participative approach.

Unfortunately, not all parts of an organization will necessarily embrace a proposed change equally, especially when there will be "winners" and "losers." Resistance surfaces first through nit-picking at the analysis itself. Frequently, conflicting parties will develop different viewpoints, each supported by analysis. Further-more, the resistance does not necessarily disappear when the deci-sion is made. Often, unable to refute the logic of the analysis, people will agree to a decision. But as time unfolds, they or members of their departments will act either wittingly or unintentionally in ways that undermine the decision's effectiveness. Strategic planning in such an organization can provide an important integrating mechanism among conflicting viewpoints. However, while the function can be very influential, it is also possible that the planners' efforts will be regarded with suspicion or even downright hostility by the other executives. Frequently, they will build their own planning staffs, thus seeking to neutralize the influence of the central staff function.

In this relatively brief discussion of observed models of change, no mention has been made of several other extremely important variables, such as the individual leadership ability of key managers, the influence of organizational structural forms, or the size and diversity of the organization's operations. The intent of the review, however, has been to make two important points. First, many organizations are hampered in their ability to change because their reasoning processes rely more on intuition and judgment than on analysis. This makes it more difficult to communicate what people in the organization should do and to control their actions in pursuit of these goals. Second, successful implementation of strategy requires that attention be paid to the motivations and behavior of all members of the organization who will be expected to play a significant role in bringing change about.

While it is probably not appropriate to overgeneralize, since there are undoubtedly many situations—whether in terms of the kind of decision being faced, its urgency, or the particular charac-teristics of the management group involved—where judgmental decision making and/or an authoritarian style are superior to any other implied model of change, our thesis would in general be that the lower-right quadrant of our matrix, the informed-consensus quadrant, probably produces on average the most effective and lasting change. Even this model, however, does not adequately address another, more fundamental obstacle to change, which, we believe, is at the base of the frustrations being expressed currently by business leaders when they speak of the so-called failure of strategic planning as a way of helping to create change.

## Organizational Resistance to Change

All organizations contain within them elements that resist change. This is true because change threatens the status quo, and members of an organization by the very continuation of their membership implicitly express satisfaction with the status quo, or at least with the steady trend of evolution of that state (as described by Miller and Friesen, 1980a). It would also seem to follow logically that the greater the degree of change, the greater the resistance.

Let us now loosely classify these resistances as "discussible" and "undiscussible." Many times, people feel challenged by change but do not feel that they need to hide their reasons for resisting it. The constructive discussion of these obstacles to change is the essence of "good management." But, in other instances, people not only feel threatened by change; they also feel uncomfortable about exposing their reasons for feeling threatened. They therefore resist but also act in ways to conceal their resistance. To illustrate this, consider the following random sampling of some of the situations that we have encountered recently:

- The head of marketing in a consumer paper-products company vigorously opposed a change that would have resulted in manufacturing being more influential in decisions regarding product-line breadth and order scheduling. Many persons in the organization secretly attributed this to his feeling that the traditionally strong influence of marketing would be undermined if he gave way in this instance.
- Senior management in a bank sought to neutralize what they perceived as a threat from the individual in charge of computer systems, because he was beginning to propose changes that they had no logical basis to resist, by promoting him into another job in the company, away from his functional expertise. Man-

agement explained this move in terms of providing opportunities for others in the displaced employee's former department.

- A manufacturer of sophisticated electrical machinery realized that its engineers had for years been building costly over-design into its products (which were tailored to individual customer requirements) because a field failure of a machine was considered absolutely the worst thing that could happen to an engineer. This attitude persisted despite strenuous efforts to reduce costs, in which the issue of overdesign was explicitly raised with the engineering department.

When an organization wishes to change in direction, it is relatively easy for it to address those resistances that are discussible. If they are also influencible, then changing should not be too much of a problem. Skillful executives are often able to go even further. They find ways to deal with some of the undiscussible or uninfluencible resistances by designing around them, or "bypassing" them. The price that is paid for this effectiveness, however, is that compromises usually have to be made and also that the features of the organization that caused it to resist in the first place have been simultaneously reinforced.

In a classic example of this kind of behavior that we observed recently, an insurance company determined that its costs were badly out of line with industry norms and that, to reverse a significant and extended share loss, it needed to re-examine all its operational systems and procedures. This was a massive undertaking, since it would potentially affect the entire way the organization did business. This was, of course, threatening to many of the company's departments, which stood either to lose their autonomy or to face significant reductions in staff.

Given the importance of this issue, the president of the corporation authorized the creation of a 70-member full-time interdepartmental task force, which would spend eighteen months studying the problem. The head of this task force was a very bright young executive whom everyone realized was on a "fast track" to the top. This executive was acutely sensitive to the potential difficulties in getting a workable set of recommendations out of his task force, so he incorporated into its design, and that of the work plan it would pursue, two features that he felt virtually ensured at least some concrete output.

First, he divided the task force into subteams that corresponded to the most significant and powerful organizational units that would be affected by the change. A team leader for each subgroup was appointed from the corresponding organizational department, and members of other relevant departments were appointed to fill each subteam. Second, while large blocks of analysis were scheduled in the work plan, the task-force head was careful to ensure that the most critical steps in determining what recommendations would be produced were discussive and judgmental and would not rely directly on any of the analytical output.

It could be expected that the subgroups would produce recommendations that were compromises, while achieving some gains in forecast cost improvement (but far less than the company needed). As the task-force leader put it, "I can't afford to have too much analysis as these subgroups try to reach their recommendations, because we'll spend all our time arguing about the numbers and we'll never make any progress. Besides, all it will do is surface issues that are really undiscussible and certainly won't change as a result of our efforts." The primary purpose of the analysis itself was to provide a means of "keeping score" on the improvements to be suggested, since the company's accounting system was not well suited to this purpose.

While the results of this effort are not yet complete, there is already considerable skepticism throughout the corporation about whether it will live up to expectations. Yet most people simultaneously praise the young team leader for doing a great job "under the circumstances."

What this story illustrates is not so much that organizations resist change but that most executives seek ways to work around the hidden (or undiscussible) barriers to change. This has two effects. First, it severely limits the change that can be made, because compromises are inevitable in such consensus decision making. Also, where power structures in the organization are being challenged because their existing behavior is at the root of the company's strategic problems, the greater their current influence, the less likely it is that they will be persuaded to change.

The second, more subtle effect is caused by the fact that an approach that bypasses the organizational and cultural features resisting change is often lauded as "effective" management. Executives who use this approach, unlike some of their authoritarian counterparts, do not ride roughshod over the undiscussible blockages. They find ways to work around them. Phrases such as "the art of the possible" implicitly reward this management style. The organizational learning that results reinforces the features that resist change, since management has, by implication, condoned them. Members of the organization also learn that the way to get ahead is to manage in a bypass manner. Thus, the organization's ability to effect change is reduced, and the resistance to change is simultaneously increased. This loop can be extremely damaging if repeated and reinforced often enough.

We believe that an analytical approach to decision making and involvement of the organization in the development and execution of strategic plans are valuable but not sufficient for achieving successful change. In addition, an organization must learn to confront the behavioral issues that prevent it from perceiving the need for change, from formulating appropriate alternatives, or from implementing plans. To do this, it must first learn to identify these issues and must then create an environment in which they can be discussed. The issues must not be bypassed or compromised. They must be brought into the open to be dealt with as rationally as possible. Organizations that can learn to do this successfully will find themselves better able to adopt more ambitious strategies or, in extreme cases, to make dramatic changes in strategic direction to avoid catastrophe without having, as often happens, to change large numbers of the top management team in the process.

Figure 2 illustrates the fundamental trade-offs at work. The two axes represent the degree of change being proposed, from low to high (or "frame breaking"), and the degree of organizational resistance to be expected, also from low to frame breaking. High value/degree of change strategies that face low resistance are obvious choices and would probably already have been adopted by the organization (assuming that it had perceived their existence). Low-value strategies with high organizational resistance probably are

**Figure 2. Degree of Change and Level of Resistance.**

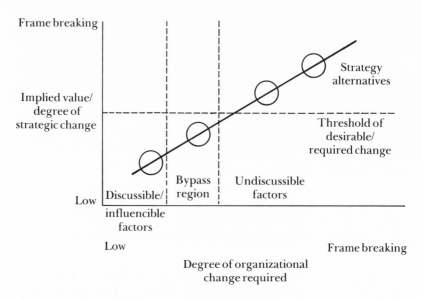

not really valid choices, if other alternatives exist. The potential array of strategic alternatives in any given situation will therefore probably display a measure of correlation between the degree of change and the level of organizational resistance.

The "discussible/influencible" resistances are at the left side of the chart in Figure 2. Strategic alternatives that fall within this area are easily attainable. By using bypass strategies, it may be possible to extend this region of permissible action (without offending the organization norms). But, frequently, there will not be a viable strategy alternative that satisfies the threshold of desirable or required change if this constraint is to be observed. If this is simply a matter of having to adopt a lower-value course of action, the choice can be rationalized in terms of going for something that is practicable, rather than attempting the impossible. But if strategic survival is at stake, the choice is not so easy. The question, therefore, is, how can an organization go beyond a level of change that is achievable without upsetting the organizational norms regarding the discussibility and/or influencibility of the embedded blockages to change? And can this be done without the kind of catharsis that so often is fatal to the careers of many of the organization's senior members?

## A New Model of Change?

We believe, on the basis of very limited experience with a handful of organizations that have begun to experiment with new ways of dealing with this fundamental dilemma, that there may be some cause for optimism. Our observations at this stage consist of two parts—a suggestion that is structural in nature and one that focuses more on the behavioral aspects. We do not yet advance these ideas as a general theory that will be helpful in all situations. Our experience thus far, however, indicates that these organizations are making significant progress in changing in ways that they would not previously have thought possible.

In considering these ideas, it is helpful first to conceptualize again, this time about the *process* of change. This process would appear to comprise three distinct activities: diagnosis, formulation, and execution. The dividing lines between these phases are, of course, blurred, and there is considerable overlap, especially in organizations that practice a participative managerial style, since movement from diagnosis to execution is often highly iterative, and it can probably be accurately argued that execution is in effect from the very beginning of the process. Another distinction that is helpful to make, although, again, there are substantial interdependencies and overlaps, is between the strategic frame and the organizational frame in which the change is being considered. Figure 3 helps to illustrate this.

The top row in this schematic is concerned with the strategic frame for the organization. This set of activities begins with diagnosing the need for change. This means determining whether the competitive and business environments remain favorable toward the business as it pursues its current mission, allowing for fine tuning of this mission as the situation evolves, or whether a dramatic shift in strategic direction is required, now or at some time in the foreseeable future. Next, alternatives for change must be evaluated. And, finally, these must be translated into a concrete action program for the new strategy to be implemented. The strategic frame, in other words, is concerned primarily with the question: what should the organization do?

**Figure 3. Change Process Model.**

|  | Diagnosis | Formulation | Execution |
|---|---|---|---|
| Strategic frame | Need for change? | Analysis of alternatives | Translation of operating programs and objectives |
| Organizational frame | Cause-and-effect models | Identifying relevant blockages | Overcoming blockages |

The organizational frame, by contrast, is more concerned with what it *can* do. There are three elements here, as well: diagnosis, in the sense of identifying the cause-and-effect models of organizational behavior (including consideration of the organizational structure and measurement and control systems); formulation, in terms of focusing on those features of organizational resistance that are likely to block change; and execution, which implies finding ways to help the organization overcome these blockages.

The structural suggestion that we are posing as part of the putative new model of change concerns itself primarily with the strategic frame elements. If change is to take place in an organization, the need for change must first be recognized. It is frequently at this point that the process breaks down. Organizations often keep information on themselves and their environment in ways that obscure the opportunities or threats that face them. One *Fortune 500* company, for example, used to encourage its divisions to report their sales and market share on the basis of what it called "served market." The idea was that this would reflect the most relevant measure of market performance. But, in at least one instance, this measure failed to record the penetration of foreign goods into the sector, because these were not captured in the industry association's reports. As a result, the threat from overseas competition was not perceived until it was too late to respond effectively.

For most organizations, the principal diagnostic measure of whether change is needed is its current financial performance. Unfortunately, an organization's financial results are not always a very good measure of its long-term health. Often, the need to consider change is most urgent when prosperity is greatest. Paradoxically, at a time when the organization still has the power and financial strength to respond effectively, and the threat is still in its infancy, anxiety about current performance is at its lowest ebb. By the time financial results begin to reflect the threat, the organization's ability to respond effectively has been reduced, and the challenge is well established. It may no longer be possible to fight back.

There is an inherent tension between management in pursuit of an existing business mission—which involves reinforcing existing cultural, organizational, structural, and measurement and control features—and considering the need for change, which will (especially if the change is frame breaking) challenge or require the reversal of many of these features. It is hard for line managers in these circumstances to develop a balanced perspective. Typically, where alternatives are required in a strategic planning process, the line managers submitting plans will propose several straw men along with the alternative that they really wish to pursue.

One possible structural approach to a more objective assessment is to legitimize some other organizational unit, or possibly an outsider, periodically to diagnose the need for change in any given business. The purpose would be less to develop new strategies than to ask these questions: Is the existing strategy working satisfactorily? Are there hitherto unperceived major threats or opportunities that suggest the need for significant change? What is the likely range of alternative responses available to the company?

The results of this evaluation would be discussed openly with both line management and the CEO. It would be the function of some permanently constituted forum of senior executives to review all of the strategic business units (SBUs) in the organization periodically, to determine the priorities among the significant strategic issues facing the organization. This body would determine the mission of different SBUs and the need to consider, by means of an intensive review, the alternatives for change.

This review is the second significant element in the structural part of our change model. In this step, ad hoc teams comprehensively examine individual issues identified as strategically significant. These teams include the business line management, who are brought into the process of formulating strategic alternatives but work with the diagnostic unit to ensure maximum objectivity. Other functional areas or organizational units can be added to the study team as appropriate.

If the decision is critical to the whole company, it may be necessary for the CEO to become personally involved in the assessment of alternatives, in order to become fully familiar with the detailed assumptions and logic upon which the new strategy is to be based. Otherwise, he or she may be faced with a decision based upon a somewhat seamless analysis and set of recommendations by whatever group has been constituted to study the issue. Should the CEO be uncomfortable with the conclusions, even if this discomfort is at an intuitive level and he or she is not able to point to explicit flaws in the logic of the analysis, he or she will be left with the unsatisfactory choices of either going along with the recommendation against his or her own instinctive judgment, disagreeing with it on grounds that he or she is unable to support logically or factually, or putting off the decision. This dilemma of the senior executive facing a major decision can only be resolved, we believe, by direct participation in the analytical build up. This problem is particularly prevalent in large, functionally organized businesses, especially when they are asset intensive (paper, steel, and so on). In more diversified organizations, the level of effective decision making may be lower (at the group level, for instance), but the same principle of direct participation applies.

Ad hoc organizations may be crystallized around less critical issues in either type of organization, but always observing the principle that the individuals represented either bring specific business experience or analytical skills or will be involved directly in implementing whatever changes are decided upon. The reasoning processes of any of these groups must be analytical rather than strictly judgmental.

As the decision is reached on the basic direction that the organization is to follow, the principle of participation by the responsible executives, which has been built into the formulation stage of the change process, is now extended to include an increasingly broad cross-section of operating management. The goal is to define and then execute programs to translate the new strategy into practice. An important device here is for the general manager to constitute a team of the relevant heads of the organizational subunits to explicitly oversee the change process. This group must discipline itself to focus on change, rather than treating its meetings as an opportunity to discuss topical business problems. It is here, too, that the greatest overlap occurs with the activities designed to overcome the organizational blockages, as described later.

Another structural suggestion is to segregate those organizational units whose mission is in the process of changing significantly from those that are pursuing an existing mission. Control systems are rarely well suited to managed status quo and change missions simultaneously. In diversified organizations, it may also be appropriate to attempt to match the characteristics of the general manager to the mission of the business. Some managers are more skilled at and certainly more comfortable with pursuing an existing mission and finding ways to fine tune it. Others are more adept at bringing about change. Most large organizations will have room for both kinds of skills, and it may be a more effective use of management resources to recognize this explicitly by giving the manager of a business unit where the need for change has been diagnosed some choice as to whether he or she or someone else would be more appropriate to develop and pursue the new mission.

The behavioral part of our change model is concerned primarily with the organizational frame. A number of activities are involved. In our experience, few companies now engage in these to any significant degree or, at least, with any explicit recognition that they consider them important. In fact, legitimizing consideration of such aspects of the change process is itself a critical feature of this model. This is because the management styles and characteristic behavior of the senior line executives—whether they are external to the business unit in question or a part of it—are inevitably an integral part of, and set the tone for, the organizational culture.

Therefore, these executives alone can create the necessary conditions for introducing consideration of behavioral and cultural resistance to change into the management process. They must do this, first, by legitimizing the subject (making the undiscussible discussible) and, second, by behaving themselves in ways that are consistent with openness to change—including the possibility that they might learn that their own behavior, as well as that of others in the organization, needs to change.

The first element in the model is actually diagnosing the cultural and organizational blockages and developing credible cause-and-effect models that illustrate how the observed behavior reinforces the current direction and practices of the organization. The same models can also explain what resistances to change may be in place in the organization's culture and characteristic behavior patterns.

An important consideration is who should be given responsibility for this diagnosis. In organizations where the behavior patterns are deeply embedded and where there are many undiscussibles, it will probably prove almost impossible for anyone who is a member of the organization to carry out this task effectively. We believe that, once an organization has learned how change can be brought about by dealing with internal blockages, it will simultaneously reduce its resistance to future changes. Eventually, an adaptive culture may emerge, in which open discussion of organizational blockages can be a normal part of internal communication.

It would be logical to expect a central staff group of some kind to play a key role as internal change agent. The strategic planning function would be advantageously positioned, since it also has responsibility for considering the potential need for and possible directions of change. The human-resource function may be a valuable complementary resource in considering the organizational frame. In the meantime, however, it is probably more effective to look to an outside agent to perform the diagnostic evaluation and to bridge the gaps between current behavior patterns and the desired future direction. We will refer to this entity as a "change agent."

In our experience, diagnosing organizational resistances to change and developing credible cause-and-effect models are both relatively straightforward exercises. An important distinction must be made between the kinds of skills required to bypass organizational resistance and those involved in addressing them openly and constructively. Inherent in the ability to bypass is a high order of "political" competence. Whether the change agent is an outsider or a member of the organization, understanding the relevant political sensitivities of any given course of action and then fashioning the necessary compromises, forging the required coalitions, and orchestrating the series of meetings in which influential executives can be induced to take a particular stance so that progress can be achieved are all activities for which few people have the capacity. It is easy to make a mistake, and this can often prove fatal to forward movement. One reason is that, in the bypass mode, the change agent assumes responsibility for guiding the process of change, including making many of the choices for the direction and means by which it is accomplished. These choices are often made either covertly and unilaterally or in collusion with senior management. This typically tends to compound the number of undiscussibles rather than reduce it, since it adds a further set along the lines of, "Why did you feel it necessary to conceal from me what you were trying to do in getting change accomplished?"

An alternative approach to addressing undiscussible resistances is to do it in an open and confrontable manner. The reasoning processes are, in fact, closely analogous to those employed in strategic analysis. The change agent first collects relevant data. This is typically done through interviews with a broad cross-section of players, observations of meetings, and examination of correspondence and other written communications. The data are thus in the form of directly observed comments on the subject of blockages in general or illustrations of particular modes of behavior in "live" circumstances, such as meetings or memoranda.

The data must now be validated. In practice, this means comparing and contrasting the views of several players (especially when they are on opposite sides of a particular issue) and then sharing the results among them. The next step is to draw the implications from these observations in a way that expresses the logic so that it can be challenged if others can make a different case and support their view with appropriate illustrations. If successfully accomplished, this process can lead to a mutual commitment on the part of the members of the organization to share responsibility for and to attempt to address the blockages, or to make the explicit choice not to address them but to live with the consequences.

In contrast to the bypass approach, the change agent can make errors and not necessarily undermine the whole process of change. The change agent is not making choices for the members of the organization, and he or she is basing his or her views of the cause-and-effect models on real, verifiable data. The change agent is not acting covertly. At all times, the change agent should be able to be completely open and comfortable about what he or she is doing and his or her motives for doing so. Through an appropriately designed series of interventions, starting with the top of the organization and working successively down, the change agent involves its members participatively in coming to grips with the blockages.

An illustration of a cause-and-effect model may be helpful at this point. The newly appointed manager of a large division of a company was concerned that the plans being prepared for his unit lacked realism. This placed him in an untenable position vis-à-vis the corporation, since he could not argue with conviction that the corporate expectations were unreasonable (his own organization's plans appeared to meet the corporation's financial goals), nor did he feel comfortable in committing with confidence to the required targets.

On closer inspection, it was discovered that previous generations of management had created and fostered a powerful "good soldier" mentality, in which everybody tried to second-guess what their bosses wanted and proposed plans to suit. The company had an elaborate performance-evaluation system based on numerical goals, which at first sight would seem to put the "good soldiers" themselves in a compromised position, since they would be committing to unreachable objectives. But it turned out that there were no real "teeth" in this system. No one was ever fired for poor performance. Salaries were affected, but only marginally. And strict application of the appraisal system was being circumvented in a multitude of small ways (for example, the weighting of goals was frequently not established until near review time; at this point, it was possible for an astute manager to decide what rating he or she wanted to give to subordinates and "work the matrix backwards," to produce the right numerical result). Only when evidence of this cause-and-effect model was brought to light was it possible to address the plan's realism problem.

Certain principles seem to be appropriate for the organizational frame activities and the behavior of the change agent. First, it is essential that the top executive in the organization be committed, if not to the entire process from the outset, at least to the initial stages, and that he or she maintain that commitment and support as the process unfolds. It will be his or her responsibility to establish a credible temporary culture in which members of the organization can feel free to act experimentally. Second, and equally important, these activities are quintessentially participative. Unblocking almost invariably means understanding the interrelationship between the behavior patterns of one set of actors and the reaction induced in others. For the process to be effective, ways must be found to explore these shared responsibilities. Third, the top executives and the organization should be able to choose as the process goes on the extent to which they feel the undiscussibles can and should be addressed.

It is not necessary to consider all of the organization's dirty linen at once—only those aspects that are directly relevant to the strategic change being contemplated. As the process of change moves from diagnosis to focus on the specific blockages, and then to finding ways to address them, participation in the organization is successively widened. As each level of management begins to address the blockage issues with the next level down, it is valuable to have them discuss what problems they expect as the next level becomes involved and how they will deal with them. This increases their involvement and commitment, while generating information for the change agent about their readiness to continue.

The effectiveness of the organizational frame activities is significantly enhanced by having them proceed in parallel with

those of the strategic frame. The same management circles that
consider strategic change are involved in the process of identifying
and discussing the impediments to change. This has an extremely
important side effect. When people talk about organizational behavior in the abstract, it is easy for them, if they so choose, to
conceal much important information about their own vulnerabilities or their perceptions of the behavior and vulnerabilities of
others. This is because little is at stake except greater understanding
of "organizational problems" in general, and many players may
choose to remove themselves from such an effort, preferring instead
to profit from the participation of others. When a real issue of
change is on the table, however, it is much harder for people to hide,
unless they are also willing to live with the consequences. There is
an inherent efficiency, in other words, in addressing organizational
obstacles to change in the context of a specifically diagnosed need
for change, rather than as a subject unto itself.

    The behavior of the change agent should be a model for that
of the other participants. Thus, the change agent must take care to
stay close to observable data. He or she must avoid attributing
motives to people unless the attributions can be tested. The change
agent must not focus on the counterproductive actions of one set of
actors only but must instead look for interrelationships between
behavior patterns and talk in terms of the responsibilities of both
parties. This enables the change agent to draw out the undesirable
consequences of these cause-and-effect loops in a constructive and
nonaccusatory way.

    When taking a point of view, the change agent should begin
with the directly observable data. He or she should state the
inferences that he or she draws from the data and should ask others
for their reactions and illustrations of their own that will help either
confirm or challenge this point of view. When people discuss their
reactions, they often educate each other about the issues raised by
the change agent. This helps build a degree of mutual commitment.

    Finally, the change agent must act in ways that, while tough-
minded in terms of presenting data and drawing out the implications, always leave open to the organization the choice of how it
wishes to proceed. He or she should take responsibility for pointing
out the consequences of a particular choice and might attempt to

argue for a different course of action, but the essential principle is one of informed choice.

## Summary

It is too early to know whether this new model of change, which combines a structural element isolating responsibility for diagnosis of the need for change with a new approach to addressing organizational resistance, will be successful in bringing about genuinely frame-breaking change. It seems clear, however, that alternative models have not yet provided the answers to the kinds of resistances or distortions that characterize the way that most organizations either determine how to change or, more important, bring change about. Furthermore, many companies seem to be frustrated with the strategic management process and appear to be placing at least part of the responsibility for their frustration on the mechanisms and functional organizations that were put in place originally to overcome other problems with the change process.

It is entirely appropriate that top management should assume the principal responsibility for strategic planning and direction. But this should, we believe, be pursued through combined attention to the strategic and the organizational frames. The analytical capabilities in both areas can significantly improve the likelihood that change can be accomplished successfully, even when such change threatens to violate the organization's cultural constraints.

# ❧ SIXTEEN ❧

# Dealing with Threat
# and Defensiveness

## *Chris Argyris*

Richard Hermon-Taylor (Chapter Fifteen of this volume) is a thoughtful senior practitioner of strategy and strategy consulting. The content of what he practices is related to such fields as economics, finance, and marketing. His approach is concerned with (1) what a business is doing now, (2) what is happening in the environment, and (3) what the business should be doing (Porter, 1980). It typically examines (1) the current strategy, (2) the major economic opportunities and threats emanating from the environment, (3) the skills and resources available to close the economic strategic gaps, (4) the evaluation of new economic options, and (5) the selection of one or more of these options for implementation (Hofer and Schendel, 1978).

Most writers on strategy agree that implementation is a crucial problem (Lorange and Vancil, 1977; Yavitz and Newman, 1982). Some have tried to specify what may be required to get genuine involvement (Ansoff, 1965; Bourgeois and Brodwin, 1982; Mason and Mitroff, 1981a). Naylor (1978) and Pettigrew (1973) have described intergroup rivalries and political infighting within organizations. Ansoff suggests that strategy formulation and development will threaten managers (1) who hold personal power by virtue of private knowledge, (2) who may be incompetent, and (3) who may not be able to make the required shifts in outlook from an introverted, historically familiar view of the world to an extroverted, unfamiliar, and therefore threatening perspective (Ansoff, 1979b, p. 179). It is these types of conditions that help to create the organizational defenses such as "the undiscussibles" that Hermon-Taylor identifies in his chapter. If we can help organizations to face up to and reduce the undiscussibles, we may provide them with help that is rarely offered, namely, the ability of the organization to learn to detect and correct errors and continue to do so.

In my chapter, I should like to describe what we are learning when we try to teach strategy professionals the framework that Hermon-Taylor has described as well as the skills that are required to implement it, especially in dealing with organizational defenses.

## A Puzzle

Early in my observations of strategy professionals at work in case teams and with the clients, I discovered a puzzle. The reasoning that they used to develop high-quality technical work was the same type of reasoning that I believed was required to reduce the organizational defenses. The puzzle was that the strategy professionals were (initially) reluctant to use these reasoning skills when dealing with human and organizational defenses. Why should they resist using these skills?

Elsewhere, I have tried to suggest two different but interdependent answers for the reluctance. First, most human beings are programmed from early life to deal with threatening issues by using reasoning strategies that are bound to be ineffective. Second, they create organizational cultures to reinforce these counterproductive strategies (Argyris and Schön, 1978; Argyris, 1982). Hence, when we ask the strategy professionals to transfer their technical reasoning skills to the human domain, they are acting as our theories predict that they would act. Let us explore this in more depth.

### Observations of Reactions to Defensiveness

During the past three years, I have been observing strategy professionals in a consulting firm and several who are internal planners in large corporations. The material that I will use in this

chapter comes primarily from my work with the external consultants. They are, in my opinion, an extremely bright and highly
competent group of professionals who have shown themselves to be
fast learners in dealing with client (and their own) defensiveness.

The first illustration as to how they deal with client defensiveness comes from a discussion among twenty-five consultants. I
selected this case because the consultants describe the strategies that
they use with their clients when the latter act defensively. Another
value of the case is that, when discussing among themselves how to
deal with client defensiveness, the consultants began to make each
other defensive. Hence, we obtained first-hand data of how they may
unrealizingly create defensiveness and how they act to reduce it.

The discussion began with a senior officer presenting the
reactions of their clients to a report. Briefly, the clients had begun
a new venture that they believed could become a billion-dollar-plus
business. The consulting team was asked to help the clients position
themselves to take advantage of the opportunity. The team worked
cooperatively with the client organization. After several months of
work and periodic lengthy discussions, the consulting team presented to the client hard data to show that it was unlikely that the
business would be more than a $75 million one (at least in the
immediate future). "As the presentation wore on," the officer stated,
"we became aware that there was a lot of nit-picking of analytical
points. For the first time, we were asked questions such as 'When
did you get that number?' or 'How do you know your assumptions
are correct?' "

The officer then asked his colleagues how they would
diagnose what was going on. An analysis of the tape-recorded
discussion indicated that all agreed that the clients' nit-picking
behavior was caused by the clients' defensiveness. "What would
make the clients defensive?" asked the officer. Three reasons were
given:

1.  The consultants had come to a different and much more
    pessimistic solution than had the clients using the same data.
    The nit-picking was caused by the feelings of embarrassment
    on the part of the clients, as well as the fact that they did not
    know how else to react.

2.  The consultants had not only just told the clients that their projections were wrong, they had also created the possibility that at least some of the people brought in to build the new business might not have jobs.
3.  The surprise itself could be the cause of the client defensiveness. If the consultants had spoken with some of the key individuals before the meeting, they could have prepared them for the surprise.

As one consultant said, "Their nit-picking is a survival process to be expected by anyone who is threatened" (many nodded their heads approvingly or said "yes," "correct," "right on"). He added, "Would we not act in the same way if we had an outsider tell us that our practice was wrong?" Again, many nodded their heads approvingly, and several said "yes." Hence, we have an example where the consultants agreed that the clients were acting defensively. They disagreed that the "causes" of the defensiveness were that the consultants had arrived at a different conclusion from what the clients expected and that they had done so using the very data that the clients had used to develop the wrong conclusion.

The officer leading the discussion asked what actions they would recommend. The responses could be categorized as follows:

1.  Ask the clients to "raise their sights and help them to see the big picture."
2.  Encourage the clients to examine "our numbers any way they wish and see what happens to the analysis. If we are correct, they will eventually realize it."
3.  Invite the clients to express all their views. "We then promise to think about them and promise to respond. In the meantime, let us get on with the presentation."
4.  Begin the presentation with more positive findings and then ease into the negative conclusions.

The first feature about this advice is that it made sense to most of the participants. By making sense, I mean that (1) the participants appeared to agree with the hypothesized positive impact of such actions on the client, and (2) they appeared to know how to implement the advice.

There is a second feature about the advice that is more complex and problematical than the easy agreement implies. All these strategies assume that clients who are feeling defensive have the capacity to reduce their defensiveness either by being asked "to raise their sights," by being promised a response, or by being given some positive examples. It is as if human beings can distance themselves from their feelings of threat and then continue to focus dispassionately on the data that are causing the threat in the first place. There was also a plea for suppressing the defensiveness in order to overcome it. The clients are expected to place their defensiveness "on hold" and discuss threatening subjects with dispassion. These strategies were being recommended even though many of the consultants had earlier agreed that they, too, would have reacted defensively if someone had told them something that was equally surprising about their practice, using their data to make the point.

A third feature of the strategies is that all of the participants attempted to bypass the defensiveness. There was no attempt to discuss it. Moreover, there was no suggestion that they should state to the client that this was what they were doing. This is understandable, because to discuss a covert bypass strategy overtly is to violate its face-saving features. Hence, the defensiveness is undiscussible, and the undiscussibility of the defensiveness is also undiscussible.

During the discussion, Consultant *A* said that he would have asked the client "to temporarily suspend disbelief, to focus less on the details and more on the major pieces of analysis." Consultant *B* responded, "But that would be adding insult to injury. Moreover, the clients could experience *A* as acting in a patronizing manner." There were a few moments of awkward silence, since this was the first time one of the participants had evaluated negatively the contributions of another.

The officer asked *A* how he felt about *B's* response. *A* said that he felt that *B* had not understood him. The officer then asked, "If the conversation continued as it did, would you have felt that *B* and others would be nit-picking?" *A* responded "yes." The officer then pointed out that *A* had concluded that his colleagues were wrong, acted as if that were not the case, and continued to hold his views more strongly, while discounting the views of his critics. *B* smiled when he heard *A's* comments and said, "To be honest, and I guess that's the idea of these sessions, I would probably have reacted the same way as you did."

The point is that the moment the threat occurred in the seminar, the participants also acted in ways to bypass the threat and to distance themselves from it. These strategies make it unlikely that individuals will ever test publicly their inferences and attributions to understand the defensiveness or will ever obtain the cooperation that they seek to overcome it. Hence, the strategies that clients may use when they become defensive may also be used by the consultants when they, too, become defensive.

In this connection, it is interesting to note how the consultants tended to react if the clients questioned their conclusions, analyses, or models in a way that did not begin with defensiveness. The fundamental strategy, as one consultant stated it, was "to up the level of proof and overcome them with evidence." The clients' reactions, at best, were of feeling the brilliance and rigor of the consultants (but not necessarily their sense of concern or compassion). At worst, they felt put down and ignored. Both consequences would tend to lead to defensiveness, and then the consultant would switch to the strategies described earlier.

In another example, a team with the objective of collecting valid financial data met with fifteen key middle managers (line and staff). They were unable to get from the managers relatively clear and unambiguous answers about the meaning of the numbers. After many hours of frustration, they assigned tasks to various individuals and scheduled individual meetings to get the answers. When the team was alone, the members made comments such as "unbelievable," "They're all screwed up," "Have you ever seen such a defensive group," "No wonder the top management does not trust the planning process." After the catharsis was finished, they laid plans for the future meetings. The team leader admonished the members to deal "sensitively" with the client members, because they and the organization were obviously defensive, and "we don't want to get mired down in their organizational garbage."

What happened? The team members observed the reactions of the line and staff managers to their questions. The team members inferred that the clients and the client system were acting defensively: that they were "screwed up" and "defensive." These inferences were not made explicit, nor were they tested publicly. The only "testing" that occurred was when the team members met by themselves and evaluated the clients' actions, hardly a valid test.

The conclusion of defensiveness then became the premise for guiding the team's actions. The team members' design for dealing with the clients included such strategies as (1) do not discuss the defensiveness in order to test or understand it, because (2) that will most likely make the clients more defensive; therefore, (3) act as if the clients are not judged as being defensive and (4) cover up the diagnosis with a bypass strategy.

There are several important consequences of this strategy. First, the consultants may never learn the extent to which their diagnosis may have been incorrect. Second, the clients may never learn the extent to which their defensiveness inhibits the formulation, development, and execution of a strategy. Third, if the clients' reactions are indeed defensive, and if they are spontaneous and automatic, then they must have been used previously, and they will probably be used in the future. If this is the case, then the players will tend to use these reactions automatically when they are asked to accept and implement the new strategy that the team may develop. Fourth, if the clients react defensively, and if the consultants bypass that defensiveness, then the consultants have been induced into an organizational routine for dealing with defensiveness—bypass the defensiveness and act as if this is not being done; hence, cover up the cover-up.

Some may say that the consultants would not have got themselves into such a predicament if they had involved the clients more in the process. But the example was precisely of a meeting where the team and the clients were working cooperatively to produce data. The team members were trying to act participatively and cooperatively from the outset. Indeed, the consultants would maintain that they dealt with the defensiveness as they did in order to protect and encourage a sense of cooperation and participation. The clients would probably maintain that they had learned to use their defensive actions because that is the way to survive, as well as the way to make the planning process work as well as possible. They could provide examples of the actions of superiors that led them to develop these automatic defensive reactions for individual and organizational survival.

We have, therefore, a situation where the clients exist in an organizational context that makes it unlikely that they can detect and correct important errors in the planning process and important cultural constraints to learning. The consultants act in ways to bypass these conditions and act as if they are not doing so. The clients' defensive routines are therefore protected. Hence, the ultimate effective implementation may be inhibited.

Perhaps more importantly, the client organization is not being helped to understand that its defensive routines designed for survival also inhibit it from learning how to learn. One consequence of this is related to the reactions of the executives at the top. They created the team (an internal task force with outside consultants) precisely because they did not believe that the present organization could produce the analysis necessary for a sound strategy. They reached that conclusion after several years of experience with the planning process that resulted in all sorts of incomplete or incorrect plans, which the top concluded were the result of the defensiveness of the organization. Like everyone else involved in this case, they, too, kept their diagnoses secret; they, too, covered up; they, too, covered up the cover-up; and they, too, bypassed the entire issue by hiring the outside consultants to work with the "best" individuals from within that they could identify.

In sum, the automatic reaction to defensiveness in both cases is to ignore or bypass the defensiveness. But the act of ignoring reality is itself defensive, because individuals who are charged with producing a new strategy eventually will have to deal with the existing organizational defensive routines, which will operate to reduce the effectiveness of the new planning processes. Bypassing and distancing do not encourage the production of valid information with which to formulate and develop a strategy, not to mention to implement it.

## Automatic Reactions of Bypass and Distancing

The automatic reactions of dealing with defensiveness by such actions as bypassing and distancing are by no means limited to strategy professionals. Executives and managers that we have studied to date, in large or small organizations, of whatever structure, private or public, volunteer or nonvolunteer, appear to act in the same way. Indeed, most individuals deal with defensiveness in the same way. There are two reactions most often used. The first is to bypass. The second, used most often when the first does not work, is to confront the issue head on in a way that usually produces the predicted defensiveness. In organizations, this reaction is usually dealt with by asking the top "to take a stand," "read the riot act," and tell the people to "shape up or ship out" (Argyris and Schön, 1978; Argyris, 1982). These types of reactions are often accompanied by the firing or transferring of key actors who are believed to inhibit progress. The reactions may solve the problem temporarily, but they do not help the organization to get control over its defensive routines, to help the organization learn how to deal effectively with defensiveness for whatever problem or whatever level.

Why is this so, when most line executives and strategy professionals believe that reducing organizational defensive routines is a good idea, and learning how to learn is a noble aspiration? The answer, I suggest, is *not* because they believe that the noble aspiration is not noble, but because they believe that it is not realistic. If the examples given earlier are illustrative, then one can understand why there is the doubt. The threatening factors and defensive reactions were so interdependent and complex that it would be very difficult to figure out how to untangle them without, as one executive said, "creating more problems." This fear is the most frequent one that is expressed by line executives. It acts to reinforce the distancing and the predisposition to bypass, because the fear is itself threatening.

If no one wants this state of affairs, why is it so prevalent? To answer this question, we must examine the reasoning processes that people use to make sense of and to remain in some degree of control over their own and others' defensiveness. We must also explore the impact of these highly skilled modes of coping with defensiveness upon the organization.

## Theory of Individual and Organizational Learning

Whenever actors are participating in economic decision-making processes, they are designing the consequences that they intend to implement. The same is true when actors are participating in managing people. Whenever actors produce a match between intentions and outcomes, or whenever they detect and correct errors (mismatches), they may be said to be learning. Organizational learning is produced through the actions of individuals acting as agents for the organization. A theory of individual and organizational learning can therefore be the basis for understanding actions, be they intendedly economic or human relationships or both.

Behavior is designed to achieve tacit or explicit intentions. It is not possible to design every action from the beginning, nor is it likely that actors will have all the knowledge that is relevant in every situation. Thus, individuals carry around with them beliefs and values about how they and others ought to behave. These beliefs and values can be stated in the form of propositions about effectiveness. "If I behave in such and such a manner, then the following consequences should occur." Since these propositions have the same structure as propositions in any scientific theory, we have called them *theories of action*. (The major concepts and empirical findings on this theory are described in Argyris, 1976c, 1982; Argyris and Schön, 1978.)

Individuals hold two types of theories of action. The one that they describe, their *espoused* theory, contains their explicit beliefs and values. Empirically speaking, espoused theories rarely inform human actions when the problem is threatening and difficult. If people behave differently from what they espouse ("Do as I say, not as I do"), if behavior is designed, and if the behavior does not fit the espoused design, then there must be another theory that individuals are using. We call it their *theory-in-use*.

In order to design ways to change theories-in-use, we must first be able to define them. Research to date indicates a result that it took us a long time to accept. Individuals vary widely in the way they act; they vary somewhat less widely in the theories of action they espouse, but (this was unexpected) there is almost no variance in the theory-in-use (for an explanation of this finding, see Argyris, 1982). This enabled us to develop a theory-in-use model that is highly generalizable, which we called *Model I*. Model I has the structure implicit in the preceding discussion. It contains the values and beliefs that govern actions, which we call the governing variables. It also contains the action strategies that individuals use to satisfy the governing variables. Finally, it contains the consequences that will result for learning and problem-solving effectiveness when the first two factors are used jointly to design and implement action.

Figure 1 summarizes the major features of Model I. Individuals will tend to deal with threatening issues by creating conditions of miscommunications, self-fulfilling prophecies, self-sealing processes, and, hence, escalation of error. Moreover, we have found that people tend to be blind when they themselves are responsible for such defensive consequences and accurately aware when others are the causes of such defensive consequences. Finally, the unawareness is not equivalent to a hole in their heads or a gap in their minds. Quite the contrary; the unawareness is programmed (Argyris, 1982).

Individuals who use Model I also create predictable social contexts that influence the nature and quality of the learning that will occur within the organization. Since these contexts appear in all organizations so far studied, and since they seem to be self-maintaining patterns, we call them Model O-I (O for *organization*) learning systems. Whenever Model I individuals strive to solve issues that are ambiguous and threatening, they will tend to produce poor resolution of conflict, win-lose dynamics, and self-fulfilling, self-sealing processes. Conditions such as these in turn increase the probability that search processes will be limited and that information distortion will occur as people scramble to cover themselves. In short, Model O-I predicts the politicking and limited problem solving that often exist in organizations. With these conditions prevailing, it is unlikely that participants engaged in economic decisions will strive to produce valid information when it may threaten their position, to test their views publicly, or to make themselves vulnerable in decisions regarding economic issues.

Figure 1. Model I Theory-in-Use.

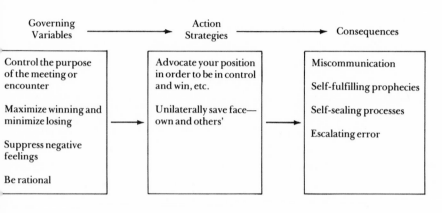

To summarize, human beings hold theories-in-use that make it likely that they will deal with threat by bypassing it. The bypass strategies will all tend to lead to escalation of defensiveness and error and, hence, are not genuinely corrective. Strategy professionals are in the difficult position of dealing with clients who could become even more defensive if the threat is not bypassed. Defensive clients might easily decide, for example, to deal with their threat by projecting all the blame onto the consultants for acting in such "obviously immature" ways. They are also in a difficult situation because, whatever strategy they may devise, it is highly likely that it will be consistent with Model I, so that it, too, would lead to escalation of defensiveness and error.

## Organizational Learning

Strategy professionals may not have to worry about these dilemmas if their strategies are not threatening and if the organization is capable of implementing them. However, even when the strategies are accepted, if they are difficult for the organization to implement, then the issue of dealing with threat becomes important.

Another major issue is the ultimate purpose of strategy formulation and implementation. What if the purpose is to implement a strategy in a way that not only reduces the organizational defensive routines but also helps the organization to learn how to deal with future threat? In order to accomplish this objective, the participants will have to learn how to reflect upon and reduce the organizational defensive routines. But, in doing this effectively, they will also reflect upon how they learned to detect and correct these defensive routines and the errors that they produced. If this occurs, strategic formulation, development, and implementation become even more important and comprehensive than described at the outset. They now become not only the vehicle for defining where the business is going but also a new management process that encourages organizational learning and learning how to learn.

### Helping Clients Learn How to Learn

The first step is for strategy professionals to learn to deal with threat in other ways than Model I. They require an additional theory-in-use, which may be called Model II (see Figure 2). Briefly, this theory-in-use is designed to enhance the kind of individual and organizational learning to which we have been alluding. The Model II governing variables are valid information, free and informed choice, and internal commitment to choices made in order to monitor the effectiveness of their implementation. Model II, therefore, is not the opposite of Model I. These governing variables, combined with stipulated action strategies, should lead to consequences where search is enhanced and deepened, where ideas are tested publicly, where individuals collaborate to enlarge inquiry, and where trust and risk taking are enhanced. These consequences should lead, in turn, to an O-II learning system, whose consequences are to reduce the dysfunctional aspects of Models I and O-I and, hence, to reduce the dysfunctional features described by the critics of the economic theory of the firm.

Figure 2. Model II Theory-in-Use.

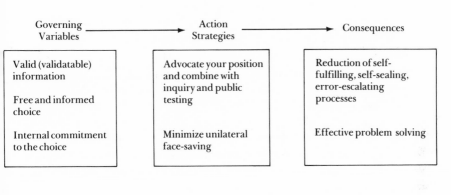

| Governing Variables | Action Strategies | Consequences |
|---|---|---|
| Valid (validatable) information | Advocate your position and combine with inquiry and public testing | Reduction of self-fulfilling, self-sealing, error-escalating processes |
| Free and informed choice | | |
| Internal commitment to the choice | Minimize unilateral face-saving | Effective problem solving |

Research is in progress to develop usable theories of intervention to help individuals and organizations bring about these changes. To date, the results are encouraging. It appears possible to teach individuals Model II action strategies in the service of Model II governing variables and to produce O-II learning systems. (Model II action strategies, if used in the service of Model I governing variables, would result in gimmicks and trickery) (Argyris 1976c; 1982; Argyris and Schön, 1978). In designing the intervention theories to get from here to there, Models II and O-II act as guideposts or criteria for the processes that would be used and the conditions that would have to be created. Models II and O-II are ideals. It is unlikely that anyone will ever have all the valid information required, that choices will be completely free and informed, or that monitoring will be perfect. The models, however, can serve to keep the participants' eyes on the objectives to be attained and to offer some strategies to use in working toward the ideal, even though the attainment will never be perfect.

At the outset of this chapter, I described many of the consultants that I work with as fast learners. There is an important reason for their capacity to learn fast—a reason that, in a few cases, can be at the core of their having difficulty learning.

First, why can strategy professionals be fast learners? The answer is related to the analytical and research skills that they learned to be rigorous planners. For example, the group with whom I work have a high respect for valid and reliable data. They prefer quantitative data but understand the importance of qualitative data. The key criterion in deciding what type of data to use is related to what will describe the world most accurately and what will be best understood by the clients. Second, all the reasoning processes used are made as explicit as possible. Their inferences are made and their conclusions reached in a way that encourages inquiry into them. Third, all the inferences, and especially the conclusions, are subject to public testing. No matter how much they believe in and advocate a way of reasoning or a particular set of conclusions, these are formulated as hypotheses subject to being empirically disconfirmed. Fourth, they are learners and experimenters and, as such, are almost always willing to be playful with technical ideas. They appear to be able to defend them vigorously while, at the same time, they are capable of dropping them with minimal defensiveness if it appears that they should do so. Finally, they are always seeking to conceptualize their ideas into patterns and the patterns into models, and, whenever possible, the models are related to known and tested models in such fields as economics of the firm.

I believe that these observations should surprise few readers who are planners. They represent ways of reasoning and acting that help planners to be rigorous and tough minded. When I asked these individuals to explain why they used tough-minded reasoning, almost all responded that they wanted to do their best to make sure that they were not knowingly kidding themselves or others. Embedded in this reply are, I suggest, three values. First is the value to seek to obtain valid information. Second, the reason for getting valid information is to make an informed choice. Third, validity of the choices should be continually tested, especially as those choices are being implemented.

If we examine carefully the five action strategies and the three values, we see that they are consistent with Model II. Thus, the strategy professionals have the values and the skills to act consistently with Model II. But they are also programmed not to use their skills but to use Model I to deal with threatening issues. Those who are willing to use these values and skills when they examine their personal strategies for dealing with threat become the fast learners. They recognize the importance of getting and examining directly observable data, of making their inferences explicit, of testing them, and so on.

A key issue, therefore, is their ability to use, when dealing with threat, the reasoning processes that they have mastered in dealing with the technical side of their activities. So far, it appears that the ones who learn fast are those who are willing to inquire into their defensive actions, to take risks, and to experiment with new ways of behaving. Those who are slower learners appear to be good at diagnosing their defensive actions but resist taking risks and experimenting (in training sessions) because they believe that Model II actions can produce defensiveness in clients. Their fear is, of course, well founded. Model II actions can make Model I clients defensive. However, this very defensiveness can be used as a fulcrum for change and learning.

### Using Model II Strategies with Clients

We are just beginning to collect examples of how strategy professionals may use Model II interventions to solve strategy problems and to help the clients learn how to learn. For example, a strategy consultant was participating in a discussion on critical economic issues with the top management of a firm. As the executives spoke, he noted three important inconsistencies in their reasoning processes. He reported that, before learning the new skills, his predisposition would have been to take note of the inconsistencies, think about them after the meeting, and bring back some kind of presentation as to how to deal with them. If the clients agreed with the ideas, he would gladly accept their praise and feel that he had built up his credibility with the client.

He behaved somewhat differently now than he would have previously. First, he noted the inconsistencies. Second, he waited for the opportunity to state them and ask whether the clients agreed.

In this case, they agreed and praised the officer for his insight. The new feature of his strategy was then to go into the mode of helping the clients learn how to learn. First, he said, in effect, "I am glad that you found this valuable. I would like, if I may, to ask one further question. What is it in this context that prevented you from recognizing the inconsistencies in the first place?" There was a momentary slience. The chief executive officer (CEO) said, "That's an interesting question." Another client said, "Well, it sounds as if some of us did not recognize it. The inconsistencies have been known."

The consultant then asked, "And could you describe what would lead individuals not to act on what they have known to be inconsistent; indeed, if I understand you correctly, to act as if they are not aware of an inconsistency?" There was laughter among some of the executives, one of whom noted that the consultant might be opening up a can of worms. The consultant responded that he thought that it would be important to explore the can of worms and gave his reasons. However, he added that, if the group did not wish to discuss the issue, he certainly was not trying to push them to do so. The CEO thought that a discussion should be held, because the comments suggested that "Our consensus decision-making process that we pride ourselves in having may have flaws in it. If so, then correcting that would be of as much value, if not more, than the present planning study we are doing."

The consultant took a risk that, in this case, added value to the relationship. The clients learned more about the intimate relationship between effective formulation, development, and implementation, on the one hand, and learning how to learn, on the other. In other cases, the clients may not respond as cooperatively. The key issue is how confident the consultant feels in dealing with client defensiveness, including helping them to choose not to discuss the issues. As a behavioral scientist intervening in organizations, I am impressed with the power of using economic issues to open up the organizational defensive routines. It is difficult for the clients to ignore issues of trust, groupthink, and intergroup rivalries when these issues can be connected directly to the way they reason, conceive, and implement business plans as well as corporate strategy.

In another case, the CEO of a decentralized organization felt that he was not receiving adequate information from his immediate subordinates. He felt that, unless he took some action, he might become not only distanced from the operations but, indeed, disconnected. The subordinates, on the other hand, felt that, if the CEO trusted them, he should leave them alone and act only if they did not meet their commitments. After several months of operating under these conditions, the CEO decided to act. He requested that, with the help of a consulting firm, a new set of managerial processes be instituted that provided him an opportunity to know what was going on before it was so late that a change would upset the people below him.

The consultants who studied the situation concluded that they could, with the cooperation of the relevant people, devise some useful reporting processes and forms. They also concluded that the effectiveness of the new processes could be blunted by the values and actions of the executives involved. For example, the subordinates might now believe that they were not trusted or that their superior did not really mean to run a decentralized organization. The superior, on the other hand, who genuinely wanted to decentralize, might feel that subordinates were blind to the issue of distancing and disconnecting the superior. At the time of this writing, the CEO and his immediate subordinates have agreed to this analysis and have scheduled a meeting to discuss the issue with a larger group of senior executives. The idea is to involve most of the senior executives who are relevant in the design and implementation of planning in such a way that they discuss the existing behavioral features that get in the way of implementing an effective planning process and then to jointly examine and redesign the planning process.

Bourgeoiss and Brodwin (1982) have recommended a bottom-up process of strategy formulation and development where the relevant managers design and send to the top the new plans. If such a process were in place in this organization, it is likely that the ideas would reach the top only to be "mangled" (as one subordinate described it) by the defensive behavioral dynamics at the top. Indeed, if my experience is valid, defensive dynamics exist at all levels. Hence, the distortions could occur in many places in the organization. If these distortions are covered up, and the cover-up is undiscussible, then it is unlikely that they will ever be corrected.

## Conclusion

Individuals and organizations tend to deal with threat in ways that will increase defensiveness and reduce the probability of learning to learn. These features will tend to make it difficult for strategy professionals to help clients implement strategies that are genuinely new and require frame breaking. To compound the problem, strategy professionals are also humans; hence, they, too, have learned the same counterproductive ways to deal with defensiveness (the clients' or their own).

There are several reasons to be optimistic. First, we are developing concepts and skills to deal effectively with threat at the individual through the organizational levels. Second, the reasoning skills required to deal effectively with human defensiveness are congruent with those required to produce rational, rigorous strategy plans. Third, it may be easier to get clients to examine their defensiveness by relating it to economic and strategy issues than by arguing for the goodness of such features as openness and trust in the name of organizational effectiveness. The strategy professionals who learn to integrate the technical (for example, economic) issues with the behavioral ones will, I believe, be at the forefront of practice.

# ❦ SEVENTEEN ❦

# Formulating an Integrated View of Strategic Management

## *William H. Newman*

This volume has stirred up many provocative ideas. To attempt to summarize them all in a few pages would be presumptuous. Instead, my assignment is to suggest ways to "integrate" the diverse concepts presented. The following selective comments focus on three related themes that can help weave together many of the ideas that have been discussed. Very briefly, the suggestions for shaping a mutually helpful synthesis are: (1) Make "strategic change" the unit of analysis, and treat "strategic decision making" as only a vital part of this broader process. (2) Incorporate research on strategy content as a significant input to the nature of change that may be required. (3) Give substantial attention to the distinction between "convergence" and "frame-breaking" strategic changes.

### "Strategic Change" as the Unit of Analysis

Many of us like to talk about *decision making*. The term is still in fashion. It is obviously important in guiding the organized efforts of humanity. It appeals to academics who are concerned with

431

cultivation of the intellect. Then, when we link it with another fashionable term, *strategy*, the combination is almost irresistible.

But *strategic decision making* may not be the most productive concept for either scholarly research or managerial action. The drawbacks are clearly illustrated in Pettigrew's insightful chapter on "Examining Change in the Long-Term Context of Culture and Politics" (Chapter Eleven). He shows that important decisions are often long in the making. They have a history and a context that strongly influence what issues are considered and what choices are made. The specific act of making a choice, if it can be isolated at all, can be understood (and improved) best as part of a stream of events.

Moreover, a strategic decision by itself is of little avail. It must be implemented. (For some mysterious reason, strategies are implemented, while more humble decisions are carried out.) Repeatedly throughout this volume, questions about "doability," resources, commitment, understanding, measurement, and control are tied to the choice of a desired end or course of action. And the advocates of incrementalism could contend that a decision is never quite complete until the execution is finished. The reported research clearly indicates that, unless we attend to implementation as well as to formulation, our strategies will bear little fruit.

What, then, is the phenomenon that we are addressing? Predominantly, it is a *change* in the intended results of an organization's united efforts. It embraces the total process of such a change—from the early discontent with the way things are going to vigorous effort directed toward a revised set of desired outcomes. The scope of such strategic change is succinctly indicated in Hermon-Taylor's change-process model (Chapter Fifteen). Choice (decision making) of operational goals and a course of action to achieve them is a crucial step in this process, but it is only one of the steps.

Broadening our unit of analysis from strategic decision making to strategic change is an easy shift for most of the authors of this volume. In fact, seven already do so explicitly—Argyris, Gladstein and Quinn, Hermon-Taylor, Normann, Pettigrew, and Starbuck. One can argue that this distinction between strategic decision making and strategic change is merely semantics. By broadening the definition of decision making (or any other step in the change process) to include recognition of need and diagnosis and definition of the problem, at the start, and implementation, at the other end, we can make the terms synonymous. Such stretching of the meaning of a well-established term, however, would be a source of confusion. Just how much *decision making* covered would have to be ascertained each time the term was used.

Using *strategic change* as the unit of analysis has several advantages: (1) It puts an emphasis on the outcome—a change—and thereby raises questions about the utility of various intermediate steps. (2) It readily embraces longitudinal analysis, starting with perception of a need (opportunity) for change and extending through to carrying out a change program; vertical relationships within the organization among doers, middle managers, division heads, staff, corporate officers, and a governing board; behavioral and political issues as well as "rational" choice; and external constraints and supports. (3) Because the potential impact of forces just listed in (2) are much easier to identify with bringing about a change than with decision making, integration of the diverse forces is more likely to occur.

The suggestion here is not to forgo focused attention on decision making per se; such analysis can improve the quality of decisions substantially (as is evident in Janis's "Sources of Error in Strategic Decision Making," Chapter Seven). However, the concept of *strategic change* ties together the topics discussed in this volume much better than does *decision making*. It can well serve a similar role in many other explorations of strategy.

### Incorporating Research on Strategy Content

A focus on strategic change, as just recommended, will be nebulous unless we have a clear idea of the nature of change that is contemplated. What kind of a change is "strategic"? Unfortunately, the word *strategy* has become so popular that it can mean anything that is important or merely any alternative, no matter how trivial. Indeed, there is no consistent use of the word in the chapters in this volume. (In my view, when the purpose is managerial action, a business-unit strategy should include four parts: domain sought differential advantage in serving that domain, strategic thrusts necessary and their approximate timing, and target results expected. (See Yavitz and Newman, 1982.)

Even an agreed-upon general definition of strategy is inadequate. The task of strategic change will vary with the specific content of the strategy adopted. To integrate backward into new material supply, for instance, will be much less traumatic than cutting output in half. The dimensions and character of a proposed change have a profound influence on the change process that is optimal. Therefore, if we seek to integrate research approaches to strategic change, we should include research on the *content* of strategy. Research on strategy content is increasing rapidly, much of it with a "hard" empirical base. The basic issue addressed is what strategy (content) is effective in a given environment. For purposes of our immediate discussion, it will be sufficient to indicate the kind of problems usually studied.

The general model has three parts: (1) an environment in which the action takes place, (2) an enterprise—or organization—with particular capabilities and values, and (3) an array of variables that the enterprise can manipulate in a strategic manner. Implicit in such a model is the presumption that an effective strategy will be contingent upon the enterprise selecting moves that are suited to its capabilities to make a desired impact in the prevailing environment.

*Environment.* Identifying and describing the relative environment is a bit tricky, because cognitive limitations call for parsimony in the number of dimensions considered, whereas useful insight requires that all the primary active forces be recognized. In practice, industry characteristics are almost always considered—such things as growth rate, profitability, nature of competition, ease of entry, capital intensity, technological change, volatility, concentration and power of competition, and the like. Often, government support and regulation must be weighed. Sometimes special interest groups are potent. Then, underlying these characteristics are broader political, social, economic, and technological trends.

A complicating aspect is that the impact of a selected strategy usually lasts for years into the future. Consequently, it is the future environments that matter most. Thus, the effectiveness of a strategy depends, in part, upon the skill (or luck) of enterprise managers to forecast their relative environment.

*Enterprise.* The main capability questions are how the focal enterprise measures up to other key actors in the arena. Key actors include, first, symbionts—customers and resource suppliers who have direct transactions with the enterprise; they benefit along with the enterprise from a continuing stream of transaction. A second set of key actors are rivals—those who compete with the enterprise for resource inputs or patronage from the symbionts. Each symbiont and rival has its own strategy and capabilities. They vary in importance and in power in relation to each other and to the focal enterprise. Strategy is played out largely in the responses of these symbionts and rivals to moves of the focal enterprise or in its responses to their moves.

*Variables.* The strategic variables that the focal enterprise can manipulate are both external and internal. External variables are the terms of the transactions with preferred symbionts—quantity, quality, delivery dates, service, price risk reduction, and the like. Internal variables relate to the building of capabilities to provide outputs desired by preferred symbionts and the allocation or real-location of scarce resources to achieve this.

Research studies built around the model just outlined vary a lot in focus, which is not surprising, considering the many permutations and combinations that are possible. Some studies explore a particular issue, such as under what environmental and enterprise conditions it is wise for an enterprise to integrate backward. Or perhaps particular industry conditions will be singled out, such as negative growth—in which case, the research question is what strategic moves make sense for enterprises in different relative positions in their industries.

Another type of study varies the model by adding joint action to the strategic variables. Then the issue becomes under what environmental conditions and company-relative capabilities it is wise to join (or promote) coalitions, alliances and other forms of cooperative action. Labor legislation, for instance, may make joint collective bargaining difficult for some enterprises to resist. Fruit growers may completely turn over their marketing activities to a marketing co-op. A further variation is to examine *sets* of strategic moves. For example, under some conditions, heavy consumer advertising makes sense only when it is combined with higher allocation of resources to quality control and to new product development.

Studies of the sort just illustrated are usually based on cross-sectional analysis, with observations made of a large number of enterprises at a single point in time. In contrast, longitudinal studies are concerned with changes over time. A classic example is how does (should) an enterprise modify its strategy as its main product moves through a product life cycle? In the steel industry, demand has matured, the structure of competition has changed, and U.S. Steel's relative capabilities have shifted; what does this imply for an appropriate strategy of an American steel enterprise?

A different sort of longitudinal study focuses on interaction among key actors. Strategy becomes a whole sequence of moves; when *B* responds to *A*'s first moves, *A* takes another tack, which provokes *B* and *C* to respond, and so on. In this sort of a game, contingency planning and prepared opportunism are added to the array of strategic options.

In summary, research on the content of strategy changes underscores the diversity among strategic moves and the diversity of reasons for undertaking such moves. The processes that are appropriate for designing and for implementing such moves should be tailored to fit this diversity. Unless we incorporate such content considerations into studies of strategic change (or "decision making," for those readers who cling to that formulation), we will miss good integration.

### Convergence and Frame-Breaking Strategic Change

Related to the content of strategic change is its magnitude. Big changes pose fundamentally different problems from incremental ones. Two chapters in this book deal eloquently with this distinction. In Chapter Eleven, Pettigrew traces the prolonged and painful process of a basic reorientation in ICI that took years and a record-breaking deficit to accomplish. Hermon-Taylor, in Chapter Fifteen, describes the transition difficulties of acceptable versus frame-breaking changes as a generalized phenomenon, provides us with several insightful matrixes for understanding the process, and then suggests an approach for overcoming the obstacles. Moreover, Normann, in Chapter Nine, identifies three levels of strategic action that pose distinctions that are very similar to those drawn by Hermon-Taylor and Pettigrew. (I believe all three authors come to this distinction quite independently.) Recent papers by Miller and Friesen (1980a) and by Tushman and Romanelli (1985) also flag the comprehensiveness of frame-breaking change. This distinction between convergence and frame breaking is so vital to understanding strategic change that a repetition of the concept is warranted here.

Often, strategic change is not traumatic. It may involve a significant refinement in services provided or in the technology of creating these services; it may be an extension to new markets or a step in vertical integration; or it may be an incremental adaptation to changes in customer or resource markets. Most organizations can absorb shifts of these sorts without a major internal upset. Indeed, Tushman and Romanelli (1985) and Miller and Friesen (1980a) suggest that a reinforcing convergence occurs during this sort of change. In many operations, learning-curve improvements lead not only to individual skills but also to organizational routines, expectations, and known dependencies. As the enterprise succeeds, its mission is internalized by people who stay with it. Lore, success symbols, and beliefs are institutionalized. The environment is not static; changes of the sort listed here are part of the expected pattern.

However, the changes fall within a "10 degree range." They don't upset the basic structure or many of the skills. Moreover, Hermon-Taylor observes that some touchy subjects are "undiscussible," and artful managers find compromises that bypass these subjects. The net result is that, as an organization follows a convergence path, it insulates itself from parts of its environment. The efficiency, success, and esprit de corps add to narrowness of perception. As a consequence, the organization fails to perceive threats and opportunities; the options that are considered for the few acknowledged threats are comfortably compatible with existing technology, power structures, and beliefs; and execution of programs relies on existing people and incentives. The inertia is so strong that, sooner or later, the organization becomes poorly adapted to its dynamic environment. Then, the argument runs, only an internal revolution can put the business onto a new, productive, frame-breaking course.

The transformation necessary to make the strategic change at this stage is so great that new managers will probably be recruited; power and status will surely change; many skills will be obsolete; uncertainty will prevail until a viable new strategy is developed and another period of convergence is begun—or death occurs.

Note that convergence with a subsequent need for a frame-breaking change may take place in a young organization as it passes from entrepreneurship to functionalized bureaucracy or from rapid growth to efficiency-demanding maturity. Reorientation difficulties are not confined to mature businesses that have trouble recognizing that their mousetrap is no longer in demand. Several questions about this convergence/frame-breaking model have only begun to be researched. For instance:

- Under what circumstances do incremental adaptations build one on the other in a manner that achieves major strategic change (as described by Quinn, 1980)? In other words, can a frame-breaking episode be entirely avoided?
- What kinds of pressures are typically necessary to induce an organization to break out of a convergence mode? Is it likely, or fair, to expect an operation division to launch a frame-breaking change, or must the initiative come from corporate executives?
- Why, when frame breaking occurs, are simultaneous changes made in strategy, organization structure, power relationships, control mechanisms, and probably executive personnel?
- Does experience indicate that postponement of major reorientation increases its cost—cost of internal disruption and/or cost of tardy environmental adjustment? That is, how long should an organization stick with what has been a winning strategy?
- What techniques are available to speed up frame-breaking transition and to minimize the associated disruption? (Hermon-Taylor does deal with this issue at the end of his chapter, and Argyris's chapter is primarily concerned with it.)

Although we still have much to learn about it, this convergence/frame-breaking model provides a very useful basis for categorizing different sorts of strategic change and for predicting obstacles that are likely to arise in the various categories.

At least a majority of the chapters in this book can be "integrated" by following the three lines sketched earlier: Think in terms of strategic change, add strategic content considerations to grasp the nature of the change involved, and, especially, distinguish between convergence and frame-breaking changes. These suggestions do more than provide a convenient way to talk about our research; they orient the research toward important phenomena in the effective running of organizations. They help make the research more relevant and potentially useful.

# ♔ EIGHTEEN ♕

# Increasing Organizational Attention to Strategic Choices

## *Andrew H. Van de Ven, Roger Hudson*

Fundamentally, strategic decision making is concerned with making and implementing choices that represent major departures from existing practices for an organization. As Pennings states in his Introduction, such decisions tend to be "significant, unstructured, complex, collective, and consequential." Ironically, while we would expect such decisions to attract a lot of attention by organizational participants, the basic human problem in strategic decision making is the management of attention. This is because human beings and their organizations are designed mostly to focus on, harvest, and protect existing practices rather than to pave new directions. A practical theory of strategic decision making should, therefore, begin with an appreciation of the physiological limitations of human beings in paying attention to nonroutine issues and their corresponding inertial forces in organizational life.

Unfortunately, as witnessed by many of the presentations and commentaries presented in this volume, many strategic decision-making scholars have ignored much of the research by cognitive psychologists and social-psychologists about the limited capacity of human beings to handle complexity and pay attention. As a consequence, one often gets the impression either that effective strategic decision makers have superhuman abilities to "walk on water," as MacCrimmon (Chapter Three) implies, or that managers are not able to recognize, exercise, or implement opportunities for strategic choice, as Starbuck (Chapter Thirteen) suggests. This commentary will conclude that, while both of these two positions have merit for analytical purposes, a practical theory of strategic choice needs to challenge the former but not conclude with the latter.

### Cognitive Limitations of Individuals

It is well established empirically that individuals lack the capability and inclination to deal with complexity (Tversky and Kahneman, 1974; March, 1981a; Johnson, 1983). Individuals have very short spans of attention—the average individual can retain raw data in short-term memory for only a few seconds. Memory, it turns out, requires relying on "old friends," which Simon (1947) describes as a process of linking raw data with pre-existing schemata and world views that an individual has stored in long-term memory. Individuals are also very efficient processors of routine tasks. They do not concentrate on repetitive tasks, once they are mastered. Skills for performing repetitive tasks are repressed in subsconscious memory, permitting individuals to pay attention to things other than performance of repetitive tasks (Johnson, 1983). Ironically, as a result, what individuals think about the most is what they will do, but what they do the most is what they think about the least.

In complex decision situations, individuals create stereotypes as a defense mechanism to deal with the complexity. For the average person, stereotyping is likely to begin when seven (plus or minus two) factors, steps, or individuals are involved in a decision—this number being the information-processing capacity of the average individual (Miller, 1956). As decision complexity increases beyond this point, people become more conservative and apply more subjective criteria, which are further and further removed from reality. Moreover, since the correctness of outcomes to complex strategic decisions can rarely be judged, the perceived legitimacy of the decision *process* becomes the dominant evaluation criterion. Thus, as Janis (Chapter Seven) points out, as decision complexity increases, solutions become increasingly error prone, means become more important than ends, and rationalization replaces rationality.

It is generally believed that crises, dissatisfaction, tension, and significant external stress are the major preconditions for stimulating strategic action. March and Simon (1958) set forth the most widely accepted model by arguing that dissatisfaction with existing conditions stimulates people to search for improved conditions, and they will search only until a satisfactory result is found. A satisfactory result is a function of a person's aspiration level, which Lewin (1947) indicated is a product of all past successes and failures that people have experienced. If this model is correct (and we believe it is), then strategic choice theorists must wrestle with another basic predicament.

This model assumes that, when people reach a threshold of dissatisfaction with existing conditions, they will initiate action to resolve their dissatisfaction. However, individuals are amazingly adaptable to their environment, often without recognizing that they are adapting. In this sense, individuals are much like frogs. The frog story goes as follows: When frogs are placed into a boiling pail of water, they jump out—they don't want to boil to death. However, when frogs are placed into a cold pail of water, and the pail is placed on a stove with the heat turned very low, over time the frogs will boil to death.

Cognitive psychologists have found that individuals have widely varying and manipulable adaptation levels (Helson, 1948, 1964). When exposed over time to a set of stimuli that deteriorate very gradually, people do not perceive the gradual changes—they unconsciously adapt to the worsening conditions. Their threshold to tolerate pain, discomfort, or dissatisfaction is not reached. As a consequence, they do not move into action to correct their situation, which over time may become deplorable.

Unfortunately, many problems calling for strategic action are similar in that they have accumulated gradually over many years as the unplanned and unanticipated consequences of independent and competitive actions of many organizations, interest groups, and stakeholders. Because of changing adaptation levels, these growing problems often do not reach a threshold of awareness or tension to trigger strategic action. As a result, opportunities for making strategic decisions are not recognized, problems swell into meta-problems, and catastrophes or tragedies are sometimes necessary for the action threshold to be reached (Van de Ven, 1980).

These worsening conditions are sometimes monitored by various corporate planning and management-information units and distributed to managers in quantitative Management Information Systems (MIS) reports of financial and performance trends. However, these impersonal statistical reports only increase the numbness of organizational participants and raise the false expectation that, if someone is measuring the trends, then someone must be doing something about them.

By this logic, when situations have deteriorated to the point of actually triggering the action threshold levels of managers, strategic choices turn out to be crisis decisions. As Janis describes, such decision processes are dominated by defense mechanisms of isolation, projection, stereotyping, displacement, and retrospective rationalizations to avoid negative evaluations. As a result, the substantive conclusions that emerge from such strategic decisions are likely to be poor choices.

### Limitations of Collective Decision Making

Collective strategic decision making adds the problems of organizational inertia and incompatible preferences to the physiological limitations of human beings summarized earlier. As Janis has clearly shown, groups place strong conformity pressures on members, who collectively conform to one another without knowing it. Indeed, the classic study by Pelz and Andrews (1966) found that a heterogeneous group of interdisciplinary scientists when working together daily became homogeneous in perspective and approach to problems in as little as three years. Groups minimize internal conflict and focus on issues that maximize consensus. "Groupthink" is partly a product not only of these internal conformity pressures but also of external conflict—"out-group" conflict stimulates "in-group" cohesion (Coser, 1959). Consequently, as Janis (Chapter Seven) and Argyris (Chapter Sixteen) point out, it is exceedingly difficult for groups to entertain threatening information that is critical for strategic decision making.

While MacCrimmon, like many model builders of strategic choice, asssumed that a consensus exists among a collectivity of corporate decision makers, the case studies by Pettigrew clearly point out that many strategic decisions in complex organizations are characterized by problematical preferences, unclear technologies, and fluid participation among partisan interest groups. Pettigrew appreciates that politics and culture are not neutral toward change—they can either hinder or encourage change. Political processes can either shift or focus attention on decision topics and can easily be used to protect the interests of the groups in power. Under these conditions, a garbage-can model of choice (March and Olsen, 1976) replaces the rational model of decision making.

Indeed, under these conditions, even if a central strategic decision unit had sufficient power to force a rational choice process, it would produce an irrational outcome for technical and political reasons. Technically, because a single decision unit seldom commands sufficient competence and information to obtain an overview of the complex situation, whatever decisions it makes will be arbitrary (Simon, 1947). Politically, there are few commonly accepted values and criteria among the many partisan stakeholders affected by a given strategic decision. Therefore, whatever decisions are reached by an elite unit will be used for partisan purposes— usually heralded by some, attacked and sabotaged by some, and apathetically ignored by the majority of political constituents (Dahl and Lindblom, 1976). Finally, given the ambiguity of most strategic decision situations and the great potential for decision failures, it is doubtful that consistency or transitivity in a series of decisions implied by the rational-choice model can be achieved or is even desired (Lindblom, 1965). Instead, when coping with complex strategic situations, incremental, reconstructed, and loosely coupled collective decisions are less likely to result in significant policy failures.

Many decision scientists may find it difficult to accept this description of the seeming inability of individual and collective choice behavior to be rational for strategic decisions in ambiguous situations (as the situations usually are, or the decisions would be routine). This is because it describes many decision situations for which classical assumptions of rational decision behavior do not apply. However, Starbuck is a notable exception.

By focusing on the process of change, which he states that the garbage-can model largely ignores, Starbuck is able to more accurately describe logic in use in organizations. Where the garbage-can model implied stalemate and inaction, Starbuck predicts programs that will generate action (but not change) even without decisions or problems. Organizations develop behavior programs to repeat the actions that led to earlier success—but the programs do not necessarily address causal factors. Instead, the programs tend to be more like superstitious learning, recreating actions that may have little to do with previous success and nothing to do with future success.

Moreover, behavior programs are attention managers, focusing efforts in some areas and blinding managers to other issues by influencing perceptions, values, and beliefs. The older, more bureaucratized, larger, and more successful that organizations become, the more likely they are to have a large repertoire of automatic or semiautomatic behavior programs that discourage change while encouraging tinkering. For example, strategic planning *systems* often drive out strategic thinking as participants "go through the numbers" of completing yearly planning forms and review cycles. The implication is that age, size, formalization, and success carry with them the seeds of organizational destruction.

Thus, for all the rational virtues that Winter (Chapter Four) and Hickson and his colleagues (Chapter Five) describe of programs for maintaining existing organizational practices, Starbuck most clearly shows how these "action generators" make decision makers inattentive to shifts in organizational environments and the need for strategic change. The consequence, as Gladstein and Quinn (Chapter Eight) point out, is that, while organizations may be built brick by brick, they assuredly destroy themselves drop by drop.

### Managing Attention to Strategic Decision Making

For all the limitations of individuals and inertial forces in organizations, it is surprising that we know so little about the management of attention. At the conference on which this book is based, several useful suggestions were made. Lawrence reported that in his consulting practice he usually focuses on what management is *not* paying attention to. Similarly, on the basis of his observations in consulting with large organizations, Normann observed that well-managed companies not only are close to their customers, but they search out and focus on their most demanding customers. Being exposed face to face with demanding customers or consultants increases the likelihood that the action threshold of organizational participants will be triggered and will stimulate them to pay attention to changing environmental conditions or customer needs. In general, we would expect that *direct personal confrontations with the problem sources* are needed to reach the threshold of concern and appreciation required to motivate people to act.

However, while face-to-face confrontations with problems may trigger action thresholds, they also create stress. One must therefore address the major problem that Janis examines: Under what conditions does stress have favorable versus unfavorable effects on the quality of decision making? Janis outlines five basic patterns of coping with stress and states that only the vigilance pattern generally leads to decisions that meet the main criteria for sound decision making. Janis proposes that vigilance tends to occur under conditions of moderate stress and when there may be sufficient time to search and deliberate before a decision. Under conditions of high stress and immediate deadlines, the decision process will resemble the characteristics of crisis decisions summarized earlier and result in errors arising from stereotyping, uncritical use of heuristics, and losses of mental efficiency from information overload.

Hermon-Taylor, Argyris, and Normann focus on single-loop, double-loop, and deutero learning models for managing attention and improving strategic decision processes. In single-loop learning, no change in criteria of effective performance takes place. Single-loop learning represents conventional monitoring activity, with actions taken on the basis of the findings of the monitoring system. Double-loop learning involves a change in the criteria of evaluation. Past practices are called into question, new assumptions about the organization are raised, and significant changes in strategy are believed to be possible. Deutero learning is basically the ability to achieve repeated double-loop learning—organizational participants learn how to learn by watching themselves repeatedly using double-loop learning.

Because it does not question the criteria of evaluation, single-loop learning leads to the type of inertial behavior programs that Starbuck indicates must be unlearned before change can occur. Single-loop learning is the basis of most organizational control systems and tactics. If this is correct, it would explain why behavior programs must be unlearned and single-loop learning must be replaced by double-loop learning before significant change can occur. After all, the purpose of a control system is to detect and eliminate change, and tactics are means for ensuring attention on existing strategies.

As Hermon-Taylor and Argyris suggest, double-loop learning manages attention by unlearning Starbuck's action generators. Evaluation criteria are questioned, strategies are criticized, and top management competence is debated. While this could lead to change, it could also lead to low trust, defensive behavior, undiscussibles, and bypass tactics. Thus, the management of attention must be concerned not only with triggering the action thresholds of organizational participants but also with channeling that action toward constructive ends.

Normann suggests ways of containing the possible negative consequences of double-loop learning by elaborating organizational constitution, culture, and philosophy. Constitutions provide a framework for structural change, limiting the degree of change to tolerable levels. Culture, by storing and communicating past learning, also provides a tempering force. Finally, philosophy, which includes a mission statement, provides yet another anchor on change. Importantly, Normann states that philosophy is a double-edged sword. It constrains inappropriate change by holding some beliefs as unquestionable, yet, if they are too tightly held, it will not allow appropriate change.

## Conclusion

Many strategic choice scholars have ignored the management of attention, which recognizes the limitations of human beings to handle complexity, appreciate and pay attention to nonroutine issues, and focus energy toward new directions for organizations that are preoccupied with inertial forces. A practical theory of strategic choice must not begin with the assumption that people can "walk on water" but must not end with the conclusion that managers are unable to make strategic choices. Useful practical ideas for developing such a theory were suggested, including having consultants ask questions about what management is not paying attention to, searching out and focusing on the most demanding customers in order to trigger the action thresholds of organizational participants, adopting vigilant strategic decision processes, developing methods and tolerance for deutero learning to occur, and elaborating organizational constitution, culture, and philosophy. While these suggestions appear to go in the right direction, it is clear that they are only partially developed to cope with the significant problem of organizational inertia and limitations of human beings. The management of attention remains a major problem to be systematically addressed if a practical theory of strategic decision making is to develop.

# NINETEEN

# Strengthening Organizational Capacity to Execute Strategic Change

*Peter Lorange*

Many of the issues raised in this book seem in some way or another to relate to how an organization can enhance its capacity to execute strategic change. This chapter reviews some central issues that might be important to someone concerned with business policy. First, I delineate a conceptual model with four classes of tasks as means to carry out strategic change. These steps outline an organization's approach to creating the ability to carry out strategic change. Second, I examine eleven issues surrounding the four specific phases in the conceptual model.

I introduce this four-phased conceptual model for strategic change not to introduce a novel and alternative model for perceiv-

*Note:* The author wishes to thank Edward Bowman, Bala Chakravarthy, and Graham Astley for helpful comments on an earlier version of this chapter.

ing strategic change phenomena per se; rather, the model serves as a useful device or framework around which to organize the discussion. The eleven issues all coincide to some extent with issues raised in different contexts by several of the authors of this volume.

Coping with the eleven issues of the model will likely enhance an organization's ability to effect strategic change. In fact, I propose that the ability to handle strategic change is a function of how well an organization can handle these eleven factors. In this connection, it is also important to understand the high cost of lost opportunity that results from being unable to carry out change at all or from carrying it out only after great delays or after overcoming strong organizational resistance and turbulence. This chapter attempts to show how an organization can maintain a productive business climate suited to carrying out strategic change.

### Delineation of Organizational Tasks

In order to change strategy, the special talents within an organization must be motivated to rally behind the particular strategic development. Any discussion of strategic change thus touches on an organization's ability to undertake strategic self-renewal. The organization must determine which organizational actions are needed to realize the strategy change and how to implement them. The four stages of this process are as follows: (1) sensitizing the organization to the needs for strategic change, (2) identifying critical blockages to strategic change, (3) strategic problem solving, and (4) securing the implementation effort. This conceptualization was inspired by earlier models of this kind, such as those proposed by Schein (1969), Kolb and Frohman (1970), and Beckhard and Harris (1977). Within each of the stages, there are a number of critical issues that have to be dealt with. These issues are as follows:

- *Sensitizing the Organization to the Need for Strategic Change*
  1. Decision rules for strategic auditing
  2. Environmental scanning and the institutionalization of information gathering
- *Identifying Blockages Critical to Strategic Change*

3. Political blockages
4. Myopic blockages
5. Resource blockages
- *Strategic Problem Solving*
  6. Team versus individuals
  7. Top-down versus bottom-up
  8. Manipulation versus confrontation
- *Securing the Implementation Effort*
  9. Assigning responsibilities for change and monitoring
  10. Managing key stakeholders
  11. Managing the strategic system and evolution of strategic processes

The first stage involves becoming more sensitive to the need for changing strategically. This can be done partially by imposing *decision rules* for assessing a particular strategic situation; for instance, assessing potential imbalances in a strategy according to a particular strategy paradigm. Sensitivity to strategic change can also be built by instituting an *environmental scanning* process to look for changes in the business environment. The environmental information is applied in the context of the decision rules in order to reveal early indications about a need for change. The second stage of the conceptual scheme involves identifying and neutralizing blockages that might be critical to the organization's ability to commit itself to change. *Political blockages* deal with the organization's internal power constellation, in which change may constitute a threat to the power of some constituents and an opportunity for others. *Myopic blockages* are caused by individuals who are trapped in traditional ways of doing things. These "traditionalists" may think in terms that are too narrow for them to see the need for change. Finally, *resource blockages,* such as lack of relevant human resources, lack of relevant new technologies, or scarcity of funds, can hinder change. In general, identifying blockages is a realism-sensitizing stage that attempts to highlight and clarify factors internal to the organization that might hamper strategic change.

The third stage of the strategic change model is the problem-solving stage, which examines how members of the organization go about analyzing and solving the particular challenge for change. I identify three dimensions of problem-solving modes. First, the problem-solving process may differ depending upon whether the problem is dealt with from a *team* approach or from an approach based more on *individuals*. Second, the degree of *"top-down"* versus *"bottom-up"* impetus for problem solving affects the level of ability to undertake strategic change. Third, the style of management may be predominantly either *manipulative* or *confrontational*. The final stage of the conceptual scheme attempts to secure the implementation of the strategic change. Again, three factors intervene. One factor calls for proper delineation of *internal responsibility* for monitoring and effecting change. Another calls for *stakeholder management*, to ensure that the various constituencies affected by the change are likely to accept it. *Management systems* and/or *processes* may need to be modified to better correspond with the needs of the new strategic setting. This four-stage conceptual scheme with its eleven subgroupings does not pretend to represent a complete model of the strategic change process. The model portrays a general decision-making context within which specific decisions are made; it does not attempt to portray the actual strategic choices that are made. Second, the model is clearly too simplistic, partly because the process is portrayed as being sequential and stepwise. Concern for each step does not follow a neat linear sequence; rather, the process evolves dynamically, with iterative feedback loops and changes in the sequence of attention. Depending upon the situation at hand, some factors may be more important in some circumstances than in others. A contingency framework must therefore be incorporated into the model. (A preliminary attempt is given in the concluding section of this chapter.) It follows that the model is, of course, incomplete. Several new dimensions might conceivably be added. Also, from an expository point of view, given that a major purpose of this chapter is to synthesize what the authors registered as relevant issues relating to strategic change, some critical dimensions will be extensively discussed, while uncontroversial dimensions will be dealt with only briefly.

## Sensitizing the Organization

*Decision Rules for Making a Strategic Audit.* One important aspect of increasing an organization's capacity for carrying out strategic change is increasing the organization's sensitivity to emerging and potential needs for strategic change. Sensitization can be achieved partially by establishing decision rules for auditing the business environment, allowing the organization to establish its relative strategic profile. Strategy models may point out discrepancies between the actual situation and the desired situation, or they may point out an unsatisfactory developmental trend.

Policy literature has pointed out that there are at least three alternative ways to build internal pressures in organizations to eliminate imbalances uncovered through strategic audits (Ferguson, 1974; Steiner, 1977; Lorange, 1983). First, such self-renewal might, in part, center around the development of businesses with unique, defendable competitive positions (Hofer and Schendel, 1978; Henderson, 1979; Porter, 1981). Another approach would be to build "business family" strategies by developing synergies among the various "business elements" in a business family; that is, by creating an explicitly developed strategic field (Strategic Planning Associates, 1982; Lorange, 1980). A third way to create awareness of strategic imbalances is to assess how the businesses in the firm's overall portfolio might best create full value for the shareholder. Rather than holding onto less productive assets in an attempt to maintain the status quo, the firm might, for instance, divest (Marakon Associates, 1980; Woo, 1983; Burgelman, 1983a).

All of these three types of decision rules require willingness within an organization to be analyzed according to such rules, with the realization that strategic shifts might result. It is thus useful to examine how an organization's willingness to accept the relevant strategy assessment models can be improved. Without an understanding of the various strategic paradigms, the effectiveness of the strategic profiling may be questionable.

A strategic analysis should be related to the economic reality that the organization faces. An in-depth understanding of economic reality (and the bottom line) might help strengthen top management's willingness to initiate change earlier rather than later. Adequate management control systems may play an important role in this respect (Anthony, Dearden, and Bedford, 1984). Less sophisticated organizations, however, typically rely unilaterally on economic-indicator-based control signals, often neglecting other types of signals, both environmental and internal. Given their unidimensional emphasis, such organizations typically tend to face up to strategic reality too late. Analysis of a firm's strategic position may provide an "early warning." For instance, noticeable changes in a business's growth rate or in its relative market share may lead to early sensitivity to the need for change—hence the label *strategic control* (Bowman, 1974; Newman, 1975; Horowitz, 1979; Lorange and Murphy, 1984). Thus, we see the value of coordinated use of several decision rules, underscoring the complementary relationships between strategy paradigms and budgetary decision rules.

A final technique for sensitizing managers to the need for strategic changes is the use of scenarios, which force managers to think ahead to detect emerging strategic imbalances. Scenario building may serve as a vehicle for sufficiently alarming managers by what they see that they face up to the need to revise their strategies (Beck, 1977).

*Environmental Scanning and Formalized Information Gathering.* An organization must be able to identify economic, strategic, and behavioral considerations that provide early warning that change may be needed. By making certain types of information gathering routine (that is, creating more "mechanistic" data inputs to the strategic decision-making process), the organization may become more efficient at scanning and decision making. Such formal scanning rules may be necessary to ensure that the organization can process large amounts of often relatively repetitive environmental data and thereby help to free managers to devote more attention to other critical environmental developments. It thus becomes critical to choose which scanning rules and processes lend themselves to formalization and routine. Does this way of formulating environmental scanning apply, given the environmental realities? What types of opportunities can it enhance, and what environmental sensitivities are lost through routine? Even though a more routine and formal scanning process can probably be implemented easily within the organization and strategic plans formulated, one may question whether such plans can be sufficiently vital, creative, and relevant (Camillus, 1981). Parts of the formal strategic planning process will probably have to remain informal so that plans can be updated to prevent them from becoming mechanistic. A formalized approach to environmental scanning, because it involves routine, will lead to an "indoctrination" of managers to a particular way of providing information. The opportunity cost incurred by such formalization must be offset by the time and energy it saves managers, but an inherent drawback of formalization is that routinized decision rules sometimes are the reasons that organizations are so poor at redefining themselves and extracting themselves from stagnating, increasingly unattractive environments. Formalization might thus preserve unfavorable patterns of business activities, given that the routine scanning and analysis take place within this contextual base.

An important question, therefore, is how to modify formal decision rules and routine environmental scanning in light of changing environmental conditions. Such revisions might take place during periods of perceived crisis, when managers more easily perceive that they are in trouble and do not have the luxury to "play games" in their strategic scanning. When there is not a crisis, managers are less impelled to take serious steps to improve scanning. Top management should thus take advantage of crises in a constructive, proactive manner to strengthen the formalized scanning processes.

One might ask how an organization might modify its formal scanning routine without having to go as far as actually facing a crisis. The control process should be structured such that managers better understand the dynamics of responses from the environment—from competitors, customers, environmental agencies, and so forth. In this way, the firm may be able to achieve a more harmonious evolutionary process for changing its decision rules and routine scanning, rather than a stop-and-go pattern of "major overhaul," then stability and decay, then new revolution, new degeneration, and so on.

In conclusion, an organization may strengthen its sensitivity to the need for strategic change in several ways. Strategic audits using strategy paradigms have been recommended; similarly, routine scanning might be institutionalized. Furthermore, firms have been warned against too much formalization of decision rules and scanning that might itself prove insensitive to needs that fall outside of the context of the rules and routine.

## Critical Blockages

*Political Blockages.* Blockages against change sometimes occur when taboos are associated with change. Politics within the organization, the motives of people in power, and the culture, norms, and values of the organization may all make discussion of change impossible. Power, a major source of political blockage, comes from many sources. In the context of strategic planning, however, power has to do with the possession of exclusive information and expertise. Requests for new expertise and information when major strategic reorientations must take place may thus be read as an attempt to change the existing balance of power. Resistance from those in power may render an organization unable to undertake major strategic shifts (Pfeffer, 1981c). Sensitivity to how strategic change might potentially be seen as a threat to the power of particular constituencies is therefore important.

Prestige and vested interest may also cause managers to misperceive their environments (Grinyer and Norburn, 1974). In attempting to avoid responsibility for bad decisions and to protect their prestige, managers render the strategic decision-making process impotent by becoming unwilling to make decisions. Calling for further study and referring decisions upward are characteristic of such decision climates. In line with this, managers prefer to interact with people at their own level or the level above, often paying little attention to input from lower levels. An overly bureaucratic managerial tradition may thus limit an organization's ability to perceive the environment dynamically and realistically (Crozier, 1964; Hummel, 1982). How, in practice, does management decide which such power blockages to confront and which to ignore when it pursues change? Addressing such political dilemmas involves ethical considerations as well as managerial competence, experience, and judgment. Self-serving motives should not be allowed to interfere.

*Myopic Blockages.* Another sort of blockage against change arises when management becomes trapped in a framework of established practices (Brockner, Rubin, and Lang, 1981), coupled with limited perceptive and managerial skills. An important dimension for facilitating change, then, is breaking the old framework to escape old routines, fixed ways of doing things, and frozen mind-sets. In this connection, it may be useful to distinguish between large, fundamental changes and small, incremental changes. Ordinarily, one might expect organizations to resist changes according to the difficulty of achieving them. In cases of myopic blockage, the converse is true: an organization is more willing to face change during a crisis than when faced with small environmental disturbances. It can opt for the luxury of myopic complacency in the latter case, not in the former.

Momentum from existing business success may add to the difficulty that a firm faces in changing. Businesses may become complacent over time and lose touch with the reality of the business environment. Most managers tend to categorize the business world in a set way; perhaps only entrepreneurs are able to see different patterns and to redefine businesses (Vesper, 1980). Ameliorating myopic blockage to change requires that business people be able to move outside their own domain, something that many managers may not comprehend and may be uncomfortable with. How does an organization cope with myopic blockage? Management culture and philosophy seem to play an important role. Human resource management in the form of recruitment, training, job reassignment, and procedures for providing feedback and incentives tends to be important in keeping the organizational culture relevant and up to par (Tichy, 1983; Lorange and Murphy, 1983).

Another approach to avoiding myopic blockage, suggested by MacCrimmon in Chapter Three of this book, calls for concurrent use of several extreme decision models in order to gain insight by looking at the problem from several angles. This approach is effective, for instance, when analyzing a major competitor as part of a contract negotiation process; MacCrimmon's super-rational, mechanistic, and Machiavellian models shed different lights on the competitor and provide a more complete understanding. These model types, often very different and even contradictory in character, may help managers to see issues from different perspectives. Examining the diverse premises that can lead to a decision may thus help managers avoid becoming trapped in habitual and often one-sided ways of thinking. At some point, of course, it will be necessary to choose among the alternatives provided by the various decision models (or to integrate the results of the various models into a compromise). A manager's beliefs, insights, and biases still apply but are now part of a "narrowing" process after exposure to alternatives.

*Resource Blockages.* Blockages against strategic change may also arise from insufficient relevant resources. Resource constraints and resource allocation have been seen as central in the strategy literature (Andrews, 1980; Bower, 1972); these blockage issues consequently do not need much discussion in our present context. One underemphasized strategic resource barrier, however, is the human resource dimension. Examples of this problem are lack of appropriate talent and lack of executive time (Tichy, 1983; Fombrun, 1983). Identifying human resource constraints and assigning tasks to deal with these constraints are important. These human resource constraints usually are not assessed together, and no integrated means of dealing with them is devised. Too often, one set of implementational constraints tends to be overemphasized, and others are neglected. Furthermore, human resource constraints tend to be dealt with too sequentially, as part of the discussion of one given strategic program that happens to be in focus at the time. Insufficient time on the part of top management may be the most serious human resource constraint, but it may be hard to correct a situation such as one in which the chief executive officer (CEO) "spreads himself too thin" (Lorange, 1985).

## Problem Solving

Having now discussed three classes of blockages that can prevent the organization from "seeing" what the decision models and relevant environmental data imply and how these blockages may impede change, we turn to the next stage in our strategic change model. This section discusses various modes of problem solving and specifically assesses how different problem-solving characteristics may strengthen (or potentially weaken) organizational strategic change capability. Three dimensions of problem-solving modes are a team versus more individualistic approach, top-down versus bottom-up decision-making initiative, and manipulative versus confrontational problem-solving style.

*Teams Versus Individuals.* One dimension of strategic problem solving has to do with the extent to which the strategic process is driven by an individual or a more group-oriented effort. We claim that a good strategic problem-solving process must be composed of *both* individualistic and group emphasis. On one hand, it is important that responsibilities be clearly delineated when it comes to strategic decision making and implementation of decisions. It must be clear *who* is doing *what* in terms of executing change. Line managers must have clear and undivided responsibility for implementing strategies, in parallel with their operating responsibilities. It is also critical that strategic problem solving be a creative process. Varied viewpoints should be brought to bear on the issues at hand. It would, therefore, be beneficial to have an eclectic team of managers (both line and staff), or possibly a set of teams, to address the issues—a strategic planning structure, complementing the normal organizational structure. The strategic structure thus can be perceived as a think tank that assists line managers of the operating structure in developing better strategies. The line managers themselves are, of course, also part of the strategic structure.

It is important that the organizational culture allow the strategic teams to function. There must be sufficient team spirit and willingness to live up to a realization that a manager's responsibility is broader than his or her formal operational authority (Vancil, 1979). Incentives should be tied not only to operating performance but also, to some extent, to whether each person provides useful input to the strategic process. This calls for, within moderation, a willingness to take some time away from near-term operating concerns and fire fighting in order to participate in the strategic process (Lorange, 1984a).

*Top-Down Versus Bottom-Up.* Another aspect of the problem-solving planning style has to do with where within the organization the locus of decision-making initiative is, whether the planning emphasis is from the top down or from the bottom up. New opportunities in the environment might be seen both from a business context, by those closest to the business, and from a broader portfolio context, from the top; therefore, *both* top-down *and* bottom-up initiatives are relevant.

Planning approaches that are predominantly bottom-up tend to be relatively well understood and are exemplified by annual multicycle, multilevel formal planning schemes (Lorange and

Vancil, 1977). When it comes to top-down planning approaches, there is less of a consensus regarding what is critical. The CEO can influence change through *power*. Members of the organization may receive leadership impulses from the CEO both from direct top-down interventions and from more indirect encouragement of change in bottom-up processes. The CEO therefore must know how to conceive, understand, and carry out his or her decision-making acts in context and must appreciate the interplay among political, behavioral, and rational factors. An often central issue for the CEO attempting to institute change is how to accelerate the process. Faster results may often be achieved by executing many small moves rather than resorting to infrequent "mega-moves." In this way, the organization can be led through a virtually continuous process of conditioning to the necessity for change, as discussed by Normann in Chapter Nine of this book (Gellerman, 1976; Jelinek, 1979).

As pointed out by Gladstein and Quinn in Chapter Eight, a crisis may also accelerate the change process in a positive manner; it is even conceivable that management might selectively induce a minor crisis to prompt such change. Managing such crises requires skill, however, so that the situation can be restabilized and not degenerate into permanent destabilization. Early intervention is likely to increase management's control. Practiced effectively, inducing crises can prepare an organization to recognize pending crises so that the organization will be able to react to crises earlier and more forcefully.

A general danger inherent in such action intervention is organizational fatigue. Managers can easily begin to view such crisis inducement and resolution as too much of a game. The CEO must avoid creating cynicism in management and maintain the organization's momentum by remaining open about his or her intentions; the CEO must be able to explain simply and plausibly what he or she is attempting to do. It is thus important that the CEO emphasize a simple strategy that can be communicated effectively to the organization and that can be translated into a relatively small series of specific actions. Highly focused messages communicated to a large segment of the organization over a relatively short period of time can help bring about a consistent understanding of the intended strategic shift in a large portion of the organization. To instill more of a sense of direct, personalized, even entrepreneurial leadership, the CEO may push for flatter organizational models with fewer levels of supervisors and maintain a consistent philosophy and credibility. *Visible* charismatic management through simple but key messages is essential. The cultural climate of the organization can also be manipulated to achieve change. Developing good feelings and pride in the organization is probably a major factor in successful strategic change (Carlzon and Hubendick, 1983). Peters and Waterman (1982) stress the importance of style, values, and a corporate culture committed to excellence and good management practices. The CEO must be committed to building and evolving such a culture.

The CEO must play a top-down role in the planning process, maintaining visibility, providing feedback, and avoiding seeming aloof. The interplay between the bottom-up, business-driven initiatives and the top-down, broader vision is critical. Top management acts as an accelerator and a catalyst and must see issues in a broader context. This role is necessary to match and counterbalance the momentum and self-renewal effort generated by a good bottom-up strategic process.

*Manipulation Versus Confrontation.* The third dimension of planning style examines whether problems are being approached in a relatively manipulative manner or are confronted head-on. One approach to problems is to create "bypasses" that institute change, perhaps indirectly, while avoiding confrontation over topics that are not open to discussion. Over time, difficult and sensitive blockages might be manipulated such that they are overcome. Such an approach emphasizes the political power negotiations involved in overcoming resistance to change (Quinn, 1971; Allison, 1971); it underscores a need for managers who can realign the members of the organization to avoid stalemates. Such managers are usually skillful at negotiation, manipulation, and persuasion.

Argyris (Chapter Sixteen) and Hermon-Taylor (Chapter Fifteen) have argued in this book that the key to creating a culture in which difficult changes can be made successfully is *not* creating bypasses but is instead confronting barriers more directly and openly. (See also Argyris, 1976c.) Instead of avoiding, smoothing over, and camouflaging, management should deal explicitly with problems that cause organizational conflict. In order to break the barriers, managers should attempt to share the responsibility and discuss the blockages with the CEO and top management. In other words, the "undiscussible" must be discussed.

It seems critical that the problem-solving style be issue orientation and willingness to face the problem. Too often, the planning process tends to be weighed down by endless bureaucratic reports, presentations providing background material and "padding" of key issues, and peripheral reviews and discussions. Most important in this context may be development of a style based on sufficient job security, sufficient maturity, and sufficient team spirit to allow issues to be raised without fear of threatening others.

### Securing Implementation

A fourth set of issues bearing upon an organization's capacity for strategic change has to do with securing implementation efforts after sensitization, blockage identification, and problem solving. Three aspects of securing implementation involve assignment of explicit tasks for carrying out and monitoring change processes, managing stakeholders, and managing the strategic process to evolve business strategy tailored to the new business environment.

*Assigning Responsibilities for Changing and Monitoring.* A critical step in implementation is to clearly define *who* is responsible for doing *what.* Three critical types of responsibilities are carrying out specific assignments, monitoring progress toward attaining the strategic programs and the continued appropriateness of critical environmental factors, and assigning support roles for staff executives to assist in executing the strategic changes.

Assigning responsibility for subtasks among managers is typically a major undertaking (Andrews, 1980; Steiner, 1979; Hrebiniak and Joyce, 1983). Managers must know specifically who is doing what to carry out each aspect of strategic change. Managers must also sensitize themselves to potential barriers, such as the earlier-mentioned political, myopic, and resource blockages. It is important to be able to identify implementational barriers associated with a particular pattern of task assignments.

Another set of managerial tasks that will likely affect a corporation's ability to adapt strategically has to do with how the organization "links up" with its environment (Cameron, 1978). Someone must be responsible for monitoring the environmental factors that are essential for success, and this calls for explicit delineation of these tasks in the context of each strategy (Andrews, 1980; Rockhart and Treacy, 1982; Lorange, 1984a). The formulated strategic plans should be the basis for such strategic control. The prominence of classical management-control approaches may tend to keep managers from turning to such environmental-factor control (Lorange and Murphy, 1984). Managers may not understand that a budgetary control system is not enough of a monitor and must be supplemented by proper strategic control. Good strategic control processes should precondition the organization for learning, for better synthesis of what the evolving strategy should be, for seeing the need for change, and for enhancing creativity. It should thus generate both thought and action. Normann's discussion in Chapter Nine of this book of how to increase an organization's capability to carry out strategic action through organizational learning is relevant in this context. He looks at learning on several levels. One level involves working within an existing strategy. A somewhat higher level of learning may come about through paradigm shifts (synthesis), as exemplified by shifts in power relationships and the development of new strategies. An even superior form of learning is "deutero," or second-order, learning, or learning how to learn (Argyris and Schön, 1981), which ensures an organization's ability to learn over time and thus enhances its strategic management capacity. Most important, such a learning process might create a better recognition within the organization that strategic change will take place at times through bottom-up evolutionary steps and at other times through more radical, disrupting intervention from the top. Both instances show that managers interpret the need for change according to the position in the organization that conditions their view on what changes are needed.

Let us now turn to the role of staff as change agent. One scenario calls for the staff member to be heavily involved in actually making the change; another scenario calls for the staff to play a less direct, more catalytic role. The nature of the change agent's role under these two scenarios differs; a person who negotiates political solutions internally operates differently from someone who emphasizes unblocking behavioral barriers (Gellerman, 1976). Depending upon the nature of the needed approach for change—catalyst or power broker—executives may be assigned separate tasks, some being in charge of the strategic planning process, others diagnosing what needs to be changed, and still others pursuing the change per se (Lorange and Vancil, 1977; Ackerman, 1970).

*Managing Stakeholders.* Strategic change may affect various stakeholders, some external to the organization and others internal. For instance, during realignment of business activities, such as closing of a plant, both the local work force and external local community constituents will be affected. Reactions from internal and/or external stakeholder groups might frustrate or even paralyze the implementation of a strategic change. Consequently, contact with such stakeholder groups must be managed. Objective economic figures and strategic facts should be kept at hand as reference points regarding what is relevant in such interactions. Face-to-face interactions are essential to this process. It seems particularly important to develop an ability to cast conflicts and crises in terms that people can understand (Freeman, 1983). Without such a broad understanding of the justification for change, stakeholders may find it hard to act positively.

Top executives must possess integrity, maturity, and sound, balanced judgment. Donaldson and Lorsch (1983), in particular, stress the importance of management sensitivity to outside constituencies and constraints. Top management should, of course, also be sensitive to internal constraints that may be cultural or psychological. The role of the CEO in the stakeholder-management context is thus not based on simple, rational theories; it is multifaceted and requires an understanding of political, behavioral, and cognitive considerations. This is critical for sheltering the strategic program implementation from potential stakeholder obstacles (Mason and Mitroff, 1981a; Freeman, 1983; Mitroff, 1983).

*Managing the Strategic Systems and the Evolution of Strategic Processes.* A final set of issues regarding a firm's capacity to undertake and implement strategic change involves its ability to proactively manage its evolution in order to maintain consistency with the firm's emerging needs. While well-designed and well-managed formal strategic planning systems can typically cope well with the strategic self-renewal of existing businesses, major, radically new business directions typically cannot be so well served by an existing formal planning process (Lorange, 1980). The formulation of the process, the delineation of a planning structure, and the assignment of executives to specific tasks within this structure tend to reinforce the evolution of the existing business thrust. New systems or process rules may have to be designed to facilitate the creation of new businesses in the organization, however. New ideas may thereby be disseminated faster and with more specific attention than if they had passed through the established bureaucratic channels. Both Pettigrew and Normann have touched on these issues in this book.

This leads us back to a related issue that we have already discussed: how to maintain efficient and effective decision-making standards that facilitate efficient use of executive time and thereby allow more time and effort for diffuse and unstructured scanning. Increasing managers' ability to deal with such unstructured, adaptive issues in addition to routine activities is clearly advantageous for the organization's capacity to undertake strategic change (assuming, however, that the standard operating procedures remain relevant in the face of changing environmental circumstances). Thus, managing the standard operating procedures so that they remain tailored to the environment and internally consistent becomes essential. The CEO's role may be particularly important in managing the systems and process context, through revising the firm's management procedures, changing planning formats, tailoring review sessions, refocusing feedback to managers, and so forth. This pattern for CEO involvement in the strategic change process (that is, working more indirectly) may have potentially constraining consequences. Planning, therefore, involves following certain "rules of the game," which may limit the CEO's options to develop and pursue radical change. How, then, can the CEO fulfill a role as entrepreneur and still operate within the managerial processes? What is the role of the nonconformist top leader? Strategic planning may, in fact, be seen as inherently antientrepreneurial, because entrepreneurialism involves seeing things in radically different ways, defying existing rules, and creating new ones. An entrepreneur may have to be a nonconformist; the problem is to reconcile this with the bottom-up, process-oriented approach that calls for planning rules to be followed by the CEO.

## Emergence of a Contingency Approach

In this chapter, we have attempted to highlight and discuss a few issues that seem to have bearing on strategic change and that may help to shed light on how to formulate and implement more realistic business strategies and how to rally an organization's resources around a particular organizational change to pursue some new, desired direction. To attempt to synthesize such a diverse set of thoughts as those presented in this volume is, of course, difficult. It is potentially risky, as well, in that one's ability to make inferences may be myopic. The attempt in this chapter, however, has been to fit many of these issues into a conceptual scheme for better understanding strategic change. The set of eleven different categories that thereby emerged may be fit into an even more general four-stage change model, which we have also attempted to portray. The output of this chapter, then, is a conceptual model that attempts to synthesize and shed light on a number of different issues raised by others, often in different contexts. The model is not derived from an a priori set of propositions.

Two issues should be raised at this point. Of the eleven factors that we have pointed out, two are fundamentally beyond the direct influence of management. Management will have to live with the strategic profile of the company, at least in the short term; the resource availability of the company (financial, managerial, and know-how) is also a given. The remaining nine conditions, however, are all controllable to some extent. These nine conditions present administrative levers for managers to induce strategic change.

At this point, it is relevant to ask whether contingency conditions might be postulated to prevail as subsets of the nine factors. Chakravarthy (1982) states three contingencies: *simple organizations,* which do not pursue a multiplicity of strategies or possess a multitude of organizational levels; *reactive organizations,* which are more elaborate in that they follow several closely related strategies and possess somewhat more complex structures and management processes; and, finally, *fully diversified organizations,* which can be portrayed as a multiplicity of organizational levels and structural arrangements, following a portfolio strategy. One might speculate that, in the case of the simple organization, factors such as the political dimension would typically be less important. Similarly, the issue of team versus individual efforts in the planning process would probably also be less critical, given the "smallness" of the management cadre. The issue of manipulative versus confrontational style would similarly not apply. Issues for this type of firm would be how to avoid myopic thinking and to undertake environmental scanning to avoid becoming trapped in "provincialism." A good environmental control for maintaining sensitivity to environmental changes is crucial.

For a reactive organization, developing synergistic strategies is probably essential. This may call for putting particular emphasis on how to generate strategic alternatives, such as team versus individual efforts, top-down versus bottom-up locus of strategic initiative, manipulative versus confrontational problem-solving styles, and so on. Similarly, sensitizing stakeholders to the implications of change would probably be relatively more critical.

Finally, for the fully diversified corporation, all nine conditions for change would play more full-fledged roles. We thus might have a contingency model wherein simpler organizations with less complex structures and strategies will find it relevant to actively deal with a smaller subset of factors affecting strategic change. The more complex the organization, the greater the need to make use of a melange of all change factors.

#  TWENTY

---

# Toward Convergence
# in Strategic Theory
# and Practice

## *Johannes M. Pennings*

The Introduction to this book listed five critical issues that should be addressed by individuals who deal with research and praxis of strategic decision making: the process versus outcome aspects of strategic decision making, the proper unit of analysis, the interdisciplinary nature of pertinent research, description versus prescription, and preferred modes of research orientation. All of these issues elicit strong advocacy and strong challenges. From the chapters of this book, we could extract position statements on these issues and proceed toward an attempt to map the area of strategic decision making.

The authors of this book were prompted to discuss the issues from their own diverse vantage points. In the aggregate, they provide a fairly good synopsis of the way a communi-

*Note:* Preparation of this manuscript was supported by a grant from the Reginald Jones Center, the Wharton School, University of Pennsylvania, and completed at Netherlands Institute for Advanced Study, Wassenaar, The Netherlands.

ty of scholars examines these issues in the 1980s. Naturally, this claim hinges on the assumption that the group of authors represents the field of strategic decision making. However, as mentioned earlier, this field is highly interdisciplinary. It has diffuse boundaries, and these boundaries are further blurred by the numerous disciplines intersecting in various ways. Thus, it is a rather bold claim that this set of contributions is representative. Some critics might perceive an underrepresentation of economists or a neglect of content questions as illustrated by portfolio or product-matrix theories. But the authors do exhibit diverse disciplinary backgrounds, employment, and degrees of practical exposure. In view of the eclectic nature of the field, the relative disjointedness of its subfields, and the need for complementarity, the set of contributions is best evaluated in toto, examining where they show the potential for integration or present opportunities for cross-fertilization.

This chapter complements the three previous chapters in trying to describe the forest derived from the collection of trees. Picturing the field might help in identifying where authors are redundant and where they are complementary. The chapters examine the issues sufficiently for a map to be drawn.

Table 1 classifies the authors with respect to the dichotomized biases on the five issues. Naturally, this is a gross simplification, since most authors are sufficiently prudent not to adhere stringently to one side or the other. However, by considering not only the content of the chapters but also the literature quoted, the history of their research, and their present interests, we can make rough judgments on their positions. It is clear, however, that this approach is only suggestive and that we have to qualify those judgments.

### Position on Five Issues

*Nature of Strategic Decision Making.* As already alluded to, the concern for process as opposed to content or outcome of strategic decisions predominates. Some authors (for example, Winter, Teece, MacCrimmon) refer to content considerations, but in most cases, the discussion of content only serves to clarify processes. It almost seems as if processes are *content-neutral* and that certain

**Table 1. Classification of Authors According to Five Global Attributes.**

| Name of Author | Nature of Decision Making | Unit of Analysis | Discipline Covered | Bias[a] | Research Approach |
|---|---|---|---|---|---|
| Hickson and colleagues | Process | Decision | Sociology, anthropology, political science | P | Empirical/variance theory |
| Dutton | Process | Decision | Psychology, economics, anthropology, sociology | P | Empirical/process theory |
| Starbuck | Process | Organization | Economics, Sociology, Psychology | P/N | Empirical/process theory |
| Lawrence | Process | Organization | Sociology, psychology | P/N | Empirical/process theory |
| MacCrimmon | Outcome | Decision | Economics, psychology, political science | P | Theoretical/process theory |
| Winter | Outcome | Markets | Economics | P | Theoretical/process theory |
| Camerer | Outcome | Markets | Economics | N | Empirical/variance theory |
| Teece | Outcome | Markets | Economics, sociology | P | Theoretical/variance theory |
| Janis | Process | Group | Psychology, political science | P/N | Empirical/Process theory |
| Gladstein and Quinn | Process | Organization | Psychology, political science, economics | P/N | Theoretical/process theory |
| Normann | Process | Organization | Psychology, anthropology, sociology | N | Empirical/process theory |
| Mohr | Process | Decision | Political science, psychology | P | Theoretical/process theory |
| Pettigrew | Process | Organization and its context | Sociology, psychology, anthropology | P | Empirical/process theory |
| Bowman | Outcome | Organization and its context | Economics, sociology | P/N | Empirical/variance theory |
| Hermon-Taylor | Outcome | Organization | Economics, sociology | N | Empirical/process theory |
| Argyris | Process | Organization | Psychology, economics, sociology | P/N | Empirical/process theory |
| Van de Ven | Process | Organization | Sociology, economics | P | Empirical/variance theory |
| Newman | Outcome | Organization | Economics, psychology, sociology | N | Empirical/process theory |
| Lorange | Process | Organization | Economics, sociology | P/N | Empirical/process theory |

[a]P = positive; N = normative.

processes are not necessarily more likely associated with certain outcomes than are others. One would draw the analogy with research methodology, which is equally appropriate for any scientific effort; for example, the experiment can be designed for studies in physics, biology, psychology, or anthropology and is invariant with respect to the idiosyncracies of theories espoused in each of those disciplines.

The implication of such statements is that processual patterns leading up to a particular outcome are not traceable to that outcome; likewise, an engineering of choice is not contingent upon any particular commitment, such as the decision to stay put, to expand, or to retrench. The difficulty lies partly in attempts to impose a model of causality upon a teleological phenomenon, as if we are taking a mirror image of goal-directed behavior to infer causality. Furthermore, the goal attainment is equifinal; part of the failure to relate outcomes to prevailing processes might be due to the inability to consider global objectives. In the Introduction, it was maintained that there are a near-infinite number of processes that would lead to a global outcome; different modes of processes within an outcome class could coexist and be equally effective. Really, in order to identify the prevalence of certain processes within a type of outcomes, we would need an inventory of processes associated with each type. Because of the earlier-mentioned "infinite regress" problem, the construction of such process-content matrixes does not appear to be feasible. Whether or not processes are outcome-neutral, it would therefore be impossible to expect the authors of this volume to arrive at such cross-classifications.

When discussing the issue of "process" versus "outcome," it is important to distinguish between the process of formulation and implementation. While one can conceptualize strategic decision making as an evolving set of events, a stream of decisions, thus obviating the need for such distinctions, it still may be useful to maintain them, because actions of individuals involved in the formulation may precede over time the actions of individuals who are more involved in the implementation stage. Even if the implementors engage in formulation, it is useful to allow for the possibility of a two-stage process. Strategy formulation is often cast in terms of the content of strategic decision making, but, obviously, this first stage also embodies a process in that it entails such activities as communication, search, and the development of commitment. The actual statement of strategic intent, whether carved out in granite or displayed in some other form, is often considered as the culmination of that process but not very interesting to examine (Mintzberg, 1978). Mintzberg even suggests dropping the term *formulation*, thus further de-emphasizing the issue of content.

Virtually all authors in the current volume deal with the process of decision making. Some focus on the processes during the early stages—say, before a formal commitment to a course of action is made (for example, Janis, Gladstein and Quinn, Pettigrew, Argyris, and Mohr)—while others center on the implementation "games," that is, the latter stages of the decision-making process (for example, Starbuck, MacCrimmon, and Dutton). It is also interesting to note that Gladstein and Quinn turn the question of cognitive commitment under conditions of groupthink around. That commitment, which might impede the search for new information, can be valuable in the implementation stages, when top decision makers can rally their organization behind a new course of action. Such practical (and theoretical) differences during the different stages of the strategic decision-making process might be an interesting challenge for future research to consider. Different concerns for process seem to contrast the current authors much more than does a concern with process versus outcome.

*Unit of Analysis.* More interesting contrasts can be derived from the treatment of strategic decision making in terms of what constitutes the proper unit of analysis. The treatment appears to vary depending upon whether one adopts a cross-sectional and, perhaps, discrete perspective or whether one sees decision making as a continuous developmental process in which successive stages follow on each other. In the first case, one tends to make a snapshot or a retrospective overview (for example, Hickson and his colleagues and Janis), while, in the second case, one tries to construct a moving scenario with fluid and variable beginning and ending points (for example, Starbuck and Pettigrew). There is a second aspect that has unit-of-analysis ramifications. Some authors define organizations as identical to strategic decision-making systems (for example, Starbuck, MacCrimmon), while others view the two as not being identical (for example, Pettigrew). Pettigrew identifies various relevant events that occur outside the organizational boundaries but that have ramifications for the unfolding of what he calls strategic change.

If one combines the discrete-indefinite stance with whether or not the organization is taken as the decision-making system, one can classify the various contributors by the way that they treat decision making as a unit of study. Figure 1 describes the four modes that derive from this combination.

The first view (View A in Figure 1) takes essentially a snapshot of a development in progress. It is best illustrated by Burns and Stalker's (1961) well-known classification of organizations as management regimes, that is, mechanistic and organic regimes. These authors examined the transformation of the British electronics industry during and after the Second World War and arrived at the construction of two configurations of structural and processual attributes that characterized the decision-making behavior of the various firms they studied. The pattern that is displayed in View A is especially appropriate to depict the various studies of strategic content, including the so-called Profit Impact of Marketing Strategies (PIMS) studies and Porter's generic types (Schoeffler, Buzzell, and Heany, 1974; Porter, 1980). For example, a generic strategic type refers to business organizations as strategic decision systems. It represents the enduring disposition of a firm toward its environment, as inferred from its degree of external specialization and the degree to which it has established a distinct product/service image or cost efficiency.

The second mode (View B in Figure 1) focuses on decisions within organizations by disaggregating from the level of organization to a bewildering array of "amalgams," such as sets of cognitions shared by a subset of members (groupthink), event histories, or clusters of actors (strategic "game" players), where the disaggregation centers around the content of strategic decisions (for example, decision type, decision outcome, topics, and so on). It appears that authors such as Hickson and his colleagues and Janis identify specific decision topics, such as "takeover" or "internal restructuring" and the Bay of Pigs or Watergate fiascoes, and subsequently proceed to describe the antecedent conditions and the relevant

**Figure 1. Classification of Strategic Decision Making by Unit of Analysis.**

| Discrete View | | Dynamic View | |
|---|---|---|---|
| View A<br>Organization Equals<br>Decision System | View B<br>Organization Does Not<br>Equal Decision System | View C<br>Organization Equals<br>Decision System | View D<br>Organization Does Not<br>Equal Decision System |

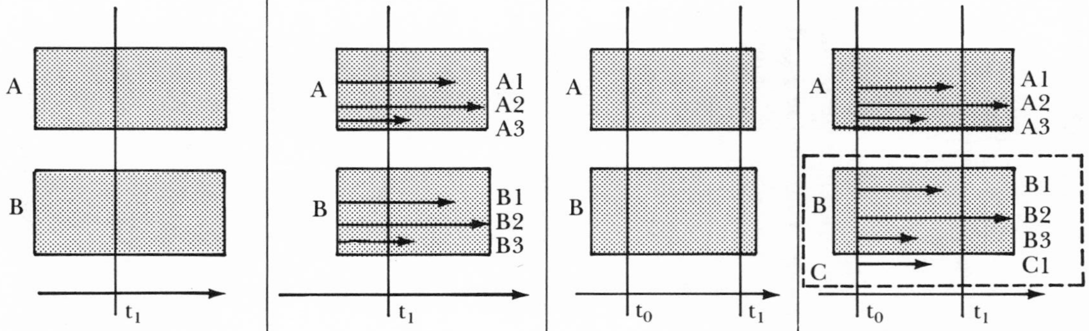


| | | | |
|---|---|---|---|
| For example,<br>Teece | For example,<br>Hickson<br>and others,<br>Janis | For example,<br>Starbuck,<br>Normann<br>Herman-Taylor,<br>MacCrimmon | For example,<br>Pettigrew |

interacting participants, with their interrelationships, their shared beliefs and attitudes, or their conflicting and overlapping interests. Since they do recognize strategic decision making to be a process, they disaggregate not only vertically (from organization to divisions, departments, or clusters of individuals) but also horizontally (from an organization's life to a limited sequence of events with a distinct beginning and ending). Naturally, these two forms of disaggregation entail an arbitrary judgment about which individuals or which time chunks to include or not to include, but they furnish us some tentative rules of thumb for delineating the vertical and horizontal bounds. Because they acknowledge strategic decisions to be processes, we should not write an arbitrary $t$ as we did on the time axis of View B in Figure 1, since these authors typically seek to develop a decision imagery when the decision has reached its terminal point—for example, when the fiasco has occurred. Their approach requires them to accommodate variable origins and destination points in the analysis of strategic event histories to its very end. It is clear that both Hickson and his colleagues and Janis do not equate strategic decision-making systems with organizations. By decomposing decision making into discernible chunks, they provide an appropriate procedure for examining event histories as manageable units of study. New methodological developments to study events or discrete dependent variables in a dynamic perspective are currently blossoming (for example, Carroll, 1983; Tuma, Hannan, and Groeneveld, 1979). It may be the analysis of well-bounded event histories that can provide a first step toward the design of superior strategic planning systems.

The third mode (View C in Figure 1) seems to be the predominant one. The chapters by Starbuck, Normann, Hermon-Taylor, and MacCrimmon lean toward equating the strategic decision system with organization and placing it in a longitudinal context. They are unambiguous in their dynamic focus and perceive strategic decision making as the embodiment of the entire organization in all its ramifications. In fact, their view of organizations, in spite of subtle differences, is so encompassing that they prefer to speak about strategic change and strategic development rather than specific socially and temporally bounded actions. They appear to hint at the futility of efforts to artificially lift a specific decision, however defined, out of its context because of the ubiquitous continuity of organizational behavior.

Finally, the last mode (View D in Figure 1) overlaps considerably with the previous one, except that authors fitting this class deny the possibility of sharply segregating an organization from its larger context. The contextual flavor of Pettigrew's strategic change model is a case in point. Stressing the open-systems nature of complex organizations, he considers it rather tenuous to claim that strategic decision making resides inside the organization. Such authors refuse to limit the study of strategic decision making to the inner confines of organizations and elaborate on the concurrence of events inside and outside the organization, which follow a pattern of confluence in a certain direction. The implication is that organizations and strategic decision-making systems are not identical.

The bias in defining the unit of analysis is, to some extent, to be expected, given the authors' epistemological and theoretical orientations. For example, authors such as Normann, Starbuck, and Pettigrew have a rather pronounced phenomenological or ethnographic disposition toward the reality that they study. One might say that these authors deal with the so-called "rationalized strategy" as described in the beginning of the Introduction. They are strongly preoccupied with the concrete, vivid, and rich aspects of organizational behavior—in particular, the experiences of organizational members. In their view, strategic decision making is the result of a social construction, so that a community of organizational members share a set of beliefs, endowed with rich meaning, that is not readily amenable to quantitative or analytical analysis. In fact, they deny the assumption that the opinions, attitudes, or values of decision-making participants at various locations in the organization are inconsequential for the content or implementation of strategic decisions. They consider it absurd to isolate the strategic decision process from the impact of the individuals who in the implementation phase become a party to it. Rather, they depict strategic choice as an intuitive, conflictual, disorderly, and fluid reality. The use of case studies and the quasi-anthropological affinity toward qualitative methodologies further exacerbate the inclination to treat strategic decision-making systems in holistic and fluid terms. Boundaries of strategic decision making are hard to draw, because concepts of time and place as they exist in the minds of organizational members are inherently fuzzy and equivocal.

In contrast, highly positivistic authors, such as Teece and Hickson and his colleagues, have a strong affinity for quantitative analytical and comparative research methodologies. They dissect their observations and construct "objective" models of strategic decision making that are fairly far removed from the interpretative "level" of organizational reality. They impose permutations and combinations to fit their analytical and conceptual needs.

Somehow, there is an overlap in the analytical schemes of their scientific work and the flavor of the rational model with its logic for providing a conceptual framework for strategic action. The implied analytical vigor of the decision process is presumed to ensure that the outcome is to be drawn from a well-defined, comprehensive set of alternatives. The conceptual framework of the decision-making research permits the dissection of the ingredients that make up the sequential logical paths toward that outcome.

In the dialectics of scientific advancements, we can expect ups and downs in prevalent modes of research. There will be studies that treat strategy as if it can be captured as a snapshot or a videotape, or as if *strategic decision-making system* is equivalent or nonequivalent with *organization*. Some investigators prefer qualitative, hypothesis-generating research, while others have an inclination toward quantitative, more hypothesis-testing research. It would appear that all modes of research can make claims for validity. It may be fruitful to have different views on the unit of analysis coexist such that hypothesis formulation is accomplished by qualitative researchers, who view strategic decision making in holistic terms, while hypothesis testing is achieved by more quantitative researchers, who punctuate the process into events whose attributes permit analytical and evaluative approaches. This is also one of the messages in Chapter Seven, where Janis suggests that qualitative research of the kind that he has been engaged in should be followed by correlational and experimental research. Such shifts inevitably lead to an alteration of the definition of the unit of analysis. It seems also fair to argue that outcome-oriented strategy research, which tends to have a static bias (see View A in Figure 1), is often more quantitive/analytical but is not necessarily more advanced; its results will rest on shaky grounds unless and until the processes leading up to outcomes are incorporated in subsequent research designs.

In conclusion, one might therefore argue that the differences in conceptualization in this volume are not as disturbing as they might seem. Punctuating or delineating decision-making processes or systems will present different problems, depending upon the stage of research or the theoretical or methodological inclination of the researchers. Case studies that tend to treat strategic decision making as a holistic concept and to treat decision-making systems as organization equivalent are more appropriate at the early stages of research—for example, for the development of new hypotheses. More limited and empirically more confined views of strategic decision making, such as "steps" in an incremental process or events triggered in a crisis situation, are more likely the forms of research that have progressed down the road and that rely on the maps that have been drawn by holistic conceptions of strategic decision making. As mentioned in the introductory chapter, research that eventually will decompose such a process into reasonable chunks might be more conducive to predictive theory, having a greater generalizability, and will enhance the development of an engineering of choice. Proposals such as those by Janis, Gladstein and Quinn, or Argyris might be suggestive for future dissections along those lines.

*Interdisciplinary Orientation.* The multitude of disciplines represented by this book's cast of characters is a major factor in accounting for the diversity of treatments of the appropriate unit of analysis. Thus, we should anticipate not only variations in quantitative versus qualitative methodologies but also differences in the choice of pertinent variables. This is to be expected in a field that is inherently eclectic.

Although the mapping of authors into some representation is bound to have the elements of a Procrustean bed, one could arrange the location of disciplines around an imaginary clock, with economics at 12, psychology at 3, anthropology at 6, sociology at 9, and political science at 10. In a thought experiment, it would then be feasible to position the various authors on this clock, assuming that one cannot excell in two disciplines at the same time. Rather, they are attached to one of these disciplines with some degree of variation, exploiting their talents, skills, and energy in a relatively narrow realm. Thus, the authors of the chapters could be roughly classified by positioning them on the face of a clock as illustrated by Figure 2.

To resolve some of the Procrustean problems, we would position some authors closer to the center of the imaginary face. For example, Pettigrew points to power aspects of strategic decision making and the central relevance of political structures to affect strategic change. MacCrimmon presents special problems in that he also provides a map of the field, thereby positioning himself away from his original disciplines, which are economics and psychology. Naturally, the present author ought to be positioned in the center of the face. Although he has been trained in sociology and psychol-

**Figure 2. The Interdisciplinary Clock of Strategic Decision Making.**

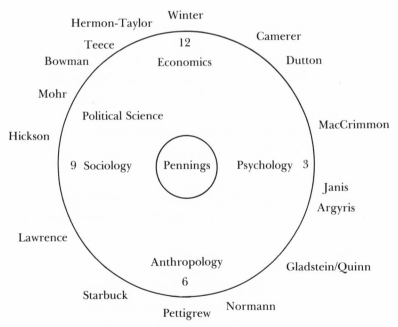

ogy, he attempts to take a bird's-eye view over the current list of characters. Therefore, his discipline background is not an issue here. Such metaphorical efforts have obviously limited value for bringing order in the field. However, it is important to recognize that most strategic decision-making researchers have a primary discipline affiliation. It is also important to recognize that they have acquired an interest in adjacent disciplines.

As Table 1 shows, sociology, economics, psychology, anthropology, and political science are both dominant and secondary disciplines for most authors. However, as already stated, the labeling of various authors in terms of their discipline background might be hazardous. Apart from their original education—for example, the earning of their doctorate—there are subsequent exposures to alternative scientific traditions that have transformed the original discipline identity. Furthermore, this original identity might be interdisciplinary in that many strategy researchers have moved through different discipline departments. During their doctorate training, they might have been exposed to academic teachers who themselves might be eclectic in their training. Conversely, researchers trained in business or public-policy schools might have been socialized into the field by people who had a strong singular discipline bias. All these considerations suggest that the identification of a community of scholars as represented in this volume might be tenuous, as the classification criteria have become equivocal. It is rather striking that many authors whose discipline identity is quite clear—as indicated by journal subscription, professional-association affiliation, or training—are currently associated with interdisciplinary institutions, such as business schools, schools of public affairs or public policy, and schools of education. Others have joined the ranks of practitioners and have become exposed to alternative theoretical perspectives as well (compare Normann and Hermon-Taylor).

Such manifestations of eclecticism have positive and negative implications. On the one hand, eclectism has diminished the parochialism that is often pervasive among many academic researchers. That parochialism could be highly damaging for the strategic decision-making field. Multidisciplinary orientations have broadened their perspective, which might not have happened if they had stayed within the confines of their discipline. For example, many economists who deal with strategic issues in decision making no longer accept blindly the simplistic rational model that was fashionable in the early decades of strategy thinking—and still predominates in a great deal of the current business-policy textbooks (for example, Andrews, 1980; Porter, 1980). Thus, they assume that information about strategic alternatives is costly and in short supply, that goods are not always known, or that choice does not always follow logically from the purposeful analysis of preferences and alternatives (compare the chapters of Teece and Winter).

On the other hand, the interdisciplinary trend has drawbacks in that individuals have drifted away from the mainstream activities of disciplines such that their work in those disciplines has become less well recognized, less legitimate, and increasingly more peripheral. As was stated in the first chapter, such individuals deal with "disturbance terms" of main-discipline research, where these terms are outside the purview of that research. Their isolation from their original community of scholars might impede their ability to serve as boundary-spanning individuals who go beyond the rolling over of old and perhaps obsolete models (Teece) and add dimensions to models that are current.

In this vein, one might consider various interesting juxtapositions in which different paradigms become merged even though they are seemingly incompatible because of the conceptual luggage that they are saddled with. Take, for example, the case of organizational inertia as an important feature of strategic decision making. In industrial economics, there are several treatments of "commitment," such as "contract specific assets," which increase dependence of the firm upon external contractual partners (Teece, Chapter One of this volume; Klein, Crawford, and Alchian, 1978). Organizations become entrapped when they make investments for the purpose of meeting specific obligations toward a client organization. The client organization, as a result, has the incentive to behave opportunistically. After the commitment, there is a reality that differs from the conditions that prevailed at the time of the contract. In social psychology, we have also witnessed a strong increase in the study of cases where commitments entrap a decision maker, whose decisions begin to lead a life of their own, creating for the decision maker a new reality that was nonexistent prior to the commitment. This emerging new reality often sets the stage for escalating the commitment, thus rendering the decision maker further captive to his or her chosen alternative (Staw, 1976). Knowing that strategic decision makers are paralyzed by their commitments in undertaking certain actions presents interesting strategic options for other organizations that are strategically interdependent with their organization. Staw claims that this entrapment is particularly likely to occur when a single decision maker is personally held accountable for the consequences of his or her decision. Group decision making would diffuse the commitment and leave the members more at liberty to reverse the course. Such a finding would, in turn, be challenged by group-induced inertia, as discussed by Janis but possibly corroborated by the recent admissions on Japanese styles of decision making (Ouchi, 1981). Many opportunities for cross-fertilization exist here.

Naturally, the question of commitment is a relatively minor aspect of the decision process. Other minor aspects could be listed as well. It is important to contrast, to interrelate, or to combine the different treatments of such decisional aspects. It is even more important to consider such expressions of "normal science" (Kuhn, 1970) with more encompassing models as they have become the hallmark of divergent disciplines. Such models may include well-established ones, such as the rational, intended-rational, political, or garbage-can ones (Allison, 1971; Mohr, 1976), as well as such others as attribution (Nisbett and Ross, 1980), learning (Argyris, Chapter Sixteen; Normann, Chapter Nine; Bateson, 1972), and game theories (Schelling, 1960). The field is in dire need of "generative theories" (Gergen, 1978) that help direct and combine the incremental empirical efforts in establishing cumulative knowledge.

Critical among the implications of different disciplines and the strategic decision-making propositions that they provide are the contradictory assumptions of their theories with regard to the process or content of strategic decision making. It is clear that no one discipline alone can adequately capture the different aspects that become differentially salient across the disciplines. Recognizing these differences avoids the vicious circle of process-versus-outcome analysis. In view of the extraordinary complexity of strategic decision making, it is safe to argue that the perspectives of more than one discipline are needed to capture the various aspects in its content or process. While the various models in the different disciplines are useful for identifying and interpreting strategic aspects, there is obviously also a great need for integrative models that incorporate the accomplishment of different disciplines in order to endow the field with theoretical advancement.

If one exposes oneself to the accomplishments of other disciplines, whether it is in their conduct of normal science or in the articulation of the associated, more encompassing theories, one will notice the limited value of one's parochial efforts in contributing to generative theories of strategic decision making. That recognition is a first step toward a more mature area of inquiry that yields a more complete understanding of the complexity of strategic decision making while maintaining primary loyalty to original disciplines—to cope with each scientist's own bounded rationality—hopefully to greatly enrich the scientist and help that advancement. While all authors in this book displayed that loyalty, they also showed courage by exposing their work to critiques from other disciplines and set an example in the field.

*Description Versus Prescription.* A major point of contention is the bridge between descriptive and prescriptive statements about strategic decision making. Among all types of social science research, decision making is one of the most salient subjects in terms of linking the realm of facts with the realm of norms. After all, researchers in this area deal with the practical person par excellence; his or her actions have material consequences, with value or ideological implications. It seems, therefore, quite difficult to be a dispassionate investigator who stays aloof when describing or interpreting the facts of strategic decision making.

The normative implications of strategic decision-making descriptions can be reviewed on several levels. There are practical research matters, such as the rules of scientific conduct when studying event histories. Some authors (for example, Normann, Chapter Nine; Mohr, 1982) argue that decision making is a process that ought to be studied with methodologies that fit its developmental nature. They prescribe norms for conducting strategy research. Cross-sectional, comparative analyses and interpretation are inappropriate if they do not consider the time-dependent, sequential flows of events. Decision making is a successive set of steps or "stages" whose pattern might resemble "flowcharts" of one or another kind and that lead up to a terminal point. The correct approach entails, therefore, longitudinal methods of data collection and analysis, such as repeated measurement designs, time-series analyses, and learning- or development-oriented theories. The normative flavor of such methodological statements is obvious.

Other authors in this volume claim that we should analyze strategic choice as a holistic process, as illustrated by the case studies of Pettigrew and Starbuck. Implicitly, they contend that "objective" modes of research are not as legitimate as "subjective," in the sense of "interpretive," modes of research. The issue of "objective" versus "subjective" modes of research has stirred heated debates and continues to be a contentious issue in the social sciences (Campbell, 1977; Ben-Yehuda, 1983).

Regardless of what methodologies or research modes one prescribes, there are at least two ways in which one can review the normative implications of the chapters in this volume. The normative implications manifest themselves either in the espousal of a particular view of social reality or in the prescriptive pronouncements that are extracted from that view.

First of all, there is the model that one subscribes to and that, implicitly or explicitly, reveals a view of the social reality. Espousal of a model implies an affinity to a particular value system or ideology. Even if they present themselves as detached, dispassionate theorists, researchers express values that are linked to the phenomena selected for study, the labels and meanings attached to these phenomena, and the selectively obtained new findings. The result is that all "valuational inferences serve as 'ought' expressions for the recipient of knowledge" (Gergen, 1978; p. 1354). The results of neutrality and lack of passion in some science research are not value free and dispassionate in their consequences.

I believe that these statements are rather germane for evaluating the rational model of strategic choice, which has become so well established in the business-policy textbooks and which also surfaces in the chapter by Teece. It also predominates in the current product-matrix research as reviewed before (for example, Schoeffler, Buzzell, and Heany, 1974). One would have thought that the recognition of other models (Allison, 1971) would have challenged the quasi-sacred nature of rational representations in the strategic choice literature. Rational-model advocates are inclined to emphasize economic-performance criteria when they pursue research on the content of organizational strategies. They ignore noneconomic criteria, or they relegate them to a perfunctory treatment of "corporate social responsibility" (Pennings, 1981). Their model and their "value-neutral" research induce one to evaluate strategic choices by exclusive reliance on criteria such as profitability, market share, or cost effectiveness. The popularity of rational models has led to a large volume of literature that serves as an impressive monument for free-market neoclassical economics. The content-oriented, economic-oriented literature has formed an imagery of the firm and its decision-making infrastructure that is an organizational carica-ture. The profound neglect of psychological, social, and political considerations renders such treatments shallow and incomplete. The strong preoccupation with outcomes of strategic choice has led to a neglect of its antecedent process, which typically is depicted in mechanistic and overly simplistic terms. As MacCrimmon has demonstrated, it is helpful to contrast the rational model with other models to disclose the one-sided view of reality that it espouses.

Some of the chapters in this book make a practical contribu-tion by providing suggestions about how decision makers make explicit the premises of their actions such that they can transcend the limits of their current platform and possibly arrive at better decisions. In particular, the chapters by Normann, Starbuck, Hermon-Taylor, and Argyris stand out in "excavating" the presup-positions of strategic decision makers. Argyris's chapter is exem-plary for the sort of critical thinking that should be used by any researcher in this field. Normann, who, like Argyris, acknowledged indebtedness to Bateson (1972), likewise tries to articulate the point that we have to transcend our traditional modes of thinking by initially self-examining those modes. We tend to ascribe undisputed legitimacy to our theories and the representation of reality that is sustained by them. Compare also Hermon-Taylor's "undiscussi-bles." By trying to step outside the cognitive cage that we have constructed for ourselves in order to describe the reality that fits our preconceptions, we reach a level of learning that helps us to put our theories in proper perspective. It is also conducive to scrutinizing and evaluating the basic premises that we hold and that we might begin to dispute, to no longer obliterate the critical questions of social ethics or to obscure other hard problems.

Argyris suggests that moving from the field of study to the field of praxis and vice versa will aid in transcending single-loop learning. We liberate ourselves from reconfirming our espoused models and reach a level of knowledge that provides us with a broader perspective. There are both epistemological and pragmatic elements in this line of thinking. On the one hand, we espouse models even if we are not aware of them. Our perceptions are shaped by those models. In fact, they affect the kind of data we collect to further corroborate our models and, as a result, have an undue influence upon the way we interpret the data. On the other hand, the espoused models also affect the way we act upon our reality. In cases of decision making, we can even argue that people in organizations are constantly engaged in "interventions" or self-created field experiments that are "designed" according to the espoused model; the experimental results generate new but biased data, which will be perceived and interpreted in such a way as to further solidify the foundations of our models. Decision makers find themselves captives of their own creations. If they want to learn from their actions, they have to transcend their models—for example, by experimenting with alternate models or by simply challenging the premises of the original one. They can acquire alternative views of themselves and their decisional realities by considering other models, perhaps models that hitherto have not been known to exist. Argyris's chapter is a practical proposal to overcome the "undiscussibles" that Hermon-Taylor enumerates when he seeks to explain why organizations are unable to overhaul their institutional habits and traditional ways of seeing things.

At a more general level in the Argyris, Hermon-Taylor, and Normann Chapters, there is a definite Habermasian twist to these ideas about strategic decision making (Habermas, 1971). Decision scientists ought to perform an "emancipatory" mission to expose and possibly to uncouple the factors that bind the decision maker to a certain view of reality and to a perfunctory role. They should challenge the well-established notions about decision making, perhaps by starting with the espoused scientific paradigms. The researcher has three distinct cognitive interests (Habermas, 1972). He or she has a technical cognitive interest whenever social reality, including strategic decision making, is studied as objectified processes without direct reference to any actors and under conditions of scientific control. Individuals are treated as objects, thus denying them their status as agents with free wills. Secondly, the researcher has practical cognitive interests when he or she attempts to comprehend the actors, the meaning that they attribute to their behavior, and the way that they share those meanings by acts of communication. Finally, the researcher has an emancipatory interest that leads to the formation of a critical social science and that exposes the conceptual shackles that unduly bias the perspectives of reality that we can hold. The emancipatory interest should induce us to demythologize our established views of organizations and the decision makers that they employ—in particular, to debunk popularly held beliefs about rational decision making and, more generally, to challenge major scientific paradigms.

Researchers should not try to resolve the applicability of strategic decision-making research by moving from the "is" realm to the "ought" realm—for example, by formulating a set of decision heuristics as derived from their program of research. If they did that, they would be merely contributing to the existing status quo, whether in the confines of university departments conducting decision-making research or the corporate or public decision systems that are the subject of research and practice. Decision scientists should be cognizant of the fact that they might contribute to the preservation of the status quo; they should be involved in "consciousness raising" by examining both for themselves and for their subject matter the deeper implications of their theoretical and practical implications.

This brief digression may not only help in putting all chapters into perspective but may also help in demythologizing the rational model that still enjoys such a high degree of acceptance as "the" model for strategic decision making. It fully endorses the attempts of this book's contributors, who, either in the present volume or previously, have courageously challenged the well-established and widely accepted premises of their disciplines. Almost without exception, the authors have written statements that could be classified as somewhat "outlandish" or nonconformist, as debunking assumptions or paradigms, or that have added dimensions to existing paradigms such that they fundamentally altered their meaning or implications.

The metaphor of the mental cage that was used earlier to expose the entrapment of strategic decision-making research in its own framework can also be extended to describe the entrapment of decision makers in their own idiosyncratic cage. One of the best treatments of this condition—which, incidentally, also serves as an illustration of outlandish theorizing as mentioned earlier—is the concept of *groupthink* from Janis. This concept makes references to cognitive schemata that decision makers have acquired and that prevent them from optimal decision making. The chapter by Janis presents a set of proposals to overcome the deleterious effects of groupthink in order to improve decision-making quality. Somehow, he offers practical remedies for decision makers. The pragmatic aspects of Axelrod's (1976b) study on public-policy decisions as constrained by prior preconceptions is a neat illustration of Janis's precepts for improving strategic decisions. It should be pointed out that his chapter is the most explicit one in stressing the second aspect of pragmatics: to derive prescriptive pronouncements from a conceptual and empirical body of research.

*Research Approach.* The fifth issue that was raised in the first chapter was the choice of research orientation. This choice was further differentiated with respect to variance versus process theory and deductive-inductive approaches. As Table 1 shows, most authors espouse a process-theoretical orientation and lean toward induction. The terms *variance* and *process theory* are derived from Mohr (1982), who suggested that decision making is inherently a processual phenomenon that must be investigated with commensurate methodologies. However, while he elaborates on variance methodologies (correlational techniques such as regression analysis and analysis of variance), he does not spell out which process methodologies he has in mind.

The most unambiguous use of variance theory and its methodology is displayed in the chapter of Hickson and his colleagues. They compare a large number of strategic decision processes on a broad array of attributes, such as direction and degree of power equalization among their stakeholders and the degree to which such processes are smooth or constricted. The attributes are examined on this covariation—for example, whether certain types of decisions show a higher incidence of "disjointed incrementalism." Camerer and Teece do not present research findings in their chapters, but most of their published work to which they make reference is likewise of the variance type. Bowman, when he cites his own research in his chapter, similarly adheres to this mode of research. For example, he has investigated whether degree of strategic commitment to nonfinancial criteria of performance is associated with higher levels of profitability.

The overwhelming majority of authors in this volume are advocates of process theory—whether implicitly or explicitly. Mohr did not provide examples of process theory in organization theory, but one can surmise that investigators who isolate states in a process in order to trace the pathways through which it unfolds are coming close to illustrating one mode. However, the ideographic, descriptive research that tends to focus on one and only one case can preclude the identification of numerous flowcharts through which the process takes place. By way of illustration, the Pettigrew narrative on the strategic transformation of Imperial Chemical Industries is punctuated with specific historic milestones, but one would not know whether similar transmutations in other corporations would unfold analogously. In line with Mohr's arguments, one would need numerous observations over time in order to discuss patterns in the flows of events (cause maps), since he implies that, as in variance theory, process theory can evolve only with stochastic assumptions about reality. The implication is that we have to ascertain the probabilistic joint occurrence of sequential stages before we can draw the maps of developments and changes that have a generality or lawlike nature. Only after such empirical research will we be able to determine the relative appropriateness of "cause maps," because their final cause permits us to conclude which should be retained and which should be discarded. This determination might render process theory of strategy in decision making more relevant from a practical point of view by presenting certain cause maps and eliminating others. Axelrod (1976b) provides some hints on the practicality of such recommendations, although he restricts the evaluation of cause maps to those that have accumulated and have been stored in the cognitive repertoire of a single decision-making system.

Apart from the variance-process distinction, there are many other angles from which one can cluster analyze the chapters of this volume. Consider widely known distinctions such as induction-deduction (Blaug, 1980), emic-etic, ideographic-nomethetic (Witte, 1972), or, more generally, theoretical-descriptive. The chapters not only tend to lean toward process approaches, but they also tend to be heavily descriptive, ideographic, and inductive.

Among the eight "main" chapters, there is not a single contribution that comes close to being formally deductive, trying to establish a decision calculus as we know to exist in applied mathematics and operations research (for example, Wagner, 1969). The chapter by MacCrimmon is fairly abstract but relies heavily on a case study that is analyzed in its concrete, vivid manifestation. His three holistic models are used to organize different aspects of that case and to highlight differences and similarities of insights.

Decision models in operations research assume that the constraints of decision are known such that we can optimally choose among the alternatives. Strategic decisions never display this certainty; rather, they are unstructured, complex, and collective. The enormous uncertainty that surrounds such decisions defies formal, logically systematic inductive models. Nevertheless, as was argued earlier, theoretical, more deductively driven research might be more conducive for the advancement of science on strategic decisions—if this is something that can be inferred from looking at other disciplines. At this stage of research, it might be acceptable to have a preponderance of empirical, descriptive investigations in the hope that eventually they will generate the more generalizable insights from which we can erect deductive-formal models of strategic decision making.

## An Epilogue

In spite of the relatively small size of the community of scholars involved in strategic decision making, there is an incredible diversity of viewpoints, which are anchored in disciplines, paradigms, scientific lingo, and professional identities. The diversity is so profound that one sometimes may wonder whether all the contributors in this book were discussing one and the same phenomenon. It is essential that the diversity of disciplines is represented in this volume but also essential that their paradigmatic or linguistic idiosyncracies do not result in a Babylonian confusion.

We should heed the moral of the fable on the weaver and the worm, where the story goes that the former watched a silkworm spinning its cocoon: "Where do you get that stuff?" asked the weaver. "Do you want to make something out of it?" asked the silkworm. This short dialogue ends in the two going their separate ways, each one annoyed and feeling slighted by the other. The implied lesson is that we live in a world where virtually everything can mean almost anything, because we live in a time of "gobbledygook, double talk, and guddy." The moral from this fable by James Thurber (1956) is "A word to the wise is not sufficient, if it does not make any sense."

With such a moral in mind, writers were invited to comment on the chapters of eight authors, who were invited because of their diversity in viewpoints. They were given several opportunities to revise their chapters, partly to enable them to better communicate with people outside their own community of scholars. In spite of the diversity, there is an unmistakably clear manifestation of convergence and a greater ability to identify areas of complementarity or "synergy." The convergence might be local in scope in that various contributors show an awareness of paradigms, weltanschauung, or viewpoints that are associated with "adjacent" areas. *Adjacent* might be understood in terms of the earlier-mentioned clock metaphor. Thus, several 12 o'clock authors are willing to examine 10 o'clock or 2 o'clock theories, research findings, or concepts but are rather reluctant to venture into more distant regions. The adjacent cross-fertilization of theories and research broadens the theoretical and pragmatic scope of these authors and the area they represent.

For example, we have noticed that authors with a profound cross-sectional comparative bias and a propensity toward variance research (Mohr, 1982) have ventured into the conduct of longitudinal research, developing or acquiring a methodological apparatus that fits a process theory of strategy. Likewise, authors were included who typically have an affinity toward strategy-content research and who have adopted a greater awareness of the antecedent processes, which cannot and should not be "bracketed"—even though it might be more expedient and convenient to limit oneself to content of strategy questions such as the product portfolio of a private firm or the retrenchment strategy of governmental bureaucracies. The bracketing of process questions such as search, internal conflict and conflict resolutions, inertial barriers, and so on reduces the organization to a black box. It is necessary to peek into that black box to gain a fuller understanding of strategic choices. It is encouraging that authors such as Teece, Winter, MacCrimmon, Bowman, and Hermon-Taylor are no longer prepared to limit themselves to outcomes or content of strategy research and practice.

Practitioners in this volume have also recognized that one should proceed beyond mechanical decision heuristics in order to better design strategic decision systems and to implement strategic change. It is most revealing that one of the practitioners re-examined that mode of strategic management consultancy that centered around content issues such as the optimality of product portfolios. The well-known Boston Consulting Group's product matrix seeks to identify a firm's most appropriate product matrix by positioning the offerings with respect to relative market share and growth rate of markets and to make resource-allocation recommendations to stimulate those products that ensure the future soundness of the firm. It is one thing, however, to make recommendations—especially those that touch upon the so-called "undiscussibles"—but it is quite something else to have an organization implement such recommendations. Practitioners will, therefore, focus increased attention on questions of implementation and design and legitimize processes that induce strategic change.

Conversely, academic researchers, with their proverbial ivory-tower shields, which protect them from having to deal with the praxis of strategic decision making, have been willing to extrapolate from the realm of science to the realm of praxis and the corresponding enlargement of the theoretical/conceptual language that they carry along in their scientific endeavors. Normann and

Argyris, in particular, have made strong endorsements for merging descriptive and normative science if the field of strategic decision making is to have any benefit for scientists and practitioners alike.

Such lines of convergence and points of complementarity are encouraging and might eventually become more prominent. However, it is equally clear that many additional bridges need to be built to forge a greater unity in diversity. Consider the sharp discrepancies between Starbuck and Newman or between Hickson and Pettigrew, where not only does one detect linguistic or philosophical differences but one might also wonder whether or not research and theory on strategic decision making are possible and might yield pragmatic results. The diversity of viewpoints, with their possible ideological undertones, could be so divisive that dialogues are strained and unproductive. Clearly, the field of strategic decision making is in need of a more or less crystallized unifying idea around which the contributors can rally. Perhaps the publication of this volume might be a little step toward the emergence of such an idea.

Several times we have speculated whether some line of research has a greater conduciveness to a cumulative body of knowledge and the obtainment of a critical mass. As a matter of conjecture, it has been suggested that a focus on relatively well-bounded, discrete decisions might be more successful than an orientation on decision making that avoids decomposition into cross-sectional and intertemporal chunks (because "everything hangs together with everything else"). As Dutton has well articulated, the focus on discrete, artificially bounded decision processes is not without risk, because it isolates such processes from the context in which they unfold. Those contexts, whether internal (for example, managerial succession) or external (for example, shifts in governmental regulation), might not be ignored in the research on such analytically defined processes.

Committing oneself to one specific research avenue almost automatically will evoke such reactions, and even more so in the eclectic field of strategic decision making, where it is unlikely that researchers will make such a commitment unless there is a persuasive statement that will bring them over the threshold. The feasibility of such a statement hinges very much on the ability to span boundaries between different disciplines and to establish a vocabulary and syntax that will facilitate communication across boundaries. Perhaps the mere exposure to different disciplines might homogenize, albeit slightly, the members of different disciplines such that they acquire a common ground within which such communication is feasible.

Scientific developments often occur in a quasi-random fashion, and the equifinality of research in strategic decision making could quite well lead to other avenues of future research. Perhaps this pathway of research and theory on discrete decisions will be overgrown by other ones. Let it be so. What should be learned, however, from the moral of the weaver and the silkworm is that individuals active in this area should be able to understand and to communicate each other's accomplishments, rather than accusing each other that, like Monsieur Jourdain, they are speaking prose without realizing so.

# References

Aaker, D. A. "How to Select a Business Strategy." *California Management Review*, 1984, *26* (3), 167–175.

Abel, E. *The Missile Crisis.* New York: Bantam Books, 1966.

Abell, P. "Organizations as Bargaining and Influence Systems: Measuring Intra-Organizational Power and Influence." In P. Abell (Ed.), *Organizations as Bargaining and Influence Systems.* London: Heinemann; New York: Halstead Press/Wiley, 1975.

Ackerman, R. W. "Influence of Integration and Diversity of Investment Process." *Administrative Science Quarterly*, 1970, *15*, 341–352.

Ackoff, R. L. *A Concept of Corporate Planning.* New York: Wiley, 1970.

Adams, J. S. "The Structure and Dynamics of Behavior in Organizational Boundary Roles." In M. D. Dunnette (Ed.), *Handbook of Industrial and Organizational Psychology.* Chicago: Rand McNally, 1976.

Aharoni, Y. *The Foreign Investment Decision Process.* Cambridge, Mass.: Harvard University Press, 1966.

Alchian, A. "Costs and Outputs." In M. Abramovitz (Ed.), *The Allocation of Economic Resources: Essays in Honor of B. F. Haley.* Berkeley: University of California Press, 1959.

Aldrich, H. E. *Organizations and Environments.* Englewood Cliffs, N.J.: Prentice-Hall, 1979.

Aldrich, H. E., and Herker, D. "Boundary Spanning Roles and Organization Structure." *Academy of Management Review,* 1977, *2* (2), 217–230.

Aldrich, H. E., and Whetten, D. A. "Organization-Sets, Action-Sets and Networks: Making the Most of Simplicity." In P. C. Nystrom and W. H. Starbuck (Eds.), *Handbook of Organizational Design.* Vol. 1. *Adapting Organizations to Their Environments.* New York: Oxford University Press, 1981.

Alexander, C. *Notes on the Synthesis of Form.* Cambridge, Mass.: Harvard University Press, 1964.

Alexander, E. R. "The Design of Alternatives in Organizational Contexts: A Pilot Study." *Administrative Science Quarterly,* 1979, *24,* 382–404.

Allison, G. T. "Conceptual Models and the Cuban Missile Crisis." *American Political Science Review,* 1969, *63* (3), 689–718.

Allison, G. T. *Essence of Decisions: Explaining the Cuban Missile Crisis.* Boston: Little, Brown, 1971.

Allison, G. T., and Halperin, M. "Bureaucratic Politics: A Paradigm and Some Policy Implications." *World Politics,* 1972, *24,* 40–79.

Altheide, D. L., and Johnson, J. M. *Bureaucratic Propaganda.* Boston: Allyn & Bacon, 1980.

Anderson, C., and Paine, F. T. "PIMS: A Reexamination." *Academy of Management Review,* 1978, *3,* 602–612.

Anderson, P. A. "Decision Making by Objection and the Cuban Missile Crisis." *Administrative Science Quarterly,* 1983, *28,* 201–222.

Andrews, K. *The Concept of Corporate Strategy.* Homewood, Ill.: Irwin, 1980.

Ansoff, H. I. *Corporate Strategy: An Analytic Approach to Business*

*Policy for Growth and Expansion.* New York: McGraw-Hill, 1965.

Ansoff, H. I. *Strategic Management.* New York: Wiley, 1979a.

Ansoff, H. I. "The State of Practice in Planning Systems." In W. R. Dill and G. Kh. Popov (Eds.), *Organization for Forecasting and Planning.* Chichester, England: Wiley, 1979b.

Anthony, R. N., Dearden, J., and Bedford, N. *Management Control Systems.* (5th ed.) Homewood, Ill.: Irwin, 1984.

Antonio, R. J. "The Contradiction of Domination and Production in Bureaucracy: The Contribution of Organizational Efficiency to the Decline of the Roman Empire." *American Sociological Review,* 1979, *44,* 895–912.

Argyris, C. *Intervention Theory and Method.* Reading, Mass.: Addison-Wesley, 1970.

Argyris, C. "Some Limits of Rational Man in Organizational Theory." *Public Administration Review,* May/June 1973, 253–267.

Argyris, C. *Increasing Leadership Effectiveness.* New York: Wiley-Interscience, 1976a.

Argyris, C. "Leadership, Learning, and Changing the Status Quo." *Organizational Dynamics,* 1976b, *4,* 29–44.

Argyris, C. "Single-Loop and Double-Loop Models in Research on Decision Making." *Administrative Science Quarterly,* 1976c, *21* (3), 363–375.

Argyris, C. *Inner Contradictions of Rigorous Research.* New York: Academic Press, 1980.

Argyris, C. *Reasoning, Learning, and Action: Individual and Organizational.* San Francisco: Jossey-Bass, 1982.

Argyris, C., and Schön, D. A. *Theory in Practice: Increasing Professional Effectiveness.* San Francisco: Jossey-Bass, 1978.

Argyris, C., and Schön, D. A. *Organizational Learning.* Reading, Mass.: Addison-Wesley, 1981.

Armour, H. O., and Teece, D. J. "Organizational Structure and Economic Performance: A Test of the Multidivisional Hypothesis." *Bell Journal of Economics,* 1978, *9* (1), 106–122.

Armstrong, J. S. "The Value of Formal Planning for Strategic Decisions: Review of Empirical Research." *Strategic Management Journal,* 1982, *3,* 197–211.

Astley, W. G., and others. "Complexity and Cleavage: Dual Explanations of Strategic Decision-Making." *Journal of Management Studies*, 1982, *19* (4), 357-375.

Axelrod, R. M. "Results." In R. M. Axelrod (Ed.), *Structure of Decision: The Cognitive Maps of Political Elites*. Princeton, N.J.: Princeton University Press, 1976a.

Axelrod, R. M. *The Structure of Decision: The Cognitive Maps of Political Elites*. Princeton, N.J.: Princeton University Press, 1976b.

Axelsson, R., and Rosenberg, L. "Decision-Making and Organizational Turbulence." *Acta Sociologica*, 1979, *22* (1), 45-62.

Bacharach, S. B., and Lawler, E. J. *Power and Politics in Organizations: The Social Psychology of Conflict, Coalitions, and Bargaining*. San Francisco: Jossey-Bass, 1980.

Bachrach, P. *The Implementation Game*. Cambridge, Mass.: MIT Press, 1977.

Bachrach, P., and Baratz, M. S. "Two Faces of Power." *American Political Science Review*, 1962, *56*, 947-952.

Bacon, R. *Novum Organum*. Part 2: *Instauratio Magna*. London: J. Billium, 1620.

Bain, J. S. *Barriers to New Competition*. Cambridge, Mass.: Harvard University Press, 1956.

Baldridge, J. *Power and Conflict in the University*. New York: Wiley, 1971.

Bass, B. M. "When Planning for Others." *Journal of Applied Behavioral Science*, 1970, *6*, 151-171.

Bateson, G. *Steps Toward an Ecology of Mind*. New York: Ballantine, 1972.

Baumol, W. J. *Business Behavior, Value, and Growth*. New York: Macmillan, 1959.

Baumol, W. J., Panzar, J. C., and Willig, R. D. *Contestable Markets and the Theory of Industry Structure*. New York: Harcourt Brace Jovanovich, 1982.

Beck, P. W. "Strategic Planning in the Royal Dutch/Shell Group." Paper presented at TIMS/ORSA Conference, New Orleans, March 1977.

Beckhard, R., and Harris, R. T. *Organizational Transitions: Managing Complex Change*. Reading, Mass.: Addison-Wesley, 1977.

Beer, M. *Organizational Change and Development.* Santa Monica, Calif.: Goodyear, 1980.

Belden, T. G., and Belden, M. R. *The Lengthening Shadow.* Boston: Little, Brown, 1962.

Bennis, W. *Organization Development: Its Nature, Origins and Prospects.* Reading, Mass.: Addison-Wesley, 1969.

Ben-Yehuda, N. "History, Selection and Randomness: Towards an Analysis of Social Historical Explanations." *Quality and Quantity,* 1983, *17,* 347-367.

Berg, P. O. *Emotional Structures in Organizations: A Study of the Process of Change in a Swedish Company.* Lund, Sweden: Student Literature, 1979.

Berger, P. L., and Luckmann, T. *The Social Construction of Reality.* Garden City, N.Y.: Doubleday, 1966.

Berkowitz, L., and Donnerstein, E. "External Validity Is More than Skin Deep." *American Psychologist,* 1982, *37* (3), 245-257.

Berkowitz, L., and Green, J. A. "The Stimulus Qualities of the Scapegoat." *Journal of Abnormal and Social Psychology,* 1962, *64,* 293-301.

Bettman, J., and Weitz, B. A. "Attributions in the Boardroom: Causal Reasoning in Corporate Annual Reports." *Administrative Science Quarterly,* 1983, *28* (2), 165-183.

Beyer, J. M. "Ideologies, Values, and Decision Making in Organizations." In P. C. Nystrom and W. H. Starbuck (Eds.), *Handbook of Organizational Design.* Vol. 2: *Remodeling Organizations and Their Environments.* New York: Oxford University Press, 1981.

Biggadike, R. "The Risky Business of Diversification." *Harvard Business Review,* 1979, *57* (3), 103-111.

Black, M. *Margins of Precision: Essays in Logic and Language.* Ithaca, N.Y.: Cornell University Press, 1970.

Blau, P. M., and Scott, W. R. *Formal Organizations.* San Francisco: Chandler, 1962.

Blaug, M. *The Methodology of Economics.* London: Cambridge University Press, 1980.

Bobrow, D. G., and Norman, D. A. "Some Principles of Memory Schemata." In D. G. Bobrow and A. Collins (Eds.), *Representation and Understanding.* New York: Academic Press, 1975.

Boland, R. J., Jr. "Myth and Technology in the American Accounting Profession." *Journal of Management Studies*, 1982, *19*, 109-127.

Bonini, C. P. *Simulation of Information and Decision Systems in the Firm*. Englewood Cliffs, N.J.: Prentice-Hall, 1963.

Boswell, J. S. *Business Policies in the Making*. London: Allen & Unwin, 1983.

Bougon, M., Weick, K. E., and Binkhorst, D. "Cognition in Organizations: An Analysis of the Utrecht Jazz Orchestra." *Administrative Science Quarterly*, 1977, *22*, 606-639.

Bourgeois, L. J., III, and Brodwin, D. R. "Strategy Implementation: Five Approaches to an Elusive Phenomenon." Working paper, Stanford University, 1982.

Bower, J. L. *Managing the Resource Allocation Process*. Boston: Division of Research, Harvard Business School, 1971.

Bower, J. L. *Managing the Resource Allocation Process*. Cambridge, Mass.: Harvard University Press, 1972.

Bower, J. L. "The Business of Business Is Serving Markets." *American Economic Review*, 1978, *68*, 322-327.

Bowers, D. G. "OD Techniques and Their Results in Twenty-Three Organizations: The Michigan ICL Study." *Journal of Applied Behavioral Science*, 1973, *9* (1), 21-43.

Bowman, E. H. "Epistemology, Corporate Strategy, and Academe." *Sloan Management Review*, 1974, *15* (2), 35-51.

Bowman, E. H. "Strategy and the Weather." *Sloan Management Review*, 1976, *17* (2), 49-62.

Bowman, E. H. "Strategy, Annual Reports, and Alchemy." *California Management Review*, 1978, *20* (3), 64-71.

Bowman, E. H. "A Risk/Return Paradox for Strategic Management." *Sloan Management Review*, 1980, *21* (3), 17-31.

Bowman, E. H. "Risk Seeking by Troubled Firms." *Sloan Management Review*, 1982, *23* (4), 33-42.

Bowman, E. H. "Content Analysis of Annual Reports for Corporate Strategy and Risk." *Interfaces*, February 1984, pp. 61-71.

Bowman, E. H., and Haire, M. "A Strategic Posture Toward Corporate Social Responsibility." *California Management Review*, 1975, *18* (2), 49-58.

Bowman, E. H., and Haire, M. "Social Impact Disclosure and

Corporate Annual Reports." *Accounting, Organizations, and Society,* 1976, *1,* 11-21.

Box, G.E.P., and Draper, N. R. *Evolutionary Operation.* New York: Wiley, 1969.

Braybrooke, D., and Lindblom, C. E. *A Strategy of Decision.* New York: Free Press, 1963.

Bresser, R. K., and Bishop, R. C. "Dysfunctional Effects of Formal Planning: Two Theoretical Explanations." *Academy of Management Review,* 1983, *8,* 588-599.

Brittain, J. W., and Freeman, J. H. "Organizational Proliferation and Density Dependent Selection." In J. R. Kimberly, R. H. Miles, and Associates, *The Organizational Life Cycle: Issues in the Creation, Transformation, and Decline of Organizations.* San Francisco: Jossey-Bass, 1980.

Brockner, J., Rubin, J., and Lang, E. "Face Saving and Entrapment." *Journal of Experimental Social Psychology,* 1981, *17,* 68-79.

Broms, H., and Gamberg, H. "Communication to Self in Organizations and Cultures." *Administrative Science Quarterly,* 1983, *28,* 482-495.

Brown, R. H. "Bureaucracy as Praxis: Toward a Political Phenomenology of Formal Organizations." *Administrative Science Quarterly,* 1978, *23,* 365-382.

Browne, P. "The Role of Top Management in Shaping Organizational Design." Unpublished doctoral dissertation, Harvard Business School, 1981.

Brugman, R. J. "A Strategic Explanation of Corporate Acquisition Success." Unpublished doctoral dissertation, Purdue University, 1983.

Brunsson, N. "The Irrationality of Action and Action Rationality: Decisions, Ideologies and Organizational Actions." *Journal of Management Studies,* 1982, *19* (1), 29-44.

Brzezinski, Z. *Power and Principle: Memoirs of the National Security Advisor.* New York: Farrar, Straus & Giroux, 1983.

Buckley, W. *Sociology and Modern Systems Theory.* Englewood Cliffs, N.J.: Prentice-Hall, 1967.

Buckley, W. *Modern Systems Research for the Behavioral Scientist.* Chicago: Aldine, 1968.

Burgelman, R. A. "A Model of the Interaction of Strategic Behavior, Corporate Context and the Concept of Strategy." *Academy of Management Review*, 1983a, *8* (1), 61–70.

Burgelman, R. A. "A Process Model of Internal Corporate Venturing in the Diversified Major Firm." *Administrative Science Quarterly*, 1983b, *28* (2), 223–244.

Burns, T., and Stalker, G. M. *The Management of Innovation.* London: Tavistock, 1961.

Butler, R. J., and others. "Organizational Power, Politicking and Paralysis." *Organization and Administrative Sciences*, 1977–78, *8* (4), 45–60.

Butler, R. J., and others. "Strategic Decision Making: Concepts of Content and Process." *International Studies of Management and Organization*, 1979–80, *9* (4), 5–36.

Camerer, C. "Redirecting Policy and Strategy Research: A Manifesto." Unpublished paper, Graduate School of Management, Northwestern University, 1982.

Camerer, C. "Redirecting Research in Business Policy and Strategy." *Strategic Management Journal*, 1984, *5* (4).

Camerer, C., and Fahey, L. "The Regression Paradigm in Strategy Research: A Critical Appraisal and Suggested Directions." In J. Grant (Ed.), *Significant Developments in Business Policy Research.* Greenwich, Conn.: JAI Press, 1985.

Cameron, K. "Measuring Organizational Effectiveness in Institutions of Higher Education." *Administrative Science Quarterly*, 1978, *23* (4), 604–632.

Camillus, J. C. "Corporate Strategy and Executive Action: Transition Stages and Linkage Dimensions." *Academy of Management Review*, 1981, *6* (2), 253–259.

Campbell, D. T. "Variation and Selective Retention in Sociocultural Evolution." *General Systems*, 1969, *16*, 69–85.

Campbell, D. T. "On the Conflicts Between Biological and Social Evolution and Between Psychology and Moral Tradition." *American Psychologist*, 1975, *30*, 1103–1126.

Campbell, J. P. "On the Nature of Organizational Effectiveness." In P. S. Goodman, J. M. Pennings, and Associates, *New Perspectives on Organizational Effectiveness.* San Francisco: Jossey-Bass, 1977.

Carlzon, J., and Hubendick, V. "Kulturrevolutionen i SAS" ["Cultural Revolution in Scandinavian Airlines"]. In L. Arvedson and B. Ryden (Eds.), *Vaga Leda.* Stockholm: Business and Social Research Institute, 1983.

Carroll, G. R. "Dynamic Analysis of Discrete Dependent Variables: A Didactic Essay." *Quality and Quantity,* 1983, *17,* 425-460.

Carroll, G. R., and Delacroix, J. "Organizational Mortality in the Newspaper Industries of Argentina and Ireland: An Ecological Approach." *Administrative Science Quarterly,* 1982, *27* (2), 169-198.

Carter, E. E. "The Behavioral Theory of the Firm and Top Level Corporate Decisions." *Administrative Science Quarterly,* 1971, *16,* 413-428.

Cassirer, E. *An Essay on Man.* Garden City, N.Y.: Anchor Books, 1953.

Casson, M. *The Entrepreneur: An Economic Theory.* Totowa, N.J.: Barnes & Noble, 1982.

Caves, R. E. "Industrial Organization, Corporate Strategy and Structure." *Journal of Economic Literature,* 1980, *18,* 64-92.

Caves, R. E. "Economic Analysis and the Quest for Competitive Advantage." *American Economic Review,* 1984.

Caves, R. E., and Porter, M. E. "From Entry Barriers to Mobility Barriers." *Quarterly Journal of Economics,* 1977, *91,* 241-262.

Chakravarthy, B. S. "Adaptation: A Promising Metaphor for Strategic Management." *Academy of Management Review,* 1982, 7 (1), 35-44.

Chamberlin, T. C. "The Method of Multiple Working Hypotheses." *Journal of Geology,* 1897, *5,* 837-848.

Chandler, A. D. *Strategy and Structure.* Cambridge, Mass.: MIT Press, 1962.

Chandler, A. D. *Strategy and Structure.* (2nd ed.) New York: Cambridge, Mass.: MIT Press, 1969.

Chandler, A. D. *The Visible Hand.* New York: McGraw-Hill, 1977.

Chang, Y. N., and Campo-Flores, F. *Business Policy and Strategy.* Santa Monica, Calif.: Goodyear, 1980.

Channon, D. *The Strategy and Structure of British Enterprise.* Boston: Harvard Business School, 1973.

Charters, W. W., Jr., and Pellegrin, R. J. "Barriers to the Innovation

Process: Four Case Studies of Differential Staffing." *Education Administration Quarterly*, 1972, *9* (1), 3-14.

Chew, S. H., and MacCrimmon, K. R. "Alpha-Nu Choice Theory: A Generalization of Expected Utility Theory." Working paper 669, University of British Columbia, July 1979.

Child, J. "Organizational Structure, Environment and Performance: The Role of Strategic Choice." *Sociology*, 1972, *6*, 1-22.

Christensen, C. R., Berg, N. A., and Salter, M. S. *Policy Formulation and Administration.* (8th ed.) Homewood, Ill.: Irwin, 1980.

Christensen, S. "Decision Making and Socialization." In J. G. March and J. P. Olsen, *Ambiguity and Choice in Organizations.* Bergen, Norway: Universitetsforlaget, 1976.

Clarkson, A. *Toward Effective Strategic Analysis: New Applications of Information Technology.* Boulder, Colo.: Westview Press, 1981.

Clegg, S. *Power, Rule and Domination.* London and Boston: Routledge & Kegan Paul, 1975.

Coase, R. "The Nature of the Firm." *Econometrica*, 1937, *4*, 386-405.

Coch, L., and French, J. P. R. "Overcoming Resistance to Change." *Human Relations*, 1948, *1*, 512-532.

Coffey, W. *303 of the World's Worst Predictions.* New York: Tribeca, 1983.

Cohen, K. J., and Cyert, R. M. "Strategy: Formulation, Implementation, and Monitoring." *Journal of Business*, 1973, *46* (3), 349-367.

Cohen, M. D., and March, J. G. *Leadership and Ambiguity: The American College President.* New York: McGraw-Hill, 1974.

Cohen, M. D., March, J. G., and Olsen, J. P. "A Garbage Can Model of Organizational Choice." *Administrative Science Quarterly*, 1972, *17*, 1-25.

Cohen, M. D., March, J. G., and Olsen, J. P. "People, Problems, Solutions and the Ambiguity of Relevance." In J. G. March and J. P. Olsen, *Ambiguity and Choice in Organizations.* Bergen, Norway: Universitetsforlaget, 1976.

Colignon, R., and Cray, D. "Critical Organizations." *Organization Studies*, 1980, *1* (3), 349-366.

Coser, L. *The Functions of Social Conflict*. New York: Routledge & Kegan Paul, 1959.

Cray, D., and others. "Sporadic, Constricted and Fluid Processes: Three Empirical Types of Strategic Decision Making in Organizations." Unpublished manuscript, University of Bradford, England, 1983.

Crozier, M. *The Bureaucratic Phenomenon*. London: Tavistock, 1964.

Crozier, M. "Comparing Structures and Comparing Games." In G. Hofstede and M. S. Kassem (Eds.), *European Contributions to Organization Theory*. Amsterdam: Van Gorcum, 1976.

Crozier, M., and Friedberg, E. *Actors and Systems*. Chicago: University of Chicago Press, 1980.

Crozier, M., Normann, R., and Tardy, G. "L'innovation dans les services" ["Innovation in the Service Industry"]. Paris: *Mission á l'Innovation*, Rapport no. 8, 1982.

Cyert, R. M., and March, J. G. *A Behavioral Theory of the Firm*. Englewood Cliffs, N.J.: Prentice-Hall, 1963.

Cyert, R. M., Simon, H. A., and Trow, D. B. "Observation of a Business Decision." *Journal of Business*, 1956, *29*, 237-248.

Dahl, R. A., and Lindblom, C. E. *Politics, Economics, and Welfare*. Chicago: University of Chicago Press, 1976.

Danielsson, C. *Studier i företags tillväxtförlopp eller Historien om Gox, Fox, Pox och de fyra telefondirektörerna [Studies in the Growth of Corporations, on the History of Gox, Fox, Pox and the Four Telephone Corporation Vice-Presidents]*. Stockholm: SIAR Dokumentation AB, 1974.

Davis, O. A., Dempster, M. A. H., and Wildavsky, A. "A Theory of the Budgeting Process." *American Political Science Review*, 1966, *60*, 529-547.

Deal, T. E., and Kennedy, A. A. *Corporate Cultures: The Rites and Rituals of Corporate Life*. Reading, Mass.: Addison-Wesley, 1982.

DIO International Research Team. "A Contingency Model of Participative Decision Making: An Analysis of Fifty-Six Decisions in Three Dutch Organizations." *Journal of Occupational Psychology*, 1983, *56* (1), 1-18.

Ditton, J. *Contrology*. London: Macmillan, 1979.

Donaldson, G., and Lorsch, J. *Decision Making at the Top: The Shaping of Strategic Decision.* New York: Basic Books, 1983.

Downey, H. K., Hellriegel, D., and Slocum, J. W., Jr. "Environmental Uncertainty: The Construct and Its Application." *Administrative Science Quarterly,* 1975, *20,* 613–629.

Downey, H. K., Hellriegel, D., and Slocum, J. W., Jr. "Individual Characteristics as Sources of Perceived Uncertainty." *Human Relations,* 1977, *30,* 161–174.

Downs, A. *Inside Bureaucracy.* Boston: Little, Brown, 1967.

Downs, G. W., Jr., and Mohr, L. B. "Conceptual Issues in the Study of Innovation." *Administrative Science Quarterly,* 1976, *21* (4), 700–714.

Dray, W. "The Historical Explanation of Actions Reconsidered." In S. Hook (Ed.), *Philosophy and History: A Symposium.* New York: New York University Press, 1963.

Drenth, P. J. D., and others. "Participative Decision Making: A Comparative Study." *Industrial Relations,* 1979, *18* (3), 295–309.

Drucker, P. F. *Concept of the Corporation.* New York: John Day, 1946.

Drucker, P. F. *The Effective Executive.* New York: Harper & Row, 1964.

Dubin, R. *Theory Building.* New York: Free Press, 1968.

Dunbar, R. L. M. "Designs for Organizational Control." In P. C. Nystrom and W. H. Starbuck (Eds.), *Handbook of Organizational Design.* Vol. 2: *Remodeling Organizations and Their Environments.* New York: Oxford University Press, 1981.

Dunbar, R. L. M., Dutton, J. M., and Torbert, W. R. "Crossing Mother: Ideological Constraints on Organizational Improvements." *Journal of Management Studies,* 1982, *19,* 91–108.

Dunn, E. S., Jr. *Economic and Social Development: A Process of Social Learning.* Baltimore, Md.: Johns Hopkins University Press, 1971.

Dutton, J. M., and Starbuck, W. H. "Finding Charlie's Run-Time Estimator." In J. M. Dutton and W. H. Starbuck (Eds.), *Computer Simulation of Human Behavior.* New York: Wiley, 1971a.

Dutton, J. M., and Starbuck, W. H. (Eds.). *Computer Simulation and Human Behavior.* New York: Wiley, 1971b.

Dutton, J., Thomas, A., and Butler, J. E. "The History of Progress

Functions as a Managerial Technology." Unpublished manuscript, Graduate School of Business Administration, New York University, October 1983.

Edelman, M. *Political Language: Words That Succeed and Policies That Fail.* New York: Academic Press, 1977.

Edwards, W. "Conservatism in Human Information Processing." In B. Kleinmuntz (Ed.), *Formal Representation of Human Judgment.* New York: Wiley, 1968.

Einstein, A. *Essays in Science.* New York: Philosophical Library, 1934.

Etzioni, A. *The Active Society.* New York: Free Press, 1968.

Etzioni, A. *A Comparative Analysis of Complex Organizations.* New York: Free Press, 1975.

Ferguson, C. R. *Measuring Corporate Strategy.* Homewood, Ill.: Irwin, 1974.

Festinger, L. "A Theory of Social Comparison Processes." *Human Relations,* 1956, *7,* 117-140.

Fischhoff, B., and Beyth, R. " 'I Knew It Would Happen': Remembered Probabilities of Once-Future Things." *Organization Behavior and Human Performance,* 1975, *13,* 1-16.

Fombrun, C. "Strategic Management: Integrating the Human Resource Systems into Strategic Planning." In. R. B. Lamb, *Advances in Strategic Management.* Vol. 2. Greenwich, Conn.: JAI Press, 1983.

Fox, A. *Beyond Contract.* London: Faber, 1974.

Frankenberg, R. J. "Taking the Blame and Passing the Buck, or, the Carpet of Agamemnon." In M. Gluckman (Ed.), *The Allocation of Responsibility.* Manchester, England: Manchester University Press, 1972.

Franklin, J. L. "Characteristics of Successful and Unsuccessful Organization Development." *Journal of Applied Behavioral Science,* 1976, *12* (4), 471-492.

Frederickson, J. W., and Mitchell, T. R. "Strategic Decision Processes: Comprehensiveness and Performance in an Industry with an Unstable Environment." *Academy of Management Journal,* 1984, *27,* n.p.

Freeman, E. *Stakeholder Management.* Marshfield, Mass.: Pitman, 1983.

Freeman, J. H. "The Unit of Analysis in Organizational Research." In M. W. Meyer and Associates, *Environments and Organizations: Theoretical and Empirical Perspectives.* San Francisco: Jossey-Bass, 1978.

French, W. L., and Bell, C. H. *Organization Development.* Englewood Cliffs, N.J.: Prentice-Hall, 1973.

Galbraith, J. R. *Designing Complex Organizations.* Reading, Mass.: Addison-Wesley, 1973.

Galbraith, J. R. *Organization Design.* Reading, Mass.: Addison-Wesley, 1977.

Galbraith, J. R., and Nathanson, D. A. *Strategy Implementation: The Role of Structure and Process.* St. Paul, Minn.: West, 1978.

Gale, B. T., and Branch, B. "Concentration Versus Market Share: Which Determines Performance and Why Does It Matter?" Unpublished working paper. Boston: Strategic Planning Institute, 1979.

Gamson, W. A. "Understanding the Careers of Challenging Groups: A Commentary on Goldstone." *American Journal of Sociology,* 1980, *85* (5), 1043–1060.

Garfinkel, H. *Studies in Ethnomethodology.* Englewood Cliffs, N.J.: Prentice-Hall, 1967.

Geertz, C. *The Interpretation of Cultures.* New York: Basic Books, 1973.

Gellerman, S. W. *Managers and Subordinates.* Hinsdale, Ill.: Dryden Press, 1976.

Gellner, E. A. "Explanations in History." *Proceedings of the Aristotelian Society,* 1956, Suppl. Vol. *30,* 157–176.

George, A. *Presidential Decisionmaking in Foreign Policy: The Effective Use of Information and Advice.* Boulder, Colo.: Westview, 1980.

George, A., and Smoke, R. *Deterrence in American Foreign Policy: Theory and Practice.* New York: Columbia University Press, 1974.

Gergen, K. J. "Toward Generative Theory." *Journal of Personality and Social Psychology,* 1978, *36,* 1344–1360.

Gibbard, A. "Manipulation of Voting Schemes: A General Result." *Econometrica,* 1973, *41,* 587–601.

Giddens, A. *Central Problems in Social Theory*. London: Macmillan, 1979.

Gluck, F. W., Kaufman, S. P., and Walleck, A. S. "Strategic Management for Competitive Advantage." *Harvard Business Review, 58* (4), 154.

Golden, A. S. "Groupthink in Japan Inc." *New York Times Magazine*, Dec. 5, 1982, pp. 132-139.

Golding, D. "Establishing Blissful Clarity in Organizational Life: Managers." *Sociological Review*, 1980, *28*, 763-782.

Goldstone, J. A. "The Weakness of Organization: A New Look at Gamson's *The Strategy of Social Protest*." *American Journal of Sociology*, 1980, *85* (5), 1017-1042.

Goodman, P. S., Pennings, J. M., and Associates. *New Perspectives on Organizational Effectiveness*. San Francisco: Jossey-Bass, 1977.

Grabowski, H. G., and Baxter, N. D. "Rivalry in Industrial Research and Development: An Empirical Study." *Journal of Industrial Economics*, 1973, *21*, 209-235.

Green, Ð., and Conolley, E. "'Groupthink' and Watergate." Paper presented to annual meeting of the American Psychological Association, Washington, D.C.: 1974.

Grinyer, P. H., and Norburn, D. "Strategic Planning in Twenty-One U.K. Companies." *Long Range Planning*, 1974, 7 (4), 80-88.

Grinyer, P. H., and Norburn. D. "Planning for Existing Markets: Perceptions of Executives and Financial Performance." *Journal of the Royal Statistical Society, Series A*, 1975, *138* (1), 70-97.

Grossman, S. J., and Hart, O. "The Costs and Benefits of Ownership: A Theory of Vertical Integration." Unpublished working paper, Department of Economics, University of Chicago, 1984.

Gusfield, J. "The Problems of Generations in an Organization Structure." *Social Forces*, 1957, *35*, 323-330.

Guth, W. D. "Formulating Organization Objectives and Strategy." *Journal of Business Policy*, 1971a, *2* (1), 24-31.

Guth, W. D. "The Growth and Profitability of the Firm: A Managerial Explanation." *Journal of Business Policy*, 1971b, *2* (3), 31-36.

Habermas, J. *Knowledge and Human Interests*. New York: Beacon Press, 1971.

Hafner, D. L. "Bureaucratic Politics and Those Frigging Missiles." *Orbis*, 1977, *21*, 307–333.

Hage, J. *Theories of Organizations: Form, Process and Transformation.* New York: Wiley, 1980.

Hahn, F. H. *On the Notion of Equilibrium in Economics.* Cambridge, England: Cambridge University Press, 1973.

Halberstam, D. *The Best and the Brightest.* New York: Random House, 1972.

Hall, D. J., and Saias, M. A. "Strategy Follows Structure." *Strategic Management Journal*, 1980, *1*, 149–163.

Hall, P. M., and Hewitt, J. P. "The Quasi-Theory of Communication and the Management of Dissent." *Social Problems*, 1970, *18*, 17–27.

Hall, R. I. "A System Pathology of an Organization: The Rise and Fall of the Old *Saturday Evening Post.*" *Administrative Science Quarterly*, 1976, *21*, 185–211.

Halperin, M. *Bureaucratic Politics and Foreign Policy.* Washington, D.C.: Brookings Institution, 1974.

Halperin, M., and Kanter, A. *Readings in American Foreign Policy: A Bureaucratic Perspective.* Boston: Little, Brown, 1973.

Hannan, M. T., and Freeman, J. H. "The Population Ecology of Organizations." *American Journal of Sociology*, 1977, *82* (5), 929–965.

Hardy, C. "The Contribution of Political Science to Organisational Behaviour." Unpublished paper, Faculty of Management, McGill University, 1983.

Harsanyi, J. C. *Bargaining Equilibrium in Games and Social Situations.* Cambridge, England: Cambridge University Press, 1977.

Hart, J. A. "Comparative Cognition: Politics of International Control of the Oceans." In R. M. Axelrod (Ed.), *Structure of Decision: The Cognitive Maps of Political Elites.* Princeton, N.J.: Princeton University Press, 1976.

Hart, J. A. "Cognitive Maps of Three Latin American Policy Makers." *World Politics*, 1977, *30*, 115–140.

Hatvany, N. G., and Gladstein, D. "A Perspective on Group Decision Making." In D. A. Nadler, M. L. Tushman, and N. Hatvany (Eds.), *Approaches to Managing Organizational Behavior.* Boston: Little, Brown, 1982.

Hedberg, B. L. T. "How Organizations Learn and Unlearn." In P. C. Nystrom and W. H. Starbuck (Eds.), *Handbook of Organizational Design*. Vol. 1: *Adapting Organizations to Their Environments*. New York: Oxford University Press, 1981.

Hedberg, B. L. T., and Jönsson, S. A. "Strategy Formulation as a Discontinuous Process." *International Studies of Management and Organization*, 1977, *7*, 89–109.

Hedberg, B. L. T., Nystrom, P. C., and Starbuck, W. H. "Camping on Seesaws: Prescriptions for a Self-Designing Organization." *Administrative Science Quarterly*, 1976, *21*, 41–65.

Helson, H. "Adaptation-Level as a Basis for a Quantitative Theory of Frames of Reference." *Psychological Review*, 1948, *55*, 294–313.

Helson, H. "Current Trends and Issues in Adaptation-Level Theory." *American Psychologist*, 1964, *19*, 23–68.

Hempel, C. "The Functions of General Laws in History." In P. Gardner (Ed.), *Theories of History*. Glencoe, Ill.: Free Press, 1959.

Hempel, C. "Reasons and Covering Laws in Historical Explanations." In S. Hook (Ed.), *Philosophy and History: A Symposium*. New York: New York University Press, 1963.

Henderson, B. D. *Henderson on Corporate Strategy*. Cambridge, Mass.: Abt Books, 1979.

Herold, D. M. "Long-Range Planning and Organizational Performance: A Cross-Valuation Study." *Academy of Management Journal*, 1972, *15*, 91–102.

Hersch, S. *The Price of Power*. New York: Simon & Schuster, 1983.

Hewitt, J. P., and Hall, P. M. "Social Problems, Problematic Situations, and Quasi-Theories." *American Sociological Review*, 1973, *38*, 367–374.

Hewitt, J. P., and Stokes, R. "Disclaimers." *American Sociological Review*, 1975, *40*, 1–11.

Hickson, D. J., and others. "A Strategic Contingencies Theory of Intra-Organizational Power." *Administrative Science Quarterly*, 1971, *16*, 216–229.

Hickson, D. J., and others. "Decisive Coalitions." In B. King, S. Streufort, and F. E. Fiedler (Eds.), *Managerial Control and Organizational Democracy*. New York: Wiley, 1978.

Hickson, D. J., and others. "Organization as Power." In L. L. Cummings and B. M. Staw (Eds.), *Research in Organizational Behavior.* Vol. 3. Greenwich, Conn.: JAI Press, 1981.

Hickson, D. J., and others. *Top Decisions: Strategic Decision Making in Organizations.* San Francisco: Jossey-Bass; Oxford, England: Martin Robertson, 1985.

Hilsman, R. *To Move a Nation.* New York: Doubleday, 1967.

Hinings, C. R., and others. "Structural Conditions of Intraorganizational Power." *Administrative Science Quarterly,* 1974, *19* (1), 22–44.

Hirsch, P. "Organizational Analysis and Industrial Sociology: An Instance of Cultural Lag." *American Sociologist,* 1975, *10,* 3–12.

Hirschleifer, J. "The Firm's Cost Function: A Successful Reconstruction." *Journal of Business,* 1962, *35,* 235–253.

Hofer, C. W. "Turnaround Strategies." *Journal of Business Strategy,* 1980, *1* (1), 19–31.

Hofer, C. W., and Schendel, D. E. *Strategy Formulation: Analytical Concepts.* St. Paul, Minn.: West, 1978.

Hoffman, L. R. "Group Problem Solving." In L. Berkowitz (Ed.), *Advances in Experimental Social Psychology.* Vol. 2. New York: Academic Press, 1965.

Hofstede, G. H. *The Game of Budget Control.* Assen, Netherlands: Van Gorcum, 1967.

Hollis, M. *Models of Man.* New York: Cambridge University Press, 1977.

Homans, G. *The Human Group.* San Diego, Calif.: Harcourt Brace Jovanovich, 1950.

Homans, G. *Social Behaviour: Its Elementary Forms.* London: Routledge & Kegan Paul, 1961.

Hopwood, A. G. "An Empirical Study of the Role of Accounting Data in Performance Evaluation." *Empirical Research in Accounting: Selected Studies, Supplement to the Journal of Accounting Research,* 1972, *10,* 156–182.

Horowitz, J. H. "Strategic Control: A New Task for Management." *Long Range Planning,* 1979, *12* (3), 2–7.

Howard, R. "The Foundations of Decision Analysis." *IEEE Transactions on Systems Science and Cybernetics,* 1968, *4* (3), 1–9.

Hrebiniak, L. G., and Joyce, W. F. *Implementing Strategy.* New York: Macmillan, 1983.

Huff, A. S. "Industry Influences on Strategy Reformulation." *Strategic Management Journal,* 1982, *3,* 119–131

Hummel, R. P. *The Bureaucratic Experience.* New York: St. Martin's Press, 1982.

IDE International Research Group. "Industrial Democracy in Europe: Differences and Similarities Across Countries and Hierarchies." *Organization Studies,* 1981, *2* (2), 113–130.

Janis, I. L. *Victims of Groupthink.* Boston: Houghton Mifflin, 1972.

Janis, I. L. *Groupthink: Psychological Studies of Policy Decisions and Fiascoes.* (Rev. and enlarged ed. of *Victims of Groupthink,* 1972) Boston: Houghton Mifflin, 1982a.

Janis, I. L. "Counteracting the Adverse Effects of Concurrence-Seeking in Policy Planning Groups: Theory and Research Perspectives." In H. Brandstatter, J. H. Davis, and G. Stocker-Kreichgauer (Eds.), *Group Decision Making.* New York: Academic Press, 1982b.

Janis, I. L., and Mann, L. *Decision-Making: A Psychological Analysis of Conflict, Choice and Commitment.* New York: Free Press, 1977.

Jaques, E. *The Changing Culture of a Factory.* London: Tavistock, 1951.

Jelinek, M. *Institutionalizing Innovation: A Study of Organizational Learning.* New York: Praeger, 1979.

Jemison, D. B. "The Contributions of Administrative Behavior to Strategic Management." *Academy of Management Review,* 1981, *6,* 601–608.

Johnson, P. E. "The Expert Mind: A New Challenge for the Information Scientist." In M. A. Bemmelmans (Ed.), *Beyond Productivity: Information Systems Development for Organizational Effectiveness.* Amsterdam: North-Holland, 1983.

Johnston, A. V. "Organisation Development and the Natural Process of Change and Its Management." Unpublished paper, 1978.

Jones, G. R. "Transaction Costs, Property Rights, and Organizational Culture: An Exchange Perspective." *Administrative Science Quarterly*, 1983, *28* (3), 454–467.

Jönsson, S. A., and Lundin, R. A. "Myths and Wishful Thinking as Management Tools." In P. C. Nystrom and W. H. Starbuck (Eds.), *Prescriptive Models of Organizations*. Amsterdam: North-Holland, 1977.

Kahn, R. L., and others. *Organizational Stress: Studies in Role Conflict and Ambiguity*. New York: Wiley, 1964.

Kahneman, D., and Tversky, A. "Prospect Theory: Analysis of Decision Under Risk." *Econometrica*, 1979, *47*, 263–291.

Kaplan, A. *The Conduct of Inquiry*. San Francisco: Chandler, 1964.

Karpik, L. "Les Politiques et les Logiques d'Action de la Grande Entreprise Industrielle" ["The Politics and the Action Logics of the Large Industrial Corporation"]. *Sociologie du Travail*, 1972, *14*, 82–105.

Katz, D., and Kahn, R. L. *The Social Psychology of Organizations*. New York: Wiley, 1966.

Kaufman, H. *The Forest Ranger*. Baltimore: Johns Hopkins University Press, 1960.

Keeney, R. L., and Raiffa, H. *Decisions with Multiple Objectives: Preferences and Value Tradeoffs*. New York: Wiley, 1976.

Kemeny, J., and Snell, J. L. *Mathematical Models in the Social Sciences*. Cambridge, Mass.: MIT Press, 1972.

Kennedy, R. F. *Thirteen Days*. New York: Norton, 1969.

Kepner, C. H., and Tregoe, B. B. *The Rational Manager*. New York: McGraw-Hill, 1965.

Kervasdoué, J., and Kimberly, J. "Are Organization Structures Culture Free?" In G. W. England and others (Eds.), *Organizational Functioning in a Cross Cultural Perspective*. Kent, Ohio: Kent State University Press, 1979.

Kieser, A., and Kubicek, H. *Organisationstheorien I*. Stuttgart: Verlag W. Kohlhammer, 1978a.

Kieser, A., and Kubicek, H. *Organisationstheorien II*. Stuttgart: Verlag W. Kohlhammer, 1978b.

Kiesler, C. A. *The Psychology of Commitment*. New York: Academic Press, 1971.

King, W. R., and Cleland, D. I. *Strategic Planning and Policy*. New York: Van Nostrand, 1978.

Kirsch, W., and Kutschker, M. "Marketing and Buying Decisions in Industrial Markets." In M. Irle and L. B. Katz (Eds.), *Studies in Decision Making*. Berlin and New York: Walter de Gruyter, 1982.

Kirzner, I. M. *Competition and Entrepreneurship*. Chicago: University of Chicago Press, 1973.

Klein, B., Crawford, R. G., and Alchian, A. A. "Vertical Integration, Appropriable Rents, and the Competitive Contracting Process." *Journal of Law and Economics*, 1978, *21*, 297-326.

Kleinginna, P. R., Jr., and Kleinginna, A. M. "A Categorized List of Motivation Definitions, with a Suggestion for a Consensual Definition." *Motivation and Emotion*, 1981, *5* (3), 263-289.

Kolb, D., and Frohman, A. L. "An Organization Development Approach to Consulting." *Sloan Management Review*, 1970, *12* (1), 16-27.

Kreps, D. M., and Wilson, R. "Reputation and Imperfect Information." *Journal of Economic Theory*, 1982a, *27*, 245-252.

Kreps, D. M., and Wilson, R. "Sequential Equilibria." *Econometrica*, 1982b, *50* (4), 863-894.

Kudla, R. J. "The Effects of Strategic Planning on Common Stock Returns." *Academy of Management Journal*, 1980, *23*, 5-20.

Kuhn, T. S. *The Structure of Scientific Revolution*. Chicago: University of Chicago Press, 1962.

Kuhn, T. S. *The Structure of Scientific Revolution*. (2nd ed.) Chicago: University of Chicago Press, 1970.

Lambert, P. "Selecting Japanese Management Practices for Import." *Personnel Management*, January 1982, 38-41.

Langer, E. J. "The Illusion of Control." *Journal of Personality and Social Psychology*, 1975, *32*, 311-328.

Langer, E. J., and Roth, J. "Heads I Win, Tails It's Chance: The Illusion of Control as a Function of the Sequence Outcomes in a Purely Chance Task." *Journal of Personality and Social Psychology*, 1975, *32*, 951-955.

Lave, C. A., and March, J. G. *An Introduction to Models in the Social Sciences*. New York: Harper & Row, 1975.

Lawler, E. E. III, and Hackman, J. R. "Impact of Employee Participation in the Development of Pay Incentive Plans: A Field Experiment." *Journal of Applied Psychology*, 1969, *53*, 467-471.

Lawrence, P. R. "The Organization and Environment Perspective."

In A. H. Van de Ven and W. Joyce (Eds.), *Perspectives on Organization Design and Behavior.* New York: Wiley-Interscience, 1981.

Lawrence, P. R., and Dyer, D. *Renewing American Industry.* New York: Free Press, 1983.

Lawrence, P. R., and Lorsch, J. W. *Organization and Environment: Managing Differentiation and Integration.* Cambridge, Mass.: Harvard University Press, 1967.

Leach, E. R. "Anthropological Aspects of Language: Animal Categories and Verbal Abuse." In E. H. Lenneberg (Ed.), *New Directions in the Study of Language.* Cambridge, Mass.: MIT Press, 1964.

Lewin, K. "Group Decision and Social Change." In T. Newcomb and E. Hartley (Eds.), *Readings in Social Psychology.* New York: Holt, Rinehart and Winston, 1947.

Lewin, R. "Santa Rosalia Was a Goat." *Science,* 1983a, *221* (4611), 636–639.

Lewin, R. "Predators and Hurricanes Change Ecology." *Science,* 1983b, *221* (4612), 737–740.

Liebenstein, H. *Beyond Economic Man.* Cambridge, Mass.: Harvard University Press, 1976.

Lindblom, C. E. "The Science of Muddling Through." *Public Administration Review,* 1959, *19*, 79–88.

Lindblom, C. E. *The Intelligence of Democracy.* New York: Free Press, 1965.

Lippman, S. A., and Rumelt, R. P. "Uncertain Imitability: An Analysis of Interfirm Differences in Efficiency Under Competition." *Bell Journal of Economics,* 1982, *13* (2), 418–438.

Loftus, E. F. "The Malleability of Human Memory." *American Scientist,* 1979, *67*, 312–320.

Longley, J., and Pruitt, D. G. "Groupthink: A Critique of Janis's Theory." In L. Wheeler (Ed.), *Review of Personality and Social Psychology.* Beverly Hills, Calif.: Sage, 1980.

Lorange, P. *Corporate Planning: An Executive Viewpoint.* Englewood Cliffs, N.J.: Prentice-Hall, 1980.

Lorange, P. "Designing a Strategic Planning System." In T. S. Dudick and R. V. Gorski, *Handbook of Business Planning and Budgeting.* New York: Van Nostrand, 1983.

Lorange, P. "Organizational Structure and Management Processes: Implications for Effective Strategic Management." In W. Guth (Ed.), *Handbook on Strategic Management.* New York: Van Nostrand, 1984a.

Lorange, P. "Implementing Strategic Planning at Two Philippine Companies." *Wharton Annual,* 1984b, *8,* 165–176.

Lorange, P. *The CEO's Perspective on Strategic Planning.* Reading, Mass.: Addison-Wesley, 1985.

Lorange, P., and Murphy D. C. "Strategic and Human Resources: Concepts and Practice." *Human Resource Management,* 1983, *22* (1/2), 111–135.

Lorange, P., and Murphy, D.C. "Considerations in Implementing Strategic Control." *Journal of Business Strategy,* 1984, *4* (4), 27–35.

Lorange, P., and Vancil, R. F. *Strategic Planning Systems.* Englewood Cliffs, N.J.: Prentice-Hall, 1977.

Lukes, S. *Power: A Radical View.* London: Macmillan, 1974.

Lyles, M. A., and Mitroff, I. I. "Organizational Problem Formulation: An Empirical Study." *Administrative Science Quarterly,* 1980, *25,* 102–119.

McCall, M. W., Jr. "Making Sense with Nonsense: Helping Frames of Reference Clash." In P. C. Nystrom and W. H. Starbuck (Eds.), *Prescriptive Models of Organizations.* Amsterdam: North-Holland, 1977.

MacCrimmon, K. R. "Elements of Decision." In W. Goldberg (Ed.), *Behavioral Approaches to Modern Management.* Gothenburg, Sweden: BAS, 1970.

MacCrimmon, K. R. "Theories of Collective Decision." Paper presented to the International Conference on Subjective Probability, Utility and Decision Making, Rome, Italy, 1973.

MacCrimmon, K. R. "Essence of Strategy: Means and Conditions." In J. Grant (Ed.), *Research in Strategic Management.* Chicago: JAI Press, 1984.

MacCrimmon, K. R., and Larsson, S. "Utility Theory: Axioms Versus Paradoxes." In M. Allais and O. Hagen (Eds.), *Expected Utility Theory and the Allais Paradox.* Dordrecht, Netherlands: Reidel, 1979.

McGregor, D. *The Human Side of Enterprise.* New York: McGraw-Hill, 1960.

Machiavelli, N. *The Prince.* (G. Bull, Trans.) Harmondsworth, England: Penguin, 1961. (Originally published 1515.)

McKelvey, B. *Organizational Systematics.* Los Angeles: University of California Press, 1982.

MacMillan, I. C., Hambrick, D. C., and Day, D. "The Product Portfolio and Profitability: A PIMS-Based Analysis of Industrial-Product Businesses." *Academy of Management Journal,* 1982, *25,* 733-755.

McPherson, M. "An Ecology of Affiliation." *American Sociological Review,* 1983, *48* (4), 519-532.

Magaziner, I., and Reich, R. B. *Minding America's Business: The Decline and Rise of the American Economy.* New York: Harcourt Brace Jovanovich, 1982.

Maier, N. R. F. *Problem-Solving Discussions and Conferences: Leadership Methods and Skills.* New York: McGraw-Hill, 1963.

Maier, N. R. F. "Group Problem Solving." *Psychological Review,* 1967, *74,* 239-249.

Malik, Z. A., and Karger, D. W. "Does Long-Range Planning Improve Company Performance?" *Management Review,* 1975, *64* (9), 27-31.

Mallory, G. R., and others. "Implanted Decision-Making: American Owned Firms in Britain." *Journal of Management Studies,* 1983, *20* (2), 191-211.

Manning, P. K. "Rules in Organizational Context: Narcotics Law Enforcement in Two Settings." *Sociological Quarterly,* 1977, *18,* 44-61.

Marakon Associates. "The Role of Finance in Strategic Planning." Paper presented to *Business Week* Conference, New York, 1980.

March, J. G. "The Technology of Foolishness." In H. J. Leavitt and L. R. Pondy (Eds.), *Readings in Managerial Psychology.* (2nd ed.) Chicago: University of Chicago Press, 1973.

March, J. G. "Bounded Rationality, Ambiguity, and the Engineering of Choice." *Bell Journal of Economics,* 1978, *9* (2), 587-608.

March, J. G. "Decision Making Perspectives." In A. H. Van der Ven and W. F. Joyce (Eds.), *Perspectives on Organization Design and Behavior.* New York: Wiley-Interscience, 1981a.

March, J. G. "Decisions in Organizations and Theories of Choice." In A. H. Van de Ven and W. F. Joyce (Eds.), *Perspectives on Organization Design and Behavior.* New York: Wiley-Interscience, 1981b.

March, J. G. "Footnotes to Organizational Change." *Administrative Science Quarterly,* 1981c, *26* (4), 563–577.

March, J. G., and Olsen, J. P. *Ambiguity and Choice in Organizations.* Bergen, Norway: Universitetsforlaget, 1976.

March, J. G., and Olsen, J. P. "Organizing Political Life: What Administrative Reorganization Tells Us About Governing." Paper presented to the International Political Science Association's World Congress, Rio de Janeiro, August 1982.

March, J. G., and Simon, H. A. *Organizations.* New York: Wiley, 1958.

Marris, R. *The Economic Theory of Managerial Capitalism.* New York: Free Press, 1964; London: Macmillan, 1966.

Mason, R. O. "A Dialectical Approach to Strategic Planning." *Management Science,* 1969, *15* (8), 403–414.

Mason, R. O., and Mitroff, I. I. "Complexity: Nature of Real World Problems." In R. O. Mason and I. I. Mitroff, *Challenging Strategic Planning Assumptions: Theory, Cases, and Techniques.* New York: Wiley-Interscience, 1981a.

Mason, R. O., and Mitroff, I. I. *Challenging Strategic Planning Assumptions: Theory, Cases, and Techniques.* New York: Wiley-Interscience, 1981b.

Mason, R. O., and Mitroff, I. I. "Toward a Theory of Practice." In R. O. Mason and I. I. Mitroff, *Challenging Strategic Planning Assumptions: Theory, Cases, and Techniques.* New York: Wiley-Interscience, 1981c.

Mayr, E. *Animal Species and Evolution.* Cambridge, England: Belknap, 1966.

Mehan, H. "Practical Decision Making in Naturally Occurring Institutional Settings." In B. Rogoff and J. C. Lave (Eds.), *Everyday Cognition: Its Development in Social Context.* Cambridge, Mass.: Harvard University Press, 1984.

Metcalf, L. "Designing Precarious Partnerships." In P. C. Nystrom and W. H. Starbuck (Eds.), *Handbook of Organizational Design.*

Vol. 1: *Adapting Organizations to Their Environments.* New York: Oxford University Press, 1981.

Meyer, J. W., and Rowan, B. "Institutionalized Organizations: Formal Structure as Myth and Ceremony." *American Journal of Sociology,* 1977, *83,* 340–363.

Meyer, M. W., and Associates. *Environments and Organizations: Theoretical and Empirical Perspectives.* San Francisco: Jossey-Bass, 1978.

Middleton, D. "Going the Military Route." *New York Times Magazine,* May 17, 1981, pp. 103–112.

Mihalka, M. "Soviet Strategic Deception, 1955–1981." *Journal of Strategic Studies,* 1982, *5,* 40–93.

Miles, R. E., and Snow, C. C. *Organizational Strategy, Structure, and Processes.* New York: MacGraw-Hill, 1978.

Miles, R. E., Snow, C. C., and Pfeffer, J. "Organization-Environment: Concepts and Issues." *Industrial Relations,* 1974, *13,* 244–264.

Miles, R. H. *Macro Organizational Behavior.* Santa Monica, Calif: Goodyear, 1980a.

Miles, R. H. "Organization Boundary Roles." In C. Cooper and R. Payne (Eds.), *Current Concerns in Occupational Stress.* London: Wiley, 1980b.

Miles, R. H., and Cameron, K. S. "Coffin Nails and Corporate Strategies: A Quarter Century View of Organizational Adaptation to Environment in the U.S. Tobacco Industry." Working paper no. 3, Research Program on Business and Government Relations, Yale School of Organization and Management, Yale University, 1977.

Miles, R. H., and Cameron, K. S. *Coffin Nails and Corporate Strategy.* Englewood Cliffs, N.J.: Prentice-Hall, 1982.

Milgram, S. *Obedience to Authority.* New York: Harper & Row, 1974.

Milgrom, P., and Roberts, J. "Predation, Reputation and Entry Deterrence." *Journal of Economic Theory,* 1982, *27,* 280–312.

Miller, D. "Evolution and Revolution: A Quantum View of Structural Change in Organizations." *Journal of Management Studies,* 1982, *19,* 131–151.

Miller, D., and Friesen, P. "Momentum and Revolution in Organizational Adaptation." *Academy of Management Journal*, 1980a, *23*, 591-614.

Miller, D., and Friesen, P. "Archetypes of Organizational Transition." *Administrative Science Quarterly*, 1980b, *25* (2), 268-299.

Miller, D., and Friesen, P. "Structural Change and Performance: Quantum Versus Piecemeal—Incremental Approaches." *Academy of Management Journal*, 1982, *25* (4), 67-92.

Miller, E. J., and Rice, A. K. *Systems of Organization: The Control of Task and Sentient Boundaries.* London: Tavistock, 1967.

Miller, G. A. "The Magical Number Seven, Plus or Minus Two: Some Limits on Our Capacity for Processing Information." *Psychological Review*, 1956, *63*, 81-97.

Miller, G. A., Galanter, E., and Pribam, K. *Plans and the Structure of Behavior.* New York: Holt, Rinehart and Winston, 1960.

Mills, C. W. "Situated Actions and Vocabularies of Motive." *American Sociological Review*, 1940, *5*, 904-913.

Mintzberg, H. "Strategy Making in Three Modes." *California Management Review*, 1973a, *16*, (2), 44-53.

Mintzberg, H. *The Nature of Managerial Work.* New York: Harper & Row, 1973b.

Mintzberg, H. "Patterns in Strategy Formation." *Management Science*, 1978, *24* (9), 934-948.

Mintzberg, H. *The Structuring of Organizations.* Englewood Cliffs, N.J.: Prentice-Hall, 1979.

Mintzberg, H., Rasinghani, D., and Théorêt, A. "The Structure of 'Unstructured' Decision Processes." *Administrative Science Quarterly*, 1976, *21*, 246-275.

Mintzberg, H., and Waters, J. A. "Tracking Strategy in an Entrepreneurial Firm." Working paper 80-82. Faculty of Management, McGill University, 1980.

Mischel, T. "Psychology and Explanations of Human Behavior." In N. Care and C. Landesman (Eds.), *Readings in the Theory of Action.* Bloomington: Indiana University Press, 1968.

Mitroff, I. I. *Stakeholders of the Organizational Mind: Toward a New View of Organizational Policy Making.* San Francisco: Jossey-Bass, 1983.

Mitroff, I. I., and Kilmann, R. H. "The Stories Managers Tell: A New Tool for Organizational Problem Solving." *Management Review*, 1975, *64* (7), 18-28.

Mohr, L. B. "Organizations, Decisions and Courts." *Law and Society Review,* 1976, *10* (4), 621-642.

Mohr, L. B. *Explaining Organizational Behavior: The Limits and Possibilities of Theory and Research.* San Francisco: Jossey-Bass, 1982.

Monteverde, K., and Teece, D. J. "Supplier Switching Costs and Vertical Integration in the U.S. Automobile Industry." Research paper no. 575, Graduate School of Business, Stanford University, 1980.

Mook, D. G. "In Defense of External Invalidity." *American Psychologist,* 1983, *38* (4), 379-387.

Morgan, G. "The Schismatic Metaphor and Its Implications for Organizational Analysis." *Organizational Studies,* 1981, *2* (1), 23-44.

Mumford, E., and Pettigrew, A. M. *Implementing Strategic Decisions.* London: Longman, 1975.

Murray, E. A. "Strategic Choice as a Negotiated Outcome." *Management Science,* 1978, *24* (9), 960-972.

Nadler, D. A., and Tushman, M. L. "A Diagnostic Model for Organizational Behavior." In J. R. Hackman, E. E. Lawler, and L. W. Porter (Eds.), *Perspectives on Behavior in Organizations.* New York: McGraw-Hill, 1977.

Nadler, D. A., and Tushman, M. L. "A Model for Diagnosing Organizational Behavior: Applying a Congruence Perspective." In D. A. Nadler, M. L. Tushman, and N. G. Hatvany, *Managing Organizations: Readings and Cases.* Boston: Little, Brown, 1982.

Nagel, E. *The Structure of Science.* New York: Harcourt Brace Jovanovich, 1961.

Narayanan, V. K., and Fahey, L. "The Micro Politics of Strategic Formulation." *Academy of Management Review,* 1982, *7* (1), 25-34.

Naylor, T. H. (Ed.). *The Politics of Corporate Planning and Modeling.* Oxford, Ohio: Planning Executives Institute, 1978.

Nelson, R. R., and Winter, S. G. *An Evolutionary Theory of Economic Change.* Cambridge, Mass.: Harvard University Press, 1982.

Newell, A., and Simon, H. A. *Human Problem Solving.* Englewood Cliffs, N.J.: Prentice-Hall, 1972.

Newman, W. H. *Constructive Control.* Englewood Cliffs, N.J.: Prentice-Hall, 1975.

Newman, W. H., and Logan, J. P. *Management of Expanding Enterprises.* New York: Columbia University Press, 1955.

Newman, W. H., and Logan, J. P. *Business Policies and Management.* Cincinnati: South-Western, 1959.

Newman, W. H., and Logan, J. P. *Strategy, Policy, and Central Management.* (8th ed.) Cincinnati: South-Western, 1981.

Nisbett, R. E., and Ross, L. *Human Inference: Strategies and Shortcomings in Social Judgment.* Englewood Cliffs, N.J.: Prentice-Hall, 1980.

Nisbett, R. E., and Wilson, T. D. "Telling More Than We Can Know: Verbal Reports on Mental Processes." *Psychological Review,* 1977, *84,* 231–259.

Normann, R. "Organizational Innovativeness: Product Variation and Reorientation." *Administrative Science Quarterly,* 1971, *16* (2), 203–215.

Normann, R. *Management for Growth.* London: Wiley, 1977.

Normann, R. *Effektiva servicesystem. Serviceföretag och kund i framgangsrik samverkan [Effective Service Systems: Service Corporations and Customers in Positive Cooperation].* Stockholm: Servicesamhället, 1980.

Normann, R. *Service Management: Strategy and Leadership in Service Businesses.* New York: Wiley, 1984.

O'Reilly, C. A. III. "The Use of Information in Organizational Decision Making: A Model and Some Propositions." In L. L. Cummings and B. M. Staw (Eds.), *Research in Organizational Behavior.* Vol. 5. Greenwich, Conn.: JAI Press, 1983.

Ouchi, W. G. "Markets, Bureaucracies and Clans." *Administrative Science Quarterly,* 1980, *25* (1), 129–141.

Ouchi, W. G. *Theory Z: How American Business Can Meet the Japanese Challenge.* Reading, Mass.: Addison-Wesley, 1981.

Ouchi, W. G., and Price, R. L. "Hierarchies, Clans, and Theory Z: 'A New Perspective on Organizational Development.'" In J. R. Hackman, E. E. Lawler III, and L. W. Porter (Eds.), *Perspectives on Behavior in Organizations.* (Rev. ed.) New York: McGraw-Hill, 1983.

Padgett, J. F. "Bounded Rationality in Budgetary Research." *American Political Science Review,* 1980, *74,* 354–372.

Pascale, R. T. "Perspectives on Strategy: The Real Story Behind Honda's Success." *California Management Review,* 1984, *26,* 3.

Payne, R. L., and Pugh, D. S. "Organizational Structure and Climate." In M. D. Dunnette (Ed.), *Handbook of Industrial and Organizational Psychology.* Chicago: Rand McNally, 1976.

Pelz, D. C., and Andrews, F. M. *Scientists in Organizations.* New York: Wiley, 1966.

Pennings, J. M. "Corporate Social Responsibility: A Must or a Virtue." *New Catholic World,* 1980, *223* (1338), 260–262.

Pennings, J. M. "Strategically Interdependent Organizations." In P. C. Nystrom and W. H. Starbuck (Eds.), *Handbook of Organizational Design.* Vol. I: *Adapting Organizations to Their Environments.* New York: Oxford University Press, 1981.

Pennings, J. M. *Implementing Strategy.* Marshfield, Mass.: Pitman, 1985.

Pennings, J. M., and Goodman, P. S. "Toward a Workable Framework." In P. S. Goodman, J. M. Pennings, and Associates, *New Perspectives on Organizational Effectiveness.* San Francisco: Jossey-Bass, 1977.

"Periscope." *Newsweek,* Aug. 8, 1983, p. 19.

Peters, R. S. *The Concept of Motivation.* (Rev. ed.) London: Routledge & Kegan Paul, 1969.

Peters, T. J. "Symbols, Patterns, and Settings: An Optimistic Case for Getting Things Done." *Organizational Dynamics,* 1978, *7* (2), 3–23.

Peters, T. J. "Putting Excellence into Management." *Business Week,* 1980, *2646,* 196–197, 200, 205.

Peters, T. J. "Strategy Follows Structure: Developing Distinctive Skills." *California Management Review,* 1984, *26* (3).

Peters, T. J., and Waterman, R. H., Jr. *In Search of Excellence: Lessons from America's Best-Run Companies.* New York: Harper & Row, 1982.

Pettigrew, A. M. "Information Control as a Power Resource." *Sociology,* 1972, *6,* 187–204.

Pettigrew, A. M. *The Politics of Organisational Decision Making.* London: Tavistock, 1973.

Pettigrew, A. M. "Strategic Aspects of the Management of Specialist Activity." *Personnel Review,* 1975a, *4,* 5–13.

Pettigrew, A. M. "Towards a Political Theory of Organizational Intervention." *Human Relations,* 1975b, *28* (3), 191–208.

Pettigrew, A. M. "Strategy Formulation as a Political Process." *International Studies of Management and Organization,* 1977, 7 (2), 78–87.

Pettigrew, A. M. "On Studying Organizational Cultures." *Administrative Science Quarterly,* 1979, *24,* 570–581.

Pettigrew, A. M. "The Politics of Organizational Change." In N. B. Anderson (Ed.), *The Human Side of Information Processing.* Amsterdam: North-Holland, 1980.

Pettigrew, A. M. "Patterns of Managerial Response as Organisations Move from Rich to Poor Environments." *Educational Management Administration,* 1983, *2,* 104–114.

Pettigrew, A. M. *Context and Politics in Organizational Change.* Englewood Cliffs, N.J.: Prentice-Hall; Oxford, England: Basil Blackwell, 1984.

Pettigrew, A. M. *The Awakening Giant: Continuity and Change in Imperial Chemical Industries.* Oxford, England: Basil Blackwell, 1985.

Pfeffer, J. "The Micropolitics of Organizations." In M. W. Meyer and Associates, *Environments and Organizations: Theoretical and Empirical Perspectives.* San Francisco: Jossey-Bass, 1978.

Pfeffer, J. "Four Laws of Organizational Research." In A. H. Van de Ven and W. F. Joyce (Eds.), *Perspectives on Organization Design and Behavior.* New York: Wiley-Interscience, 1981a.

Pfeffer, J. "Management as Symbolic Action: The Creation and Maintenance of Organizational Paradigms." In L. L. Cummings and B. M. Staw (Eds.), *Research in Organizational Behavior.* Vol. 3. Greenwich, Conn.: JAI Press, 1981b.

Pfeffer, J. *Power in Organizations.* Marshfield, Mass.: Pitman, 1981c.

Pfeffer, J. *Organizational and Organization Theory.* Marshfield, Mass.: Pitman, 1982.

Pfeffer, J., and Salancik, G. R. *The External Control of Organizations: A Resource Dependence Perspective.* New York: Harper & Row, 1978.

Platt, J. R. "Strong Inference." *Science,* 1964, *146* (3642), 347–349.

Poggi, G. "A Main Theme of Contemporary Sociological Analysis:

It Achievements and Eliminations." *British Journal of Sociology*, 1965, *16*, 283-294.

Polanyi, M. *Knowing and Being*. London: Routledge & Kegan Paul; Chicago, University of Chicago Press, 1969.

Popper, K. *The Logic of Scientific Discovery*. New York: Basic Books, 1959.

Popper, K. *Conjectures and Refutations: The Growth of Scientific Knowledge*. New York: Basic Books, 1962.

Porter, L. W., and Roberts, K. H. "Communication in Organizations." In M. D. Dunnette (Ed.), *Handbook of Industrial and Organizational Psychology*. Chicago: Rand McNally, 1976.

Porter, M. E. "The Structure Within Industries and Companies' Performance." *Review of Economics and Statistics*, 1979, *61* (2), 214-226.

Porter, M. E. *Competitive Strategy: Techniques for Analyzing Industries and Competitors*. New York: Free Press, 1980.

Porter, M. E. "The Contributions of Industrial Organizations to Strategic Management." *Academy of Management Review*, 1981, *6* (4), 609-620.

Pugh, D. S., and others. "The Context of Organization Structures." *Administrative Science Quarterly*, 1969, *14*, 91-114.

Quinn, J. B. *The Logic of Strategic Incrementalism*. Homewood, Ill.: Irwin, 1971

Quinn, J. B. "Strategic Change: Logical Incrementalism." *Sloan Management Review*, 1978, *20*, 7-21.

Quinn, J. B. *Strategies for Change: Logical Incrementalism*. Homewood, Ill.: Irwin, 1980.

Quinn, J. B. "Managing Strategies Incrementally." *Omega*, 1982, *10* (6), 613-627.

Raiffa, H. *The Art and Science of Negotiation*. Cambridge, Mass.: Harvard University Press, 1982.

Ranson, S., Hinings, C. R., and Greenwood, R. "The Structuring of Organizational Structures." *Administrative Science Quarterly*, 1980, *25* (1), 1-17.

Raven, B. H. "The Nixon Group." *Journal of Social Issues*, 1974, *30*, 297-320.

Raven, B. H., and Rubin, J. Z. *Social Psychology: People in Groups*. New York: Wiley, 1976.

Reader, W. J. *Imperial Chemical Industries: A History.* Vol. 2. Oxford, England: Oxford University Press, 1975.

Rhenman, E. *Organization Theory for Long-Range Planning.* London and New York: Wiley, 1973.

Richardson, G. B. *Information and Investment.* Oxford, England: Oxford University Press, 1960.

Roberts, K. H., Hulin, C. L., and Rousseau, D. M. *Developing an Interdisciplinary Science of Organizations.* San Francisco: Jossey-Bass, 1978.

Rockhart, J. F., and Treacy, E. "The CEO Goes On-Line." *Harvard Business Review,* 1982, *60* (1), 82–88.

Romanelli, E., and Tushman, M. L. "Executive Leadership and Organizational Outcomes: An Evolutionary Perspective." Unpublished manuscript, Columbia University, 1983.

Rosenhan, D. L. "On Being Sane in Insane Places." In J. M. Neale, G. C. Davison, and K. P. Price (Eds.), *Contemporary Readings in Psychopathology.* New York: Wiley, 1978.

Rothschild, W. E. *Putting It All Together.* New York: AMACOM, 1976.

Rue, L. W., and Fulmer, R. M. "Is Long-Range Planning Profitable?" *Academy of Management Proceedings, Thirty-Third Annual Meeting, Boston,* 1974, 66–73.

Ruefli, T., and Sarrazin, J. "Strategic Control of Corporate Development Under Ambiguous Circumstances." *Management Science,* 1981, *27* (10), 1158–1170.

Rumelt, R. P. *Strategy, Structure and Economic Performance.* Boston, Mass.: Harvard Business School, 1974.

Ryan, A. *The Philosophy of the Social Sciences.* London: Macmillan, 1970.

Ryle, G. *The Concept of Mind.* London: Hutchinson, 1949.

Sahal, D. "A Unified Theory of Self-Organization." *Journal of Cybernetics,* 1979, *9,* 127–142.

Sahal, D. *Patterns of Technological Innovation.* Lexington, Mass.: Lexington Books, 1981.

Sahal, D. "Structure and Self-Organization." *Behavioral Science,* 1982, *27* (3), 249–258.

Salancik, G. R. "Commitment and the Control of Organizational Behavior and Belief." In B. M. Staw and G. R. Salancik (Eds.),

*New Directions in Organizational Behavior.* Chicago: St. Clair, 1977.

Salthouse, T. A. "The Skill of Typing." *Scientific American,* 1984, *250* (2), 128–135.

Satterthwaite, M. A. "Strategy-Proofness and Arrow's Conditions." *Journal of Economic Theory,* 1975, *10,* 187–217.

Savage, L. J. *The Foundations of Statistics.* New York: Wiley, 1954.

Schank, R. C. "The Structure of Episodes in Memory." In D. G. Bobrow and A. Collins (Eds.), *Representation and Understanding.* New York: Academic Press, 1975.

Schein, E. H. *Process Consultation: Its Role in Organizational Design.* Reading, Mass.: Addison-Wesley, 1969.

Schelling, T. C. *Strategy of Conflict.* Cambridge, Mass.: Harvard University Press, 1960.

Schelling, T. C. *Micromotives and Macrobehavior.* New York and London: Norton, 1978.

Schendel, D. E., and Hofer, C. W. (Eds.). *Strategic Management: A New View of Business Policy and Planning.* Boston: Little, Brown, 1979.

Scherer, F. M. *Industrial Market Structure and Economic Performance.* Chicago: Rand McNally, 1970.

Schoeffler, S., Buzzell, R. D., and Heany, D. F. "Impact of Strategic Planning on Profit Performance." *Harvard Business Review,* 1974, *52* (2), 137–145.

Schön, D. A. *The Reflective Practitioner: How Professionals Think in Action.* London: Temple Smith; New York: Basic Books, 1983.

Schreyögg, G. "Contingency and Choice in Organization Theory." *Organization Studies,* 1980, *1* (4), 305–326.

Schroder, H. M., Driver, M. J., and Streufert, S. *Human Information Processing.* New York: Holt, Rinehart and Winston, 1967.

Schumpeter, J. A. *Capitalism, Socialism, and Democracy.* New York: Harper & Row, 1950.

Scott, B. R. "The Industrial State: Old Myths and New Realities." 1973, *51* (2), 133.

Scriven, M. "Maximizing the Power of Causal Investigations: The Modus Operandi Method." In G. V. Glass (Ed.), *Evaluation*

*Studies.* Review annual Vol. 1. Beverly Hills, Calif.: Sage, 1976.

Selekman, B. M., Selekman, S. K., and Fuller, S. H. *Problems in Labor Relations.* New York: McGraw-Hill, 1958.

Selznick, P. *Leadership in Administration: A Sociological Interpretation.* New York: Harper & Row, 1957.

Shell Chemicals. *The Directional Policy Matrix: A New Aid to Corporate Planning.* London: Shell International Chemical Co., 1975.

Shepard, R. N., and Cooper, L. A. *Mental Images and Their Transformations.* Cambridge, Mass.: MIT Press, 1982.

Shepherd, W. G. *The Economics of Industrial Organization.* Englewood Cliffs, N.J.: Prentice-Hall, 1979.

Shrivastava, P., and Mitroff, I. I. "Frames of Reference Managers Use." In R. Lamb (Eds.), *Advances in Strategic Management.* Vol. 1. Greenwich, Conn.: JAI Press, 1983.

Siehl, C., and Martin, J. "The Role of Symbolic Management: How Can Managers Effectively Transmit Organizational Culture?" Paper presented at International Symposium on Managerial Behavior and Leadership Research, Cleveland, Ohio, July 1982.

Simon, H. A. *Administrative Behavior.* New York: Macmillan, 1947.

Simon, H. A. "A Behavioral Model of Rational Choice." *Quarterly Journal of Economics,* 1955, *64,* 129–138.

Simon, H. A. "Rational Choice and the Structure of the Environment." *Psychological Review,* 1956, *63,* 129–138.

Simon, H. A. *Administrative Behavior: A Study of Decision-Making Processes in Administrative Organization.* (2nd ed.) New York: Macmillan, 1957a.

Simon, H. A. "A Behavioral Model of Rational Choice." In H. A. Simon, *Models of Man.* New York: Wiley, 1957b.

Simon, H. A. *Models of Man.* New York: Wiley, 1957c.

Simon, H. A. *The New Science of Management Decision.* New York: Harper & Row, 1960.

Simon, H. A. "The Architecture of Complexity." *Proceedings of the American Philosophical Society,* 1962, *106,* 467–482.

Simon, H. A. *Administrative Behavior: A Study of Decision-Making Processes in Administrative Organization.* (3rd ed.) New York: Free Press, 1976.

Simon, H. A. "On How to Decide What to Do." *Bell Journal of Economics,* 1978a, *9,* 494–507.

Simon, H. A. "Rationality as Process and as Product of Thought." *American Economic Review,* 1978b, *68* (2), 1–16.

Simon, H. A. *Models of Thought.* New Haven, Conn.: Yale University Press, 1979.

Singer, B., and Benassi, V. A. "Occult Beliefs." *American Scientist,* 1981, *69* (1): 49–55.

Skinner, B. F. *About Behaviorism.* New York: Knopf, 1974.

Skinner, B. F. "Selection by Consequences." *Science,* 1981, *213* (4507), 501–504.

Sloan, A. P., Jr. *My Years with General Motors.* Garden City, N.Y.: Doubleday, 1963.

Slovic, P., Fischhoff, B., and Lichtenstein, S. C. "Behavioral Decision Theory." *Annual Review of Psychology,* 1977, *28,* 1–39.

Slovic, P., and Lichtenstein, S. C. "Comparison of Bayesian and Regression Approaches to Study of Information-Processing in Judgment." *Organizational Behavior and Human Performance,* 1971, *6,* 649–744.

Smoke, R., and George, A. "Theory for Policy in International Affairs." *Policy Sciences,* 1973, *4,* 387–413.

Snyder, G. H., and Diesing, P. *Conflict Among Nations.* Princeton, N.J.: Princeton University Press, 1977.

Sofer, C. *Men in Mid-Career: A Study of British Managers and Technical Specialists.* Cambridge, England: Cambridge University Press, 1970.

Spence, A. M. *Market Signaling.* Cambridge, Mass.: Harvard University Press, 1974.

Spence, A. M. "Entry, Capacity, Investment and Oligopolistic Pricing." *Bell Journal of Economics,* 1977, *8,* 534–544.

Sproull, L. S. "Beliefs in Organizations." In P. C. Nystrom and W. H. Starbuck (Eds.), *Handbook of Organizational Design.* Vol. 2: *Remodeling Organizations and Their Environments.* New York: Oxford University Press, 1981.

Starbuck, W. H. "Organizational Growth and Development." In J. G. March (Ed.), *Handbook of Organizations.* Chicago: Rand McNally, 1965.

Starbuck, W. H. "Organizational Metamorphosis." In R. W. Millman and M. P. Hottenstein (Eds.), *Promising Research Directions*. State College, Penn.: Academy of Management, 1968.

Starbuck, W. H. "Tadpoles into Armageddon and Chrysler into Butterflies." *Social Science Research*, 1973, *2*, 81–109.

Starbuck, W. H. "Organizations and Their Environments." In M. D. Dunnette (Ed.), *Handbook of Industrial and Organizational Psychology*. Chicago: Rand McNally, 1976.

Starbuck, W. H. "A Trip to View the Elephants and Rattlesnakes in the Garden of Aston." In A. H. Van de Ven and W. F. Joyce (Eds.), *Perspectives on Organization Design and Behavior*. New York: Wiley-Interscience, 1981.

Starbuck, W. H. "Congealing Oil: Inventing Ideologies To Justify Acting Ideologies Out." *Journal of Management Studies*, 1982, *19*, 3–27.

Starbuck, W. H. "Organizations as Action Generators." *American Sociological Review*, 1983, *48* (1), 91–102.

Starbuck, W. H., Greve, A., and Hedberg, B. L. T. "Responding to Crises." *Journal of Business Administration*, 1978, *9* (2), 111–137.

Starbuck, W. H., and Hedberg, B. L. T. "Saving an Organization from a Stagnating Environment." In H. B. Thorelli (Ed.), *Strategy + Structure = Performance: The Strategic Planning Imperative*. Bloomington: Indiana University Press, 1977.

Starbuck, W. H., and Nystrom, P. C. "Designing and Understanding Organizations." In P. C. Nystrom and W. H. Starbuck (Eds.), *Handbook of Organizational Design*. Vol. 1: *Adapting Organizations to Their Environments*. New York: Oxford University Press, 1981.

Staw, B. M. "Knee-Deep in Big Muddy: A Study of Escalating Commitment to a Chosen Course of Action." *Organizational Behavior and Human Performance*, 1976, *16*, 27–44.

Staw, B. M. "Rationality and Justification in Organizational Life." In L. L. Cummings and B. M. Staw (Eds.), *Research in Organizational Behavior*. Vol. 2. Greenwich, Conn.: JAI Press, 1980.

Staw, B. M., McKenzie, P. I., and Puffer, S. M. "The Justifications of Organizational Performance." *Administrative Science Quarterly*, 1983, *28* (4), 582–600.

Staw, B. M., and Ross, J. "Commitment to a Policy Decision: A Multi-Theoretical Perspective." *Administrative Science Quarterly*, 1978, *23*, 40–64.

Straw, B. M., Sandelands, L. E., and Dutton, J. E. "Threat-Rigidity Effects in Organizational Behavior: A Multilevel Analysis." *Administrative Science Quarterly*, 1981, *26* (4), 501–524.

Stein J. "Contextual Factors in the Selection of Strategic Decision Methods." *Human Relations*, 1981a, *34* (10), 819–834.

Stein, J. "Strategic Decision Methods." *Human Relations*, 1981b, *34* (11), 917–933.

Steinbruner, J. D. *The Cybernetic Theory of Decision*. Princeton, N.J.: Princeton University Press, 1974.

Steiner, G. A. *Top Management Planning*. New York: Macmillan, 1969.

Steiner, G. A. *Strategic Managerial Planning*. Oxford, England: Planning Research Institute, 1977.

Steiner, G. A. *Strategic Planning*. New York: Free Press, 1979.

Steiner, I. "Heuristic Models of Groupthink." In H. Brandstatter, J. H. Davis, and G. Stocker-Kreichgauer (Eds.), *Group Decision Making*. New York: Academic Press, 1982.

Stopford, J. M., and Wells, L. T. *Managing the Multinational Enterprise*. London: Longman, 1972.

Strategic Planning Associates. *Beyond The Portfolio*. Washington, D.C.: Strategic Planning Associates, 1982.

Stretton, H. *The Political Sciences*. London: Routledge & Kegan Paul, 1969.

Sutton, C. J. *Economics and Corporate Strategy*. Cambridge, England: Cambridge University Press, 1980.

Swinburne, R. "Introduction." In R. Swinburne (Ed.), *The Justification of Induction*. Oxford, England: Oxford University Press, 1974.

Tannenbaum, A. S. (Ed.). *Control in Organizations*. New York: McGraw-Hill, 1968.

Taylor, D. W. "Decision Making and Problem Solving." In J. G. March (Ed.), *Handbook of Organizations*. Chicago: Rand McNally, 1965.

Teece, D. J. *Vertical Integration and Vertical Divestiture in the U.S. Oil Industry*. Palo Alto, Calif.: Institute for Energy Studies, Stanford University, 1976.

Teece, D. J. "Technology Transfer by Multinational Firms: The

Resource Cost of Transferring Technological Know-How." *Economic Journal*, 1977, *87* (346), 242-261.

Teece, D. J. "The Diffusion of Administrative Innovation." *Management Science*, 1980, *26*, 464-470.

Teece, D. J. "Internal Organization and Economic Performance: An Empirical Analysis of the Profitability of Principal Firms." *Journal of Industrial Economics*, 1981a, *30* (2), 173-199.

Teece, D. J. "The Market for Knowhow and the Efficient International Transfer of Technology." *Annals of the Academy of Political and Social Science*, 1981b, *26*, 81-96.

Teece, D. J., and Winter, S. G. "The Limits of Neoclassical Theory in Management Education." *American Economic Review*, 1984, *74* (2), 116-126.

Tetlock, P. E. "Psychological Research on Foreign Policy: A Methodological Overview." In L. Wheeler (Ed.), *Review of Personality and Social Psychology*. Vol. 4. Beverly Hills, Calif.: Sage, 1983.

Teulings, A. W. M. "Interlocking Interests and Collaboration with the Enemy: Corporate Behavior in the Second World War." *Organization Studies*, 1982, *3* (2), 99-118.

Teulings, A. W. M. "The Social, Cultural and Political Setting of Industrial Democracy." In *International Yearbook of Industrial Democracy*. Vol. 2: *International Perspectives on Organizational Democracy*. Chichester, England: Wiley, 1985.

Thompson, H. A., Jr., and Strickland, A. J. III. *Strategy Formulation and Implementation*. Dallas: Business Publications, 1980.

Thompson, J. D. *Organizations in Action*. New York: McGraw-Hill, 1967.

Thompson, J. D., and Tuden, A. "Strategies, Structures and Processes of Organizational Decision." In H. J. Leavitt and L. R. Pondy (Eds.), *Readings in Managerial Psychology*. Chicago: University of Chicago Press, 1964.

Thorelli, H. B. *Strategy + Structure = Performance: The Strategic Planning Imperative*. Bloomington: Indiana University Press, 1977.

Thorngate, W. "'In General' Versus 'It Depends': Some Comments on the Gergen-Schlenker Debate." *Personality and Social Psychology Bulletin*, 1976, *2*, 404-410.

Thorson, J., and Sylvan, D. A. "Couterfactuals and the Cuban

Missile Crisis." *International Studies Quarterly,* 1982, *26* (4), 539-571.

Thune, S. S., and House, R. J. "Where Long-Range Planning Pays Off." *Business Horizons,* 1970, *13* (4), 81-87.

Thurber, J. *Further Fables for Our Time.* New York: Simon and Schuster, 1956.

Thurow, L. C. *Dangerous Currents: The State of Economics.* New York: Random House, 1983.

Tichy, N. M. "Managing Organizational Transformation." *Human Resource Management,* 1983, 22 (1/2), 45-60.

Tosi, H., Aldag, R., and Storey, R. "On the Measurement of the Environment: An Assessment of the Lawrence and Lorsch Environental Uncertainty Subscale." *Administrative Science Quarterly,* 1973, *18,* 27-36.

Tuchman, G. "Making News by Doing Work: Routinizing the Unexpected." *American Journal of Sociology,* 1973, *79,* 110-131.

Tuma, N. B., Hannan, M. T., and Groeneveld, L. P. "Approaches to the Censoring Problem in Analysis of Event Histories." In K. F. Schuessler (Ed.), *Sociological Methodology.* San Francisco: Jossey-Bass, 1979.

"Turnover at the Top." *Business Week,* Dec. 19, 1983, pp. 104-110.

Tushman, M. L., and Romanelli, E. "Organizational Evolution: A Metamorphosis Model of Convergence and Reorientation." In L. L. Cummings and B. M. Staw (Eds.), *Research in Organizational Behavior.* Vol. 7. Greenwich, Conn.: JAI Press, 1985.

Tversky, A., and Kahneman, D. "Availability: Heuristic for Judging Frequency and Probability." *Cognitive Psychology,* 1973, *5,* 207-232.

Tversky, A., and Kahneman, D. "Judgment Under Uncertainty: Heuristics and Biases." *Science,* 1974, *195,* 1124-1131.

Tversky, A., and Kahneman, D. "The Framing of Decisions and the Psychology of Choice."*Science,* 1981, *221,* 453-458.

Ungson, G. R., Braunstein, D. N., and Hall, P. D. "Managerial Information Processing: A Research Review." *Administrative Science Quarterly,* 1981, *26,* 116-134.

Vancil, R. F. *Decentralization: Managing Ambiguity by Design.* Homewood, Ill.: Dow Jones Irwin, 1979.

Van de Ven, A. H. "Problem Solving, Planning, and Innovation:

Part 2. Speculations for Theory and Practice." *Human Relations,* 1980, *33,* 757–779.

Van de Ven, A. H., and Joyce, W. (Eds.). *Perspectives on Organization Design and Behavior.* New York: Wiley-Interscience, 1981.

Verba, S. "Some Dilemmas in Comparative Research." *World Politics,* 1967, *20,* 114.

Vesper, K. "New Venture Planning." *Journal of Business Strategy,* 1980, *1* (2), 73, 75.

Von Hipple, E. A. "The Dominant Role of the User in Semiconductor and Electronic Process Innovation." *IEEE Transactions on Engineering Management,* 1977, *24,* 1977.

Von Neumann, J., and Morgenstern, O. *Theory of Games and Economic Behavior.* (Rev. ed.) Princeton, N.J.: Princeton University Press, 1947.

Wachter, M. L., and Wachter, S. M. *Toward a New U.S. Industrial Policy?* Philadelphia: University of Pennsylvania Press, 1983.

Wagner, H. M. *Principles of Operations Research.* Englewood Cliffs, N.J.: Prentice-Hall, 1969.

Watkins, J. "Ideal Types and Historical Explanation." *British Journal for the Philosophy of Science,* 1952. Reprinted in H. Feigl and M. Brodbeck (Eds.), *Readings in the Philosophy of Science.* New York: Appleton-Century-Crofts, 1953.

Watkins, J. "Imperfect Rationality." In R. Borger and F. Cioffi (Eds.), *Explanation in the Behavioural Sciences.* New York: Cambridge University Press, 1970.

Watson, J. B. "Psychology as the Behaviorist Views It." *Psychological Review,* 1913, *20,* 158–177.

Watzlawick, P., Weakland, J. H., and Fisch, R. *Change: Principles of Problem Formation and Problem Resolution.* New York: Norton, 1974.

Weick, K. E. "Laboratory Organizations and Unnoticed Causes." *Administrative Science Quarterly,* 1969a, *14* (2), 294–303.

Weick, K. E. *The Social Psychology of Organizing.* Reading, Mass.: Addison-Wesley, 1969b.

Weick, K. E. "Educational Organizations as Loosely Coupled Systems." *Administrative Science Quarterly,* 1976, *21,* 1–19.

Weick, K. E. "Punctuating the Concept." In P. S. Goodman, J. M.

Pennings, and Associates, *New Perspectives on Organizational Effectiveness.* San Francisco: Jossey-Bass, 1977.

Weick, K. E. *The Social Psychology of Organizing.* (2nd ed.) Reading, Mass.: Addison-Wesley, 1979.

Weick, K. E. "Managerial Thought in the Context of Action." In S. Srivastva and Associates, *The Executive Mind: New Insights on Managerial Thought and Action.* San Francisco: Jossey-Bass, 1983.

Weick, K. E. "Perspectives on Action in Organizations." In J. W. Lorsch (Ed.), *Handbook of Organizational Behavior.* Englewood Cliffs, N.J.: Prentice-Hall, 1984.

Weil, M. "Can Bureaucracies Be Rational Actors?" *International Studies Quarterly,* December 1975, 432–468.

Weiss, W. "The Historical and Political Perspective on Organizations of Lucien Karpik." In M. Zey-Ferrell and M. Aiken (Eds.), *Complex Organizations: Critical Perspectives.* Glenview, Ill.: Scott, Foresman, 1981.

Wensley, R. "PIMS and BCG: New Horizons or False Dawn?" *Strategic Management Journal,* 1982, *3,* 147–158.

Westerlund, G., and Sjöstrand, S. E. *Organizational Myths.* London and New York: Harper & Row, 1978.

Wheeler, D. D., and Janis, I. L. *A Practical Guide for Making Decisions.* New York: Free Press, 1980.

White, L. *The Science of Culture.* New York: Grove Press, 1949.

Wildavsky, A. B. "The Self-Evaluating Organization." *Public Administration Review,* 1972, *32,* 509–520.

Wildavsky, A. B. *The Politics of the Budgetary Process.* (3rd ed.) Boston: Little, Brown, 1979.

Wilensky, H. L. *Organizational Intelligence.* New York: Basic Books, 1967.

Wilkins, A. L., and Ouchi, W. G. "Efficient Cultures: Exploring the Relationship Between Culture and Organizational Performance." *Administrative Science Quarterly,* 1983, *28* (3), 468–481.

Williamson, O. E. *The Economics of Discretionary Behavior: Managerial Objectives in a Theory of the Firm.* Englewood Cliffs, N.J.: Prentice-Hall, 1964.

Williamson, O. E. *Markets and Hierarchies: Analysis and Antitrust Implications.* New York: Free Press, 1975.

Williamson, O. E. "Transaction-Cost Economics: The Governance of Contractual Relations." *Journal of Law and Economics*, 1979, *22*, 233-261.

Williamson, O. E. "The Modern Corporation: Origins, Evolution, Attributes." *Journal of Economic Literature*, 1981, *19* (4), 1537-1568.

Wilson, D. C. "Organizational Strategy." Unpublished doctoral dissertation, Management Centre, University of Bradford, England, 1980.

Wilson, D. C. "Electricity and Resistance: A Case Study of Innovation and Politics." *Organization Studies*, 1982, *3*, (2), 119-140.

Wilson, D. C., and others. "The Limits of Trade Union Power in Organizational Decision Making." *British Journal of Industrial Relations*, 1982, *20*, (3), 322-341.

Wilson, D. C., and others. "Sources of Power in Strategic Decision Making: The Selective Embodiment of Power." Unpublished manuscript, Management Centre, University of Bradford, England, 1984.

Wilson, E. *On Human Nature.* Cambridge, Mass.: Harvard University Press, 1978.

Winter, S. G. "Concepts of Rationality in Behavioral Theory." Working paper, Institute of Public Policy Studies, University of Michigan, 1969.

Witte, E. "Field Research on Complex Decision-Making Processes: The Phase Theorem." *International Studies on Management and Organization*, 1972, *2*, 156-182.

Woo, C. Y. Y. *Strategic and Financial Management: An Integrative View.* Working paper, Purdue University, 1983.

Woo, C. Y. Y., and Cooper, A. C. "Strategies of Effective Low Share Businesses." *Strategic Management Journal*, 1981, *2*, 301-318.

Wood, D. R., Jr., and LaForge, R. L. "The Impact of Comprehensive Planning on Financial Performance." *Academy of Management Journal*, 1979, *22*, 516-526.

Wrigley, L. *Diversification and Divisional Autonomy.* Boston: Harvard Business School, 1970.

Wynne, J. M., and Zaleznik, A. *"The Saturday Evening Post."* Unpublished paper, Graduate School of Business Administration, Harvard University, 1972.

Yavitz, B., and Newman, W. H. *Strategy in Action.* New York: Free Press, 1982.

Young, S. *Management: A Systems Analysis.* Glenview, Ill.: Scott, Foresman, 1966.

Zald, M. N., and McCarthy, J. D. *The Dynamics of Social Movements: Resource Mobilization, Social Control and Tactics.* Boston: Little Brown, 1979.

Zaleznik, A. *Human Dilemmas of Leadership.* New York: Harper & Row, 1966.

# Name Index

# Subject Index